Anonymous

The Service of Song for Baptist Churches

Anonymous

The Service of Song for Baptist Churches

ISBN/EAN: 9783337849542

Printed in Europe, USA, Canada, Australia, Japan

Cover: Foto ©Lupo / pixelio.de

More available books at **www.hansebooks.com**

Tunes in New Collections — Pages

105	196	296	347
106	197	298	352
107	198	299	354
112	199	300	386
114	200	301	389
116	202	302	392
117	204	303	400
119	206	307	402
120	210	308	412
121	212	309	414
123	213	310	415
124	216	312	422
126	219	314	430
129	220	315	
130	221	316	187 Tunes
131	223	317	
132	224	320	List of
133	226	324	New Tunes
134	227	327	16 101
135	230	329	18 103
138	233	331	20 108
139	234	332	21 109
140	236	333	29 111
141	241	334	31 113 — 2 tune
142	244	336	32 125 — 2 tune
144	246	338	35 127
147	248	340	36 149
150	249	342	37 162
154	250	344	38 168 both
155	251	346	39 169
157	252	352	40 182
158	253	355	41 185
167	259	358	43 195
171	267	359	45 205
172	270	361	46 215
174	272	362	47. 1 tune 229
176	274	365	49 — both " 239
177	275	367	57 245
178	276	370	61 262
181	280	371	71 268
183	288	373	72 277
184	292	374	82 287
187	295		94 290
188			95 291, 295
193			96 297
194			97 325
			335 January 29
			348
			365
			380

THE

SERVICE OF SONG

FOR

BAPTIST CHURCHES.

"THE SERVICE OF SONG IN THE HOUSE OF THE LORD."
— *I. Chronicles* vi. 31.

BOSTON:
GOULD AND LINCOLN,
59 WASHINGTON STREET.
NEW YORK: SHELDON AND COMPANY.
1873.

Entered according to Act of Congress, in the year 1871, by
GOULD & LINCOLN,
In the office of the Librarian of Congress, at Washington.

PREFACE.

THIS collection of hymns is made for use in Baptist churches. While limited in number, it will be found to be catholic in selection. Hymnology is a harp of many strings, and we have tried to strike them all. We have drawn from a wide variety of sources, and with reference to all occasions of the Christian life, all the moods of Christian experience, and all the forms of Christian doctrine. It would be easy to select hymns which should be all in one vein, or in fact written by one person. But as the Bible, the manual of Christian knowledge, inspired by one and the self-same Spirit, is in the varied style of so many different writers, so our manuals of Christian song should partake of a similar variety, which is possible by drawing from the singers of all times, countries, and communions.

But while the field of research is so wide and various, a hymn-book is not necessarily useful in proportion to the number of hymns it contains. We have not attempted to include all hymns which even an enlightened judgment might call good. We have excluded some which have their merit, and indeed hallowed associations, in many minds. But we have omitted many on account of some weakness or defect which would subtract from the general tone of strength both in doctrine and style which we have desired this selection should possess. A single defect may spoil an otherwise good hymn. We hope that what is omitted is more than made up by the quality of that which is retained.

So far as practicable the original text of hymns has been given, for the simple reason that in most cases it is superior to the alterations to which it has been subjected. A few alterations have been universally accepted, and justify themselves. But in the innumerable variations which have found their way into the different collections, it has seemed to us the wiser rule to fall back on the original and uncorrupted text. Where departures are made from the author's text, in most cases, and unless in slight verbal changes, the fact is indicated.

A few of the hymns in this collection exceed the length usually prescribed for singing. Verses which seemed necessary to the unity and effectiveness of a hymn, or for whose omission there seemed to be no reason which would not apply to the other verses, have been given, even where all the verses would not be sung at one time, giving the opportunity of selection to the minister. For a true hymn is vital in every part, and cannot be cut down to given dimensions without injury. Abridgment or mutilation is often the worst alteration a hymn can suffer. A hymn-book is not used in public worship alone. Its hymns may be studied by the young, and by all Christians, and committed to memory with great profit. Moreover, the conductor of public worship, making his selections carefully and in advance, may be left to use his own taste and judgment in selecting the verses to be sung, instead of having an exact number fixed for him, beyond which he cannot go. Therefore, while selections have been made from some hymns which could not be given at their full length, the selection has been governed by the quality and the relation of the verses, rather than their number. We have often regretted that there seemed to be a necessity for any abridgment at all. This necessity, it will not be concealed, has been enforced, in part, by the attempt to combine a collection of music for congregational singing with the collection of hymns. To preserve the natural order, and a uniform numbering of the hymns in both collections, as well as an unbroken page in the book of tunes, we have submitted to occasional elisions or additions which had no other sufficient reason.

In the arrangement of the music in this work two ideas have been kept steadily in view, viz., the maintenance of sacred and long-established associations between old hymns and old tunes, and the introduction with less familiar hymns of such new music as shall meet the constant demand among the younger portion of our congregations for something fresh and attractive.

Of course it is impossible to carry out the first idea uniformly, since some much-used tunes have scores of hymns associated with them in common use, and some hymns have become identified with a not less number of different tunes. It only needs a glance at the book, however, to show that it is largely stored with those familiar and favorite tunes which can be sung at sight, and that these are always accompanied by one or more equally familiar hymns.

While a large and just requirement is thus met, we are persuaded that the other is not less imperative. Congregational singing will fail of success without constant practice in rehearsal. The interest in such rehearsal will fail to be kept up, unless there is fresh and modern music to be learned and enjoyed. Provision has been made for the want, by the introduction of a considerable number of original tunes by the best composers, and a still larger number of not new, but less familiar ones, from the best American, English, and German sources. It is believed, however, that there is not a single tune that may not be readily learned and sung by a congregation, and not one that will not amply repay the pains of such learning. The grateful acknowledgments of the compilers are tendered to George Hews, Esq., of Boston, the well-known composer, for a large number of original tunes, and also for the free use of his valuable manuscript music, from which they have drawn some of the best tunes in the collection. Their sincere thanks are also tendered to Leonard Marshall, Esq., for the use of many of his excellent compositions.

We have endeavored to avail ourselves of the progress made in hymnology in late years, and to use its researches and its ampler resources, in preparing a book adapted to the service of song in the house of the Lord. Our labor has given us a fresh impression of the difficulty and the responsibility of selecting out of such abundant materials a body of hymns which, while not large in number, shall serve all the needs of the people of God in public worship, and be also an aid in their private spiritual culture. It has made us aware of the defects which exist after the best endeavors. But believing that the Spirit of the Lord in the hearts of his people can make it sufficient, we have only to commit it to their use and to His blessing.

S. L. CALDWELL,
A. J. GORDON.

JULY 15, 1871.

THE
SERVICE OF SONG.

WORSHIP.

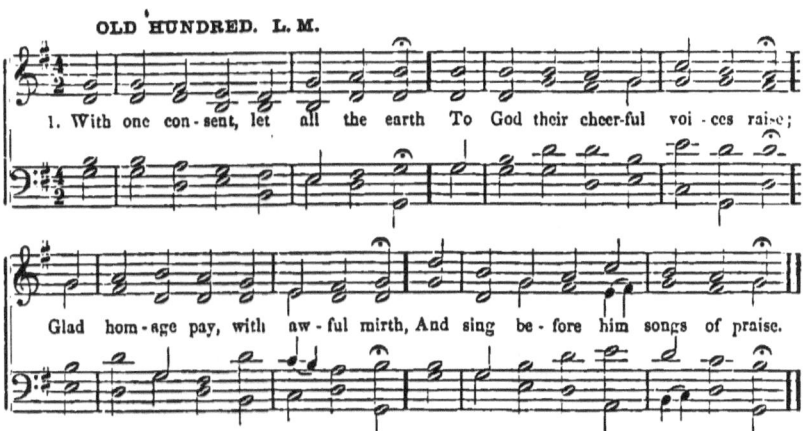

OLD HUNDRED. L. M.

1. With one con-sent, let all the earth To God their cheerful voi-ces raise; Glad hom-age pay, with aw-ful mirth, And sing be-fore him songs of praise.

1.

PSALM 100.

1 With one consent, let all the earth
  To God their cheerful voices raise;
  Glad homage pay with awful mirth,
  And sing before him songs of praise:

2 Convinced that he is God alone,
  From whom both we and all proceed;
  We, whom he chooses for his own,
  The flock that he vouchsafes to feed.

3 Oh enter, then, his temple gate,
  Thence to his courts devoutly press,
  And still your grateful hymns repeat,
  And still his name with praises bless,

4 For he's the Lord, supremely good;
  His mercy is forever sure;
  His truth, which always firmly stood,
  To endless ages shall endure.

  Tate and Brady, 1696.

2.

PSALM 100.

1 Before Jehovah's awful throne,
  Ye nations, bow with sacred joy;
  Know that the Lord is God alone;
  He can create, and he destroy.

2 His sovereign power, without our aid,
  Made us of clay, and formed us men;
  And when, like wandering sheep, we strayed,
  He brought us to his fold again.

3 We are his people, we his care,
  Our souls, and all our mortal frame:
  What lasting honors shall we rear,
  Almighty Maker, to thy name?

4 We'll crowd thy gates with thankful songs,
  High as the heaven our voices raise;
  And earth, with her ten thousand tongues,
  Shall fill thy courts with sounding praise.

5 Wide as the world is thy command,
  Vast as eternity thy love:
  Firm as a rock thy truth must stand,
  When rolling years shall cease to move.

  Isaac Watts, 1719; alt. by *J. Wesley*, 1741.

WORSHIP.

DUKE STREET. L. M.

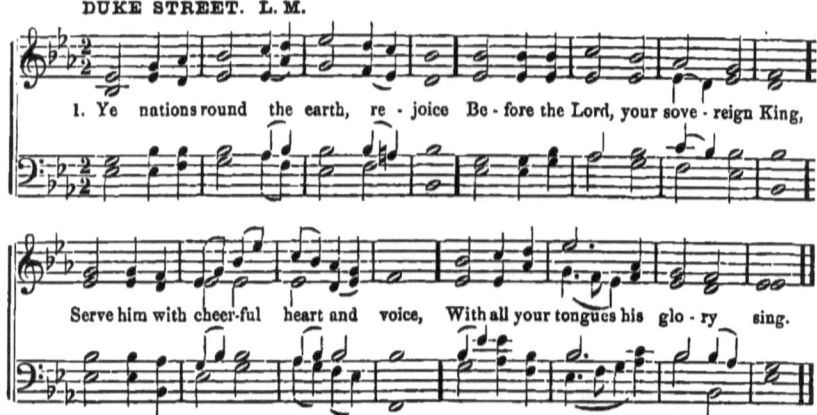

1. Ye nations round the earth, re-joice Be-fore the Lord, your sove-reign King, Serve him with cheer-ful heart and voice, With all your tongues his glo-ry sing.

3.   PSALM 100.

1 YE nations round the earth, rejoice
   Before the Lord, your sovereign King,
Serve him with cheerful heart and voice,
   With all your tongues his glory sing.

2 The Lord is God; 'tis he alone
   Doth life and breath and being give;
We are his work, and not our own;
   The sheep that on his pastures live.

3 Enter his gates with songs of joy,
   With praises to his courts repair,
And make it your divine employ
   To pay your thanks and honors there.

4 The Lord is good; the Lord is kind;
   Great is his grace, his mercy sure;
And the whole race of man shall find
   His truth from age to age endure.

Isaac Watts, 1719.

4.   PSALM 65.

1 FOR thee, O God, our constant praise
   In Zion waits, thy chosen seat;
Our promised altars we will raise,
   And there our zealous vows complete.

2 O thou, who to my humble prayer
   Didst always bend thy listening ear,
To thee shall all mankind repair,
   And at thy gracious throne appear.

3 Our sins, though numberless, in vain,
   To stop thy flowing mercy try;
Whilst thou o'erlook'st the guilty stain,
   And washest out the crimson dye.

4 Blest is the man, who, near thee placed,
   Within thy sacred dwelling lives!
While we, at humbler distance, taste
   The vast delights thy temple gives.

Tate and Brady, 1696.

5.   PSALM 65.

1 PRAISE, Lord, for thee in Zion waits;
   Prayer shall besiege thy temple gates;
All flesh shall to thy throne repair,
   And find, through Christ, salvation there.

2 Our spirits faint; our sins prevail;
   Leave not our trembling hearts to fail:
O Thou that hearest prayer, descend,
   And still be found the sinner's friend.

3 How blest thy saints! how safely led!
   How surely kept! how richly fed!
Saviour of all in earth and sea,
   How happy they who rest in thee!

4 Thy hand sets fast the mighty hills,
   Thy voice the troubled ocean stills!
Evening and morning hymn thy praise,
   And earth thy bounty wide displays.

5 The year is with thy goodness crowned;
   Thy clouds drop wealth the world around;
Through thee the deserts laugh and sing,
   And Nature smiles and owns her king.

6 Lord, on our souls thy Spirit pour;
   The moral waste within restore;
Oh let thy love our spring-tide be,
   And make us all bear fruit to thee.

Henry Francis Lyte, 1834.

WORSHIP.

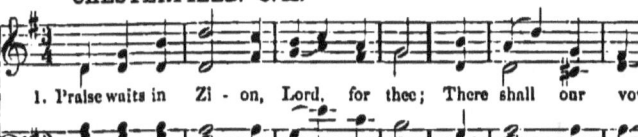

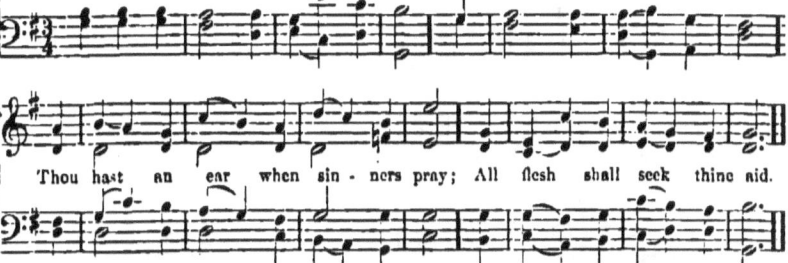

6.   PSALM 65.

1 PRAISE waits in Zion, Lord, for thee;
   There shall our vows be paid:
   Thou hast an ear when sinners pray;
   All flesh shall seek thine aid.

2 Lord, our iniquities prevail.
   But pardoning grace is thine;
   And thou wilt grant us power and skill
   To conquer every sin.

3 Blest are the men whom thou wilt choose
   To bring them near thy face;
   Give them a dwelling in thy house,
   To feast upon thy grace.

4 In answering what thy church requests,
   Thy truth and terror shine;
   And works of dreadful righteousness
   Fulfil thy kind design.

5 Thus shall the wondering nations see
   The Lord is good and just;
   And distant islands fly to thee,
   And make thy name their trust.
   Isaac Watts, 1719.

7.   PSALM 84.

1 MY soul, how lovely is the place
   To which thy God resorts!
   'Tis heaven to see his smiling face,
   Though in his earthly courts.

2 There the great Monarch of the skies
   His saving power displays,
   And light breaks in upon our eyes
   With kind and quickening rays.

3 With his rich gifts the heavenly Dove
   Descends and fills the place,
   While Christ reveals his wondrous love,
   And sheds abroad his grace.

4 There, mighty God, thy words declare
   The secrets of thy will;
   And still we seek thy mercy there,
   And sing thy praises still.

5 My heart and flesh cry out for thee,
   While far from thine abode;
   When shall I tread thy courts, and see
   My Saviour and my God?
   Isaac Watts, 1719.

8.   PSALM 95.

1 SING to the Lord Jehovah's name,
   And in his strength rejoice;
   When his salvation is our theme,
   Exalted be our voice.

2 With thanks, approach his awful sight,
   And psalms of honor sing;
   The Lord's a God of boundless might,
   The whole creation's King.

3 Come, and with humble souls adore,
   Come, kneel before his face;
   Oh, may the creatures of his power
   Be children of his grace!

4 Now is the time: he bends his ear,
   And waits for your request;
   Come, lest he rouse his wrath, and swear
   ' Ye shall not see my rest.'
   Isaac Watts, 1719.

WORSHIP.

BLENDON. L. M.

1. Come, let our voices join to raise A sacred song of solemn praise;
God is a sovereign King; rehearse His honors in exalted verse.

9.   Psalm 95.

1 Come, let our voices join to raise
A sacred song of solemn praise;
God is a sovereign King; rehearse
His honors in exalted verse.

2 Come, let our souls address the Lord,
Who framed our natures with his word;
He is our shepherd; we the sheep
His mercy chose, his pastures keep.

3 Come, let us hear his voice to-day,
The counsels of his love obey;
Nor let our hardened hearts renew
The sins and plagues that Israel knew.

4 Seize the kind promise while it waits,
And march to Zion's heavenly gates;
Believe, and take the promised rest;
Obey, and be for ever blest.
Isaac Watts, 1719.

10.   Psalm 84.

1 Great God, attend, while Zion sings
The joy that from thy presence springs:
To spend one day with thee on earth,
Exceeds a thousand days of mirth.

2 Might I enjoy the meanest place
Within thy house, O God of grace,
Not tents of ease nor thrones of power
Should tempt my feet to leave thy door.

3 God is our sun, he makes our day;
God is our shield, he guards our way
From all th' assaults of hell and sin,
From foes without and foes within.

4 All needful grace will God bestow,
And crown that grace with glory too;
He gives us all things, and withholds
No real good from upright souls.
Isaac Watts, 1719.

11.

1 Lord, in the temples of thy grace
Thy saints behold thy smiling face;
And oft have seen thy glory shine,
With power and majesty divine.

2 Come, dearest Lord, thy children cry,
Our graces droop, our comforts die;
Return, and let thy glories rise
Again to our admiring eyes:

3 Till filled with light, and joy, and love,
Thy courts below, like those above,
Triumphant hallelujahs raise,
And heaven and earth resound thy praise.
Anne Steele, 1760.

12.   Psalm 141.

1 My God, accept my early vows,
Like morning incense in thy house;
And let my nightly worship rise,
Sweet as the evening sacrifice.

2 Watch o'er my lips and guard them, Lord,
From every rash and heedless word;
Nor let my feet incline to tread
The guilty path where sinners lead.

3 Oh may the righteous, when I stray,
Smite and reprove my wandering way;
Their gentle words, like ointment shed,
Shall never bruise, but cheer my head.
Isaac Watts, 1719.

WORSHIP.

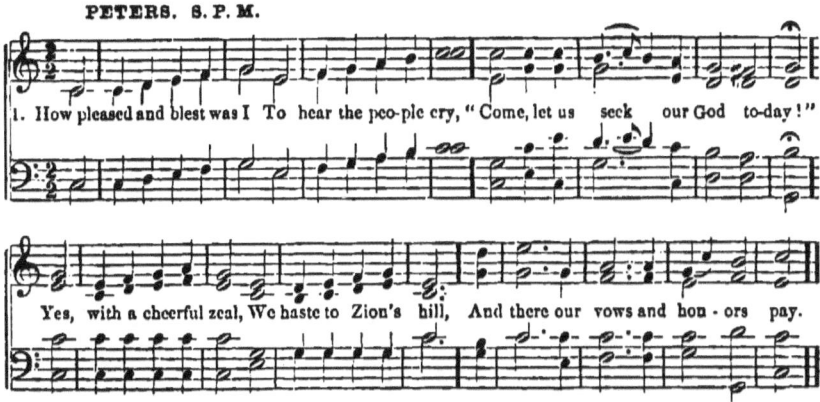

13. PSALM 122.

1 How pleased and blest was I
To hear the people cry,
"Come, let us seek our God to-day!"
Yes, with a cheerful zeal,
We haste to Zion's hill,
And there our vows and honors pay.

2 Zion, thrice happy place,
Adorned with wondrous grace,
And walls of strength embrace thee round;
In thee our tribes appear
To pray, and praise, and hear
The sacred gospel's joyful sound.

3 There David's greater Son
Has fixed his royal throne,
He sits for grace and judgment there;
He bids the saints be glad,
He makes the sinner sad,
And humble souls rejoice with fear.

4 May peace attend thy gate,
And joy within thee wait
To bless the soul of every guest!
The man that seeks thy peace,
And wishes thine increase,
A thousand blessings on him rest!

5 My tongue repeats her vows,
"Peace to this sacred house!"
For here my friends and kindred dwell;
And since my glorious God
Makes thee his blest abode,
My soul shall ever love thee well.

Isaac Watts, 1719.

WORSHIP.

CAMBRIDGE. C. M.

1. How did my heart re-joice to hear My friends de-vout-ly say, "In Zi-on let us all appear, And keep the solemn day. And keep the solemn day. And keep the sol-emn day."

14. PSALM 122.

1 How did my heart rejoice to hear
　My friends devoutly say,
"In Zion let us all appear,
　And keep the solemn day."

2 I love her gates, I love the road;
　The Church, adorned with grace,
Stands like a palace, built for God,
　To show his milder face.

3 Up to her courts, with joys unknown,
　The holy tribes repair;
The Son of David holds his throne,
　And sits in judgment there.

4 He hears our praises and complaints;
　And while his awful voice
Divides the sinners from the saints,
　We tremble and rejoice.

5 Peace be within this sacred place,
　And joy a constant guest;
With holy gifts and heavenly grace
　Be her attendants blest.

6 My soul shall pray for Zion still,
　While life or breath remains;
There my best friends, my kindred, dwell,
　There God, my Saviour reigns.

Isaac Watts, 1719.

15.

1 COME, ye that love the Saviour's name,
　And joy to make it known;
The sovereign of your heart proclaim,
　And bow before his throne.

2 Behold your King, your Saviour, crowned
　With glories all divine;
And tell the wondering nations round,
　How bright those glories shine.

3 Infinite power and boundless grace,
　In him unite their rays:
You, that have e'er beheld his face,
　Can you forbear his praise?

4 When in his earthly courts we view
　The glories of our King,
We long to love as angels do,
　And wish like them to sing.

5 And shall we long and wish in vain?
　Lord, teach our songs to rise;
Thy love can animate the strain,
　And bid it reach the skies.

6 Oh, happy period! glorious day!
　When heaven and earth shall raise,
With all their powers, the raptured lay,
　To celebrate thy praise.

Anne Steele, 1760.

DOXOLOGY.

To Father, Son, and Holy Ghost,
　One God whom we adore,
Be glory as it was, is now,
　And shall be evermore.

Tate and Brady, 1696.

WORSHIP.

16. PSALM 84.

1 How pleasant, how divinely fair,
O Lord of hosts, thy dwellings are!
With long desire my spirit faints
To meet the assemblies of thy saints.

2 My flesh would rest in thine abode,
My panting heart cries out for God;
My God, my King, why should I be
So far from all my joys and thee?

3 Blest are the saints who sit on high
Around thy throne of majesty;
Thy brightest glories shine above,
And all their work is praise and love.

4 Blest are the souls that find a place
Within the temple of thy grace;
There they behold thy gentler rays,
And seek thy face and learn thy praise.

5 Blest are the men whose hearts are set
To find the way to Zion's gate;
God is their strength, and thro' the road
They lean upon their helper, God.

6 Cheerful they walk with growing strength,
Till all shall meet in heaven at length;
Till all before Thy face appear,
And join in nobler worship there.
Isaac Watts, 1719.

17. PSALM 135.

1 PRAISE ye the Lord, exalt his name,
While in his holy courts ye wait,
Ye saints, that to his house belong,
Or stand attending at his gate.

2 Praise ye the Lord; the Lord is good;
To praise his name is sweet employ:
Israel he chose of old, and still
His church is his peculiar joy.

3 The Lord himself will judge his saints;
He treats his servants as his friends;
And when he hears their sore complaints,
Repents the sorrow that he sends.

4 Bless ye the Lord, who taste his love,
People and priests exalt his name:
Amongst his saints he ever dwells;
His church is his Jerusalem.
Isaac Watts, 1719.

18.

1 SWEET is the solemn voice that calls
The Christian to the house of prayer;
I love to stand within its walls,
For thou, O Lord, art present there.

2 I love to tread the hallowed courts,
Where two or three for worship meet;
For thither Christ himself resorts,
And makes the little band complete.

3 'Tis sweet to raise the common song,
To join in holy praise and love;
And imitate the blessed throng
That mingle hearts and songs above.

4 Within these walls may peace abound,
May all our hearts in one agree!
Where brethren meet, where Christ is found,
May peace and concord ever be!
H. F. Lyte, 1847.

WORSHIP.

HADDAM. H. M.

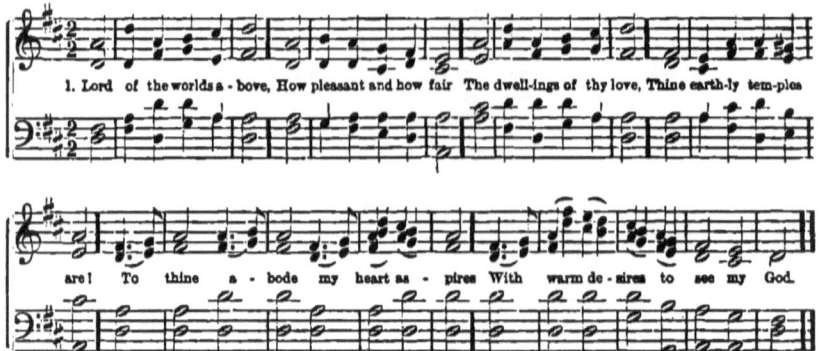

1. Lord of the worlds a-bove, How pleasant and how fair The dwell-ings of thy love, Thine earth-ly tem-ples are! To thine a-bode my heart as-pires With warm de-sires to see my God.

---

19. PSALM 84.

2 The sparrow for her young
  With pleasure seeks a nest,
And wandering swallows long
  To find their wonted rest:
My spirit faints with equal zeal
To rise and dwell among thy saints.

3 Oh happy souls that pray
  Where God appoints to hear;
Oh happy men that pay
  Their constant service there;
They praise thee still, and happy they
That love the way to Zion's hill.

4 They go from strength to strength,
  Through this dark vale of tears,
Till each arrives at length,
  Till each in heaven appears:
Oh glorious seat, when God our King
Shall thither bring our willing feet!

5 To spend one sacred day
  Where God and saints abide,
Affords diviner joy
  Than thousand days beside:
Where God resorts, I love it more
To keep the door, than shine in courts.
Isaac Watts, 1719.

20.

1 O THOU that hearest prayer,
  Attend our humble cry,
And let thy servants share
  Thy blessing from on high:
We plead the promise of thy word;
Grant us thy Holy Spirit, Lord.

2 If earthly parents hear
  Their children when they cry, —
If they, with love sincere,
  Their varied wants supply,
Much more wilt thou thy love display,
And answer when thy children pray.

3 Our heavenly Father, thou;
  We, children of thy grace:
O, let thy Spirit now
  Descend and fill the place:
So shall we feel the heavenly flame,
And all unite to praise thy name.

4 And send thy Spirit down
  On all the nations, Lord,
With great success to crown
  The preaching of thy word,
Till heathen lands shall own thy sway,
And cast their idol gods away.
John Burton, 1824.

DOXOLOGY.

To God the Father's throne
  Perpetual honors raise;
Glory to God the Son,
  To God the Spirit praise;
And while our lips their tribute bring,
Our faith adores the name we sing.
Isaac Watts, 1709.

WORSHIP.

LANESBORO'. C. M.

1. Early, my God, without delay, I haste to seek thy face; My thirsty spirit faints away, My thirsty spirit faints away Without thy cheering grace.

21.   Psalm 63.

1 Early, my God, without delay,
   I haste to seek thy face;
 My thirsty spirit faints away
   Without thy cheering grace.

2 So pilgrims on the scorching sand,
   Beneath a burning sky,
 Long for a cooling stream at hand,
   And they must drink or die.

3 I've seen thy glory and thy power
   Through all thy temple shine;
 My God, repeat that heavenly hour,
   That vision so divine.

4 Not life itself, with all its joys,
   Can my best passions move,
 Or raise so high my cheerful voice,
   As thy forgiving love.

5 Thus, till my last expiring day,
   I'll bless my God and King;
 Thus will I lift my hands to pray,
   And tune my lips to sing.
          Isaac Watts, 1719.

22.   Psalm 5.

1 Lord, in the morning thou shalt hear
   My voice ascending high;
 To thee will I direct my prayer,
   To thee lift up mine eye:

2 Up to the hills where Christ is gone
   To plead for all his saints,
 Presenting at his Father's throne
   Our songs and our complaints.

3 Thou art a God before whose sight
   The wicked shall not stand;
 Sinners shall ne'er be thy delight,
   Nor dwell at thy right hand.

4 But to thy house will I resort
   To taste thy mercies there;
 I will frequent thy holy court,
   And worship in thy fear.

5 Oh may thy Spirit guide my feet
   In ways of righteousness!
 Make every path of duty straight
   And plain before my face.
          Isaac Watts, 1719.

23.   Psalm 27.

1 The Lord of Glory is my Light,
   And my Salvation too;
 God is my Strength, nor will I fear
   What all my foes can do.

2 One privilege my heart desires:
   Oh grant me an abode
 Among the churches of thy saints,
   The temples of my God.

3 There shall I offer my requests,
   And see thy beauty still;
 Shall hear thy messages of love,
   And there inquire thy will.

4 When troubles rise, and storms appear,
   There may his children hide;
 God has a strong pavilion where
   He makes my soul abide.

5 Now shall my head be lifted high
   Above my foes around,
 And songs of joy and victory
   Within thy temple sound.
          Isaac Watts, 1719.

WORSHIP.

HUMMEL. C. M.

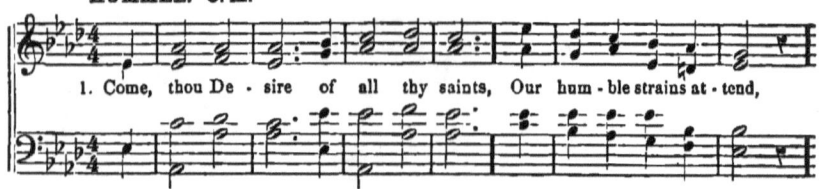

While with our prais-es and com-plaints Low at thy feet we bend.

24.

1 Come, thou Desire of all thy saints,
  Our humble strains attend,
  While with our praises and complaints
  Low at thy feet we bend.

2 When we thy wondrous glories hear,
  And all thy sufferings trace,
  What sweetly awful scenes appear,
  What rich unbounded grace!

3 How should our songs, like those above,
  With warm devotion rise!
  How should our souls, on wings of love,
  Mount upward to the skies!

4 Come, Lord, thy love alone can raise
  In us the heavenly flame,
  Then shall our lips resound thy praise,
  Our hearts adore thy name.

5 Dear Saviour, let thy glory shine
  And fill thy dwellings here,
  Till life, and love, and joy divine
  A heaven on earth appear.

6 Then shall our hearts enraptured say,
  Come, great Redeemer, come,
  And bring the bright, the glorious day,
  That calls thy children home!

Anne Steele, 1760.

25.

1 Whilst thee I seek, protecting Power,
  Be my vain wishes stilled;
  And may this consecrated hour
  With better hopes be filled.

2 Thy love the power of thought bestowed,
  To thee my thoughts would soar:
  Thy mercy o'er my life has flowed;
  That mercy I adore.

3 In each event of life, how clear
  Thy ruling hand I see!
  Each blessing to my soul more dear,
  Because conferred by thee.

4 In every joy that crowns my days,
  In every pain I bear,
  My heart shall find delight in praise,
  Or seek relief in prayer.

5 When gladness wings the favored hour,
  Thy love my thoughts shall fill;
  Resigned, when storms of sorrow lower,
  My soul shall meet thy will.

6 My lifted eye, without a tear,
  The gathering storm shall see;
  My steadfast heart shall know no fear;
  That heart will rest on thee.

Helen Maria Williams, 1786.

WORSHIP.

BROWNELL. L. M. 6 LINES.

1. Forth from the dark and stormy sky, Lord, to thine altar's shade we fly;
Forth from the world, its hope and fear, Saviour, we seek thy shelter here;
Weary and weak, thy grace we pray; Turn not, O Lord, thy guests away.

26.

1 Forth from the dark and stormy sky,
Lord, to thine altar's shade we fly;
Forth from the world, its hope and fear,
Saviour, we seek thy shelter here;
Weary and weak, thy grace we pray;
Turn not, O Lord, thy guests away.

2 Long have we roamed in want and pain;
Long have we sought thy rest in vain;
Wildered in doubt, in darkness lost,
Long have our souls been tempest-tost:
Low at thy feet our sins we lay;
Turn not, O Lord, thy guests away.
Reginald Heber, 1827.

27.

1 Lo! God is here! Let us adore,
  And own, how dreadful is this place!
Let all within us feel his power,
  And silent bow before his face;
Who know his power, his grace who prove,
Serve him with awe, with reverence love.

2 Lo! God is here! him day and night
  The united choirs of angels sing:
To him, enthroned above all height,
  Heaven's hosts their noblest praises bring:
Disdain not, Lord, our meaner song,
Who praise thee with a stammering tongue.

3 Gladly the toys of earth we leave,
  Wealth, pleasure, fame, for thee alone:
To thee our will, soul, flesh, we give;
  Oh take, oh seal them for thine own!
Thou art the God; thou art the Lord;
Be thou by all thy works adored.

4 Being of beings, may our praise
  Thy courts with grateful fragrance fill;
Still may we stand before thy face,
  Still hear and do thy sovereign will;
To thee may all our thoughts arise,
Ceaseless, accepted sacrifice!
Gerhard Tersteegen, 1730. Tr. *by John Wesley,* 1739.

WORSHIP.

HUMMEL. C. M.

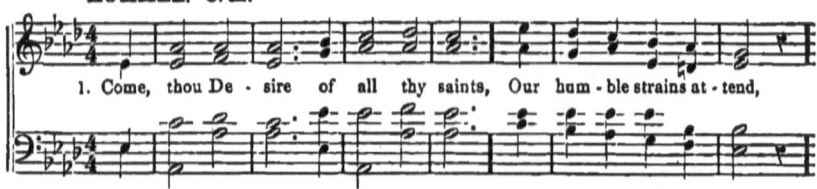

1. Come, thou Desire of all thy saints, Our humble strains attend, While with our praises and complaints Low at thy feet we bend.

24.

1 Come, thou Desire of all thy saints,
  Our humble strains attend,
  While with our praises and complaints
  Low at thy feet we bend.

2 When we thy wondrous glories hear,
  And all thy sufferings trace,
  What sweetly awful scenes appear,
  What rich unbounded grace!

3 How should our songs, like those above,
  With warm devotion rise!
  How should our souls, on wings of love,
  Mount upward to the skies!

4 Come, Lord, thy love alone can raise
  In us the heavenly flame,
  Then shall our lips resound thy praise,
  Our hearts adore thy name.

5 Dear Saviour, let thy glory shine
  And fill thy dwellings here,
  Till life, and love, and joy divine
  A heaven on earth appear.

6 Then shall our hearts enraptured say,
  Come, great Redeemer, come,
  And bring the bright, the glorious day,
  That calls thy children home!

Anne Steele, 1760.

25.

1 Whilst thee I seek, protecting Power,
  Be my vain wishes stilled;
  And may this consecrated hour
  With better hopes be filled.

2 Thy love the power of thought bestowed,
  To thee my thoughts would soar:
  Thy mercy o'er my life has flowed;
  That mercy I adore.

3 In each event of life, how clear
  Thy ruling hand I see!
  Each blessing to my soul more dear,
  Because conferred by thee.

4 In every joy that crowns my days,
  In every pain I bear,
  My heart shall find delight in praise,
  Or seek relief in prayer.

5 When gladness wings the favored hour,
  Thy love my thoughts shall fill;
  Resigned, when storms of sorrow lower,
  My soul shall meet thy will.

6 My lifted eye, without a tear,
  The gathering storm shall see;
  My steadfast heart shall know no fear;
  That heart will rest on thee.

Helen Maria Williams, 1786.

WORSHIP.

BROWNELL. L. M. 6 LINES.

1. Forth from the dark and stormy sky, Lord, to thine altar's shade we fly;
Forth from the world, its hope and fear, Saviour, we seek thy shelter here;
Weary and weak, thy grace we pray; Turn not, O Lord, thy guests away.

26.

1 Forth from the dark and stormy sky,
  Lord, to thine altar's shade we fly;
  Forth from the world, its hope and fear,
  Saviour, we seek thy shelter here;
  Weary and weak, thy grace we pray;
  Turn not, O Lord, thy guests away.

2 Long have we roamed in want and pain;
  Long have we sought thy rest in vain;
  Wildered in doubt, in darkness lost,
  Long have our souls been tempest-tost;
  Low at thy feet our sins we lay;
  Turn not, O Lord, thy guests away.
  Reginald Heber, 1827.

27.

1 Lo! God is here! Let us adore,
    And own, how dreadful is this place!
  Let all within us feel his power,
    And silent bow before his face;
  Who know his power, his grace who prove,
  Serve him with awe, with reverence love.

2 Lo! God is here! him day and night
    The united choirs of angels sing:
  To him, enthroned above all height,
    Heaven's hosts their noblest praises bring:
  Disdain not, Lord, our meaner song,
  Who praise thee with a stammering tongue.

3 Gladly the toys of earth we leave,
    Wealth, pleasure, fame, for thee alone:
  To thee our will, soul, flesh, we give;
    Oh take, oh seal them for thine own!
  Thou art the God; thou art the Lord;
  Be thou by all thy works adored.

4 Being of beings, may our praise
    Thy courts with grateful fragrance fill;
  Still may we stand before thy face,
    Still hear and do thy sovereign will;
  To thee may all our thoughts arise,
  Ceaseless, accepted sacrifice!
  Gerhard Tersteegen, 1730. Tr. by John Wesley, 1739.

WORSHIP.

BEMERTON. C. M.

1. What shall I ren-der to my God For all his kind-ness shown? My feet shall vi-sit thine a-bode, My songs ad-dress thy throne.

28. PSALM 116.

1 WHAT shall I render to my God
   For all his kindness shown?
   My feet shall visit thine abode,
   My songs address thy throne.

2 Among the saints that fill thine house
   My offering shall be paid;
   There shall my zeal perform the vows
   My soul in anguish made.

3 How much is mercy thy delight,
   Thou ever blesséd God!
   How dear thy servants in thy sight!
   How precious is their blood!

4 How happy all thy servants are!
   How great thy grace to me!
   My life, which thou hast made thy care,
   Lord, I devote to thee.

5 Now I am thine, for ever thine,
   Nor shall my purpose move;
   Thy hand has loosed my bonds of pain,
   And bound me with thy love.

6 Here in thy courts I leave my vow,
   And thy rich grace record;
   Witness, ye saints, who hear me now,
   If I forsake the Lord.

Isaac Watts, 1719.

29.

1 LORD, when we bend before thy throne,
   And our confessions pour,
   Teach us to feel the sins we own,
   And hate what we deplore.

2 Our broken spirits pitying see,
   And penitence impart;
   Then let a kindling glance from thee
   Beam hope upon the heart.

3 When our responsive tongues essay
   Their grateful hymns to raise,
   Grant that our souls may join the lay,
   And mount to thee in praise.

4 Then on thy glories while we dwell,
   Thy mercies we'll review,
   Till love divine transported tell
   Our God's our Father too.

5 When we disclose our wants in prayer,
   May we our wills resign,
   And not a thought our bosoms share
   Which is not wholly thine.

6 Let faith each meek petition fill,
   And waft it to the skies,
   And teach our hearts 'tis goodness, still,
   That grants it, or denies.

Joseph D. Carlyle, 1805.

WORSHIP.

NUREMBURG. 7s.

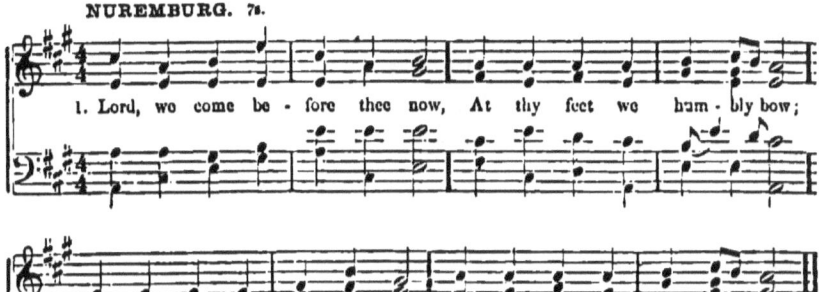
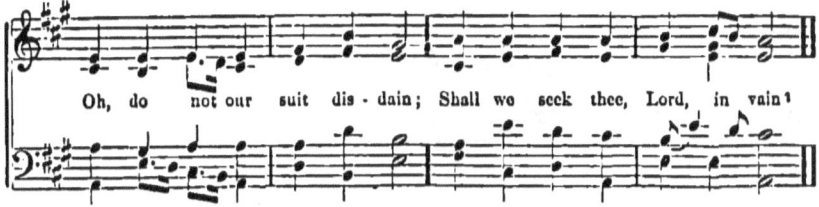

30.

1 Lord, we come before thee now,
At thy feet we humbly bow;
Oh, do not our suit disdain;
Shall we seek thee, Lord, in vain?

2 Lord, on thee our souls depend;
In compassion now descend;
Fill our hearts with thy rich grace,
Tune our lips to sing thy praise.

3 In thine own appointed way
Now we seek thee, here we stay;
Lord, we know not how to go
Till a blessing thou bestow.

4 Send some message from thy word
That may joy and peace afford;
Let thy Spirit now impart
Full salvation to each heart.

5 Comfort those who weep and mourn;
Let the time of joy return;
Those who are cast down, lift up,
Strong in faith, in love and hope.

6 Grant that all may seek and find
Thee a God supremely kind;
Heal the sick, the captive free,
Let us all rejoice in thee.
William Hammond, 1745.

31.

1 To thy temple I repair;
Lord, I love to worship there,
When within the veil I meet
Christ before the mercy-seat.

2 While thy glorious praise is sung,
Touch my lips, unloose my tongue,
That my joyful soul may bless
Thee, the Lord my Righteousness.

3 While the prayers of saints ascend,
God of love, to mine attend;
Hear me, for thy Spirit pleads;
Hear, for Jesus intercedes.

4 While I hearken to thy law,
Fill my soul with humble awe,
Till thy gospel bring to me
Life and immortality.

5 While thy ministers proclaim
Peace and pardon in thy name,
Through their voice, by faith, may I
Hear thee speaking from the sky.

6 From thy house when I return,
May my heart within me burn;
And at evening let me say,
I have walked with God to-day!
James Montgomery, 1825.

DOXOLOGY.

Holy Father, hear our cry,
Through thy Son, our Lord most High,
Whom our thankful hearts adore
With the Spirit evermore.
Charles Coffin, 1676-1749.

WORSHIP.

GERAR. S. M.

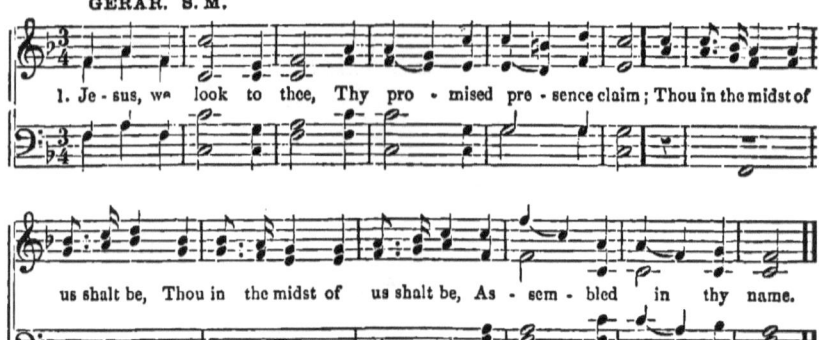

1. Je-sus, we look to thee, Thy pro-mised pre-sence claim; Thou in the midst of us shalt be, Thou in the midst of us shalt be, As-sem-bled in thy name.

32.

1 Jesus, we look to thee,
  Thy promised presence claim;
  Thou in the midst of us shalt be,
  Assembled in thy name.

2 Thy name salvation is,
  Which here we come to prove;
  Thy name is life, and health, and peace,
  And everlasting love.

3 Not in the name of pride
  Or selfishness we meet;
  From nature's paths we turn aside,
  And worldly thoughts forget.

4 We meet the grace to take
  Which thou hast freely given;
  We meet on earth for thy dear sake,
  That we may meet in heaven.

5 Present we know thou art,
  But oh thyself reveal!
  Now, Lord, let every bounding heart
  The mighty comfort feel.

6 Oh may thy quick'ning voice
  The death of sin remove,
  And bid our inmost souls rejoice
  In hope of perfect love.
    Charles Wesley, 1740.

33.

1 How charming is the place
  Where my Redeemer, God,
  Unveils the beauties of his face,
  And sheds his love abroad!

2 Not the fair palaces,
  To which the great resort,
  Are once to be compared with this,
  Where Jesus holds his court.

3 Here, on the mercy-seat,
  With radiant glory crowned,
  Our joyful eyes behold him sit,
  And smile on all around.

4 To him their prayers and cries
  Each humble soul presents;
  He listens to their broken sighs,
  And grants them all their wants.

5 To them his sovereign will
  He graciously imparts,
  And in return accepts, with smiles,
  The tribute of their hearts.

6 Give me, O Lord, a place
  Within thy blest abode,
  Among the children of thy grace,
  The servants of my God.
    Samuel Stennett, 1787.

DOXOLOGY.

1 Let God the Maker's name
  Have honor, love, and fear,
  To God the Saviour pay the same,
  And God the Comforter.

2 Father of lights above,
  Thy mercy we adore,
  The Son of thy eternal love,
  And Spirit of thy power.
    Isaac Watts, 1709.

WORSHIP.

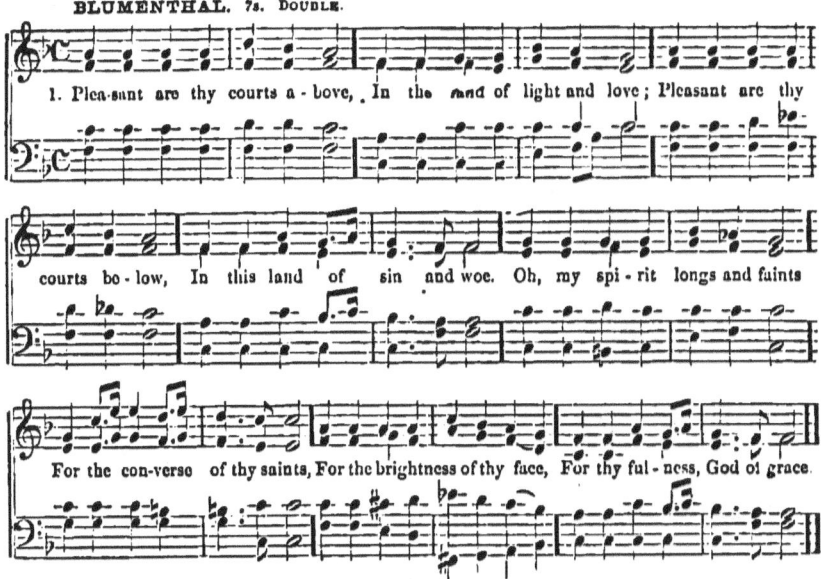

BLUMENTHAL. 7s. DOUBLE.

1. Pleasant are thy courts above, In the land of light and love; Pleasant are thy courts below, In this land of sin and woe. Oh, my spirit longs and faints For the converse of thy saints, For the brightness of thy face, For thy fulness, God of grace.

34.   PSALM 84.

1 PLEASANT are thy courts above
In the land of light and love;
Pleasant are thy courts below
In this land of sin and woe.
Oh, my spirit longs and faints
For the converse of thy saints,
For the brightness of thy face,
For thy fulness, God of grace.

2 Happy birds that sing and fly
Round thy altars, O Most High;
Happier souls that find a rest
In a heavenly Father's breast;
Like the wandering dove that found
No repose on earth around,
They can to their ark repair,
And enjoy it ever there.

3 Happy souls, their praises flow,
Even in this vale of woe;
Waters in the deserts rise,
Manna feeds them from the skies;
On they go from strength to strength,
Till they reach thy throne at length,
At thy feet adoring fall,
Who hast led them safe through all.

4 Lord, be mine this prize to win,
Guide me through a world of sin,
Keep me by thy saving grace,
Give me at thy side a place.
Sun and shield alike thou art,
Guide and guard my erring heart;
Grace and glory flow from thee;
Shower, oh shower them, Lord, on me.
H. F. Lyte, 1834.

35.

1 JESUS, God of love, attend,
From thy glorious throne descend;
Answer now some waiting heart,
Now some hardened soul convert:
To our Advocate we fly,
Let us feel Immanuel nigh;
Manifest thy love abroad,
Make us now the sons of God.

2 Prostrate at thy mercy-seat
Let us our Beloved meet,
Give us in thyself a part
Deep engraven on thine heart:
Let us hear thy pardoning voice,
Bid the broken bones rejoice;
Condemnation do away,
Oh make this the perfect day!
Augustus M. Toplady, 1759.

WORSHIP.

DUNDEE. C. M.

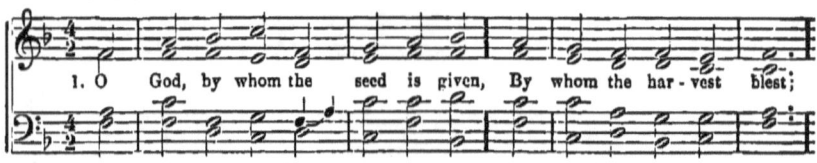

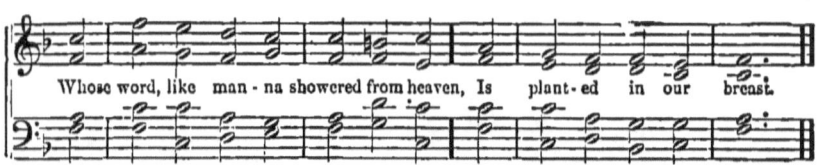

1. O God, by whom the seed is given, By whom the har-vest blest;
Whose word, like man-na showered from heaven, Is plant-ed in our breast.

36. Matt. xiii. 3–8.

1 O God, by whom the seed is given,
   By whom the harvest blest;
   Whose word, like manna showered from heaven,
   Is planted in our breast:

2 Preserve it from the passing feet,
   And plunderers of the air;
   The sultry sun's intenser heat,
   And weeds of worldly care.

3 Though buried deep, or thinly strewn,
   Do thou thy grace supply;
   The hope in earthly furrows sown
   Shall ripen in the sky.
   Reginald Heber, 1827.

37. Matt. xiii. 3–8.

1 Almighty God, thy word is cast
   Like seed into the ground;
   Oh may it grow in humble hearts,
   And righteous fruits abound.

2 Let not the foe of Christ and man
   This holy seed remove,
   But give it root in praying souls
   To bring forth fruits of love.

3 Let not the world's deceitful cares
   The rising plant destroy,
   But may it, in converted minds,
   Produce the fruits of joy.

4 Let not thy word, so kindly sent
   To raise us to thy throne,
   Return to thee, and sadly tell
   That we reject thy Son.

5 Great God, come down, and on thy word
   Thy mighty power bestow,
   That all who hear the joyful sound,
   Thy saving grace may know.
   John Cawood, 1825.

38.

1 Long have I sat beneath the sound
   Of thy salvation, Lord;
   But still how weak my faith is found,
   And knowledge of thy word!

2 Oft I frequent thy holy place,
   And hear almost in vain;
   How small a portion of thy grace
   My memory can retain!

3 How cold and feeble is my love!
   How negligent my fear!
   How low my hope of joys above!
   How few affections there!

4 Great God! thy sovereign power impart,
   To give thy word success:
   Write thy salvation in my heart,
   And make me learn thy grace.

5 Show my forgetful feet the way
   That leads to joys on high:
   There knowledge grows without decay,
   And love shall never die.
   Isaac Watts, 1709.

Doxology.

To Father, Son, and Holy Ghost,
   One God, whom we adore,
   Be glory as it was, is now,
   And shall be evermore!
   Tate and Brady, 1696.

WORSHIP.

39. PSALM 95.

1 COME, sound his praise abroad,
  And hymns of glory sing!
  Jehovah is the sovereign God,
  The universal King.

2 He formed the deeps unknown;
  He gave the seas their bound;
  The watery worlds are all his own,
  And all the solid ground.

3 Come, worship at his throne.
  Come, bow before the Lord;
  We are his work, and not our own;
  He formed us by his word.

4 To-day attend his voice,
  Nor dare provoke his rod;
  Come, like the people of his choice,
  And own your gracious God.
    Isaac Watts, 1719.

40. PSALM 48.

1 FAR as thy name is known
  The world declares thy praise;
  Thy saints, O Lord, before thy throne
  Their songs of honor raise.

2 With joy let Judah stand
  On Zion's chosen hill,
  Proclaim the wonders of thy hand,
  And counsels of thy will.

3 Let strangers walk around
  The city where we dwell,
  Compass and view the holy ground,
  And mark the building well,

4 The order of thy house,
  The worship of thy court,
  The cheerful songs, the solemn vows,
  And make a fair report.

5 How decent and how wise!
  How glorious to behold!
  Beyond the pomp that charms the eyes,
  And rites adorned with gold.

6 The God we worship now
  Will guide us till we die;
  Will be our God while here below,
  And ours above the sky.
    Isaac Watts, 1719.

41.

1 ONCE more before we part,
  O bless the Saviour's name:
  Let every tongue and every heart
  Adore and praise the same.

2 Lord, in thy grace we came,
  That blessing still impart;
  We met in Jesus' sacred name,
  In Jesus' name we part.

3 Still on thy holy word
  Help us to feed, and grow,
  Still to go on to know the Lord,
  And practise what we know.

4 Now, Lord, before we part,
  Help us to bless thy name:
  Let every tongue and every heart
  Adore and praise the same.
    Joseph Hart, 1762.

WORSHIP.

ARNHEIM. L. M.

1. Ho-san-na to the liv-ing Lord! Ho-san-na to th' In-car-nate Word!
To Christ, Cre-a-tor, Sa-viour, King, Let earth, let heav'n, ho-san-na sing.

42.

1 HOSANNA to the living Lord!
Hosanna to the Incarnate Word!
To Christ, Creator, Saviour, King,
Let earth, let heaven, hosanna sing.

2 Hosanna, Lord, thine angels cry;
Hosanna, Lord, thy saints reply;
Above, beneath us, and around,
The dead and living swell the sound.

3 O Saviour, with protecting care,
Return to this thy house of prayer;
Assembled in thy sacred name,
Here we thy parting promise claim.

4 But, chiefest, in our cleansèd breast,
Eternal, bid thy Spirit rest,
And make our secret soul to be
A temple pure, and worthy thee.

5 So, in the last and dreadful day,
When earth and heaven shall melt away,
Thy flock, redeemed from sinful stain,
Shall swell the sound of praise again.

Reginald Heber, 1811.

43.   EPH. iii. 17-23.

1 COME, dearest Lord, descend and dwell
By faith and love in every breast;
Then shall we know, and taste, and feel
The joys that cannot be expressed.

2 Come, fill our hearts with inward strength,
Make our enlargèd souls possess,
And learn the height, and breadth, and length
Of thine unmeasurable grace.

3 Now to the God whose power can do
More than our thoughts and wishes know,
Be everlasting honors done,
By all the church, through Christ his Son.

Isaac Watts, 1709.

44.

1 LORD, now we part in thy blest name,
In which we here together came;
Grant us, our few remaining days,
To work thy will and spread thy praise.

2 Teach us in life and death to bless
Thee, Lord, our strength and righteousness;
Grant that we all may meet above,
Where we shall better sing thy love.

3 To God the Father, God the Son,
And God the Spirit, three in one,
Be honor, praise, and glory given,
By all on earth, and all in heaven.

Reginald Heber, 1812.

45.

1 DISMISS us with thy blessing, Lord;
Help us to feed upon thy word;
All that has been amiss, forgive,
And let thy truth within us live.

2 Though we are guilty, thou art good:
Wash all our works in Jesus' blood;
Give every burdened soul release,
And bid us all depart in peace.

Joseph Hart, 1762.

WORSHIP.

SICILIAN HYMN. 8s, 7s & 4s.

1. In thy name, O Lord, as-sem-bling, We, thy peo-ple, now draw near;

Teach us to re-joice with trembling; Speak, and let thy ser-vants hear,
Hear with meekness, Hear with meekness, Hear thy word with god-ly fear.

46.

1 In thy name, O Lord, assembling,
  We, thy people, now draw near;
  Teach us to rejoice with trembling;
  Speak, and let thy servants hear,—
    Hear with meekness,
  Hear thy word with godly fear.

2 While our days on earth are lengthened,
  May we give them, Lord, to thee;
  Cheered by hope, and daily strengthened,
  We would run, nor weary be,
    Till thy glory,
  Without clouds, in heaven we see.

3 There, in worship purer, sweeter,
  All thy people shall adore,
  Tasting of enjoyment greater
  Than they could conceive before,—
    Full enjoyment,—
  Full, unmixed, and evermore.

Thomas Kelly, 1815.

47.

1 Lord, dismiss us with thy blessing;
  Fill our hearts with joy and peace;

Let us each, thy love possessing,
  Triumph in redeeming grace:
    Oh refresh us,
  Travelling through this wilderness.

2 Thanks we give, and adoration,
  For thy gospel's joyful sound;
  May the fruits of thy salvation
  In our hearts and lives abound;
    Ever faithful
  To the truth may we be found.

3 So, whene'er the signal's given
  Us from earth to call away,
  Borne on angels' wings to heaven,
  Glad the summons to obey,
    May we ever
  Reign with Christ in endless day!

Walter Shirley, 1779.

DOXOLOGY.

Glory be to God the Father!
  Glory be to God the Son!
Glory be to God the Spirit!
  Great Jehovah, Three in One:
    Glory, glory,
  While eternal ages run.

Horatius Bonar, 1862.

THE LORD'S DAY.

PAX DEI. 10s.

1. Saviour, again to thy dear name we raise With one accord our parting hymn of praise; We rise to bless thee ere our worship cease, And, now departing, wait thy word of peace. A-men.

48.

1 Saviour, again to thy dear name we raise
  With one accord our parting hymn of praise;
  We rise to bless thee ere our worship cease,
  And, now departing, wait thy word of peace.

2 Grant us thy peace upon our homeward way;
  With thee began, with thee shall end the day;
  Guard thou the lips from sin, the hearts from shame,
  That in this house have called upon thy name.

3 Grant us thy peace, Lord, through the coming night,
  Turn thou for us its darkness into light;
  From harm and danger keep thy children free,
  For dark and light are both alike to thee.

4 Grant us thy peace throughout our earthly life,
  Our balm in sorrow, and our stay in strife;
  Then, when thy voice shall bid our conflict cease,
  Call us, O Lord, to thine eternal peace.
    J. Ellerton, 1861.

49.
  The Lord's Day:

1 Again returns the day of holy rest,
  Which, when he made the world, Jehovah blest;
  When, like his own, he bade our labors cease,
  And all be piety, and all be peace.

2 Let us devote this consecrated day
  To learn his will, and all we learn obey;
  So shall he hear when fervently we raise
  Our choral harmony in hymns of praise.

3 Father in heaven! in whom our hopes confide,
  Whose power defends us, and whose precepts guide;
  In life our Guardian, and in death our Friend;
  Glory supreme be thine, till time shall end.
    William Mason, 1811.

THE LORD'S DAY. 27

LEIGHTON. S. M.

1. Welcome, sweet day of rest, That saw the Lord arise; Welcome to this reviving breast And these rejoicing eyes.

50.

1 WELCOME, sweet day of rest,
  That saw the Lord arise;
  Welcome to this reviving breast
  And these rejoicing eyes.

2 The King himself comes near,
  And feasts his saints to-day;
  Here we may sit, and see him here,
  And love, and praise, and pray.

3 One day amidst the place
  Where my dear God hath been,
  Is sweeter than ten thousand days
  Of pleasurable sin.

4 My willing soul would stay
  In such a frame as this,
  And sit and sing herself away
  To everlasting bliss.
      Isaac Watts, 1709.

51.

1 SWEET is the work, O Lord,
  Thy glorious acts to sing,
  To praise thy name, and hear thy word,
  And grateful offerings bring.

2 Sweet, at the dawning light,
  Thy boundless love to tell;
  And, when approach the shades of night,
  Still on the theme to dwell.

3 Sweet, on this day of rest,
  To join in heart and voice
  With those who love and serve thee best,
  And in thy name rejoice.

4 To songs of praise and joy
  Be every Sabbath given,
  That such may be our blest employ
  Eternally in heaven.
      H. F. Lyte, 1834.

52.   PSALM 118.

1 SEE what a living Stone
  The builders did refuse!
  Yet God has built his church thereon,
  In spite of envious Jews.

2 The scribe and angry priest
  Reject thine only Son;
  Yet on this Rock shall Zion rest,
  As the chief corner-stone.

3 The work, O Lord, is thine,
  And wondrous in our eyes;
  This day declares it all divine;
  This day did Jesus rise.

4 This is the glorious day
  That our Redeemer made:
  Let us rejoice, and sing, and pray;
  Let all the church be glad.

5 Hosanna to the King
  Of David's royal blood:
  Bless him, ye saints! he comes to bring
  Salvation from your God.

6 We bless thine holy word,
  Which all this grace displays,
  And offer on thine altar, Lord,
  Our sacrifice of praise.
      Isaac Watts, 1719.

THE LORD'S DAY.

RAPTURE. C. P. M.

1. The fes-tal morn, my God, is come, That calls me to thy hon-ored dome,

Thy pres-ence to a-dore; My feet the sum-mons shall at-tend,

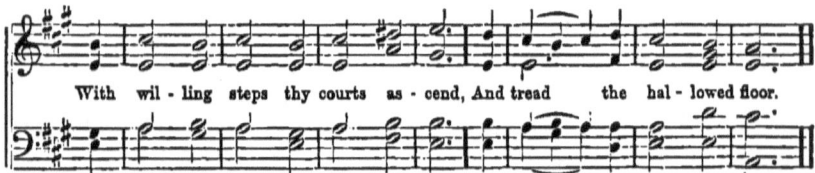
With wil-ling steps thy courts as-cend, And tread the hal-lowed floor.

---

53. PSALM 122.

1 THE festal morn, my God, is come,
   That calls me to thy honored dome,
     Thy presence to adore;
   My feet the summons shall attend,
   With willing steps thy courts ascend,
     And tread the hallowed floor.

2 Hither from Judah's utmost end
   The heaven-protected tribes ascend,
     Their offerings hither bring:
   Here, eager to attest their joy,
   In hymns of praise their tongues employ,
     And hail the immortal King.

3 Be peace implored by each on thee,
   O Zion, while with bended knee
     To Jacob's God we pray;
   How blest, who calls himself thy friend!
   Success his labor shall attend,
     And safety guard his way.

4 Seat of my friends and brethren, hail!
   How can my tongue, O Zion, fail
     To bless thy loved abode?
   How cease the zeal that in me glows,
   Thy good to seek, whose walls enclose
     The mansions of my God?

5 With joy shall I behold the day
   That calls my thirsting soul away
     To dwell among the blest!
   For lo, my great Redeemer's power
   Unfolds the everlasting door,
     And leads me to his rest!
         James Merrick, 1765. a.

DOXOLOGY.

To Father, Son, and Holy Ghost,
The God whom heaven's triumphant host
  And saints on earth adore,
Be glory as in ages past,
As now it is, and so shall last
  When time shall be no more.
         Tate and Brady, 1696.

THE LORD'S DAY.

JENNER. 7s & 6s.

O day of rest and gladness, O day of joy and light, O balm of care and sadness, Most beautiful, most bright! On thee the high and lowly Before th' eternal throne Sing Holy, Holy, Holy, To the great THREE IN ONE! A-men.

54.

1 O DAY of rest and gladness,
   O day of joy and light,
   O balm of care and sadness,
   Most beautiful, most bright!
   On thee the high and lowly,
   Before th' eternal throne,
   Sing Holy, Holy, Holy,
   To the great THREE IN ONE!

2 On thee, at the creation,
   The light first had its birth;
   On thee, for our salvation,
   Christ rose from depths of earth;
   On thee our Lord victorious
   The Spirit sent from heaven;
   And thus on thee most glorious
   A triple light was given.

3 Thou art a cooling fountain
   In life's dry, dreary sand;
   From thee, like Pisgah's mountain,
   We view our promised land;

   A day of sweet refection,
   A day of holy love,
   A day of resurrection
   From earth to things above.

4 To-day on weary nations
   The heavenly manna falls;
   To holy convocations
   The silver trumpet calls,
   Where gospel-light is glowing
   With pure and radiant beams,
   And living water flowing
   With soul-refreshing streams.

5 New graces ever gaining
   From this our day of rest,
   We reach the Rest remaining
   To spirits of the blest.
   To Holy Ghost be praises,
   To Father and to Son;
   The church her voice upraises
   To thee, blest THREE IN ONE.

Christopher Wordsworth, 1865.

THE LORD'S DAY.

DARWELL. H. M.

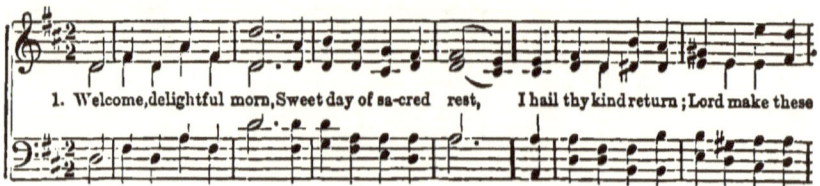

1. Welcome, delightful morn, Sweet day of sacred rest, I hail thy kind return; Lord make these moments blest. From low desires and fleeting toys, I soar to reach immortal joys.

55.

1 Welcome, delightful morn,
   Sweet day of sacred rest,
   I hail thy kind return;
   Lord, make these moments blest.
   From low desires and fleeting toys,
   I soar to reach immortal joys.

2 Now may the King descend,
   And fill his throne of grace;
   Thy sceptre, Lord, extend,
   While saints address thy face:
   Let sinners feel thy quickening word,
   And learn to know and fear the Lord.

3 Descend, celestial Dove,
   With all thy quickening powers;
   Disclose a Saviour's love,
   And bless the sacred hours:
   Then shall my soul new life obtain,
   Nor Sabbaths be indulged in vain.
   Hayward.

56.

1 Awake, our drowsy souls,
   Shake off each slothful band;
   The wonders of this day
   Our noblest songs demand.
   Auspicious morn! thy blissful rays,
   Bright seraphs hail in songs of praise.

2 At thy approaching dawn,
   Reluctant death resigned
   The glorious Prince of Life,
   In dark domains confined:
   The angelic host around him bends,
   And 'midst their shouts the God ascends.

3 All hail, triumphant Lord!
   Heaven with hosannas rings;
   While earth, in humbler strains,
   Thy praise responsive sings:
   "Worthy art thou, who once wast slain,
   Through endless years to live and reign."

4 Gird on, great God, thy sword,
   Ascend thy conquering car;
   While justice, truth, and love
   Maintain the glorious war:
   Victorious, thou thy foes shalt tread,
   And sin and hell in triumph lead.

5 Make bare thy potent arm,
   And wing the unerring dart,
   With salutary pangs,
   To each rebellious heart:
   Then dying souls for life shall sue,
   Numerous as drops of morning dew.
   Elizabeth Scott, 1763.

THE LORD'S DAY.

MISSIONARY CHANT. L. M.

1. Sweet is the work, my God, my King, To praise thy name, give thanks and sing, To show thy love by morning light, And talk of all thy truth at night.

57.   *Psalm 92.*

1 Sweet is the work, my God, my King,
To praise thy name, give thanks, and
   sing,
To show thy love by morning light,
And talk of all thy truth at night.

2 Sweet is the day of sacred rest;
No mortal care shall seize my breast;
Oh, may my heart in tune be found,
Like David's harp of solemn sound!

3 My heart shall triumph in my Lord,
And bless his works, and bless his word:
Thy works of grace, how bright they
   shine!
How deep thy counsels, how divine!

4 Fools never raise their thoughts so high:
Like brutes they live, like brutes they die;
Like grass they flourish, till thy breath
Blasts them in everlasting death.

5 But I shall share a glorious part,
When grace hath well refined my heart,
And fresh supplies of joy are shed,
Like holy oil, to cheer my head.

6 Then shall I see, and hear, and know
All I desired or wished below;
And every power find sweet employ
In that eternal world of joy.
Isaac Watts, 1719.

58.

1 Another six days' work is done,
Another Sabbath is begun;
Return, my soul, enjoy thy rest,
Improve the day thy God hath blest.

2 Oh, that our thoughts and thanks may
   rise,
As grateful incense, to the skies;
And draw from heaven that sweet repose
Which none but he that feels it knows!

3 This heavenly calm within the breast
Is the dear pledge of glorious rest,
Which for the church of God remains:
The end of cares, the end of pains.

4 In holy duties let the day,
In holy pleasures, pass away:
How sweet a Sabbath thus to spend,
In hope of one that ne'er shall end!
Joseph Stennett, 1734.

59.

1 Blest hour when mortal man retires
To hold communion with his God,
To send to heaven his warm desires,
And listen to the sacred word.

2 Blest hour when earthly cares resign
Their empire o'er his anxious breast;
While, all around, the calm divine
Proclaims the holy day of rest.

3 Blest hour when God himself draws nigh,
Well pleased his people's voice to hear,
To hush the penitential sigh,
And wipe away the mourner's tear.

4 Blest hour! for, where the Lord resorts,
Foretastes of future bliss are given;
And mortals find his earthly courts
The house of God, the gate of heaven.
Thomas Raffles, 1788-1863.

THE LORD'S DAY.

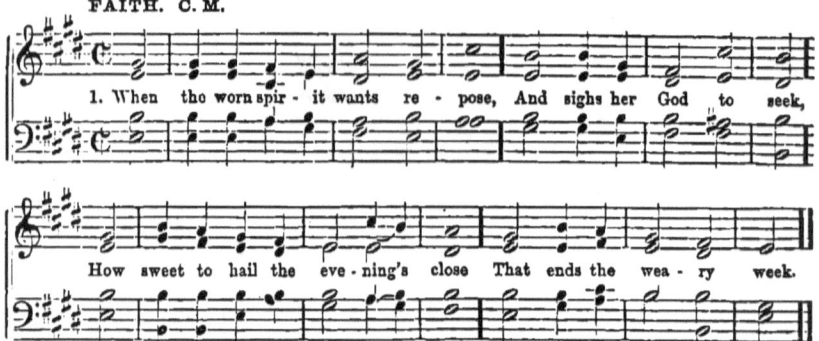

FAITH. C. M.

1. When the worn spir-it wants re-pose, And sighs her God to seek, How sweet to hail the eve-ning's close That ends the wea-ry week.

60.

1 When the worn spirit wants repose,
  And sighs her God to seek,
  How sweet to hail the evening's close
  That ends the weary week!

2 How sweet to hail the early dawn,
  That opens on the sight,
  When first that soul-reviving morn
  Sheds forth new rays of light!

3 Sweet day, thine hours too soon will cease;
  Yet, while they gently roll,
  Breathe, heavenly Spirit, source of peace,
  A Sabbath o'er my soul.

4 When will my pilgrimage be done;
  The world's long week be o'er;
  That Sabbath dawn which needs no sun;
  That day which fades no more?
  James Edmeston, 1820.

61.

1 Frequent the day of God returns
  To shed its quickening beams;
  And yet how slow devotion burns!
  How languid are its flames!

2 Accept our faint attempts to love;
  Our follies, Lord, forgive:
  We would be like thy saints above,
  And praise thee while we live.

3 Increase, O Lord, our faith and hope;
  And fit us to ascend
  Where the assembly ne'er breaks up,
  And Sabbaths never end;

4 Where we shall breathe in heavenly air,
  With heavenly lustre shine,
  Before the throne of God appear,
  And feast on love divine.

5 There shall we join, and never tire,
  To sing immortal lays;
  And, with the bright, seraphic choir,
  Sound forth Immanuel's praise.
  Simon Browne, 1720.

62.

1 O Father, though the anxious fear
  May cloud to-morrow's way,
  Nor fear nor doubt shall enter here:
  All shall be thine to-day.

2 We will not bring divided hearts
  To worship at thy shrine;
  But each unholy thought departs,
  And leaves the temple thine.

3 Sleep, sleep to-day, tormenting cares,
  Of earth and folly born;
  Ye shall not dim the light that streams
  From this celestial morn.

4 To-morrow will be time enough
  To feel your harsh control;
  Ye shall not violate this day,
  The Sabbath of my soul.

5 Sleep, sleep forever, guilty thoughts;
  Let fires of vengeance die;
  And purged from sin, may I behold
  A God of purity.
  Anna Laetitia Barbauld, 1825.

THE LORD'S DAY.

SABBATH. 7s. 6 LINES.

63.

1 SAFELY through another week
    God has brought us on our way;
  Let us now a blessing seek,
    Waiting in his courts to-day:
  Day of all the week the best,
  Emblem of eternal rest.

2 While we pray for pardoning grace,
    Through the dear Redeemer's name,
  Show thy reconciled face,
    Take away our sin and shame;
  From our worldly care set free,
  May we rest, this day, in thee.

3 Here we come thy name to praise;
    Let us feel thy presence near;
  May thy glory meet our eyes,
    While we in thy house appear;
  Here afford us, Lord, a taste
  Of our everlasting feast.

4 May thy gospel's joyful sound
    Conquer sinners, comfort saints,
  Make the fruits of grace abound,
    Bring relief from all complaints:
  Thus may all our Sabbaths prove,
  Till we join the church above.

John Newton, 1779.

64.

1 ON this day, the first of days,
  God the Father's name we praise;
  Who, creation's Fount and Spring,
  Did the world from darkness bring.

2 On this day th' Eternal Son
  Over death his triumph won;
  On this day the Spirit came
  With his gifts of living flame.

3 Father, who didst fashion me
  Image of thyself to be,
  Fill me with thy love divine,
  Let my every thought be thine.

4 Holy Jesus, may I be
  Dead and buried here with thee;
  And, by love inflamed, arise
  Unto thee a sacrifice.

5 Thou who dost all gifts impart,
  Shine, sweet Spirit, in my heart;
  Best of gifts, thyself, bestow;
  Make me burn thy love to know.

6 God, the blessed THREE IN ONE,
  Dwell within my heart alone;
  Thou dost give thyself to me,
  May I give myself to thee.

From the Latin by Sir H. W. Baker, 1860.

THE LORD'S DAY.

WARWICK. C. M.

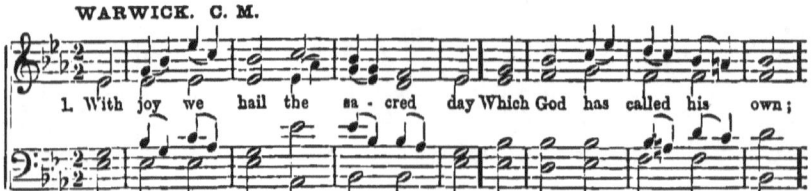
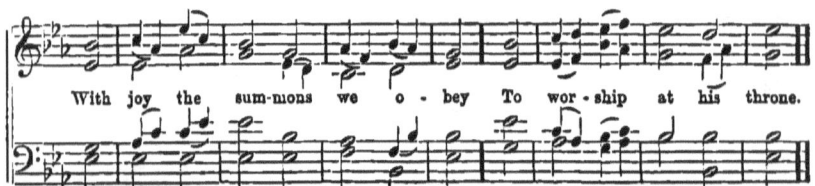

1. With joy we hail the sacred day Which God has called his own;
With joy the summons we obey To worship at his throne.

65.

1 With joy we hail the sacred day
   Which God has called his own;
   With joy the summons we obey
   To worship at his throne.

2 Thy chosen temple, Lord, how fair!
   Where willing votaries throng
   To breathe the humble, fervent prayer,
   And pour the choral song.

3 Spirit of grace! oh, deign to dwell
   Within thy church below;
   Make her in holiness excel,
   With pure devotion glow.

4 Let peace within her walls be found;
   Let all her sons unite,
   To spread with grateful zeal around
   Her clear and shining light.

5 Great God, we hail the sacred day
   Which thou hast called thine own;
   With joy the summons we obey
   To worship at thy throne.
   H. F. Lyte, 1834.

66. PSALM CXVIII. 24-26.

1 This is the day the Lord hath made;
   He calls the hours his own;
   Let heaven rejoice, let earth be glad,
   And praise surround the throne.

2 To-day he rose and left the dead,
   And Satan's empire fell;
   To-day the saints his triumphs spread,
   And all his wonders tell.

3 Hosanna to th' anointed King,
   To David's holy Son;
   Help us, O Lord; descend and bring
   Salvation from thy throne.

4 Blest be the Lord, who comes to men
   With messages of grace;
   Who comes in God the Father's name,
   To save our sinful race.

5 Hosanna in the highest strains
   The Church on earth can raise!
   The highest heavens, in which he reigns,
   Shall give him nobler praise.
   Isaac Watts, 1719.

67.

1 Blest morning, whose young dawning rays
   Beheld our rising God;
   That saw him triumph o'er the dust,
   And leave his dark abode!

2 In the cold prison of a tomb
   The dead Redeemer lay,
   Till the revolving skies had brought
   The third, th' appointed day.

3 Hell and the grave unite their force
   To hold our God in vain;
   The sleeping Conqueror arose,
   And burst their feeble chain.

4 To thy great name, Almighty Lord,
   These sacred hours we pay;
   And loud hosannas shall proclaim
   The triumph of the day.
   Isaac Watts, 1709.

THE LORD'S DAY. 85

DOWNS. C. M.

1. Again the Lord of life and light Awakes the kindling ray, Unseals the eyelids of the morn, And pours increasing day.

68.

1 Again the Lord of life and light
Awakes the kindling ray,
Unseals the eyelids of the morn,
And pours increasing day.

2 Oh, what a night was that which wrapt
The heathen world in gloom!
Oh, what a sun, which broke this day
Triumphant from the tomb!

3 This day be grateful homage paid,
And loud hosannas sung;
Let gladness dwell in every heart,
And praise on every tongue.

4 Jesus, the friend of human kind,
Was crucified and slain;
Behold, the tomb its prey restores!
Behold, he lives again!

5 Exalted high at God's right hand,
The Lord of all below,
Through him is pardoning love dispensed,
And boundless blessings flow.

6 And still for erring, guilty man
A brother's pity flows;
And still his bleeding heart is touched
With memory of our woes.

7 To thee, my Saviour and my King,
Glad homage let me give;
And stand prepared like thee to die,
With thee that I may live.

Anna Laetitia Barbauld, 1773 a.

69.

1 My Lord, my love, was crucified,
He all the pains did bear;
But in the sweetness of his rest
He makes his servants share.

2 How sweetly rest thy saints above
Which in thy bosom lie!
The church below doth rest in hope
Of that felicity.

3 Thou, Lord, who daily feed'st thy sheep,
Mak'st them a weekly feast;
Thy flocks meet in their several folds
Upon this day of rest.

4 Welcome and dear unto my soul
Are these sweet feasts of love;
But what a Sabbath shall I keep
When I shall rest above!

5 I bless thy wise and wondrous love,
Which binds us to be free:
Which makes us leave our earthly snares,
That we may come to thee!

6 I come, I wait, I hear, I pray;
Thy footsteps, Lord, I trace;
I sing to think this is the way
Unto my Saviour's face!

John Mason, 1683.

DOXOLOGY.

Let God the Father, and the Son,
And Spirit be adored,
Where there are works to make him known,
Or saints to love the Lord.

Isaac Watts, 1709.

THE LORD'S DAY.

CREATION. L. M.

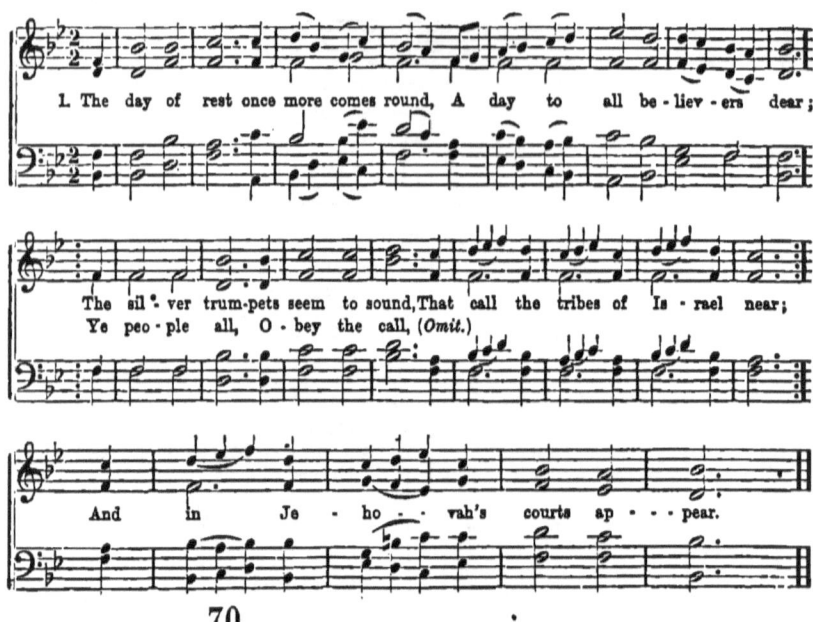

70.

1 THE day of rest once more comes round,
    A day to all believers dear;
  The silver trumpets seem to sound,
    That call the tribes of Israel near;
      Ye people all,
      Obey the call,
    And in Jehovah's courts appear.

2 Obedient to thy summons, Lord,
    We to thy sanctuary come;
  Thy gracious presence here afford,
    And send thy people joyful home;
      Of thee our King
      Oh may we sing,
    And none with such a theme be dumb!

3 Oh hasten, Lord, the day when those
    Who know thee here shall see thy face;
  When suffering shall forever close,
    And they shall reach their destined place;
      Then shall they rest
      Supremely blest,
    Eternal debtors to thy grace!

Thomas Kelly, 1806.

THE LORD'S DAY.

SOLITUDE. 7s.

1. Ere another Sabbath's close, Ere again we seek repose, Lord, our song ascends to thee; At thy feet we bow the knee.

71.

1 Ere another Sabbath's close,
Ere again we seek repose,
Lord, our song ascends to thee;
At thy feet we bow the knee.

2 For the mercies of the day,
For this rest upon our way,
Thanks to thee alone be given,
Lord of earth, and King of heaven!

3 Cold our services have been;
Mingled every prayer with sin;
But thou canst and wilt forgive;
By thy grace alone we live!

4 Let these earthly Sabbaths prove
Foretastes of our joys above;
While their steps thy pilgrims bend
To the rest which knows no end!

Anon., 1833.

72.

1 Softly fades the twilight ray
Of the holy Sabbath day;
Gently as life's setting sun,
When the Christian's course is run.

2 Peace is on the world abroad;
'Tis the holy peace of God;
Symbol of the peace within,
When the spirit rests from sin.

3 Still the Spirit lingers near,
Where the evening worshipper
Seeks communion with the skies,
Pressing onward to the prize.

4 Saviour, may our Sabbaths be
Days of peace and joy in thee!
Till in heaven our souls repose,
Where the Sabbath ne'er shall close.

S. F. Smith, 1840.

73.

1 Holy Father, whom we praise
With imperfect accents here;
Ancient of eternal days,
Lord of heaven and earth and air;
Stooping from amid the blaze
Of the flaming seraphim,
Hear and help us, while we raise
This our Sabbath evening hymn.

2 We have trod thy temple, Lord;
We have joined the public praise;
We have heard thy holy word;
We have sought thy heavenly grace;
All thy goodness we record;
All our powers to thee we bring;
Let thy faithfulness afford
Now the shadow of thy wing.

3 We have seen thy dying love,
Jesus! once for sinners slain;
We would follow thee above;
We, like thee, would rise and reign.
Let revolving Sabbaths prove
Seasons of delight in thee;
Let thy presence, Holy Dove,
Fit us for eternity.

Thomas Binney, 1825.

MORNING AND EVENING.

GERMANY. L. M.

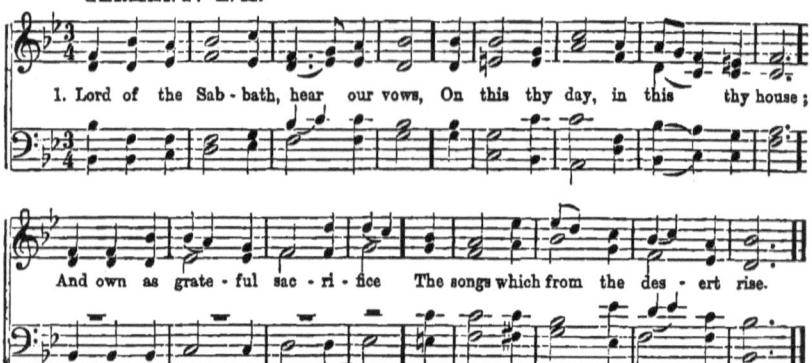

1. Lord of the Sab-bath, hear our vows, On this thy day, in this thy house;
And own as grate-ful sac-ri-fice The songs which from the des-ert rise.

74. HEB. iv. 9.

1 LORD of the Sabbath, hear our vows,
On this thy day, in this thy house;
And own as grateful sacrifice
The songs which from the desert rise.

2 Thine earthly Sabbaths, Lord, we love,
But there's a nobler rest above;
To that our laboring souls aspire
With ardent pangs of strong desire.

3 No more fatigue, no more distress;
Nor sin, nor hell, shall reach the place;
No groans to mingle with the songs
Which warble from immortal tongues:

4 No rude alarms of raging foes,
No cares to break the long repose,
No midnight shade, no clouded sun;
But sacred, high, eternal noon.

5 O long-expected day, begin;
Dawn on these realms of woe and sin;
Fain would we leave this weary road,
And sleep in death to rest with God.
Philip Doddridge, 1737.

75.

1 SWEET is the light of Sabbath eve,
And soft the sunbeams lingering there;
For these blest hours the world I leave,
Wafted on wings of faith and prayer.

2 Season of rest! the tranquil soul [love;
Feels the sweet calm, and melts in
And while these sacred moments roll,
Faith sees a smiling heaven above.

3 Nor will our days of toil be long:
Our pilgrimage will soon be trod;
And we shall join the ceaseless song,
The endless Sabbath of our God.
James Edmeston, 1820.

76. MORNING AND EVENING.

1 NEW every morning is the love
Our wakening and uprising prove;
Through sleep and darkness safely brought,
Restored to life, and power, and thought.

2 New mercies each returning day
Hover around us while we pray;
New perils past, new sins forgiven,
New thoughts of God, new hopes of heaven.

3 If, on our daily course, our mind
Be set to hallow all we find,
New treasures still, of countless price,
God will provide for sacrifice.

4 Old friends, old scenes, will lovelier be,
As more of heaven in each we see;
Some softening gleam of love and prayer
Shall dawn on every cross and care.

5 The trivial round, the common task,
Will furnish all we ought to ask;
Room to deny ourselves; a road
To bring us daily nearer God.

6 Only, O Lord, in thy dear love,
Fit us for perfect rest above,
And help us this, and every day,
To live more nearly as we pray.
John Keble, 1827.

MORNING AND EVENING.

CAREY. L. M. 6 LINES. (Omit repeat for 4 lines.)

1. When, streaming from the eastern skies, The morning light salutes mine eyes,
O Sun of Righteousness divine, On me with beams of mercy shine;
Oh chase the shades of guilt away, And turn my darkness in-to day.

77.

1 WHEN, streaming from the eastern skies,
The morning light salutes mine eyes,
O Sun of Righteousness divine,
On me with beams of mercy shine;
Oh, chase the shades of guilt away,
And turn my darkness into day!

2 When to heaven's great and glorious King
My morning sacrifice I bring,
And, mourning o'er my guilt and shame,
Ask mercy in my Saviour's name;
Then, Jesus, sprinkle with thy blood,
And be my Advocate with God.

3 As every day thy mercy spares
Will bring its trials and its cares;
O Saviour, till my life shall end,
Be thou my counsellor and friend:
Teach me thy precepts, all divine,
And be thy great example mine.

4 When each day's scenes and labors close,
And wearied nature seeks repose,
With pardoning mercy richly blest,
Guard me, my Saviour, while I rest;
And as each morning's sun shall rise,
Oh, lead me onward to the skies!

5 And, at my life's last setting sun,
My conflicts o'er, my labors done,

Jesus, thy heavenly radiance shed,
To cheer and bless my dying bed;
And from death's gloom my spirit raise
To see thy face, and sing thy praise.
William Shrubsole, Jr., 1813.

78.

1 GOD of the morning, at whose voice
The cheerful sun makes haste to rise,
And like a giant doth rejoice
To run his journey through the skies:

2 From the fair chambers of the east
The circuit of his race begins;
And, without weariness or rest,
Round the whole earth he flies and shines.

3 Oh, like the sun, may I fulfil
The appointed duties of the day;
With ready mind and active will
March on and keep my heavenly way!

4 But I shall rove, and lose the race,
If God, my Sun, should disappear,
And leave me in this world's wide maze,
To follow every wandering star.

5 Give me thy counsel for my guide,
And then receive me to thy bliss:
All my desires and hopes beside
Are faint and cold compared with this.
Isaac Watts, 1709.

MORNING AND EVENING.

GILEAD. L. M.

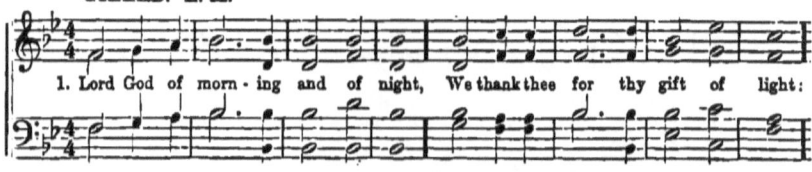
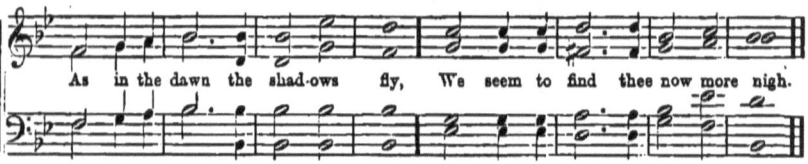

1. Lord God of morn-ing and of night, We thank thee for thy gift of light: As in the dawn the shad-ows fly, We seem to find thee now more nigh.

79.

1. LORD God of morning and of night,
   We thank thee for thy gift of light:
   As in the dawn the shadows fly,
   We seem to find thee now more nigh.

2. Fresh hopes have wakened in our hearts,
   Fresh force to do our daily parts ;
   Thy thousand sleeps our strength restore
   A thousand-fold to serve thee more.

3. Yet, whilst thy will we would pursue,
   Oft what we would we cannot do ;
   The sun may stand in zenith skies,
   But on the soul thick midnight lies.

4. O Lord of lights, 'tis thou alone
   Canst make our darkened hearts thine own ;
   Though this new day with joy we see,
   O Dawn of God, we cry for thee !
   Francis Turner Palgrave, 1862.

80.

1. AWAKE, my soul, and with the sun
   Thy daily stage of duty run ;
   Shake off dull sloth, and joyful rise
   To pay thy morning sacrifice.

2. Wake and lift up thyself, my heart,
   And with the angels bear thy part,
   Who, all night long, unwearied sing
   High praise to the eternal King.

3. All praise to thee who safe hast kept,
   And hast refreshed me whilst I slept !
   Grant, Lord, when I from death shall wake,
   I may of endless life partake !

4. Lord, I my vows to thee renew ;
   Disperse my sins as morning dew ;
   Guard my first springs of thought and will,
   And with thyself my spirit fill.

5. Direct, control, suggest, this day,
   All I design, or do, or say ;
   That all my powers, with all their might,
   In thy sole glory may unite.
   Bishop Thomas Ken, 1700.

81.

1. O JESUS, Lord of heavenly grace,
   Thou brightness of thy Father's face,
   Thou fountain of eternal light,
   Whose beams disperse the shades of night !

2. Come, holy Sun of heavenly love,
   Shower down thy radiance from above,
   And to our inward hearts convey
   The Holy Spirit's cloudless ray !

3. And we the Father's help will claim,
   And sing the Father's glorious name ;
   His powerful succor we implore,
   That we may stand, to fall no more.

4. Oh, hallowed be the approaching day !
   Let meekness be our morning ray,
   And faithful love our noonday light,
   And hope our sunset, calm and bright !

5. O Christ ! with each returning morn
   Thine image to our hearts is borne ;
   Oh, may we ever clearly see
   Our Saviour and our God in thee !
   Ambrose, 307-397 ; trans. by John Chandler, 1837.

MORNING AND EVENING. 41

HURSLEY. L. M.

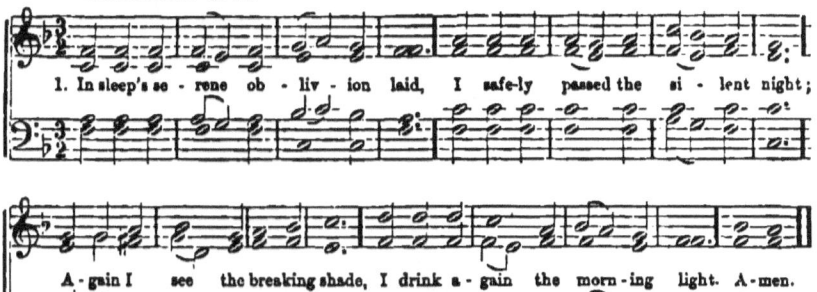

82.
1 In sleep's serene oblivion laid,
 I safely passed the silent night;
 Again I see the breaking shade,
 I drink again the morning light.

2 New-born, I bless the waking hour;
 Once more, with awe, rejoice to be;
 My conscious soul resumes her power,
 And springs, my guardian God, to thee!

3 Oh, guide me through the various maze
 My doubtful feet are doomed to tread;
 And spread thy shield's protecting blaze,
 When dangers press around my head.

4 A deeper shade will soon impend;
 A deeper sleep mine eyes oppress;
 Yet then thy strength shall still defend,
 Thy goodness still delight to bless.

5 That deeper shade shall break away;
 That deeper sleep shall leave mine eyes;
 Thy light shall give eternal day;
 Thy love, the rapture of the skies.
  John Hawkesworth, 1773.

83.
1 My God, how endless is thy love!
 Thy gifts are every evening new;
 And morning mercies from above
 Gently distil like early dew.

2 Thou spread'st the curtains of the night,
 Great Guardian of my sleeping hours;
 Thy sovereign word restores the light,
 And quickens all my drowsy powers.

3 I yield my powers to thy command;
 To thee I consecrate my days;
 Perpetual blessings from thy hand
 Demand perpetual songs of praise.
  Isaac Watts, 1709.

84.
1 Sun of my soul, thou Saviour dear,
 It is not night if thou be near;
 Oh, may no earth-born cloud arise
 To hide thee from thy servant's eyes!

2 When the soft dews of kindly sleep
 My wearied eyelids gently steep,
 Be my last thought, How sweet to rest
 Forever on my Saviour's breast!

3 Abide with me from morn till eve,
 For without thee I cannot live;
 Abide with me when night is nigh,
 For without thee I dare not die.

4 If some poor wandering child of thine
 Have spurned to-day the voice divine,
 Now, Lord, the gracious work begin;
 Let him no more lie down in sin.

5 Watch by the sick, enrich the poor
 With blessings from thy boundless store;
 Be every mourner's sleep to-night
 Like infant's slumbers, pure and light!

6 Come near and bless us when we wake,
 Ere through the world our way we take;
 Till in the ocean of thy love
 We lose ourselves in heaven above.
  John Keble, 1827.

MORNING AND EVENING.

TALLIS' EVENING HYMN. L. M.

1. All praise to thee, my God, this night, For all the bless-ings of the light; Keep me, oh keep me, King of kings, Be-neath thine own al - - mighty wings!

85.

1 ALL praise to thee, my God, this night,
   For all the blessings of the light;
   Keep me, oh, keep me, King of kings,
   Beneath thine own almighty wings!

2 Forgive me, Lord, for thy dear Son,
   The ill that I this day have done;
   That with the world, myself, and thee,
   I, ere I sleep, at peace may be.

3 Teach me to live that I may dread
   The grave as little as my bed;
   To die, that this vile body may
   Rise glorious at the awful day!

4 Oh may my soul on thee repose;
   And may sweet sleep mine eyelids close;
   Sleep, that may me more vigorous make
   To serve my God when I awake!
   Bishop Thomas Ken, 1700.

86.

1 GREAT God, to thee my evening song
   With humble gratitude I raise;
   Oh, let thy mercy tune my tongue,
   And fill my heart with lively praise.

2 My days, unclouded as they pass,
   And every gently rolling hour,
   Are monuments of wondrous grace,
   And witness to thy love and power.

3 And yet this thoughtless, wretched heart,
   Too oft regardless of thy love,
   Ungrateful, can from thee depart,
   And, fond of trifles, vainly rove.

4 Seal my forgiveness in the blood
   Of Jesus; his dear name alone
   I plead for pardon, gracious God,
   And kind acceptance at thy throne.

5 Let this blest hope mine eyelids close;
   With sleep refresh my feeble frame;
   Safe in thy care may I repose,
   And wake with praises to thy name!
   Anne Steele, 1760

87.

1 THUS far the Lord hath led me on,
   Thus far his power prolongs my days;
   And every evening shall make known
   Some fresh memorials of his grace.

2 Much of my time has run to waste,
   And I perhaps am near my home;
   But he forgives my follies past,
   And gives me strength for days to come.

3 I lay my body down to sleep:
   Peace is the pillow for my head,
   While well-appointed angels keep
   Their watchful stations round my bed.

4 Faith in his name forbids my fear;
   Oh, may thy presence ne'er depart!
   And, in the morning, make me hear
   The love and kindness of thy heart.

5 Thus, when the night of death shall come,
   My flesh shall rest beneath the ground;
   And wait thy voice to rouse my tomb,
   With sweet salvation in the sound.
   Isaac Watts, 1709.

MORNING AND EVENING.   43

KEDRON CHANT. C. M.

1. Dread Sovereign, let my eve-ning song, Like ho-ly in - - cense rise;
As - sist the offerings of my tongue To reach the lof - - - ty skies.

88.

1 Dread Sovereign, let my evening song,
    Like holy incense, rise;
  Assist the offerings of my tongue
    To reach the lofty skies.

2 Through all the dangers of the day
    Thy hand was still my guard;
  And still, to drive my wants away,
    Thy mercy stood prepared.

3 Perpetual blessings from above
    Encompass me around,
  But, oh, how few returns of love
    Hath my Creator found!

4 What have I done for him that died
    To save my wretched soul?
  How are my follies multiplied,
    Fast as my minutes roll!

5 Lord, with this guilty heart of mine,
    To thy dear cross I flee,
  And to thy grace my soul resign,
    To be renewed by thee.

6 Sprinkled afresh with pardoning blood,
    I lay me down to rest,
  As in th' embraces of my God,
    Or on my Saviour's breast.
            Isaac Watts, 1709.

89.

1 O Lord, another day is flown,
    And we, a lonely band,
  Are met once more before thy throne,
    To bless thy fostering hand.

2 And wilt thou bend a listening ear
    To praises low as ours?
  Thou wilt; for thou dost love to hear
    The song which meekness pours.

3 And, Jesus, thou thy smiles wilt deign
    As we before thee pray;
  For thou didst bless the infant train,
    And we are less than they.

4 Oh, let thy grace perform its part,
    And let contention cease;
  And shed abroad in every heart
    Thine everlasting peace.

5 Thus chastened, cleansed, entirely thine,
    A flock by Jesus led,
  The sun of holiness shall shine
    In glory on our head.

6 And thou wilt turn our wandering feet,
    And thou wilt bless our way,
  Till worlds shall fade, and faith shall greet
    The dawn of lasting day.
            Henry Kirke White, 1803.

90. Tune, "Woodstock," p. 44.

1 I love to steal awhile away
    From every cumbering care,
  And spend the hours of setting day
    In humble, grateful prayer.

2 I love in solitude to shed
    The penitential tear,
  And all his promises to plead
    Where none but God is near.

MORNING AND EVENING.

WOODSTOCK. C. M.

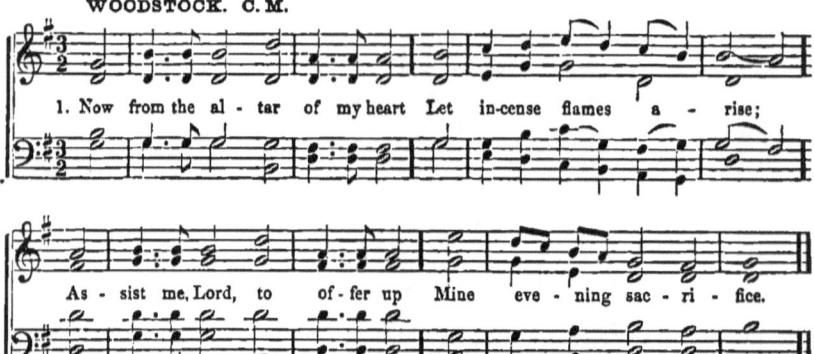

1. Now from the al-tar of my heart Let in-cense flames a-rise;
As-sist me, Lord, to of-fer up Mine eve-ning sac-ri-fice.

3 I love to think on mercies past,
  And future good implore;
  And all my cares and sorrows cast
  On him whom I adore.

4 I love by faith to take a view
  Of brighter scenes in heaven;
  The prospect doth my strength renew,
  While here by tempests driven.

5 Thus, when life's toilsome day is o'er,
  May its departing ray
  Be calm as this impressive hour,
  And lead to endless day.
   Phœbe H. Brown, 1825.

91.

1 Now from the altar of my heart
  Let incense-flames arise;
  Assist me, Lord, to offer up
  Mine evening sacrifice.

2 Awake, my love; awake, my joy;
  Awake, my heart and tongue!
  Sleep not: when mercies loudly call,
  Break forth into a song.

3 This day God was my sun and shield,
  My keeper and my guide:
  His care was on my frailty shown,
  His mercies multiplied.

4 Minutes and mercies multiplied
  Have made up all this day:
  Minutes came quick, but mercies were
  More fleet and free than they.

5 New time, new favor, and new joys
  Do a new song require;
  Till I shall praise thee as I would,
  Accept my heart's desire.

6 Lord of my time, whose hand hath set
  New time upon my score,
  Then shall I praise for all my time,
  When time shall be no more.
   John Mason, 1683.

92.

1 BEFORE thy throne, O Lord of heaven,
  We kneel at close of day;
  Look on thy children from on high,
  And hear us while we pray.

2 The sorrows of thy servants, Lord,
  Oh, do not thou despise!
  But let the incense of our prayers
  Before thy mercy rise.

3 Slowly the rays of daylight fade;
  So fade, within our heart,
  The hopes in earthly love and joy,
  That one by one depart.

4 Let peace, O Lord, thy peace, O God,
  Upon our souls descend;
  From midnight fears and perils, thou
  Our trembling hearts defend.

5 Give us a respite from our toil;
  Calm and subdue our woes;
  Through the long day we suffer, Lord;
  Oh, give us now repose!
   Adelaide A. Proctor, 1858.

MORNING AND EVENING.

EVENING. L. M.

93.

1 Sweet Saviour, bless us ere we go;
   Thy word into our minds instil;
   And make our lukewarm hearts to glow
   With lowly love and fervent will.
   Through life's long day and death's dark
         night,
   O gentle Jesus, be our Light.

2 The day is gone, its hours have run,
   And thou hast taken count of all,
   The scanty triumphs grace hath won,
   The broken vow, the frequent fall.
   Through life's long day and death's dark
         night,
   O gentle Jesus, be our Light.

3 Labor is sweet, for thou hast toiled,
   And care is light, for thou hast cared;
   Ah! never let our works be soiled
   With strife, or by deceit ensnared.
   Through life's long day and death's dark
         night,
   O gentle Jesus, be our Light.

4 For all we love, the poor, the sad,
   The sinful, unto thee we call;
   Oh, let thy mercy make us glad;
   Thou art our Jesus, and our All.
   Through life's long day and death's dark
         night,
   O gentle Jesus, be our Light.

Frederick W. Faber, 1849.

MORNING AND EVENING.

PROTECTION. 8s. DOUBLE.

94.

1 INSPIRER and hearer of prayer,
  Thou Shepherd and Guardian of thine,
 My all to thy covenant care
  I, sleeping or waking. resign.
 If thou art my Shield and my Sun,
  The night is no darkness to me;
 And, fast as my moments roll on,
  They bring me but nearer to thee.

2 From evil secure, and its dread,
  I rest, if my Saviour be nigh;
 And songs his kind presence indeed
  Shall in the night season supply.
 His smiles and his comforts abound;
  His grace like the dew shall descend;
 And walls of salvation surround
  The soul he delights to defend.

3 Thy ministering spirits descend
  To watch while thy saints are asleep;
 By day and by night they attend,
  The heirs of salvation to keep.
 Bright seraphs, dispatched from the throne,
  Repair to their stations assigned;
 And angels elect are sent down
  To guard the elect of mankind.

4 Their worship no interval knows;
  Their fervor is still on the wing;
 And, while they protect my repose,
  They chant to the praise of my King.
 I, too, at the season ordained,
  Their chorus forever shall join;
 And love and adore, without end,
  Their faithful Creator and mine.

Augustus M. Toplady, 1776.

MORNING AND EVENING.

RATHBUN. 8s & 7s.

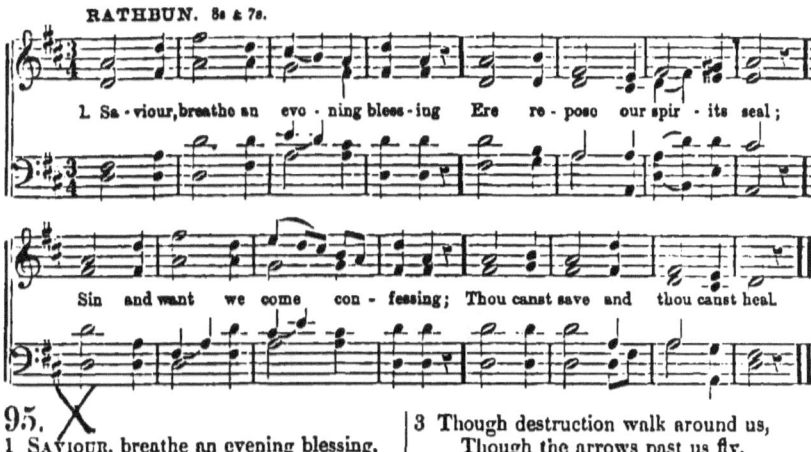

95.

1 Saviour, breathe an evening blessing,
  Ere repose our spirits seal;
  Sin and want we come confessing:
  Thou canst save, and thou canst heal.

2 Though the night be dark and dreary,
  Darkness cannot hide from thee;
  Thou art he who, never weary,
  Watchest where thy people be.

3 Though destruction walk around us,
  Though the arrows past us fly,
  Angel guards from thee surround us;
  We are safe if thou art nigh.

4 Should swift death this night o'ertake us,
  And command us to the tomb,
  May the morn in heaven awake us,
  Clad in light and deathless bloom.

James Edmeston, 1820.

HASTINGS. 8s, 6s & 8s.

96.

1 Lord of my life, whose tender care
  Hath led me on till now,
  Here lowly, at the hour of prayer,
  Before thy throne I bow;
  I bless thy gracious hand, and pray
  Forgiveness for another day.

2 Oh, may I daily, hourly strive
  In heavenly grace to grow;
  To thee and to thy glory live,
  Dead else to all below;
  Tread in the path my Saviour trod,—
  Though thorny, yet the path to God!

3 With prayer, my humble praise I bring,
  For mercies day by day;
  Lord, teach my heart thy love to sing;
  Lord, teach me how to pray:
  All that I have, I am, to thee
  I offer through eternity.

Anon., 1818.

MORNING AND EVENING.

BOYLSTON. S. M.

1. The day is past and gone, The eve-ning shades ap-pear;
Oh may I ev-er keep in mind, The night of death draws near.

97.

1 THE day is past and gone;
    The evening shades appear:
  Oh, may I ever keep in mind,
    The night of death draws near!

2 I lay my garments by,
    Upon my bed to rest:
  So death shall soon disrobe us all
    Of what we've here possessed,

3 Lord, keep me safe this night,
    Secure from all my fears;
  May angels guard me while I sleep,
    Till morning light appears.

4 And when I early rise,
    To view the unwearied sun,
  May I set out to win the prize,
    And after glory run.

5 And when my days are past,
    And I from time remove,
  Oh, may I in thy bosom rest,
    The bosom of thy love!
            John Leland, 1804.

98.

1 THE day, O Lord, is spent;
    Abide with us, and rest;
  Our hearts' desires are fully bent
    On making thee our guest!

2 We have not reached that land,
    That happy land, as yet,
  Where holy angels round thee stand,
    Whose sun can never set.

3 Our sun is sinking now;
    Our day is almost o'er;
  O Sun of Righteousness, do thou
    Shine on us evermore!
            John Mason Neale, 1854.

99. Tune, "Olivet." 6s & 8s.

1 FATHER of love and power,
    Guard thou our evening hour,
      Shield with thy might:
  For all thy care this day
  Our grateful thanks we pay,
  And to our Father pray:
      Bless us to-night.

2 Jesus Immanuel,
    Come in thy love to dwell
      In hearts contrite.
  For many sins we grieve;
  But we thy grace receive,
  And in thy word believe:
      Bless us to-night.

3 Spirit of truth and love,
    Life-giving, holy Dove,
      Shed forth thy light!
  Heal every sinner's smart;
  Still every throbbing heart;
  And thine own peace impart:
      Bless us to-night.
            George Rawson, 1853.

MORNING AND EVENING.

HOLLEY. 7s.

1. Softly now the light of day Fades upon my sight away;
Free from care, from labor free, Lord, I would commune with thee.

100.

2 Thou, whose all-pervading eye
Naught escapes without, within,
Pardon each infirmity,
Open fault, and secret sin.

3 Soon, for me, the light of day
Shall forever pass away:

Then, from sin and sorrow free,
Take me, Lord, to dwell with thee.

4 Thou who, sinless, yet hast known
All of man's infirmity;
Then, from thine eternal throne,
Jesus, look with pitying eye.

George W. Doane, 1824.

NIGHTFALL. 6s, 4s & 6s.

1. The sun is sinking fast, The day-light dies;
Let love awake, and pay Her evening sacrifice.

101.

2 As Christ upon the cross
His head inclined,
And to his Father's hands
His parting soul resigned;

3 So now herself my soul
Would wholly give
Into his sacred charge,
In whom all spirits live;

4 So now, beneath his eye,
Would calmly rest,
Without a wish or thought
Abiding in the breast;

5 Save that his will be done,
Whate'er betide;
Dead to herself, and dead
In him to all beside.

6 Thus would I live; yet now
Not I, but he,
In all his power and love,
Henceforth alive in me.

7 One Sacred Trinity!
One Lord Divine!
May I be ever his,
And he forever mine.

Trans. from the Latin by E. Caswall, 1848.

GOD.—THE TRINITY.

LOUVAN. L. M.

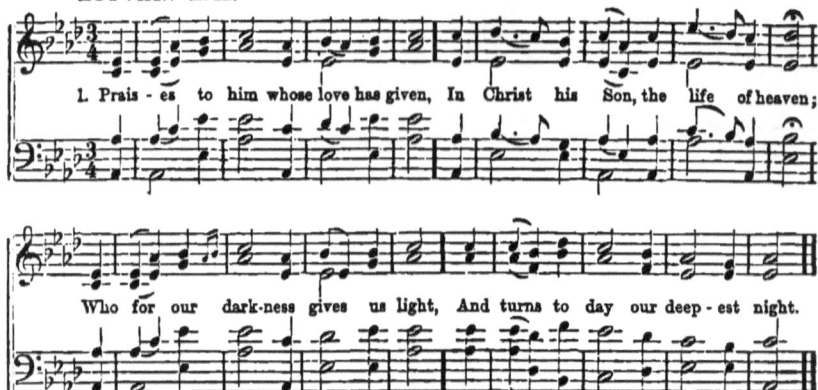

1. Praises to him whose love has given, In Christ his Son, the life of heaven; Who for our darkness gives us light, And turns to day our deepest night.

102.

1 Praises to him whose love has given,
In Christ his Son, the life of heaven;
Who for our darkness gives us light,
And turns to day our deepest night.

2 Praises to him, in grace, who came,
To bear our woe and sin and shame;
Who lived to die, who died to rise,
The God-accepted sacrifice.

3 Praises to him the chain who broke,
Opened the prison, burst the yoke,
Sent forth the captives glad and free,
Heirs of an endless liberty.

4 Praises to him who sheds abroad
Within our hearts the love of God;
The Spirit of all truth and peace,
Fountain of joy and holiness.

5 To Father, Son, and Spirit, now
The hands we lift, the knees we bow;
To thee, Jehovah, thus we raise
The sinner's endless song of praise!
Horatius Bonar, 1856.

103.

1 Blest be the Father and his love,
To whose celestial source we owe
Rivers of endless joy above,
And rills of comfort here below.

2 Glory to thee, Great Son of God,
From whose dear wounded body rolls
A precious stream of vital blood,
Pardon and life for dying souls.

3 We give the sacred Spirit praise,
Who, in our hearts of sin and woe,
Makes living springs of grace arise,
And into boundless glory flow.

4 Thus, God the Father, God the Son,
And God the Spirit, we adore:
That sea of life and love unknown,
Without a bottom or a shore.
Isaac Watts, 1709.

104.

1 Father of heaven! whose love profound
A ransom for our souls hath found,
Before thy throne we sinners bend:
To us thy pardoning love extend.

2 Almighty Son! incarnate Word!
Our Prophet, Priest, Redeemer, Lord!
Before thy throne we sinners bend;
To us thy saving grace extend.

3 Eternal Spirit! by whose breath
The soul is raised from sin and death,
Before thy throne we sinners bend:
To us thy quick'ning power extend.

4 Jehovah! Father, Spirit, Son!
Mysterious Godhead! Three in One!
Before thy throne we sinners bend·
Grace, pardon, life, to us extend!
J. Cooper, 1812.

DOXOLOGY.

Praise we the Father and the Son,
And Holy Spirit, with them One;
And may the Son on us bestow
The gifts that from the Spirit flow.
Hymns, Ancient and Modern, 1861.

GOD.—THE TRINITY.

51

WARSAW. H. M.

1. I give immortal praise To God the Father's love, For all my comforts here, And better hopes above: He sent his own Eternal Son, To die for sins That man had done.

105.

1 I GIVE immortal praise
 To God the Father's love,
For all my comforts here,
 And better hopes above:
He sent his own | To die for sins
Eternal Son | That man had done.

2 To God the Son belongs
 Immortal glory too,
Who bought us with his blood
 From everlasting woe:
And now he lives, | And sees the fruit
And now he reigns, | Of all his pains.

3 To God the Spirit's name
 Immortal worship give,
Whose new-creating power
 Makes the dead sinner live:
His work completes | And fills the soul
The great design, | With joy divine.

4 Almighty God, to thee
 Be endless honors done,
The undivided Three,
 And the mysterious One:
Where reason fails | There faith prevails,
With all her powers, | And love adores.

Isaac Watts, 1709.

106.

1 To him that chose us first,
 Before the world began;
To him that bore the curse
 To save rebellious man;
To him that formed | Is endless praise
Our hearts anew, | And glory due.

2 The Father's love shall run
 Through our immortal songs;
We bring to God the Son
 Hosannas on our tongues:
Our lips address | With equal praise,
The Spirit's name, | And zeal the same.

3 Let every saint above,
 And angel round the throne,
Forever bless and love
 The sacred Three in One:
Thus heaven shall | When earth and
 raise | time
His honors high, | Grow old and die.

Isaac Watts, 1709.

DOXOLOGY.

To God the Father's throne
 Perpetual honors raise;
 Glory to God the Son;
 To God the Spirit praise:
With all our powers, | Thy name we sing,
Eternal King, | While faith adores.

Isaac Watts, 1719.

GOD,—THE TRINITY.

ITALIAN HYMN. 6s & 4s.

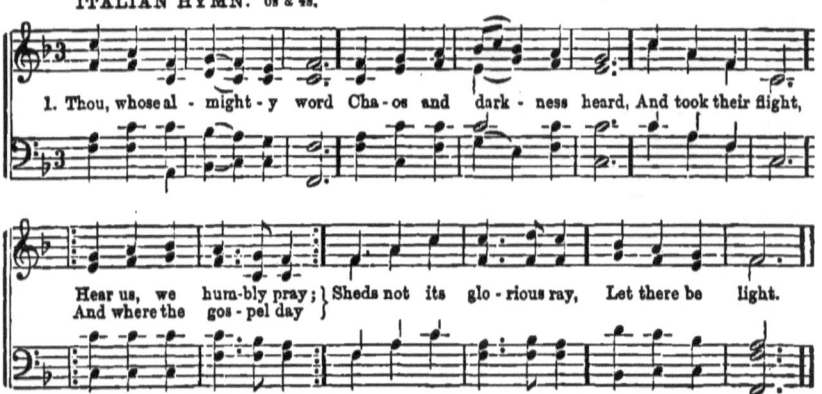

1. Thou, whose almighty word Chaos and darkness heard, And took their flight, Hear us, we humbly pray; And where the gospel day Sheds not its glorious ray, Let there be light.

107.

1 Thou, whose almighty word
  Chaos and darkness heard,
    And took their flight,
  Hear us, we humbly pray;
  And where the gospel's day
  Sheds not its glorious ray,
    Let there be light!

2 Thou, who didst come to bring,
  On thy redeeming wing,
    Healing and sight:
  Health to the sick in mind;
  Sight to the inly blind;
  Oh, now, to all mankind,
    Let there be light!

3 Spirit of truth and love,
  Life-giving, Holy Dove,
    Speed forth thy flight:
  Move o'er the water's face,
  Bearing the lamp of grace;
  And, in earth's darkest place,
    Let there be light!

4 Blesséd and Holy Three,
  Glorious Trinity,
    Wisdom, Love, Might!
  Boundless as ocean's tide,
  Rolling in fullest pride,
  Through the world, far and wide,
    Let there be light!
              John Marriott, 1813.

108.

1 Come, thou almighty King,
  Help us thy name to sing,
    Help us to praise:
  Father all-glorious,
  O'er all victorious,
  Come, and reign over us,
    Ancient of Days.

2 Jesus, our Lord, arise;
  Scatter our enemies,
    And make them fall;
  Let thine almighty aid
  Our sure defence be made;
  Our souls on thee be stayed;
    Lord, hear our call.

3 Come, thou incarnate Word,
  Gird on thy mighty sword,
    Our prayer attend:
  Come, and thy people bless,
  And give thy word success:
  Spirit of holiness,
    On us descend.

4 Come, holy Comforter,
  Thy sacred witness bear,
    In this glad hour:
  Thou who almighty art,
  Now rule in every heart;
  And ne'er from us depart,
    Spirit of power.

5 To the great One in Three,
  Eternal praises be
    Hence, evermore.
  His sovereign majesty
  May we in glory see,
  And to eternity
    Love and adore.
              Charles Wesley, 1757.

GOD,—HIS PRAISE.

FARRANT. C. M.

1. Let them neg-lect thy glo-ry, Lord, Who nev-er knew thy grace; But our loud songs shall still re-cord The won-ders of thy praise.

109.

1 Let them neglect thy glory, Lord,
  Who never knew thy grace;
  But our loud songs shall still record
  The wonders of thy praise.

2 We raise our shouts, O God, to thee,
  And send them to thy throne:
  All glory to th' united Three,
  The undivided One!

3 'Twas he (and we'll adore his name)
  That formed us by a word;
  'Tis he restores our ruined frame:
  Salvation to the Lord!

4 Hosanna! let the earth and skies
  Repeat the joyful sound;
  Rocks, hills, and vales reflect the voice
  In one eternal round!
  Isaac Watts, 1709.

110.   Psalm 9.

1 To celebrate thy praise, O Lord,
  I will my heart prepare;
  To all the listening world thy works,
  Thy wondrous works declare.

2 The thought of them shall to my soul
  Exalted pleasure bring;
  Whilst to thy name, O thou Most High,
  Triumphant praise I sing.

3 All those who have his goodness proved
  Will in his truth confide,
  Whose mercy ne'er forsook the man
  That on his help relied.

4 His suffering saints, when most distressed,
  He ne'er forgets to aid;
  Their expectations shall be crowned,
  Though for a time delayed.

5 Sing praises, therefore, to the Lord,
  From Zion, his abode;
  Proclaim his deeds, till all the world
  Confess no other God.
  Tate and Brady, 1696.

111.   Psalm 145.

1 Long as I live I'll bless thy name,
  My King, my God of love;
  My work and joy shall be the same
  In the bright world above.

2 Great is the Lord, his power unknown,
  And let his praise be great:
  I'll sing the honors of thy throne,
  Thy works of grace repeat.

3 Thy grace shall dwell upon my tongue;
  And while my lips rejoice,
  The men that hear my sacred song
  Shall join their cheerful voice.

4 Fathers to sons shall teach thy name,
  And children learn thy ways;
  Ages to come thy truth proclaim,
  And nations sound thy praise.

5 The world is managed by thy hands;
  Thy saints are ruled by love;
  And thy eternal kingdom stands,
  Though rocks and hills remove.
  Isaac Watts, 1719.

GOD,—HIS PRAISE.

LYONS. 10s & 11s.

1. Oh worship the King, all glorious above, Oh grateful-ly sing his power and his love! Our Shield and Defender, the Ancient of Days, Pavilioned in splendor and girded with praise.

112. Psalm 104.

2 Oh, tell of his might! oh, sing of his grace!
Whose robe is the light; whose canopy,
   space; [clouds form,
His chariots of wrath the deep thunder
And dark is his path on the wings of the
   storm.

3 The earth, with its store of wonders untold,
Almighty, thy power hath founded of old;
Hath 'stablished it fast by a changeless
   decree; [the sea.
And round it hath cast, like a mantle,

4 Thy bountiful care what tongue can re-
   cite? [light,
It breathes in the air, it shines in the
It streams from the hills, it descends to
   the plain, [rain.
And sweetly distils in the dew and the

5 Frail children of dust, and feeble as frail,
In thee do we trust, nor find thee to fail;
Thy mercies how tender, how firm to the
   end, [Friend!
Our Maker, Defender, Redeemer, and

6 O measureless Might! ineffable Love!
While angels delight to hymn thee above,
The humbler creation, though feeble their
   lays, [praise,
With true adoration shall lisp to thy
              Sir Robert Grant, 1830.

CHROME. 11s & 8s.

1. Be joyful in God, all ye lands of the earth; Oh, serve him with gladness and fear; Exult in his presence with music and mirth, With love and devotion draw near.

113. Psalm 75.

2 Jehovah is God, and Jehovah alone,
Creator and Ruler o'er all; [own;
And we are his people, his sceptre we
His sheep, and we follow his call.

3 O, enter his gates with thanksgiving and
   song;
Your vows in his temple proclaim;
His praise in melodious accordance pro-
And bless his adorable name. [long;
              James Montgomery, 1771-1854.

GOD,—HIS PRAISE.

SILVER STREET. S. M.

1. Stand up, and bless the Lord, Ye people of his choice; Stand up, and bless the Lord your God, With heart, and soul, and voice.

114.

1 STAND up, and bless the Lord,
  Ye people of his choice;
  Stand up, and bless the Lord your God
  With heart, and soul, and voice.

2 Though high above all praise,
  Above all blessing high,
  Who would not fear his holy name,
  And laud, and magnify?

3 Oh, for the living flame
  From his own altar brought,
  To touch our lips, our souls inspire,
  And wing to heaven our thought!

4 There, with benign regard,
  Our hymns he deigns to hear;
  Though unrevealed to mortal sense,
  The spirit feels him near.

5 God is our strength and song,
  And his salvation ours;
  Then be his love in Christ proclaimed
  With all our ransomed powers.

6 Stand up, and bless the Lord;
  The Lord your God adore;
  Stand up, and bless his glorious name,
  Henceforth for evermore.
  James Montgomery, 1825.

115. PSALM 67.

1 To bless thy chosen race,
  In mercy, Lord, incline;
  And cause the brightness of thy face
  On all thy saints to shine:

2 That so thy wondrous way
  May through the world be known,
  While distant lands their homage pay,
  And thy salvation own.

3 Let differing nations join
  Their Saviour to proclaim;
  Let all the world, O Lord, combine
  To praise thy glorious name.

4 Oh, let them shout and sing
  With joy and pious mirth;
  For thou, the righteous Judge and King,
  Shalt govern all the earth.

5 Then God, upon our land,
  Shall constant blessings shower:
  And all the world in awe shall stand
  Of his resistless power.
  Tate and Brady, 1696.

116.

1 THY name, almighty Lord,
  Shall sound through distant lands;
  Great is thy grace, and sure thy word,
  Thy truth forever stands.

2 Far be thine honor spread,
  And long thy praise endure,
  Till morning light and evening shade
  Shall be exchanged no more.
  Isaac Watts, 1719.

GOD,—HIS PRAISE.

GILEAD. L. M.

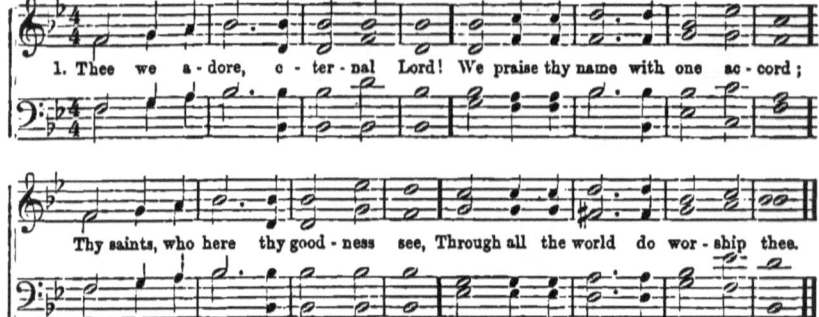

1. Thee we adore, eternal Lord! We praise thy name with one accord;
Thy saints, who here thy goodness see, Through all the world do worship thee.

117.

1 THEE we adore, eternal Lord!
We praise thy name with one accord;
Thy saints who here thy goodness see,
Through all the world do worship thee.

2 To thee aloud all angels cry,
And ceaseless raise their songs on high,
Both cherubim and seraphim,
The heavens and all the powers therein.

3 The apostles join the glorious throng;
The prophets swell the immortal song;
The martyrs' noble army raise
Eternal anthems to thy praise.

4 From day to day, O Lord, do we
Highly exalt and honor thee!
Thy name we worship and adore,
World without end, for evermore!
Thomas Cotterill, 1810.

118.   PSALM 145.

1 MY God, my King, thy various praise
Shall fill the remnant of my days;
Thy grace employ my humble tongue,
Till death and glory raise the song.

2 The wings of every hour shall bear
Some thankful tribute to thine ear;
And every setting sun shall see
New works of duty done for thee.

3 Thy truth and justice I'll proclaim,
Thy bounty flows, an endless stream;
Thy mercy swift; thine anger slow,
But dreadful to the stubborn foe.

4 Thy works with sovereign glory shine
And speak thy majesty divine;
Let every realm with joy proclaim
The sound and honor of thy name.

5 Let distant times and nations raise
The long succession of thy praise;
And unborn ages make my song
The joy and labor of their tongue.

6 But who can speak thy wondrous deeds?
Thy greatness all our thoughts exceeds:
Vast and unsearchable thy ways,
Vast and immortal be thy praise.
Isaac Watts, 1719.

119.

1 COME, O my soul! in sacred lays,
Attempt thy great Creator's praise:
But, oh, what tongue can speak his fame?
What mortal verse can reach the theme?

2 Enthroned amid the radiant spheres,
He glory like a garment wears;
To form a robe of light divine,
Ten thousand suns around him shine.

3 In all our Maker's grand designs
Almighty power with wisdom shines;
His works, thro' all this wondrous frame,
Declare the glory of his name.

4 Raised on devotion's lofty wing,
Do thou, my soul, his glories sing;
And let his praise employ thy tongue,
Till listening worlds shall join the song!
Thomas Blacklock, 1754.

GOD,—HIS PRAISE.

FADEN. 8s & 7s. DOUBLE.

120.

1 MIGHTY God, while angels bless thee,
   May an infant lisp thy name?
  Lord of men as well as angels,
   Thou art every creature's theme.
  Lord of every land and nation,
   Ancient of eternal days,
  Sounded through the wide creation
   Be thy just and lawful praise.

2 For the grandeur of thy nature,
   Grand beyond a seraph's thought;
  For created works of power, [wrought;
   Works with skill and kindness
  For thy providence, that governs
   Through thine empire's wide domain,
  Wings an angel, guides a sparrow;
   Blessed be thy gentle reign.

3 But thy rich, thy free redemption,
   Dark through brightness, all along:
  Thought is poor, and poor expression;
   Who dare sing that awful song?
  Brightness of the Father's glory,
   Shall thy praise unuttered lie?
  Fly, my tongue, such guilty silence!
   Sing the Lord who came to die.

4 From the highest throne in glory,
   To the cross of deepest woe,
  All to ransom guilty captives;
   Flow, my praise, forever flow.
  Go, return, immortal Saviour;
   Leave thy footstool, take thy throne;
  Thence return, and reign forever;
   Be the kingdom all thy own.
                    Robert Robinson, 1774.

121.

1 PRAISE to thee, thou great Creator!
   Praise to thee from every tongue.
  Join, my soul, with every creature,
   Join the universal song.
  Father, Source of all compassion,
   Pure, unbounded grace is thine:
  Hail the God of our salvation!
   Praise him for his love divine.

2 For ten thousand blessings given,
   For the hope of future joy, [heaven
  Sound his praise through earth and
   Sound Jehovah's praise on high.
  Joyfully on earth adore him,
   Till in heaven our song we raise;
  There, enraptured, fall before him,
   Lost in wonder, love, and praise.
                    John Fawcett, 1782. a.

GOD,—HIS PRAISE.

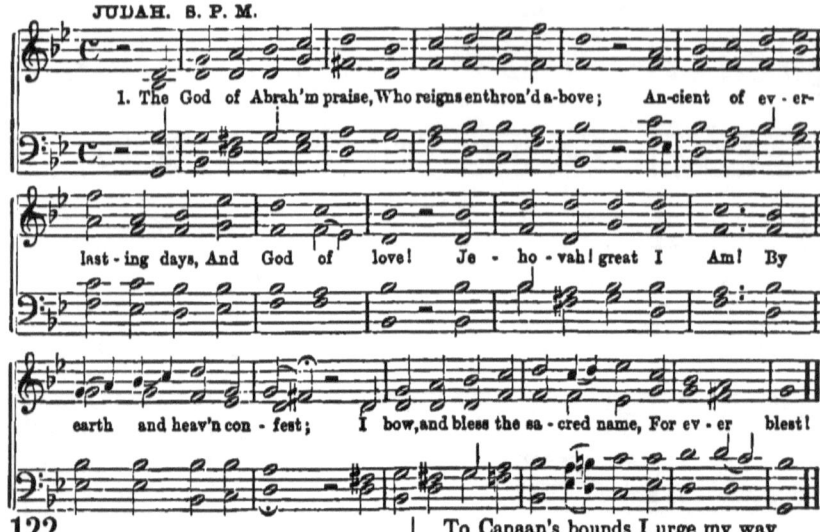

JUDAH. S. P. M.

1. The God of Abrah'm praise, Who reigns enthron'd a-bove; An-cient of ev-er-last-ing days, And God of love! Je-ho-vah! great I Am! By earth and heav'n con-fest; I bow, and bless the sa-cred name, For ev-er blest!

122.

2 The God of Abrah'm praise!
   At whose supreme command
   From earth I rise, and seek the joys
     At his right hand:
   I all on earth forsake,
   Its wisdom, fame and power,
   And him my only portion make,
     My Shield and Tower.

3 The God of Abrah'm praise!
   Whose all-sufficient grace
   Shall guide me all my happy days
     In all his ways:
   He calls a worm his friend!
   He calls himself my God!
   And he shall save me to the end,
     Through Jesus' blood.

4 He by himself hath sworn;
   I on his oath depend;
   I shall, on eagle's wings upborne,
     To heaven ascend:
   I shall behold his face;
   I shall his power adore,
   And sing the wonders of his grace
     For evermore!
          Thomas Olivers, 1772.

123.

1 Though nature's strength decay,
   And earth and hell withstand,
   To Canaan's bounds I urge my way
     At his command:
   The watery deep I pass,
   With Jesus in my view;
   And, through the howling wilderness,
     My way pursue.

2 The goodly land I see,
   With peace and plenty blest;
   A land of sacred liberty
     And endless rest:
   There milk and honey flow,
   And oil and wine abound;
   And trees of life forever grow,
     With mercy crowned.

3 There dwells the Lord our King,
   The Lord our righteousness;
   Triumphant o'er the world and sin,
     The Prince of peace,
   On Zion's sacred height,
   His kingdom still maintains;
   And, glorious with his saints in light,
     Forever reigns.

4 The whole triumphant host
   Give thanks to God on high;
   "Hail! Father, Son, and Holy Ghost!"
     They ever cry;
   Hail! Abraham's God and mine!
   I join the heavenly lays;
   All might and majesty are thine,
     And endless praise!
          Thomas Olivers, 1772.

GOD,—HIS PRAISE.

NOTTINGHAM. C. M.

1. My God, how wonderful thou art, Thy majesty how bright! How beautiful thy mercy-seat In depths of burning light!

124.

1 My God, how wonderful thou art,
  Thy majesty how bright!
  How beautiful thy mercy-seat
  In depths of burning light!

2 Oh, how I fear thee, living God,
  With deepest, tenderest fears;
  And worship thee with trembling hope,
  And penitential tears!

3 Yet I may love thee, too, O Lord,
  Almighty as thou art;
  For thou hast stooped to ask of me
  The love of my poor heart.

4 No earthly father loves like thee;
  No mother, half so mild,
  Bears and forbears, as thou hast done
  With me thy sinful child.

5 Only to sit and think of God,
  Oh, what a joy it is! [name,
  To think the thought, to breathe the
  Earth has no higher bliss.

6 Father of Jesus, love's reward,
  What rapture will it be,
  Prostrate before thy throne to lie,
  And ever gaze on thee!
  Frederick W. Faber, 1849.

125.

1 My soul shall praise thee, O my God,
  Through all my mortal days;
  And to eternity prolong
  Thy vast, thy boundless praise.

2 In each bright hour of peace and hope,
  Be this my sweet employ!
  Devotion heightens all my bliss,
  And sanctifies my joy.

3 When gloomy care or keen distress
  Invades my throbbing breast,
  My tongue shall learn to speak thy praise,
  And soothe my pains to rest.

4 Nor shall my tongue alone proclaim
  The honors of my God:
  My life, with all its active powers,
  Shall spread thy praise abroad.

5 And though these lips shall cease to move,
  Though death shall close these eyes,
  Yet shall my soul to nobler heights
  Of joy and transport rise.

6 Then shall my powers, in endless strains,
  Their grateful tribute pay:
  The theme demands an angel's tongue,
  And an eternal day.
  Ottiwell Heginbotham, 1765.

DOXOLOGY.

1 The God of mercy be adored,
  Who calls our souls from death,
  Who saves by his redeeming word
  And new-creating breath.

2 To praise the Father, and the Son,
  And Spirit all divine,
  The One in Three and Three in One,
  Let saints and angels join.
  Isaac Watts, 1709.

GOD,—HIS PRAISE.

NEWCOURT. L. P. M.

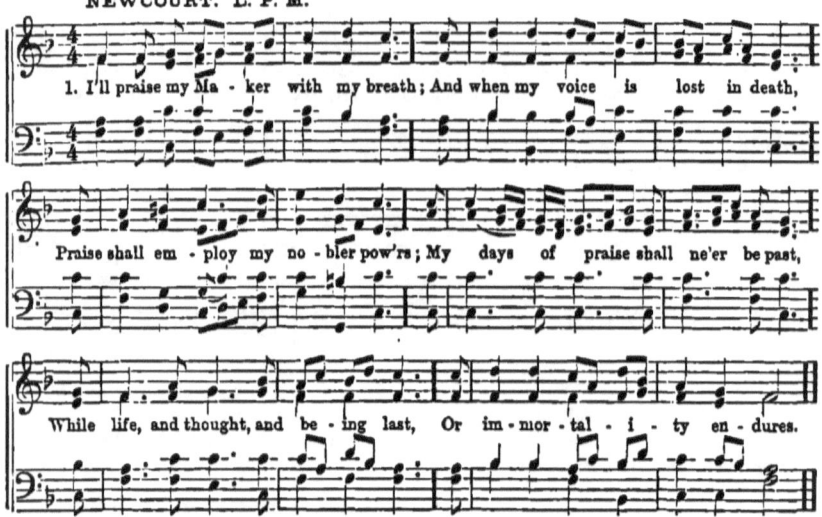

I'll praise my Maker with my breath; And when my voice is lost in death, Praise shall employ my nobler pow'rs; My days of praise shall ne'er be past, While life, and thought, and being last, Or immortality endures.

126.   PSALM 146.

1 I'LL praise my Maker with my breath;
And when my voice is lost in death,
Praise shall employ my nobler powers;
My days of praise shall ne'er be past,
While life, and thought, and being last,
Or immortality endures.

2 Happy the man whose hopes rely
On Israel's God; he made the sky,
And earth, and seas, with all their train;
His truth forever stands secure;
He saves the opprest, he feeds the poor,
And none shall find his promise vain.

3 The Lord hath eyes to give the blind;
The Lord supports the sinking mind;
He sends the laboring conscience peace:
He helps the stranger in distress,
The widow and the fatherless,
And grants the prisoner sweet release.

4 I'll praise him while he lends me breath;
And when my voice is lost in death,
Praise shall employ my nobler powers:
My days of praise shall ne'er be past,
While life and thought and being last,
Or immortality endures.
Isaac Watts, 1719.

127.   PSALM 96.

1 LET all the earth their voices raise
To sing the choicest psalms of praise,
To sing and bless Jehovah's name:
His glory let the heathen know,
His wonders to the nations show,
And all his saving works proclaim.

2 The heathen know thy glory, Lord;
The wondering nations read thy word;
Among us is Jehovah known:
Our worship shall no more be paid
To gods which mortal hands have made;
Our Maker is our God alone.

3 He framed the globe, he built the sky,
He made the shining worlds on high,
And reigns complete in glory there:
His beams are majesty and light;
His beauties how divinely bright!
His temple how divinely fair!

4 Come, the great day, the glorious hour,
When earth shall feel his saving power,
And barbarous nations fear his name;
Then shall the race of man confess
The beauty of his holiness,
And in his courts his grace proclaim.
Isaac Watts, 1719.

GOD,—HIS PRAISE.

BLOOMFIELD CHANT. L. M.

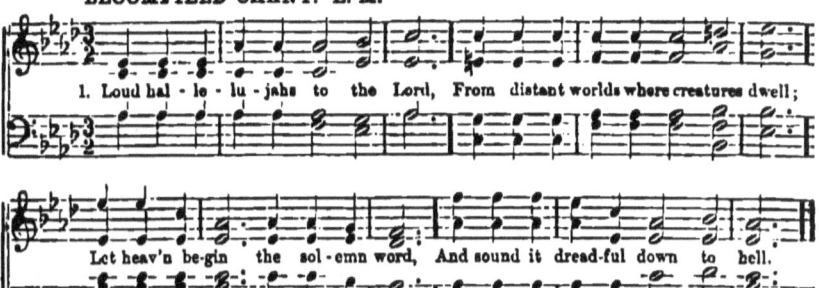

1. Loud hallelujahs to the Lord, From distant worlds where creatures dwell; Let heav'n begin the solemn word, And sound it dreadful down to hell.

128. PSALM 148.

1 LOUD hallelujahs to the Lord, [dwell,
From distant worlds, where creatures
Let heaven begin the solemn word,
And sound it dreadful down to hell.

2 Wide as his vast dominion lies,
Make the Creator's name be known;
Loud as his thunder shout the praise,
And sound it lofty as his throne.

3 Jehovah! 't is a glorious word;
Oh, may it dwell on every tongue;
But saints, who best have known the Lord,
Are bound to raise the noblest song.

4 Speak of the wonders of that love
Which Gabriel plays on every chord;
From all below and all above,
Loud hallelujahs to the Lord.
Isaac Watts, 1719.

129. PSALM 133.

1 WITH all my powers of heart and tongue,
I'll praise my Maker in my song;
Angels shall hear the notes I raise,
Approve the song, and join the praise.

2 I'll sing thy truth and mercy, Lord;
I'll sing the wonders of thy word;
Not all thy works and names below
So much thy power and glory show.

3 To God I cried when troubles rose;
He heard me and subdued my foes;
He did my rising fears control, [soul.
And strength diffused through all my

4 Amidst a thousand snares I stand,
Upheld and guarded by thy hand;
Thy words my fainting soul revive,
And keep my dying faith alive.

5 Grace will complete what grace begins,
To save from sorrows or from sins;
The work that wisdom undertakes,
Eternal mercy ne'er forsakes.
Isaac Watts, 1719.

130. PSALM 63.

1 GREAT God, indulge my humble claim;
Thou art my hope, my joy, my rest;
The glories that compose thy name
Stand all engaged to make me blest.

2 Thou great and good, thou just and wise,
Thou art my Father and my God;
And I am thine by sacred ties, [blood.
Thy son, thy servant, bought with

3 With heart and eyes and lifted hands,
For thee I long, to thee I look;
As travellers in thirsty lands
Pant for the cooling water-brook.

4 With early feet I love t' appear
Among thy saints, and seek thy face;
Oft have I seen thy glory there,
And felt the power of sovereign grace.

5 I'll lift my hands, I'll raise my voice,
While I have breath to pray or praise;
This work shall make my heart rejoice,
And spend the remnant of my days.
Isaac Watts, 1712.

GOD,—HIS PRAISE.

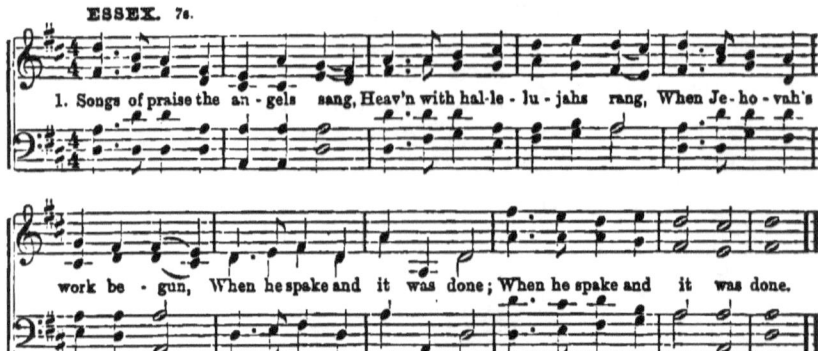

ESSEX. 7s.

1. Songs of praise the angels sang, Heav'n with hal-le-lu-jahs rang, When Jehovah's work begun, When he spake and it was done; When he spake and it was done.

131.

1 Songs of praise the angels sang,
Heaven with hallelujahs rang,
When Jehovah's work begun,
When he spake, and it was done.

2 Songs of praise awoke the morn
When the Prince of peace was born;
Songs of praise awoke when he
Captive led captivity.

3 Heaven and earth must pass away,
Songs of praise shall crown that day;
God will make new heavens, new earth,
Songs of praise shall hail their birth.

4 And can man alone be dumb,
Till that glorious kingdom come?
No: the church delights to raise
Psalms, and hymns, and songs of praise.

5 Saints below, with heart and voice,
Still in songs of praise rejoice;
Learning here, by faith and love,
Songs of praise to sing above.

6 Borne upon their latest breath,
Songs of praise shall conquer death;
Then, amidst eternal joy,
Songs of praise their powers employ.
James Montgomery, 1825.

132.   Psalm 150.

1 Praise the Lord, his glories show,
Saints within his courts below,
Angels round his throne above,
All that see and share his love.

2 Earth to heaven, and heaven to earth,
Tell his wonders, sing his worth;
Age to age, and shore to shore,
Praise him, praise him, evermore!

3 Praise the Lord, his mercies trace;
Praise his providence and grace;
All that he for man hath done,
All he sends us through his Son:

4 Strings and voices, hands and hearts,
In the concert bear your parts;
All that breathe, your Lord adore,
Praise him, praise him, evermore!
H. F. Lyte, 1834.

133.   Psalm 92.

1 Thou, who art enthroned above;
Thou, by whom we live and move;
Thou, who art most great, most high,
God from all eternity!

2 Oh, how sweet, how excellent,
When all tongues and hearts consent,
Grateful hearts and joyful tongues,
Hymning thee in tuneful songs!

3 When the morning paints the skies,
When the stars of evening rise,
We thy praises will record,
Sovereign Ruler, mighty Lord!

4 Decks the spring with flowers the field?
Harvest rich doth autumn yield?
Giver of these blessings, we
Pour the grateful song to thee.
George Sandys, 1648. a.

GOD,—HIS PRAISE.

WARE. L. M.

1. Not un-to us, al-might-y Lord, But to thy-self the glo-ry be! Cre-a-ted by thy aw-ful word, We on-ly live to hon-or thee.

134. PSALM 115.
1 NOT unto us, almighty Lord,
   But to thyself the glory be!
   Created by thy awful word,
   We only live to honor thee.

2 Where is their God, the heathen cry,
   And bow to senseless wood and stone;
   Our God, we tell them, fills the sky,
   And calls ten thousand worlds his own.

3 Vain gods! vain men! the Lord alone
   Is Israel's worship. Israel's friend;
   Oh, fear his power, his goodness own,
   And love him, trust him, to the end.

4 Who lean on him, from strength to strength,
   From light to light, shall onward move,
   Till through the grave they pass at length,
   To sing on high his saving love.
   H. F. Lyte, 1834

135.
1 GOD of my life, through all its days
   My grateful powers shall sound thy praise;
   The song shall wake with opening light,
   And warble to the silent night.

2 When anxious cares would break my rest,
   And grief would tear my throbbing breast,
   Thy tuneful praises, raised on high,
   Shall check the murmur and the sigh.

3 When death o'er nature shall prevail,
   And all its powers of language fail,
   Joy through my swimming eyes shall break,
   And mean the thanks I cannot speak.

4 But, oh, when that last conflict's o'er,
   And I am chained to flesh no more,
   With what glad accents shall I rise
   To join the music of the skies!

5 Soon shall I learn the exalted strains
   Which echo o'er the heavenly plains,
   And emulate, with joy unknown,
   The glowing seraphs round thy throne.

6 The cheerful tribute will I give,
   Long as a deathless soul can live;
   A work so sweet, a theme so high,
   Demands and crowns eternity.
   Philip Doddridge, 1755.

136. PSALM 103.
1 BLESS, O my soul, the living God;
   Call home thy thoughts that rove abroad;
   Let all the powers within me join
   In work and worship so divine.

2 Bless, O my soul, the God of grace;
   His favors claim thy highest praise:
   Why should the wonders he hath wrought
   Be lost in silence and forgot?

3 'Tis he, my soul, that sent his Son
   To die for crimes which thou hast done;
   He owns the ransom, and forgives
   The hourly follies of our lives.

4 Let the whole earth his power confess,
   Let the whole earth adore his grace;
   The Gentile with the Jew shall join
   In work and worship so divine.
   Isaac Watts, 1719.

GOD.—HIS PRAISE.

DUKE STREET. L. M.

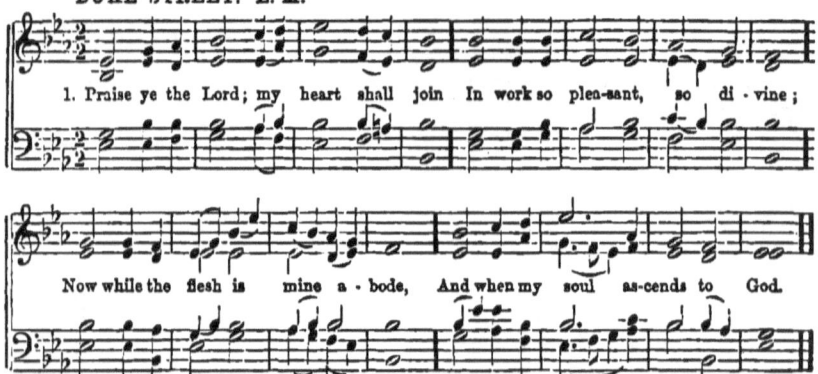

1. Praise ye the Lord; my heart shall join In work so pleasant, so divine; Now while the flesh is mine abode, And when my soul ascends to God.

137. PSALM 146.

1 Praise ye the Lord; my heart shall join
In work so pleasant, so divine;
Now while the flesh is mine abode,
And when my soul ascends to God.

2 Praise shall employ my noblest powers,
While immortality endures:
My days of praise shall ne'er be past
While life, and thought, and being last.

3 Happy the man whose hopes rely
On Israel's God; he made the sky,
And earth, and seas, with all their train;
And none shall find his promise vain.

4 His truth forever stands secure;
He saves th' oppressed, he feeds the poor;
He sends the laboring conscience peace,
And grants the prisoner sweet release.

5 The Lord hath eyes to give the blind;
The Lord supports the sinking mind;
He helps the stranger in distress,
The widow and the fatherless.

6 He loves his saints, he knows them well,
But turns the wicked down to hell;
Thy God, O Zion, ever reigns!
Praise him in everlasting strains.
Isaac Watts, 1719.

138. PSALM 57.

1 My God, in whom are all the springs
Of boundless love and grace unknown;
Hide me beneath thy spreading wings,
Till the dark cloud is overblown.

2 Up to the heavens I send my cry;
The Lord will my desires perform;
He sends his angels from the sky,
And saves me from the threatening storm.

3 Be thou exalted, O my God,
Above the heavens, where angels dwell;
Thy power on earth be known abroad,
And land to land thy wonders tell.

4 My heart is fixed; my song shall raise
Immortal honors to thy name;
Awake, my tongue, to sound his praise;
My tongue, the glory of my frame.

5 High o'er the earth his mercy reigns,
And reaches to the utmost sky;
His truth to endless years remains,
When lower worlds dissolve and die.

6 Be thou exalted, O my God,
Above the heavens, where angels dwell;
Thy power on earth be known abroad,
And land to land thy wonders tell.
Isaac Watts, 1719.

139. PSALM 117.

1 From all that dwell below the skies,
Let the Creator's praise arise;
Let the Redeemer's name be sung,
Through every land, by every tongue.

2 Eternal are thy mercies, Lord!
Eternal truth attends thy word; [shore,
Thy praise shall sound from shore to
Till suns shall rise and set no more.
Isaac Watts, 1719.

GOD,—HIS ATTRIBUTES.

YORK. C. M.

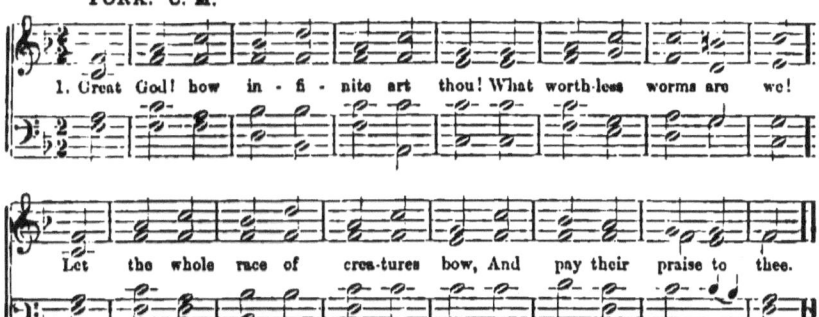

1. Great God! how in-fi-nite art thou! What worth-less worms are we! Let the whole race of crea-tures bow, And pay their praise to thee.

140.

1 GREAT God, how infinite art thou!
  What worthless worms are we!
  Let the whole race of creatures bow,
  And pay their praise to thee.

2 Thy throne eternal ages stood,
  Ere seas or stars were made;
  Thou art the ever-living God,
  Were all the nations dead.

3 Eternity, with all its years,
  Stands present in thy view;
  To thee there's nothing old appears,
  Great God, there's nothing new.

4 Our lives through various scenes are drawn,
  And vexed with trifling cares;
  While thine eternal thought moves on
  Thine undisturbed affairs.

5 Great God, how infinite art thou!
  What worthless worms are we!
  Let the whole race of creatures bow,
  And pay their praise to thee.
  Isaac Watts, 1709.

141.   PSALM 90.

1 OUR God, our help in ages past,
  Our hope for years to come,
  Our shelter from the stormy blast,
  And our eternal home:

2 Under the shadow of thy throne
  Thy saints have dwelt secure;
  Sufficient is thine arm alone,
  And our defence is sure.

3 Before the hills in order stood,
  Or earth received her frame,
  From everlasting thou art God,
  To endless years the same.

4 Thy word commands our flesh to dust,
  " Return, ye sons of men;"
  All nations rose from earth at first,
  And turn to earth again.

5 A thousand ages in thy sight
  Are like an evening gone;
  Short as the watch that ends the night
  Before the rising sun.

6 Time, like an ever-rolling stream,
  Bears all its sons away;
  They fly, forgotten, as a dream
  Dies at the opening day.

7 Our God, our help in ages past,
  Our hope for years to come,
  Be thou our guard while troubles last,
  And our eternal home.
  Isaac Watts, 1719.

142.   PSALM 89.

1 WITH reverence let the saints appear,
  And bow before the Lord;
  His high commands with reverence hear,
  And tremble at his word.

2 How terrible thy glories be!
  How bright thine armies shine!
  Where is the power that vies with thee,
  Or truth compared with thine?

GOD,—HIS ATTRIBUTES.

LONDON-NEW. C. M.

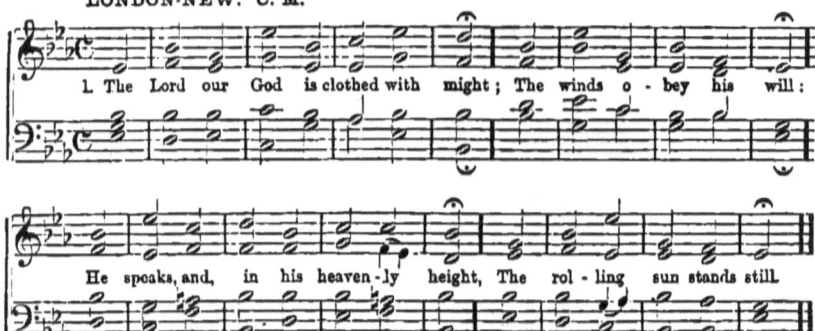

1. The Lord our God is clothed with might; The winds obey his will: He speaks, and, in his heavenly height, The rolling sun stands still.

3 The northern pole and southern, rest
On thy supporting hand;
Darkness and day from east to west
Move round at thy command.

4 Thy words the raging winds control,
And rule the boisterous deep;
Thou mak'st the sleeping billows roll,
The rolling billows sleep.

5 Justice and judgment are thy throne,
Yet wondrous is thy grace;
While truth and mercy, joined in one,
Invite us near thy face.
Isaac Watts, 1719.

143.

1 The Lord our God is clothed with might;
The winds obey his will;
He speaks, and in his heavenly height
The rolling sun stands still.

2 Rebel, ye waves, and o'er the land
With threatening aspect roar:
The Lord uplifts his awful hand,
And chains you to the shore.

3 Howl, winds of night, your force combine;
Without his high behest
Ye shall not, in the mountain pine,
Disturb the sparrow's nest.

4 His voice sublime is heard afar,
In distant peals it dies;
He yokes the whirlwind to his car,
And sweeps the howling skies.

5 Ye nations bend, in reverence bend;
Ye monarchs, wait his nod,
And bid the choral song ascend
To celebrate our God.
Henry Kirke White, 1806.

144. Psalm 18.

1 In my distress I sought my God,
I sought Jehovah's face;
My cry before him came; he heard
Out of his holy place.

2 The Lord descended from above,
And bowed the heavens most high;
And underneath his feet he cast
The darkness of the sky.

3 On cherub and on cherubim,
Full royally, he rode;
And, on the wings of mighty winds,
Came flying all abroad.

4 He sat serene upon the floods,
Their fury to restrain;
And he, as sovereign Lord and King,
For evermore shall reign.

5 The Lord will give his people strength,
Whereby they shall increase;
And he will bless his chosen flock
With everlasting peace.

6 Give glory to his awful name,
And honor him alone;
Give worship to his majesty
Upon his holy throne.
Thomas Sternhold, 1540.

GOD,—HIS ATTRIBUTES.

WOODLAND. C. M.

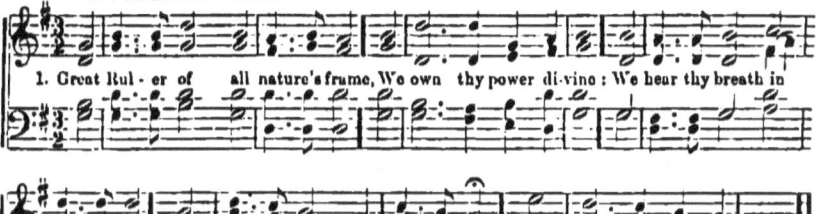
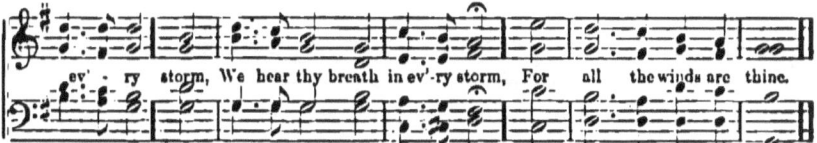

1. Great Ruler of all nature's frame, We own thy power divine: We hear thy breath in ev'ry storm, We hear thy breath in ev'ry storm, For all the winds are thine.

145.

1 Great Ruler of all nature's frame,
  We own thy power divine:
  We hear thy breath in every storm,
  For all the winds are thine.

2 Wide as they sweep their sounding way,
  They work thy sovereign will;
  And awed by thy majestic voice
  Confusion shall be still.

3 Thy mercy tempers every blast
  To them that seek thy face,
  And mingles with the tempest's roar
  The whispers of thy grace.

4 Those gentle whispers let me hear
  Till all the tumult cease;
  And gales of paradise shall lull
  My weary soul to peace.
  Philip Doddridge, 1755.

146. Psalm 139.

1 In all my vast concerns with thee,
  In vain my soul would try
  To shun thy presence, Lord, or flee
  The notice of thine eye.

2 Thine all-surrounding sight surveys
  My rising and my rest,
  My public walks, my private ways,
  And secrets of my breast.

3 My thoughts lie open to the Lord
  Before they're formed within;
  And, ere my lips pronounce the word,
  He knows the sense I mean.

4 Oh, wondrous knowledge, deep and high!
  Where can a creature hide?

  Within thy circling arms I lie
  Enclosed on every side.

5 So let thy grace surround me still,
  And like a bulwark prove,
  To guard my soul from every ill,
  Secured by sovereign love.
  Isaac Watts, 1719.

147.

1 Eternal light! eternal light!
  How pure the soul must be,
  When, placed within thy searching sight,
  It shrinks not, but with calm delight
  Can live and look on thee!

2 The spirits that surround thy throne
  May bear the burning bliss;
  But that is surely theirs alone,
  Since they have never, never known
  A fallen world like this.

3 Oh, how shall I, whose native sphere
  Is dark, whose mind is dim,
  Before the Ineffable appear,
  And on my naked spirit bear
  That uncreated beam?

4 There is a way for man to rise
  To that sublime abode;
  An Offering and a Sacrifice,
  A Holy Spirit's energies,
  An Advocate with God.

5 These, these, prepare us for the light
  Of majesty above:
  The sons of ignorance and night
  Can stand in the eternal light,
  Through the eternal love.
  Thomas Binney, 1826.

GOD,—HIS ATTRIBUTES.

ALMIN. L. M.

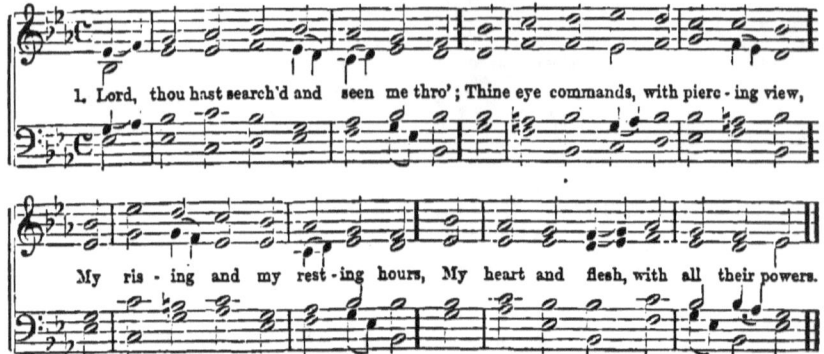

1. Lord, thou hast search'd and seen me thro'; Thine eye commands, with pierc-ing view, My ris-ing and my rest-ing hours, My heart and flesh, with all their powers.

148.   Psalm 139.

1 Lord, thou hast searched and seen me through;
Thine eye commands, with piercing view,
My rising and my resting hours,
My heart and flesh, with all their powers.

2 My thoughts, before they are my own,
Are to my God distinctly known;
He knows the words I mean to speak,
Ere from my opening lips they break.

3 Within thy circling power I stand;
On every side I find thy hand:
Awake, asleep, at home, abroad,
I am surrounded still with God.

4 Amazing knowledge, vast and great!
What large extent! what lofty height!
My soul, with all the powers I boast,
Is in the boundless prospect lost.

5 Oh, may these thoughts possess my breast,
Where'er I rove, where'er I rest!
Nor let my weaker passions dare
Consent to sin, for God is there.
Isaac Watts, 1719.

149.

1 Lord, thou hast formed mine every part,
Mine inmost thought is known to thee;
Each word, each feeling of my heart,
Thine ear doth hear, thine eye can see.

2 Though I should seek the shades of night,
And hide myself in guilty fear,
To thee the darkness seems as light,
The midnight as the noonday clear.

3 The heavens, the earth, the sea, the sky,
All own thee ever present there;
Where'er I turn thou still art nigh,
Thy Spirit dwelling everywhere.

4 Oh, may that Spirit, ever blest,
Upon my soul in radiance shine,
Till, welcomed to eternal rest,
I taste thy presence, Lord divine!
Robert Allan Scott, 1839.

150.

1 What secret place, what distant star,
Is like, dread Lord, to thine abode?
Why dwellest thou from us so far?
We yearn for thee, thou hidden God.

2 Vain searchers! but we need not mourn:
We need not stretch our weary wings;
Thou meetest us, where'er we turn;
Thou beamest, Lord, from all bright things.

3 But sweetest, Lord, dost thou appear
In the dear Saviour's smiling face:
The heavenly Majesty draws near,
And offers us its kind embrace.

4 To us, vain searchers after God,
To us the Holy Ghost doth come;
From us thou hidest thine abode;
But thou wilt make our souls thy home.

5 O Glory that no eye may bear!
O Presence bright, our soul's sweet guest!
O farthest off, O ever near!
Most hidden and most manifest!
Thomas H. Gill, 1860.

GOD,—HIS ATTRIBUTES.

PARK PLACE. H. M.

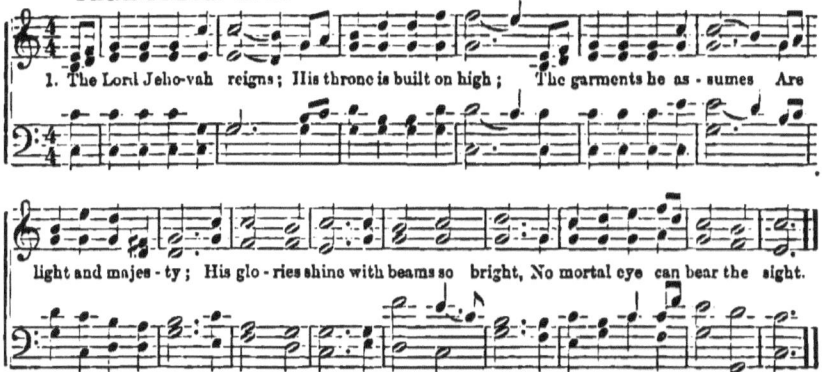

1. The Lord Jehovah reigns; His throne is built on high; The garments he assumes Are light and majesty; His glo-ries shine with beams so bright, No mortal eye can bear the sight.

151.

1 THE Lord Jehovah reigns;
His throne is built on high;
The garments he assumes
Are light and majesty;
His glories shine with beams so bright,
No mortal eye can bear the sight.

2 The thunders of his hand
Keep the wide world in awe;
His wrath and justice stand
To guard his holy law;
And where his love resolves to bless,
His truth confirms and seals the grace.

3 Through all his ancient works
Surprising wisdom shines,
Confounds the powers of hell,
And breaks their cursed designs;
Strong is his arm, and shall fulfil
His great decrees, his sovereign will.

4 And can this mighty King
Of glory condescend,
And will he write his name,
My Father and my Friend?
I love his name, I love his word;
Join all my powers, and praise the Lord.
Isaac Watts, 1709.

152. PSALM 93. Tune, "Peters," p. 11. S. P. M.

1 THE Lord Jehovah reigns,
And royal state maintains,

His head with awful glories crowned;
Arrayed in robes of light,
Begirt with sovereign might,
And rays of majesty around.

2 Upheld by thy commands,
The world securely stands,
And skies and stars obey thy word:
Thy throne was fixed on high
Before the starry sky:
Eternal is thy kingdom, Lord.

3 In vain the noisy crowd,
Like billows fierce and loud,
Against thine empire rage and roar;
In vain, with angry spite,
The surly nations fight,
And dash like waves against the shore.

4 Let floods and nations rage,
And all their powers engage;
Let swelling tides assault the sky;
The terrors of thy frown
Shall beat their madness down;
Thy throne forever stands on high.

5 Thy promises are true,
Thy grace is ever new;
'There fixed, thy church shall ne'er remove:
Thy saints, with holy fear,
Shall in thy courts appear,
And sing thine everlasting love.
Isaac Watts, 1719.

GOD,—HIS ATTRIBUTES.

OCTAVIUS. L. M.

1. The Lord is King! lift up thy voice, O earth; and all ye heav'ns rejoice; From world to world the joy shall ring, The Lord omnipotent is King.

153.

1 The Lord is King! lift up thy voice,
   O earth; and all ye heavens, rejoice;
   From world to world the joy shall ring,
   The Lord omnipotent is King.

2 The Lord is King! who then shall dare
   Resist his will, distrust his care,
   Or murmur at his wise decrees,
   Or doubt his royal promises?

3 Oh, when his wisdom can mistake,
   His might decay, his love forsake,
   Then may his children cease to sing,
   The Lord omnipotent is King!

4 One Lord, one empire all secures;
   He reigns, and life and death are yours:
   Through earth and heaven one song shall ring,
   The Lord omnipotent is King.
   Josiah Conder, 1850.

154.

1 Awake, my tongue, thy tribute bring
   To him who gave thee power to sing:
   Praise him who is all praise above,
   The source of wisdom and of love.

2 How vast his knowledge! how profound!
   A depth where all our thoughts are drowned!
   The stars he numbers, and their names
   He gives to all those heavenly flames.

3 Through each bright world above, behold
   Ten thousand thousand charms unfold;
   Earth, air, and mighty seas combine,
   To speak his wisdom all divine.

4 But in redemption, oh, what grace!
   Its wonders, oh, what thought can trace!
   Here wisdom shines forever bright:
   Praise him, my soul, with sweet delight.
   John Needham, 1768.

155.   Psalm 19.

1 The spacious firmament on high,
   With all the blue ethereal sky,
   And spangled heavens, a shining frame,
   Their great Original proclaim.

2 The unwearied sun, from day to day,
   Does his Creator's power display,
   And publishes to every land
   The work of an almighty hand.

3 Soon as the evening shades prevail,
   The moon takes up the wondrous tale,
   And nightly to the listening earth
   Repeats the story of her birth;

4 While all the stars that round her burn,
   And all the planets in their turn,
   Confirm the tidings as they roll,
   And spread the truth from pole to pole.

5 What though in solemn silence all
   Move round the dark terrestrial ball?
   What though no real voice nor sound
   Amidst their radiant orbs be found?

6 In reason's ear they all rejoice,
   And utter forth a glorious voice;
   Forever singing, as they shine,
   "The hand that made us is divine."
   Joseph Addison, 1712.

GOD,—HIS PROVIDENCE. 71

DALLAS. 7s.

156. Psalm 113.
1 Hallelujah! raise, oh raise
To our God the song of praise;
All his servants join to sing
God our Saviour and our King.

2 Blessèd be for evermore
That dread name which we adore!
Round the world his praise be sung,
Through all lands, in every tongue!

3 O'er all nations God alone,
Higher than the heavens his throne;
Who is like to God Most High,
Infinite in majesty?

4 Yet to view the heavens he bends,
Yea, to earth he condescends;
Passing by the rich and great
For the low and desolate.

5 He can raise the poor to stand
With the princes of the land;
Wealth upon the needy shower,
Set the meanest high in power.

6 He the broken spirit cheers;
Turns to joy the mourner's tears;
Such the wonders of his ways;
Praise his name, forever praise.
Josiah Conder, 1854.

157. Psalm 136.
1 Let us with a gladsome mind
Praise the Lord, for he is kind;
For his mercy shall endure,
Ever faithful, ever sure.

2 Let us sound his name abroad,
For of gods he is the God;
For his mercies shall endure,
Ever faithful, ever sure.

3 He, with all-commanding might,
Filled the new-made world with light
For his mercy shall endure,
Ever faithful, ever sure.

4 All things living he doth feed,
His full hand supplies their need;
For his mercy shall endure,
Ever faithful, ever sure.

5 He his chosen race did bless
In the wasteful wilderness;
For his mercy shall endure,
Ever faithful, ever sure.

6 He hath with a piteous eye
Looked upon our misery;
For his mercy shall endure,
Ever faithful, ever sure.

7 Let us, then, with gladsome mind,
Praise the Lord, for he is kind;
For his mercy shall endure,
Ever faithful, ever sure.
John Milton, 1623, a.

DOXOLOGY.
Sing we to our God above
Praise eternal as his love:
Praise him, all ye heavenly host;
Father, Son, and Holy Ghost.

GOD,—HIS PROVIDENCE.

ENMORE. C. M.

1 O Lord, how good, how great art thou, In heaven and earth the same! There angels at thy footstool bow, Here babes thy grace proclaim.

158. Psalm 8.

1 O Lord, how good, how great art thou,
  In heaven and earth the same!
  There angels at thy footstool bow,
  Here babes thy grace proclaim.

2 When glorious in the nightly sky
  Thy moon and stars I see,
  Oh, what is man! I wondering cry,
  To be so loved by thee!

3 To him thou hourly deign'st to give
  New mercies from on high;
  Didst quit thy throne with him to live,
  For him in pain to die.

4 Close to thine own bright seraphim
  His favored path is trod;
  And all beside are serving him,
  That he may serve his God.

5 O Lord, how good, how great art thou,
  In heaven and earth the same!
  There angels at thy footstool bow,
  Here babes thy grace proclaim.
  H. F. Lyte, 1834.

159.

1 Since all the downward tracts of time
  God's watchful eye surveys;
  Oh, who so wise to choose our lot,
  Or regulate our ways!

2 I cannot doubt his bounteous love,
  Immeasurably kind;
  To his unerring, gracious will,
  Be every wish resigned.

3 Good when he gives, supremely good,
  Nor less when he denies;
  E'en crosses from his sovereign hand
  Are blessings in disguise.
  James Hervey, 1745.

160.

1 God moves in a mysterious way
  His wonders to perform;
  He plants his footsteps in the sea,
  And rides upon the storm.

2 Deep in unfathomable mines
  Of never-failing skill
  He treasures up his bright designs,
  And works his sovereign will.

3 Ye fearful saints, fresh courage take,
  The clouds ye so much dread
  Are big with mercy, and shall break
  In blessings on your head.

4 Judge not the Lord by feeble sense,
  But trust him for his grace;
  Behind a frowning providence,
  He hides a smiling face.

5 His purposes will ripen fast,
  Unfolding every hour;
  The bud may have a bitter taste,
  But sweet will be the flower.

6 Blind unbelief is sure to err,
  And scan his works in vain;
  God is his own interpreter,
  And he will make it plain.
  William Cowper, 1774.

GOD,—HIS PROVIDENCE.

MARTYRS. C. M.

1. Keep silence, all created things, And wait your Maker's nod;
My soul stands trembling while she sings The honors of her God.

161.

1 KEEP silence, all created things,
   And wait your Maker's nod;
My soul stands trembling while she sings
   The honors of her God.

2 Life, death, and hell, and worlds unknown,
   Hang on his firm decree;
He sits on no precarious throne,
   Nor borrows leave to be.

3 Chained to his throne, a volume lies,
   With all the fates of men,
With every angel's form and size,
   Drawn by the eternal pen.

4 His providence unfolds the book,
   And makes his counsels shine;
Each opening leaf, and every stroke,
   Fulfils some deep design.

5 My God, I would not long to see
   My fate with curious eyes,
What gloomy lines are writ for me,
   Or what bright scenes may rise.

6 In thy fair book of life and grace,
   Oh, may I find my name
Recorded in some humble place,
   Beneath my Lord the Lamb!

Isaac Watts, 1709.

162.

1 How shall I praise th' eternal God,
   That Infinite Unknown?
Who can ascend his high abode,
   Or venture near his throne?

2 The great Invisible! He dwells
   Concealed in dazzling light;
But his all-searching eye reveals
   The secrets of the night.

3 Those watchful eyes, that never sleep,
   Survey the world around;
His wisdom is a boundless deep,
   Where all our thoughts are drowned.

4 He knows no shadow of a change,
   Nor alters his decrees;
Firm as a rock his truth remains
   To guard his promises.

5 Justice, upon a dreadful throne,
   Maintains the rights of God;
While mercy sends her pardons down,
   Bought with a Saviour's blood.

6 Now to my soul, immortal King,
   Speak some forgiving word;
Then 'twill be double joy to sing
   The glories of my Lord.

Isaac Watts, 1709.

GOD,—HIS PROVIDENCE.

HAMBURG. L. M.

1. Lord, how mysterious are thy ways! How blind are we! how mean our praise! Thy steps can mortal eyes explore? 'Tis ours to wonder and adore.

163.

1 LORD, how mysterious are thy ways!
How blind are we! how mean our praise!
Thy steps can mortal eyes explore?
'Tis ours to wonder and adore.

2 Thy deep decrees from creature sight
Are hid in shades of awful night;
Amid the lines, with curious eye,
Not angel minds presume to pry.

3 Great God! I would not ask to see
What in futurity shall be;
If light and bliss attend my days,
Then let my future hours be praise.

4 Is darkness and distress my share?
Then, let me trust thy guardian care;
Enough for me if love divine [shine.
At length through every cloud shall

5 Yet this my soul desires to know,
Be this my only wish below,
That Christ is mine; this great request
Grant, bounteous God, and I am blest.
Anne Steele, 1760.

164.

1 THY ways, O Lord! with wise design,
Are framed upon thy throne above,
And every dark and bending line
Meets in the centre of thy love.

2 With feeble light, and half obscure,
Poor mortals thy arrangements view;
Not knowing that the least are sure,
And the mysterious just and true.

3 Thy flock, thy own peculiar care,
Though now they seem to roam uneyed,
Are led or driven only where
They best and safest may abide.

4 They neither know nor trace the way;
But, trusting to thy piercing eye,
None of their feet to ruin stray,
Nor shall the weakest fail or die.

5 My favored soul shall meekly learn
To lay her reason at thy throne;
Too weak thy secrets to discern,
I'll trust thee for my guide alone.
Ambrose Serle, 1787.

165.

1 WAIT, O my soul, thy Maker's will;
Tumultuous passions, all be still!
Nor let a murmuring thought arise;
His ways are just, his counsels wise.

2 He in the thickest darkness dwells,
Performs his work, the cause conceals;
But, though his methods are unknown,
Judgment and truth support his throne.

3 In heaven, and earth, and air, and seas,
He executes his firm decrees;
And by his saints it stands confest,
That what he does is ever best.

4 Wait, then, my soul, submissive wait,
Prostrate before his awful seat;
And, 'midst the terrors of his rod,
Trust in a wise and gracious God.
Benjamin Beddome, 1818.

GOD,—HIS PROVIDENCE.

UXBRIDGE. L. M.

1. Lord, we adore thy vast de-signs, Th' obscure a-byss of prov-i-dence,
Too deep to sound with mor-tal lines, Too dark to view with fee-ble sense.

166.

1 LORD, we adore thy vast designs,
  The obscure abyss of providence,
  Too deep to sound with mortal lines,
  Too dark to view with feeble sense.

2 Now thou array'st thine awful face
  In angry frowns without a smile;
  We through the clouds believe thy grace,
  Secure of thy compassion still.

3 Through seas and storms of deep distress,
  We sail by faith, and not by sight;
  Faith guides us in the wilderness
  Through all the terrors of the night.

4 Dear Father, if thy lifted rod
  Resolve to scourge us here below,
  Still let us lean upon our God,
  Thine arm shall bear us safely through.
  Isaac Watts, 1709.

167.

1 LORD, my weak thought in vain would climb
  To search the starry vault profound;
  In vain would wing her flight sublime,
  To find creation's utmost bound.

2 But weaker yet that thought must prove
  To search thy great eternal plan,
  Thy sovereign counsels born of love
  Long ages ere the world began.

3 When my dim reason would demand
  Why that or this thou dost ordain,
  By some vast deep I seem to stand,
  Whose secrets I must ask in vain.

4 When doubts disturb my troubled breast,
  And all is dark as night to me,
  Here, as on solid rock, I rest;
  That so it seemeth good to thee.

5 Be this my joy, that evermore
  Thou rulest all things at thy will:
  Thy sovereign wisdom I adore,
  And calmly, sweetly trust thee still.
  Ray Palmer, 1858.

168.

1 UP to the Lord, that reigns on high,
  And views the nations from afar,
  Let everlasting praises fly,
  And tell how large his bounties are.

2 God, that must stoop to view the skies,
  And bow to see what angels do,
  Down to our earth he casts his eyes,
  And bends his footsteps downwards too.

3 He overrules all mortal things,
  And manages our mean affairs;
  On humble souls the King of kings
  Bestows his counsels and his cares.

4 Our sorrows and our tears we pour
  Into the bosom of our God;
  He hears us in the mournful hour,
  And helps to bear the heavy load.

5 Oh, could our thankful hearts devise
  A tribute equal to thy grace,
  To the third heaven our song should rise,
  And teach the golden harps thy praise.
  Isaac Watts, 1709.

GOD,—HIS PROVIDENCE.

BELGRAVE. C. M.

1. Sweet is the mem'ry of thy grace, My God, my heavenly King; Let age to age thy right-eous-ness In sounds of glo-ry sing.

169. PSALM 145.

1 SWEET is the memory of thy grace,
  My God, my heavenly King;
  Let age to age thy righteousness
  In sounds of glory sing.

2 God reigns on high, but ne'er confines
  His goodness to the skies;
  Through the whole earth his bounty shines,
  And every want supplies.

3 With longing eyes thy creatures wait
  On thee for daily food:
  Thy liberal hand provides their meat,
  And fills their mouth with good.

4 How kind are thy compassions, Lord!
  How slow thine anger moves!
  But soon he sends his pardoning word
  To cheer the souls he loves.

5 Creatures, with all their endless race,
  Thy power and praise proclaim;
  But saints that taste thy richer grace
  Delight to bless thy name.
  Isaac Watts, 1719.

170. PSALM 73.

1 GOD my supporter and my hope,
  My help forever near,
  Thy arm of mercy held me up
  When sinking in despair.

2 Thy counsels, Lord, shall guide my feet
  Through this dark wilderness;
  Thy hand conduct me near thy seat,
  To dwell before thy face.

3 Were I in heaven without my God,
  'Twould be no joy to me;
  And whilst this earth is my abode,
  I long for none but thee.

4 Behold, the sinners that remove
  Far from thy presence die;
  Not all the idol gods they love
  Can save them when they cry.

5 But to draw near to thee, my God,
  Shall be my sweet employ;
  My tongue shall sound thy works abroad,
  And tell the world my joy.
  Isaac Watts, 1719.

171. PSALM 121.

1 To heaven I lift my waiting eyes;
  There all my hopes are laid;
  The Lord, that built the earth and skies,
  Is my perpetual aid.

2 Their feet shall never slide nor fall
  Whom he designs to keep:
  His ear attends the softest call;
  His eyes can never sleep.

3 Israel, rejoice, and rest secure;
  Thy keeper is the Lord;
  His wakeful eyes employ his power
  For thine eternal guard.

4 He guards thy soul, he keeps thy breath,
  Where thickest dangers come;
  Go and return, secure from death,
  Till God commands thee home.
  Isaac Watts, 1719.

GOD,—HIS PROVIDENCE.

VANHALL'S HYMN. L. M.

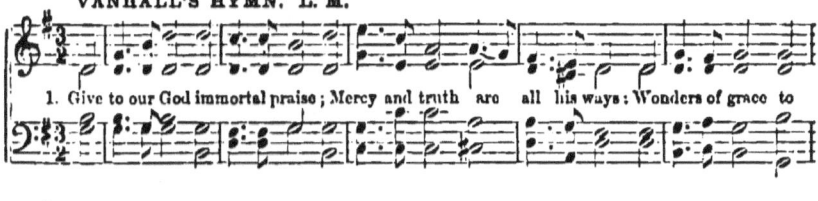
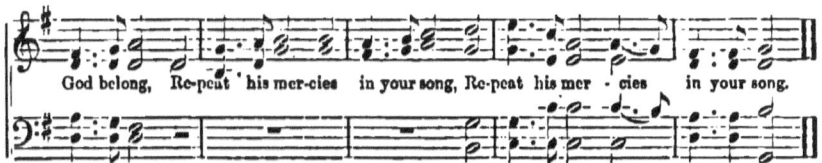

1. Give to our God immortal praise; Mercy and truth are all his ways: Wonders of grace to God belong, Repeat his mercies in your song, Repeat his mercies in your song.

172. PSALM 136.

1 GIVE to our God immortal praise;
Mercy and truth are all his ways:
Wonders of grace to God belong;
Repeat his mercies in your song.

2 Give to the Lord of lords renown,
The King of kings with glory crown:
His mercies ever shall endure,
When lords and kings are known no more.

3 He built the earth, he spread the sky,
And fixed the starry lights on high:
Wonders of grace to God belong;
Repeat his mercies in your song.

4 He fills the sun with morning light,
He bids the moon direct the night:
His mercies ever shall endure,
When suns and moons shall shine no more.

5 He sent his Son with power to save
From guilt, and darkness, and the grave:
Wonders of grace to God belong;
Repeat his mercies in your song.

6 Through this vain world he guides our feet,
And leads us to his heavenly seat:
His mercies ever shall endure,
When this vain world shall be no more.
Isaac Watts, 1719.

173. PSALM 107.

1 GIVE thanks to God; he reigns above,
Kind are his thoughts, his name is love:
His mercy ages past have known,
And ages long to come shall own.

2 Let the redeemed of the Lord
The wonders of his grace record;
Israel, the nation whom he chose,
And rescued from their mighty foes.

3 He feeds and clothes us all the way,
He guides our footsteps lest we stray,
He guards us with a powerful hand,
And brings us to the heavenly land.

4 Oh, let the saints with joy record
The truth and goodness of the Lord!
How great his works! how kind his ways!
Let every tongue pronounce his praise.
Isaac Watts, 1719.

174. PSALM 116.

1 RETURN, my soul, and sweetly rest
On thy almighty Father's breast;
The bounties of his grace adore,
And count his wondrous mercies o'er.

2 Thy mercy, Lord, preserved my breath,
And snatched my fainting soul from death,
Removed my sorrows, dried my tears,
And saved me from surrounding snares.

3 What shall I render to the Lord,
Or how his wondrous grace record?
To him my grateful voice I'll raise
With just thanksgiving to his praise.

4 O Zion! in thy sacred courts,
Where glory dwells and joy resorts,
To notes divine I'll tune the song,
And praise shall flow from every tongue.
John A. Latrobe, 1850.

GOD,—HIS PROVIDENCE.

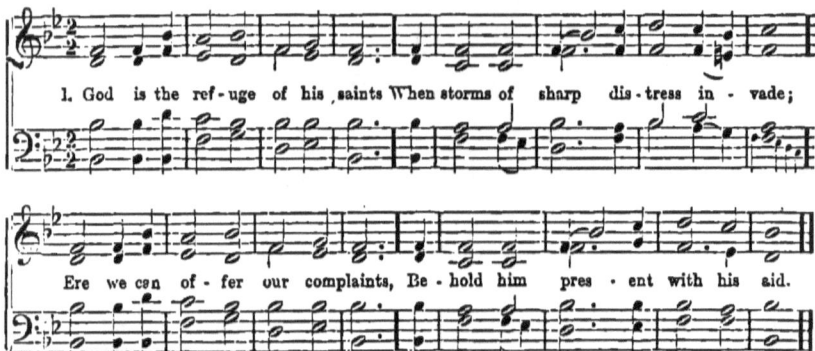

175. PSALM 46.
1 GOD is the refuge of his saints,
  When storms of sharp distress invade;
  Ere we can offer our complaints,
  Behold him present with his aid.

2 Let mountains from their seats be hurled
  Down to the deep, and buried there;
  Convulsions shake the solid world;
  Our faith shall never yield to fear.

3 Loud may the troubled ocean roar;
  In sacred peace our souls abide,
  While every nation, every shore,
  Trembles, and dreads the swelling tide.

4 There is a stream whose gentle flow
  Supplies the city of our God;
  Life, love, and joy still gliding through,
  And watering our divine abode.

5 That sacred stream, thine holy word,
  Our grief allays, our fear controls;
  Sweet peace thy promises afford, [souls.
  And give new strength to fainting

6 Zion enjoys her Monarch's love,
  Secure against a threatening hour;
  Nor can her firm foundations move,
  Built on his truth, and armed with power.
      Isaac Watts, 1719.

176. PSALM 18.
1 No change of times shall ever shock
  My firm affections, Lord, to thee;
  For thou hast always been my Rock,
  A fortress and defence to me.

2 Thou my deliverer art, O God;
  My trust is in thy mighty power;
  Thou art my shield from foes abroad;
  At home, my safeguard and my tower.

3 To thee will I address my prayer,
  To whom all praise we justly owe;
  So shall I, by thy watchful care,
  Be guarded safe from every foe.

4 Let the eternal Lord be praised,
  The Rock on whose defence I rest!
  O'er highest heavens his name be raised,
  Who me with his salvation blest.

5 Therefore, to celebrate his fame,
  My grateful voice to heaven I'll raise;
  And nations, strangers to his name,
  Shall thus be taught to sing his praise.
      Tate and Brady, 1696.

177. PSALM 103.
1 THE Lord! how wondrous are his ways!
  How firm his truth! how large his grace!
  He takes his mercy for his throne,
  And thence he makes his glories known.

2 Not half so high his power hath spread
  The starry heavens above our head,
  As his rich love exceeds our praise,
  Exceeds the highest hopes we raise.

3 Not half so far hath nature placed
  The rising morning from the west,
  As his forgiving grace removes
  The daily guilt of those he loves.

4 How slowly doth his wrath arise!
   On swifter wings salvation flies:
   Or, if he lets his anger burn,
   How soon his frowns to pity turn!

5 His everlasting love is sure
   To all his saints, and shall endure;
   From age to age his truth shall reign,
   Nor children's children hope in vain.
Isaac Watts, 1719.

178.   PSALM 36.   L. M.

1 HIGH in the heavens, eternal God,
   Thy goodness in full glory shines:
   Thy truth shall break thro' every cloud
   That vails and darkens thy designs.

2 Forever firm thy justice stands,
   As mountains their foundations keep;
   Wise are the wonders of thy hands;
   Thy judgments are a mighty deep.

3 My God, how excellent thy grace,
   Whence all our hope and comfort springs!
   The sons of Adam in distress
   Fly to the shadow of thy wings.

4 From the provisions of thy house
   We shall be fed with sweet repast;
   There mercy like a river flows,
   And brings salvation to our taste.

5 Life, like a fountain rich and free,
   Springs from the presence of the Lord!
   And in thy light our souls shall see
   The glories promised in thy word.
Isaac Watts, 1719.

179.   PSALM 103.   L. M.

1 MY soul, inspired with sacred love,
   God's holy name forever bless!
   Of all his favors mindful prove,
   And still thy grateful thanks express.

2 The Lord abounds with tender love,
   And unexampled acts of grace;
   His wakened wrath doth slowly move,
   His willing mercy flows apace.

3 As high as heaven its arch extends
   Above this little spot of clay,
   So much his boundless grace transcends
   The best obedience we can pay.

4 As far as 'tis from east to west,
   So far has he our sins removed,
   Who, with a father's tender breast,
   Has such as fear him always loved.

5 Let every creature join to bless
   The mighty Lord; and thou, my heart,
   With grateful joy thy thanks express,
   And in this concert bear thy part.
Tate and Brady, 16/s a.

180.   PSALM 136.   L. M.

1 MY God, what monuments I see,
   In all around, of thine and thee!
   I view thee in the heavens above;
   More high than these is heavenly love.

2 I mark the strong eternal hill,
   Thy faithfulness is stronger still;
   I gaze on ocean deep and broad,
   More deep thy counsels are, O God.

3 Oh, give me 'neath thy wings to rest;
   To lean on thy parental breast;
   To feed on thee, the living bread,
   And drink at mercy's fountain head!

4 The springs of life are all thine own,
   They flow from thy eternal throne;
   Light in thy light alone we see;
   Oh, save us, for we rest on thee!
H. F. Lyte, 1834.

181.   PSALM 103.   L. M.

1 AWAKE, my soul, awake my tongue;
   My God demands the grateful song;
   Let all my inmost powers record
   The wondrous mercy of the Lord.

2 Divinely free his mercy flows,
   Forgives my sins, allays my woes,
   And bids approaching death remove,
   And crowns me with indulgent love.

3 His mercy, with unchanging rays,
   Forever shines, while time decays;
   And children's children shall record
   The truth and goodness of the Lord.

4 While all his works his praise proclaim,
   And men and angels bless his name,
   Oh, let my heart, my life, my tongue
   Attend, and join the blissful song!
Anne Steele, 1760.

182.   L. M.

1 OH, for a strong, a lasting faith,
   To credit what the Almighty saith!
   To embrace the message of his Son,
   And call the joys of heaven our own.

2 Then, should the earth's old pillars shake,
   And all the wheels of nature break,
   Our steady souls would fear no more
   Than solid rocks when billows roar.
Isaac Watts, 1709.

GOD,—HIS PROVIDENCE.

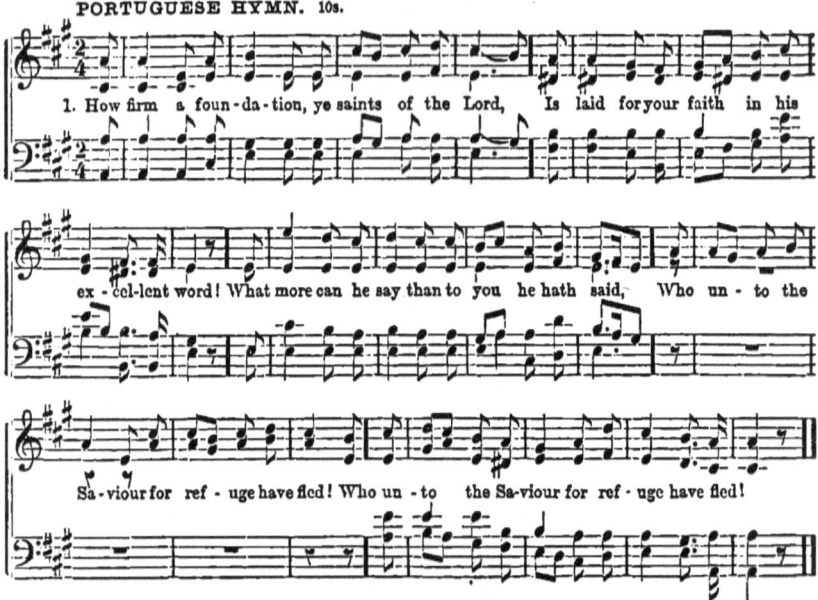

PORTUGUESE HYMN. 10s.

1. How firm a foun-da-tion, ye saints of the Lord, Is laid for your faith in his ex-cel-lent word! What more can he say than to you he hath said, Who un-to the Sa-viour for ref-uge have fled! Who un-to the Sa-viour for ref-uge have fled!

183.

1 How firm a foundation, ye saints of the Lord,
Is laid for your faith in his excellent word!
What more can he say than to you he hath said,
Who unto the Saviour for refuge have fled?

2 "Fear not, I am with thee; oh, be not dismayed!
I, I am thy God, and will still give thee aid;
I'll strengthen thee, help thee, and cause thee to stand,
Upheld by my righteous, omnipotent hand.

3 "When through the deep waters I call thee to go,
The rivers of sorrow shall not overflow;
For I will be with thee thy troubles to bless,
And sanctify to thee thy deepest distress.

4 "When through fiery trials thy pathway shall lie,
My grace all-sufficient shall be thy supply;
The flame shall not hurt thee; I only design
Thy dross to consume, and thy gold to refine.

5 "E'en down to old age, all my people shall prove
My sovereign, eternal, unchangeable love;
And then, when gray hairs shall their temples adorn,
Like lambs they shall still in my bosom be borne.

6 "The soul that on Jesus hath leaned for repose
I will not, I will not desert to his foes; [shake,
That soul, though all hell should endeavor to
I'll never, no never, no never forsake."

K.—*Rippon's Selection*, 1787.

184.

1 THY mercy, my God, is the theme of my song,
The joy of my heart, and the boast of my tongue;
Thy free grace alone, from the first to the last,
Hath won my affections, and bound my soul fast.

2 Without thy sweet mercy I could not live here,
Sin soon would reduce me to utter despair;
But, through thy free goodness, my spirits revive,
And he that first made me, still keeps me alive.

3 Thy mercy is more than a match for my heart,
Which wonders to feel its own hardness depart;
Dissolved by thy goodness, I fall to the ground,
And weep to the praise of the mercy I found.

4 Dear Father, thy merciful word is my all;
Thy promise supports me when ready to fall;
When enemies crowd, to cause doubt and despair,
I conquer them all by the spirit of prayer.

5 Thy mercy in Jesus exempts me from hell;
Its glories I'll sing, and its wonders I'll tell;
'Twas Jesus, my friend, when he hung on the tree,
Who opened the channel of mercy for me.

6 Great Father of mercies! thy goodness I own,
And the covenant love of thy crucified Son:
All praise to the Spirit, whose whisper divine
Seals mercy and pardon and righteousness mine!

John Stocker, 1776.

GOD,—HIS PROVIDENCE.   81

LISCHER. H. M.

185.   Psalm 121.

1 UPWARD I lift my eyes;
    From God is all my aid;
    The God who built the skies,
    And earth and nature made:
God is the tower | His grace is nigh
To which I fly; | In every hour.

2 My feet shall never slide,
    And fall in fatal snares,
    Since God, my guard and guide,
    Defends me from my fears:
Those wakeful eyes | Shall Israel keep
That never sleep | When dangers rise.

3 No burning heats by day,
    Nor blasts of evening air,
    Shall take my breath away,
    If God be with me there:
Thou art my sun | To guard my head
And thou my shade, | By night or noon.

4 Hast thou not given thy word
    To save my soul from death?
    And I can trust my Lord
    To keep my mortal breath:
I'll go and come, | Till from on high
Nor fear to die, | Thou call me home.
                                Isaac Watts, 1719.

186.

1 THE promises I sing,
    Which sovereign love hath spoke;
    Nor will th' eternal King
    His words of grace revoke:
They stand secure | Not Zion's hill
And steadfast still: | Abides so sure.

2 The mountains melt away,
    When once the Judge appears;
    And sun and moon decay
    That measure mortal years;
But still the same, | The promise shines
In radiant lines, | Thro' all the flame.

3 Their harmony shall sound
    Through my attentive ears,
    When thunders cleave the ground
    And dissipate the spheres;
Midst all the shock | I stand serene,
Of that dread scene, | Thy word my rock.
                            Philip Doddridge, 1755.

DOXOLOGY.

1 To God the Father's throne
    Your highest honors raise;
    Glory to God the Son,
    To God the Spirit praise:
And while our lips | Our faith adores
Their tributes bring, | The name we sing.
                            Isaac Watts, 1709.

82   GOD,—HIS PROVIDENCE.

BRISTOL. C. M.

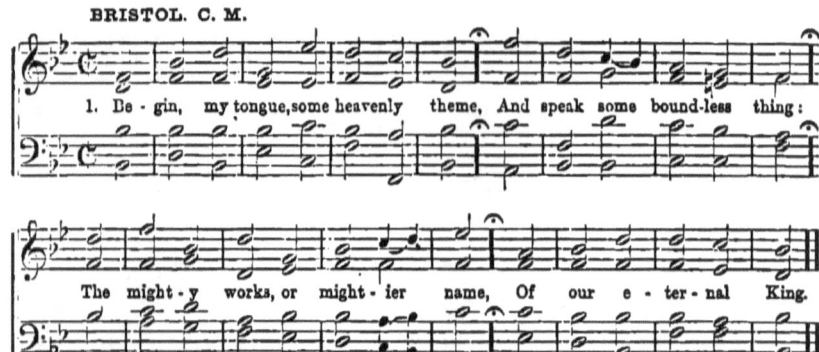

1. Be-gin, my tongue, some heavenly theme, And speak some bound-less thing: The might-y works, or might-ier name, Of our e-ter-nal King.

187.

1 Begin, my tongue, some heavenly theme,
   And speak some boundless thing:
The mighty works, or mightier name,
   Of our eternal King.

2 Tell of his wondrous faithfulness,
   And sound his power abroad;
Sing the sweet promise of his grace,
   And the performing God.

3 His very word of grace is strong
   As that which built the skies;
The voice that rolls the stars along
   Speaks all the promises.

4 Oh, might I hear thy heavenly tongue
   But whisper "Thou art mine!"
Those gentle words would raise my song
   To notes almost divine. .
            Isaac Watts, 1709.

188.   Psalm 33.

1 Let all the just, to God with joy
   Their cheerful voices raise;
For well the righteous it becomes
   To sing glad songs of praise.

2 For, faithful is the word of God;
   His works with truth abound:
He justices loves, and all the earth
   Is with his goodness crowned.

3 Whate'er the mighty Lord decrees,
   Shall stand forever sure;
The settled purpose of his heart
   To ages shall endure.

4 Our soul on God with patience waits;
   Our help and shield is he:
Then, Lord, let still our hearts rejoice,
   Because we trust in thee.

5 The riches of thy mercy, Lord,
   Do thou to us extend;
Since we, for all we want or wish,
   On thee alone depend.
            Tate and Brady, 1696.

189.   Psalm 89.

1 My never-ceasing songs shall show
   The mercies of the Lord,
And make succeeding ages know
   How faithful is his word.

2 The sacred truths his lips pronounce
   Shall firm as heaven endure;
And if he speaks a promise once,
   The eternal grace is sure.

3 How long the race of David held
   The promised Jewish throne!
But there's a nobler covenant sealed
   To David's greater Son.

4 His seed forever shall possess
   A throne above the skies;
The meanest subject of his grace
   Shall to that glory rise.

5 Lord God of hosts, thy wondrous ways
   Are sung by saints above;
And saints on earth their honors raise
   To thy unchanging love.
            Isaac Watts, 1719.

GOD,—HIS PROVIDENCE.

190. 2 Samuel 23, 5. C. M.
1 My God, the covenant of thy love
   Abides for ever sure,
And in its matchless grace I feel
   My happiness secure.

2 What though my house be not with thee,
   As nature could desire;
To nobler joys than nature gives,
   Thy servants all aspire.

3 Since thou, the everlasting God,
   My Father art become;
Jesus, my guardian and my friend,
   And heaven my final home;

4 I welcome all thy sovereign will,
   For all that will is love;
And when I know not what thou dost,
   I wait the light above.

5 Thy covenant the last accent claims
   Of this poor faltering tongue;
And that shall the first notes employ
   Of my celestial song.
Philip Doddridge, 1755.

191. C. M.
1 How rich thy favors, God of grace!
   How various and divine!
Full as the ocean they are poured,
   And bright as heaven they shine.

2 He to eternal glory calls,
   And leads the wondrous way
To his own palace, where he reigns
   In uncreated day.

3 Jesus, the herald of his love,
   Displays the radiant prize,
And shows the purchase of his blood
   To our admiring eyes.

4 He perfects what his hand begins,
   And stone on stone he lays,
Till firm and fair the building rise
   A temple to his praise.

5 The songs of everlasting years
   That mercy shall attend,
Which leads, thro' sufferings of an hour,
   To joys that never end.
Philip Doddridge, 1755.

192. C. M.
1 The mercies of my God and King
   My tongue shall still pursue:
Oh, happy they who, while they sing
   Those mercies, share them too!

2 As bright and lasting as the sun,
   As lofty as the sky,
From age to age thy word shall run,
   And chance and change defy.

3 The covenant of the King of kings
   Shall stand forever sure;
Beneath the shadow of thy wings
   Thy saints repose secure.

4 Thine is the earth, and thine the skies,
   Created at thy will;
The waves at thy command arise,
   At thy command are still.

5 In earth below, in heaven above,
   Who, who is Lord like thee?
Oh, spread the gospel of thy love
   Till all thy glories see.
H. F. Lyte, 1834.

193. Psalm 107. C. M.
1 How are thy servants blessed, O Lord,
   How sure is their defence!
Eternal wisdom is their guide,
   Their help, Omnipotence.

2 In foreign realms and lands remote,
   Supported by thy care,
Through burning climes they pass unhurt,
   And breathe in tainted air.

3 When by the dreadful tempest borne
   High on the broken wave,
They know thou art not slow to hear,
   Nor impotent to save.

4 The storm is laid, the winds retire,
   Obedient to thy will:
The sea that roars at thy command,
   At thy command is still.

5 In midst of dangers, fears, and deaths,
   Thy goodness we'll adore;
We'll praise thee for thy mercies past,
   And humbly hope for more.

6 Our life, while thou preserv'st that life,
   Thy sacrifice shall be;
And death, when death shall be our lot,
   Shall join our souls to thee.
Joseph Addison, 1712. a.

Doxology. C. M.
Let God the Father, and the Son,
   And Spirit, be adored,
Where there are works to make him known,
   Or saints to love the Lord!
Isaac Watts, 1719.

GOD,—HIS PROVIDENCE.

GENEVA. C. M.

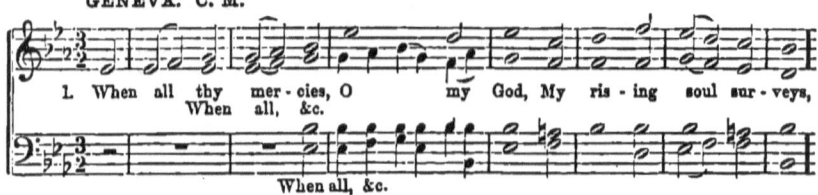
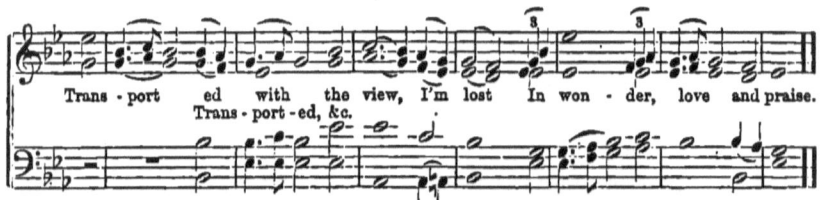

1. When all thy mercies, O my God, My rising soul surveys,
Transported with the view, I'm lost In wonder, love and praise.

194.

1 WHEN all thy mercies, O my God,
   My rising soul surveys,
Transported with the view, I'm lost
   In wonder, love, and praise.

2 Unnumbered comforts to my soul
   Thy tender care bestowed,
Before my infant heart conceived
   From whom those comforts flowed.

3 When in the slippery paths of youth
   With heedless steps I ran,
Thine arm, unseen, conveyed me safe,
   And led me up to man.

4 When worn with sickness oft hast thou
   With health renewed my face,
And when in sin and sorrow sunk,
   Revived my soul with grace.

5 Ten thousand thousand precious gifts
   My daily thanks employ;
Nor is the least a cheerful heart,
   That tastes those gifts with joy.

6 Through every period of my life
   Thy goodness I'll pursue;
And after death, in distant worlds,
   The glorious theme renew.

7 Through all eternity to thee
   A grateful song I'll raise:
But, oh, eternity's too short
   To utter all thy praise.

Joseph Addison, 1712.

195.

1 THY goodness, Lord, our souls confess;
   Thy goodness we adore:
A spring whose blessings never fail;
   A sea without a shore!

2 Sun, moon, and stars thy love attest
   In every cheerful ray;
Love draws the curtains of the night,
   And love restores the day.

3 Thy bounty every season crowns
   With all the bliss it yields;
With joyful clusters bend the vines,
   With harvests wave the fields.

4 But chiefly thy compassions, Lord,
   Are in the gospel seen;
There, like the sun, thy mercy shines,
   Without a cloud between.

5 Thy Son, thy noblest, richest gift,
   Was from thy bosom sent,
To bear from off our guilty world
   Its load of punishment.

6 Pardon, acceptance, peace, and joy
   Are published in his name;
Ours is the life, the glory ours,
   And his the death and shame.

7 Of sovereign grace, how wide the reign!
   How strong the current rolls,
That bears to heaven's unbounded bliss
   Our hell-deserving souls!

Thomas Gibbons, 1784.

GOD,—HIS PROVIDENCE. 85

CLARENDON. C. M.

1. O God of Beth-el, by whose hand Thy peo-ple still are fed;
Who thro' this wea-ry pil-grim-age Hast all our fa-thers led:

196. Gen. xxviii. 20-22.

1 O God of Bethel, by whose hand
  Thy people still are fed;
  Who through this weary pilgrimage
  Hast all our fathers led;

2 Our vows, our prayers, we now present
  Before thy throne of grace:
  God of our fathers, be the God
  Of their succeeding race.

3 Through each perplexing path of life
  Our wandering footsteps guide;
  Give us each day our daily bread,
  And raiment fit provide.

4 Oh, spread thy covering wings around,
  Till all our wanderings cease,
  And at our Father's loved abode
  Our souls arrive in peace.

5 Such blessings from thy gracious hand
  Our humble prayers implore;
  And thou shalt be our chosen God,
  And portion evermore.
  Doddridge, 1737; alt. by J. Logan, or M. Bruce, 1781.

197. Psalm 34.

1 Through all the changing scenes of life,
  In trouble and in joy,
  The praises of my God shall still
  My heart and tongue employ.

2 Of his deliverance I will boast,
  Till all who are distressed,
  From my example comfort take,
  And charm their griefs to rest.

3 Oh, magnify the Lord with me,
  With me exalt his name!
  When in distress to him I called,
  He to my rescue came.

4 Oh, make but trial of his love:
  Experience will decide
  How blest are they, and only they,
  Who in his truth confide.

5 Fear him, ye saints, and ye will then
  Have nothing else to fear;
  Make you his service your delight,
  Your wants shall be his care.
  Tate and Brady, 1696.

198.

1 Faithful, O Lord, thy mercies are,
  A rock that cannot move;
  A thousand promises declare
  Thy constancy of love.

2 Thou waitest to be gracious still;
  Thou dost with sinners bear;
  That, saved, we may thy goodness feel,
  And all thy grace declare.

3 Its streams the whole creation reach,
  So plenteous is the store;
  Enough for all, enough for each,
  Enough for evermore.

4 Throughout the universe it reigns,
  Unalterably sure;
  And while the truth of God remains,
  The goodness shall endure.
  Charles Wesley, 1708-1788.

GOD,—HIS PROVIDENCE.

WATCHMAN. S. M.

1. My soul, re-peat his praise, Whose mer-cies are so great; Whose an-ger is so slow to rise, So read-y to a-bate.

199. *Psalm 103.*

1 My soul, repeat his praise,
   Whose mercies are so great;
Whose anger is so slow to rise,
   So ready to abate.

2 God will not always chide;
   And when his strokes are felt,
His strokes are fewer than our crimes,
   And lighter than our guilt.

3 High as the heavens are raised
   Above the ground we tread,
So far the riches of his grace
   Our highest thoughts exceed.

4 His power subdues our sins,
   And his forgiving love,
Far as the east is from the west,
   Doth all our guilt remove.

5 The pity of the Lord
   To those that fear his name,
Is such as tender parents feel;
   He knows our feeble frame.

6 He knows we are but dust,
   Scattered by every breath;
His anger, like a rising wind,
   Can send us swift to death.

7 Our days are as the grass,
   Or like the morning flower;
If one sharp blast sweep o'er the field,
   It withers in an hour.

8 But thy compassions, Lord,
   To endless years endure;
And children's children ever find
   Thy words of promise sure.
Isaac Watts, 1719.

200. *Psalm 103.*

1 Oh, bless the Lord, my soul!
   Let all within me join,
And aid my tongue to bless his name,
   Whose favors are divine.

2 Oh, bless the Lord, my soul!
   Nor let his mercies lie
Forgotten in unthankfulness,
   And without praises die.

3 'Tis he forgives thy sins;
   'Tis he relieves thy pain;
'Tis he that heals thy sicknesses,
   And makes thee young again.

4 He crowns thy life with love,
   When ransomed from the grave;
He, who redeemed my soul from hell,
   Hath sovereign power to save.

5 He fills the poor with good;
   He gives the sufferers rest:
The Lord hath judgments for the proud,
   And justice for th' oppressed.

6 His wondrous works and ways
   He made by Moses known;
But sent the world his truth and grace
   By his beloved Son.
Isaac Watts, 1719.

GOD,—HIS PROVIDENCE.

201. *Psalm 91.*

1 Call Jehovah thy salvation;
  Rest beneath the Almighty's shade;
  In his secret habitation
  Dwell, nor ever be dismayed.

2 There no tumult can alarm thee,
  Thou shalt dread no hidden snare;
  Guile nor violence can harm thee,
  In eternal safeguard there.

3 From the sword at noonday wasting
  From the noisome pestilence,
  In the depth of midnight blasting,
  God shall be thy sure defence.

4 He shall charge his angel legions
  Watch and ward o'er thee to keep,
  Though thou walk through hostile regions,
  Though in desert wilds thou sleep.

5 Since with firm and pure affection
  Thou on God hast set thy love,
  With the wings of his protection
  He will shield thee from above.

6 Thou shalt call on him in trouble,
  He will hearken, he will save;
  Here for grief reward thee double,
  Crown with life beyond the grave.
  James Montgomery. 1822.

202.

1 God is love; his mercy brightens
  All the path in which we rove;
  Bliss he wakes, and woe he lightens;
  God is wisdom, God is love.

2 Chance and change are busy ever;
  Man decays, and ages move;
  But his mercy waneth never;
  God is wisdom, God is love.

3 E'en the hour that darkest seemeth,
  Will his changeless goodness prove;
  From the gloom his brightness streameth;
  God is wisdom, God is love.

4 He with earthly cares entwineth
  Hope and comfort from above:
  Everywhere his glory shineth;
  God is wisdom, God is love.
  Sir John Bowring, 1825.

203. *Psalm 23.* 7s.

1 To thy pastures fair and large,
  Heavenly Shepherd, lead thy charge;
  And my couch, with tend'rest care,
  'Mid the springing grass prepare.

2 When I faint with summer's heat,
  Thou shalt guide my weary feet
  To the streams that, still and slow,
  Through the verdant meadows flow.

3 Safe the dreary vale I tread,
  By the shades of death o'erspread,
  With thy rod and staff supplied,
  This my guard, and that my guide.

4 Constant to my latest end,
  Thou my footsteps shalt attend;
  Thou shalt bid thy hallowed dome
  Yield me an eternal home.
  James Merrick, 1765.

GOD,—HIS PROVIDENCE.

PASTORAL HYMN. L. M. 6 lines.

1. The Lord my pas-ture shall pre-pare, And feed me with a shep-herd's care;
His pres-ence shall my wants sup-ply, And guard me with a watch-ful eye;
My noon-day walks he shall at-tend, And all my mid-night hours de-fend.

204. PSALM 23.

1 THE Lord my pasture shall prepare,
And feed me with a shepherd's care;
His presence shall my wants supply,
And guard me with a watchful eye;
My noonday walks he shall attend,
And all my midnight hours defend.

2 When in the sultry glebe I faint,
Or on the thirsty mountain pant,
To fertile vales and dewy meads
My weary, wandering steps he leads,
Where peaceful rivers, soft and slow,
Amid the verdant landscape flow.

3 Though in the paths of death I tread,
With gloomy horrors overspread,
My steadfast heart shall fear no ill,
For thou, O Lord, art with me still;
Thy friendly rod shall give me aid,
And guide me through the dreadful shade.

4 Though in a bare and rugged way
Through devious, lonely wilds I stray,
Thy bounty shall my wants beguile;
The barren wilderness shall smile,
With sudden greens and herbage crowned,
And streams shall murmur all around.

Joseph Addison, 1712.

205. PSALM 23. Tune, "Watchman," p. 86. S. M.

1 THE Lord my Shepherd is,
I shall be well supplied;
Since he is mine, and I am his,
What can I want beside?

2 He leads me to the place
Where heavenly pasture grows,
Where living waters gently pass,
And full salvation flows.

3 If e'er I go astray,
He doth my soul reclaim;
And guides me in his own right way,
For his most holy name.

4 While he affords his aid,
I cannot yield to fear; [dark shade,
Though I should walk through death's
My Shepherd's with me there.

5 In spite of all my foes,
Thou dost my table spread;
My cup with blessings overflows,
And joy exalts my head.

6 The bounties of thy love
Shall crown my following days;
Nor from thy house will I remove,
Nor cease to speak thy praise.

Isaac Watts, 1719.

GOD,—HIS PROVIDENCE.

CHESTNUT STREET. C. M.

1. My Shepherd will supply my need; Jehovah is his name;
In pastures fresh he makes me feed, Beside the living stream.

206. *PSALM 23.*

1 My Shepherd will supply my need;
  Jehovah is his name;
In pastures fresh he makes me feed,
  Beside the living stream.

2 He brings my wandering spirit back,
  When I forsake his ways;
And leads me, for his mercy's sake,
  In paths of truth and grace.

3 When I walk through the shades of death,
  Thy presence is my stay;
A word of thy supporting breath
  Drives all my fears away.

4 Thy hand, in spite of all my foes,
  Doth still my table spread;
My cup with blessings overflows;
  Thine oil anoints my head.

5 The sure provisions of my God
  Attend me all my days;
Oh, may thine house be mine abode,
  And all my works be praise.

6 There would I find a settled rest,
  While others go and come;
No more a stranger or a guest,
  But like a child at home.

Isaac Watts, 1709.

207.

1 To thee, my Shepherd and my Lord,
  A grateful song I'll raise;
Oh, let the feeblest of thy flock
  Attempt to speak thy praise!

2 My life, my joy, my hope, I owe
  To thine amazing love;
Ten thousand thousand comforts here,
  And nobler bliss above.

3 To thee my trembling spirit flies,
  With sin and grief oppressed;
Thy gentle voice dispels my fears,
  And lulls my cares to rest.

4 Nay, should I walk thro' death's dark vale
  With double horrors spread,
Thy rod would guide my doubtful steps,
  And guard my drooping head.

5 Lead on, dear Shepherd; led by thee,
  No evil shall I fear:
Soon shall I reach thy fold above,
  And praise thee better there.

Ottiwell Heginbotham, 1765.

DOXOLOGY.

To Father, Son, and Holy Ghost,
  One God, whom we adore,
Be glory as it was, is now,
  And shall be evermore!

Tate and Brady, 1696.

CHRIST,—HIS ADVENT.

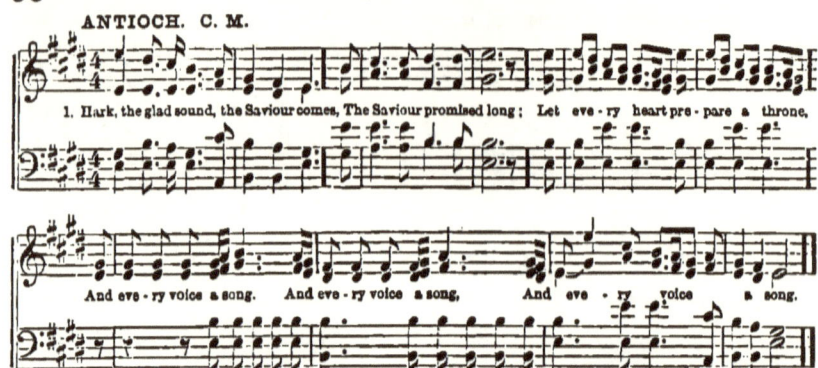

ANTIOCH. C. M.

1. Hark, the glad sound, the Saviour comes, The Saviour promised long; Let eve-ry heart pre-pare a throne, And eve-ry voice a song. And eve-ry voice a song, And eve-ry voice a song. And eve-ry voice a song.

208.

1 HARK, the glad sound! the Saviour comes,
The Saviour promised long;
Let every heart prepare a throne,
And every voice a song.

2 He comes the prisoners to release,
In Satan's bondage held;
The gates of brass before him burst,
The iron fetters yield.

3 He comes from thickest films of vice
To clear the mental ray,
And on the eyeballs of the blind
To pour celestial day.

4 He comes the broken heart to bind;
The bleeding soul to cure;
And, with the treasures of his grace,
To enrich the humble poor.

5 Our glad hosannas, Prince of Peace,
Thy welcome shall proclaim,
And heaven's eternal arches ring
With thy belovéd name.
Philip Doddridge, 1735.

209. PSALM 98.

1 JOY to the world! the Lord is come!
Let earth receive her King;
Let every heart prepare him room,
And heaven and nature sing.

2 Joy to the earth! the Saviour reigns;
Let men their songs employ;
While fields, and floods, rocks, hills, and plains
Repeat the sounding joy.

3 No more let sins and sorrows grow,
Nor thorns infest the ground;
He comes to make his blessings flow
Far as the curse is found.

4 He rules the world with truth and grace,
And makes the nations prove
The glories of his righteousness,
And wonders of his love.
Isaac Watts, 1719.

210.

1 PLUNGED in a gulf of dark despair,
We wretched sinners lay,
Without one cheerful beam of hope,
Or spark of glimmering day.

2 With pitying eyes the Prince of grace
Beheld our helpless grief;
He saw, and, oh, amazing love!
He ran to our relief.

3 Down from the shining seats above
With joyful haste he fled,
Entered the grave in mortal flesh,
And dwelt among the dead.

4 He spoiled the powers of darkness thus,
And brake our iron chains;
Jesus has freed our captive souls
From everlasting pains.

5 Oh, for his love, let rocks and hills
Their lasting silence break,
And all harmonious human tongues
The Saviour's praises speak.
Isaac Watts, 1709.

CHRIST,—HIS ADVENT.

ZERAH. C. M.

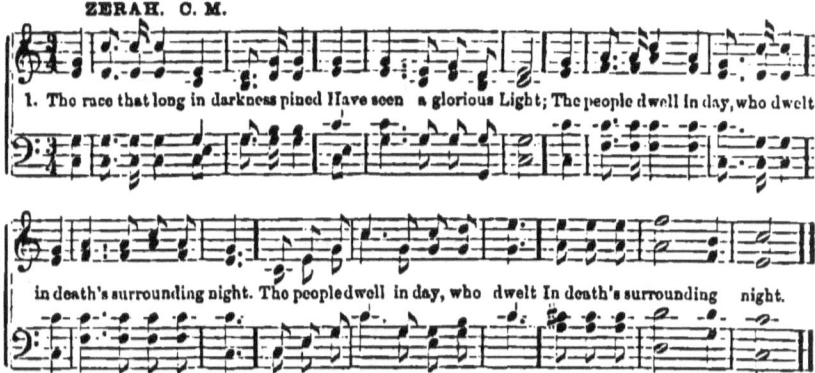

1. The race that long in darkness pined Have seen a glorious Light; The people dwell in day, who dwelt in death's surrounding night. The people dwell in day, who dwelt In death's surrounding night.

211.
ISAIAH ix. 1-7.

1 THE race that long in darkness pined
Have seen a glorious Light;
The people dwell in day, who dwelt
In death's surrounding night.

2 To hail thy rise, thou better Sun,
The gathering nations come,
Joyous as when the reapers bear
The harvest-treasures home.

3 For thou our burden hast removed,
And quelled th' oppressor's sway,
Quick as the slaughtered squadrons fell
In Midian's evil day.

4 To us a Child of hope is born,
To us a Son is given;
Him shall the tribes of earth obey,
Him all the hosts of heaven.

5 His name shall be the Prince of Peace,
For evermore adored;
The Wonderful, the Counsellor,
The great and mighty Lord!

6 His power, increasing, still shall spread;
His reign no end shall know;
Justice shall guard his throne above,
And peace abound below.
John Morrison, 1770.

212.

1 MORTALS, awake, with angels join,
And chant the solemn lay;
Joy, love, and gratitude combine
To hail the auspicious day.

2 In heaven the rapturous song began;
And sweet seraphic fire
Through all the shining legions ran,
And strung and tuned the lyre.

3 Swift through the vast expanse it flew,
And loud the echo rolled;
The theme, the song, the joy was new,
'Twas more than heaven could hold.

4 Down from the portals of the sky
The impetuous torrent ran;
And angels flew, with eager joy,
To bear the news to man.

5 Hark! the cherubic armies shout,
And glory leads the song;
Good-will and peace are heard throughout
The harmonious heavenly throng.

6 Oh, for a glance of heavenly love,
Our hearts and songs to raise,
Sweetly to bear our souls above,
And mingle with their lays!

7 With joy the chorus we repeat,
" Glory to God on high!
Good-will and peace are now complete;
Jesus was born to die."

8 Hail, Prince of life! forever hail,
Redeemer, Brother, Friend!
Tho' earth, and time, and life should fail,
Thy praise shall never end.
Samuel Medley, 1787.

CHRIST,—HIS ADVENT.

COLCHESTER. C. M.

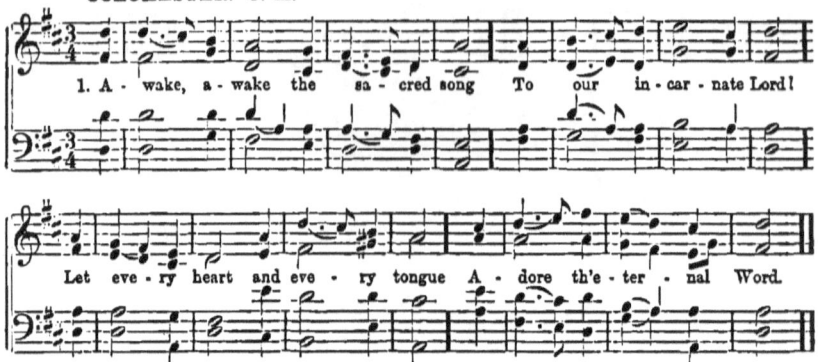

1. Awake, awake the sacred song To our incarnate Lord! Let every heart and every tongue Adore th' eternal Word.

213.

1 Awake, awake the sacred song
   To our incarnate Lord!
Let every heart and every tongue,
   Adore th' eternal Word.

2 That awful Word, that sovereign Power,
   By whom the worlds were made,
Oh, happy morn! illustrious hour!
   Was once in flesh arrayed.

3 Then shone almighty power and love,
   In all their glorious forms,
When Jesus left his throne above,
   To dwell with sinful worms.

4 Adoring angels tuned their songs
   To hail the joyful day;
With rapture, then, let mortal tongues
   Their grateful worship pay.
   Anne Steele, 1760.

214.

1 While shepherds watched their flocks
      by night,
   All seated on the ground,
The angel of the Lord came down,
   And glory shone around.

2 " Fear not," said he,—for mighty dread
   Had seized their troubled mind,—
" Glad tidings of great joy I bring
   To you and all mankind.

3 " To you, in David's town, this day,
   Is born of David's line
The Saviour, who is Christ the Lord;
   And this shall be the sign :

4 " The heavenly babe you there shall find
   To human view displayed,
All meanly wrapped in swathing bands,
   And in a manger laid."

5 Thus spake the seraph; and forthwith
   Appeared a shining throng
Of angels praising God, and thus
   Addressed their joyful song :

6 " All glory be to God on high,
   And to the earth be peace;
Good-will henceforth from heaven to men
   Begin, and never cease !"
   Nahum Tate, 1703.

215.

1 Bright was the guiding star that led,
   With mild, benignant ray,
The Gentiles to the lowly shed
   Where the Redeemer lay.

2 But, lo! a brighter, clearer light
   Now points to his abode;
It shines through sin and sorrow's night,
   To guide us to our God.

3 Oh, haste to follow where it leads;
   The gracious call obey,
Be rugged wilds, or flowery meads,
   The Christian's destined way.

4 Oh, gladly tread the narrow path,
   While light and grace are given;
Who meekly follow Christ on earth
   Shall reign with him in heaven.
   Harriet Auber, 1829.

CHRIST,—HIS ADVENT.

VESPER HYMN. 8s & 7s. (Omit repeat for Hymn 218.)

1. Hark! what mean those ho-ly voi-ces, Sweetly warbling thro' the skies?
Sure th' an-gel-ic host re-joic-es; Loudest hal-le-lu-jahs rise.
2. Lis-ten to the wondrous sto-ry, Which they chant in hymns of joy: "Glo-ry in the highest, glory! Glo-ry be to God most high!

216.

1 HARK! what mean those holy voices,
   Sweetly warbling through the skies?
   Sure, the angelic host rejoices;
   Loudest hallelujahs rise.

2 Listen to the wondrous story,
   Which they chant in hymns of joy:
   "Glory in the highest, glory!
   Glory be to God most high!

3 "Peace on earth, good-will from heaven,
   Reaching far as man is found;
   Souls redeemed, and sins forgiven!
   Loud our golden harps shall sound.

4 "Christ is born, the great Anointed:
   Heaven and earth his praises sing!
   Glad receive whom God appointed
   For your Prophet, Priest, and King!

5 "Hasten, mortals, to adore him;
   Learn his name, and taste his joy:
   Till in heaven you sing before him,
   "Glory be to God most high!'"

6 Let us learn the wondrous story
   Of our great Redeemer's birth;
   Spread the brightness of his glory
   Till it cover all the earth.
John Cawood, 1819.

217.

1 COME, thou long-expected Jesus,
   Born to set thy people free;
   From our fears and sins release us,
   Let us find our rest in thee.

2 Israel's Strength and Consolation,
   Hope of all the earth thou art;
   Dear desire of every nation,
   Joy of every longing heart.

3 Born thy people to deliver,
   Born a child, and yet a King,
   Born to reign in us forever,
   Now thy gracious kingdom bring.

4 By thine own eternal Spirit,
   Rule in all our hearts alone;
   By thine all-sufficient merit,
   Raise us to thy glorious throne.
Charles Wesley, 1744.

218.

1 ANGELS, from the realms of glory,
   Wing your flight o'er all the earth:
   Ye, who sang creation's story,
   Now proclaim Messiah's birth:
   ‖: Come and worship :‖
   Worship Christ, the new-born King.

2 Shepherds in the field abiding,
   Watching o'er your flocks by night,
   God with man is now residing;
   Yonder shines the heavenly light:
   ‖: Come and worship :‖ etc.

3 Saints before the altar bending,
   Watching long in hope and fear,
   Suddenly the Lord, descending,
   In his temple shall appear:
   ‖: Come and worship :‖ etc.

4 Sinners, wrung with true repentance,
   Doomed for guilt to endless pains,
   Justice now revokes the sentence;
   Mercy calls you; break your chains:
   ‖: Come and worship :‖ etc.
James Montgomery, 1819.

CHRIST,—HIS ADVENT.

FOLSOM. 11s & 10s.

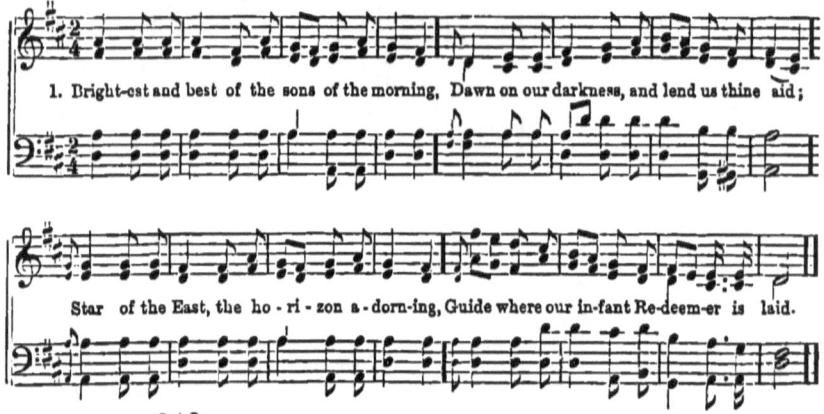

219.

1 BRIGHTEST and best of the sons of the morning,
  Dawn on our darkness, and lend us thine aid;
  Star of the East, the horizon adorning,
  Guide where our infant Redeemer is laid.

2 Cold on his cradle the dew-drops are shining;
  Low lies his head with the beasts of the stall:
  Angels adore him, in slumber reclining,
  Maker, and Monarch, and Saviour of all!

3 Say, shall we yield him, in costly devotion,
  Odors of Edom, and offerings divine?
  Gems of the mountain, and pearls of the ocean,
  Myrrh from the forest, or gold from the mine?

4 Vainly we offer each ample oblation,
  Vainly with gold would his favor secure:
  Richer, by far, is the heart's adoration;
  Dearer to God are the prayers of the poor.

Reginald Heber, 1811.

220.

1 ZION, the marvellous story be telling,
  The Son of the Highest, how lowly his birth!
  The brightest archangel in glory excelling,
  He stoops to redeem thee, he reigns upon earth.

2 Tell how he cometh; from nation to nation,
  The heart-cheering news let the earth echo round;
  How free to the faithful he offers salvation,
  How his people with joy everlasting are crowned.

3 Mortals, your homage be gratefully bringing,
  And sweet let the gladsome hosanna arise;
  Ye angels, the full hallelujah be singing;
  One chorus resound through the earth and the skies.

W. A. Muhlenberg, 1823.

CHRIST,—HIS ADVENT.

WATCHMAN, TELL US OF THE NIGHT. 7s. DOUBLE.

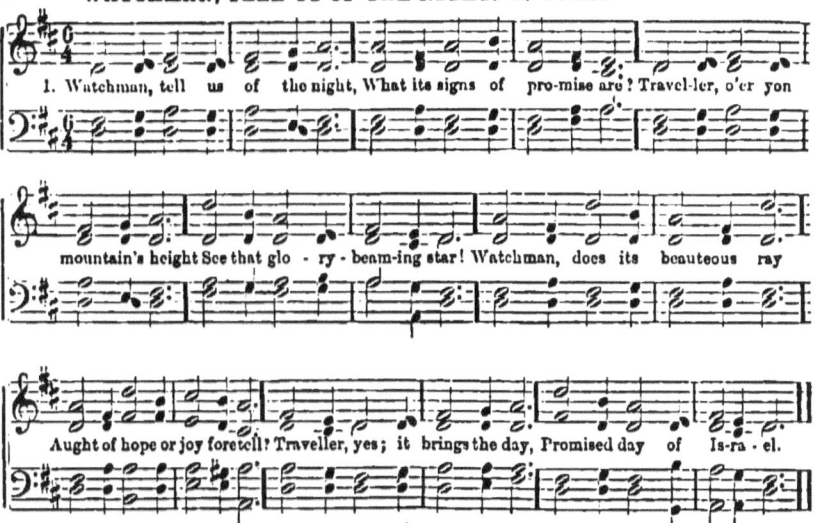

221.
ISAIAH xxi. 11.

1 WATCHMAN, tell us of the night,
  What its signs of promise are.
  Traveller, o'er yon mountain height
  See that glory-beaming star!
  Watchman, does its beauteous ray
  Aught of joy or hope foretell?
  Traveller, yes; it brings the day,
  Promised day of Israel.

2 Watchman, tell us of the night;
  Higher yet that star ascends.
  Traveller, blessedness and light,
  Peace and truth its course portends.
  Watchman, will its beams alone
  Gild the spot that gave them birth?
  Traveller, ages are its own;
  See, it bursts o'er all the earth!

3 Watchman, tell us of the night,
  For the morning seems to dawn.
  Traveller, darkness takes its flight,
  Doubt and terror are withdrawn.
  Watchman, let thy wanderings cease;
  Hie thee to thy quiet home!
  Traveller, lo! the Prince of peace,
  Lo! the Son of God is come!

Sir John Bowring, 1825.

222.

1 LET the earth now praise the Lord,
  Who hath truly kept his word,
  And the sinner's Help and Friend
  Now at last to us doth send.
  What the fathers most desired,
  What the prophets' hearts inspired,
  What they longed for many a year,
  Stands fulfilled in glory here.

2 Abram's promised great reward,
  Zion's helper, Jacob's Lord,
  Him of twofold race, behold;
  Truly come, as long foretold.
  Welcome, O my Saviour now!
  Hail! my portion, Lord, art thou!
  Here, too, in my heart I pray:
  Oh, prepare thyself a way!

3 Enter, King of glory, in;
  Purify the wastes of sin,
  As thou hast so often done;
  This belongs to thee alone.
  And when thou dost come again,
  As a glorious King to reign,
  I with joy may see thy face,
  Freely ransomed by thy grace.

H. Held, 1643; tr. by C. Winkworth, 1862.

CHRIST,—HIS ADVENT.

ADVENT. 7s. 6 LINES.

223.

1 As with gladness men of old
Did the guiding star behold;
As with joy they hailed its light,
Leading onward beaming bright;
So, most gracious God, may we
Evermore be led by thee.

2 As with joyful steps they sped
To that lowly manger-bed,
There to bend the knee before
Him whom heaven and earth adore;
So may we with willing feet
Ever seek thy mercy-seat.

3 As they offered gifts most rare
At that manger rude and bare;
So may we with holy joy,
Pure, and free from sin's alloy,
All our costliest treasures bring,
Christ, to thee, our heavenly King.

4 Holy Jesus! every day
Keep us in the narrow way;
And, when earthly things are past,
Bring our ransomed souls at last
Where they need no star to guide,
Where no clouds thy glory hide.

5 In the heavenly country bright
Need they no created light;
Thou its light, its joy, its crown,
Thou its Sun, which goes not down;
There forever may we sing
Hallelujahs to our King.
William Chatterton Dix, 1860.

DOXOLOGY.

BLESSING, honor, glory, might,
And dominion infinite,
To the Father of our Lord,
To the Spirit and the Word:
As it was all worlds before,
Is, and shall be evermore.
Josiah Conder, 1824.

CHRIST,—HIS ADVENT.   97

NATIVITY 7s. DOUBLE.

Hark! the her-ald an-gels sing, Glo-ry to the new-born King! Peace on earth, and mer-cy mild, God and sin-ners re-con-ciled! Joy-ful all ye na-tions, rise, Join the tri-umph of the skies; Un-i-ver-sal na-ture say, Christ the Lord is born to-day!

224.

1 HARK! the herald angels sing,
Glory to the new-born King!
Peace on earth, and mercy mild,
God and sinners reconciled!
Joyful, all ye nations, rise,
Join the triumph of the skies;
Universal nature say,
Christ the Lord is born to-day!

2 Christ, by highest heaven adored;
Christ, the everlasting Lord;
Late in time behold him come,
Offspring of a virgin's womb:
Veiled in flesh the Godhead see;
Hail, the Incarnate Deity,
Pleased as man with men to appear,
Jesus, our Immanuel here!

3 Hail! the heavenly Prince of peace!
Hail! the Sun of righteousness!
Light and life to all he brings,
Risen with healing in his wings.
Mild he lays his glory by,
Born that man no more may die,
Born to raise the sons of earth,
Born to give them second birth.

4 Come, desire of nations, come,
Fix in us thy humble home!
Rise, the woman's conquering seed,
Bruise in us the serpent's head!
Now display thy saving power,
Ruined nature now restore,
Now in mystic union join
Thine to ours, and ours to thine!

5 Adam's likeness, Lord, efface;
Stamp thy image in its place;
Second Adam from above,
Reinstate us in thy love!
Let us thee, though lost, regain,
Thee, the Life, the heavenly Man:
Oh, to all thyself impart,
Formed in each believing heart!
Charles Wesley, 1739: *altered by Martin Madan,* 1760.

DOXOLOGY.

HALLELUJAH! joyful raise
Heart and voice our God to praise!
Praise the Father! praise the Son!
Praise the Spirit! Three in One.
One to perfect all the plan
Of redeeming ruined man!
Triune God, to thee be given
Praise on earth and praise in heaven.
Newman Hall, 1857.

CHRIST,—HIS ADVENT.

STERLING. L. M.

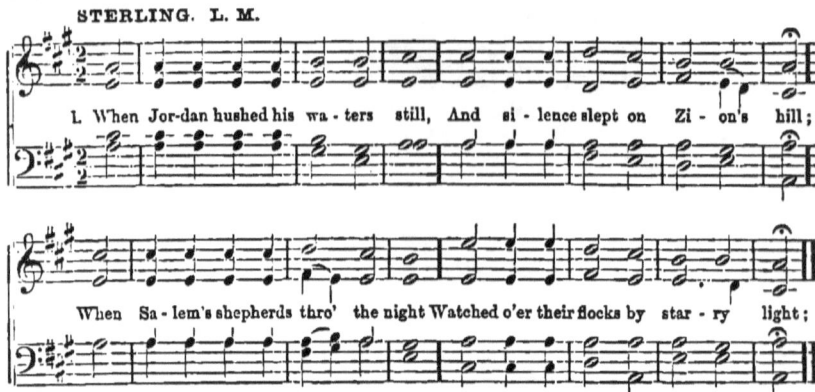

1. When Jor-dan hushed his wa-ters still, And si-lence slept on Zi-on's hill;
When Sa-lem's shepherds thro' the night Watched o'er their flocks by star-ry light;

225.

1 When Jordan hushed his waters still,
And silence slept on Zion's hill;
When Salem's shepherds thro' the night
Watched o'er their flocks by starry light;

2 Hark! from the midnight hills around,
A voice of more than mortal sound
In distant hallelujahs stole,
Wild murmuring o'er the raptured soul.

3 On wheels of light, on wings of flame,
The glorious hosts of Zion came;
High heaven with songs of triumph rung,
While thus they struck their harps and sung:

4 "O Zion, lift thy raptured eye;
The long-expected hour is nigh;
The joys of nature rise again,
The Prince of Salem comes to reign.

5 "He comes to cheer the trembling heart,
Bids Satan and his host depart;
Again the Daystar gilds the gloom,
Again the bowers of Eden bloom."

6 O Zion! lift thy raptured eye;
The long-expected hour is nigh;
The joys of nature rise again:
The Prince of Salem comes to reign.
Thomas Campbell, 1799.

226.

1 On Jordan's bank the Baptist's cry
Announces that the Lord is nigh;
Come, then, and hearken, for he brings
Glad tidings from the King of kings.

2 Then cleansed be every Christian breast,
And furnished for so great a guest!
Yea, let us each our hearts prepare
For Christ to come and enter there.

3 For thou art our salvation, Lord,
Our refuge, and our great reward;
Without thy grace, our souls must fade,
And wither like a flower decayed.

4 Stretch forth thy hand to heal our sore,
And make us rise, to fall no more;
Once more upon thy people shine,
And fill the world with love divine.

5 To Him who left the throne of heaven
To save mankind, all praise be given!
Like praise be to the Father done,
And Holy Spirit, Three in One!
Translated from the Latin by J. Chandler, 1837.

227. JOHN III. 16-18.

1 Not to condemn the sons of men
Did Christ the Son of God appear;
No weapons in his hands are seen,
No flaming sword nor thunder there.

2 Such was the pity of our God,
He loved the race of man so well,
He sent his Son to bear our load
Of sins, and save our souls from hell.

3 Sinners, believe the Saviour's word;
Trust in his mighty name, and live:
A thousand joys his lips afford,
His hands a thousand blessings give.
Isaac Watts, 1709.

CHRIST,—HIS ADVENT.

MIGDOL. L. M.

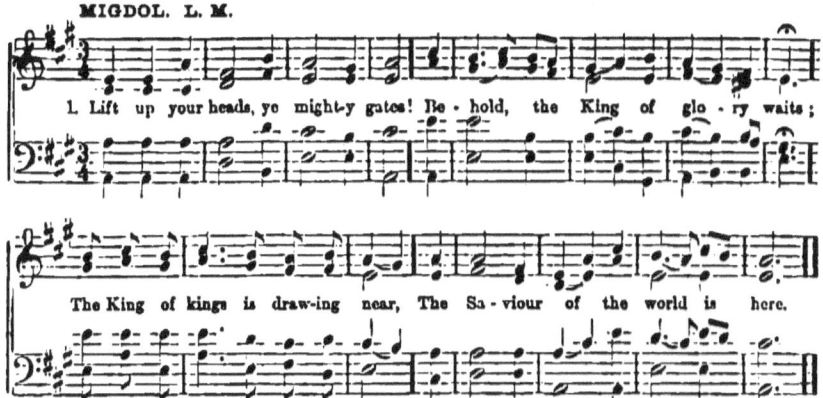

1. Lift up your heads, ye mighty gates! Be-hold, the King of glo-ry waits; The King of kings is draw-ing near, The Sa-viour of the world is here.

228.

1 LIFT up your heads, ye mighty gates!
Behold, the King of glory waits;
The King of kings is drawing near,
The Saviour of the world is here.

2 The Lord is just, a helper tried,
Mercy is ever at his side;
His kingly crown is holiness;
His sceptre, pity in distress.

3 Oh, blest the land, the city blest,
Where Christ the ruler is confessed!
Oh, happy hearts and happy homes,
To whom this King of triumph comes.

4 Fling wide the portals of your heart,
Make it a temple set apart
From earthly use for heaven's employ,
Adorned with prayer and love and joy.

5 Redeemer, come! I open wide
My heart to thee: here, Lord, abide!
Let me thy inner presence feel;
Thy grace and love in me reveal.

6 So come, my Sovereign, enter in;
Let new and nobler life begin:
Thy Holy Spirit guide us on,
Until the glorious crown be won.
George Weissel, 1630.

229.

1 How sweetly flowed the gospel sound
From lips of gentleness and grace,
When listening thousands gathered round,
And joy and reverence filled the place!

2 From heaven he came, of heaven he spoke,
To heaven he led his followers' way;
Dark clouds of gloomy night he broke,
Unvailing an immortal day.

3 " Come, wanderers, to my Father's home;
Come, all ye weary ones, and rest;"
Yes, sacred Teacher, we will come,
Obey thee, love thee, and be blest.
Sir John Bowring, 1825.

230.

1 ALL praise to thee, eternal Lord,
Clothed in a garb of flesh and blood;
Choosing a manger for thy throne,
While worlds on worlds are thine alone!

2 Once did the skies before thee bow;
A virgin's arms contain thee now;
Angels, who did in thee rejoice,
Now listen for thine infant voice.

3 A little child, thou art our guest,
That weary ones in thee may rest;
Forlorn and lowly is thy birth,
That we may rise to heaven from earth.

4 Thou comest in the darksome night
To make us children of the light;
To make us, in the realms divine,
Like thine own angels round thee shine.

5 All this for us thy love hath done;
By this to thee our love is won;
For this we tune our cheerful lays,
And shout our thanks in ceaseless praise.
Martin Luther, 1523

CHRIST,—HIS LIFE.

HEBRON. L. M.

1. My dear Redeemer and my Lord, I read my duty in thy word; But in thy life the law appears, Drawn out in living characters.

231.

1 My dear Redeemer and my Lord,
I read my duty in thy word;
But in thy life the law appears,
Drawn out in living characters.

2 Such was thy truth, and such thy zeal,
Such deference to thy Father's will,
Such love and meekness so divine,
I would transcribe and make them mine.

3 Cold mountains and the midnight air
Witnessed the fervor of thy prayer;
The desert thy temptations knew,
Thy conflict, and thy victory too.

4 Be thou my pattern; make me bear
More of thy gracious image here:
Then God, the Judge, shall own my name
Among the followers of the Lamb.
Isaac Watts, 1709.

232.

1 WHEN, like a stranger on our sphere,
The lowly Jesus wandered here,
Where'er he went, affliction fled,
And sickness reared her fainting head.

2 The eye that rolled in irksome night
Beheld his face, for God is light;
The opening ear, the loosened tongue,
His precepts heard, his praises sung.

3 With bounding steps, the halt and lame
To hail their great deliverer came;
O'er the cold grave he bowed his head,
He spake the word, and raised the dead.

4 Despairing madness, dark and wild,
In his inspiring presence smiled;
The storm of horror ceased to roll,
And reason lightened through the soul.

5 Through paths of loving-kindness led,
Where Jesus triumphed, we would tread;
To all with willing hands dispense
The gifts of our benevolence.
James Montgomery, 1825.

233.

1 How beauteous were the marks divine
That in thy meekness used to shine,
That lit thy lonely pathway trod
In wondrous love, O Son of God!

2 Oh, who like thee, so calm, so bright,
Thou God of God, thou Light of Light;
Oh, who like thee did ever go
So patient through a world of woe?

3 Oh, who like thee so humbly bore
The scorn, the scoffs of men, before?
So meek, forgiving, godlike, high,
So glorious in humility?

4 E'en death, which sets the prisoner free,
Was pang and scoff and scorn to thee;
Yet love through all thy torture glowed,
And mercy with thy life-blood flowed.

5 Oh, in thy light be mine to go,
Illuming all my way of woe!
And give me ever on the road
To trace thy footsteps, Son of God!
Arthur C. Coxe, 1838.

CHRIST,—HIS LIFE.

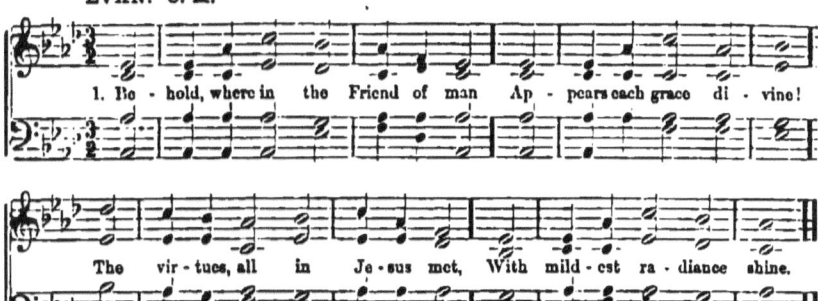

EVAN. C. M.

1. Behold, where in the Friend of man Appears each grace divine! The virtues, all in Jesus met, With mildest radiance shine.

234.

1 BEHOLD, where in the Friend of man
Appears each grace divine!
The virtues, all in Jesus met,
With mildest radiance shine.

2 To spread the rays of heavenly light,
To give the mourner joy,
To preach glad tidings to the poor,
Was his divine employ.

3 Lowly in heart, to all his friends
A friend and servant found:
He washed their feet, he wiped their tears,
And healed each bleeding wound.

4 'Mid keen reproach and cruel scorn,
Patient and meek he stood;
His foes, ungrateful, sought his life;
He labored for their good.

5 In the last hour of deep distress,
Before his Father's throne,
With soul resigned, he bowed, and said,
"Thy will, not mine, be done!"

6 Be Christ our pattern and our guide;
His image may we bear;
Oh, may we tread his holy steps,
And his bright glories share!

William Enfield, 1770.

235.

1 O LORD, when we the path retrace
Which thou on earth hast trod;

To man thy wondrous love and grace,
Thy faithfulness to God:

2 Thy love, by man so sorely tried,
Proved stronger than the grave;
The very spear that pierced thy side
Drew forth the blood to save.

3 Faithful amid unfaithfulness,
'Midst darkness only light,
Thou didst thy Father's name confess,
And in his will delight.

4 Unmoved by Satan's subtle wiles,
Or suffering, shame, and loss,
Thy path, uncheered by earthly smiles,
Led only to the cross.

5 O Lord, with sorrow and with shame,
We meekly would confess
How little we, who bear thy name,
Thy mind, thy ways express.

6 Give us thy meek, thy lowly mind;
We would obedient be,
And all our rest and pleasure find
In fellowship with thee.

James G. Deck, 1838.

DOXOLOGY.

PRAISE to the Father and the Son
Who dwell aloft in heaven;
And to the Spirit, Three in One,
Let equal praise be given.

From the Latin, tr. by J. Chandler.

CHRIST,—HIS LIFE.

WARRINGTON. L. M.

1. O wondrous type, O vision fair, Of glory that the church shall share, Which Christ upon the mountain shows, Where brighter than the sun he glows!

236. MATT. xvii. 1-9.

1 O WONDROUS type, O vision fair
Of glory that the church shall share,
Which Christ upon the mountain shows,
Where brighter than the sun he glows!

2 From age to age the tale declare,
How with the three disciples there,
Where Moses and Elias meet,
The Lord holds converse high and sweet.

3 The Law and Prophets there have place,
Two chosen witnesses of grace;
The Father's voice from out the cloud
Proclaimed his only Son aloud.

4 With shining face and bright array,
Christ deigns to manifest to-day,
What glory shall be theirs above
Who joy in God with perfect love.

5 And faithful hearts are raised on high
By this great vision's mystery;
For which in joyful strains we raise
The voice of prayer, the hymn of praise.

6 O Father, with the eternal Son,
And Holy Spirit, ever one,
Vouchsafe to bring us by thy grace
To see thy glory face to face.
Translated from the Latin by J. M. Neale, 1851.

237. MATT. xxi. 1-10.

1 RIDE on! ride on in majesty!
Hark! all the tribes Hosanna cry!
Thine humble beast pursues his road,
With palms and scattered garments strewed.

2 Ride on! ride on in majesty!
In lowly pomp ride on to die!

O Christ! thy triumphs now begin
O'er captive death and conquered sin.

3 Ride on! ride on in majesty!
The winged squadrons of the sky
Look down with sad and wondering eyes
To see the approaching sacrifice.

4 Ride on! ride on in majesty!
Thy last and fiercest strife is nigh;
The Father on his sapphire throne
Expects his own anointed Son.

5 Ride on! ride on in majesty!
In lowly pomp ride on to die!
Bow thy meek head to mortal pain!
Then take, O God, thy power, and reign!
Henry Hart Milman, 1827.

238. MATT. xxiii. 36. Tune "Ashwell," p. 322.

1 'TIS midnight, and on Olive's brow
The star is dimmed that lately shone;
'Tis midnight; in the garden now
The suffering Saviour prays alone.

2 'Tis midnight; and from all removed,
Immanuel wrestles lone with fears;
E'en that disciple whom he loved
Heeds not his Master's grief and tears.

3 'Tis midnight; and, for others' guilt,
The Man of Sorrows weeps in blood;
Yet he, who hath in anguish knelt,
Is not forsaken by his God.

4 'Tis midnight; and from ether plains
Is borne the song that angels know:
Unheard by mortals are the strains
That sweetly soothe the Saviour's woe.
William B. Tappan, 1819.

CHRIST,—HIS SUFFERINGS AND DEATH. 103

GETHSEMANE. 7s. 6 LINES.

1. Go to dark Gethsemane, Ye that feel the tempter's power; Your Redeemer's conflict see: Watch with him one bitter hour: Turn not from his griefs away; Learn of Jesus Christ to pray.

239.

1 Go to dark Gethsemane,
  Ye that feel the tempter's power;
  Your Redeemer's conflict see:
  Watch with him one bitter hour:
  Turn not from his griefs away;
  Learn of Jesus Christ to pray.

2 Follow to the judgment-hall;
  View the Lord of life arraigned.
  Oh the wormwood and the gall!
  Oh the pangs his soul sustained!
  Shun not suffering, shame, or loss:
  Learn of him to bear the cross.

3 Calvary's mournful mountain climb;
  There, adoring at his feet,
  Mark that miracle of time,
  God's own sacrifice complete.
  "It is finished!" hear him cry;
  Learn of Jesus Christ to die.

4 Early hasten to the tomb,
  Where they laid his breathless clay;
  All is solitude and gloom:
  Who hath taken him away?
  Christ is risen, he seeks the skies;
  Saviour, teach us so to rise.
  James Montgomery, 1822.

240.

1 Wouldst thou learn the depth of sin,
  All its bitterness and pain?
  What it cost thy God to win
  Sinners to himself again?
  Come, poor sinner, come with me;
  Visit sad Gethsemane.

2 Wouldst thou know God's wondrous love?
  Seek it not beside the throne;
  List not angels' praise above;
  Come and hear the heavy groan
  By the Godhead heaved for thee,
  Sinner, in Gethsemane.

3 When his tears and bloody sweat,
  When his passion and his prayer,
  When his pangs on Olivet
  Wake within thee thoughts of care,
  Think, O sinner, 'twas for thee
  He suffered in Gethsemane.

4 Hate the sin that cost so dear;
  Love the God that loved thee so;
  Weep thou must, but likewise fear
  Lest that fountain freshly flow,
  That once freely gushed for thee
  In sorrowful Gethsemane.
  John S. B. Monsell, 1863. a.

CHRIST,—HIS SUFFERINGS AND DEATH.

AYLESBURY. S. M.

1. O'erwhelmed in depths of woe, Upon the tree of scorn Hangs the Redeemer of mankind, With racking anguish torn.

241.

1 O'ERWHELMED in depths of woe,
  Upon the tree of scorn
Hangs the Redeemer of mankind,
  With racking anguish torn.

2 See how the nails those hands
  And feet so tender rend;
See down his face, and neck, and breast,
  His sacred blood descend.

3 Hark! with what awful cry
  His spirit takes its flight;
That cry, it pierced his mother's heart,
  And whelmed her soul in night.

4 Earth hears, and trembling quakes
  Around that tree of pain;
The rocks are rent; the graves are burst;
  The vail is rent in twain.

5 The sun withdraws his light;
  The mid-day heavens grow pale;
The moon, the stars, the universe,
  Their Maker's death bewail.

6 Shall man alone be mute?
  Come, youth and hoary hairs,
Come rich and poor, come all mankind,
  And bathe those feet in tears.

7 Come, fall before his cross,
  Who shed for us his blood;
Who died, the victim of pure love,
  To make us sons of God.

8 Jesus, all praise to thee,
  Our joy and endless rest;
Be thou our guide while pilgrims here,
  Our crown amid the blest.

Translated from the Latin by Edward Caswall, 1849.

242.

1 BEHOLD the amazing sight,
  The Saviour lifted high,
Behold the Son of God's delight
  Expire in agony.

2 For whom, for whom, my heart,
  Were all these sorrows borne?
Why did he feel that piercing smart,
  And meet that various scorn?

3 For love of us he bled,
  And all in torture died;
'Twas love that bowed his fainting head,
  And oped his gushing side.

4 I see, and I adore
  In sympathy of love;
I feel the strong, attractive power
  To lift my soul above.

5 Drawn by such cords as these,
  Let all the earth combine,
With cheerful ardor, to confess
  The energy divine.

6 In thee our hearts unite,
  Nor share thy griefs alone,
But from thy cross pursue their flight
  To thy triumphant throne.

Philip Doddridge, 1737.

CHRIST,—HIS SUFFERINGS AND DEATH.

MANOAH. C. M.

1. To Calv'ry, Lord, in spi-rit now Our wea-ry souls re-pair,
To dwell up-on thy dy-ing love, And taste its sweetness there.

243.

1 To Calv'ry, Lord, in spirit now
Our weary souls repair,
To dwell upon thy dying love,
And taste its sweetness there.

2 Sweet resting-place of every heart
That feels the plague of sin,
Yet knows that deep mysterious joy,
The peace of God within.

3 Dear suffering Lamb! thy bleeding
With cords of love divine, [wounds,
Have drawn our willing hearts to thee,
And linked our life with thine.

4 Thy sympathies and hopes are ours;
Dear Lord, we wait to see
Creation, all,—below, above,—
Redeemed and blest by thee.

5 Our longing eyes would fain behold
That bright and blessèd brow,
Once wrung with bitt'rest anguish, wear
Its crown of glory now.

6 Why linger, then? Come, Saviour,
Responsive to our call! [come.
Come, claim thine ancient power and
The heir and Lord of all. [reign
Sir Edward Denny, 1839.

244.

1 Alas! and did my Saviour bleed,
And did my Sovereign die?
Would he devote that sacred head
For such a worm as I?

2 Was it for crimes that I had done
He groaned upon the tree?
Amazing pity! grace unknown!
And love beyond degree!

3 Well might the sun in darkness hide,
And shut his glories in,
When God, the mighty Maker, died
For man, the creature's sin.

4 Thus might I hide my blushing face
While his dear cross appears,
Dissolve my heart in thankfulness,
And melt mine eyes to tears!

5 But drops of grief can ne'er repay
The debt of love I owe;
Here, Lord, I give myself away,
'Tis all that I can do.
Isaac Watts, 1707.

245.

1 In evil long I took delight,
Unawed by shame or fear,
Till a new object struck my sight,
And stopped my wild career:

2 I saw one hanging on a tree,
In agonies and blood,
Who fixed his languid eyes on me,
As near his cross I stood.

3 Sure never till my latest breath
Can I forget that look:
It seemed to charge me with his death,
Though not a word he spoke.

CHRIST,—HIS SUFFERINGS AND DEATH.

SILOAM. C. M.

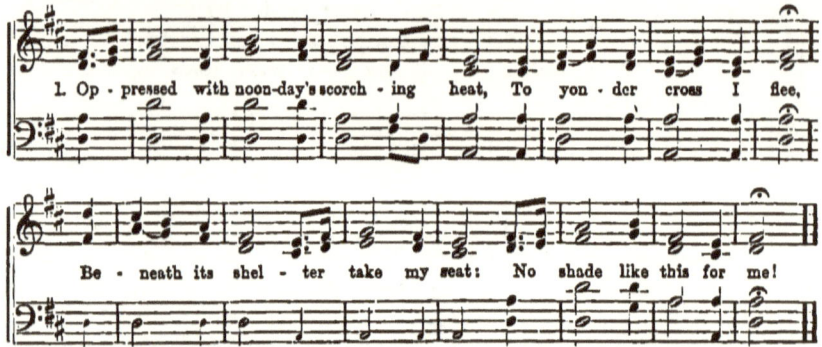

1. Op-pressed with noon-day's scorch-ing heat, To yon-der cross I flee, Be-neath its shel-ter take my seat: No shade like this for me!

4 My conscience felt and owned the guilt,
And plunged me in despair;
I saw my sins his blood had spilt,
And helped to nail him there.

5 Alas! I knew not what I did!
But now my tears are vain:
Where shall my trembling soul be hid?
For I the Lord have slain!

6 A second look he gave, which said,
"I freely all forgive;
This blood is for thy ransom paid;
I die that thou may'st live."

7 Thus, while his death my sin displays
In all its blackest hue,
Such is the mystery of grace,
It seals my pardon too.
John Newton, 1779.

246.

1 Oppressed with noon-day's scorching heat,
To yonder cross I flee,
Beneath its shelter take my seat:
No shade like this for me!

2 Beneath that cross clear waters burst,
A fountain sparkling free;
And there I quench my desert thirst:
No spring like this for me!

3 A stranger here, I pitch my tent
Beneath this spreading tree;
Here shall my pilgrim life be spent:
No home like this for me!

4 For burdened ones a resting-place
Beside that cross I see;
Here I cast off my weariness:
No rest like this for me!
Horatius Bonar, 1857.

247.

1 O Jesus! sweet the tears I shed,
While at thy cross I kneel,
Gaze on thy wounded, fainting head,
And all thy sorrows feel.

2 My heart dissolves to see thee bleed,
This heart so hard before;
I hear thee for the guilty plead,
And grief o'erflows the more.

3 'Twas for the sinful thou didst die,
And I a sinner stand:
What love speaks from thy dying eye,
And from each piercéd hand!

4 I know this cleansing blood of thine
Was shed, dear Lord, for me;
For me, for all — oh, grace divine!—
Who look by faith on thee.

5 O Christ of God! O spotless Lamb!
By love my soul is drawn;
Henceforth forever thine I am;
Here life and peace are born.

6 In patient hope the cross I'll bear,
Thine arm shall be my stay;
And thou, enthroned, my soul shalt spare
On thy great judgment-day.
Ray Palmer, 1867.

WILLIAMS. L. M.

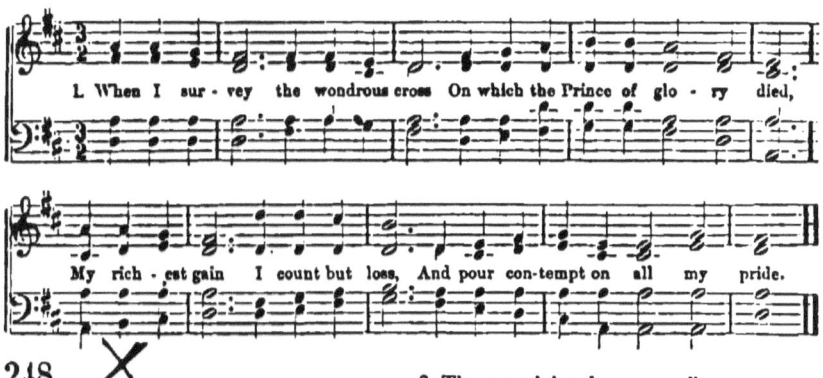

1. When I survey the wondrous cross On which the Prince of glory died, My rich-est gain I count but loss, And pour con-tempt on all my pride.

248.

1 When I survey the wondrous cross
   On which the Prince of glory died,
   My richest gain I count but loss,
   And pour contempt on all my pride.

2 Forbid it, Lord, that I should boast,
   Save in the death of Christ my God:
   All the vain things that charm me most,
   I sacrifice them to his blood.

3 See, from his head, his hands, his feet,
   Sorrow and love flow mingled down!
   Did e'er such love and sorrow meet,
   Or thorns compose so rich a crown?

4 His dying crimson, like a robe,
   Spreads o'er his body on the tree;
   Then I am dead to all the globe,
   And all the globe is dead to me.

5 Were the whole realm of nature mine,
   That were a present far too small;
   Love so amazing, so divine,
   Demands my soul, my life, my all!
                                    Isaac Watts, 1709.

249.

1 We sing the praise of Him who died,
   Of him who died upon the cross:
   The sinner's hope let men deride;
   For this we count the world but loss.

2 Inscribed upon the cross we see
   The shining letters, God is Love;
   He bears our sins upon the tree,
   He brings us mercy from above.

3 The cross! it takes our guilt away;
   It holds the fainting spirit up:
   It cheers with hope the gloomy day,
   And sweetens every bitter cup.

4 It makes the coward spirit brave,
   And nerves the feeble arm for fight;
   It takes its terror from the grave,
   And gilds the bed of death with light;

5 The balm of life, the cure of woe,
   The measure and the pledge of love;
   The sinner's refuge here below,
   The angels' theme in heaven above!
                                    Thomas Kelly, 1820.

250.

1 Nature with open volume stands
   To spread her Maker's praise abroad;
   And every labor of his hands
   Shows something worthy of a God.

2 But in the grace that rescued man
   His brightest form of glory shines;
   Here on the cross 'tis fairest drawn
   In precious blood and crimson lines.

3 Oh, the sweet wonders of that cross
   Where God the Saviour loved and died!
   Her noblest life my spirit draws [side.
   From his dear wounds and bleeding

4 I would forever speak his name
   In sounds to mortal ears unknown,
   With angels join to praise the Lamb,
   And worship at his Father's throne.
                                    Isaac Watts, 1709.

CHRIST,—HIS SUFFERINGS AND DEATH.

HAMDEN. 8s, 7s & 4s.

1. Now, my soul, thy voice up-rais-ing, Sing the cross in mourn-ful strain;
Tell the sor-rows all-a-mu-zing, Tell the wounds and dy-ing pain,
Which our Sa-viour, Sin-less, bore, for sin-ners slain.

251.

1 Now, my soul, thy voice upraising,
Sing the cross in mournful strain;
Tell the sorrows all-amazing,
Tell the wounds and dying pain,
Which our Saviour,
Sinless, bore, for sinners slain.

2 He to freedom hath restored us
By the very bonds he bare;
And his flesh and blood afford us
Each a stream of mercy rare;
So he draws us
To the cross, and keeps us there.

3 When his painful life was ended,
When the spear transfixed his side,
Blood and water thence descended,
Pouring forth a double tide;
This to cleanse us,
That to heal us is applied.

4 Jesus! may thy promised blessing
Comfort to our souls afford;
May we, now thy love possessing,
And at length our full reward,
Ever praise thee,
Thee, our ever-glorious Lord!

John Chandler, 1837. a.

252.

1 Hark! the voice of love and mercy
Sounds aloud from Calvary;
See! it rends the rocks asunder,
Shakes the earth, and vails the sky:
"It is finished!"
Hear the dying Saviour cry.

2 "It is finished!" Oh, what pleasure
Do these charming words afford!
Heavenly blessings, without measure,
Flow to us from Christ, the Lord:
"It is finished!"
Saints, the dying words record.

3 Finished all the types and shadows
Of the ceremonial law;
Finished all that God had promised;
Death and hell no more shall awe.
"It is finished!"
Saints, from hence your comfort draw

4 Tune your harps anew, ye seraphs;
Join to sing the pleasing theme:
All on earth and all in heaven,
Join to praise Immanuel's name:
Hallelujah!
Glory to the bleeding Lamb!

Jonathan Evans, 1787.

DOXOLOGY.

1 Glory be to God the Father!
Glory be to God the Son!
Glory be to God the Spirit!
Great Jehovah, Three in One:
Glory, glory,
While eternal ages run!

Horatius Bonar, 1868.

CHRIST,—HIS SUFFERINGS AND DEATH.

ECCE HOMO. 7s. & 6s.

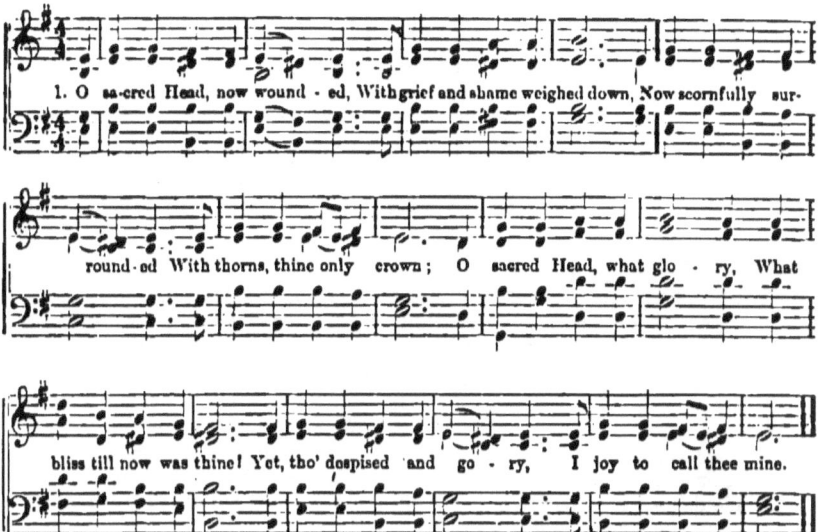

253.

1 O SACRED Head, now wounded,
  With grief and shame weighed down,
Now scornfully surrounded
  With thorns, thine only crown;
O sacred Head, what glory,
  What bliss till now was thine!
Yet, though despised and gory,
  I joy to call thee mine.

2 What thou, my Lord, hast suffered
  Was all for sinners' gain;
Mine, mine was the transgression,
  But thine the deadly pain:
Lo, here I fall, my Saviour!
  'Tis I deserve thy place;
Look on me with thy favor,
  Vouchsafe to me thy grace.

3 What language shall I borrow
  To thank thee, dearest Friend,
For this thy dying sorrow,
  Thy pity without end?
Oh, make me thine forever;
  And, should I fainting be,

Lord, let me never, never,
  Outlive my love to thee!

4 Be near me when I'm dying,
  Oh, show thy cross to me!
And for my succor flying,
  Come, Lord, and set me free!
These eyes, new faith receiving,
  From Jesus shall not move;
For he who dies believing,
  Dies safely, through thy love.

Bernard of Clairvaux, 1153; tr. by Gerhardt, 1656; J. W. Alexander, 1849.

DOXOLOGY.

To Father, Son, and Spirit,
  The God whom we adore,
Be loftiest praises given,
  Now and forever more:
Earth, join with heaven in singing
  The praise of pardoning love,
Till the loud anthem swelling
  Shall reach the courts above.

CHRIST,—HIS SUFFERINGS AND DEATH.

SPANISH HYMN. 7s.

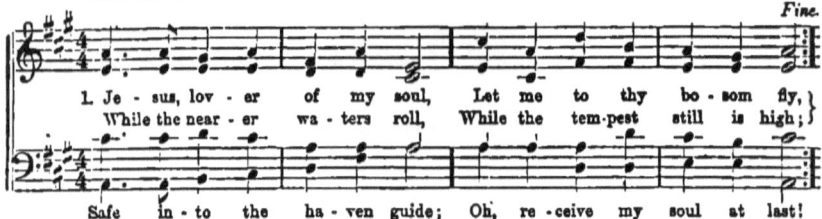

1. Jesus, lover of my soul,
Let me to thy bosom fly,
While the nearer waters roll,
While the tempest still is high;
Hide me, O my Saviour, hide,
Till the storm of life be past;
Safe into the haven guide;
Oh, receive my soul at last!

254.

1 JESUS, lover of my soul,
　Let me to thy bosom fly,
While the nearer waters roll,
　While the tempest still is high;
Hide me, O my Saviour, hide,
　Till the storm of life be past;
Safe into the haven guide;
　Oh, receive my soul at last!

2 Other refuge have I none;
　Hangs my helpless soul on thee;
Leave, ah! leave me not alone,
　Still support and comfort me;
All my trust on thee is stayed,
　All my help from thee I bring;
Cover my defenceless head
　With the shadow of thy wing.

3 Wilt thou not regard my call?
　Wilt thou not accept my prayer?
Lo! I sink, I faint, I fall!
　Lo! on thee I cast my care!
Reach me out thy gracious hand,
　While I of thy strength receive;
Hoping against hope I stand,
　Dying, and behold I live!

4 Thou, O Christ, art all I want;
　More than all in thee I find:
Raise the fallen, cheer the faint,
　Heal the sick, and lead the blind.

Just and holy is thy name;
　I am all unrighteousness;
False and full of sin I am,
　Thou art full of truth and grace.

5 Plenteous grace with thee is found,
　Grace to cover all my sin;
Let the healing streams abound;
　Make and keep me pure within.
Thou of life the fountain art,
　Freely let me take of thee;
Spring thou up within my heart!
　Rise to all eternity!
　　　　　　Charles Wesley, 1740.

255.

1 WHEN on Sinai's top I see
　God descend in majesty,
To proclaim his holy law,
　All my spirit sinks with awe.
When, in ecstacy sublime,
　Tabor's glorious height I climb,
In the too transporting light
　Darkness rushes o'er my sight.

2 When on Calvary I rest,
　God in flesh made manifest
Shines in my Redeemer's face,
　Full of beauty, truth, and grace.
Here I would forever stay,
　Weep and gaze my soul away;
Thou art heaven on earth to me,
　Lovely, mournful Calvary.
　　　　　　James Montgomery, 1812.

CHRIST,—HIS SUFFERINGS AND DEATH.

RATHBUN. 8s & 7s.

1. In the cross of Christ I glory; Towering o'er the wrecks of time, All the light of sacred story Gathers round its head sublime.

256.

1 In the cross of Christ I glory;
Towering o'er the wrecks of time,
All the light of sacred story
Gathers round its head sublime.

2 When the woes of life o'ertake me,
Hopes deceive, and fears annoy,
Never shall the cross forsake me; .
Lo! it glows with peace and joy.

3 When the sun of bliss is beaming
Light and love upon my way,
From the cross the radiance streaming
Adds new lustre to the day.

4 Bane and blessing, pain and pleasure,
By the cross are sanctified;
Peace is there that knows no measure,
Joys that through all time abide.

5 In the cross of Christ I glory;
Towering o'er the wrecks of time,
All the light of sacred story
Gathers round its head sublime.
Sir John Bowring, 1825.

257.

1 Sweet the moments, rich in blessing,
Which before the cross I spend,
Life, and health, and peace possessing
From the sinner's dying Friend.

2 Here I'll sit, forever viewing
Mercy's streams in streams of blood;
Precious drops, my soul bedewing,
Plead, and claim my peace with God.

3 Truly blessèd is this station,
Low before his cross to lie,
While I see divine compassion
Floating in his languid eye.

4 Here it is I find my heaven
While upon the Lamb I gaze;
Love I much? I've much forgiven;
I'm a miracle of grace.

5 Love and grief my heart dividing,
With my tears his feet I'll bathe,
Constant still in faith abiding,
Life deriving from his death.

6 May I still enjoy this feeling,
In all need to Jesus go;
Prove his blood each day more healing,
And himself most deeply know.
James Allen, 1757; alt. by Walter Shirley, 1776.

DOXOLOGY.

Praise the God of all creation:
Praise the Father's boundless love;
Praise the Lamb, our expiation,
Priest and King enthroned above:
Praise the Fountain of salvation,
Him by whom our spirits live;
Undivided adoration
To the One Jehovah give
Josiah Conder, 1836.

CHRIST,—HIS SUFFERINGS AND DEATH.

ROCK OF AGES. 7s. 6 lines.

1. Rock of Ages, cleft for me, Let me hide myself in thee!
Be of sin the double cure, Cleanse me from its guilt and power.
Let the water and the blood, From thy riven side that flowed, D.C.

258.

1 Rock of Ages, cleft for me,
Let me hide myself in thee:
Let the water and the blood,
From thy riven side that flowed,
Be of sin the double cure,
Cleanse me from its guilt and power.

2 Not the labors of my hands
Can fulfil thy law's demands;
Could my zeal no respite know,
Could my tears forever flow,
All for sin could not atone,
Thou must save, and thou alone.

3 Nothing in my hand I bring,
Simply to thy cross I cling;
Naked, come to thee for dress;
Helpless, look to thee for grace;
Foul, I to the fountain fly:
Wash me, Saviour, or I die!

4 Whilst I draw this fleeting breath,
When my eyelids close in death,
When I soar through tracts unknown,
See thee on thy judgment-throne,
Rock of Ages, cleft for me,
Let me hide myself in thee.
Augustus M. Toplady, 1776.

259.

1 Resting from his work to-day,
In the tomb the Saviour lay;
Still he slept, from head to feet
Shrouded in the winding sheet,
Lying in the rock alone,
Hid beneath the sealed stone.

2 Late at even there was seen,
Watching long, the Magdalene;
Early, ere the break of day,
Sorrowful she took her way
To the holy garden glade,
Where her buried Lord was laid.

3 So with thee, till life shall end,
I would solemn vigil spend;
Let me hew thee, Lord, a shrine
In this rocky heart of mine,
Where in pure embalmèd cell
None but thou may'st ever dwell.

4 Myrrh and spices I will bring,
True affection's offering;
Close the door from sight and sound
Of the busy world around;
And in patient watch remain
Till my Lord appear again.
Thomas Whytehead, 1842. a.

DOXOLOGY.

Praise the name of God most high;
Praise him, all below the sky;
Praise him, all ye heavenly host:
Father, Son, and Holy Ghost!
As through countless ages past,
Evermore his praise shall last.

CHRIST,—HIS RESURRECTION AND ASCENSION.

THEODORA. 7s.

1. Morn-ing breaks up on the tomb; Je-sus dis-si-pates its gloom; Day of triumph! through the skies, See the glo-rious Sa-viour rise!

260.

1 MORNING breaks upon the tomb;
Jesus dissipates its gloom;
Day of triumph! through the skies,
See the glorious Saviour rise!

2 Christians, dry your flowing tears;
Chase those unbelieving fears;
Look on his deserted grave;
Doubt no more his power to save.

3 Ye who are of death afraid,
Triumph in the scattered shade;
Drive your anxious cares away;
See the place where Jesus lay.

4 So the rising sun appears,
Shedding radiance o'er the spheres;
So returning beams of light
Chase the terrors of the night.
William Bengo Collyer, 1812.

261.

1 ANGELS, roll the rock away!
Death, yield up thy mighty prey!
See, the Saviour leaves the tomb,
Glowing with immortal bloom.

2 Shout, ye seraphs; Gabriel, raise
Thine eternal trump of praise;
Let the earth's remotest bound
Echo to the blissful sound.

3 Saints on earth, lift up your eyes;
Now to glory see him rise;
Troops of angels on the road,
Hail and sing th' incarnate God.

4 Heaven unfolds its portals wide:
Glorious hero, through them ride;
King of glory, mount thy throne;
Boundless empire is thine own.

5 Praise him, all ye heavenly choirs!
Praise, and sweep your golden lyres!
Shout, O earth, in rapturous song,
Let the strains be sweet and strong!

6 Every note with wonder swell,
Sin o'erthrown, and captive hell!
Where, O death, is now thy sting?
Where thy terrors, vanquished king?
Thomas Scott, 1769.

262.

1 JESUS CHRIST is risen to-day,
Our triumphant holy day,
Who did once upon the cross
Suffer to redeem our loss.

2 Hymns of praise, then, let us sing
Unto Christ, our heavenly King,
Who endured the cross and grave,
Sinners to redeem and save.

3 But the pains which he endured
Our salvation has procured;
Now above the sky he's King,
Where the angels ever sing.

4 Now be God the Father praised,
With the Son from death upraised,
And the Spirit ever blest:
One true God by all confessed.
Tr. from the Latin of 15th century.

114. CHRIST,—HIS RESURRECTION AND ASCENSION.

SUDBURY. 7s.

1. Christ the Lord is risen a-gain, Christ hath brok-en eve-ry chain; Hark, an-gel-ic voi-ces cry, Sing-ing ev-er-more on high, Hal-le-lu-jah! Praise the Lord!

263.

1 Christ the Lord is risen again;
 Christ hath broken every chain;
 Hark! angelic voices cry,
 Singing evermore on high,
  Hallelujah! Praise the Lord!

2 He who gave for us his life,
 Who for us endured the strife,
 Is our paschal Lamb to-day!
 We, too, sing for joy, and say,
  Hallelujah! Praise the Lord!

3 He who bore all pain and loss,
 Comfortless, upon the cross,
 Lives in glory now on high,
 Pleads for us, and hears our cry:
  Hallelujah! Praise the Lord!

4 He who slumbered in the grave
 Is exalted now to save;
 Now through Christendom it rings
 That the Lamb is King of kings:
  Hallelujah! Praise the Lord!

5 Now he bids us tell abroad
 How the lost may be restored,
 How the penitent forgiven,
 How we, too, may enter heaven:
  Hallelujah! Praise the Lord!

6 Thou, our paschal Lamb indeed,
 Christ, to-day thy people feed!
 Take our sins and guilt away,
 Let us sing by night and day,
  Hallelujah! Praise the Lord!

Bohemian Easter Hymn, 1531; tr. by *C. Winkworth*, 1858.

264.

1 Christ, the Lord, is risen to-day!
 Sons of men and angels say:
 Raise your joys and triumphs high;
 Sing ye heavens, and earth reply!

2 Love's redeeming work is done,
 Fought the fight, the battle won:
 Lo! our sun's eclipse is o'er;
 Lo! he sets in blood no more.

3 Vain the stone, the watch, the seal;
 Christ hath burst the gates of hell:
 Death in vain forbids his rise,
 Christ hath opened paradise.

4 Lives again our glorious King!
 Where, O death, is now thy sting?
 Once he died our souls to save;
 Where thy victory, O grave?

5 Soar we now where Christ has led,
 Following our exalted Head:
 Made like him, like him we rise,
 Ours the cross, the grave, the skies.

6 Hail the Lord of earth and heaven!
 Praise to thee by both be given;
 Thee we greet triumphant now,
 Hail! the resurrection thou.

Charles Wesley, 1739.

DOXOLOGY.

Holy Father, Holy Son,
Holy Spirit, Three in One,
Glory as of old to Thee,
Now and evermore shall be!

CHRIST,—HIS RESURRECTION AND ASCENSION. 115

EASTER HYMN. H. M.

1. The hap-py morn is come; The Saviour leaves the grave; His glorious work is done. Al-might-y now to save, Cap-tiv-i-ty is cap-tive led, Since Je-sus liv-eth that was dead.

265.

2 Who to our charge shall lay
   Iniquity and guilt?
All sin is done away,
   Since his rich blood was spilt;
Captivity is captive led,
Since Jesus liveth that was dead.

3 Now the ungodly dare
   The Holy God draw near;
Justice itself declares
   No cause remains for fear;
Captivity is captive led,
Since Jesus liveth that was dead.

4 Christ hath the ransom paid;
   The glorious work is done;
On him our help is laid,
   The victory is won;
Captivity is captive led,
Since Jesus liveth that was dead.

5 Hail the triumphant Lord!
   The resurrection thou!
We bless thy sacred word,
   Before thy throne we bow;
Captivity is captive led,
Since Jesus liveth that was dead.
Thomas Haweis, 1802.

266.

1 COME, every pious heart
   That loves the Saviour's name,
Your noblest powers exert
   To celebrate his fame:
Tell all above and all below
The debt of love to him you owe.

2 He left his starry crown,
   And laid his robes aside;
On wings of love came down,
   And wept, and bled, and died.
What he endured, oh, who can tell,
To save our souls from death and hell?

3 From the dark grave he rose,
   The mansion of the dead;
And thence his mighty foes
   In glorious triumph led:
Up thro' the sky the Conqueror rode,
And reigns on high the Saviour God.

4 From thence he'll quickly come,
   His chariot will not stay,
And bear our spirits home.
   To realms of endless day:
There shall we see his lovely face,
And ever be in his embrace.
Samuel Stennett, 1770.

116   CHRIST,—HIS RESURRECTION AND ASCENSION.

TAPPAN. C. M.

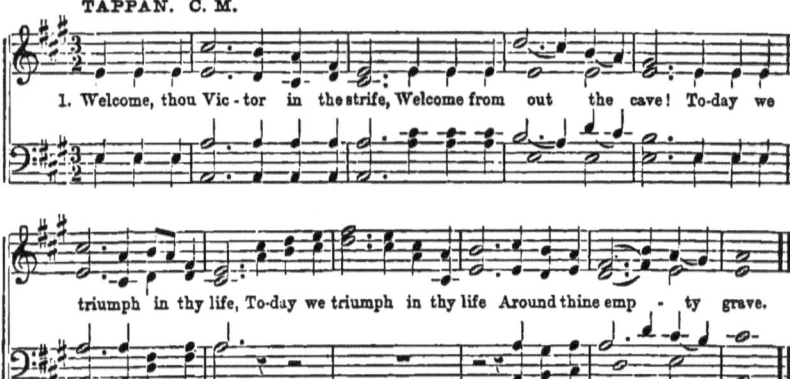

267.

1 WELCOME thou Victor in the strife,
   Welcome from out the cave!
 To-day we triumph in thy life
   Around thine empty grave.

2 Our enemy is put to shame,
   His short-lived triumph o'er;
 Our God is with us, we exclaim,
   We fear our foe no more.

3 Oh share with us the spoils, we pray,
   Thou diedst to achieve;
 We meet within thy house to-day
   Our portion to receive.

4 And let thy conquering banner wave
   O'er hearts thou makest free,
 And point the path that from the grave
   Leads heavenwards up to thee.

5 We bury all our sin and crime
   Deep in our Saviour's tomb;
 And seek the treasure there, that time
   Nor change can e'er consume.

6 We die with thee: oh, let us live
   Henceforth to thee aright!
 The blessings thou hast died to give
   Be daily in our sight.

7 Fearless we lay us in the tomb,
   And sleep the night away,
 If thou art there to break the gloom,
   And call us back to day.
     Benjamin Schmolke, 1712; tr. C. Winkworth.

268.

1 HOSANNA to the Prince of Light,
   Who clothed himself in clay,
 Entered the iron gates of death,
   And tore the bars away.

2 Death is no more the king of dread,
   Since our Immanuel rose;
 He took the tyrant's sting away,
   And spoiled our hellish foes.

3 See how the Conqueror mounts aloft,
   And to his Father flies,
 With scars of honor in his flesh,
   And triumph in his eyes.

4 There our exalted Saviour reigns,
   And scatters blessings down;
 Our Jesus fills the middle seat
   Of the celestial throne.

5 Raise your devotion, mortal tongues,
   To reach his blest abode;
 Sweet be the accents of your songs
   To our incarnate God.

6 Bright angels, strike your loudest strings,
   Your sweetest voices raise;
 Let heaven, and all created things,
   Sound our Immanuel's praise.
     Isaac Watts, 1709.

DOXOLOGY.

To Father, Son, and Holy Ghost,
   One God, whom we adore,
Be glory as it was, is now,
   And shall be evermore.
     Tate and Brady, 1696.

CHRIST,—HIS RESURRECTION AND ASCENSION.

WELTON. L. M.

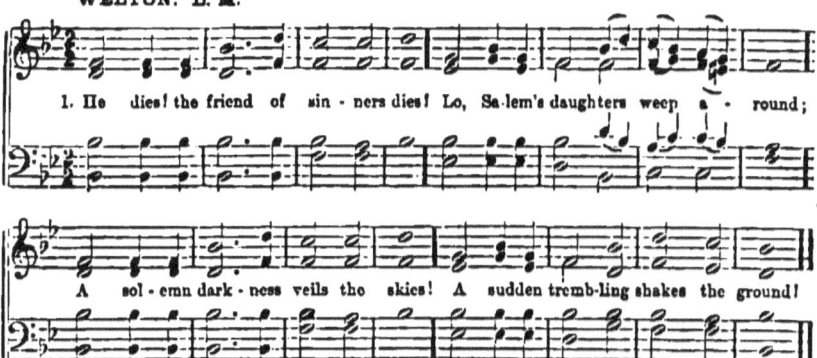

1. He dies! the friend of sinners dies! Lo, Salem's daughters weep around; A solemn darkness veils the skies! A sudden trembling shakes the ground!

269.

1 He dies! the friend of sinners dies!
Lo, Salem's daughters weep around;
A solemn darkness veils the skies!
A sudden trembling shakes the ground!

2 Here's love and grief beyond degree;
The Lord of glory dies for men!
But lo! what sudden joys we see!
Jesus the dead revives again!

3 The rising God forsakes the tomb!
Up to his Father's court he flies;
Cherubic legions guard him home,
And shout him welcome to the skies.

4 Break off your tears, ye saints, and tell
How high our great Deliverer reigns;
Sing how he spoiled the hosts of hell,
And led the monster, death, in chains!

5 Say, "Live forever, wondrous King,
Born to redeem, and strong to save!"
Then ask the monster, "Where's thy sting? [grave?"
And where's thy victory, boasting
Isaac Watts, 1706. a. by J. Wesley.

270. Psalm 86.

1 Lord, when thou didst ascend on high,
Ten thousand angels filled the sky;
Those heavenly guards around thee wait,
Like chariots, that attend thy state.

2 Not Sinai's mountain could appear
More glorious, when the Lord was there;
While he pronounced his holy law,
And struck the chosen tribes with awe.

3 How bright the triumph none can tell,
When the rebellious powers of hell,
That thousand souls had captive made,
Were all in chains, like captives, led.

4 Raised by his Father to the throne,
He sent his promised Spirit down,
With gifts and grace for rebel men,
That God might dwell on earth again.
Isaac Watts, 1719.

271.

1 Come, our indulgent Saviour, come,
Illustrious conqueror o'er the tomb;
Here thine assembled servants bless,
And fill our hearts with sacred peace.

2 Oh come thyself, most gracious Lord,
With all the joy thy smiles afford,
Reveal the lustre of thy face,
And make us feel thy vital grace.

3 With rapture kneeling round we greet
Thy pierced hands, thy wounded feet.
And from the scar that marks thy side
We see our life's warm torrent glide.

4 Enter our hearts, Redeemer blest,
Enter, thou ever honored Guest,
Not for one transient hour alone,
But there to fix thy lasting throne.

5 Own this mean dwelling as thine own;
And when our life's last hour is come,
Let us but die as in thy sight,
And death shall vanish in delight.
Philip Doddridge, 1755.

CHRIST,—HIS RESURRECTION AND ASCENSION.

272.

1 Hail the day that sees him rise,
  Ravished from our wishful eyes!
  Christ, awhile to mortals given,
  Reascends his native heaven.

2 Him though highest heaven receives,
  Still he loves the earth he leaves;
  Though returning to his throne,
  Still he calls mankind his own.

3 See, he lifts his hands above!
  See, he shows the prints of love!
  Hark, his gracious lips bestow
  Blessings on his church below!

4 Master (will we ever say),
  Taken from our head to-day,
  See thy faithful servants, see,
  Ever gazing up to thee.

5 Grant, though parted from our sight,
  High above yon azure height,
  Grant our hearts may thither rise,
  Following thee beyond the skies.

6 There we shall with thee remain,
  Partners of thy endless reign;
  There thy face unclouded see,
  Find our heaven of heavens in thee.
  Charles Wesley, 1739.

273.

1 Sons of God, triumphant rise,
  Shout the accomplished sacrifice;
  Shout your sins in Christ forgiven,
  Sons of God and heirs of heaven.

2 Love's mysterious work is done;
  Greet we now the atoning Son;
  Healed and quickened by his blood,
  Joined to Christ and one with God.

3 Him by faith we taste below,
  Mightier joys ordained to know,
  When his utmost grace we prove,
  Rise to heaven by perfect love.
  Charles Wesley, 1739.

274.

1 Sing, O heavens! O earth, rejoice!
  Angel harp and human voice,
  Round him, as he rises, raise
  Your ascending Saviour's praise.

2 Bruiséd is the serpent's head,
  Hell is vanquished, death is dead,
  And to Christ, gone up on high,
  Captive is captivity.

3 All his work and warfare done,
  He into his heaven is gone,
  And beside his Father's throne
  Now is pleading for his own:

4 Asking gifts for sinful men,
  That he may come down again,
  And, the fallen to restore,
  In them dwell forevermore.

5 Sing, O heavens! O earth, rejoice!
  Angel harp and human voice,
  Round him, in his glory, raise
  Your ascended Saviour's praise.
  John S. B. Monsell, 1863.

CHRIST,—HIS RESURRECTION AND ASCENSION. 119

ALFRETON. L. M.

1. O Christ, who hast prepared a place For us around thy throne of grace,
We pray thee, lift our hearts above, And draw them with the cords of love.

275.

1 O CHRIST, who hast prepared a place
　For us around thy throne of grace,
　We pray thee, lift our hearts above,
　And draw them with the cords of love.

2 Source of all good, thou, gracious Lord,
　Art our exceeding great reward:
　How transient is our present pain;
　How boundless our eternal gain!

3 With open face and joyful heart
　We then shall see thee as thou art;
　Our love shall never cease to glow,
　Our praise shall never cease to flow.

4 Thy never-failing grace to prove,
　A surety of thine endless love,
　Send down thy Holy Ghost to be
　The miser of our souls to thee.

Santolius Victorinus, 1630-1697; tr. by John Chandler, 1837.

276.   PSALM 24.

1 OUR Lord is risen from the dead;
　Our Jesus is gone up on high;
　The powers of hell are captive led,
　Dragged to the portals of the sky.

2 There his triumphal chariot waits,
　And angels chant the solemn lay:
　Lift up your heads, ye heavenly gates!
　Ye everlasting doors, give way!

3 Loose all your bars of massy light,
　And wide unfold the ethereal scene;
　He claims those mansions as his right;
　Receive the King of glory in.

4 Who is the King of glory,—who?
　The Lord that all his foes o'ercame;

The world, sin, death, and hell o'erthrew;
　And Jesus is the Conqueror's name.

5 Lo, his triumphal chariot waits,
　And angels chant the solemn lay:
　Lift up your heads, ye heavenly gates!
　Ye everlasting doors give way!

6 Who is the King of glory,—who?
　The Lord of glorious power possest,
　The King of saints and angels too,
　God over all, forever blest.

Charles Wesley, 1737.

277.

1 Now for a tune of lofty praise
　To great Jehovah's equal Son!
　Awake, my voice, in heavenly lays;
　Tell the loud wonders he hath done.

2 Sing how he left the worlds of light,
　And the bright robes he wore above;
　How swift and joyful was his flight
　On wings of everlasting love.

3 Deep in the shades of gloomy death,
　The almighty Captive prisoner lay;
　Th' almighty Captive left the earth,
　And rose to everlasting day.

4 Lift up your eyes, ye sons of light,
　Up to his throne of shining grace;
　See what immortal glories sit
　Round the sweet beauties of his face.

5 Amongst a thousand harps and songs,
　Jesus the God exalted reigns:
　His sacred name fills all their tongues,
　And echoes thro' the heavenly plains!

Isaac Watts, 1709.

CHRIST,—HIS GLORY.

ST. JOHN'S. C. M.

278.

1 BEYOND the glittering starry globe,
  Far as the eternal hills,
There, in the boundless worlds of light,
  Our great Redeemer dwells.

2 Immortal angels, bright and fair,
  In countless armies shine,
At his right hand, with golden harps,
  To offer songs divine.

3 Blest angels, who adoring wait
  Around the Saviour's throne,
Oh! tell us, for your eyes have seen,
  The wonders he has done.

4 In all his toils, and dangers too,
  Ye did his steps attend;
Oft paused, and wondered how at last
  This scene of love would end.

5 And when the powers of hell combined
  To fill his cup of woe,
Your pitying eyes beheld his tears
  In bloody anguish flow.

6 As on the torturing cross he hung,
  And darkness veiled the sky,
Ye saw, aghast, that awful sight,
  The Lord of glory die!

7 Anon he bursts the gates of death,
  Subdues the tyrant's power:
Ye saw th' illustrious Conqueror rise,
  And hailed the blissful hour,—

8 Tended his chariot up the sky,
  And bore him to his throne;
Then swept your golden harps and cried,
  "The glorious work is done!"

9 My soul the joyful triumph feels,
  And thinks the moments long,
Ere she her Saviour's glory sees,
  And joins your rapturous song.
  James Fanch and Daniel Turner, 1791.

279. REV. viii. 13.

1 COME, let us join our cheerful songs
  With angels round the throne;
Ten thousand thousand are their tongues,
  But all their joys are one.

2 "Worthy the Lamb that died," they cry,
  "To be exalted thus:"
"Worthy the Lamb," our lips reply,
  "For he was slain for us."

3 Jesus is worthy to receive
  Honor and power divine;
And blessings, more than we can give,
  Be, Lord, forever thine.

4 Let all that dwell above the sky,
  And air, and earth, and seas,
Conspire to lift thy glories high,
  And speak thine endless praise.

5 The whole creation join in one
  To bless the sacred name
Of Him that sits upon the throne,
  And to adore the Lamb.
  Isaac Watts, 1709.

CHRIST,—HIS GLORY.

MEAR. C. M.

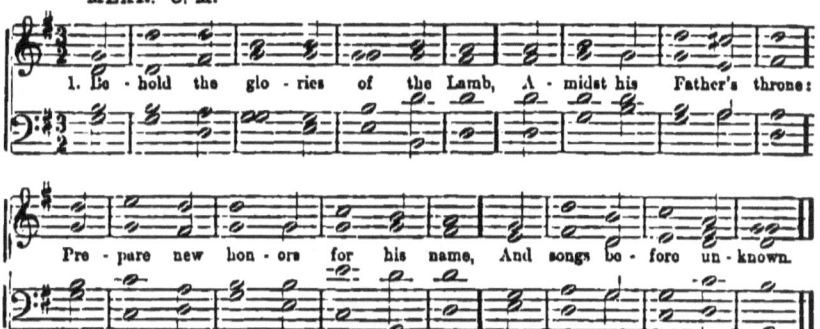

280.

1 BEHOLD the glories of the Lamb,
Amidst his Father's throne;
Prepare new honors for his name,
And songs before unknown.

2 Let elders worship at his feet,
The church adore around,
With vials full of odors sweet,
And harps of sweeter sound.

3 Those are the prayers of all the saints,
And these the hymns they raise:
Jesus is kind to our complaints,
He loves to hear our praise.

4 Now to the Lamb, that once was slain,
Be endless blessings paid;
Salvation, glory, joy remain
Forever on thy head.

5 Thou hast redeemed our souls with blood,
Hast set the prisoners free;
Hast made us kings and priests to God,
And we shall reign with thee.
Isaac Watts, 1709.

281.

1 WITH joy we meditate the grace
Of our High-Priest above;
His heart is made of tenderness,
His bosom glows with love.

2 Touched with a sympathy within,
He knows our feeble frame;
He knows what sore temptations mean,
For he has felt the same.

3 But spotless, innocent, and pure,
The great Redeemer stood;

And Satan's fiery darts he bore,
And did resist to blood.

4 He, in the days of feeble flesh,
Poured out his cries and tears;
And in his measure feels afresh
What every member bears.

5 Then let our humble faith address
His mercy and his power;
We shall obtain delivering grace
In the distressing hour.
Isaac Watts, 1709.

282.

1 Now let our cheerful eyes survey
Our great High-Priest above,
And celebrate his constant care,
And sympathetic love.

2 Though raised to a superior throne,
Where angels bow around,
And high o'er all the shining train
With matchless honor crowned;

3 The names of all his saints he bears,
Deep graven on his heart;
Nor shall the meanest Christian say
That he hath lost his part.

4 Those characters shall fair abide,
Our everlasting trust,
When gems, and monuments, and crowns,
Are mouldered down to dust.

5 So, gracious Saviour, on my breast
May thy dear name be worn,
A sacred ornament and guard,
To endless ages borne.
Philip Doddridge, 1755.

CHRIST,—HIS INTERCESSION.

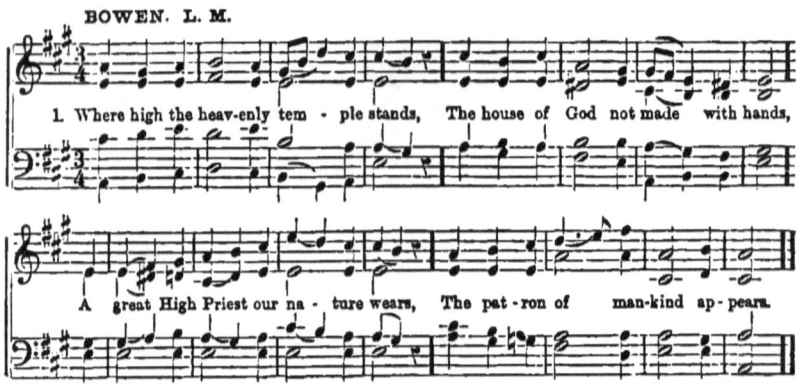

BOWEN. L. M.

1. Where high the heav-enly tem-ple stands, The house of God not made with hands, A great High Priest our na-ture wears, The pat-ron of man-kind ap-pears.

283.

1 Where high the heavenly temple stands,
  The house of God not made with hands,
  A great High Priest our nature wears,
  The patron of mankind appears.

2 He, who for men in mercy stood,
  And poured on earth his precious blood,
  Pursues in heaven his plan of grace,
  The guardian God of human race.

3 Though now ascended up on high,
  He bends on earth a brother's eye;
  Partaker of the human name,
  He knows the frailty of our frame.

4 Our fellow-sufferer yet retains
  A fellow-feeling of our pains;
  And still remembers, in the skies,
  His tears and agonies and cries.

5 In every pang that rends the heart,
  The Man of Sorrows had a part;
  He sympathizes with our grief,
  And to the sufferer sends relief.

6 With boldness therefore, at the throne,
  Let us make all our sorrows known,
  And ask the aids of heavenly power
  To help us in the evil hour.
  Michael Bruce, 1770.

284.

1 Before the throne of God above,
  I have a strong, a perfect plea:
  A great High Priest, whose name is Love,
  Who ever lives and pleads for me.

2 My name is graven on his hands;
  My name is written on his heart;
  Oh, know that while in heaven he stands
  No tongue can bid me thence depart.

3 When Satan tempts me to despair,
  And tells me of the guilt within,
  Upward I look, and see him there,
  Who made an end of all my sin.

4 Because the sinless Saviour died,
  My sinful soul is counted free;
  For God, the Just, is satisfied
  To look on him, and pardon me.

5 Behold him there, the bleeding Lamb!
  My perfect, spotless righteousness,
  The great unchangeable "I Am,"
  The King of glory and of grace.

6 One with himself, I cannot die;
  My soul is purchased by his blood;
  My life is hid with Christ on high,
  With Christ, my Saviour and my God.
  Charitie Lees Smith, 1863.

285.

1 Saviour, I lift my trembling eyes [high,
  To that bright seat where, placed on
  The great, the atoning Sacrifice,
  For me, for all, is ever nigh.

2 Be thou my guard on peril's brink;
  Be thou my guide thro' weal and woe;
  And teach me of thy cup to drink,
  And make me in thy path to go.

3 For what is earthly change or loss?
  Thy promises are still my own;
  The feeblest frame may bear thy cross,
  The lowliest spirit share thy throne.
  M. G. T. 1831.

CHRIST,—HIS INTERCESSION.

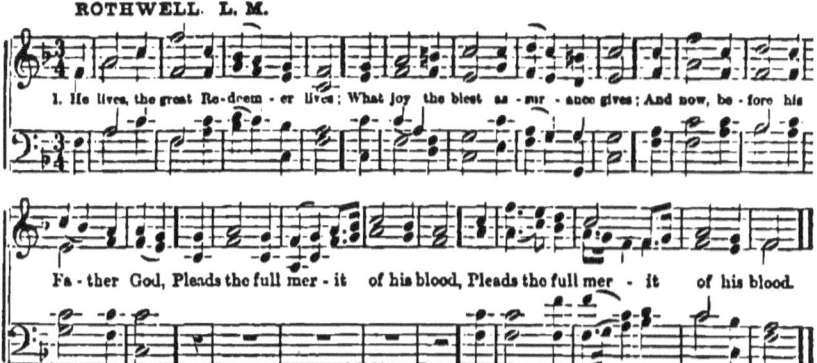

ROTHWELL. L. M.

1. He lives, the great Redeem-er lives; What joy the blest as-sur-ance gives; And now, be-fore his Father God, Pleads the full mer-it of his blood, Pleads the full mer-it of his blood.

286.

1 He lives, the great Redeemer lives;
   What joy the blest assurance gives!
   And now, before his Father God,
   Pleads the full merit of his blood.

2 Repeated crimes awake our fears,
   And justice, armed with frowns, appears;
   But in the Saviour's lovely face
   Sweet mercy smiles, and all is peace!

3 Hence, then, ye black despairing thoughts;
   Above our fears, above our faults,
   His powerful intercessions rise,
   And guilt recedes, and terror dies.

4 In every dark, distressful hour,
   When sin and Satan join their power,
   Let this dear hope repel the dart,
   That Jesus bears us on his heart.

5 Great Advocate, almighty Friend!
   On him our humble hopes depend;
   Our cause can never, never fail,
   For Jesus pleads, and must prevail.
   Anne Steele, 1760.

287.

1 Jesus, the Lord, our souls adore,
   A painful sufferer now no more;
   High on his Father's throne he reigns
   O'er earth, and heaven's extensive plains.

2 His race forever is complete;
   Forever undisturbed his seat;
   Myriads of angels round him fly,
   And sing his well-gained victory.

3 Yet, 'midst the honors of his throne,
   He joys not for himself alone;
   His meanest servants share their part,—
   Share in that royal, tender heart.

4 Raise, raise, my soul, thy raptured sight,
   With sacred wonder and delight;
   Jesus, thine own forerunner, see,
   Entered within the veil for thee.

5 Loud let the howling tempest yell,
   And foaming waves to mountains swell;
   No shipwreck can my vessel fear,
   Since hope hath fixed its anchor here.
   Philip Doddridge, 1755.

288.

1 Where is my God? does he retire
   Beyond the reach of humble sighs?
   Are these weak breathings of desire
   Too languid to ascend the skies?

2 Look up, my soul, with cheerful eye;
   See where the great Redeemer stands,
   The glorious Advocate on high,
   With precious incense in his hands!

3 He sweetens every humble groan;
   He recommends each broken prayer;
   Recline thy hope on him alone,
   Whose power and love forbid despair.

4 Teach my weak heart, O gracious Lord,
   With stronger faith to call thee mine!
   Bid me pronounce the blissful word,
   My Father God, with joy divine.
   Anne Steele, 1760.

CHRIST,—HIS INTERCESSION.

ST. PETERSBURG. L. M. 6 lines, by repeating the first two.

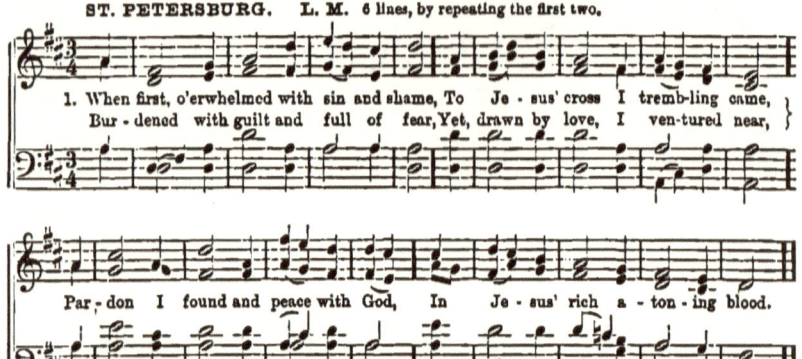

1. When first, o'erwhelmed with sin and shame, To Jesus' cross I trembling came,
Burdened with guilt and full of fear, Yet, drawn by love, I ventured near,
Pardon I found and peace with God, In Jesus' rich atoning blood.

289.

1 When first, o'erwhelmed with sin and shame,
To Jesus' cross I trembling came,
Burdened with guilt and full of fear,
Yet, drawn by love, I ventured near,
Pardon I found and peace with God,
In Jesus' rich atoning blood.

2 My sin is gone, my fears are o'er,
I shun his presence now no more;
He sits upon the throne of grace,
He bids me boldly seek his face;
Sprinkled upon the throne of God,
I see that rich atoning blood.

3 Before his face my Priest appears;
My Advocate, the Father hears;
That precious blood, before his eyes,
Both day and night for mercy cries!
It speaks, it ever speaks to God—
The voice of that atoning blood.

4 By faith that voice I also hear;
It answers doubt, it stills each fear:
The accuser seeks in vain to move
The wrath of him whose name is Love;
Each charge against the sons of God
Is silenced by the atoning blood.

5 Here I can rest without a fear;
By this, to God I now draw near;
By this I triumph over sin,
For this has made and keeps me clean;

And when I reach the throne of God,
I'll praise that rich atoning blood.
James G. Deck, 1838.

290.

1 O Saviour, who for man hast trod
The winepress of the wrath of God,
Ascend, and claim again on high
Thy glory, left for us to die.

2 A radiant cloud is now thy seat,
And earth lies stretched beneath thy feet;
Ten thousand thousands round thee sing,
And share the triumph of their King.

3 The angel-host enraptured waits;
"Lift up your heads, eternal gates!"
O God-and-Man! the Father's throne
Is now, for evermore, thine own.

4 Our great High Priest and Shepherd thou
Within the veil art entered now,
To offer there thy precious blood,
Once poured on earth a cleansing flood.

5 And thence the church, thy chosen Bride,
With countless gifts of grace supplied,
Through all her members draws from thee
Her hidden life of sanctity.

6 O Christ, our Lord, of thy dear care
Thy lowly members heavenward bear;
Be ours with thee to suffer pain,
With thee for evermore to reign.
C. Coffin; tr. by John Chandler, 1837.

CHRIST,—HIS INTERCESSION.

GOLAN. 8, 8, 8, 6.

1. O Thou, the con-trite sin-ner's Friend, Who, lov-ing, lov'st them to the end, On this a-lone my hopes de-pend, That thou wilt plead for me.

291.

2 When, weary in the Christian race,
Far off appears my resting place,
And, fainting, I mistrust thy grace,
Then, Saviour, plead for me.

3 When I have erred and gone astray,
Afar from thine and wisdom's way,
And see no glimmering, guiding ray,
Still, Saviour, plead for me.

4 When Satan, by my sins made bold,
Strives from thy cross to loose my hold,
Then with thy pitying arms enfold,
And plead, oh, plead for me!

5 And when my dying hour draws near,
Darkened with anguish, guilt, and fear,
Then to my fainting sight appear,
Pleading in heaven for me.

6 When the full light of heavenly day
Reveals my sins in dread array,
Say thou hast washed them all away;
Oh, say thou plead'st for me!

Charlotte Elliott, 1837.

ST. ALBINUS. 7s & 8s.

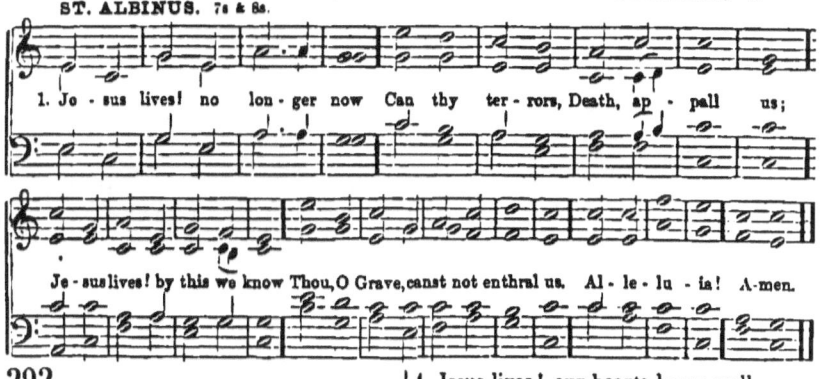

1. Je-sus lives! no lon-ger now Can thy ter-rors, Death, ap-pall us; Je-sus lives! by this we know Thou, O Grave, canst not enthral us. Al-le-lu-ia! A-men.

292.

2 Jesus lives! henceforth is death
But the gate of life immortal;
This shall calm our trembling breath,
When we pass its gloomy portal.
Alleluia!

3 Jesus lives! for us he died;
Then, alone to Jesus living,
Pure in heart may we abide,
Glory to our Saviour giving, etc.

4 Jesus lives! our hearts know well
Nought from us his love shall sever;
Life, nor death, nor powers of hell
Tear us from his keeping ever, etc.

5 Jesus lives! to him the throne
Over all the world is given:
May we go where he is gone,
Rest and reign with him in heaven.
Alleluia! Amen.

Ch. F. Gellert, 1757; tr. by *F. E. Cox,* 1841, a.

CHRIST,—HIS INTERCESSION.

BENEVENTO. 7s. DOUBLE.

293.

1 SAVIOUR, when in dust to thee
Low we bend the adoring knee;
When, repentant, to the skies
Scarce we lift our weeping eyes;
Oh, by all the pains and woe
Suffered once for man below,
Bending from thy throne on high,
Hear our solemn litany!

2 By thy helpless infant years,
By thy life of want and tears,
By thy days of sore distress
In the savage wilderness,
By the dread mysterious hour
Of the insulting tempter's power;
Turn, oh, turn a favoring eye,
Hear our solemn litany!

3 By the sacred griefs that wept
O'er the grave where Lazarus slept,
By the boding tears that flowed
Over Salem's loved abode,
By the anguished sigh that told
Treachery lurked within thy fold,
From thy seat above the sky,
Hear our solemn litany!

4 By thine hour of dire despair,
By thine agony of prayer,
By the cross, the nail, the thorn,
Piercing spear, and torturing scorn,
By the gloom that veiled the skies
O'er the dreadful sacrifice,
Listen to our humble cry,
Hear our solemn litany!

5 By thy deep expiring groan,
By the sad sepulchral stone,
By the vault, whose dark abode
Held in vain the rising God,
Oh, from earth to heaven restored,
Mighty, reascended Lord,
Listen, listen to the cry
Of our solemn litany!

Sir Robert Grant, 1815.

CHRIST,—HIS REIGN.

CORONET. 8s & 7s. DOUBLE.

1. Hail, thou once des - pis - ed Je - sus! Hail thou Ga - li - le - an King!
Thou didst suf - fer to re-lease us; Thou didst free sal - va - tion bring:
Hail! thou ag - o - niz - ing Sa-viour, Bear - er of our sin and shame!
By thy mer - its we find fa - vor; Life is giv - en through thy name.

294.

2 Paschal Lamb, by God appointed,
  All our sins on thee were laid;
By almighty love anointed,
  Thou hast full atonement made;
All thy people are forgiven
  Through the virtue of thy blood;
Opened is the gate of heaven;
  Peace is made 'twixt man and God.

3 Jesus, hail! enthroned in glory,
  There for ever to abide!
All the heavenly host adore thee,
  Seated at thy Father's side:
There for sinners thou art pleading;
  There thou dost our place prepare;
Ever for us interceding,
  Till in glory we appear.

4 Worship, honor, power, and blessing,
  Thou art worthy to receive;
Loudest praises, without ceasing,
  Meet it is for us to give:
Help, ye bright angelic spirits!
  Bring your sweetest, noblest lays!
Help to sing our Saviour's merits;
  Help to chant Immanuel's praise.

John Bakewell, 1760; alt. by A. M. Toplady, 1776.

295.

1 Crowns his head with endless blessing,
  Who, in God the Father's name,
With compassions never ceasing,
  Comes salvation to proclaim.
Hail, ye saints, who know his favor,
  Who within his gates are found;
Hail, ye saints, the exalted Saviour,
  Let his courts with praise resound.

2 Lo, Jehovah, we adore thee;
  Thee our Saviour! thee our God!
From his throne his beams of glory
  Shine through all the world abroad.
In his word his light arises,
  Brightest beams of truth and grace;
Bind, oh, bind your sacrifices,
  In his courts your offerings place.

3 Jesus, thee our Saviour hailing,
  Thee our God in praise we own;
Highest honors, never failing,
  Rise eternal round thy throne.
Now, ye saints, his power confessing,
  In your grateful strains adore;
For his mercy, never ceasing,
  Flows, and flows forevermore.

William Goode, 1811.

CHRIST,—HIS REIGN.

TAMWORTH. 8s, 7s & 4s.

1. Look, ye saints, the sight is glorious,
   From the fight re-turned vic-to-rious!
   See the Man of sor-rows now
   Every knee to him shall bow:
   Crown him! crown him! Crown him! crown him! Crowns become the Victor's brow.

296.

1 Look, ye saints, the sight is glorious;
   See the Man of sorrows now
   From the fight returned victorious!
   Every knee to him shall bow:
      Crown him! crown him!
   Crowns become the Victor's brow.

2 Crown the Saviour, angels, crown him!
   Rich the trophies Jesus brings;
   In the seat of power enthrone him,
   While the vault of heaven rings:
      Crown him! crown him!
   Crown the Saviour King of kings!

3 Sinners in derision crowned him,
   Mocking thus the Saviour's claim;
   Saints and angels, crowd around him,
   Own his title, praise his name!
      Crown him! crown him!
   Spread abroad the Victor's fame.

4 Hark, those bursts of acclamation!
   Hark, those loud, triumphant chords!
   Jesus takes the highest station;
   Oh, what joy the sight affords!
      Crown him! crown him!
   King of kings and Lord of lords!
   Thomas Kelly, 1806.

297.

1 Let us sing the King Messiah,
   King of righteousness and peace!
   Hail him, all his happy subjects;
   Never let his praises cease:
      Ever hail him!
   Never let his praises cease.

2 How transcendant are thy glories,
   Fairer than the sons of men!
   While thy blessed mediation
   Brings us back to God again:
      Blest Redeemer,
   How we triumph in thy reign!

3 Gird thy sword on, mighty Hero;
   Make the word of truth thy car;
   Prosper in thy course majestic;
   All success attend thy war:
      Gracious Victor,
   Let mankind before thee bow.

4 Majesty combines with meekness,
   Righteousness and peace unite,
   To insure thy blessèd conquests;
   On, great Prince; assert thy right:
      Ride triumphant
   All around the conquered globe!

5 Blest are all that touch thy sceptre;
   Blest are all that own thy reign;
   Freed from sin, that worst of tyrants,
   Rescued from its galling chain:
      Saints and angels,
   All who know thee, bless thy reign.
   John Ryland, 1790.

CHRIST,—HIS REIGN.

ROSEFIELD 7s. 6 LINES. (Omit repeat for 4 lines).

1. Glory, glory to our King! Crowns unfading wreathe his head; Jesus is the name we sing; Jesus risen from the dead; Jesus spoiler of the grave; Jesus mighty now to save.

298.

1 GLORY, glory to our King!
Crowns unfading wreathe his head;
Jesus is the name we sing;
Jesus risen from the dead;
Jesus spoiler of the grave;
Jesus mighty now to save.

2 Jesus is gone up on high,
Angels come to meet their King;
Shouts triumphant rend the sky,
While the Victor's praise they sing:
"Open now, ye heavenly gates!
'Tis the King of glory waits."

3 Now behold him high enthronéd,
Glory beaming from his face!
By adoring angels ownéd,
God of holiness and grace!
Oh for hearts and tongues to sing
"Glory, glory to our King!"

4 Jesus, on thy people shine; [tongues,
Warm our hearts and tune our
That with angels we may join, [songs:
Share their bliss, and swell their
Glory, honor, praise, and power,
Lord, be thine for evermore!
Thomas Kelly, 1804.

299.

1 SEE, the ransomed millions stand,
Palms of conquest in their hand;
This before the throne their strain:
"Hell is vanquished; death is slain;

2 Blessing, honor, glory, might
Are the Conqueror's native right;
Thrones and powers before him fall;
Lamb of God, and Lord of all!"

3 Hasten, Lord, the promised hour;
Come in glory and in power;
Still thy foes are unsubdued;
Nature sighs to be renewed.

4 Time has nearly reached its sum;
All things with thy bride say, Come;
Jesus, whom all worlds adore,
Come, and reign for evermore!
Josiah Conder, 1856.

300.

1 BRETHREN, let us join to bless
Christ, our peace and righteousness;
Let our praise to him be given,
High at God's right hand in heaven.

2 Son of God, to thee we bow;
Thou art Lord, and only thou;
Thou the woman's promised seed;
Thou, who didst for sinners bleed.

3 Thee the angels ceaseless sing;
Thee we praise, our Priest and King;
Worthy is thy name of praise,
Full of glory, full of grace.

4 Thee, our Lord, would we adore,
Serve and follow more and more;
Praise and bless thy matchless love,
Till we join thy saints above.
John Cennick, 1743. a.

CHRIST,—HIS REIGN.

CORONATION. C. M.

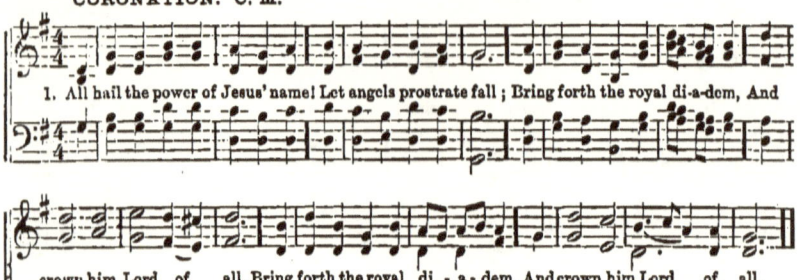

301.

1 ALL hail the power of Jesus' name!
   Let angels prostrate fall;
   Bring forth the royal diadem,
   And crown him Lord of all.

2 Let high-born seraphs tune the lyre,
   And, as they tune it, fall
   Before his face who tunes their choir,
   And crown him Lord of all.

3 Crown him, ye morning stars of light,
   Who fixed this floating ball;
   Now hail the strength of Israel's might,
   And crown him Lord of all.

4 Crown him, ye martyrs of your God,
   Who from his altar call;
   Extol the stem of Jesse's rod,
   And crown him Lord of all.

5 Ye seed of Israel's chosen race,
   Ye ransomed of the fall,
   Hail him who saves you by his grace,
   And crown him Lord of all.

6 Hail him, ye heirs of David's line,
   Whom David Lord did call;
   The God incarnate, man divine,
   And crown him Lord of all.

7 Sinners! whose love can ne'er forget
   The wormwood and the gall,
   Go, spread your trophies at his feet,
   And crown him Lord of all.

8 Let every tribe and every tongue
   That bound creation's call,
   Now shout in universal song,
   The crownéd Lord of all.
   Edward Perronet, 1785.

302.

1 THE head that once was crowned with
      thorns,
   Is crowned with glory now;
   A royal diadem adorns
   The mighty Victor's brow.

2 The highest place that heaven affords
   Is his, is his by right,
   The King of kings and Lord of lords,
   And heaven's eternal light:

3 The joy of all who dwell above,
   The joy of all below,
   To whom he manifests his love,
   And grants his name to know.

4 To them the cross, with all its shame,
   With all its grace, is given;
   Their name an everlasting name,
   Their joy the joy of heaven.

5 They suffer with their Lord below,
   They reign with him above,
   Their profit and their joy to know
   The mystery of his love.

6 The cross he bore is life and health,
   Though shame and death to him,
   His people's hope, his people's wealth,
   Their everlasting theme.
   Thomas Kelly, 1820.

CHRIST,—HIS REIGN.

TRURO. L. M.

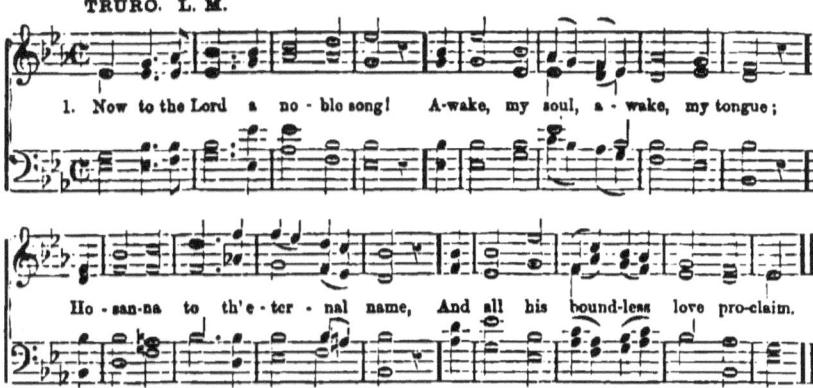

1. Now to the Lord a no-ble song! A-wake, my soul, a-wake, my tongue; Ho-san-na to th'e-ter-nal name, And all his bound-less love pro-claim.

303.

1 Now to the Lord a noble song!
  Awake, my soul, awake, my tongue;
  Hosanna to the eternal name,
  And all his boundless love proclaim.

2 See where it shines in Jesus' face
  The brightest image of his grace;
  God, in the person of his Son,
  Has all his mightiest works outdone.

3 The spacious earth and spreading flood
  Proclaim the wise, the powerful God;
  And thy rich glories from afar
  Sparkle in every rolling star.

4 But in his looks a glory stands,
  The noblest labor of thine hands;
  The pleasing lustre of his eyes
  Outshines the wonders of the skies.

5 Grace, 'tis a sweet, a charming theme;
  My thoughts rejoice at Jesus' name:
  Ye angels, dwell upon the sound,
  Ye heavens, reflect it to the ground!
  Isaac Watts, 1709.

304.

1 What equal honors shall we bring
    To thee, O Lord our God, the Lamb,
  When all the notes that angels sing
  Are far inferior to thy name?

2 Worthy is he that once was slain,
    The Prince of peace, that groaned and died;
  Worthy to rise, and live and reign
  At his almighty Father's side.

3 Honor immortal must be paid,
    Instead of scandal and of scorn;
  While glory shines around his head,
  And a bright crown without a thorn.

4 Blessings forever on the Lamb,
    Who bore the curse for wretched men,
  Let angels sound his sacred name,
  And every creature say, Amen.
  Isaac Watts, 1709.

305.

1 O Christ! our King, Creator, Lord!
  Saviour of all who trust thy word!
  To them who seek thee ever near,
  Now to our praises bend thine ear.

2 In thy dear cross a grace is found,
  It flows from every streaming wound,
  Whose power our inbred sin controls,
  Breaks the firm bond, and frees our souls.

3 Thou didst create the stars of night;
  Yet thou hast veiled in flesh thy light,
  Hast deigned a mortal form to wear,
  A mortal's painful lot to bear.

4 When thou didst hang upon the tree,
  The quaking earth acknowledged thee;
  When thou didst there yield up thy breath,
  The world grew dark as shades of death.

5 Now in the Father's glory high,
  Great Conqu'ror, never more to die,
  Us by thy mighty power defend,
  And reign through ages without end!
  Gregory, 550-604; tr. by *Ray Palmer,* 1858.

CHRIST,—HIS REIGN.

LENOX. H. M.

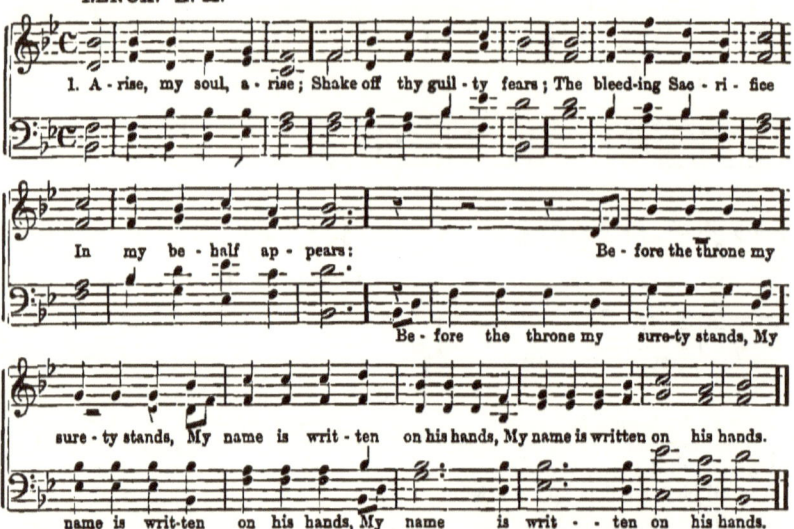

1. Arise, my soul, arise; Shake off thy guilty fears; The bleeding Sacrifice In my behalf appears: Before the throne my surety stands, My name is written on his hands.

306.

2 He ever lives above,
   For me to intercede;
His all-redeeming love,
   His precious blood, to plead;
His blood atoned for all our race,
And sprinkles now the throne of grace.

3 The Father hears him pray,
   His dear anointed one,
He cannot turn away
   The presence of his Son:
His Spirit answers to the blood,
And tells me I am born of God.

4 My God is reconciled;
   His pard'ning voice I hear:
He owns me for his child;
   I can no longer fear:
With confidence I now draw nigh,
And Father, Abba, Father, cry.

Charles Wesley, 1739.

307.

1 JOIN all the glorious names
   Of wisdom, love, and power,
That ever mortals knew,
   That angels ever bore;
All are too mean to speak his worth,
Too mean to set my Saviour forth.

2 Great Prophet of my God,
   My tongue would bless thy name;
By thee the joyful news
   Of our salvation came:
The joyful news of sins forgiven,
Of hell subdued, and peace with heaven.

3 Jesus, my great High-Priest,
   Offered his blood and died;
My guilty conscience seeks
   No sacrifice beside:
His powerful blood did once atone,
And now it pleads before the throne.

4 O thou almighty Lord!
   My Conqueror and my King!
Thy sceptre and thy sword,
   Thy reigning grace I sing;
Thine is the power; behold, I sit,
In willing bonds, before thy feet.

5 Now let my soul arise,
   And tread the tempter down;
My Captain leads me forth
   To conquest and a crown;
A feeble saint shall win the day,
Though death and hell obstruct the way.

Isaac Watts, 1709.

CHRIST,—HIS REIGN.

DARWELL. H. M.

308.

1 ALL hail, Incarnate God!
  The wondrous things foretold
  Of thee in sacred writ
  With joy our eyes behold;
Still does thine arm new trophies wear,
And monuments of glory rear.

2 To thee the hoary head
  Its silver honors pays;
  To thee the blooming youth
  Devotes his brightest days;
And every age their tribute bring,
And bow to thee, all conquering King.

3 Oh haste, victorious Prince,
  That happy, glorious day,
  When souls like drops of dew
  Shall own thy gentle sway;
Oh may it bless our longing eyes
And bear our shouts beyond the skies!

4 All hail, triumphant Lord!
  Eternal be thy reign;
  Behold the nations sue
  To wear thy gentle chain;
When earth and time are known no more,
Thy throne shall stand forever sure.

Elizabeth Scott, 1764.

309.

1 THE atoning work is done,
  The Victim's blood is shed;
  And Jesus now is gone
  His people's cause to plead;
He stands in heaven their great High-Priest,
And bears their name upon his breast.

2 He sprinkles with his blood
  The mercy-seat above;
  For justice hath withstood
  The purposes of love:
But justice now objects no more,
And mercy yields her boundless store.

3 No temple made with hands
  His place of service is;
  In heaven itself he stands,
  A heavenly priesthood his;
In him the shadows of the law
Are all fulfilled and now withdraw.

4 And though awhile he be
  Hid from the eyes of men,
  His people look to see
  Their great High Priest again:
In brightest glory he will come,
And take his waiting people home.

Thomas Kelly, 1803.

CHRIST,—HIS REIGN.

GROSTETE. L. M.

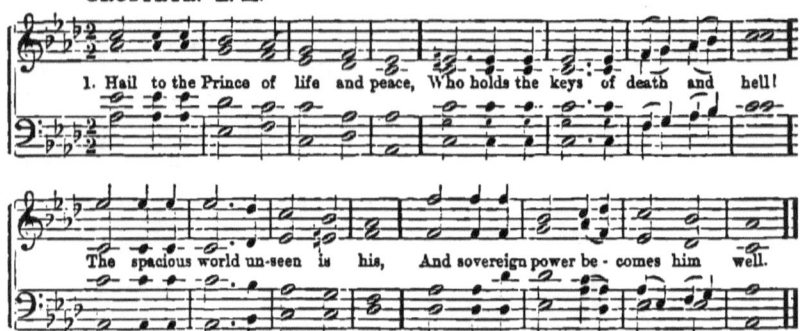

1. Hail to the Prince of life and peace, Who holds the keys of death and hell! The spacious world unseen is his, And sovereign power becomes him well.

310.

1 HAIL to the Prince of life and peace,
  Who holds the keys of death and hell!
  The spacious world unseen is his,
  And sovereign power becomes him well.

2 In shame and torment once he died;
  But now he lives for evermore:
  Bow down, ye saints around his seat,
  And, all ye angel-bands, adore.

3 So live forever glorious Lord,
  To crush thy foes and guard thy friends!
  While all thy chosen tribes rejoice
  That thy dominion never ends.

4 Worthy thy hands to hold the keys,
  Guided by wisdom and by love;
  Worthy to rule o'er mortal life,
  O'er worlds below and worlds above.

5 Forever reign, victorious King! [known;
  Wide through the earth thy name be
  And call my longing soul to sing
  Sublimer anthems near thy throne.
  Philip Doddridge, 1755.

311. PSALM 45.

1 Now be my heart inspired to sing
  The glories of my Saviour King:
  Jesus, the Lord, how heavenly fair
  His form! how bright his beauties are!

2 O'er all the sons of human race
  He shines with a superior grace;
  Love from his lips divinely flows,
  And blessings all his state compose.

3 Thy throne, O God, forever stands!
  Grace is the sceptre in thy hands:
  Thy laws and works are just and right;
  Justice and grace are thy delight.

4 God, thine own God, has richly shed
  His oil of gladness on thy head;
  And with his sacred Spirit blest
  His first-born Son above the rest.
  Isaac Watts, 1719.

312.

1 Now to the Lord, that makes us know
  The wonders of his dying love,
  Be humble honors paid below,
  And strains of nobler praise above!

2 'T was he that cleansed our foulest sins,
  And washed us in his precious blood;
  'T is he that makes us priests and kings,
  And brings us rebels near to God.

3 To Jesus, our atoning Priest,
  To Jesus, our superior King,
  Be everlasting power confessed,
  Let every tongue his glory sing.

4 Behold on flying clouds he comes,
  And every eye shall see him move;
  Tho' with our sins we pierced him once,
  He now displays his pardoning love.

5 The unbelieving world shall wail,
  While we rejoice to see the day:
  Come, Lord. nor let thy promise fail,
  Nor let thy chariot long delay.
  Isaac Watts, 1709.

CHRIST,—HIS REIGN.

CULLODEN. H. M.

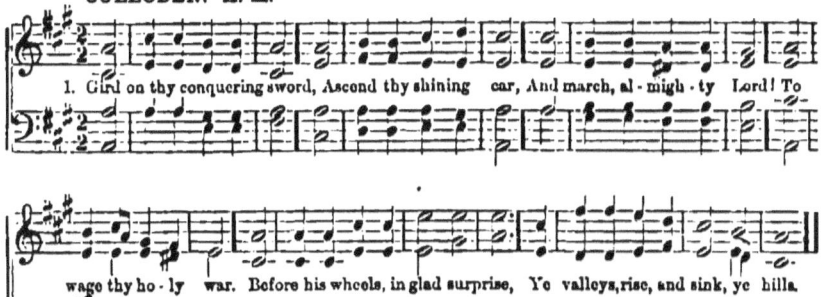

1. Gird on thy conquering sword, Ascend thy shining car, And march, almighty Lord! To wage thy holy war. Before his wheels, in glad surprise, Ye valleys, rise, and sink, ye hills.

313.

1 GIRD on thy conquering sword,
  Ascend thy shining car,
And march, almighty Lord,
  To wage thy holy war.
Before his wheels, in glad surprise,
Ye valleys, rise, and sink, ye hills.

2 Fair truth and smiling love,
  And injured righteousness,
Under thy banners move,
  And seek from thee redress;
Thou in their cause shalt prosperous ride,
And far and wide dispense thy laws.

3 Before thine awful face
  Millions of foes shall fall,
The captives of thy grace —
  That grace that conquers all.
The world shall know, great King of kings,
What wondrous things thine arm can do.

4 Here to my willing soul
  Bend thy triumphant way;
Here every foe control,
  And all thy power display;
My heart, thy throne, blest Jesus! see,
Bows low to thee, to thee alone.
          Philip Doddridge, 1736.

314.

1 REJOICE, the Lord is King.
  Your Lord and King adore;

Mortals, give thanks and sing,
  And triumph evermore:
Lift up your heart, lift up your voice;
Rejoice, again I say, rejoice.

2 Jesus the Saviour reigns,
  The God of truth and love;
When he had purged our stains,
  He took his seat above:
Lift up your heart, lift up your voice;
Rejoice, again I say, rejoice.

3 His kingdom cannot fail;
  He rules o'er earth and heaven;
The keys of death and hell
  Are to our Jesus given:
Lift up your heart, lift up your voice;
Rejoice, again I say, rejoice.

4 He all his foes shall quell,
  Shall all our sins destroy,
And every bosom swell
  With pure seraphic joy:
Lift up your heart, lift up your voice;
Rejoice, again I say, rejoice.

5 Rejoice in glorious hope;
  Jesus, the Judge, shall come,
And take his servants up
  To their eternal home:
We soon shall hear the archangel's voice;
The trump of God shall sound, Rejoice.
          Charles Wesley, 1745.

CHRIST,—HIS REIGN.

315.

1 HARK! ten thousand harps and voices
   Sound the note of praise above;
   Jesus reigns, and heaven rejoices;
   Jesus reigns, the God of love:
   See, he sits on yonder throne;
   Jesus rules the world alone.

2 Jesus, hail! whose glory brightens
   All above, and gives it worth;
   Lord of life, thy smile enlightens,
   Cheers, and charms, thy saints on earth:
   When we think of love like thine,
   Lord, we own it love divine.

3 King of glory, reign forever;
   Thine an everlasting crown:
   Nothing from thy love shall sever
   Those whom thou hast made thine own;
   Happy objects of thy grace,
   Chosen to behold thy face.

4 Saviour, hasten thine appearing;
   Bring, oh, bring the glorious day,
   When, the awful summons hearing,
   Heaven and earth shall pass away;
   Then, with golden harps, we'll sing,
   "Glory, glory to our King!"
   Thomas Kelly, 1836.

316.

1 ONE there is, above all others,
   Well deserves the name of Friend;
   His is love beyond a brother's,
   Costly, free, and knows no end.
   They who once his kindness prove
   Find it everlasting love.

2 Which of all our friends, to save us,
   Could or would have shed their blood?
   But our Jesus died to have us
   Reconciled in him to God.
   This was boundless love indeed;
   Jesus is a Friend in need.

3 When he lived on earth abased,
   Friend of sinners was his name;
   Now, above all glory raised,
   He rejoices in the same:
   Still he calls them brethren, friends,
   And to all their wants attends.

4 Could we bear from one another
   What he daily bears from us?
   Yet this glorious Friend and Brother
   Loves us though we treat him thus:
   Though for good we render ill,
   He accounts us brethren still.

5 Oh for grace our hearts to soften!
   Teach us, Lord, at length to love;
   We, alas! forget too often
   What a Friend we have above:
   But when home our souls are brought,
   We will love thee as we ought.
   John Newton, 1779.

CHRIST,—HIS CHARACTERS.

FENWORTH. L. M. 6 lines, by repeating the first two.

1. Thou hid-den source of calm re-pose, Thou all - suffi - cient Love di - vine,
My help and ref - uge from my foes, Se - cure I am if thou art mine:
And lo! from sin, and grief, and shame, I hide me, Je - sus, in thy name.

317.

1 Thou hidden source of calm repose,
Thou all-sufficient Love divine,
My help and refuge from my foes,
Secure I am if thou art mine:
And lo! from sin, and grief, and shame,
I hide me, Jesus, in thy name.

2 Thy mighty name salvation is,
And keeps my happy soul above;
Comfort it brings, and power and peace,
And joy, and everlasting love:
To me, with thy dear name, are given
Pardon, and holiness, and heaven.

3 Jesus, my all in all thou art;
My rest in toil, my ease in pain;
The med'cine of my broken heart;
In war, my peace; in loss, my gain;
My smile beneath the tyrant's frown;
In shame, my glory and my crown;

4 In want, my plentiful supply;
In weakness, my almighty power;
In bonds, my perfect liberty;
My light in Satan's darkest hour;
In grief, my joy unspeakable;
My life in death, my all in all.
Charles Wesley, 1741.

318.

1 O Love of God, how strong and true!
Eternal and yet ever new,
Uncomprehended and unbought,
Beyond all knowledge and all thought.

2 We read thee best in him who came
To bear for us the cross of shame;
Sent by the Father from on high,
Our life to live, our death to die.

3 We read thy power to bless and save
E'en in the darkness of the grave;
Still more in resurrection light
We read the fulness of thy might.

4 O Love of God, our shield and stay,
Through all the perils of our way:
Eternal Love, in thee we rest,
For ever safe, forever blest!
Horatius Bonar, 1861.

319.

1 There is none other name than thine,
Jehovah Jesus! name divine!
On which to rest for sins forgiven,
For peace with God, for hope of heaven.

2 There is none other name than thine,
When cares, and fears, and griefs are mine,
That, with a gracious power, can heal
Each care, and fear, and grief I feel.

3 There is none other name than thine,
When called my spirit to resign,
To bear me through that latest strife,
And e'en in death to be my life.

4 Name above every name! thy praise
Shall fill the remnant of my days:
Jehovah Jesus! name divine,
Rock of salvation! thou art mine.
Anon. 1858.

CHRIST,—HIS CHARACTERS.

ARIEL. C. P. M.

1. Oh, could I speak the matchless worth, Oh could I sound the glories forth, Which in my Saviour shine! I'd soar, and touch the heavenly strings, And vie with Gabriel while he sings In notes almost divine, In notes almost divine.

320.

1 OH, could I speak the matchless worth,
Oh, could I sound the glories forth,
  Which in my Saviour shine,
I'd soar, and touch the heavenly strings,
And vie with Gabriel while he sings ·
  In notes almost divine.

2 I'd sing the precious blood he spilt,
My ransom from the dreadful guilt
  Of sin and wrath divine!
I'd sing his glorious righteousness,
In which all-perfect, heavenly dress
  My soul shall ever shine.

3 I'd sing the characters he bears,
And all the forms of love he wears,
  Exalted on his throne:
In loftiest songs of sweetest praise,
I would to everlasting days
  Make all his glories known.

4 Well, the delightful day will come,
When my dear Lord will bring me home,
  And I shall see his face:
Then with my Saviour, Brother, Friend,
A blest eternity I'll spend,
  Triumphant in his grace.

Samuel Medley, 1789.

321.

1 O THOU who hast redeemed of old,
And bidst me of thy strength lay hold,
  And be at peace with thee,
Help me thy benefits to own,
And hear me tell what thou hast done,
  O dying Lamb! for me.

2 Out of myself for help I go,
Thy only love resolved to know,
  Thy love my plea I make;
Give me thy love, 'tis all I claim;
Give, for the honor of thy name,
  Give, for thy mercy's sake.

3 Love, only love, thy heart inclined,
And brought thee, Saviour of mankind,
  Down from thy throne above;
Love made my God a man of grief,
Distressed thee sore for my relief:
  Oh, mystery of love!

4 As thou hast loved and died for me,
So grant me, Saviour, love to thee,
  And gladly I resign
Whate'er I have, whate'er I am:
My life be all with thine the same,
  And all thy death be mine.

Charles Wesley, 1749.

CHRIST,—HIS CHARACTERS.

PARK STREET. L. M.

1. Awake, my soul, in joy-ful lays, And sing thy great Re-deem-er's praise; He just-ly claims a song from me; His loving-kindness is so free! His loving-kindness is so free!

322.

1 AWAKE, my soul, in joyful lays,
And sing thy great Redeemer's praise;
He justly claims a song from me,
His loving-kindness is so free.

2 He saw me ruined in the fall,
Yet loved me notwithstanding all;
He saved me from my lost estate,
His loving-kindness is so great.

3 Through mighty hosts of cruel foes,
Where earth and hell my way oppose,
He safely leads my soul along,
His loving-kindness is so strong.

4 When earthly friends forsake me quite,
And I have neither skill nor might,
He's sure my helper to appear,
His loving-kindness is so near.

5 Often I feel my sinful heart
Prone from my Jesus to depart;
And though I oft have him forgot,
His loving-kindness changes not.

6 So when I pass death's gloomy vale,
And life and mortal powers shall fail,
Oh, may my last expiring breath
His loving-kindness sing in death!

7 Then shall I mount and soar away
To the bright world of endless day;
Then shall I sing with sweet surprise
His loving-kindness in the skies!

Samuel Medley, 1787.

323.

1 HAIL, sovereign love, that first began
The scheme to rescue fallen man!
Hail, matchless, free, eternal grace,
That gave my soul a hiding-place!

2 Against the God that rules the sky
I fought with hand uplifted high;
Despised the mention of his grace,
Too proud to seek a hiding-place.

3 Enwrapped in thick Egyptian night,
And fond of darkness more than light,
Madly I ran the sinful race,
Secure, without a hiding-place.

4 Indignant justice stood in view,
To Sinai's fiery mount I flew;
But justice cried, with frowning face,
This mountain is no hiding-place.

5 Ere long a heavenly voice I heard,
And Mercy's angel form appeared;
She led me on, with placid pace,
To Jesus as my hiding-place.

6 On him almighty vengeance fell,
That must have sunk a world to hell;
He bore it for the chosen race,
And thus became their hiding-place.

7 A few more rolling suns at most
Will land me on fair Canaan's coast,
Where I shall sing the song of grace,
And see my glorious hiding-place.

Jehoiada Brewer, 1776.

CHRIST,—HIS CHARACTERS.

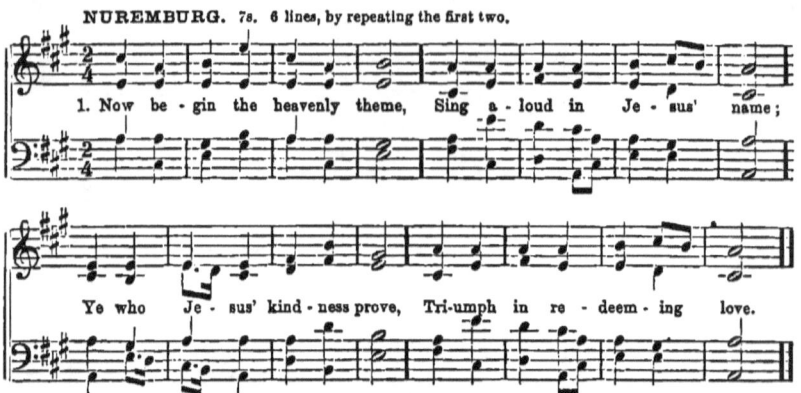

NUREMBURG. 7s. 6 lines, by repeating the first two.

1. Now begin the heavenly theme, Sing aloud in Jesus' name; Ye who Jesus' kindness prove, Triumph in redeeming love.

324.

1 Now begin the heavenly theme,
Sing aloud in Jesus' name;
Ye who Jesus' kindness prove,
Triumph in redeeming love.

2 Ye who see the Father's grace
Beaming in the Saviour's face,
As to Canaan on ye move,
Praise and bless redeeming love.

3 Mourning souls, dry up your tears,
Banish all your guilty fears;
See your guilt and curse remove,
Cancelled by redeeming love.

4 Ye, alas! who long have been
Willing slaves of death and sin,
Now from bliss no longer rove,
Stop and taste redeeming love.

5 Welcome all by sin opprest,
Welcome to his sacred rest;
Nothing brought him from above,
Nothing but redeeming love.

6 Hither, then, your music bring;
Strike aloud each joyful string:
Mortals, join the host above,
Join to praise redeeming love.
Martin Madan, 1763.

325.

1 Holy Jesus, Saviour blest,
When, by passion strong possest,
Through this world of sin we stray,
Thou to guide us art the Way.

2 Holy Jesus, when like night
Error dims our clouded sight,
Through the mists of sin to shine
Thou dost rise the Truth divine.

3 Holy Jesus, when our power
Fails us in temptation's hour,
All unequal to the strife,
Thou to aid us art the Life.

4 Who would reach his heavenly home,
Who would to the Father come,
And his glorious presence see,
Jesus, he must come by thee.
Bishop Richard Mant, 1837.

326.

1 Christ, whose glory fills the sky,
Christ the true, the only Light,
Sun of righteousness, arise,
Triumph o'er the shades of night;
Day-spring from on high, be near;
Day-star, in my heart appear.

2 Dark and cheerless is the morn,
Unaccompanied by thee;
Joyless is the day's return,
Till thy mercy's beams I see,
Till they inward light impart,
Glad my eyes and warm my heart.

3 Visit, then, this soul of mine;
Pierce the gloom of sin and grief;
Fill me, Radiancy divine;
Scatter all my unbelief;
More and more thyself display,
Shining to the perfect day.
Charles Wesley, 1740.

CHRIST,—HIS CHARACTERS.

GEER. C. M.

1. How sweet the name of Je-sus sounds In a be-liev-er's ear! It soothes his sor-rows, heals his wounds, And drives a-way his fear.

327.

1 How sweet the name of Jesus sounds
  In a believer's ear!
It soothes his sorrows, heals his wounds,
  And drives away his fear.

2 It makes the wounded spirit whole,
  And calms the troubled breast;
'Tis manna to the hungry soul,
  And to the weary, rest.

3 Dear Name! the Rock on which I build,
  My Shield and Hiding-place,
My never-failing Treasury, filled
  With boundless stores of grace!

4 By thee my prayers acceptance gain,
  Although with sin defiled;
Satan accuses me in vain,
  And I am owned a child.

5 Jesus! my Shepherd, Husband, Friend,
  My Prophet, Priest, and King;
My Lord, my Life, my Way, my End,
  Accept the praise I bring.

6 Weak is the effort of my heart,
  And cold my warmest thought;
But when I see thee as thou art,
  I'll praise thee as I ought.

7 Till then I would thy love proclaim
  With every fleeting breath;
And may the music of thy name
  Refresh my soul in death.
John Newton, 1779.

328.

1 O FOR a thousand tongues to sing
  My great Redeemer's praise;
The glories of my God and King,
  The triumphs of his grace.

2 My gracious Master, and my God,
  Assist me to proclaim,
To spread through all the earth abroad,
  The honors of thy name.

3 Jesus! the name that charms our fears,
  That bids our sorrows cease;
'Tis music in the sinner's ears,
  'Tis life, and health, and peace.

4 He breaks the power of cancelled sin,
  He sets the pris'ner free;
His blood can make the foulest clean;
  His blood availed for me.

5 He speaks, and, listening to his voice,
  New life the dead receive;
The mournful, broken hearts rejoice;
  The humble poor believe.

6 Hear him, ye deaf; his praise, ye dumb,
  Your loosened tongues employ;
Ye blind, behold your Saviour come;
  And leap, ye lame, for joy.
Charles Wesley, 1740.

DOXOLOGY.
To God the Father glory be.
  And to his only Son,
And to the Spirit, One and Three,
  While endless ages run.
John Henry Newman, 1842.

CHRIST,—HIS CHARACTERS.

BROWN. C. M.

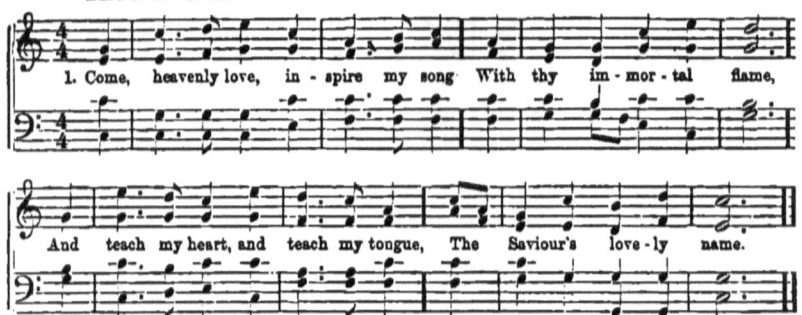

329.

1 Come, heavenly love, inspire my song
  With thy immortal flame,
And teach my heart, and teach my tongue,
  The Saviour's lovely name.

2 The Saviour! oh, what endless charms
  Dwell in that blissful sound!
Its influence every fear disarms,
  And spreads sweet comfort round.

3 Here pardon, life, and joys divine,
  In rich effusion flow,
For guilty rebels lost in sin,
  And doomed to endless woe.

4 The almighty Former of the skies
  Stooped to our vile abode;
While angels viewed with wondering eyes,
  And hailed th' incarnate God.

5 Oh, the rich depths of love divine!
  Of bliss, a boundless store!
Dear Saviour, let me call thee mine:
  I cannot wish for more.

6 On thee alone my hope relies;
  Beneath thy cross I fall;
My Lord, my life, my sacrifice,
  My Saviour, and my all!
Anne Steele, 1760.

330.

1 Jesus, the name high over all,
  In hell, or earth, or sky;
Angels and men before it fall,
  And devils fear and fly.

2 Jesus, the name to sinners dear,
  The name to sinners given;
It scatters all their guilty fear;
  It turns their hell to heaven.

3 Jesus the prisoner's fetters breaks,
  And bruises Satan's head;
Power into strengthless souls he speaks,
  And life into the dead.

4 Oh, that the world might taste and see
  The riches of his grace;
The arms of love that compass me,
  Would all mankind embrace.

5 His only righteousness I show,
  His saving truth proclaim:
'Tis all my business here below,
  To cry, Behold the Lamb!

6 Happy, if with my latest breath
  I may but gasp his name;
Preach him to all, and cry in death,
  Behold, behold the Lamb!
Charles Wesley, 1740.

DOXOLOGY.

Honor to the almighty Three
  And everlasting One;
All glory to the Father be,
  The Spirit, and the Son.
Isaac Watts, 1709.

331. PSALM 71. C. M.

1 My Saviour, my Almighty Friend,
   When I begin thy praise,
   Where will the growing numbers end,
   The numbers of thy grace!

2 Thou art my everlasting trust,
   Thy goodness I adore;
   And since I knew thy graces first,
   I speak thy glories more.

3 My feet shall travel all the length
   Of the celestial road,
   And march with courage in thy strength
   To see my Father, God.

4 When I am filled with sore distress
   For some surprising sin,
   I'll plead thy perfect righteousness,
   And mention none but thine.

5 How will my lips rejoice to tell
   The victories of my King!
   My soul, redeemed from sin and hell,
   Shall thy salvation sing.
Isaac Watts, 1719.

332. C. M.

1 JESUS, thou art my Righteousness,
   For all my sins were thine;
   Thy death hath bought of God my peace,
   Thy life hath made him mine.

2 Spotless and just in thee I am;
   I feel my sins forgiven;
   I taste salvation in thy name,
   And antedate my heaven.

3 Forever here my rest shall be,
   Close to thy bleeding side;
   This all my hope, and all my plea,
   For me the Saviour died!

4 My dying Saviour and my God,
   Fountain for guilt and sin,
   Sprinkle me ever with thy blood,
   And cleanse and keep me clean!

5 Wash me, and make me thus thine own;
   Wash me, and mine thou art;
   Wash me, but not my feet alone:
   My hands, my head, my heart!

6 Th' atonement of thy blood apply,
   Till faith to sight improve;
   Till hope in full fruition die,
   And all my soul be love.
Charles Wesley, 1740.

333. C. M.

1 To our Redeemer's glorious name
   Awake the sacred song;
   Oh, may his love, immortal flame,
   Tune every heart and tongue.

2 His love what mortal thought can reach,
   What mortal tongue display!
   Imagination's utmost stretch
   In wonder dies away.

3 Let wonder still with love unite,
   And gratitude and joy;
   Jesus be our supreme delight,
   His praise our blest employ.

4 Jesus who left his throne on high,
   Left the bright realms of bliss,
   And came to earth to bleed and die,—
   Was ever love like this?

5 Dear Lord, while we adoring pay
   Our humble thanks to thee,
   May every heart with rapture say,
   "The Saviour died for me!"

6 Oh may the sweet, the blissful theme,
   Fill every heart and tongue,
   Till strangers love thy charming name,
   And join the sacred song.
Anne Steele, 1760.

334. C. M.

1 I've found the pearl of greatest price!
   My heart doth sing for joy;
   And sing I must, for Christ is mine!
   Christ shall my song employ.

2 Christ is my Prophet, Priest, and King;
   My Prophet full of light,
   My great High Priest before the throne,
   My King of heavenly might.

3 For he indeed is Lord of lords,
   And he the King of kings;
   He is the Sun of Righteousness,
   With healing in his wings.

4 Christ is my peace; he died for me,
   For me he gave his blood,
   And as my wondrous Sacrifice
   Offered himself to God.

5 Christ Jesus is my All in All,
   My comfort and my love;
   My life below, and he shall be
   My joy and crown above.
John Mason, 1683.

ERNAN. L. M.

1. Je-sus, thy blood and right-eous-ness My beauty are, my glo-rious dress;
'Midst flaming worlds, in these ar-rayed, With joy shall I lift up my head.

335.

1 JESUS, thy blood and righteousness
My beauty are, my glorious dress;
'Midst flaming worlds, in these arrayed,
With joy shall I lift up my head.

2 Bold shall I stand in thy great day,
For who aught to my charge shall lay?
Fully absolved through these I am,
From sin and fear, from guilt and shame.

3 The holy, meek, unspotted Lamb,
Who from the Father's bosom came,
Who died for me, e'en me to atone,
Now for my Lord and God I own.

4 Lord, I believe thy precious blood,
Which, at the mercy-seat of God,
Forever doth for sinners plead,
For me, e'en for my soul, was shed.

5 Lord. I believe were sinners more
Than sand upon the ocean shore,
Thou hast for all a ransom paid,
For all a full atonement made.

6 Thus Abraham, the friend of God,
Thus all heaven's armies bought with blood,
Saviour of sinners, thee proclaim,
Sinners, the chief of whom I am.

7 Jesus, be endless praise to thee,
Whose boundless mercy hath for me,
For me and all thy hands have made,
An everlasting ransom paid.

Count Zinzendorf, 1739; tr. by John Wesley. 1740.

336.

1 JESUS, whom angel hosts adore,
Became a man of griefs for me;
In love, though rich, becoming poor,
That I through him enriched might be.

2 Though Lord of all, above, below,
He went to Olivet for me;
There drank my cup of wrath and woe,
When bleeding in Gethsemane.

3 The ever-blessèd Son of God
Went up to Calvary for me;
There paid my debt, there bore my load,
In his own body on the tree.

4 Jesus, whose dwelling is the skies,
Went down into the grave for me;
There overcame my enemies,
There won the glorious victory.

5 'T is finished all: the veil is rent,
The welcome sure, the access free;
Now, then, we leave our banishment,
O Father, to return to thee!

Horatius Bonar, 1857.

DOXOLOGY.

O FUTURE Judge, eternal Lord,
Thy name be hallowed and adored;
To God the Father, King of heaven,
And Holy Ghost, like praise be given.

From the Latin, tr. by John Chandler.

CHRIST,—HIS CHARACTERS. 145

HUMMEL. C. M.

1. The Son of God! the Lord of Life! How wondrous are his ways!
Oh for a harp of thousand strings, To sound abroad his praise!

337.
1 THE Son of God! the Lord of Life;
How wondrous are his ways!
Oh for a harp of thousand strings,
To sound abroad his praise!

2 How passing strange, to leave the seat
Of heaven's eternal throne,
And hosts of glittering seraphim,
For guilty man alone!

3 And did he bow his sacred head,
And die a death of shame?
Let men and angels magnify
And bless his holy name!

4 Oh let us live in peace and love,
And cast away our pride,
And crucify our sins afresh,
As he was crucified!

5 He rose again; then let us rise
From sin, and Christ adore,
And dwell in peace with all mankind,
And tempt the Lord no more!

6 The Son of God! the Lord of Life!
How wondrous are his ways!
Oh for a harp of thousand strings
To sound abroad his praise!
George Mogridge, 1851.

338.
1 PRAISE to the radiant Source of bliss,
Who gives the blind their sight,
And scatters round their wondering eyes
A flood of sacred light.

2 In paths unknown he leads them on
To his divine abode,
And shows new miracles of grace
Through all the heavenly road.

3 The ways all rugged and perplexed
He renders smooth and straight,
And strengthens every feeble knee
To march to Zion's gate.

4 Through all the path I'll sing his name,
Till I the mount ascend, [more.
Where toils and storms are known no
And anthems never end!
Philip Doddridge, 1755.

339. JOHN xiv. 6.
1 THOU art the Way; to thee alone
From sin and death we flee;
And he who would the Father seek,
Must seek him, Lord, by thee.

2 Thou art the Truth; thy word alone
True wisdom can impart;
Thou only canst inform the mind
And purify the heart.

3 Thou art the Life; the rending tomb
Proclaims thy conquering arm,
And those who put their trust in thee
Nor death nor hell shall harm.

4 Thou art the Way, the Truth, the Life;
Grant us that way to know,
That truth to keep, that life to win,
Whose joys eternal flow.
George W. Doane, 1824.

CHRIST,—HIS CHARACTERS.

HURSLEY. L. M.

340.

1 O Christ, our true and only light,
Illumine those who sit in night;
Let those afar now hear thy voice,
And in thy fold with us rejoice.

2 Fill with the radiance of thy grace
The souls now lost in error's maze,
And all in whom their secret mind
Some dark delusion hurts and blinds.

3 And all who else have strayed from thee
Oh, gently seek; thy healing be
To every wounded conscience given,
And let them also share thy heaven.

4 Oh make the deaf to hear thy word,
And teach the dumb to speak, dear Lord,
Who dare not yet the faith avow,
Though secretly they hold it now.

5 Shine on the darkened and the cold,
Recall the wanderers from thy fold,
Unite those now who walk apart,
Confirm the weak and doubting heart.

6 So they, with us, may evermore
Such grace with wondering thanks adore;
And endless praise to thee be given,
By all thy church in earth and heaven.

Johann Heermann, 1653; tr. by C. Winkworth, 1858.

341.

1 Jesus, the Shepherd of the sheep,
Thy little flock in safety keep, [heaven,
The flock for which thou cam'st from
The flock for which thy life was given.

2 Thou saw'st them wandering far from
Secure, as if from danger free; [thee,
Thy love did all their wanderings trace,
And brought them to a wealthy place.

3 Oh guard thy sheep from beasts of prey,
And guide them that they never stray;
Cherish the young, sustain the old,
Let none be feeble in thy fold.

4 Secure them from the scorching beam,
And lead them to the living stream;
In verdant pastures let them lie,
And watch them with a shepherd's eye.

5 Oh, may thy sheep discern thy voice,
And in its sacred sound rejoice;
From strangers may they ever flee,
And know no other guide but thee.

6 Lord, bring thy sheep that wander yet,
And let the number be complete:
Then let thy flock from earth remove,
And occupy the fold above.

Thomas Kelly, 1804-1836.

CHRIST,—HIS CHARACTERS. 147

STAR OF BETHLEHEM. L. M. DOUBLE.

342.

1 When, marshalled on the nightly plain,
The glittering host bestud the sky,
One star alone of all the train
Can fix the sinner's wandering eye.
Hark! hark! to God the chorus breaks
From every host, from every gem;
But one alone the Saviour speaks,
It is the Star of Bethlehem.

2 Once on the raging seas I rode,
The storm was loud, the night was dark,
The ocean yawned, and rudely blowed
The wind that tossed my foundering bark.
Deep horror then my vitals froze;
Death-struck, I ceased the tide to stem;
When suddenly a star arose,
It was the Star of Bethlehem!

3 It was my guide, my light, my all;
It bade my dark forebodings cease,
And through the storm and danger's thrall
It led me to the port of peace.
Now safely moored, my perils o'er,
I'll sing, first in night's diadem,
For ever and for evermore,
The Star, the Star of Bethlehem!

Henry Kirke White, 1806.

343.

1 Jesus, my All, to heaven is gone,
He that I placed my hopes upon;
His track I see, and I'll pursue
The narrow way till him I view.
The way the holy prophets went,
The road that leads from banishment,
The King's highway of holiness,
I'll go, for all the paths are peace.

2 This is the way I long have sought,
And mourned because I found it not;
My grief, my burden, long have been
Because I could not cease from sin.
The more I strove against its power,
I sinned and stumbled but the more;
Till late I heard my Saviour say,
"Come hither, soul, for I'm the Way!"

3 Lo! glad I come; and thou, dear Lamb,
Shalt take me to thee as I am:
Nothing but sin I thee can give;
Yet help me, and thy praise I'll live:
I'll tell to all poor sinners round
What a dear Saviour I have found;
I'll point to thy redeeming blood,
And say, "Behold the way to God!"

John Cennick. 1743.

CHRIST,—HIS CHARACTERS.

ST. GREGORIUS. C. M.

1. O Jesus! King most wonderful, Thou Conqueror renowned; Thou sweetness most ineffable, In whom all joys are found;

344.

1 O Jesus! King most wonderful,
Thou Conqueror renowned;
Thou sweetness most ineffable,
In whom all joys are found;

2 When once thou visitest the heart,
Then truth begins to shine,
Then earthly vanities depart,
Then kindles love divine.

3 O Jesus, Light of all below!
Thou Fount of life and fire!
Surpassing all the joys we know,
All that we can desire;

4 May every heart confess thy name,
And ever thee adore;
And, seeking thee; itself inflame
To seek thee more and more.

5 Thee may our tongues forever bless;
Thee may we love alone;
And ever in our life express
The image of thine own.

Bernard of Clairvaux, 1153; tr. E. Caswall, 1849.

345.

1 Infinite excellence is thine,
Thou lovely Prince of grace!
Thy uncreated beauties shine
With never-fading rays.

2 Sinners, from earth's remotest end,
Come bending at thy feet;
To thee their prayers and vows ascend,
In thee their wishes meet.

3 Thy name, as precious ointment shed,
Delights the church around;
Sweetly the sacred odors spread
Through all Immanuel's ground.

4 Millions of happy spirits live
On thy exhaustless store;
From thee they all their bliss receive,
And still thou givest more.

5 Thou art their triumph and their joy;
They find their all in thee;
Thy glories will their tongues employ
Through all eternity.

John Fawcett, 1782.

346.

1 To Him that loved the souls of men,
And washed us in his blood,
To royal honors raised our head,
And made us priests to God;

2 To him let every tongue be praise,
And every heart be love,
All grateful honors paid on earth,
And nobler songs above!

3 Behold, on flying clouds he comes!
His saints shall bless the day,
While they that pierced him sadly mourn
In anguish and dismay.

4 Thou art the First, and thou the Last:
Time centres all in thee,
The almighty God, who was and is,
And evermore shall be.

Isaac Watts, 1709.

CHRIST,—HIS CHARACTERS.

GUARDIAN. S. M.

1. To praise our Shepherd's care, His wisdom, love, and might, Your loudest, loftiest songs prepare, And bid the world unite.

347.

1 To praise our Shepherd's care,
  His wisdom, love, and might,
  Your loudest, loftiest songs prepare,
  And bid the world unite.

2 Supremely good and great,
  He tends his blood-bought fold;
  He stoops, tho' throned in highest state,
  The feeblest to uphold.

3 He hears their softest plaint;
  He sees them when they roam;
  And if his meanest lamb should faint,
  His bosom bears it home.

4 Kind Shepherd of the sheep,
  A weakly flock are we;
  And snares and foes are nigh; but keep
  The lambs who look to thee.

5 And if through death's dark vale
  Our feet shall early tread,
  Oh, may we reach thy fold, and hail
  The love which us hath led!
          William H. Havergal, 1868.

348.

1 While my Redeemer's near,
  My Shepherd and my Guide,
  I bid farewell to anxious fear;
  My wants are all supplied.

2 To ever-fragrant meads,
  Where rich abundance grows,
  His gracious hand indulgent leads,
  And guards my sweet repose.

3 Dear Shepherd, if I stray,
  My wandering feet restore;
  To thy fair pastures guide my way,
  And let me rove no more.
          Anne Steele, 1760.

349.

1 I bless the Christ of God,
  I rest on love divine,
  And with unfaltering lip and heart,
  I call this Saviour mine.

2 His cross dispels each doubt;
  I bury in his tomb
  Each thought of unbelief and fear,
  Each lingering shade of gloom.

3 I praise the God of peace;
  I trust his truth and might;
  He calls me his, I call him mine,
  My God, my joy, my light.

4 In him is only good,
  In me is only ill;
  My ill but draws his goodness forth,
  And me he loveth still.

5 'Tis he who saveth me,
  And freely pardon gives:
  I love because he loveth me;
  I live because he lives.

6 My life with him is hid,
  My death has passed away,
  My clouds have melted into light,
  My midnight into day.
          Horatius Bonar, 1863.

150   CHRIST,—HIS PRAISE.
MORNINGTON. S. M.

1. Jesus, the Lamb of God, Who us from hell to raise
Hast shed thy reconciling blood, We give thee endless praise!

350.

1 Jesus, the Lamb of God,
   Who us from hell to raise
Hast shed thy reconciling blood,
   We give thee endless praise.

2 God, and yet man, thou art!
   True God, true man art thou;
Of man, and of man's earth a part,
   One with us thou art now.

3 Great Sacrifice for sin,
   Giver of life for life,
Restorer of the peace within,
   True ender of the strife;

4 To thee, the Christ of God,
   Thy saints exulting sing;
The bearer of our heavy load,
   Our own anointed King.

5 True lover of the lost,
   From heaven thou camest down,
To pay for souls the righteous cost,
   And claim them for thine own.

6 Rest of the weary, thou!
   To thee our rest we come;
In thee to find our dwelling now,
   Our everlasting home.
         Horatius Bonar, 1861.

351.

1 Awake, and sing the song
   Of Moses and the Lamb;
Wake every heart and every tongue,
   To praise the Saviour's name.

2 Sing of his dying love;
   Sing of his rising power;
Sing how he intercedes above
   For those whose sins he bore.

3 Sing till we feel our heart
   Ascending with our tongue;
Sing till the love of sin depart,
   And grace inspires our song.

4 Sing on your heavenly way,
   Ye ransomed sinners, sing;
Sing on, rejoicing every day
   In Christ the eternal King.

5 Soon shall ye hear him say,
   "Ye blessed children, come;"
Soon will he call you hence away,
   And take his wanderers home.

6 Soon shall our raptured tongue
   His endless praise proclaim,
And sweeter voices tune the song
   Of Moses and the Lamb.
         William Hammond, 1745

DOXOLOGY.

We give thee glory, Lord,
   Thy Majesty adore;
Thee Father, Son, and Holy Ghost,
   We bless for evermore.
         Horatius Bonar, 1868.

CHRIST,—HIS PRAISE.

ABRIDGE. C. M.

352.

1 To Christ, the Lord, let every tongue
   Its noblest tribute bring;
   When he's the subject of the song,
   Who can refuse to sing?

2 Survey the beauties of his face,
   And on his glories dwell;
   Think of the wonders of his grace,
   And all his triumphs tell.

3 Majèstic sweetness sits enthroned
   Upon his awful brow;
   His head with radiant glories crowned,
   His lips with grace o'erflow.

4 No mortal can with him compare
   Among the sons of men;
   Fairer he is than all the fair
   That fill the heavenly train.

5 He saw me plunged in deep distress,
   He flew to my relief;
   For me he bore the shameful cross,
   And carried all my grief.

6 To heaven, the place of his abode,
   He brings my weary feet;
   Shows me the glories of my God,
   And makes my joys complete.

7 Since from his bounty I receive
   Such proofs of love divine,
   Had I a thousand hearts to give,
   Lord, they should all be thine!

Samuel Stennett, 1772.

353.

1 WE sing to thee, thou Son of God,
   Fountain of life and grace;
   We praise thee, Son of Man, whose blood
   Redeemed our fallen race.

2 Thee we acknowledge God and Lord,
   The Lamb for sinners slain,
   Who art by heaven and earth adored,
   Worthy o'er both to reign.

3 To thee all angels cry aloud,
   Through heaven's extended coasts,
   Hail! Holy, Holy, Holy Lord
   Of glory and of hosts!

4 The prophets' goodly fellowship,
   In radiant garments drest,
   Praise thee, thou Son of God, and reap
   The fulness of thy rest.

5 The apostles' glorious company
   Thy righteous praise proclaim;
   The martyred army glorify
   Thine everlasting name.

6 Throughout the world, thy churches join
   To call on thee, their Head,
   Brightness of Majesty Divine,
   Who every power hast made.

7 Among their number, Lord, we love
   To sing thy precious blood:
   Reign here and in the worlds above,
   Thou holy Lamb of God!

John Cennick, 1743.

152   CHRIST,—HIS PRAISE.

ATLANTIC. L. M.

1. Worthy the Lamb of boundless sway, In heaven or earth the Lord of all;
Ye princes, rulers, powers, obey, And low before his footstool fall.

354.

2 The deed was done; the Lamb was slain,
   The groaning earth the burden bore;
   He rose, he lives, he lives to reign,
   Nor time shall shake his endless power.

3 From heaven, from earth, loud bursts of praise
   The mighty blessings shall proclaim;
   Blessings that earth to glory raise,
   The purchase of the wounded Lamb.

4 Higher, still higher swell the strain,
   Creation's voice the note prolong;
   The Lamb shall ever, ever reign:
   Let hallelujahs crown the song.
   Walter Shirley, 1774.

355.

1 Now let us join with hearts and tongues,
   And emulate the angels' songs;
   Yea, sinners may address their King
   In songs that angels cannot sing.

2 They praise the Lamb who once was slain;
   But we can add a higher strain:
   Not only say he suffered thus,
   But that he suffered all for us.

3 Jesus, who passed the angels by,
   Assumed our flesh to bleed and die;
   And still he makes it his abode:
   As man he fills the throne of God.

4 Our next of kin, our brother now,
   Is he to whom the angels bow;
   They join with us to praise his name,
   And we the nearest interest claim.

5 But, ah! how faint our praises rise!
   Sure, 'tis the wonder of the skies,
   That we, who share his richest love,
   So cold and unconcerned should prove.

6 Oh, glorious hour! it comes with speed,
   When we, from sin and darkness freed,
   Shall see the God who died for man,
   And praise him more than angels can.
   John Newton, 1779.

356.

1 O Christ, the Lord of heaven, to thee,
   Clothed with all majesty divine,
   Eternal power and glory be;
   Eternal praise of right is thine.

2 Reign, Prince of life, who once thy brow
   Didst yield to wear the wounding thorn;
   Reign, throned beside the Father now,
   Adored the Son of God first-born.

3 From angel hosts that round thee stand,
   With forms more pure than spotless snow,
   From the bright, burning seraph band,
   Let praise in loftiest numbers flow.

4 To thee, the Lamb, our mortal songs,
   Born of deep, fervent love, shall rise;
   All honor to thy name belongs,
   Our lips would sound it to the skies.

5 Jesus! all earth shall speak the word;
   Jesus! all heaven shall sound it still;
   Immanuel, Saviour, Conqueror, Lord,
   Thy praise the universe shall fill.
   Ray Palmer, 1867.

CHRIST,—HIS PRAISE.

357. Rev. v. 9-13. L. M.

1 Come, let us sing the song of songs —
The saints in heaven began the strain;
The homage which to Christ belongs:
"Worthy the Lamb, for he was slain!"

2 Slain to redeem us by his blood,
To cleanse from every sinful stain,
And make us kings and priests to God —
"Worthy the Lamb, for he was slain!"

3 To him who suffered on the tree,
Our souls, at his soul's price, to gain,
Blessing, and praise, and glory be:
"Worthy the Lamb, for he was slain!"

4 To him, enthroned by filial right,
All power in heaven and earth proclaim,
Honor, and majesty, and might:
"Worthy the Lamb, for he was slain!"

5 Long as we live, and when we die,
And while in heaven with him we reign,
This song our song of songs shall be:
"Worthy the Lamb, for he was slain!"
James Montgomery.

358. L. M.

1 Now let us raise our cheerful strains,
And join the blissful choir above;
There our exalted Saviour reigns,
And there they sing his wondrous love.

2 While seraphs tune the immortal song,
Oh may we feel the sacred flame,
And every heart and every tongue
Adore the Saviour's glorious name.

3 Jesus, who once upon the tree
In agonizing pains expired,
Who died for rebels — yes, 'tis he!
How bright! how lovely! how admired!

4 Jesus, who died that we might live,
Died in the wretched traitor's place;
Oh what returns can mortals give
For such unmeasurable grace!

5 Were universal nature ours,
And art with all her boasted store,
Nature and art with all their powers
Would still confess the offerer poor.

6 Yet, though for bounty so divine
We ne'er can equal honors raise,
Jesus, may all our hearts be thine,
And all our tongues proclaim thy praise.
Anne Steele, 1760.

359. Rev. 5. Tune, "Lenox," p. 132. H. M.

1 Shall hymns of grateful love
Through heaven's high arches ring,
And all the hosts above
Their songs of triumph sing;
And shall not we take up the strain,
And send the echo back again?

2 Shall every ransomed tribe
Of Adam's scattered race
To Christ all power ascribe,
Who saved them by his grace?
And shall not we take up the strain,
And send the echo back again?

3 Shall they adore the Lord,
Who bought them with his blood,
And all the love record
That led them home to God;
And shall not we take up the strain,
And send the echo back again!
James J. Cummins, 1849.

360. Tune, "Lyons," p. 54. 11s.

1 Ye servants of God your Master proclaim,
And publish abroad his wonderful name;
The name all-victorious of Jesus extol;
His kingdom is glorious and rules over all

2 God ruleth on high, almighty to save;
Yet still he is nigh, his presence we have;
The great congregation his triumph shall sing,
Ascribing salvation to Jesus our King.

3 "Salvation to God who sits on the throne,"
Let all cry aloud and honor the Son;
The praises of Jesus the angels proclaim,
Fall down on their faces, and worship the Lamb.

4 Then let us adore, and give him his right,
All glory and power, and wisdom and might,
All honor and blessing, with angels above,
And thanks never ceasing, and infinite love.
Charles Wesley, 1745.

CHRIST,—HIS PRAISE.

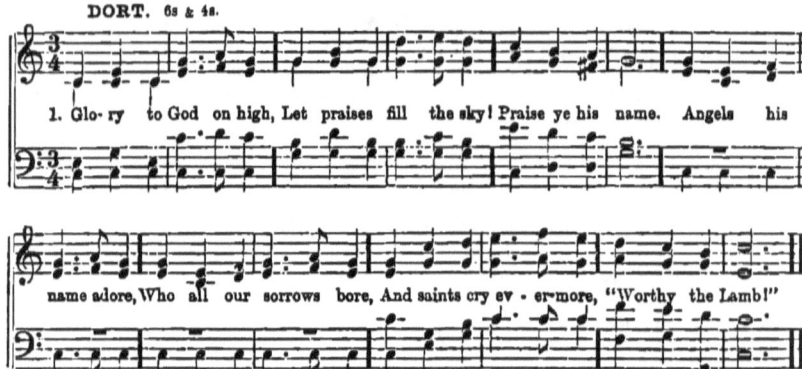

DORT. 6s & 4s.

1. Glo-ry to God on high, Let praises fill the sky! Praise ye his name. Angels his name adore, Who all our sorrows bore, And saints cry ev-er-more, "Worthy the Lamb!"

361.

1 GLORY to God on high,
   Let praises fill the sky !
      Praise ye his name.
   Angels his name adore,
   Who all our sorrows bore,
   And saints cry evermore,
      " Worthy the Lamb ! "

2 All they around the throne
   Cheerfully join in one,
      Praising his name.
   We who have felt his blood
   Sealing our peace with God,
   Spread his dear fame abroad :
      " Worthy the Lamb ! "

3 Join all the human race,
   Our Lord and God to bless ;
      Praise ye his name !
   In him we will rejoice,
   Making a cheerful noise,
   And say with heart and voice,
      " Worthy the Lamb ! "

4 Though we must change our place,
   Our souls shall never cease
      Praising his name ;
   To him we'll tribute bring,
   Laud him our gracious King,
   And without ceasing sing,
      " Worthy the Lamb ! "
                    James Allen, 1761.

362.

1 COME, all ye saints of God,
   Through all the earth abroad,
      Spread Jesus' fame :
   Tell what his love hath done ;
   Trust in his name alone ;
   Shout to his lofty throne,
      " Worthy the Lamb ! "

2 Hence, gloomy doubts and fears !
   Dry up your mournful tears ;
      Join our glad theme :
   Beauty for ashes bring ;
   Strike each melodious string ;
   Join heart and voice to sing,
      " Worthy the Lamb ! "

3 Hark ! how the choirs above,
   Filled with the Saviour's love,
      Dwell on his name !
   There, too, may we be found,
   With light and glory crowned,
   While all the heavens resound,
      " Worthy the Lamb ! "
                    James Boden, 1801.

DOXOLOGY.

To God, the Father, Son,
And Spirit, Three in One,
   All praise be given !
Crown him in every song ;
To him your hearts belong ;
Let all his praise prolong
   On earth, in heaven !

THE HOLY SPIRIT.

ST. ANN'S. C. M.

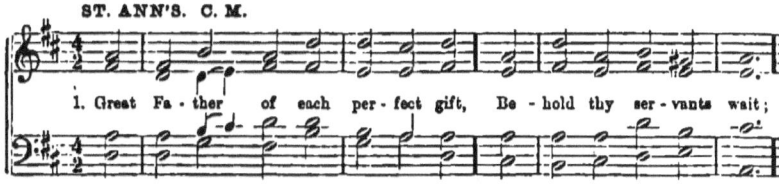
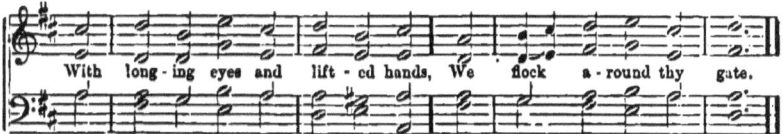

1. Great Father of each perfect gift, Behold thy servants wait; With longing eyes and lifted hands, We flock around thy gate.

363.

1 GREAT Father of each perfect gift,
　Behold thy servants wait;
　With longing eyes and lifted hands,
　We flock around thy gate.

2 Oh shed abroad that royal gift,
　Thy Spirit from above,
　To bless our eyes with sacred light,
　And fire our hearts with love.

3 With speedy flight may he descend,
　And solid comfort bring,
　And o'er our languid souls extend
　His all-reviving wing.

4 Blest earnest of eternal joy,
　Declare our sins forgiven;
　And bear with energy divine
　Our raptured thoughts to heaven.

5 Diffuse, O God, these copious showers,
　That earth its fruit may yield,
　And change this barren wilderness
　To Carmel's flowery field.
　　　　　Philip Doddridge, 1736.

364.

1 WHY should the children of a King
　Go mourning all their days?
　Great Comforter, descend and bring
　Some tokens of thy grace.

2 Dost thou not dwell in all the saints,
　And seal the heirs of heaven?
　When wilt thou banish my complaints,
　And show my sins forgiven?

3 Assure my conscience of her part
　In the Redeemer's blood;
　And bear thy witness with my heart
　That I am born of God.

4 Thou art the earnest of his love,
　The pledge of joys to come;
　And thy soft wings, celestial Dove,
　Will safe convey me home.
　　　　　Isaac Watts, 1709

365.

1 SPIRIT of truth! on this thy day,
　To thee for help we cry,
　To guide us through the dreary way
　Of dark mortality.

2 We ask not, Lord, thy cloven flame,
　Or tongues of various tone;
　But long thy praises to proclaim
　With fervor in our own.

3 We mourn not that prophetic skill
　Is found on earth no more;
　Enough for us to trace thy will
　In Scripture's sacred lore.

4 No heavenly harpings soothe our ear.
　No mystic dreams we share;
　Yet hope to feel thy comfort near,
　And bless thee in our prayer.

5 When tongues shall cease, and power
　　And knowledge empty prove, [decay,
　Do thou thy trembling servants stay,
　With faith, with hope, with love.
　　　　　Reginald Heber, 1827.

THE HOLY SPIRIT.

NEWTON. C. M.

1. Come, Holy Spirit, heavenly Dove, With all thy quickening powers, Kindle a flame of sacred love In these cold hearts of ours.

366.

1 COME, Holy Spirit, heavenly Dove,
  With all thy quickening powers,
Kindle a flame of sacred love
  In these cold hearts of ours.

2 Look how we grovel here below,
  Fond of these trifling toys;
Our souls can neither fly nor go
  To reach eternal joys.

3 In vain we tune our formal songs,
  In vain we strive to rise;
Hosannas languish on our tongues,
  And our devotion dies.

4 Dear Lord, and shall we ever live
  At this poor, dying rate!
Our love so faint, so cold to thee,
  And thine to us so great!

5 Come, Holy Spirit, heavenly Dove,
  With all thy quickening powers!
Come, shed abroad a Saviour's love,
  And that shall kindle ours.
            Isaac Watts, 1709.

367.

1 ENTHRONED on high, Almighty Lord,
  The Holy Ghost send down;
Fulfil in us thy faithful word,
  And all thy mercies crown.

2 Though on our heads no tongues of fire
  Their wondrous powers impart,
Grant, Saviour, what we more desire,—
  Thy Spirit in our heart.

3 Spirit of life, and light, and love,
  Thy heavenly influence give;
Quicken our souls, born from above,
  In Christ that we may live.

4 To our benighted minds reveal
  The glories of his grace,
And bring us where no clouds conceal
  The brightness of his face.

5 His love within us shed abroad,
  Life's ever-springing well,
Till God in us, and we in God,
  In love eternal dwell.
            Thomas Haweis, 1792.

368.

1 COME, Holy Ghost! in us arise;
  Be this thy mighty hour!
And make thy willing people wise
  To know thy day of power.

2 Pour down thy fire in us to glow,
  Thy might in us to dwell;
Again thy works of wonder show,
  Thy blessed secrets tell!

3 Bear us aloft, more glad, more strong,
  On thy celestial wing,
And grant us grace to look and long
  For our returning King.

4 He draweth near, he standeth by,
  He fills our eyes, our ears;
Come, King of Grace, thy people cry,
  And bring the glorious years!
            Thomas H. Gill, 1860.

THE HOLY SPIRIT.

WIMBORNE. L. M.

1. Eternal Spirit, we confess And sing the wonders of thy grace; Thy power conveys our blessings down From God the Father and the Son.

369.

1 Eternal Spirit, we confess
And sing the wonders of thy grace;
Thy power conveys our blessings down
From God the Father and the Son.

2 Enlightened by thine heavenly ray,
Our shades and darkness turn to day;
Thine inward teachings make us know
Our danger and our refuge too.

3 Thy power and glory works within,
And breaks the chains of reigning sin,
Doth our imperious lusts subdue,
And forms our wretched hearts anew.

4 The troubled conscience knows thy voice;
Thy cheering words awake our joys;
Thy words allay the stormy wind,
And calm the surges of the mind.
Isaac Watts, 1709.

370.

1 Come, sacred Spirit, from above,
And fill the coldest heart with love;
Soften to flesh the rugged stone,
And let thy God-like power be known.

2 Speak thou, and from the haughtiest eyes
Shall floods of pious sorrow rise,
While all their glowing souls are borne
To seek that grace which now they scorn.

3 Oh, let a holy flock await,
Numerous, around thy temple-gate;
Each pressing on with zeal to be
A living sacrifice to thee.

4 In answer to our fervent cries,
Give us to see thy church arise;
Or, if that blessing seem too great,
Give us to mourn its low estate.
Philip Doddridge, 1755.

371.

1 Come, O Creator-Spirit blest!
And in our souls take up thy rest;
Come, with thy grace and heavenly aid,
To fill the hearts which thou hast made.

2 Great Comforter! to thee we cry;
O highest gift of God most high!
O Fount of life! O Fire of love!
And sweet anointing from above!

3 Kindle our senses from above,
And make our hearts o'erflow with love,
With patience firm and virtue high,
The weakness of our flesh supply.

4 Far from us drive the foe we dread,
And grant us thy true peace instead;
So shall we not, with thee for guide,
Turn from the path of life aside.
Translated from the Latin by E. Caswall 1847

THE HOLY SPIRIT.

SHEFFIELD. S. M.

1. Blest Com-fort-er di-vine, Let rays of heav-enly love A-mid our gloom and dark-ness shine, And guide our souls a-bove.

372.

1 BLEST Comforter divine!
  Let rays of heavenly love
Amidst our gloom and darkness shine,
  And guide our souls above.

2 Draw with thy still, small voice,
  From every sinful way;
And bid the mourning saint rejoice,
  Though earthly joys decay.

3 By thine inspiring breath
  Make every cloud of care,
And e'en the gloomy vale of death,
  A smile of glory wear.

4 Oh, fill thou every heart
  With love to all our race!
Great Comforter, to us impart
  These blessings of thy grace.
              Anon.

373.

1 COME, Holy Spirit, come,
  Let thy bright beams arise;
Dispel the darkness from our minds,
  And open all our eyes.

2 Revive our drooping faith,
  Our doubts and fears remove,
And kindle in our breasts the flame
  Of never-dying love.

3 Convince us of our sin,
  Then lead to Jesus' blood,
And to our wondering view reveal
  The secret love of God.

4 Show us that loving Man
  That rules the courts of bliss,

The Lord of hosts, the mighty God,
  The eternal Prince of peace.

5 'T is thine to cleanse the heart,
  To sanctify the soul,
To pour fresh life in every part,
  And new-create the whole.

6 Dwell, therefore, in our hearts,
  Our minds from bondage free;
Then we shall know and praise and love
  The Father, Son, and thee!
              Joseph Hart, 1759.

374.

1 THE Holy Ghost is here,
  Where saints in prayer agree;
As Jesus' parting gift, he 's near
  Each pleading company.

2 Not far away is He,
  To be by prayer brought nigh;
But here in present majesty,
  As in his courts on high.

3 He dwells within our soul,
  An ever-welcome Guest;
He reigns with absolute control
  As Monarch in the breast.

4 Our bodies are his shrine,
  And he th' indwelling Lord:
All hail, thou Comforter divine!
  Be evermore adored.

5 Obedient to thy will,
  We wait to feel thy power;
O Lord of life, our hopes fulfil,
  And bless this hallowed hour.
              Charles H. Spurgeon, 1866.

375.

1 HOLY Ghost, the Infinite!
Shine upon our nature's night
With thy blessed inward light,
    Comforter divine!

2 We are sinful, cleanse us, Lord;
We are faint, thy strength afford;
Lost, until by thee restored,
    Comforter divine!

3 Like the dew thy peace distil;
Guide, subdue our wayward will,
Things of Christ unfolding still,
    Comforter divine!

4 In us, for us, intercede,
And with voiceless groanings plead
Our unutterable need,
    Comforter divine!

5 In us "Abba, Father," cry,
Earnest of our bliss on high,
Seal of immortality,
    Comforter divine!

6 Search for us the depths of God,
Bear us up the starry road
To the height of thine abode,
    Comforter divine!

Anon.

DOXOLOGY.

1 To the Father, to the Son,
And the Spirit, ever blest,
Everlasting Three in One,
Be all praise addrest.

2 Praise from all above, below,
As throughout the ages past,
Now is given, and shall be so
While the ages last.

THE HOLY SPIRIT.

WINCHELSEA. L. M.

1. Spirit of mercy, truth, and love, Oh shed thine influence from above;
And still through endless time convey The wonders of this sacred day.

376.

1 Spirit of mercy, truth, and love,
Oh shed thine influence from above;
And still through endless time convey
The wonders of this sacred day.

2 In every clime, by every tongue,
Be God's surpassing glory sung;
Let all the listening earth be taught
The wonders by our Saviour wrought.

3 Unfailing comfort, heavenly Guide,
Still in our longing hearts abide;
Still let mankind thy blessings prove,
Spirit of mercy, truth, and love.
Anon. 1775.

377.

1 O Holy Ghost who down dost come
To make each contrite heart thy home,
On me descend; within me dwell,
My soul renew, my sin expel.

2 Spirit of Truth who makest bright
All souls that long for heavenly light,
Appear and on my darkness shine,
Descend and be my Guide Divine.

3 Spirit of Power whose might doth dwell
Full in the souls thou lovest well,
Unto this fainting heart draw near,
And be my daily Quickener.

4 Spirit of Joy who makest glad
Each broken heart by sin made sad,

Pour on this mourning soul thy cheer;
Give me to bless my Comforter.

5 Oh tender Spirit who dost mourn
Whene'er from thee thy people turn,
Give me each day to grieve thee less;
Enjoy my fuller faithfulness.

6 Come mightier down! Thyself impart
More largely to this longing heart;
My Comforter more dearly be;
More sweetly guide and hallow me:

7 Till thou shalt make me meet to bear
The sweetness of heaven's holy air,
The light wherein no darkness is,
The eternal, overflowing bliss!
Thomas H. Gill, 1860.

378.

1 Come, Holy Ghost, who ever one
Art with the Father and the Son;
Come, Holy Ghost, our souls possess
With thy full flood of holiness.

2 In word and deed, by heart and tongue,
With all our powers, thy praise be sung;
May love enwrap our mortal frame,
And others catch the living flame.

3 Almighty Father, hear our cry,
Through Jesus Christ our Lord most high,
Who, with the Holy Ghost and thee,
Doth live and reign eternally.
Ambrose, 340-397; tr. by John H. Newman, 1836.

THE HOLY SPIRIT. 161

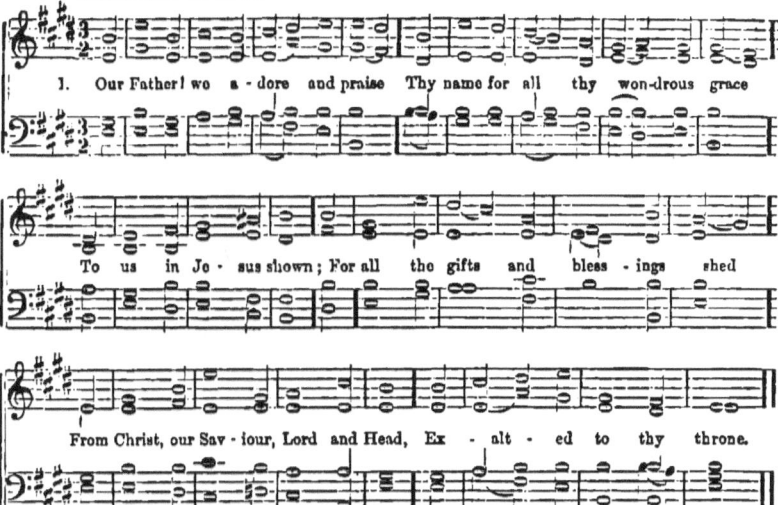

MILFORD. C. P. M.

1. Our Father! we adore and praise Thy name for all thy wondrous grace
To us in Jesus shown; For all the gifts and blessings shed
From Christ, our Saviour, Lord and Head, Exalted to thy throne.

379.

1 OUR Father! we adore and praise
Thy name for all thy wondrous grace
To us in Jesus shown;
For all the gifts and blessings shed
From Christ, our Saviour, Lord and Head,
Exalted to thy throne.

2 The promised Comforter bestowed
Now dwells in all the sons of God,
And seals them thus thine own;
Through him we "Abba, Father" cry,
With filial love to thee draw nigh,
And worship at thy throne.

3 Oh grant renewings of his grace,
That all thy glory in the face
Of Jesus we may see;
And as with unveiled face we view
That glory, to his image true
We may conformed be.

4 Oh that we thus, through grace bestowed,
In fellowship with thee, our God,
And with thy saints may be;
And thus in blest communion prove
The Father, Son, and Spirit's love,
And yield ourselves to thee.

Bristol Hymns, 1870.

380.

1 DESCEND from heaven, celestial Dove;
With flames of pure seraphic love
Our ravished breasts inspire;
Fountain of joy, blest Paraclete,
Warm our cold hearts with heavenly heat,
And set our souls on fire.

2 Breathe on these bones so dry and dead;
Thy sweetest, softest influence shed
In all our hearts abroad.
Point out the place where grace abounds;
Direct us to the bleeding wounds
Of our incarnate God.

3 Teach us for what to pray, and how;
And since, blest Spirit, only thou
The throne of grace canst move,
Pray thou for us through faith,
May feel the effects of Jesus' death,
Through faith that works by love.

4 Thou, with the Father and the Son,
Art that mysterious Three in One,
God blest for evermore;
Whom though we cannot comprehend,
Feeling thou art the sinner's Friend,
We love thee and adore.

Joseph Hart, 1759.

THE HOLY SPIRIT.

ADRIAN. S. M.

1. O Holy Spirit, come, And Jesus' love declare; Oh, tell us of our heavenly home, And guide us safely there.

381.

1 O Holy Spirit, come,
  And Jesus' love declare;
 Oh tell us of our heavenly home,
  And guide us safely there.

2 Our unbelief remove
  By thine almighty breath;
 Oh work the wondrous work of love,
  The mighty work of faith.

3 Come with resistless power,
  Come with almighty grace,
 Come with the long-expected shower,
  And fall upon this place.

4 Give us the melting soul,
  Give us the will subdued,
 Give us the streams of grace, to roll
  Over a heart renewed.

5 We bless thee for thy grace,
  And thine almighty power;
 We bless thee for thy holy place,
  And this accepted hour.
      Oswald Allen, 1860.

382.

1 Lord God the Holy Ghost,
  In this accepted hour,
 As on the day of Pentecost,
  Descend in all thy power!

2 We meet with one accord
  In our appointed place,
 And wait the promise of our Lord,
  The Spirit of all grace.

3 Like mighty rushing wind
  Upon the waves beneath,
 Move with one impulse every mind,
  One soul, one feeling breathe.

4 The young, the old inspire
  With wisdom from above,
 And give us hearts and tongues of fire
  To pray, and praise, and love.

5 Spirit of Truth, be thou
  In life and death our Guide;
 O Spirit of adoption, now
  May we be sanctified.
      James Montgomery, 1819.

383.

1 Descend, immortal Dove,
  Spread thy kind wings abroad;
 And wrapt in flames of holy love
  Bear all my soul to God.

2 Jesus, my Lord, reveal
  In charms of grace divine,
 And be thyself the sacred seal
  That pearl of price is mine.

3 Behold, my heart expands
  To catch the heavenly fire,
 It longs to feel the gentle bands,
  And groans with strong desire.

4 Thy love, my God, appears,
  And brings salvation down,
 My cordial through this vale of tears,
  In Paradise my crown.
      Philip Doddridge, 1755.

THE HOLY SPIRIT.

TELLEMAN'S CHANT. 7s.

1. Ho-ly Ghost, with light divine, Shine up-on this heart of mine;
Chase the shades of night a-way, Turn my dark-ness in-to day.

384.

1 HOLY Ghost, with light divine,
Shine upon this heart of mine;
Chase the shades of night away,
Turn my darkness into day.

2 Holy Ghost, with power divine,
Cleanse this guilty heart of mine;
Long hath sin, without control,
Held dominion o'er my soul.

3 Holy Ghost, with joy divine,
Cheer this saddened heart of mine;
Bid my many woes depart,
Heal my wounded, bleeding heart.

4 Holy Spirit, all divine,
Dwell within this heart of mine;
Cast down every idol-throne,
Reign supreme, and reign alone.
Andrew Reed, 1841.

385.

1 HOLY Spirit, from on high
Bend on us a pitying eye;
Animate the drooping heart;
Bid the power of sin depart.

2 Light up every dark recess
Of our heart's ungodliness;
Show us every devious way
Where our steps have gone astray.

3 Teach us, with repentant grief,
Humbly to implore relief;
Then the Saviour's blood reveal,
All our deep disease to heal.

4 Other ground-work should we lay,
Sweep those empty hopes away;
Make us feel that Christ alone
Can for human guilt atone.

5 May we daily grow in grace,
And pursue the heavenly race,
Trained in wisdom, led by love,
Till we reach our rest above.
W. H. Bathurst, 1831.

386.

1 HOLY Spirit, heavenly Dove,
Breathe upon us from above;
And, with sweet, celestial fire,
Zeal inflame, and love inspire.

2 On this congregation pour
Heavenly blessings, like a shower;
Streams of grace upon us shed;
Teach the living, raise the dead.

3 Bid each groundless doubt depart;
Bind up every broken heart;
Warm the frozen, cheer the faint,
Feed and comfort every saint.

4 Every soul do thou engage;
Every Christian's grief assuage;
Be our Counsellor and Guide;
Lead to Jesus crucified.
Joseph Irons, 1347.

DOXOLOGY.

HOLY Father, Holy Son,
Holy Spirit, Three in One,
Glory as of old to thee,
Now and evermore shall be.
Thomas Scott, 1769.

THE HOLY SPIRIT.

FEDERAL STREET. L. M.

1. Stay, thou in-sult-ed Spir-it, stay, Though I have done thee such de-spite,
Nor cast the sin-ner quite a-way, Nor take thine ev-er-last-ing flight.

387.

1 Stay, thou insulted Spirit, stay,
   Though I have done thee such despite;
   Nor cast the sinner quite away,
   Nor take thine everlasting flight.

2 Though I have steeled my stubborn heart,
   And shaken off my guilty fears;
   And vexed, and urged thee to depart,
   For many long rebellious years;

3 Though I have most unfaithful been
   Of all who e'er thy grace received;
   Ten thousand times thy goodness seen,
   Ten thousand times thy goodness grieved:

4 Yet, oh, the chief of sinners spare,
   In honor of my great High Priest;
   Nor in thy righteous anger swear
   I shall not see thy people's rest.

5 Now, Lord, my weary soul release;
   Upraise me with thy gracious hand,
   And guide into thy perfect peace,
   And bring me to the promised land.
   Charles Wesley, 1749.

388.

1 O Lord, and shall our fainting souls
   Thy just displeasure ever mourn?
   Thy Spirit grieved, and long withdrawn,
   Will he no more to us return?

2 Great Source of light and peace, return,
   Nor let us mourn and sigh in vain;
   Come, repossess these longing hearts
   With all the graces of thy train.

3 This temple, hallowed by thine hand,
   Once more be with thy presence blest;
   Here be thy grace anew displayed,
   Be this thine everlasting rest!
   Thomas Scott, 1773.

389.

1 Spirit of power and truth and love,
   Who sitt'st enthroned in light above,
   Descend and bear us on thy wings
   Far from these low and fleeting things.

2 Compass'd by foes on every side,
   By sin and sore temptation tried,
   Where can we look, or whither flee,
   If not, great Strengthener, to thee?

3 When faith is weak and courage fails,
   When grief or doubt our soul assails,
   Who can, like thee, our spirits cheer?
   Great Comforter, be ever near.

4 Like captives at their prison grate,
   We mourn our languishing estate;
   Thou only canst our bonds untie;
   Great Sanctifier, hear our cry.

5 Come, Holy Spirit, like the fire,
   With burning zeal our souls inspire;
   Come, like the south wind, breathing balm;
   Our joys refresh, our passions calm.

6 Come, like the sun's enlightening beam;
   Come, like the cooling, cleansing stream;
   With all thy graces present be;
   Spirit of God, we wait for thee.
   William L. Alexander, 1845.

THE HOLY SPIRIT.

ZEPHYR. L. M.

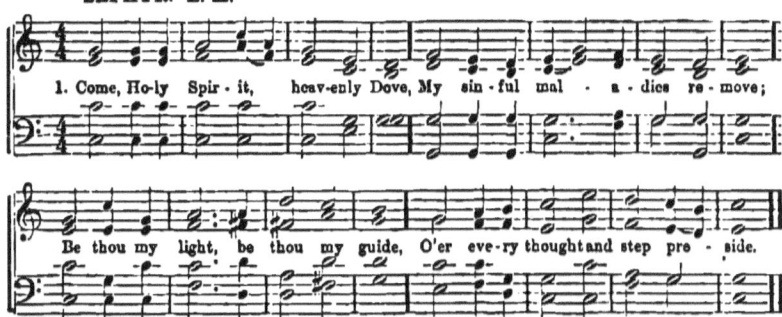

1. Come, Holy Spirit, heavenly Dove, My sinful maladies remove; Be thou my light, be thou my guide, O'er every thought and step preside.

390.

1 COME, Holy Spirit, heavenly Dove,
My sinful maladies remove;
Be thou my light, be thou my guide,
O'er every thought and step preside.

2 The light of truth to me display,
That I may know and choose my way;
Plant holy fear within my heart,
That I from God may ne'er depart.

3 Conduct me safe, conduct me far
From every sin and hurtful snare;
Lead me to God, my final rest,
In his enjoyment to be blest.

4 Lead me to Christ, the living way,
Nor let me from his pastures stray:
Lead me to heaven, the seat of bliss,
Where pleasure in perfection is.

5 Lead me to holiness, the road
That I must take to dwell with God;
Lead to thy word, that rules must give,
And sure directions how to live.

6 Thus I, conducted still by thee,
Of God a child beloved shall be,
Here to his family pertain,
Hereafter with him ever reign.
Simon Browne, 1720.

391.

1 COME, blessed Spirit, source of light,
Whose power and grace are unconfined,
Dispel the gloomy shades of night,
Remove the darkness of the mind.

2 To mine illumined eyes display
The glorious truth thy word reveals;
Chase prejudices far away,
Unclasp the book, and loose the seals.

3 By inward teachings make me know
The mysteries of redeeming love,
The vanity of things below,
The excellence of things above.

4 All through the dubious maze of life
Spread, like the sun, thy beams abroad;
Point out the dangers of the way,
And guide my wandering feet to God.
Benjamin Beddome, 1787.

392.

1 SURE the blest Comforter is nigh;
'T is he sustains my fainting heart:
Else would my hopes forever die,
And every cheering ray depart.

2 Whene'er to call the Saviour mine
With ardent wish my heart aspires,
Can it be less than power divine
That animates these strong desires?

3 And when my cheerful hope can say
I love my God and taste his grace,
Lord, is it not thy blissful ray [peace?
Which brings this dawn of sacred

4 Let thy kind Spirit in my heart
Forever dwell, O God of love;
And light and heavenly peace impart,
Sweet earnest of the joys above.
Anne Steele, 1760.

THE HOLY SPIRIT.

TONICA. 8s & 4s.

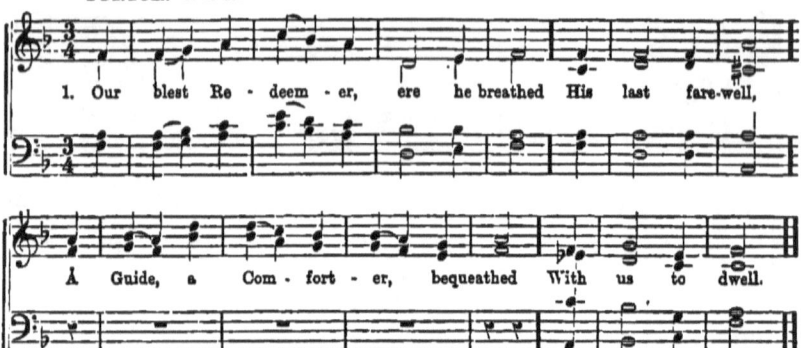

1. Our blest Redeemer, ere he breathed His last farewell,
A Guide, a Comforter, bequeathed With us to dwell.

393.

1 Our blest Redeemer, ere he breathed
   His last farewell,
A Guide, a Comforter, bequeathed
   With us to dwell.

2 He came in tongues of living flame,
   To teach, subdue;
All powerful as the wind he came,
   As viewless too.

3 He comes, his graces to impart;
   A willing guest,
While he can find one humble heart
   Wherein to rest.

4 He breathes that gentle voice we hear,
   As breeze of even,   [fear,
That checks each fault, that calms each
   And speaks of heaven.

5 And all the good that we possess,
   His gift we own;
Yea, every thought of holiness,
   And victory won.

6 Spirit of purity and grace,
   Our weakness see;
Oh make our hearts thy dwelling-place,
   And worthier thee.

Harriet Aubrr, 1829.

394. "Italian Hymn," p. 82. 6s & 4s.

1 Come, Holy Ghost, in love,
   Shed on us from above
      Thine own bright ray:
   Divinely good thou art;
   Thy sacred gifts impart
   To gladden each sad heart:
      Oh, come to-day.

2 Come, tenderest Friend, and best,
   Our most delightful guest,
      With soothing power:
   Rest, which the weary know,
   Shade 'mid the noontide glow,
   Peace, when deep griefs o'erflow,
      Cheer us, this hour.

3 Come, Light serene and still,
   Our inmost bosoms fill,
      Dwell in each breast:
   We know no dawn but thine;
   Send forth thy beams divine
   On our dark souls to shine,
      And make us blest.

4 Come, all the faithful bless;
   Let all who Christ confess,
      His praise employ;
   Give virtue's rich reward;
   Victorious death accord,
   And, with our glorious Lord,
      Eternal joy.

Trans. from the Latin, by Ray Palmer, 1858.

THE SCRIPTURES. 167

MENDON. L. M.

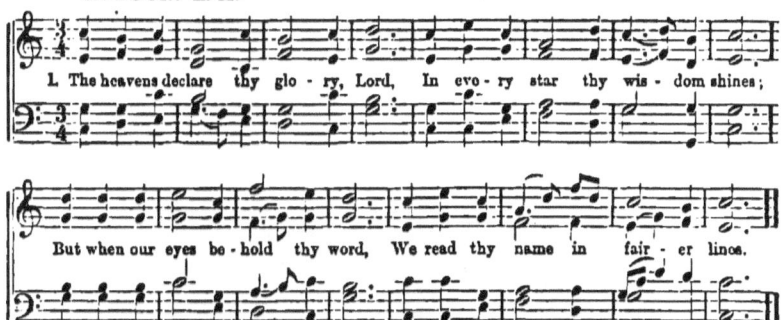

1. The heavens declare thy glo-ry, Lord, In evo-ry star thy wis-dom shines;
But when our eyes be-hold thy word, We read thy name in fair-er lines.

395.
PSALM 19.

1 THE heavens declare thy glory, Lord,
In every star thy wisdom shines;
But when our eyes behold thy word,
We read thy name in fairer lines.

2 The rolling sun, the changing light,
And nights and days, thy power confess;
But the blest volume thou hast writ
Reveals thy justice and thy grace.

3 Sun, moon, and stars convey thy praise
Round the whole earth, and never stand;
So when thy truth began its race,
It touched and glanced on every land.

4 Nor shall thy spreading gospel rest [run;
Till through the world thy truth has
Till Christ has all the nations blest,
That see the light, or feel the sun.

5 Great Sun of Righteousness, arise;
Bless the dark world with heavenly
   light;
Thy gospel makes the simple wise;
Thy laws are pure, thy judgments right.

6 Thy noblest wonders here we view
In souls renewed and sins forgiven;
Lord, cleanse my sins, my soul renew,
And make thy word my guide to
    heaven.

Isaac Watts, 1719.

396.

1 THE starry firmament on high,
And all the glories of the sky,
Yet shine not to thy praise, O Lord,
So brightly as thy written word;
The hopes that holy word supplies,
Its truths divine and precepts wise,
In each a heavenly beam I see,
And every beam conducts to thee.

2 When, taught by painful proof to know
That all is vanity below,
The sinner roams from comfort far,
And looks in vain for sun or star;
Soft gleaming then those lights divine
Through all the cheerless darkness shine,
And sweetly to the ravished eye
Disclose the Day-spring from on high.

3 Almighty Lord, the sun shall fail,
The moon forget her nightly tale,
And deepest silence hush on high
The radiant chorus of the sky;
But fixed for everlasting years,
Unmoved amid the wreck of spheres,
Thy word shall shine in cloudless day,
When heaven and earth have passed
   away.

Sir Robert Grant, 1833.

DOXOLOGY.

PRAISE God, from whom all blessings flow,
Praise him, all creatures here below;
Praise him above, ye heavenly host;
Praise Father, Son, and Holy Ghost.

Bishop Thomas Ken, 1697.

THE SCRIPTURES.

NASHVILLE. L. P. M.

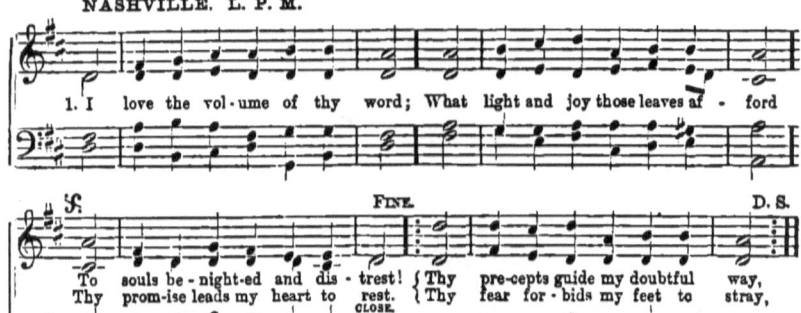

1. I love the vol-ume of thy word; What light and joy those leaves af-ford
To souls be-night-ed and dis-trest! Thy pre-cepts guide my doubtful way,
Thy prom-ise leads my heart to rest. Thy fear for-bids my feet to stray,

397. PSALM 19.

2 From the discoveries of thy law
  The perfect rules of life I draw;
    These are my study and delight;
  Not honey so invites the taste,
  Nor gold that has the furnace passed
    Appears so pleasing to the sight.

3 Thy threatenings wake my slumbering eyes,
  And warn me where my danger lies;

But 'tis thy blessèd gospel, Lord,
That makes my guilty conscience clean,
Converts my soul, subdues my sin,
And gives a free, but large reward.

4 Who knows the errors of his thoughts?
  My God, forgive my secret faults,
    And from presumptuous sins restrain;
  Accept my poor attempts to praise,
  That I have read thy book of grace,
    And book of nature, not in vain.

Isaac Watts, 1719.

ALETTA. 7s.

1. Ho-ly Bi-ble! book di-vine! Pre-cious treas-ure, thou art mine:
Mine to tell me whence I came; Mine to teach me what I am;

398.

2 Mine to chide me when I rove;
  Mine to show a Saviour's love;
  Mine art thou to guide my feet,
  Mine to judge, condemn, acquit;

3 Mine to comfort in distress,
  If the Holy Spirit bless;

Mine to show by living faith,
Man can triumph over death;

4 Mine to tell of joys to come,
  And the rebel sinner's doom:
  Holy Bible! book divine!
  Precious treasure, thou art mine!

John Burton, 1805.

THE SCRIPTURES.

MERTON. C. M.

399. PSALM 119.
1 How shall the young secure their hearts,
 And guard their lives from sin?
 Thy word the choicest rules imparts
 To keep the conscience clean.

2 When once it enters to the mind,
 It spreads such light abroad.
 The meanest souls instruction find,
 And raise their thoughts to God.

3 'T is like the sun, a heavenly light,
 That guides us all the day;
 And, through the dangers of the night,
 A lamp to lead our way.

4 Thy precepts make me truly wise;
 I hate the sinner's road;
 I hate my own vain thoughts that rise,
 But love thy law, my God!

5 Thy word is everlasting truth;
 How pure is every page!
 That holy book shall guide our youth,
 And well support our age.
Isaac Watts, 1719.

400. PSALM 119.
1 LORD, I have made thy word my choice,
 My lasting heritage;
 There shall my noblest powers rejoice,
 My warmest thoughts engage.

2 I'll read the histories of thy love,
 And keep thy laws in sight;
 While through the promises I rove,
 With ever fresh delight.

3 'T is a broad land of wealth unknown,
 Where springs of life arise,
 Seeds of immortal bliss are sown,
 And hidden glory lies.

4 The best relief that mourners have,
 It makes our sorrows blest;
 Our fairest hope beyond the grave,
 And our eternal rest.
Isaac Watts, 1719.

401.
1 LADEN with guilt, and full of fears,
 I fly to thee, my Lord;
 And not a glimpse of hope appears
 But in thy written word.

2 The volume of my Father's grace
 Does all my grief assuage;
 Here I behold my Saviour's face
 Almost in every page.

3 Here consecrated water flows,
 To quench my thirst of sin;
 Here the fair tree of knowledge grows,
 Nor danger dwells therein.

4 This is the judge that ends the strife
 Where wit and reason fail;
 My guide to everlasting life
 Through all this gloomy vale.

5 Oh may thy counsels, mighty God,
 My roving feet command:
 Nor I forsake the happy road
 That leads to thy right hand.
Isaac Watts, 1709.

THE SCRIPTURES.

NICHOLS. C. M.

1. Father of mercies! in thy word What endless glory shines;
For-ev-er be thy name adored For these ce-les-tial lines.

402.

1 FATHER of mercies! in thy word
What endless glory shines;
Forever be thy name adored
For these celestial lines.

2 Here may the wretched sons of want
Exhaustless riches find;
Riches above what earth can grant,
And lasting as the mind.

3 Here the Redeemer's welcome voice
Spreads heavenly peace around;
And life. and everlasting joys,
Attend the blissful sound.

4 Oh may these heavenly pages be
My ever dear delight;
And still new beauties may I see,
And still increasing light.

5 Divine Instructor, gracious Lord,
Be thou forever near;
Teach me to love thy sacred word,
And view my Saviour there.
Anne Steele, 1760.

403.

1 THE Spirit breathes upon the word,
And brings the truth to sight;
Precepts and promises afford
A sanctifying light.

2 A glory gilds the sacred page,
Majestic. like the sun;
It gives a light to every age;
It gives, but borrows none.

3 The hand that gave it still supplies
The gracious light and heat;
Its truths upon the nations rise,
They rise, but never set.

4 Let everlasting thanks be thine,
For such a bright display,
As makes a world of darkness shine
With beams of heavenly day.

5 My soul rejoices to pursue
The steps of him I love,
Till glory breaks upon my view,
In brighter worlds above.
William Cowper, 1779.

404. PSALM 119.

1 OH how I love thy holy law!
'T is daily my delight;
And thence my meditations draw
Divine advice by night.

2 My waking eyes prevent the day,
To meditate thy word;
My soul with longing melts away,
To hear thy gospel, Lord.

3 How doth thy word my heart engage,
How well employ my tongue!
And, in my tiresome pilgrimage,
Yields me a heavenly song.

4 When nature sinks, and spirits droop,
Thy promises of grace
Are pillars to support my hope,
And there I write thy praise.
Isaac Watts, 1719.

THE SCRIPTURES.

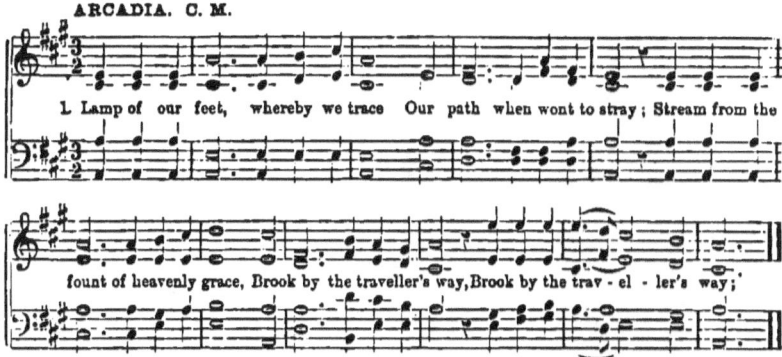

ARCADIA. C. M.

1. Lamp of our feet, whereby we trace Our path when wont to stray; Stream from the fount of heavenly grace, Brook by the traveller's way, Brook by the trav-el-ler's way;

405.

1 Lamp of our feet, whereby we trace
   Our path when wont to stray;
   Stream from the fount of heavenly grace,
   Brook by the traveller's way;

2 Bread of our souls, whereon we feed;
   True manna from on high;
   Our guide, our chart, wherein we read
   Of realms beyond the sky;

3 Pillar of fire through watches dark,
   Or radiant cloud by day;   [bark,
   When waves would whelm our tossing
   Our anchor and our stay;

4 Word of the everlasting God,
   Will of his glorious Son,
   Without thee how could earth be trod,
   Or heaven itself be won?

5 Lord, grant us all aright to learn
   The wisdom it imparts,
   And to its heavenly teaching turn
   With simple, child-like hearts.
Bernard Barton, 1827.

406.

1 How precious is the book divine,
   By inspiration given!
   Bright as a lamp its doctrines shine
   To guide our souls to heaven.

2 Its light, descending from above,
   Our gloomy world to cheer,
   Displays a Saviour's boundless love,
   And brings his glories near.

3 It shows to man his wandering ways,
   And where his feet have trod,
   And brings to view the matchless grace
   Of a forgiving God.

4 It sweetly cheers our drooping hearts
   In this dark vale of tears;
   Life, light, and joy it still imparts,
   And quells our rising fears.

5 This lamp through all the tedious night
   Of life shall guide our way,
   Till we behold the clearer light
   Of an eternal day.
John Fawcett, 1782.

407. Psalm 19. Tune, "Mornington." p. 150. S. M.

1 Behold, the morning sun
   Begins his glorious way;
   His beams through all the nations run,
   And life and light convey.

2 But where the gospel comes,
   It spreads diviner light;
   It calls dead sinners from their tombs,
   And gives the blind their sight.

3 How perfect is thy word!
   And all thy judgments just;
   Forever sure thy promise, Lord,
   And men securely trust.

4 My gracious God, how plain
   Are thy directions given!
   Oh, may I never read in vain,
   But find the path to heaven!
Isaac Watts, 1719.

THE SCRIPTURES.

ROCKINGHAM. L. M.

1. Let ev-er-last-ing glories crown Thy head, my Sáv-iour, and my Lord; Thy hands have brought sal-va-tion down, And writ the blessings in thy word.

408.

1 LET everlasting glories crown
  Thy head, my Saviour and my Lord;
  Thy hands have brought salvation down,
  And writ the blessings in thy word.

2 In vain the trembling conscience seeks
  Some solid ground to rest upon;
  With long despair the spirit breaks,
  Till we apply to Christ alone.

3 How well thy blessed truths agree!
  How wise and holy thy commands!
  Thy promises, how firm they be!
  How firm our hope and comfort stands!

4 Should all the forms that men devise
  Assault my faith with treacherous art,
  I'd call them vanity and lies,
  And bind the gospel to my heart.
  Isaac Watts, 1709.

409.

1 GOD, in the gospel of his Son,
  Makes his eternal counsels known,
  'T is here his richest mercy shines,
  And truth is drawn in fairest lines.

2 Here sinners of a humble frame
  May taste his grace and learn his name;
  May read, in characters of blood,
  The wisdom, power, and grace of God.

3 The prisoner here may break his chains;
  The weary rest from all his pains;
  The captive feel his bondage cease;
  The mourner find the way of peace.

4 Here faith reveals to mortal eyes
  A brighter world beyond the skies; ⌊way
  Here shines the light which guides our
  From earth to realms of endless day.

5 Oh, grant us grace, almighty Lord,
  To read and mark thy holy word,
  Its truths with meekness to receive,
  And by its holy precepts live.
  Benj. Beddome, 1787; alt. by Robert Hall, 1810.

410. PSALM 51.

1 LORD, I am vile, conceived in sin,
  And born unholy and unclean:
  Sprung from the man whose guilty fall
  Corrupts the race, and taints us all.

2 Soon as we draw our infant breath,
  The seeds of sin grow up for death;
  Thy law demands a perfect heart;
  But we're defiled in every part.

3 Behold, I fall before thy face;
  My only refuge is thy grace;
  No outward forms can make me clean;
  The leprosy lies deep within.

4 No bleeding bird, nor bleeding beast,
  Nor hyssop branch, nor sprinkling priest,
  Nor running brook, nor flood, nor sea,
  Can wash the dismal stain away.

5 Jesus, my God, thy blood alone
  Hath power sufficient to atone;
  Thy blood can make me white as snow;
  No Jewish types could cleanse me so.
  Isaac Watts, 1719.

SALVATION,—MAN'S NEED.

OWEN. S. M.

411.

1 Ah, how shall fallen man
 Be just before his God?
 If he contend in righteousness,
 We fall beneath his rod.

2 If he our ways should mark
 With strict, inquiring eyes,
 Could we for one of thousand faults
 A just excuse devise?

3 All-seeing, powerful God,
 Who can with thee contend?
 Or who that tries th' unequal strife
 Shall prosper in the end?

4 The mountains in thy wrath,
 Their ancient seats forsake;
 The trembling earth deserts her place;
 Her rooted pillars shake.

5 Ah, how shall guilty man
 Contend with such a God?
 None, none can meet him, and escape,
 But through the Saviour's blood.
 Isaac Watts, 1709, a.

412.

1 How heavy is the night
 That hangs upon our eyes,
 Till Christ with his reviving light
 Over our souls arise!

2 Our guilty spirits dread
 To meet the wrath of Heaven;
 But in his righteousness arrayed,
 We see our sins forgiven.

3 Unholy and impure
 Are all our thoughts and ways;
 His hands infected nature cure
 With sanctifying grace.

4 The powers of hell agree
 To hold our souls, in vain;
 He sets the sons of bondage free,
 And breaks the curséd chain.

5 Lord, we adore thy ways
 To bring us near to God;
 Thy sovereign power, thy healing grace,
 And thine atoning blood.
 Isaac Watts, 1709.

413.

1 Not all the blood of beasts
 On Jewish altars slain,
 Could give the guilty conscience peace,
 Or wash away the stain.

2 But Christ, the heavenly Lamb,
 Takes all our sins away;
 A sacrifice of nobler name,
 And richer blood than they.

3 My faith would lay her hand
 On that dear head of thine,
 While like a penitent I stand,
 And there confess my sin.

4 My soul looks back to see
 The burdens thou didst bear
 When hanging on the curséd tree,
 And hopes her guilt was there.

5 Believing, we rejoice
 To see the curse remove;
 We bless the Lamb with cheerful voice,
 And sing his bleeding love.
 Isaac Watts, 1709.

SALVATION,—MAN'S NEED.

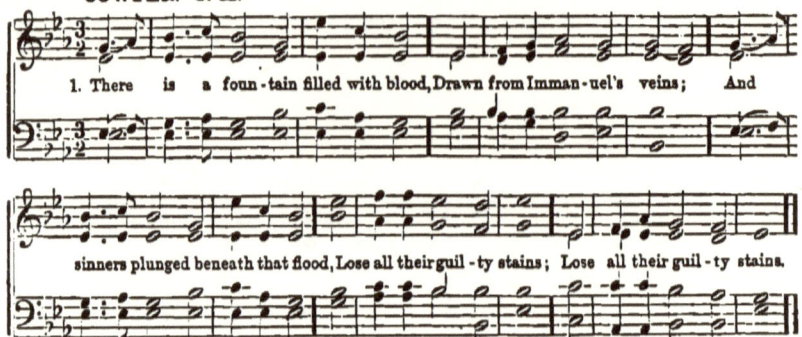

COWPER. C. M.

1. There is a foun-tain filled with blood, Drawn from Imman-uel's veins; And sinners plunged beneath that flood, Lose all their guil-ty stains; Lose all their guil-ty stains.

414.

1 There is a fountain filled with blood
  Drawn from Immanuel's veins;
 And sinners plunged beneath that flood,
  Lose all their guilty stains.

2 The dying thief rejoiced to see
  That fountain in his day;
 And there have I, as vile as he,
  Washed all my sins away.

3 Dear dying Lamb, thy precious blood
  Shall never lose its power,
 Till all the ransomed church of God
  Be saved to sin no more.

4 E'er since, by faith, I saw the stream
  Thy flowing wounds supply,
 Redeeming love has been my theme,
  And shall be till I die.

5 Then in a nobler, sweeter song,
  I'll sing thy power to save, [tongue
 When this poor lisping, stammering
  Lies silent in the grave.

6 Lord, I believe thou hast prepared,
  Unworthy though I be,
 For me a blood-bought, free reward,
  A golden harp for me.

7 'T is strung, and tuned for endless years,
  And formed by power divine,
 To sound in God the Father's ears
  No other name but thine.
          William Cowper, 1779.

415.

1 When wounded sore the stricken soul
  Lies bleeding and unbound,
 One only hand, a piercéd hand,
  Can salve the sinner's wound.

2 When sorrow swells the laden breast,
  And tears of anguish flow,
 One only heart, a broken heart,
  Can feel the sinner's woe.

3 When penitence has wept in vain
  Over some foul dark spot,
 One only stream, a stream of blood,
  Can wash away the blot.

4 'T is Jesus' blood that washes white,
  His hand that brings relief,
 His heart that 's touched with all our joy,
  And feeleth for our grief.

5 Lift up thy bleeding hand, O Lord;
  Unseal that cleansing tide;
 We have no shelter from our sin
  But in thy wounded side.
          Cecil Frances Alexander, 1858.

DOXOLOGY.

To Father, Son, and Holy Ghost,
 One God, whom we adore,
Be glory as it was, is now
 And shall be evermore!

SALVATION,—MAN'S NEED

NAOMI. C. M.

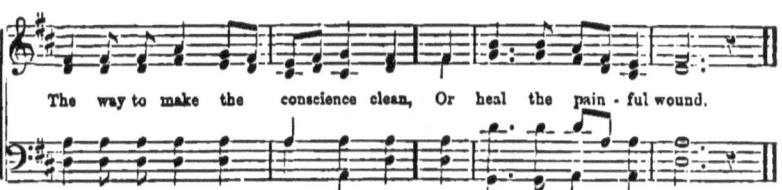

1. How is our nature spoiled by sin! Yet nature ne'er hath found
The way to make the conscience clean, Or heal the painful wound.

416.

1 How is our nature spoiled by sin!
Yet nature ne'er hath found
The way to make the conscience clean,
Or heal the painful wound.

2 In vain we seek for peace with God
By methods of our own:
Jesus, there's nothing but thy blood
Can bring us near the throne.

3 The threatenings of thy broken law
Impress our souls with dread;
If God his sword of vengeance draw,
It strikes our spirits dead.

4 But thine illustrious sacrifice
Hath answered these demands,
And peace and pardon from the skies
Come down by Jesus' hands.

5 'T is by thy death we live, O Lord;
'T is on thy cross we rest;
Forever be thy love adored,
Thy name forever blest.
Isaac Watts, 1721.

417.

1 How sad our state by nature is!
Our sin, how deep it stains!
And Satan binds our captive minds
Fast in his slavish chains.

2 But there's a voice of sovereign grace
Sounds from the sacred word:
"Ho! ye despairing sinners, come,
And trust upon the Lord!"

3 My soul obeys the almighty call,
And runs to this relief;
I would believe thy promise, Lord;
Oh, help my unbelief.

4 To the dear fountain of thy blood,
Incarnate God, I fly;
Here let me wash my spotted soul
From crimes of deepest dye.

5 A guilty, weak, and helpless worm,
On thy kind arms I fall:
Be thou my strength and righteousness,
My Jesus, and my all.
Isaac Watts, 1709.

418.

1 Prostrate, dear Jesus, at thy feet
A guilty rebel lies,
And upward to the mercy-seat
Presumes to lift his eyes.

2 If tears of sorrow would suffice
To pay the debt I owe,
Tears should from both my weeping eyes
In ceaseless torrents flow.

3 But no such sacrifice I plead
To expiate my guilt;
No tears but those which thou hast shed,
No blood but thou hast spilt.

4 Think of thy sorrows, dearest Lord,
And all my sins forgive:
Justice will well approve the word
That bids the sinner live.
Joseph Stennett, 1700.

176. SALVATION,—MAN'S NEED.

STEPHENS. C. M.

1. O God of mercy, hear my call, My load of guilt remove; Break down this separating wall That bars me from thy love.

419.

1 O God of mercy, hear my call,
My load of guilt remove;
Break down this separating wall
That bars me from thy love.

2 Give me the presence of thy grace;
Then my rejoicing tongue
Shall speak aloud thy righteousness,
And make thy praise my song.

3 No blood of goats, nor heifer slain,
For sin could e'er atone;
The death of Christ shall still remain
Sufficient and alone.

4 A soul oppressed with sin's desert
My God will ne'er despise;
A humble groan, a broken heart,
Is our best sacrifice.
Isaac Watts, 1719.

420.

1 How helpless guilty nature lies,
Unconscious of its load!
The heart, unchanged, can never rise
To happiness and God.

2 Can aught beneath a power divine
The stubborn will subdue?
'T is thine, almighty Saviour, thine,
To form the heart anew.

3 'T is thine the passions to recall,
And upward bid them rise,
And make the scales of error fall
From reason's darkened eyes;

4 To chase the shades of death away,
And bid the sinner live;
A beam of heaven, a vital ray,
'T is thine alone to give.

5 Oh change these wretched hearts of ours,
And give them life divine!
Then shall our passions and our powers,
Almighty Lord, be thine.
Anne Steele, 1760.

421.

1 Amazing grace! how sweet the sound,
That saved a wretch like me!
I once was lost, but now am found;
Was blind, but now I see.

2 'T was grace that taught my heart to fear,
And grace my fears relieved;
How precious did that grace appear,
The hour I first believed!

3 Through many dangers, toils, and snares,
I have already come;
'T is grace has brought me safe thus far,
And grace will lead me home.

4 Yes, when this flesh and heart shall fail,
And mortal life shall cease,
I shall possess, within the veil,
A life of joy and peace.

5 The earth shall soon dissolve like snow,
The sun forbear to shine;
But God, who called me here below,
Will be forever mine.
John Newton, 1779.

SALVATION,—OF GRACE.

MARLOW. C. M.

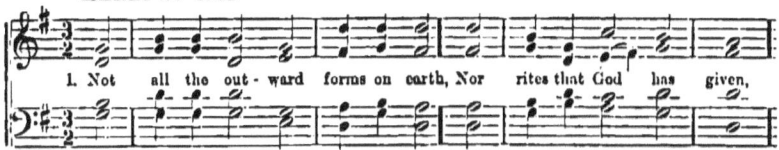

1. Not all the outward forms on earth, Nor rites that God has given, Nor will of man, nor blood, nor birth, Can raise a soul to heaven.

422.

1 Not all the outward forms on earth,
  Nor rites that God has given,
  Nor will of man, nor blood, nor birth,
  Can raise a soul to heaven.

2 The sovereign will of God alone
  Creates us heirs of grace;
  Born in the image of his Son,
  A new, peculiar race.

3 The Spirit, like some heavenly wind,
  Blows on the sons of flesh;
  New models all the carnal mind,
  And forms the man afresh.

4 Our quickened souls awake and rise
  From the long sleep of death;
  On heavenly things we fix our eyes,
  And praise employs our breath.
  Isaac Watts, 1709.

423.

1 Salvation! oh the joyful sound!
  'Tis pleasure to our ears;
  A sovereign balm for every wound,
  A cordial for our fears.

2 Buried in sorrow and in sin,
  At hell's dark door we lay;
  But we arise by grace divine
  To see a heavenly day.

3 Salvation! let the echo fly
  The spacious earth around;
  While all the armies of the sky
  Conspire to raise the sound.
  Isaac Watts, 1709.

424.

1 Father, how wide thy glory shines!
  How high thy wonders rise! [signs,
  Known through the earth by thousand
  By thousand through the skies.

2 Those mighty orbs proclaim thy power,
  Their motions speak thy skill;
  And on the wings of every hour
  We read thy patience still.

3 But when we view thy strange design
  To save rebellious worms,
  Where vengeance and compassion join
  In their divinest forms;

4 Our thoughts are lost in reverent awe;
  We love, and we adore:
  The first archangel never saw
  So much of God before.

5 Here the whole Deity is known;
  Nor dares a creature guess
  Which of the glories brightest shone,
  The justice, or the grace.

6 Now the full glories of the Lamb
  Adorn the heavenly plains;
  Bright seraphs learn Immanuel's name,
  And try their choicest strains.

7 Oh may I bear some humble part
  In that immortal song!
  Wonder and joy shall tune my heart,
  And love command my tongue.
  Isaac Watts, 1706.

SALVATION,—OF GRACE.

LENOX. H. M.

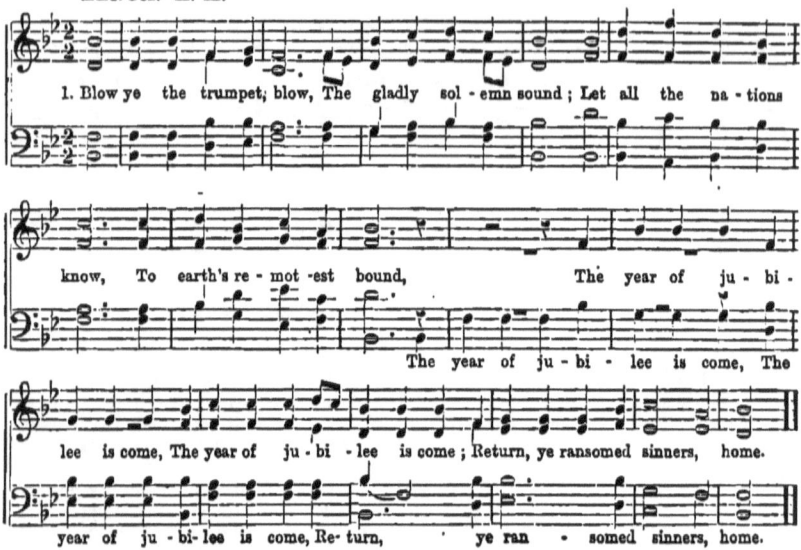

1. Blow ye the trumpet, blow, The gladly sol-emn sound; Let all the na-tions know, To earth's re-mot-est bound, The year of ju-bi-lee is come, The year of ju-bi-lee is come, The year of ju-bi-lee is come; Return, ye ransomed sinners, home.

425.

2 Jesus, our great High-Priest,
   Hath full atonement made:
Ye weary spirits, rest;
   Ye mournful souls, be glad:
The year of jubilee is come;
Return, ye ransomed sinners, home.

3 Extol the Lamb of God,
   The all-atoning Lamb;
Redemption in his blood
   Throughout the world proclaim:
The year of jubilee is come;
Return, ye ransomed sinners, home.

4 Ye slaves of sin and hell,
   Your liberty receive,
And safe in Jesus dwell,
   And blest in Jesus live:
The year of jubilee is come;
Return, ye ransomed sinners, home.

5 The gospel trumpet hear,
   The news of heavenly grace;
And, saved from earth, appear
   Before your Saviour's face:
The year of jubilee is come;
Return, ye ransomed sinners, home.
Charles Wesley, 1750.

426.

1 INDULGENT God! how kind
   Are all thy ways to me,
Whose dark benighted mind
   Was enmity with thee;
Yet now, subdued by sovereign grace,
My spirit longs for thine embrace.

2 How precious are thy thoughts,
   That o'er my bosom roll,
They swell beyond my faults,
   And captivate my soul;
How great their sum, how high they rise,
Can ne'er be known beneath the skies.

3 Preserved in Jesus when
   My feet made haste to hell,
And there I should have gone,
   But thou dost all things well;
Thy love was great, thy mercy free,
Which from the pit delivered me.

4 A monument of grace,
   A sinner saved by blood;
The streams of love I trace
   Up to the fountain, God;
And in his sacred bosom see
Eternal thoughts of love to me.
John Kent, 1803.

SALVATION,—OF GRACE.

ISRAEL. 8s. DOUBLE.

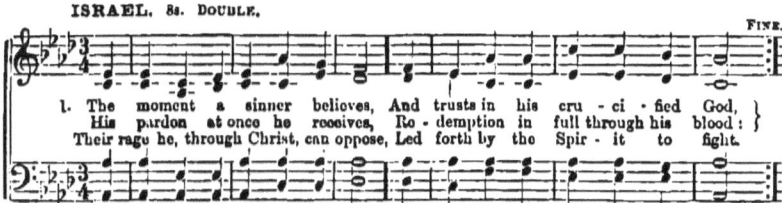

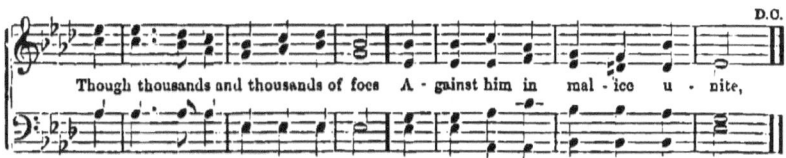

427.

1 THE moment a sinner believes,
And trusts in his crucified God,
His pardon at once he receives,
Redemption in full through his blood;
Though thousands and thousands of foes
Against him in malice unite,
Their rage he, through Christ, can oppose,
Led forth by the Spirit to fight.

2 The faith that unites to the Lamb,
And brings such salvation as this,
Is more than mere notion or name;
The work of God's Spirit it is;
A principle, active and young,
That lives under pressure and load;
That makes out of weakness more strong,
And draws the soul upward to God.

3 It treads on the world and on hell;
It vanquishes death and despair;
And, oh, what is stranger to tell,
It overcomes heaven by prayer;
Permits a vile worm of the dust
With God to commune as a friend;
To hope his forgiveness as just,
And look for his love to the end.

4 It says to the mountains, "Depart,"
That stand betwixt God and the soul,
It binds up the broken in heart,
And makes wounded consciences whole;

Bids sins of a crimson-like dye
Be spotless as snow, and as white,
And makes such a sinner as I
As pure as an angel of light.
Joseph Hart, 1759.

428.

1 A DEBTOR to mercy alone,
Of covenant mercy I sing;
Nor fear, with thy righteousness on,
My person and offering to bring:
The terrors of law and of God
With me can have nothing to do;
My Saviour's obedience and blood
Hide all my transgressions from view.

2 The work which his goodness began,
The arm of his strength will complete;
His promise is yea and amen,
And never was forfeited yet:
Things future, nor things that are now,
Not all things below nor above,
Can make him his purpose forego,
Or sever my soul from his love.

3 My name from the palms of his hands,
Eternity will not erase:
Imprest on his heart it remains,
In marks of indelible grace:
Yes, I to the end shall endure,
As sure as the earnest is given;
More happy, but not more secure,
The glorified spirits in heaven.
A. M. Toplady, 1776.

SALVATION,—OF GRACE.

MELCOMBE. L. M. (Repeat for 6 lines.)

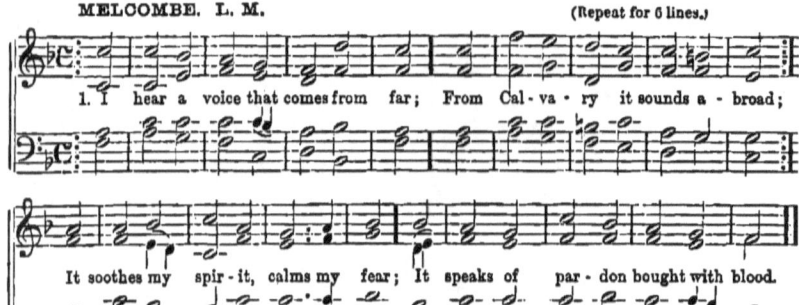

1. I hear a voice that comes from far; From Calvary it sounds abroad;
It soothes my spirit, calms my fear; It speaks of pardon bought with blood.

429.

1 I HEAR a voice that comes from far;
  From Calvary it sounds abroad;
  It soothes my spirit, calms my fear;
  It speaks of pardon bought with blood.

2 And is it true that many fly
  The sound that bids my soul rejoice,
  And rather choose in sin to die
  Than turn an ear to mercy's voice?

3 Alas for those! the day is near
  When mercy will be heard no more;
  Then may they ask in vain to hear
  The voice they would not hear before.

4 With such, I own, I once appeared;
  But now I know how great their loss;
  For sweeter sounds were never heard
  Than mercy utters from the cross.

5 But let me not forget to own
  That, if I differ aught from those,
  'T is due to sovereign grace alone,
  That conquers oft its proudest foes.
  Thomas Kelly, 1769-1855.

430.

1 GREAT God of wonders! all thy ways
  Are matchless, godlike and divine;
  But the fair glories of thy grace
  More godlike and unrivalled shine:
  Who is a pardoning God like thee,
  Or who has grace so rich and free!

2 Crimes of such horror to forgive,
  Such guilty daring worms to spare;
  This is thy grand prerogative,
  And none shall in the honor share:
  Who is a pardoning God like thee,
  Or who has grace so rich and free!

3 In wonder lost, with trembling joy
  We take the pardon of our God,
  Pardon for crimes of deepest dye.
  A pardon bought with Jesus' blood:
  Who is a pardoning God like thee,
  Or who has grace so rich and free!

4 Oh may this strange, this matchless grace,
  This god-like miracle of love,
  Fill the wide earth with grateful praise,
  And all the angelic choirs above:
  Who is a pardoning God like thee,
  Or who has grace so rich and free!
  Samuel Davies, 1769.

431.

1 WHO shall the Lord's elect condemn?
  'T is God that justifies their souls;
  And mercy, like a mighty stream,
  O'er all their sins divinely rolls.

2 Who shall adjudge the saints to hell?
  'T is Christ that suffered in their stead;
  And, their salvation to fulfil,
  Behold him rising from the dead!

3 He lives! he lives! and sits above,
  Forever interceding there;
  Who shall divide us from his love,
  Or what should tempt us to despair?

4 Not all that men on earth can do,
  Nor powers on high, nor powers below,
  Shall cause his mercy to remove, [love.
  Or wean our hearts from Christ our
  Isaac Watts, 1709.

SALVATION,—OF GRACE.

GANGES. C. P. M.

1. Let Zion in her songs record The honors of her dying Lord, Triumphant over sin; How sweet the song there's none can say, But he whose sins are washed away, Who feels the same with - in.

432.

1 Let Zion in her songs record
 The honors of her dying Lord,
 Triumphant over sin:
How sweet the song there's none can say,
But he whose sins are washed away,
 Who feels the same within.

2 We claim no merit of our own,
 But self-condemned, before thy throne,
  Our hopes on Jesus place,
Though once in heart and life depraved,
We now can sing as sinners saved,
 And praise redeeming grace.

3 We'll sing the same while life shall last,
And when, at the archangel's blast,
 Our sleeping dust shall rise,
Then, in a song forever new,
The glorious theme we'll still pursue
 Throughout the azure skies.

4 Prepared of old, at God's right hand
Bright everlasting mansions stand
 For all the blood-bought race;
And till we reach those seats of bliss,
We'll sing no other song but this —
 Salvation all of grace.

John Kent, 1803. a.

433.

1 Awaked by Sinai's awful sound,
 My soul in bonds of guilt I found,
  And knew not where to go;
Eternal truth did loud proclaim
 "The sinner must be born again,"
  Or sink to endless woe.

2 I heard the law its thunders roll.
 While guilt lay heavy on my soul —
  A vast oppressive load;
All creature-aid I saw was vain;
 "The sinner must be born again,"
  Or drink the wrath of God.

3 The saints I heard with rapture tell
How Jesus conquered death and hell,
 And broke the fowler's snare;
Yet, when I found this truth remain,
 "The sinner must be born again,"
  I sunk in deep despair.

4 But while I thus in anguish lay,
Jesus of Nazareth passed that way,
 And felt his pity move:
The sinner, by his justice slain,
 Now by his grace is born again,
  And sings redeeming love.

Samson Occum, 1760. a.

SALVATION,—OF GRACE.

HAYDN'S HYMN. 8s, 7s & 4s.

Sons we are through God's e-lec-tion, Who in Je-sus Christ be-lieve;
By e-ter-nal des-ti-na-tion, Sove-reign grace we here re-ceive:
Lord, thy mer-cy, Lord, thy mer-cy Does both grace and glo-ry give.

434.

1 Sons we are through God's election,
Who in Jesus Christ believe;
By eternal destination,
Sovereign grace we here receive:
Lord, thy mercy
Does both grace and glory give.

2 Every fallen soul, by sinning,
Merits everlasting pain;
But thy love, without beginning,
Has restored thy sons again:
Countless millions
Shall in life through Jesus reign.

3 Pause, my soul, adore and wonder!
Ask, "Oh why such love to me?"
Grace hath put me in the number
Of the Saviour's family:
Hallelujah!
Thanks, eternal thanks to thee!

4 Since that love had no beginning,
And shall never, never cease;
Keep, oh keep me, Lord, from sinning!
Guide me in the way of peace;
Make me walk in
All the paths of holiness.

5 When I quit this feeble mansion,
And my soul returns to thee;

Let the power of thy ascension
Manifest itself in me:
Through thy Spirit,
Give the final victory!

6 When in that blest habitation,
Which my God has fore-ordained;
When, in glory's full possession,
I with saints and angels stand;
Free grace only
Shall resound through Canaan's land.
S. P. R., 1777.

435.   Tune "Jenner," p. 29.   7s & 6s.

1 'Tis not that I did choose thee,
For, Lord, that could not be;
This heart would still refuse thee;
But thou hast chosen me:
Hast, from the sin that stained me,
Washed me and set me free,
And to this end ordained me,
That I should live to thee.

2 'T was sovereign mercy called me,
And taught my opening mind;
The world had else enthralled me,
To heavenly glories blind.
My heart owns none above thee;
For thy rich grace I thirst;
This knowing,—if I love thee,
Thou must have loved me first.
Josiah Conder, 1789-1855.

SALVATION,—OF GRACE. 183
THATCHER. S. M.

1. Grace! 'tis a charm-ing sound, Har-mo-nious to the ear!

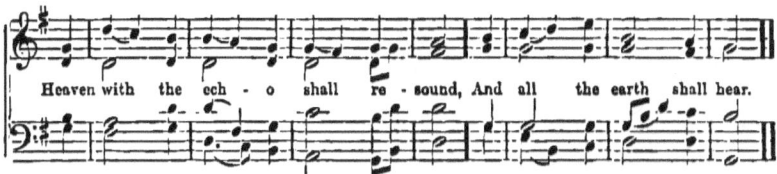
Heaven with the ech-o shall re-sound, And all the earth shall hear.

436.
1 GRACE! 'tis a charming sound,
  Harmonious to the ear!
  Heaven with the echo shall resound,
  And all the earth shall hear.

2 Grace first contrived the way
  To save rebellious man;
  And all the steps that grace display
  Which drew the wondrous plan.

3 Grace taught my roving feet
  To tread the heavenly road;
  And new supplies each hour I meet,
  While pressing on to God.

4 Grace all the work shall crown,
  Through everlasting days;
  It lays in heaven the topmost stone,
  And well deserves the praise.
  Philip Doddridge, 1740.

437.
1 RAISE your triumphant songs
  To an immortal tune;
  Let the wide earth resound the deeds
  Celestial grace has done.

2 Sing how eternal love
  Its chief belovéd chose,
  And bid him raise our wretched race
  From their abyss of woes.

3 His hand no thunder bears,
  No terror clothes his brow;
  No bolts to drive our guilty souls
  To fiercer flames below.

4 'T was mercy filled the throne,
  And wrath stood silent by,
  When Christ was sent with pardons down
  To rebels doomed to die.

5 Now, sinners, dry your tears,
  Let hopeless sorrow cease;
  Bow to the sceptre of his love,
  And take the offered peace.

6 Lord, we obey thy call;
  We lay an humble claim
  To the salvation thou hast brought,
  And love and praise thy name.
  Isaac Watts, 1719.

438.
1 DID Christ o'er sinners weep,
  And shall our cheeks be dry?
  Let floods of penitential grief
  Burst forth from every eye.

2 The Son of God in tears
  Angels with wonder see:
  Be thou astonished, O my soul!
  He shed those tears for thee.

3 He wept that we might weep,—
  Each sin demands a tear;
  In heaven alone no sin is found,
  And there's no weeping there.
  Benjamin Beddome, 1818.

DOXOLOGY.

THE Father and the Son
  And Spirit we adore;
  We praise, we bless, we worship thee,
  Both now and evermore!

SALVATION,—OF GRACE.

PASCAL. H. M.

1. From thy dear, pierc-ed side, Un-spot-ted Lamb of God,
Came forth a min-gled stream Of wa-ter and of blood:
My sin-ful soul there I would lay, Till eve-ry stain is washed a-way.

439.

1 From thy dear, piercéd side,
  Unspotted Lamb of God,
Came forth a mingled stream
  Of water and of blood:
My sinful soul there I would lay,
Till every stain is washed away.

2 'T is from this sacred spring
  A sovereign virtue flows,
To heal my painful wounds,
  And cure my deadly woes:
Here, then, I'll bathe, and bathe again,
Till not a wound or woe remain.

3 A fountain 't is unsealed,
  Divinely rich and free,
Open for all who come,
  And open, too, for me:
To this pure fount will I repair; [there.
Come, sinners, come; there's mercy

Benjamin Beddome, 1818.

440.

1 Thy works, not mine, O Christ!
  Speak gladness to this heart:
They tell me all is done,
  They bid my fear depart:
To whom, save thee who canst alone
For sin atone, Lord, shall I flee?

2 Thy wounds, not mine, O Christ,
  Can heal my bruiséd soul;
Thy stripes, not mine, contain
  The balm that makes me whole:
To whom, save thee who canst alone
For sin atone, Lord, shall I flee?

3 Thy cross, not mine, O Christ,
  Has borne the awful load
Of sins that none could bear
  But the incarnate God:
To whom, save thee who canst alone
For sin atone, Lord, shall I flee?

4 Thy death, not mine, O Christ,
  Has paid the ransom due;
Ten thousand deaths like mine
  Would have been all too few:
To whom, save thee who canst alone
For sin atone, Lord, shall I flee?

5 Thy righteousness alone
  Can clothe and beautify;
I wrap it round my soul,
  In this I'll live and die:
To whom, save thee who canst alone
For sin atone, Lord, shall I flee?

Horatius Bonar, 1856.

SALVATION,—CALLS.

HUMILITY. L. M.

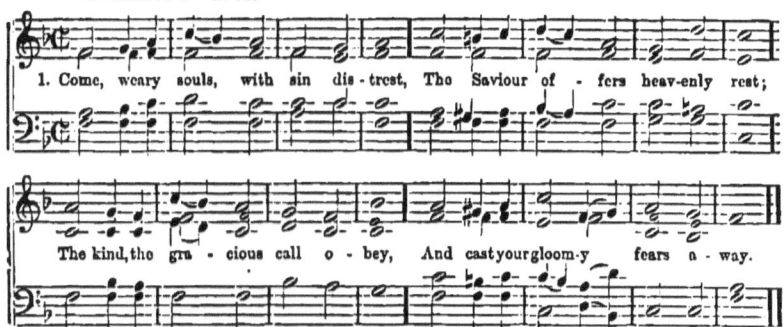

1. Come, weary souls, with sin dis-trest, The Saviour of-fers heav-enly rest; The kind, the gra-cious call o-bey, And cast your gloom-y fears a-way.

441.

1 Come, weary souls with sin distrest,
The Saviour offers heavenly rest;
The kind, the gracious call obey,
And cast your gloomy fears away.

2 Oppressed with guilt, a painful load,
Oh come and bow before your God!
Divine compassion, mighty love,
Will all that painful load remove.

3 Here mercy's boundless ocean flows
To cleanse your guilt and heal your woes;
Pardon, and life, and endless peace;
How rich the gift, how free the grace!

4 Lord we accept, with thankful heart,
The hope thy gracious words impart;
We come with trembling, yet rejoice,
And bless the kind inviting voice.

5 Dear Saviour, let thy powerful love
Confirm our faith, our fears remove,
And sweetly influence every breast,
And guide us to eternal rest.
Anne Steele, 1760.

442. Matt. xl. 28-30.

1 "Come hither, all ye weary souls,
Ye heavy-laden sinners, come;
I'll give you rest from all your toils,
And raise you to my heavenly home,

2 "They shall find rest who learn of me;
I'm of a meek and lowly mind;
But passion rages like the sea,
And pride is restless as the wind.

3 "Blest is the man whose shoulders take
My yoke, and bear it with delight;
My yoke is easy to his neck,
My grace shall make the burden light.

4 Jesus, we come at thy command;
With faith, and hope, and humble zeal,
Resign our spirits to thy hand,
To mould and guide us at thy will.
Isaac Watts, 1709.

443.

1 Behold! a Stranger's at the door!
He gently knocks, has knocked before,
Has waited long, is waiting still;
You treat no other friend so ill.

2 Oh lovely attitude! he stands
With melting heart, and laden hands!
Oh matchless kindness! and he shows
This matchless kindness to his foes.

3 Admit him, for the human breast
Ne'er entertained so kind a guest:
Admit him, for you can't expel;
Where'er he comes, he comes to dwell.

4 Admit him, ere his anger burn,
His feet depart, and ne'er return!
Admit him; or the hour's at hand,
When at his door denied you'll stand.

5 Sovereign of souls, thou Prince of Peace,
Oh may thy gentle reign increase!
Throw wide the door, each willing mind;
And be his empire all mankind!
Joseph Grigg, 1765.

SALVATION,—CALLS.

LANGDON. 7s. 6 LINES.

1. From the cross up-lift-ed high, Where the Saviour deigns to die,
What me-lo-dious sounds I hear, Bursting on my ravished ear!
Love's redeeming work is done; Come and welcome, sinner, come!

444.

2 " Sprinkled now with blood the throne,
Why beneath thy burdens groan?
On my pierced body laid,
Justice owns the ransom paid;
Bow the knee, and kiss the Son:
Come and welcome, sinner, come!

3 " Spread for thee, the festal board
See with richest dainties stored;
To thy Father's bosom prest,
Yet again a child confest,
Never from his house to roam:
Come and welcome, sinner, come!

4 " Soon the days of life shall end;
Lo I come, your Saviour, Friend,
Safe your spirit to convey
To the realms of endless day,
Up to my eternal home:
Come and welcome, sinner, come!"

Thomas Haweis, 1792.

445. Tune, "Seymour," p. 193.

1 COME, said Jesus' sacred voice,
Come, and make my paths your choice;
I will guide you to your home,
Weary pilgrim, hither come!

2 Thou who, houseless, sole, forlorn,
Long hast borne the proud world's scorn,
Long hast roamed the barren waste,
Weary pilgrim, hither haste.

3 Ye who, tossed on beds of pain,
Seek for ease, but seek in vain;
Ye, by fiercer anguish torn,
In remorse for guilt who mourn;

4 Hither come! for here is found
Balm that flows for every wound,
Peace that ever shall endure,
Rest eternal, sacred, sure.

Anna Laetitia Barbauld, 1825.

446.

1 YE who in his courts are found,
Listening to the joyful sound,
Lost and helpless as ye are,
Sons of sorrow, sin, and care,
Glorify the King of kings;
Take the peace the gospel brings.

2 Turn to Christ your longing eyes;
View this bleeding sacrifice;
See in him your sins forgiven,
Pardon, holiness, and heaven;
Glorify the King of kings;
Take the peace the gospel brings.

Rowland Hill, 1774.

SALVATION,—CALLS. 187

AVA. 6s & 4s.

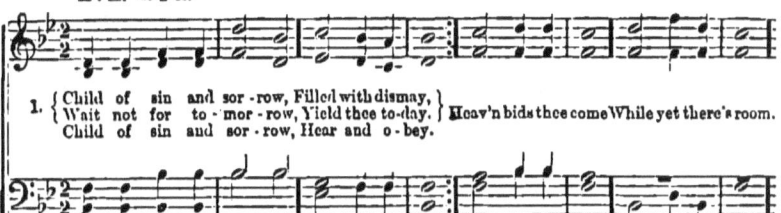

447.

1 Child of sin and sorrow,
 Filled with dismay,
 Wait not for to-morrow,
 Yield thee to-day:
 Heaven bids thee come,
 While yet there's room.
 Child of sin and sorrow,
 Hear and obey.

2 Child of sin and sorrow,
 Why wilt thou die?
 Come while thou canst borrow
 Help from on high;
 Grieve not that love
 Which from above,
 Child of sin and sorrow,
 Would bring thee nigh.

3 Child of sin and sorrow,
 Thy moments glide
 Like the flitting arrow
 Or the rushing tide;
 Ere time is o'er,
 Heaven's grace implore;
 Child of sin and sorrow,
 In Christ confide.

Thomas Hastings, 1842.

AMOY. 6s & 4s.

448.

1 To-day the Saviour calls:
 Ye wanderers, come!
 Oh, ye benighted souls,
 Why longer roam?

2 To-day the Saviour calls:
 Oh, listen now!
 Within these sacred walls
 To Jesus bow.

3 To-day the Saviour calls;
 For refuge fly;
 The storm of justice falls,
 And death is nigh.

4 The Spirit calls to-day,
 Yield to his power;
 Oh, grieve him not away!
 'T is mercy's hour.

Thomas Hastings, 1838.

SALVATION,—CALLS.

BELMONT. 8s, 7s & 4s.

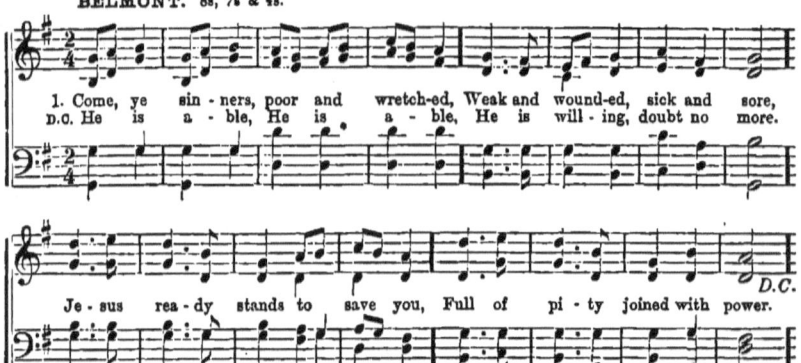

449.

1 COME, ye sinners, poor and wretched,
  Weak and wounded, sick and sore,
 Jesus ready stands to save you,
  Full of pity joined with power:
   He is able,
   He is willing; doubt no more.

2 Come, ye thirsty, come and welcome;
  God's free bounty glorify;
 True belief, and true repentance,
  Every grace that brings us nigh —
   Without money,
   Come to Jesus Christ, and buy.

3 Let not conscience make you linger,
  Nor of fitness fondly dream;
 All the fitness he requireth
  Is to feel your need of him;
   This he gives you;
   'T is his Spirit's rising beam.

4 Come, ye weary, heavy laden,
  Bruised and mangled by the fall;
 If you tarry till you're better,
  You will never come at all, —
   Not the righteous,
   Sinners Jesus came to call.

5 Lo, the incarnate God ascended,
  Pleads the merit of his blood;
 Venture on him, venture wholly,
  Let no other trust intrude;
   None but Jesus
   Can do helpless sinners good.
       Joseph Hart, 1759, a.

450.

1 SINNERS, will you scorn the message
  Sent in mercy from above?
 Every sentence, oh how tender!
  Every line is full of love:
   Listen to it;
   Every line is full of love.

2 Hear the heralds of the gospel
  News from Zion's King proclaim,
 "Pardon to each rebel sinner;
  Free forgiveness in his name:"
   How important!
   "Free forgiveness in his name."

3 Tempted souls, they bring you succor;
  Fearful hearts, they quell your fears,
 And, with news of consolation,
  Chase away the falling tears;
   Tender heralds!
   Chase away the falling tears.

4 Who hath our report believed?
  Who received the joyful word?
 Who embraced the news of pardon
  Offered to you by the Lord?
   Can you slight it?
   Offered to you by the Lord.

5 O ye angels, hovering round us,
  Waiting spirits, speed your way;
 Haste ye to the court of heaven,
  Tidings bear without delay;
   Rebel sinners
   Glad the message will obey.
       Jonathan Allen, 1801.

SALVATION,—CALLS. 189

COOLEY. L. M.

1. Return, O wanderer, return, And seek an injured Father's face; Those warm desires that in thee burn Were kindled by reclaiming grace.

451.

1 RETURN, O wanderer, return,
And seek an injured Father's face;
Those warm desires that in thee burn
Were kindled by reclaiming grace.

2 Return, O wanderer, return,
And seek a Father's melting heart,
Whose pitying eyes thy grief discern,
Whose hand can heal thy inward smart.

3 Return, O wanderer, return;
He hears thy deep, repentant sigh;
He sees thy softened spirit mourn,
When no intruding ear is nigh.

4 Return, O wanderer, return;
Thy Saviour bids thy spirit live;
Go to his bleeding feet, and learn
How freely Jesus can forgive.

5 Return, O wanderer, return,
And wipe away the falling tear;
Thy Father calls, no longer mourn;
'T is mercy's voice invites thee near.
William B. Collyer, 1812.

452.

1 GOD calling yet! shall I not hear?
Earth's pleasures shall I still hold dear?
Shall life's swift passing years all fly,
And still my soul in slumbers lie?

2 God calling yet! shall I not rise?
Can I his loving voice despise,
And basely his kind care repay?
He calls me still; can I delay?

3 God calling yet! and shall he knock,
And I my heart the closer lock?
He still is waiting to receive,
And shall I dare his Spirit grieve?

4 God calling yet! and shall I give
No heed, but still in bondage live?
I wait, but he does not forsake;
He calls me still; my heart, awake!

5 God calling yet! I cannot stay;
My heart I yield without delay:
Vain world, farewell! from thee I part;
The voice of God hath reached my heart.
G. Tersteegen, 1750; tr. by Jane Borthwick, 1853.

453.

1 BROAD is the road that leads to death,
And thousands walk together there;
But wisdom shows a narrow path,
With here and there a traveller.

2 "Deny thyself, and take thy cross,"
Is the Redeemer's great command;
Nature must count her gold but dross.
If she would gain this heavenly land.

3 The fearful soul that tires and faints,
And walks the ways of God no more,
Is but esteemed almost a saint,
And makes his own destruction sure.

4 Lord! let not all my hopes be vain,
Create my heart entirely new;
Which hypocrites could ne'er attain,
Which false apostates never knew.
Isaac Watts, 1709.

SALVATION,—CALLS.

CALM. C. M.

1. Let eve-ry mor-tal ear at-tend, And eve-ry heart re-joice, The trum-pet of the gos-pel sounds With an in-vit-ing voice.

454.

1 LET every mortal ear attend,
  And every heart rejoice,
  The trumpet of the gospel sounds
  With an inviting voice.

2 Ho, all ye hungry, starving souls,
  That feed upon the wind,
  And vainly strive with earthly toys
  To fill an empty mind;

3 Eternal wisdom has prepared
  A soul-reviving feast,
  And bids your longing appetites
  The rich provision taste.

4 Ho, ye that pant for living streams,
  And pine away and die,
  Here you may quench your raging thirst
  With springs that never dry.

5 Rivers of love and mercy here
  In a rich ocean join;
  Salvation in abundance flows,
  Like floods of milk and wine.

6 Great God, the treasures of thy love
  Are everlasting mines,
  Deep as our helpless miseries are,
  And boundless as our sins.

7 The happy gates of gospel grace
  Stand open night and day;
  Lord, we are come to seek supplies,
  And drive our wants away.
  Isaac Watts, 1706.

455.

1 COME, humble sinner, in whose breast
  A thousand thoughts revolve;
  Come with your guilt and fear oppressed,
  And make this last resolve:

2 "I'll go to Jesus, though my sin
  Hath like a mountain rose;
  I know his courts, I'll enter in,
  Whatever may oppose.

3 "Prostrate I'll lie before his throne,
  And there my guilt confess;
  I'll tell him I'm a wretch undone,
  Without his sovereign grace.

4 "I'll to the gracious King approach,
  Whose sceptre pardon gives;
  Perhaps he may command my touch,
  And then the suppliant lives.

5 "Perhaps he will admit my plea,
  Perhaps will hear my prayer;
  But if I perish, I will pray,
  And perish only there.

6 "I can but perish if I go,
  I am resolved to try;
  For if I stay away, I know
  I must forever die.

7 "But if I die with mercy sought,
  When I the King have tried,
  This were to die (delightful thought!)
  As sinner never died."
  Edmund Jones, 1777.

456. C. M.

1 SEE, Jesus stands with open arms;
   He calls, he bids you come;
   Guilt holds you back, and fear alarms,
   But, see, there yet is room:

2 Room in the Saviour's bleeding heart,
   There love and pity meet;
   Nor will he bid the soul depart
   That trembles at his feet.

3 In him the Father, reconciled,
   Invites your souls to come;
   The rebel shall be called a child,
   And kindly welcomed home.

4 Oh come, and with his children taste
   The blessings of his love,
   While hope attends the sweet repast
   Of nobler joys above.

5 There with united heart and voice,
   Before the eternal throne,
   Ten thousand thousand souls rejoice,
   In ecstasies unknown.

6 And yet ten thousand thousand more
   Are welcome still to come;
   Ye longing souls, the grace adore,
   Approach, there yet is room.
   Anne Steele, 1760.

457. C. M.

1 THE Saviour calls; let every ear
   Attend the heavenly sound;
   Ye doubting souls, dismiss your fear;
   Hope smiles reviving round.

2 For every thirsty, longing heart,
   Here streams of bounty flow;
   And life, and health, and bliss impart,
   To banish mortal woe.

3 Here springs of sacred pleasure rise
   To ease your every pain;
   Immortal fountain! full supplies!
   Nor shall you thirst in vain.

4 Ye sinners, come; 't is mercy's voice,
   The gracious call obey;
   Mercy invites to heavenly joys,
   And can you yet delay?

5 Dear Saviour, draw reluctant hearts!
   To thee let sinners fly,
   And take the bliss thy love imparts
   And drink, and never die.
   Anne Steele, 1760.

458. LUKE xiv. 22. C. M.

1 THE King of Heaven his table spreads,
   And dainties crown the board;
   Not paradise with all its joys
   Could such delight afford.

2 Pardon and peace to dying men,
   And endless life, are given,
   And the rich blood that Jesus shed
   To raise the soul to heaven.

3 Ye hungry poor, that long have strayed
   In sin's dark mazes, come;
   Come, from the hedges and highways,
   And grace shall find you room.

4 Millions of souls, in glory now,
   Were fed and feasted here;
   And millions more, still on the way,
   Around the board appear.

5 Yet are his house and heart so large,
   That millions more may come;
   Nor could the wide assembling world
   O'erfill the spacious room.

6 All things are ready, come away,
   Nor weak excuses frame;
   Crowd to your places at the feast,
   And bless the Founder's name.
   Philip Doddridge, 1755.

459. C. M.

1 SINNERS, the voice of God regard,
   'T is mercy speaks to-day;
   He calls you by his sovereign word
   From sin's destructive way.

2 Why will you in the crooked ways
   Of sin and folly go?
   In pain you travel all your days,
   To reap immortal woe!

3 But he that turns to God shall live,
   Through his abounding grace;
   His mercy will the guilt forgive
   Of those that seek his face.

4 Bow to the sceptre of his word,
   Renouncing every sin;
   Submit to him, your sovereign Lord,
   And learn his will divine.

5 His love exceeds your highest thoughts;
   He pardons like a God;
   He will forgive your numerous faults,
   Through a Redeemer's blood.
   John Fawcett, 1782.

SALVATION,—CALLS.

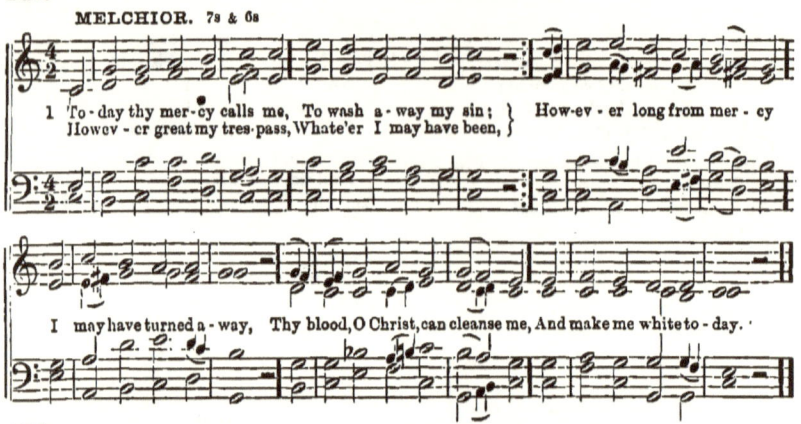

MELCHIOR. 7s & 6s

1 To-day thy mer-cy calls me, To wash a-way my sin;
   Howev-er great my tres-pass, Whate'er I may have been,
   How-ev-er long from mer-cy I may have turned a-way,
   Thy blood, O Christ, can cleanse me, And make me white to-day.

460.
2 To-day thy gate is open,
   And all who enter in
Shall find a Father's welcome,
   And pardon for their sin.
The past shall be forgotten,
   A present joy be given,
A future grace be promised,
   A glorious crown in heaven.

3 To-day the Father calls me,
   The Holy Spirit waits;
The blessed angels gather
   Around the heavenly gates;
No question will be asked me,
   How often I have come;
Although I oft have wandered,
   It is my Father's home.

4 O all-embracing mercy,
   Thou ever-open door,
What should I do without thee,
   When heart and eyes run o'er?
When all things seem against me,
   To drive me to despair,
I know one gate is open,
   One ear will hear my prayer.
Oswald Allen, 1862.

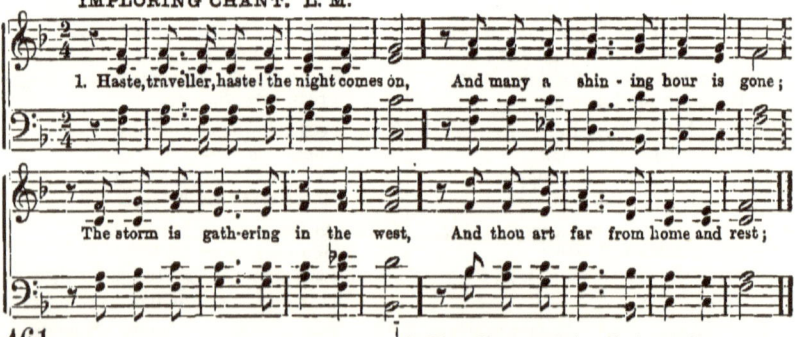

IMPLORING CHANT. L. M.

1. Haste, traveller, haste! the night comes on, And many a shin-ing hour is gone;
The storm is gath-ering in the west, And thou art far from home and rest;

461.
2 The rising tempest sweeps the sky;
The rains descend, the winds are high;
The waters swell, and death and fear
Beset thy path, nor refuge near:

3 Then linger not in all the plain,
Flee for thy life, the mountain gain;
Look not behind, make no delay,
O speed thee, speed thee on thy way!
William B. Collyer, 1829.

SALVATION,—CALLS.

SEYMOUR. 7s.

1. Hasten, sinner! to be wise, Stay not for the morrow's sun; Wisdom if you still despise, Harder is it to be won.

462.

1 HASTEN, sinner! to be wise,
   Stay not for the morrow's sun;
   Wisdom if you still despise,
   Harder is it to be won.

2 Hasten mercy to implore,
   Stay not for the morrow's sun,
   Lest thy season should be o'er,
   Ere this evening's stage be run.

3 Hasten, sinner! now return;
   Stay not for the morrow's sun,
   Lest thy lamp should cease to burn
   Ere salvation's work is done.

4 Hasten, sinner! to be blest,
   Stay not for the morrow's sun,
   Lest perdition thee arrest,
   Ere the morrow is begun.
   Thomas Scott, 1773.

463.

1 SINNERS, turn, why will ye die?
   God, your Maker, asks you why;
   God, who did your being give,
   Made you with himself to live,

2 He the fatal cause demands,
   Asks the work of his own hands,
   Why, ye thankless creatures, why
   Will ye cross his love, and die?

3 Sinners, turn, why will ye die?
   God, your Saviour, asks you why;
   God who did your souls retrieve,
   Died himself that ye might live;

4 Will you let him die in vain?
   Crucify your Lord again;
   Why, ye ransomed sinners, why
   Will you slight his grace, and die?

5 Sinners, turn, why will ye die?
   God, the Spirit, asks you why;
   He, who all your lives hath strove,
   Wooed you to embrace his love:

6 Will you not his grace receive?
   Will you still refuse to live?
   Why, ye long-sought sinners, why
   Will you grieve your God, and die?
   Charles Wesley, 1756.

464.

1 SOVEREIGN Ruler, Lord of all,
   Prostrate at thy feet I fall;
   Hear, oh, hear my earnest cry;
   Frown not, lest I faint and die.

2 Vilest of the sons of men,
   Chief of sinners I have been;
   Oft have sinned before thy face,
   Trampled on thy richest grace.

3 Justly might thy fatal dart
   Pierce this bleeding, broken heart;
   Justly might thy angry breath
   Blast me in eternal death.

4 Jesus, save my dying soul;
   Make my broken spirit whole;
   Humbled in the dust I lie;
   Saviour, leave me not to die.
   Thomas Raffles, 1812.

SALVATION,—CALLS.

BETHESDA. H. M.

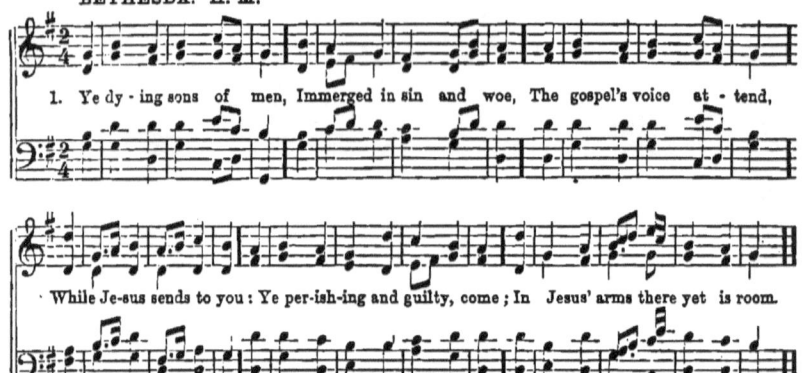

1. Ye dying sons of men, Immerged in sin and woe, The gospel's voice attend, While Jesus sends to you: Ye perishing and guilty, come; In Jesus' arms there yet is room.

465.

1 YE dying sons of men,
  Immerged in sin and woe,
  The gospel's voice attend,
  While Jesus sends to you:
  Ye perishing and guilty, come;
  In Jesus' arms there yet is room.

2 No longer now delay,
  Nor vain excuses frame;
  He bids you come to-day,
  Though poor, and blind, and lame:
  All things are ready; sinner, come;
  For every trembling soul there's room.

3 Believe the heavenly word
  His messengers proclaim;
  He is a gracious Lord,
  And faithful is his name:
  Backsliding souls, return and come;
  Cast off despair; there yet is room.

4 Compelled by bleeding love,
  Ye wandering sheep, draw near;
  Christ calls you from above;
  His charming accents hear:
  Let whosoever will now come,
  In Mercy's breast there still is room.
  James Boden, 1777.

466.

1 COME, my fond, fluttering heart,
  Come, struggle to be free;

Thou and the world must part,
  However hard it be;
  My trembling spirit owns it just,
  But cleaves yet closer to the dust.

2 Ye tempting sweets, forbear;
  Ye dearest idols, fall;
  My love ye must not share,
  Jesus shall have it all:
  'T is bitter pain, 't is cruel smart,
  But, ah! thou must consent, my heart!

3 Ye fair, enchanting throng,
  Ye golden dreams, farewell!
  Earth has prevailed too long,
  And now I break the spell:
  Farewell, ye joys of earthly years!
  Jesus! forgive these parting tears.

4 In Gilead there is balm,
  A kind Physician there,
  My fevered mind to calm,
  And bid me not despair:
  Aid me, dear Saviour! set me free;
  My all I would resign to thee.

5 Oh! may I feel thy worth,
  And let no idol dare,
  No vanity of earth,
  With thee, my Lord, compare;
  Now bid all worldly joys depart,
  And reign supremely in my heart.
  Jane Taylor, 1812.

SALVATION,—CALLS.

CLARENDON STREET. 7s.

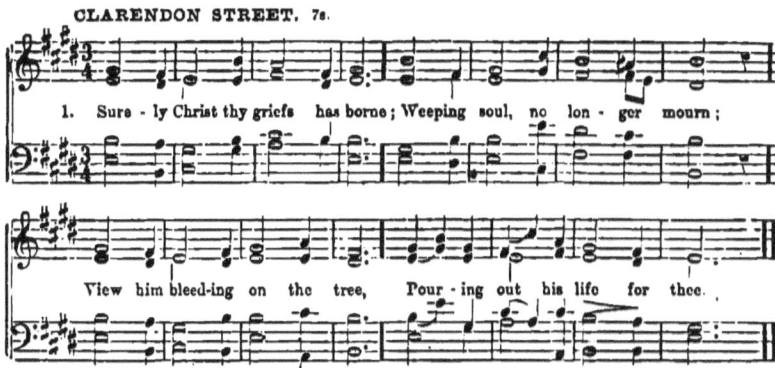

1. Sure-ly Christ thy griefs has borne; Weeping soul, no lon-ger mourn;
View him bleed-ing on the tree, Pour-ing out his life for thee.

467.

1 Surely Christ thy griefs has borne;
Weeping soul, no longer mourn;
View him bleeding on the tree,
Pouring out his life for thee.

2 Weary sinner, keep thine eyes
On the atoning Sacrifice;
There the Incarnate Deity
Numbered with transgressors see.

3 Cast thy guilty soul on him,
Find him mighty to redeem;
At his feet thy burden lay,
Look thy doubts and cares away.

4 Lord, thine arm must be revealed,
Ere I can by faith be healed;
Since I scarce can look to thee,
Cast a gracious eye on me.
A. M. Toplady, 1770.

468.

1 Lord, a better heart bestow;
Hear a sinner's broken prayer;
Full of weariness and woe,
To thy mercies I repair.

2 Once I thought I could amend
All the evil of my ways,
To thy throne my steps could bend,
Do thy will and gain thy praise.

3 But in vain I toiled and prayed,
Still I did but sin the more,
All the efforts that I made
Left me weaker than before.

4 Now I find no hand but one
Can deliver me from guilt;
On the merits of thy Son
All my confidence is built.

5 Ruined, helpless, and forlorn,
To the Saviour's cross I flee;
Oh, since Christ my sins hath borne,
Let my burdened soul go free.
W. H. Bathurst, 1830.

469.

1 When thy mortal life is fled,
When the death-shades o'er thee spread;
When is finished thy career,
Sinner, where wilt thou appear?

2 When the world has passed away,
When draws near the judgment day,
When the awful trump shall sound,
Say, oh, where wilt thou be found?

3 When the Judge descends in light,
Clothed in majesty and might,
When the wicked quail with fear,
Where, oh, where wilt thou appear?

4 What shall soothe thy bursting heart,
When the saints and thou must part?
When the good with joy are crowned,
Sinner, where wilt thou be found?

5 While the Holy Ghost is nigh,
Quickly to the Saviour fly;
Then shall peace thy spirit cheer;
Then in heaven shalt thou appear.
S. F. Smith, 1832.

SALVATION,—SOUGHT AND FOUND.

DENNIS. S. M.

1. Like Noah's weary dove, That soared the earth around, But not a resting-place above The cheerless waters found;

470.

1 Like Noah's weary dove,
   That soared the earth around,
But not a resting-place above
   The cheerless waters found;

2 Oh cease, my wandering soul,
   On restless wing to roam;
All the wide world, to either pole,
   Has not for thee a home.

3 Behold the ark of God,
   Behold the open door!
Hasten to gain that dear abode,
   And rove, my soul, no more.

4 There safe thou shalt abide,
   There, sweet shall be thy rest,
And every longing satisfied,
   With full salvation blest.
             W. A. Muhlenberg, 1823.

471.

1 Oh where shall rest be found,
   Rest for the weary soul?
'T were vain the ocean's depths to sound,
   Or pierce to either pole.

2 The world can never give
   The bliss for which we sigh;
'T is not the whole of life to live,
   Nor all of death to die.

3 Beyond this vale of tears
   There is a life above,
Unmeasured by the flight of years;
   And all that life is love.

4 There is a death whose pang
   Outlasts the fleeting breath:

Oh what eternal horrors hang
   Around the second death!

5 Lord God of truth and grace,
   Teach us that death to shun;
Lest we be banished from thy face,
   And evermore undone.

6 Here would we end our quest;
   Alone are found in thee,
The life of perfect love, the rest
   Of immortality.
             James Montgomery, 1819.

472.

1 My former hopes are fled,
   My terror now begins;
I feel, alas! that I am dead
   In trespasses and sins.

2 Ah! whither shall I fly?
   I hear the thunder roar;
The law proclaims destruction nigh,
   And vengeance at the door.

3 When I review my ways,
   I dread impending doom;
But sure a friendly whisper says,
   " Flee from the wrath to come."

4 I see, or think I see,
   A glimmering from afar;
A beam of day that shines for me,
   To save me from despair.

5 Forerunner of the sun,
   It marks the pilgrim's way;
I'll gaze upon it while I run,
   And watch the rising day.
             William Cowper, 1779.

SALVATION,—SOUGHT AND FOUND. 197
LEBANON. S. M. DOUBLE.

1. I was a wandering sheep, I did not love the fold, I did not love my Shepherd's voice, I would not be con-trolled; I was a way-ward child, I did not love my home, I did not love my Fa-ther's voice, I loved a-far to roam.

473.
2 The Shepherd sought his sheep,
   The Father sought his child;
They followed me o'er vale and hill,
   O'er deserts waste and wild;
They found me nigh to death,
   Famished, and faint, and lone;
They bound me with the bands of love,
   They saved the wandering one.

3 I was a wandering sheep,
   I would not be controlled;
But now I love the Shepherd's voice,
   I love, I love the fold!
I was a wayward child;
   I once preferred to roam;
But now I love my Father's voice,
   I love, I love his home!
Horatius Bonar, 1857.

474.
1 AH! what avails my strife,
   My wandering to and fro?
Thou hast the words of endless life;
   Ah! whither should I go?

2 Thy condescending grace
   To me did freely move;
It calls me still to seek thy face,
   And stoops to ask my love.

3 And can I yet delay
   My little all to give?
To tear my soul from earth away
   For Jesus to receive?

4 Nay, but I yield, I yield;
   I can hold out no more,
I sink, by dying love compelled,
   And own thee conqueror.
Charles Wesley, 1740.

475.
1 THOU Lord of all above,
   And all below the sky,
Before thy feet I prostrate fall,
   And for thy mercy cry.

2 Forgive my follies past,
   The crimes which I have done;
Oh bid a contrite sinner live,
   Through thy incarnate Son.

3 The burden which I feel,
   Thou only canst remove;
Do thou display thy pardoning grace,
   And thine unbounded love.

4 One gracious look of thine
   Will ease my troubled breast;
Oh, let me know my sins forgiven,
   And I shall then be blest!
Benjamin Beddome, 1818.

SALVATION,—SOUGHT AND FOUND.

COVENTRY. C, M.

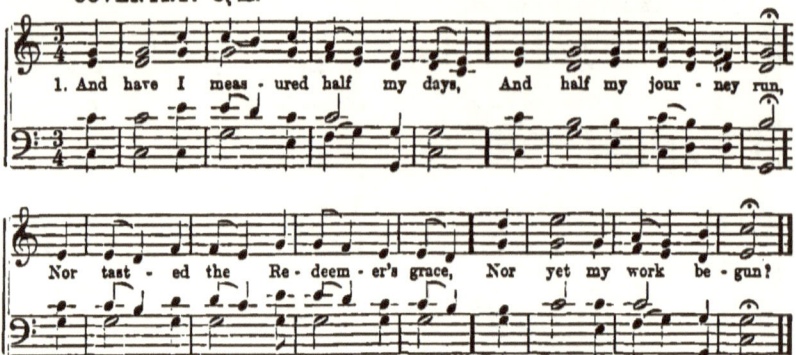

1. And have I measured half my days, And half my journey run, Nor tasted the Redeemer's grace, Nor yet my work begun?

476.

1 And have I measured half my days,
  And half my journey run,
  Nor tasted the Redeemer's grace,
  Nor yet my work begun?

2 The morning of my life is past,
  The noon is almost o'er;
  The night of death approaches fast
  When I can work no more.

3 O'er earth a banished man I rove,
  But cannot feel him nigh;
  Where is the pardoning God of Love,
  Who stooped for me to die?

4 Still every means in vain I try;
  I seek him far and near;
  Where'er I come, constrained to cry,
  "My Saviour is not here."

5 Empty of him, who all things fills,
  Till he his light impart,
  Till he his glorious self reveals,
  The veil is on my heart.

6 O thou, who seest and know'st my grief,
  Thyself unseen, unknown,
  Pity my helpless unbelief,
  And take away the stone.

7 Regard me with a gracious eye,
  The long-sought blessing give;
  And bid me, at the point to die,
  Behold thy face and live.

8 A darker soul did never yet
  Thy promised aid implore;
  Oh that I now my Lord might meet,
  And never lose him more.

  Charles Wesley, 1749.

477.

1 When rising from the bed of death,
  O'erwhelmed with guilt and fear,
  I see my Maker face to face,
  Oh how shall I appear!

2 If yet, while pardon may be found,
  And mercy may be sought,
  My heart with inward horror shrinks,
  And trembles at the thought;

3 When thou, O Lord, shalt stand disclosed
  In majesty severe,
  And sit in judgment on my soul,
  Oh how shall I appear!

4 But thou hast told the troubled soul,
  Who does her sins lament.
  The timely tribute of her tears
  Shall endless woe prevent.

5 Then see my sorrows, gracious Lord!
  Let mercy set me free.
  While in the confidence of prayer
  My heart takes hold of thee.

6 For never shall my soul despair
  Her pardon to procure,
  Who knows thy only Son has died
  To make that pardon sure.

  Joseph Addison, 1719 a.

SALVATION,—SOUGHT AND FOUND.

ARLINGTON. C. M.

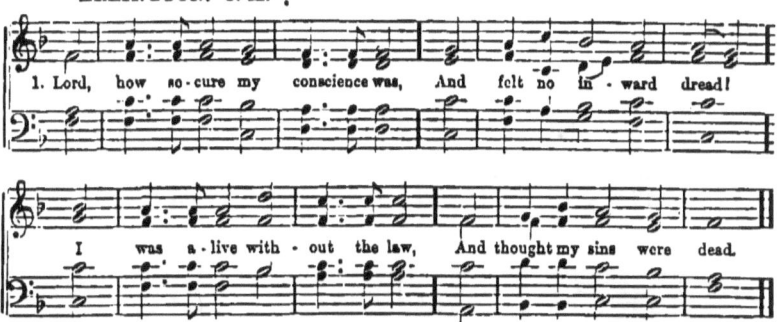

478. Romans vii. 7-13.

1 LORD, how secure my conscience was,
   And felt no inward dread!
   I was alive without the law,
   And thought my sins were dead.

2 My hopes of heaven were firm and bright;
   But since the precept came
   With a convincing power and light,
   I find how vile I am.

3 My guilt appeared but small before,
   Till I with terror saw
   How perfect, holy, just, and pure
   Was thine eternal law.

4 Then felt my soul the heavy load;
   My sins revived again;
   I had provoked a dreadful God,
   And all my hopes were slain.

5 My God! I cry with every breath
   For some kind power to save;
   To break the yoke of sin and death,
   And thus redeem the slave.
              Isaac Watts, 1709.

479.

1 As o'er the past my memory strays,
   Why heaves the secret sigh?
   'T is that I mourn departed days,
   Still unprepared to die.

2 The world and worldly things beloved
   My anxious thoughts employed;
   And time, unhallowed, unimproved,
   Presents a fearful void.

3 Yet, holy Father, wild despair
   Chase from my laboring breast;
   Thy grace it is which prompts the prayer,
   That grace can do the rest.

4 My life's brief remnant all be thine;
   And when thy sure decree
   Bids me this fleeting breath resign,
   Oh, speed my soul to thee.
            Thomas F. Middleton, 1831.

480.

1 ALL that I was, my sin and guilt,
   My death was all mine own;
   All that I am, I owe to thee,
   My gracious God, alone.

2 The evil of my former state
   Was mine, and only mine;
   The good in which I now rejoice
   Is thine, and only thine.

3 The darkness of my former state,
   The bondage, all was mine;
   The light of life in which I walk,
   The liberty, is thine.

4 Thy grace first made me feel my sin,
   It taught me to believe;
   Then, in believing, peace I found;
   And now I live, I live!

5 All that I am, e'en here on earth,
   All that I hope to be,
   When Jesus comes, and glory dawns,
   I owe it, Lord, to thee.
            Horatius Bonar, 1856.

SALVATION,—SOUGHT AND FOUND.

SELBORNE. 7s & 6s.

1. I lay my sins on Jesus, The spotless Lamb of God; He bears them all and frees us From the accursed load: I bring my guilt to

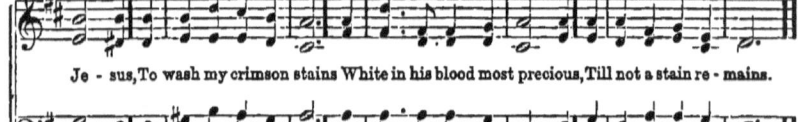

Jesus, To wash my crimson stains White in his blood most precious, Till not a stain remains.

481.

1 I LAY my sins on Jesus,
   The spotless Lamb of God;
He bears them all and frees us
   From the accursèd load;
I bring my guilt to Jesus,
   To wash my crimson stains
White in his blood most precious,
   Till not a stain remains.

2 I lay my wants on Jesus.
   All fulness dwells in him;
He healeth my diseases,
   He doth my soul redeem;
I lay my griefs on Jesus,
   My burdens and my cares;
He from them all releases,
   He all my sorrow shares.

3 I rest my soul on Jesus,
   This weary soul of mine;
His right hand me embraces,
   I on his breast recline.
I love the name of Jesus,
   Immanuel, Christ, the Lord;
Like fragrance on the breezes,
   His name abroad is poured.

4 I long to be like Jesus,
   Meek, loving, lowly, mild;
I long to be like Jesus,
   The Father's holy child;
I long to be with Jesus
   Amid the heavenly throng,
To sing with saints his praises,
   To learn the angels' song.
Horatius Bonar, 1857.

482.

1 How lost was my condition
   Till Jesus made me whole!
There is but one Physician
   Can cure a sin-sick soul;
Next door to death he found me,
   And snatched me from the grave,
To tell to all around me
   His wondrous power to save.

2 A dying, risen Jesus,
   Seen by the eye of faith,
At once from danger frees us,
   And saves the soul from death.
Come, then, to this Physician;
   His help he'll freely give;
He makes no hard condition,
   'T is only, Look and live.
John Newton, 1779.

SALVATION,—SOUGHT AND FOUND.

MOUNT CALVARY. 7s. 6 LINES.

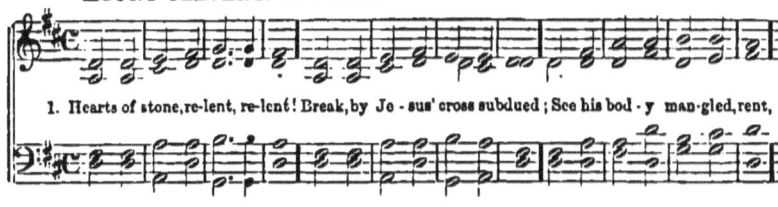

1. Hearts of stone, relent, relent! Break, by Jesus' cross subdued; See his body mangled, rent,

Stain'd and cover'd with his blood! Sinful soul, what hast thou done? Crucified th' eternal Son.

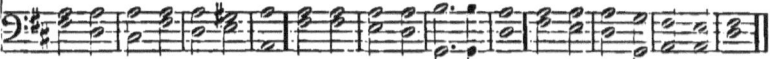

483.

1 Hearts of stone, relent, relent!
   Break, by Jesus' cross subdued;
 See his body mangled, rent,
   Stained and covered with his blood!
 Sinful soul, what hast thou done?
   Crucified th' eternal Son.

2 Yes, thy sins have done the deed:
   Driven the nails that fixed him there,
 Crowned with thorns his sacred head;
   Plunged into his side the spear;
 Made his soul a sacrifice,
   While for sinful man he dies.

3 Wilt thou let him bleed in vain, —
   Still to death thy Lord pursue?
 Open all his wounds again,
   And the shameful cross renew?
 No; with all my sins I'll part, —
   Saviour, take my broken heart.
   John Kruger, 1640; tr. by Charles Wesley.

484.

1 Jesus, Lamb of God, for me,
   Thou, the Lord of life, didst die;
 Whither, whither, but to thee,
   Can a trembling sinner fly!
 Death's dark waters o'er me roll,
 Save, oh, save my sinking soul!

2 Never bowed a martyr's head
   Weighed with equal sorrow down;
 Never blood so rich was shed,
   Never king wore such a crown;
 To thy cross and sacrifice
 Faith now lifts her tearful eyes.

3 All my soul, by love subdued,
   Melts in deep contrition there;
 By thy mighty grace renewed,
   New-born hope forbids despair;
 Lord! thou canst my guilt forgive,
 Thou hast bid me look and live.

4 While with broken heart I kneel
   Sinks the inward storm to rest;
 Life, immortal life, I feel
   Kindled in my throbbing breast!
 Thine, forever thine, I am;
 Glory to the bleeding Lamb!
   Ray Palmer, 1865.

SALVATION,—SOUGHT AND FOUND.

485.

1 JESUS, full of all compassion,
    Hear thy humble suppliant's cry;
    Let me know thy great salvation;
    See, I languish, faint, and die.
    Guilty, but with heart relenting,
    Overwhelmed with helpless grief,
    Prostrate at thy feet repenting,
    Send, oh send me quick relief!

2 Whither should a wretch be flying,
    But to him who comfort gives?
    Whither, from the dread of dying,
    But to him who ever lives?
    While I view thee, wounded, grieving,
    Breathless, on the curséd tree,
    Fain I'd feel my heart believing
    That thou suffer'dst thus for me.

3 Hear, then, blessed Saviour, hear me!
    My soul cleaveth to the dust;
    Send the Comforter to cheer me;
    Lo! in thee I put my trust.
    On the word thy blood hath sealed
    Hangs my everlasting all;
    Let thy arm be now revealed,—
    Stay, oh stay me, lest I fall!

4 In the world of endless ruin,
    Let it never, Lord, be said,
    "Here's a soul that perished suing
    For the boasted Saviour's aid!"

    Saved — the deed shall spread new glory
    Through the shining realms above!
    Angels sing the pleasing story,
    All enraptured with thy love!
Daniel Turner, 1787.

486.

1 LORD, I hear of showers of blessing
    Thou art scattering full and free;
    Showers the thirsty land refreshing;
    Let some droppings fall on me!
    Pass me not, O gracious Father!
    Sinful though my heart may be,
    Thou might'st curse me, but the rather
    Let thy mercy light on me.

2 Pass me not, O tender Saviour!
    Let me love and cling to thee;
    I am longing for thy favor;
    When thou comest, call for me.
    Pass me not, O mighty Spirit!
    Thou canst make the blind to see;
    Witnesser of Jesus' merit,
    Speak the word of power to me.

3 Have I long in sin been sleeping?
    Long been slighting, grieving thee?
    Has the world my heart been keeping?
    Oh! forgive and rescue me!
    Pass me not; this lost one bringing,
    Satan's slave thy child shall be;
    All my heart to thee is springing:
    Blessing others, oh bless me!
Elizabeth Codner, 1860.

SALVATION,—SOUGHT AND FOUND.

AGNUS DEI. 8s & 6s.

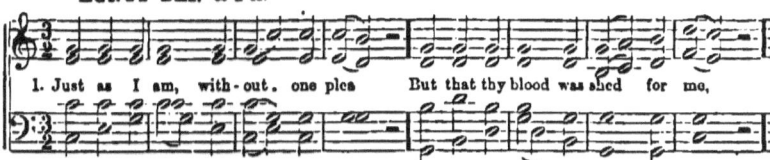
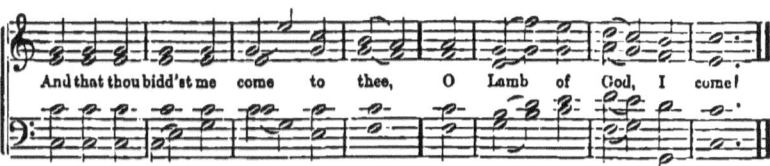

487.

1. Just as I am, without one plea
But that thy blood was shed for me,
And that thou bidd'st me come to thee,
O Lamb of God, I come!

2. Just as I am, and waiting not
To rid my soul of one dark blot, [spot,
To thee, whose blood can cleanse each
O Lamb of God, I come!

3. Just as I am, though tossed about
With many a conflict, many a doubt,
Fightings and fears within, without,
O Lamb of God, I come!

4. Just as I am, poor, wretched, blind,
Sight, riches, healing of the mind,
Yea, all I need, in thee to find,
O Lamb of God, I come!

5. Just as I am, thou wilt receive,
Wilt welcome, pardon, cleanse, relieve!
Because thy promise I believe,
O Lamb of God, I come!

6. Just as I am, thy love unknown
Has broken every barrier down;
Now, to be thine, yea, thine alone,
O Lamb of God, I come!

7. Just as I am, of that free love   [prove,
The breadth, length, depth, and height to
Here for a season, then above,
O Lamb of God, I come!

Charlotte Elliott, 1836.

488.

1. The wanderer no more will roam,
The lost one to the fold hath come,
The prodigal is welcomed home,
O Lamb of God, in thee!

2. Though clothed with shame, by sin defiled,
The Father hath embraced his child,
And I am pardoned, reconciled,
O Lamb of God, in thee!

3. It is the Father's joy to bless,
His love provides for me a dress,
A robe of spotless righteousness,
O Lamb of God, in thee!

4. Now shall my famished soul be fed,
A feast of love for me is spread,
I feed upon the children's bread,
O Lamb of God, in thee!

5. Yea, in the fulness of his grace,
He put me in the children's place,
Where I may gaze upon his face,
O Lamb of God, in thee!

6. I cannot half his love express,
Yet, Lord, with joy my lips confess
This blessed portion I possess,
O Lamb of God, in thee!

7. And when I in thy likeness shine,
The glory and the praise be thine,
That everlasting joy is mine,
O Lamb of God, in thee!

Mary Jane Deck, 1841.

SALVATION,—SOUGHT AND FOUND.

WINDHAM. L. M.

1. Show pi-ty, Lord, O Lord, for-give; Let a re-pent-ing reb-el live; Are not thy mer-cies large and free? May not a sin-ner trust in thee?

489.   Psalm 51.

1 Show pity, Lord, O Lord, forgive;
Let a repenting rebel live;
Are not thy mercies large and free?
May not a sinner trust in thee?

2 My crimes, though great, do not surpass
The power and glory of thy grace;
Great God, thy nature hath no bound,
So let thy pardoning love be found.

3 Oh, wash my soul from every sin,
And make my guilty conscience clean;
Here on my heart the burden lies,
And past offences pain mine eyes.

4 My lips with shame my sins confess,
Against thy law, against thy grace;
Lord, should thy judgment grow severe,
I am condemned, but thou art clear.

5 Should sudden vengeance seize my breath,
I must pronounce thee just in death;
And if my soul were sent to hell,
Thy righteous law approves it well.

6 Yet save a trembling sinner, Lord,
Whose hope, still hovering round thy word,
Would light on some sweet promise there,
Some sure support against despair.
Isaac Watts, 1719.

490.

1 Father! if I may call thee so,
Regard my fearful heart's desire;
Lift up this load of guilty woe,
Nor let me in my sins expire!

2 I tremble, lest the wrath divine,
Which bruises now my sinful soul,
Should bruise this wretched soul of mine
Long as eternal ages roll.

3 I deprecate that death alone,
That endless banishment from thee!
Oh, save, and give me to thy Son,
Who trembled, wept, and bled for me!
Charles Wesley, 1740.

491.

1 With broken heart and contrite sigh,
A trembling sinner, Lord, I cry;
Thy pardoning grace is rich and free,—
O God, be merciful to me!

2 I smite upon my troubled breast,
With deep and conscious guilt oppressed,
Christ and his cross my only plea;
O God, be merciful to me!

3 Far off I stand with tearful eyes,
Nor dare uplift them to the skies;
But thou dost all my anguish see;
O God, be merciful to me!

4 Nor alms, nor deeds that I have done,
Can for a single sin atone;
To Calvary alone I flee;
O God, be merciful to me!

5 And when, redeemed from sin and hell,
With all the ransomed throng I dwell,
My raptured song shall ever be,
God has been merciful to me!
Cornelius Elven, 1852.

SALVATION,—SOUGHT AND FOUND.

GRACE CHURCH. L. M.

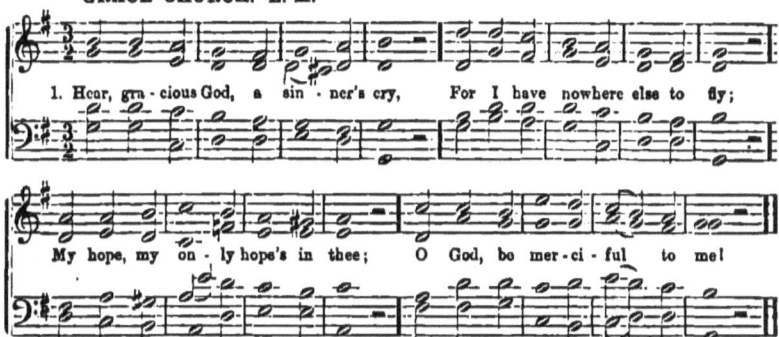

1. Hear, gracious God, a sinner's cry, For I have nowhere else to fly; My hope, my only hope's in thee; O God, be merciful to me!

492.

1 HEAR, gracious God, a sinner's cry,
For I have nowhere else to fly;
My hope, my only hope's in thee;
O God, be merciful to me!

2 To thee I come, a sinner poor,
And wait for mercy at thy door;
Indeed, I've nowhere else to flee;
O God, be merciful to me!

3 To thee I come, a sinner weak,
And scarce know how to pray or speak;
From fear and weakness set me free;
O God, be merciful to me!

4 To thee I come a sinner vile;
Upon me, Lord, vouchsafe to smile!
Mercy alone I make my plea;
O God, be merciful to me!

5 To thee I come, a sinner great,
And well thou knowest all my state;
Yet full forgiveness is with thee;
O God, be merciful to me!

6 To thee I come, a sinner lost,
Nor have I aught wherein to trust;
But where thou art, Lord, I would be;
O God, be merciful to me!

7 To glory bring me, Lord, at last;
And there, when all my fears are past,
With all the saints I'll then agree,
God has been merciful to me!

Samuel Medley, 1789.

493. PSALM 51.

1 O THOU who hear'st when sinners cry,
Though all my crimes before thee lie,
Behold them not with angry look,
But blot their memory from thy book.

2 Create my nature pure within,
And form my soul averse to sin;
Let thy good Spirit ne'er depart,
Nor hide thy presence from my heart.

3 A broken heart, my God, my King,
Is all the sacrifice I bring;
The God of grace will ne'er despise
A broken heart for sacrifice.

4 My soul is humbled in the dust,
And owns thy dreadful sentence just;
Look down, O Lord, with pitying eye,
And save the soul condemned to die.

5 Then will I teach the world thy ways;
Sinners shall learn thy sovereign grace;
I'll lead them to my Saviour's blood,
And they shall praise a pardoning God.

6 Oh, may thy love inspire my tongue!
Salvation shall be all my song;
And all my powers shall join to bless
The Lord, my strength and righteousness.

Isaac Watts, 1719.

DOXOLOGY.

Now to the Father, to the Son,
And to the Spirit, Three in One,
Be praise and thanks and glory given
By men on earth, by saints in heaven.

John Henry Newman, 1842.

SALVATION,—SOUGHT AND FOUND.

FEDERAL STREET. L. M.

1. I left the God of truth and light, I left the God who gave me breath, To wander in the wilds of night, And perish in the snares of death!

494.

1 I LEFT the God of truth and light,
  I left the God who gave me breath,
  To wander in the wilds of night,
  And perish in the snares of death!

2 Sweet was his service, and his yoke
  Was light and easy to be borne,—
  Through all his bonds of love I broke;
  I cast away his gifts with scorn!

3 Heart-broken, friendless, poor, cast down,
  Where shall the chief of sinners fly,
  Almighty Vengeance! from thy frown,
  Eternal Justice! from thy eye?

4 Lo! through the gloom of guilty fears,
  My faith discerns a dawn of grace;
  The Sun of Righteousness appears
  In Jesus' reconciling face!

5 Prostrate before the mercy-seat,
  I dare not, if I would, despair;
  None ever perished at thy feet,
  And I will lie forever there.
  James Montgomery, 1809.

495.

1 No more, my God, I boast no more
  Of all the duties I have done;
  I quit the hopes I held before,
  To trust the merits of thy Son.

2 Now, for the love I bear his name,
  What was my gain I count my loss;
  My former pride I call my shame,
  And nail my glory to his cross.

3 Yes, and I must and will esteem
  All things but loss for Jesus' sake;
  Oh may my soul be found in him,
  And of his righteousness partake!

4 The best obedience of my hands
  Dares not appear before thy throne;
  But faith can answer thy demands,
  By pleading what my Lord has done.
  Isaac Watts, 1709.

496.

1 JESUS, my Lord, my life, my all!
  Prostrate before thy throne I fall;
  Fain would my soul look up and see
  My hope, my heaven, my all in thee.

2 Here in this world of sin and woe
  I'm filled with tossings to and fro,
  Burdened with sin, with fear oppressed,
  And nothing here can give me rest.

3 Oh speak, and bid my soul rejoice;
  I long to hear thy pardoning voice
  Say, " Peace, be still! look up and live;
  Life, peace, and heaven are mine to give."

4 Without thy peace and presence, Lord,
  Not all the world can help afford;
  Oh, do not frown my soul away,
  Lord, smile my darkness into day.

5 Then, filled with grateful, holy love,
  My soul in praise shall soar above,
  And with delightful joy record
  The wondrous goodness of my Lord.
  Samuel Medley, 1789.

SALVATION,—SOUGHT AND FOUND. 207

BERA. L. M.

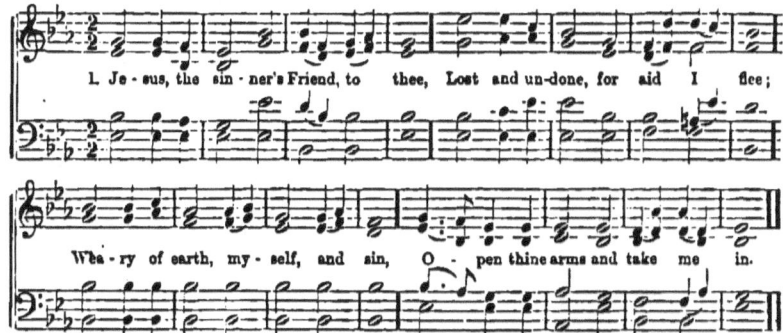

1. Jesus, the sinner's Friend, to thee, Lost and undone, for aid I flee; Weary of earth, myself, and sin, Open thine arms and take me in.

497.

1 JESUS, the sinner's Friend, to thee,
Lost and undone, for aid I flee;
Weary of earth, myself, and sin,
Open thine arms and take me in.

2 Pity and heal my sin-sick soul;
'T is thou alone canst make me whole;
Fall'n, till in me thine image shine,
And lost I am, till thou art mine.

3 Long have I vainly hoped and strove
To force my hardness into love,
To give thee all thy laws require,
And labored in the purging fire.

4 Frail, dark, impure, I still remain,
Nor hope to break my nature's chain;
The fond, self-emptying scheme is past,
And lo! constrained, I yield at last.

5 At last I own it cannot be
That I should fit myself for thee;
Here, then, to thee I all resign, —
Thine is the work, and only thine.

6 What can I say thy grace to move?
Lord, I am sin, but thou art love;
I give up every plea beside,
Lord, I am lost, but thou hast died!
Charles Wesley, 1739.

498.

1 BENEATH thy cross I lay me down,
And mourn to see thy bloody crown;
Love drops in blood from every vein,
Love is the spring of all his pain.

2 Here, Jesus, I shall ever stay,
And spend my longing hours away,
Think on thy bleeding wounds and pain,
And contemplate thy woes again.

3 The rage of Satan and of sin,
Of foes without and fears within,
Shall ne'er my conquering soul remove
Or from thy cross, or from thy love.

4 O unmolested, happy rest!
Where inward fears are all suppressed;
Here I shall love, and live secure,
And patiently my cross endure.
William Williams, 1772.

499.

1 HERE, at thy cross, my dying God,
I lay my soul beneath thy love,
Beneath the droppings of thy blood,
Jesus, nor shall it e'er remove.

2 Should worlds conspire to drive me hence,
Moveless and firm this heart should lie;
Resolved, for that's my last defence,
If I must perish, here to die.

3 But speak, my Lord, and calm my fear;
Am I not safe beneath thy shade?
Thy vengeance will not strike me here,
Nor Satan dares my soul invade.

4 Yes, I'm secure beneath thy blood,
And all my foes shall lose their aim;
Hosanna to my dying God,
And my best honors to his name!
Isaac Watts, 1709.

SALVATION,—SOUGHT AND FOUND.

ZALENA. C. P. M.

500.

1 O THOU that hear'st the prayer of faith,
   Wilt thou not save a soul from death
   That casts itself on thee?
   I have no refuge of my own,
   But fly to what my Lord hath done
   And suffered once for me.

2 Slain in the guilty sinner's stead,
   His spotless righteousness I plead
   And his availing blood:
   Thy merit, Lord, my robe shall be,
   Thy merit shall atone for me,
   And bring me near to God.

3 Then save me from eternal death,
   The Spirit of adoption breathe,
   His consolations send;
   By him some word of life impart,
   And sweetly whisper to my heart,
   "Thy Maker is thy friend."

4 The king of terrors then would be
   A welcome messenger to me,
   To bid me come away;
   Unclogged by earth or earthly things,
   I'd mount upon his sable wings
   To everlasting day.

   A. M. Toplady, 1776.

501.

1 LORD, thou hast won, at length I yield;
   My heart, by mighty grace compelled,
   Surrenders all to thee:
   Against thy terrors long I strove,
   But who can stand against thy love?
   Love conquers even me.

2 Yes, since thou hast thy love revealed,
   And shown my soul a pardon sealed,
   I can resist no more;
   Couldst thou for such a sinner bleed?
   Canst thou for such a rebel plead?
   I wonder and adore!

3 If thou hadst bid thy thunders roll,
   And lightnings flash to blast my soul,
   I still had stubborn been;
   But mercy has my heart subdued,
   A bleeding Saviour I have viewed,
   And now I hate my sin.

4 Now, Lord, I would be thine alone,
   Come, take possession of thine own,
   For thou hast set me free;
   Released from Satan's hard command,
   See all my powers in waiting stand,
   To be employed by thee.

   John Newton, 1779.

SALVATION,—SOUGHT AND FOUND.

HABAKKUK. C. P. M.

1. Author of faith, to thee I cry, To thee, who wouldst not have me die, But know the truth and live: O - pen mine eyes to see thy face; Work in my heart the sav-ing grace; The life e-ter-nal give.

502.

2 Shut up in unbelief, I groan,
And blindly serve a God unknown,
Till thou the veil remove;
The gift unspeakable impart,
And write thy name upon my heart,
And manifest thy love.

3 I know the work is only thine;
The gift of faith is all divine;
But if on thee we call,
Thou wilt the benefit bestow,
And give us hearts to feel and know
That thou hast died for all.

4 Thou bidd'st us knock and enter in,
Come unto thee, and rest from sin,
The blessing seek and find:
Thou bidd'st us ask thy grace, and have;
Thou canst, thou wouldst, this moment
Both me and all mankind. [save

5 Be it according to thy word;
Now let me find my pardoning Lord;
Let what I ask be given:
The bar of unbelief remove;
Open the door of faith and love,
And take me into heaven.

Charles Wesley, 1749.

503.

1 Lo! on a narrow neck of land,
'Twixt two unbounded seas, I stand,
Secure, insensible!
A point of time, a moment's space.
Removes me to yon heavenly place,
Or shuts me up in hell.

2 O God, mine inmost soul convert,
And deeply on my thoughtful heart
Eternal things impress;
Give me to feel their solemn weight,
And tremble on the brink of fate,
And wake to righteousness.

3 Before me place, in dread array,
The pomp of that tremendous day
When thou with clouds shalt come
To judge the nations at thy bar;
And tell me, Lord, shall I be there
To meet a joyful doom?

4 Then, Saviour, then my soul receive,
Transported from this vale, to live
And reign with thee above,
Where faith is sweetly lost in sight,
And hope in full, supreme delight,
And everlasting love.

Charles Wesley, 1749.

SALVATION,—SOUGHT AND FOUND.

ERNAN. L. M.

1. Oh, sweetly breathe the lyres a-bove, When an-gels touch the quiv-ering string, And wake, to chant Im-man-uel's love, Such strains as an-gel-lips can sing!

504.

1 Oh, sweetly breathe the lyres above,
  When angels touch the quivering string,
And wake, to chant Immanuel's love,
  Such strains as angel-lips can sing!

2 And sweet, on earth, the choral swell,
  From mortal tongues, of gladsome lays,
When pardoned souls their raptures tell,
  And, grateful, hymn Immanuel's praise.

3 Jesus, thy name our souls adore;
  We own the bond that makes us thine;
And carnal joys, that charmed before,
  For thy dear sake we now resign.

4 Our hearts, by dying love subdued,
  Accept thine offered grace to-day;
Beneath the cross, with blood bedewed,
  We bow, and give ourselves away.

5 In thee we trust, on thee we rely;
  Though we are feeble, thou art strong;
Oh, keep us till our spirits fly
  To join the bright, immortal throng!

Ray Palmer, 1858.

505.

1 TREMBLING before thine awful throne,
  O Lord! in dust my sins I own:
Justice and mercy for my life
  Contend; oh, smile and heal the strife!

2 The Saviour smiles, upon my soul
  New tides of hope tumultuous roll;
His voice proclaims my pardon found;
  Seraphic transport wings the sound.

3 Earth has a joy unknown in heaven,
  The new-born peace of sin forgiven;
Tears of such pure and deep delight,
  Ye angels, never dimmed your sight.

4 But I amid your choirs shall shine,
  And all your knowledge will be mine:
Ye on your harps must lean to hear
  A secret chord that mine will bear.

Augustus L. Hillhouse, 1816.

506.

1 To God, my Saviour and my King,
  Fain would my soul her tribute bring;
Join me, ye saints, in songs of praise,
  For ye have known and felt his grace.

2 Wretched and helpless once I lay,
  Just breathing all my life away;
He saw me weltering in my blood,
  And felt the pity of a God.

3 With speed he flew to my relief, [grief,
  Bound up my wounds and soothed my
Poured joy divine into my heart,
  And bade each anxious fear depart.

4 These proofs of love, my dearest Lord,
  Deep in my breast I will record:
The life which I from thee receive,
  To thee, behold, I freely give.

5 My heart and tongue shall tune thy praise
  Through the remainder of my days;
And when I join the powers above,
  My soul shall better sing thy love.

Samuel Stennett, 1778.

507. L. M.

1 LORD, didst thou die, but not for me?
   Am I forbid to trust thy blood?
   Hast thou not pardons, rich and free,
   And grace, an overwhelming flood?

2 Who, then, shall drive my trembling soul
   From thee, to regions of despair?
   Who has surveyed the sacred roll,
   And found my name not written there?

3 Presumptuous thought! to fix the bound,
   To limit mercy's sovereign reign:
   What other happy souls have found,
   I'll seek; nor shall I seek in vain.

4 I own my guilt; my sins confess;
   Can men or devils make them more?
   Of crimes already numberless,
   Vain the attempt to swell the score.

5 Were the black list before my sight,
   While I remember thou hast died,
   'T would only urge my speedier flight,
   To seek salvation at thy side.

6 Low at thy feet I'll cast me down,
   To thee reveal my guilt and fear;
   And, if thou spurn me from thy throne,
   I'll be the first who perished there.
        Rippon's Selection, 1787.

508. L. M.

1 I SEND the joys of earth away;
   Away, ye tempters of the mind,
   False as the smooth, deceitful sea,
   And empty as the whistling wind!

2 Your streams were floating me along,
   Down to the gulf of black despair;
   And while I listened to your song,
   Your streams had e'en conveyed me there.

3 Lord, I adore thy matchless grace,
   Which warned me of that dark abyss,
   Which drew me from those treacherous seas,
   And bade me seek superior bliss.

4 Now to the shining realms above
   I stretch my hands and glance my eyes;
   Oh for the pinions of a dove,
   To bear me to the upper skies!

5 There, from the bosom of my God,
   Oceans of endless pleasure roll;
   There would I fix my last abode,
   And drown the sorrows of my soul!
        Isaac Watts, 1709.

509. L. M.

1 OH, happy day, that fixed my choice
   On thee, my Saviour, and my God!
   Well may this glowing heart rejoice,
   And tell its raptures all abroad.

2 Oh, happy bond, that seals my vows
   To him who merits all my love!
   Let cheerful anthems fill his house,
   While to that sacred shrine I move.

3 'T is done, the great transaction's done.
   I am my Lord's, and he is mine:
   He drew me, and I followed on,
   Charmed to confess the voice divine.

4 Now, rest, my long-divided heart;
   Fixed on this blissful centre, rest;
   With ashes who would grudge to part,
   When called on angel's bread to feast?

5 High Heaven, that heard the solemn vow,
   That vow renewed shall daily hear;
   Till in life's latest hour I bow,
   And bless in death a bond so dear.
        Philip Doddridge, 1755.

510. L. M.

1 LORD, I am thine, entirely thine,
   Purchased and saved by blood divine;
   With full consent thine I would be,
   And own thy sovereign right in me.

2 Grant one poor sinner more a place
   Among the children of thy grace;
   A wretched sinner, lost to God,
   But ransomed by Immanuel's blood.

3 Thine would I live, thine would I die,
   Be thine through all eternity;
   The vow is passed beyond repeal;
   And now I set the solemn seal.

4 Here at that cross where flows the blood
   That bought my guilty soul for God,
   Thee my new Master now I call,
   And consecrate to thee my all.

5 Do thou assist a feeble worm
   The great engagement to perform;
   Thy grace can full assistance lend,
   And on that grace I dare depend.
        Samuel Davies, 1760.

212. SALVATION,—SOUGHT AND FOUND.

AVON. C. M.

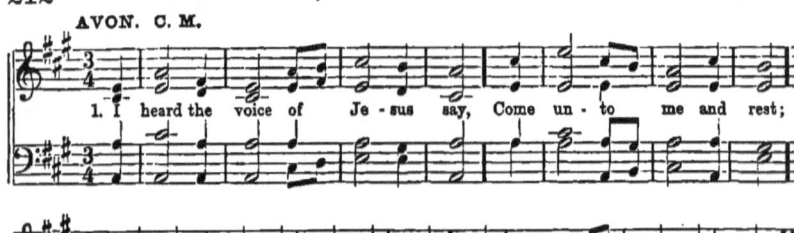
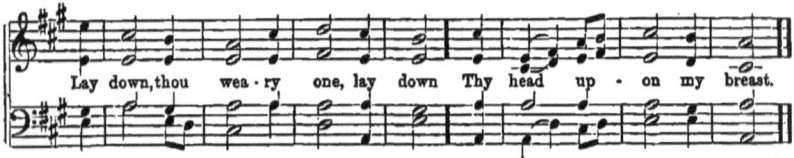

1. I heard the voice of Jesus say, Come unto me and rest;
Lay down, thou weary one, lay down Thy head upon my breast.

511.

1 I HEARD the voice of Jesus say,
"Come unto me and rest;
Lay down, thou weary one, lay down
Thy head upon my breast."

2 I came to Jesus as I was,
Weary, and worn, and sad;
I found in him a resting-place,
And he has made me glad.

3 I heard the voice of Jesus say,
"Behold, I freely give
The living water; thirsty one,
Stoop down, and drink, and live."

4 I came to Jesus, and I drank
Of that life-giving stream;
My thirst was quenched, my soul revived,
And now I live in him.

5 I heard the voice of Jesus say,
"I am this dark world's Light;
Look unto me, thy morn shall rise,
And all thy day be bright."

6 I looked to Jesus, and I found
In him my Star, my Sun;
And in that light of life I'll walk
Till travelling days are done.
Horatius Bonar, 1857.

512.   PSALM 126.

1 WHEN God revealed his gracious name,
And changed my mournful state,
My rapture seemed a pleasing dream,
The grace appeared so great.

2 The world beheld the glorious change,
And did thy hand confess;
My tongue broke out in unknown strains,
And sung surprising grace.

3 "Great is the work," my neighbors cried,
And owned thy power divine;
"Great is the work," my heart replied,
"And be the glory thine."

4 The Lord can clear the darkest skies,
Can give us day for night;
Make drops of sacred sorrow rise
To rivers of delight.

5 Let those that sow in sadness wait
Till the fair harvest come;
They shall confess their sheaves are great,
And shout the blessings home.
Isaac Watts, 1719.

513.   Tune, "Ernan," p. 210.   L. M.

1 WHO can describe the joys that rise
Through all the courts of paradise,
To see a prodigal return,
To see an heir of glory born!

2 With joy the Father doth approve
The fruit of his eternal love;
The Son with joy looks down and sees
The purchase of his agonies.

3 The Spirit takes delight to view
The holy soul he formed anew;
And saints and angels join to sing
The growing empire of their King.
Isaac Watts, 1709.

THE CHRISTIAN LIFE,—UNION WITH CHRIST.

ST. THOMAS. S. M.

1. Who can forbear to sing, Who can refuse to praise, When Zion's high, celestial King His saving power displays?—

514.

1 Who can forbear to sing,
 Who can refuse to praise,
When Zion's high, celestial King
 His saving power displays? —

2 When sinners at his feet,
 By mercy conquered, fall?
When grace, and truth, and justice meet,
 And peace unites them all?

3 When heaven's opening gates
 Invite the pilgrims feet;
And Jesus at their entrance waits,
 To place them on his seat?

4 Who can forbear to praise
 Our high, celestial King,
When sovereign, rich, redeeming grace
 Invites our tongues to sing?
  Joseph Swain, 1792.

515. THE CHRISTIAN LIFE.

1 Dear Saviour! I am thine,
 By everlasting bands ;
My name, my heart, I would resign ;
 My soul is in thy hands.

2 To thee I still would cleave
 With ever growing zeal ;
Let millions tempt me Christ to leave,
 They never shall prevail!

3 His Spirit shall unite
 My soul to him, my head ;
Shall form me to his image bright,
 And teach his paths to tread.

4 Death may my soul divide
 From this abode of clay ;
But love shall keep me near his side,
 Through all the gloomy way.

5 Since Christ and we are one,
 What should remain to fear ?
If he in heaven has fixed his throne,
 He'll fix his members there.
  Philip Doddridge, 1755.

516. 1 John L 3.

1 Our heavenly Father calls,
 And Christ invites us near ;
With both our friendship shall be sweet,
 And our communion dear.

2 God pities all our griefs ;
 He pardons every day,
Almighty to protect our souls,
 And wise to guide our way.

3 How large his bounties are!
 What various stores of good,
Diffused from our Redeemer's hand.
 And purchased with his blood !

4 Jesus, our living Head,
 We bless thy faithful care,
Our Advocate before the throne,
 And our Forerunner there.

5 Here fix, my roving heart ;
 Here wait, my warmest love ;
Till the communion be complete,
 In nobler scenes above.
  Philip Doddridge, 1755.

THE CHRISTIAN LIFE,—UNION WITH CHRIST.

WIRTH. C. M.

1. Lord Jesus, are we one with thee? Oh height! oh depth of love! With thee we died upon the tree, In thee we live above.

517.

1 Lord Jesus, are we one with thee?
  Oh height! oh depth of love!
  With thee we died upon the tree,
  In thee we live above.

2 Such was thy grace, that for our sake
  Thou didst from heaven come down,
  Thou didst of flesh and blood partake,
  In all our sorrows one.

3 Our sins, our guilt, in love divine,
  Confessed and borne by thee;
  The gall, the curse, the wrath were thine,
  To set thy members free.

4 Ascended now, in glory bright,
  Still one with us thou art;
  Nor life, nor death, nor depth, nor height,
  Thy saints and thee can part.

5 Oh, teach us, Lord, to know and own
  This wondrous mystery,
  That thou with us art truly one,
  And we are one with thee!

6 Soon, soon shall come that glorious day,
  When, seated on thy throne,
  Thou shalt to wondering worlds display,
  That thou with us art one.
  James G. Deck, 1837.

518.

1 Lord, in thy people dost thou dwell,
  And do they dwell in thee?
  Oh blessedness unspeakable!
  Oh wondrous unity!

2 One with thee, all thy life they know,
  And all thou hast possess;
  In thee they underwent all woe,
  And wrought all righteousness.

3 One with them still thou walkest here,
  And all their life dost know;
  When they are glad, thou makest cheer;
  Thou weepest in their woe.

4 When Satan tempts thy people sore,
  Again he tempteth thee;
  And when he flees from them, once more
  Thou makest him to flee.

5 In every gift and grace of theirs,
  Thy beauty, Lord, doth shine;
  Their faithfulness thine own declares;
  Their righteousness is thine.

6 When thou thy kingdom shalt obtain,
  And put thy glory on,
  Thine endless reign shall be their reign:
  The King and they are one.

7 Lord Jesus, grant me all this grace;
  Abide, be one with me;
  Give me to dwell in thine embrace,
  Forever one with thee!
  T. H. Gill, 1860.

DOXOLOGY.

Praise to the Father, as is meet,
Praise to the only Son,
Praise to the Holy Paraclete,
While endless ages run.
J. H. Newman, 1836.

THE CHRISTIAN LIFE,—UNION WITH CHRIST.

BURLINGTON. C. M.

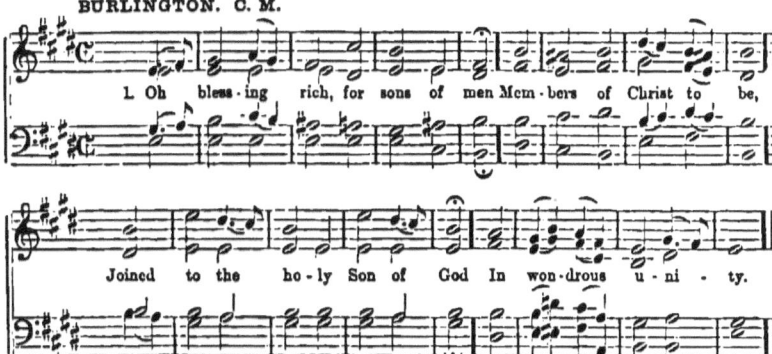

1. Oh bless-ing rich, for sons of men Mem-bers of Christ to be, Joined to the ho-ly Son of God In won-drous u-ni-ty.

519.

1 O BLESSING rich, for sons of men
  Members of Christ to be,
  Joined to the holy Son of God
  In wondrous unity.

2 O Jesus, our great Head divine,
  From whom most freely flow
  The streams of life and strength and
  To all the frame below :   [warmth

3 Keep us as members sound and whole
  Within thy body true;
  Build us into a temple fair,
  Meet stones in order due.

4 Keep us good branches of thy vine,
  Large store of fruit to yield;
  Keep us as sheep that wander not
  From thy most pleasant field.

5 For one with God, O Jesus blest,
  We are, when one with thee,
  With saints on earth and saints at rest
  A glorious company.
  Hymnologia Christiana, 1863.

520.

1 JESUS, immutably the same,
  Thou true and living Vine,
  Around thy all-supporting stem
  My feeble arms I twine.

2 Quickened by thee, and kept alive,
  I flourish and bear fruit;
  My life I from thy sap derive,
  My vigor from thy root.

3 I can do nothing without thee;
  My strength is wholly thine;

Withered and barren should I be,
  If severed from the Vine.

4 Upon my leaf, when parched with heat,
  Refreshing dew shall drop;
  The plant which thy right hand hath set,
  Shall ne'er be rooted up.

5 Each moment watered by thy care,
  And fenced with power divine,
  Fruit to eternal life shall bear
  The feeblest branch of thine.
  Augustus M. Toplady, 1771.

521.

1 JESUS, I sing thy matchless grace,
  That calls a worm thy own;
  Gives me among thy saints a place
  To make thy glories known.

2 Allied to thee, our vital Head,
  We act, and grow, and thrive;
  From thee divided, each is dead
  When most he seems alive.

3 Thy saints on earth and those above
  Here join in sweet accord;
  One body all in mutual love,
  And thou our common Lord.

4 Oh, may my faith each hour derive
  Thy Spirit with delight;
  While death and hell in vain shall strive
  This bond to disunite.

5 Thou the whole body wilt present
  Before thy Father's face,
  Nor shall a wrinkle or a spot
  Its beauteous form disgrace.
  Philip Doddridge, 1755.

216 THE CHRISTIAN LIFE,—UNION WITH CHRIST.

ELIZABETHTOWN. C. M.

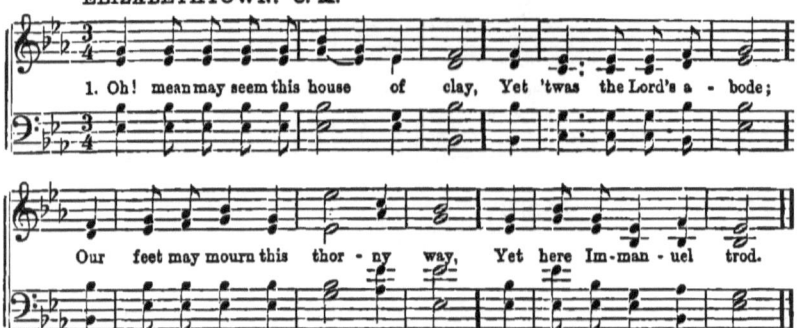

522.

1 Oh! mean may seem this house of clay,
  Yet 'twas the Lord's abode;
  Our feet may mourn this thorny way,
  Yet here Immanuel trod.

2 This fleshly robe the Lord did wear;
  This watch the Lord did keep;
  These burdens sore the Lord did bear;
  These tears the Lord did weep!

3 Our very frailty brings us near
  Unto the Lord of heaven;
  To every grief, to every tear,
  Such glory strange is given.

4 But not this fleshly robe alone
  Shall link us, Lord, to thee;
  Nor always in the tear and groan
  Shall the dear kindred be.

5 We shall be reckoned for thine own,
  Because thy heaven we share;
  Because we sing around thy throne,
  And thy bright raiment wear.

6 Oh, mighty grace! our life to live,
  To make our earth divine;
  Oh, mighty grace! thy heaven to give,
  And lift our life to thine!
  T. H. Gill, 1860.

523.

1 Compared with Christ, in all beside
  No comeliness I see;

  The one thing needful, dearest Lord,
  Is to be one with thee.

2 The sense of thy expiring love
  Into my soul convey;
  Thyself bestow: for thee alone
  I absolutely pray.

3 Whatever else thy will withholds,
  Here grant me to succeed:
  Oh let thyself my portion be,
  And I am blest indeed!

4 Less than thyself will not suffice
  My comfort to restore;
  More than thyself I cannot have,
  And thou canst give no more.

5 Loved of my God, for him again
  With love intense I burn;
  Chosen of thee ere time began,
  I choose thee in return.

6 Whate'er consists not with thy love,
  Oh teach me to resign;
  I'm rich to all th' intents of bliss,
  If thou, O God, art mine!
  Augustus M. Toplady, 1772.

DOXOLOGY.

Honor and glory, power and praise,
  To Father and to Son,
And Holy Ghost, be paid always,
  The Eternal Three in One.
  J. H. Newman, 1840.

EMMAUS. L. M.

1. Jesus, thou joy of loving hearts, Thou fount of life, thou Light of men! From the best bliss that earth imparts, We turn unfilled to thee again.

524.

1 JESUS, thou joy of loving hearts,
 Thou fount of life! thou light of men!
 From the best bliss that earth imparts,
 We turn unfilled to thee again.

2 Thy truth unchanged hath ever stood;
 Thou savest those that on thee call;
 To them that seek thee, thou art good,
 To them that find thee, All in All!

3 We taste thee, O thou Living Bread,
 And long to feast upon thee still;
 We drink of thee, the Fountain Head,
 And thirst our souls from thee to fill!

4 Our restless spirits yearn for thee,
 Where'er our changeful lot is cast;
 Glad, when thy gracious smile we see,
 Blest, when our faith can hold thee fast.

5 O Jesus, ever with us stay;
 Make all our moments calm and bright;
 Chase the dark night of sin away,
 Shed o'er the world thy holy light!
 Bernard of Clairvaux; tr. by Ray Palmer, 1858.

525.

1 WHEN sins and fears prevailing rise,
 And fainting hope almost expires,
 Jesus, to thee I lift mine eyes,
 To thee I breathe my soul's desires.

2 Art thou not mine, my living Lord?
 And can my hope, my comfort die,
 Fixed on thine everlasting word, [sky!
 That word which built the earth and

3 If my immortal Saviour lives,
 Then my immortal life is sure;
 His word a firm foundation gives;
 Here let me build and rest secure.

4 Here let my faith unshaken dwell;
 Immovable the promise stands;
 Not all the powers of earth or hell
 Can e'er dissolve the sacred bands.

5 Here, O my soul, thy trust repose;
 If Jesus is forever mine,
 Not death itself, that last of foes,
 Shall break a union so divine.
 Anne Steele, 1760.

526.
Tune, "Boylston," p. 48. S. M.

1 BLEST be thy love, dear Lord,
 That taught us this sweet way,
 Only to love thee for thyself,
 And for that love obey.

2 O thou, our souls' chief hope,
 We to thy mercy fly;
 Where'er we are, thou canst protect,
 Whate'er we need, supply.

3 Whether we sleep or wake,
 To thee we both resign:
 By night we see, as well as day,
 If thy light on us shine.

4 Whether we live or die,
 Both we submit to thee;
 In death we live, as well as life,
 If thine in death we be.
 John Austin, 1668.

THE CHRISTIAN LIFE,—LOVE TO CHRIST.

ST. MARY'S ABBEY. S. M.

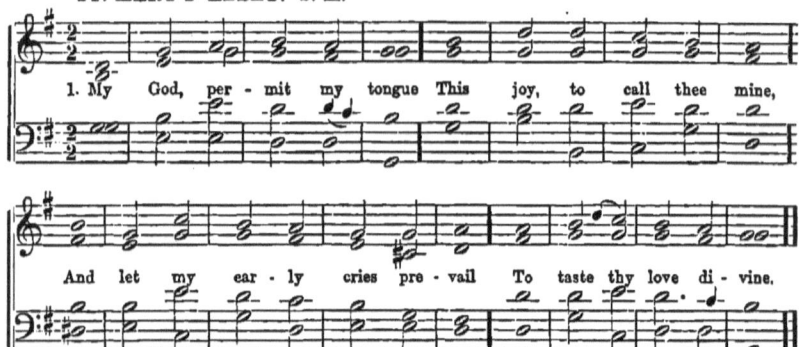

1. My God, per-mit my tongue This joy, to call thee mine, And let my ear-ly cries pre-vail To taste thy love di-vine.

527.   Psalm 63.

1 My God, permit my tongue
   This joy, to call thee mine,
And let my early cries prevail
   To taste thy love divine.

2 My thirsty, fainting soul
   Thy mercy doth implore;
Not travellers in desert lands
   Can pant for water more.

3 For life without thy love
   No relish can afford;
No joy can be compared to this,
   To serve and please the Lord.

4 In wakeful hours of night,
   I call my God to mind;
I think how wise thy counsels are,
   And all thy dealings kind.

5 Since thou hast been my help,
   To thee my spirit flies,
And on thy watchful providence
   My cheerful hope relies.

6 The shadow of thy wings
   My soul in safety keeps;
I follow where my Father leads,
   And he supports my steps.
                    Isaac Watts, 1719.

528.

1 My God, my Life, my Love,
   To thee, to thee I call;
I cannot live if thou remove,
   For thou art all in all.

2 To thee, and thee alone,
   The angels owe their bliss;
They sit around thy gracious throne,
   And dwell where Jesus is.

3 Not all the harps above
   Can make a heavenly place,
If God his residence remove,
   Or but conceal his face.

4 Nor earth, nor all the sky,
   Can one delight afford;
No, not a drop of real joy
   Without thy presence, Lord.

5 Thou art the sea of love,
   Where all my pleasures roll;
The circle where my passions move,
   And centre of my soul.
                    Isaac Watts, 1709.

529.

1 Not with our mortal eyes
   Have we beheld the Lord;
Yet we rejoice to hear his name,
   And love him in his word.

2 On earth we want the sight
   Of our Redeemer's face;
Yet, Lord, our inmost thoughts delight
   To dwell upon thy grace.

3 And when we taste thy love,
   Our joys divinely grow
Unspeakable, like those above,
   And heaven begins below.
                    Isaac Watts, 1709.

THE CHRISTIAN LIFE,—LOVE TO CHRIST. 219

MARTYN. 7s. DOUBLE.

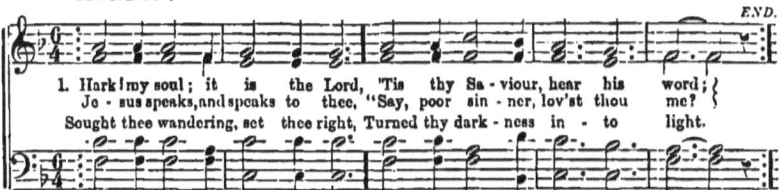

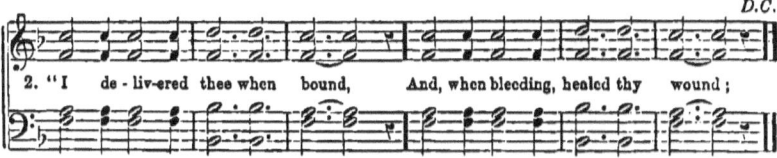

530.

1 HARK! my soul; it is the Lord,
'T is thy Saviour; hear his word;
Jesus speaks, and speaks to thee,
"Say, poor sinner, lov'st thou me?

2 " I delivered thee when bound,
And, when bleeding, healed thy wound;
Sought thee wandering, set thee right,
Turned thy darkness into light.

3 " Can a woman's tender care
Cease toward the child she bare?
Yes, she may forgetful be,
Yet will I remember thee.

4 " Mine is an unchanging love,
Higher than the heights above,
Deeper than the depths beneath,
Free and faithful, strong as death.

5 " Thou shalt see my glory soon,
When the work of grace is done;
Partner of my throne shalt be:
Say, poor sinner, lov'st thou me?"

6 Lord, it is my chief complaint,
That my love is weak and faint;
Yet I love thee, and adore;
Oh! for grace to love thee more.
William Cowper, 1779.

531.

1 'T IS a point I long to know,
Oft it causes anxious thought,
Do I love the Lord or no?
Am I his, or am I not?

2 If I love, why am I thus?
Why this dull, this lifeless frame?
Hardly, sure, can they be worse
Who have never heard his name.

3 Could my heart so hard remain,
Prayer a task and burden prove,
Every trifle give me pain,
If I knew a Saviour's love?

4 When I turn my eyes within
All is dark, and vain, and wild;
Filled with unbelief and sin,
Can I deem myself a child?

5 Yet I mourn my stubborn will,
Find my sin a grief and thrall;
Should I grieve for what I feel
If I did not love at all?

6 Could I joy his saints to meet,
Choose the ways I once abhorred,
Find at times the promise sweet,
If I did not love the Lord?

7 Lord, decide the doubtful case;
Thou who art thy people's sun,
Shine upon thy work of grace,
If it be indeed begun.

8 Let me love thee more and more,
If I love at all, I pray;
If I have not loved before,
Help me to begin to-day.
John Newton, 1779.

THE CHRISTIAN LIFE,—LOVE TO CHRIST.

ARIEL. C. P. M.

1. O love divine, how sweet thou art! When shall I find my willing heart All taken up by thee? I thirst, I faint, I die to prove The greatness of redeeming love, The love of Christ to me; The love of Christ to me.

532.

2 Stronger his love than death or hell;
  Its riches are unsearchable;
  The first-born sons of light
  Desire in vain its depths to see;
  They cannot reach the mystery,
  The length, the breadth, the height.

3 God only knows the love of God;
  Oh that it now were shed abroad
  In this poor stony heart:
  For love I sigh, for love I pine;
  This only portion, Lord, be mine;
  Be mine this better part.

4 Oh that I could forever sit
  With Mary at the Master's feet!
  Be this my happy choice;
  My only care, delight, and bliss,
  My joy, my heaven on earth, be this,
  To hear the Bridegroom's voice.

5 Oh that I could, with favored John,
  Recline my weary head upon
  The dear Redeemer's breast:
  From care, and sin, and sorrow free,
  Give me, O Lord, to find in thee
  My everlasting rest.

  Charles Wesley, 1746.

533.   Tune, "Stockwell," p. 391.   8s & 7s.

1 I WOULD love thee, God and Father!
  My Redeemer, and my King!
  I would love thee; for, without thee,
  Life is but a bitter thing.

2 I would love thee; every blessing
  Flows to me from out thy throne:
  I would love thee — he who loves thee
  Never feels himself alone.

3 I would love thee; look upon me,
  Ever guide me with thine eye:
  I would love thee; if not nourished
  By thy love, my soul would die.

4 I would love thee; may thy brightness
  Dazzle my rejoicing eyes!
  I would love thee; may thy goodness
  Watch from heaven o'er all I prize.

5 I would love thee, I have vowed it;
  On thy love my heart is set:
  While I love thee, I will never
  My Redeemer's blood forget.

  Tr. from French "Christian Songs," 1854.

THE CHRISTIAN LIFE,—LOVE TO CHRIST. 221

EASTON. L. M. 6 LINES.

1. Je-sus, thy boundless love to me No thought can reach, no tongue de-clare;
Oh knit my thankful heart to thee, And reign with-out a ri-val there:
Thine whol-ly, thine a-lone, I am; Be thou a-lone my con-stant flame.

534.

1 JESUS, thy boundless love to me [clare;
 No thought can reach, no tongue de-
Oh knit my thankful heart to thee,
 And reign without a rival there:
Thine wholly, thine alone, I am;
Be thou alone my constant flame.

2 Oh grant that nothing in my soul
 May dwell, but thy pure love alone:
Oh may thy love possess me whole,—
 My joy, my treasure, and my crown:
Strange flames far from my heart remove;
My every act, word, thought, be love.

3 Oh Love! how cheering is thy ray!
 All pain before thy presence flies;
Care, anguish, sorrow, melt away,
 Where'er thy healing beams arise:
O Jesus! nothing may I see,
Nothing desire, or seek but thee!

4 In suff'ring be thy love my peace;
 In weakness be thy love my power;
And when the storms of life shall cease,
 Jesus, in that important hour,
In death as life be thou my guide,
And save me, who for me hast died.

Paul Gerhard, 1653; *tr. by John Wesley,* 1739.

535.

1 THOU hidden love of God, whose height,
 Whose depth, unfathomed, no man
  knows,
I see from far thy beauteous light:
 Inly I sigh for thy repose;
My heart is pained; nor can it be
At rest till it find rest in thee.

2 Thy secret voice invites me still
 The sweetness of thy yoke to prove;
And fain I would; but though my will
 Seems fixed, yet wide my passions rove;
Yet hind'rances strow all the way;
I aim at thee, yet from thee stray.

3 Is there a thing beneath the sun [share?
 That strives with thee my heart to
Ah, tear it thence, and reign alone,
 The Lord of every motion there;
Then shall my heart from earth be free,
When it hath found repose in thee.

4 O Love, thy sovereign aid impart
 To save me from low-thoughted care;
Chase this self-will through all my heart,
 Through all its latent mazes there;
Make me thy duteous child, that I,
Ceaseless, may Abba, Father, cry.

Gerhard Tersteegen, 1731; *tr. by John Wesley,* 1739.

THE CHRISTIAN LIFE,—LOVE TO CHRIST.

CADDO. C. M.

1. Talk with us, Lord, thy-self re-veal, While here o'er earth we rove;
Speak to our hearts, and let us feel The kind-ling of thy love.

536.

1 TALK with us, Lord, thyself reveal,
    While here o'er earth we rove ;
Speak to our hearts, and let us feel
    The kindling of thy love.

2 With thee conversing, we forget
    All time, and toil, and care ;
Labor is rest, and pain is sweet,
    If thou, my God, art here.

3 Here then, my God, vouchsafe to stay,
    And bid my heart rejoice ;
My bounding heart shall own thy sway,
    And echo to thy voice.

4 Thou callest me to seek thy face ;
    'T is all I wish to seek ;
T' attend the whispers of thy grace,
    And hear thee inly speak.

5 Let this my every hour employ,
    Till I thy glory see ;
Enter into my Master's joy,
    And find my heaven in thee.
                    Charles Wesley, 1739.

537.

1 THOU lovely Source of true delight,
    Whom I unseen adore,
Unveil thy beauties to my sight,
    That I may love thee more.

2 Thy glory o'er creation shines ;
    But in thy sacred word
I read in fairer, brighter lines,
    My bleeding, dying Lord.

3 'T is here, whene'er my comforts droop,
    And sins and sorrows rise,
Thy love with cheerful beams of hope
    My fainting heart supplies.

4 Jesus, my Lord, my life, my light,
    Oh come with blissful ray, [night,
Break radiant through the shades of
    And chase my fears away.

5 Then shall my soul with rapture trace
    The wonders of thy love ;
But the full glories of thy face
    Are only known above.
                    Anne Steele, 1760.

538.

1 O JESUS, thou the beauty art
    Of angel-worlds above ;
Thy name is music to the heart,
    Enchanting it with love.

2 Celestial sweetness unalloyed !
    Who eat thee hunger still ;
Who drink of thee, still feel a void,
    Which nought but thou can fill.

3 O my sweet Jesus, hear the sighs
    Which unto thee I send ;
To thee mine inmost spirit cries,
    My being's hope and end.

4 Stay with us Lord, and let thy light
    Illume the soul's abyss,
Scatter the darkness of our night,
    And fill the world with bliss.
    Bernard of Clairvaux, 1140; tr. by E. Caswall, 1849. a.

THE CHRISTIAN LIFE,—LOVE TO CHRIST.

BRADFORD. C. M.

539.

1 Jesus! the very thought of thee
With sweetness fills my breast;
But sweeter far thy face to see,
And in thy presence rest.

2 Nor voice can sing, nor heart can frame,
Nor can the memory find
A sweeter sound than thy blest name,
O Saviour of mankind!

3 O Hope of every contrite heart,
O Joy of all the meek!
To those who fall, how kind thou art,
How good to those who seek!

4 But what to those who find? Ah! this
Nor tongue nor pen can show:
The love of Jesus, what it is,
None but his loved ones know.

5 Jesus, our only joy be thou!
As thou our prize wilt be;
Jesus, be thou our glory now,
And through eternity!
Bernard of Clairvaux, 1153; tr. by E. Caswall, 1849.

540.

1 Jesus, I love thy charming name,
'T is music to mine ear;
Fain would I sound it out so loud
That earth and heaven should hear.

2 Yes, thou art precious to my soul,
My transport, and my trust;
Jewels to thee are gaudy toys,
And gold is sordid dust.

3 All my capacious powers can wish,
In thee doth richly meet;
Nor to mine eyes is light so dear,
Nor friendship half so sweet.

4 Thy grace still dwells upon my heart,
And sheds its fragrance there;
The noblest balm of all its wounds,
The cordial of its care.

5 I'll speak the honors of thy name
With my last laboring breath;
Then, speechless, clasp thee in mine arms,
The antidote of death.
Philip Doddridge, 1755.

541.

1 My God, I love thee; not because
I hope for heaven thereby,
Nor yet because who love thee not
Must burn eternally.

2 Thou, O my Jesus, thou didst me
Upon the cross embrace;
For me didst bear the nails, and spear,
And manifold disgrace,

3 And griefs and torments numberless,
And sweat of agony;
Yea, death itself; and all for me
Who was thine enemy.

4 Then why, O blessèd Jesus Christ,
Should I not love thee well?
Not for the hope of winning heaven,
Nor of escaping hell.

THE CHRISTIAN LIFE,—LOVE TO CHRIST.

DENFIELD. C. M.

1. Do not I love thee, O my Lord? Behold my heart and see;
And turn each cursèd idol out That dares to rival thee.

5 Not with the hope of gaining aught,
   Not seeking a reward;
   But as thyself hast lovèd me,
   O ever-loving Lord,

6 So would I love thee, dearest Lord,
   And in thy praise will sing;
   Solely because thou art my God,
   And my Eternal King.
   Francis Xavier, 1552; tr. by Edward Caswall, 1849.

542.

1 Do not I love thee, O my Lord?
   Behold my heart and see;
   And turn each cursèd idol out
   That dares to rival thee.

2 Is not thy name melodious still
   To mine attentive ear?
   Doth not each pulse with pleasure bound
   My Saviour's voice to hear?

3 Hast thou a lamb in all thy flock
   I would disdain to feed?
   Hast thou a foe before whose face
   I fear thy cause to plead?

4 Would not my ardent spirit vie
   With angels round the throne
   To execute thy sacred will
   And make thy glory known?

5 Would not my heart pour forth its blood
   In honor of thy name,
   And challenge the cold hand of death
   To damp th' immortal flame?

6 Thou know'st I love thee, dearest Lord;
   But, oh! I long to soar
   Far from the sphere of mortal joys,
   And learn to love thee more.
   Philip Doddridge, 1755.

543.

1 Ye souls for whom the Son did die,
   In whom the Spirit dwells,
   Your sweet amazement riseth high,
   And strong your rapture swells.

2 Who sparéd not that Son Divine?
   Who sent that Spirit sweet?
   Father, the work of love is thine,
   The wonder is complete.

3 Thrice blessed souls, by heavenly love
   Elect, redeemed, renewed;
   Through endless years, below, above,
   By heavenly Love pursued!

4 Lord! wouldst thou set thy love on me
   And choose me in thy Son?
   Lord! hath my heart been given to thee?
   Hath love in me begun?

5 Ne'er let thy smile from me depart,
   My heart from thee remove!
   Eternal Lover, teach my heart
   Thine own eternal love.

6 As on the endless ages roll
   Let my glad song still be,
   "Forever hast thou loved my soul;
   Lord! thou hast chosen me."
   Thomas H. Gill, 1860.

THE CHRISTIAN LIFE,—LOVE TO CHRIST.

ETHELBERG. L. M.

1. O God! thou art my God alone, Early to thee my soul shall cry, A pilgrim in a land unknown, A thirsty land, whose springs are dry.

544.
PSALM 63.

1 O God! thou art my God alone,
Early to thee my soul shall cry,
A pilgrim in a land unknown,
A thirsty land, whose springs are dry.

2 Yet through this rough and thorny maze
I follow hard on thee, my God;
Thine hand, unseen, upholds my ways,
I safely tread where thou hast trod.

3 Better than life itself thy love,
Dearer than all beside to me,
For whom have I in heaven above,
Or what on earth, compared with thee?

4 Praise with my heart, my mind, my voice,
For all thy mercy I will give;
My soul shall still in God rejoice,
My tongue shall bless thee while I live.

James Montgomery, 1822.

545.

1 O God, my God, my all thou art;
Ere shines the dawn of rising day,
Thy sovereign light within my heart,
Thy all enlivening power display.

2 For thee my thirsty soul doth pant,
While in this desert land I live;
And hungry as I am, and faint,
Thy love alone can comfort give.

3 More dear than life itself, thy love
My heart and tongue shall still employ;
And to declare thy praise will prove
My peace, my glory, and my joy.

4 In blessing thee with grateful songs
My happy life shall glide away;
The praise that to thy name belongs
Hourly with lifted hands I'll pay.

5 Abundant sweetness, while I sing
Thy love, my ravished heart o'erflows,
Secure in thee, my God and King,
Of glory that no period knows.

Translated from the Spanish by John Wesley.

546.

1 O thou, by long experience tried,
Near whom no grief can long abide;
My Lord, how full of sweet content
I pass my years of banishment.

2 All scenes alike engaging prove
To souls impressed with sacred love;
Where'er they dwell, they dwell in thee,
In heaven, in earth, or on the sea.

3 To me remains nor place nor time:
My country is in every clime;
I can be calm and free from care
On any shore, since God is there.

4 While place we seek, or place we shun,
The soul finds happiness in none;
But with our God to guide the way,
'T is equal joy to go or stay.

5 Could I be cast where thou art not,
That were indeed a dreadful lot;
But regions none remote I call,
Secure of finding God in all.

Jeanne Marie Guyon, 1790; tr. by William Cowper, 1801.

226 THE CHRISTIAN LIFE,—LOVE TO CHRIST.

HEBRON. L. M.

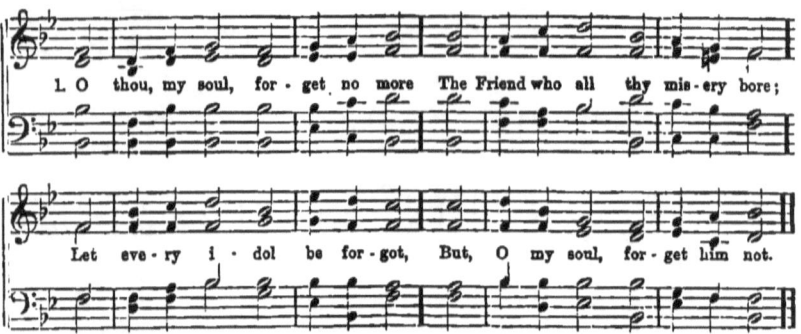

1. O thou, my soul, for-get no more The Friend who all thy mis-e-ry bore;
Let eve-ry i-dol be for-got, But, O my soul, for-get him not.

547.

1 O THOU, my soul, forget no more
The Friend who all thy misery bore;
Let every idol be forgot,
But, O my soul, forget him not.

2 Jesus for thee a body takes,
Thy guilt assumes, thy fetters breaks,
Discharging all thy dreadful debt;
And canst thou e'er such love forget?

3 Renounce thy works and ways, with grief,
And fly to this most sure relief;
Nor him forget, who left his throne
And for thy life gave up his own.

4 Infinite truth and mercy shine
In him, and he himself is thine:
And canst thou then, with sin beset,
Such charms, such matchless charms forget?

5 Ah, no: when all things else expire,
And perish in the general fire,
This name all others shall survive,
And through eternity shall live.

Khrisnu Pâl, tr. by Joshua Marshman, 1801.

548.

1 NOT yet, ye people of his grace,
Ye see your Saviour face to face;
Not yet enamored eyes ye bring
Unto the glory of your King.

2 Ye follow in his steps below,
Along his thorny way ye go,
Ye stand his bitter cross beside,
Ye cling to him, the crucified.

3 Upon his grace ye banquet here;
Ye know him true, ye feel him near;
The balm of his dear blood ye bless;
Ye wear his robe of righteousness.

4 But greater shall the wonder grow,
But mightier shall the joy o'erflow;
Upon your Lord ye yet shall gaze
And look your love and sweet amaze.

5 Oh make me meet for joy like this!
Oh grant me grace to bear the bliss,
To set my heart on thee below,
Nor other lord or love to know.

6 Then shall I set mine eyes on thee,
The King in all his beauty see,
And gazing on for evermore,
Glow with the beauty I adore.

Thomas H. Gill, 1859.

549.

1 LORD, with a grieved and aching heart,
To thee I look, to thee I cry;
Supply my wants, and ease my smart;
Oh help me soon, or else I die.

2 Here, on my soul, a burden lies!
No human power can it remove;
My numerous sins like mountains rise;
Do thou reveal thy pardoning love.

3 Break off these adamantine chains;
From cruel bondage set me free;
Rescue from everlasting pains,
And bring me safe to heaven and thee.

Benjamin Beddome, 1778.

THE CHRISTIAN LIFE,—PENITENCE.

WELLS. L. M.

1. Jesus demands this heart of mine, Demands my love, my joy, my care;
But ah! how dead to things divine, How cold my best affections are!

550.

1 Jesus demands this heart of mine,
Demands my love, my joy, my care;
But ah! how dead to things divine,
How cold my best affections are!

2 'Tis sin, alas! with dreadful power,
Divides my Saviour from my sight;
Oh, for one happy, shining hour
Of sacred freedom, sweet delight!

3 Lord! let thy love shine forth and raise
My captive powers from sin and death,
And fill my heart and life with praise,
And tune my last expiring breath.
Anne Steele, 1760.

551. PSALM 130.

1 From deep distress and troubled thoughts,
To thee, my God, I raise my cries;
If thou severely mark our faults,
No flesh can stand before thine eyes.

2 But thou hast built thy throne of grace,
Free to dispense thy pardons there;
That sinners may approach thy face,
And hope and love, as well as fear.

3 As the benighted pilgrims wait,
And long and wish for breaking day,
So waits my soul before thy gate:
When will my God his face display?

4 My trust is fixed upon thy word,
Nor shall I trust thy word in vain;
Let mourning souls address the Lord,
And find relief from all their pain.

5 Great is his love, and large his grace,
Through the redemption of his Son;
He turns our feet from sinful ways,
And pardons what our hands have done.
Isaac Watts, 1719.

552.

1 Oh that my load of sin were gone!
Oh that I could at last submit
At Jesus' feet to lay it down,
To lay my soul at Jesus' feet!

2 When shall mine eyes behold the Lamb,
The God of my salvation see?
Weary, O Lord, thou know'st I am;
Yet still I cannot come to thee.

3 Rest for my soul I long to find;
Saviour of all, if mine thou art,
Give me thy meek and lowly mind,
And stamp thy image on my heart!

4 Fain would I learn of thee, my God,
Thy light and easy burden prove,
The cross, all stained with hallowed blood,
The labor of thy dying love.

5 This moment would I take it up,
And after my dear Master bear;
With thee ascend to Calvary's top,
And bow my head and suffer there.

6 I would; but thou must give the power,
My heart from every sin release;
Bring near, bring near the joyful hour,
And fill me with thy perfect peace!
Charles Wesley, 1742.

THE CHRISTIAN LIFE,—PENITENCE.

PRINCE. L. M. 6 LINES. (Omit repeat for four lines.)

553.

1 WEARY of wandering from my God,
  And now made willing to return,
I hear, and bow me to the rod;
  For thee not without hope I mourn:
I have an advocate above,
A friend before the throne of love.

2 O Jesus, full of pardoning grace,
  More full of grace than I of sin;
Yet once again I seek thy face,
  Open thine arms and take me in,
And freely my backslidings heal,
And love the faithless sinner still!

3 Thou know'st the way to bring me back,
  My fallen spirit to restore;
Oh, for thy truth and mercy's sake,
  Forgive, and bid me sin no more!
The ruins of my soul repair,
And make my heart an house of prayer!

4 Ah! give me, Lord, the tender heart,
  That trembles at th' approach of sin;
A godly fear of sin impart,
  Implant, and root it deep within;
That I may dread thy gracious power,
And never dare offend thee more!
Charles Wesley, 1749.

554.

1 JESUS, our souls' delightful choice,
  In thee, believing, we rejoice;
Yet still our joy is mixed with grief,
While faith contends with unbelief.

2 Thy promises our hearts revive,
And keep our fainting hopes alive;
But guilt, and fears, and sorrows rise,
And hide the promise from our eyes.

3 Oh let not sin and Satan boast,
While saints lie mourning in the dust;
Nor see that faith to ruin brought,
Which thy own gracious hand hath wrought.

4 Do thou the dying spark inflame;
Reveal the glories of thy name;
And put all anxious doubts to flight,
As shades dispersed by opening light.
Philip Doddridge, 1755.

555.

1 OH, where is now that glowing love,
  That marked our union with the Lord?
Our hearts were fixed on things above,
  Nor could the world a joy afford.

2 Where is the zeal that led us then
  To make our Saviour's glory known?
That freed us from the fear of men,
  And kept our eye on him alone?

3 Where are the happy seasons spent
  In fellowship with him we loved?
The sacred joy, the sweet content,
The blessedness that then we proved?

4 Behold! again we turn to thee;
  Oh, cast us not away, though vile!
No peace we have, no joy we see,
  O Lord our God, but in thy smile.
Thomas Kelly, 1806.

THE CHRISTIAN LIFE,—PENITENCE.

SEIR. S. M.

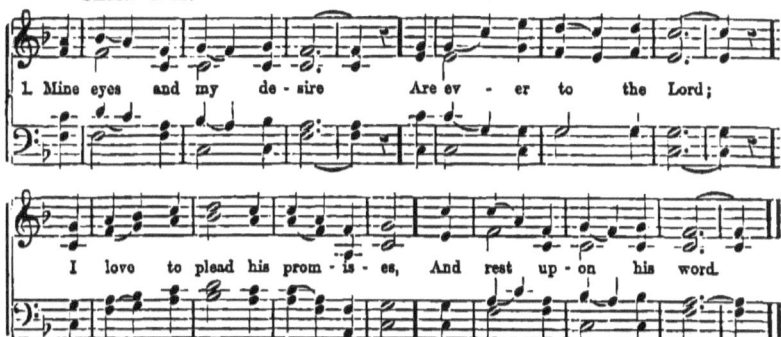

1. Mine eyes and my de-sire Are ev-er to the Lord; I love to plead his prom-is-es, And rest up-on his word.

556. PSALM 25.

1 MINE eyes and my desire
  Are ever to the Lord;
  I love to plead his promises,
  And rest upon his word.

2 Lord, turn thee to my soul;
  Bring thy salvation near:
  When will thy hand release my feet
  Out of the deadly snare?

3 When shall the sovereign grace
  Of my forgiving God
  Restore me from those dangerous ways
  My wandering feet have trod?

4 Oh keep my soul from death,
  Nor put my hope to shame,
  For I have placed my only trust
  In my Redeemer's name.

5 With humble faith I wait
  To see thy face again:
  Of Israel it shall ne'er be said,
  He sought the Lord in vain.
                    Isaac Watts, 1719.

557.

1 Is this the kind return,
  And these the thanks we owe?
  Thus to abuse eternal Love,
  Whence all our blessings flow!

2 To what a stubborn frame
  Hath sin reduced our mind!
  What strange, rebellious wretches we,
  And God as strangely kind!

3 Turn, turn us, mighty God,
  And mould our souls afresh; [stone,
  Break, sovereign grace, these hearts of
  And give us hearts of flesh.

4 Let past ingratitude
  Provoke our weeping eyes,
  And hourly, as new mercies fall,
  Let hourly thanks arise.
                    Isaac Watts, 1709.

558.

1 OH that I could repent,
  With all my idols part;
  And to thy gracious eyes present
  A humble, contrite heart;

2 A heart with grief oppressed
  For having grieved my God;
  A troubled heart, that cannot rest
  Till sprinkled with thy blood.

3 With softening pity look,
  And melt my hardness down;
  Strike with thy love's resistless stroke,
  And break this heart of stone!

4 Saviour and Prince of Peace,
  The double grace bestow;
  Unloose the bands of wickedness,
  And let the captive go.

5 Grant me my sins to feel,
  And then the load remove;
  Wound, and pour in, my wounds to heal,
  The balm of pardoning love.
                    Charles Wesley, 1740.

THE CHRISTIAN LIFE,—PENITENCE.

PLEYEL'S HYMN. 7s.

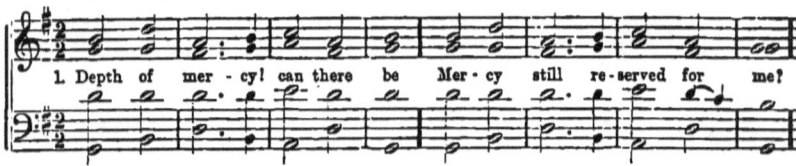
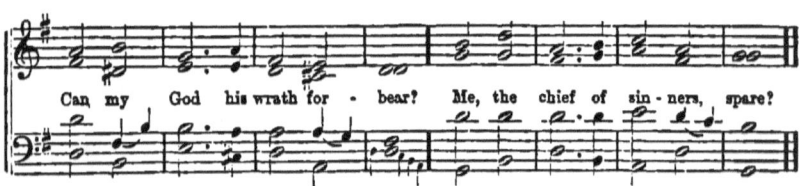

559.

1 Depth of mercy! can there be
Mercy still reserved for me?
Can my God his wrath forbear?
Me, the chief of sinners, spare?

2 I have long withstood his grace;
Long provoked him to his face;
Would not hearken to his calls;
Grieved him by a thousand falls.

3 Kindled his relentings are;
Me he now delights to spare;
Cries, How shall I give thee up?
Lets the lifted thunder drop.

4 There for me the Saviour stands;
Shows his wounds, and spreads his hands;
God is love! I know, I feel;
Jesus weeps, and loves me still.

5 Jesus, answer from above;
Is not all thy nature love?
Wilt thou not the wrong forget?
Suffer me to kiss thy feet?

6 Now incline me to repent;
Let me now my sins lament;
Now my foul revolt deplore,
Weep, believe, and sin no more.

Charles Wesley, 1740.

560. Psalm 6.

1 Gently, gently lay thy rod
On my sinful head, O God!
Stay thy wrath, in mercy stay,
Lest I sink before its sway!

2 Heal me, for my flesh is weak;
Heal me, for thy grace I seek:
This, my only plea, I make,
Heal me for thy mercy's sake!

3 Who within the silent grave
Shall proclaim thy power to save?
Lord, my trembling soul reprieve;
Speak! and I shall rise and live.

4 Lo! he comes; he heeds my plea;
Lo! he comes; the shadows flee;
Glory round me dawns once more,
Rise, my spirit, and adore!

H. F. Lyte, 1834.

561.

1 Prince of peace, control my will;
Bid this struggling heart be still;
Bid my fears and doubtings cease,
Hush my spirit into peace.

2 Thou hast bought me with thy blood,
Opened wide the gate to God:
Peace I ask, but peace must be,
Lord, in being one with thee.

3 May thy will, not mine, be done;
May thy will and mine be one:
Chase these doubtings from my heart;
Now thy perfect peace impart.

4 Saviour! at thy feet I fall;
Thou my life, my God, my all!
Let thy happy servant be
One for evermore with thee!

Anon.

THE CHRISTIAN LIFE,—PENITENCE. 231

MENDELSSOHN. L. M.

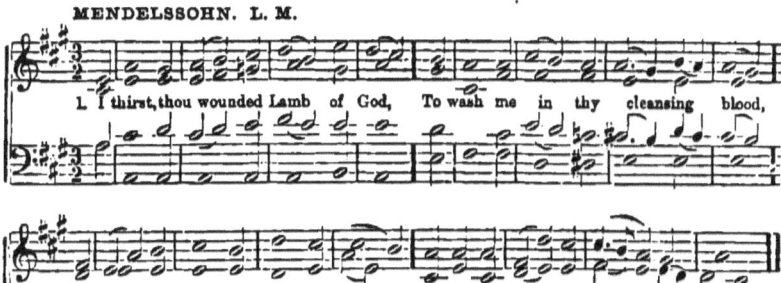

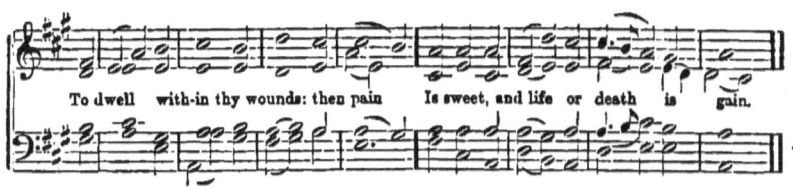

562.

1 I THIRST, thou wounded Lamb of God,
To wash me in thy cleansing blood,
To dwell within thy wounds: then pain
Is sweet, and life or death is gain.

2 Take my poor heart, and let it be
Forever closed to all but thee;
Seal thou my breast, and let me wear
That pledge of love forever there.

3 How blest are they who still abide
Close sheltered in thy bleeding side;
Who life and strength from thence derive,
And by thee move, and in thee live.

4 What are our works but sin and death,
Till thou thy quickening Spirit breathe?
Thou giv'st the power thy grace to move,
Oh wondrous grace! Oh boundless love!

5 Ah, Lord! enlarge our scanty thought,
To know the wonders thou hast wrought!
Unloose our stammering tongues to tell
Thy love immense, unsearchable!

6 First-born of many brethren thou,
To thee, lo, all our souls we bow;
To thee our hearts and hands we give;
Thine may we die, thine may we live.

Count Zinzendorf, John and Anna Nitschman, 1737–8; tr. by J. Wesley, 1740.

563.

1 THOU Prince of glory, slain for me,
Breathing forgiveness in thy prayer;
That loving, melting look I see,
That bursting sigh, that tender tear.

2 Can I behold that closing eye,
Still fixed on me, still beaming love!
And can I see my Saviour die,
Nor feel one holy passion move?

3 Let me but hear thy dying voice
Pronounce forgiveness in my breast;
My trembling spirit shall rejoice,
And feel the calm of heavenly rest.

4 Lord, thine atoning blood apply,
And life or death is sweet to me:
In life's last hour, thy presence, nigh,
From fear shall set my spirit free.

Wm. Bengo Collyer, 1812.

564.

1 O LORD, thy heavenly grace impart,
And fix my frail, inconstant heart:
Henceforth my chief delight shall be
To dedicate myself to thee.

2 Whate'er pursuits my time employ,
One thought shall fill my soul with joy;
That silent, secret thought shall be,
That all my hopes are fixed on thee.

3 Thy glorious eye pervadeth space:
Thou'rt present, Lord, in every place;
And, wheresoe'er my lot may be,
Still shall my spirit cleave to thee.

4 Renouncing every worldly thing,
And safe beneath thy spreading wing,
My sweetest thought henceforth shall be,
That all I want I find in thee.

J. F. Oberlin, 1820; tr. by Mrs. Daniel Wilson, 1830.

THE CHRISTIAN LIFE,—PENITENCE.

HURSLEY. L. M.

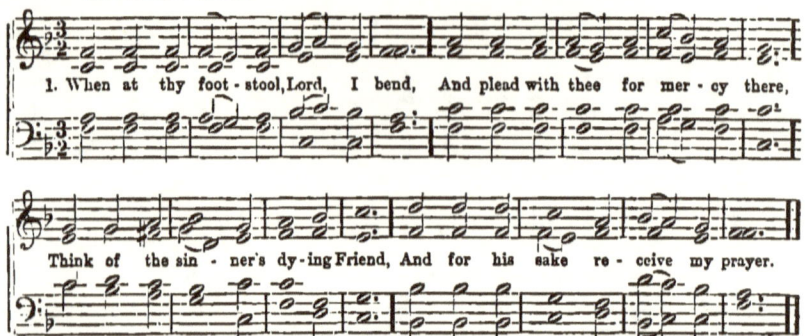

1. When at thy foot-stool, Lord, I bend, And plead with thee for mer-cy there, Think of the sin-ner's dy-ing Friend, And for his sake re-ceive my prayer.

565.

1 WHEN at thy footstool, Lord, I bend,
   And plead with thee for mercy there,
   Think of the sinner's dying Friend,
   And for his sake receive my prayer.

2 Oh think not of my shame and guilt,
   My thousand stains of deepest dye;
   Think of the blood which Jesus spilt,
   And let that blood my pardon buy.

3 Think, Lord, how I am still thy own,
   The trembling creature of thy hand;
   Think how my heart to sin is prone,
   And what temptations round me stand.

4 Oh think upon thy holy word,
   And every plighted promise there;
   How prayer should evermore be heard,
   And how thy glory is to spare.

5 Oh think not of my doubts and fears,
   My strivings with thy grace divine:
   Think upon Jesus' woes and tears,
   And let his merits stand for mine.

6 Thine eye, thine ear, they are not dull;
   Thine arm can never shortened be;
   Behold me here; my heart is full;
   Behold, and spare, and succor me!

Henry Francis Lyte, 1833.

566.

1 THOU only Sovereign of my heart,
   My Refuge, my Almighty Friend,
   And can my soul from thee depart,
   On whom alone my hopes depend?

2 Whither, ah! whither shall I go,
   A wretched wanderer from my Lord?
   Can this dark world of sin and woe
   One glimpse of happiness afford?

3 Eternal life thy words impart;
   On these my fainting spirit lives:
   Here sweeter comforts cheer my heart
   Than all the round of nature gives.

4 Let earth's alluring joys combine;
   While thou art near, in vain they call;
   One smile, one blissful smile, of thine,
   My gracious Lord, outweighs them all.

5 Low at thy feet my soul would lie;
   Here safety dwells, and peace divine;
   Still let me live beneath thine eye,
   For life, eternal life, is thine.

Anne Steele, 1760.

567.

1 MY only Saviour! when I feel
   O'erwhelmed in spirit, faint, oppressed,
   'T is sweet to tell thee, while I kneel
   Low at thy feet, thou art my rest.

2 I'm weary of the strife within;
   Strong powers against my soul contest;
   Oh, let me turn from self and sin
   To thy dear cross, for there is rest!

3 Oh! sweet will be the welcome day,
   When, from her toils and woes released,
   My parting soul in death shall say,
   "Now, Lord! I come to thee for rest."

Anon.

THE CHRISTIAN LIFE,—PENITENCE.

GRATITUDE. L. M.

1. My God, permit me not to be A stranger to myself and thee; Amidst a thousand thoughts I rove, Forgetful of my highest love.

568.

1 My God, permit me not to be
A stranger to myself and thee;
Amidst a thousand thoughts I rove,
Forgetful of my highest love.

2 Why should my passions mix with earth,
And thus debase my heavenly birth?
Why should I cleave to things below,
And let my God, my Saviour, go?

3 Call me away from flesh and sense;
One sovereign word can draw me thence;
I would obey the voice divine,
And all inferior joys resign.

4 Be earth, with all her scenes, withdrawn;
Let noise and vanity be gone;
In secret silence of the mind,
My heaven, and there my God, I find.
Isaac Watts, 1709.

569.

1 Return, my roving heart, return,
And chase these shadowy forms no more;
Seek out some solitude to mourn,
And thy forsaken God implore.

2 And thou, my God, whose piercing eye
Distinct surveys each deep recess;
In these abstracted hours draw nigh,
And with thy presence fill the place.

3 Through all the mazes of my heart,
My search let heavenly wisdom guide,
And still its radiant beams impart
Till all be searched and purified.

4 Then, with the visits of thy love,
Vouchsafe my inmost soul to cheer;
Till every grace shall join to prove
That God has fixed his dwelling there.
Philip Doddridge, 1755.

570.

1 My soul before thee prostrate lies,
To thee, her Source, my spirit flies:
My wants I mourn, my chains I see;
Oh, let thy presence set me free!

2 Undone and lost, for aid I cry;
In thy death. Saviour, let me die; [pain,
Grieved with thy grief, pained with thy
Ne'er let me live for self again.

3 In life's short day, let me yet more
Of thine enlivening love implore;
My mind must deeper sink in thee,
My foot stand firm, from wandering free.
Christian Friedrich Richter, 1676-1711.

571.

1 Oh, turn, great Ruler of the skies!
Turn from my sin thy searching eyes;
Nor let th' offenses of my hand
Within thy book recorded stand.

2 Give me a will to thine subdued,
A conscience pure, a soul renewed;
Nor let me, wrapt in endless gloom,
An outcast from thy presence roam.

3 Oh, let thy Spirit to my heart
Once more its quickening aid impart;
My mind from every fear release,
And soothe my troubled thoughts to peace.
James Merrick, 1763.

THE CHRISTIAN LIFE,—PENITENCE.

BOWDOIN SQUARE. C. M.

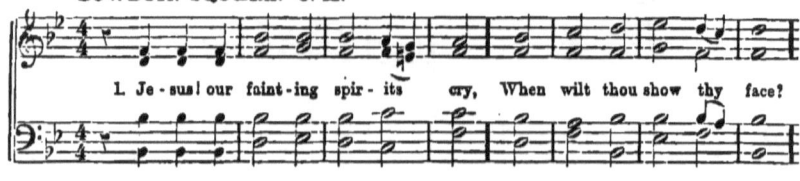
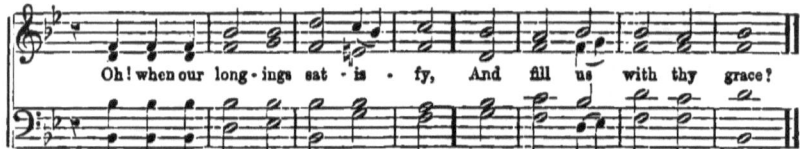

572.

1 Jesus! our fainting spirits cry,
　When wilt thou show thy face?
　Oh! when our longings satisfy,
　And fill us with thy grace?

2 We sinners, Lord, with earnest heart,
　With sighs and prayers and tears,
　To thee our inmost cares impart,
　Our burdens and our fears.

3 Thy sovereign grace can give relief,
　Thou Source of peace and light!
　Dispel the gloomy cloud of grief,
　And make our darkness bright.

4 Around thy Father's throne on high,
　All heaven thy glory sings;
　And earth, for which thou cam'st to die,
　Loud with thy praises rings.

5 Dear Lord! to thee our prayers ascend;
　Our eyes thy face would see:
　Oh! let our weary wanderings end,
　Our spirits rest in thee!
　　　Bernard of Clairvaux: tr. by R. P. Dunn, 1858.

573.

1 Dear Saviour, when my thoughts recall
　The wonders of thy grace,
　Low at thy feet, ashamed, I fall,
　And hide this wretched face.

2 Shall love like thine be thus repaid?
　Ah, vile, ungrateful heart!
　By earth's low cares so oft betrayed
　From Jesus to depart.

3 But he, for his own mercy's sake,
　My wandering soul restores;
　He bids the mourning heart partake
　The pardon it implores.

4 Oh, while I breathe to thee, my Lord,
　The penitential sigh,
　Confirm the kind, forgiving word,
　With pity in thine eye!

5 Then shall the mourner at thy feet
　Rejoice to seek thy face;
　And grateful, own how kind, how sweet
　Thy condescending grace.
　　　Anne Steele, 1760.

574.

1 Oh for that tenderness of heart
　Which bows before the Lord,
　Acknowledging how just thou art,
　And trembling at thy word;

2 Oh for those humble, contrite tears,
　Which from repentance flow;
　That consciousness of guilt, which fears
　The long-suspended blow.

3 Saviour, to me, in pity, give
　The sensible distress;
　The pledge thou wilt at last receive,
　And bid me die in peace:

4 Wilt from the dreadful day remove,
　Before the evil come;
　My spirit hide with saints above,
　My body, in the tomb.
　　　Charles Wesley, 1708-1788.

575. C. M. Double.

1 O Lord, turn not thy face away
From them that lowly lie,
Lamenting sore their sinful life
With tears and bitter cry;
Thy mercy-gates are open wide
To them that mourn their sin;
Oh shut them not against us, Lord,
But let us enter in.

2 We need not to confess our fault,
For surely thou canst tell;
What we have done, and what we are,
Thou knowest very well;
Wherefore, to beg and to entreat,
With tears we come to thee,
As children that have done amiss
Fall at their father's knee.

3 And need we then, O Lord, repeat
The blessing which we crave,
When thou dost know, before we speak,
The thing that we would have?
Mercy, O Lord, mercy we ask,
This is the total sum;
For mercy, Lord, is all our prayer;
Oh let thy mercy come!

John Mardley, 1562; alt. by Reginald Heber, 1827.

576. C. M.

1 Lord, at thy feet we sinners lie,
And knock at mercy's door;
With heavy heart and downcast eye
Thy favor we implore.

2 On us the vast extent display
Of thy forgiving love;
Take all our heinous guilt away,
This heavy load remove.

3 We sink with all this weight oppressed,
Sink down to death and hell;
Oh give our troubled spirits rest,
Our numerous fears dispel.

4 Oh for thy own, for Jesus' sake,
Our many sins forgive!
Thy grace our rocky hearts can break;
And, breaking, soon relieve.

5 Thus melt us down; thus make us bend,
And thy dominion own;

Nor let a rival more pretend
To repossess thy throne.

Simon Browne, 1720.

577. C. M.

1 When shall I, Lord, a journey take
Through my departed years,
And not a mournful visit make,
And not return in tears?

2 Hath not thy mercy made me whole?
Hath not thy grace forgiven?
Yet still the grief regains my soul:
Yet still my heart is riven.

3 Those buried sins of mine arise;
Again my heart runs o'er:
Once more those deep repentant sighs
Those bitter tears once more!

4 Oh, shall these drops of sadness make
The light celestial dim,
And memory's mournful music break
On heaven's eternal hymn?

5 My Saviour's powerful blood I know;
My pardoning God I bless;
But send thy Spirit down; bestow
Of thine own holiness.

6 Those sins so bitter to my soul,
Lord, let me not repeat:
So make my past less sorrowful;
So make my heaven more sweet!

Thomas H. Gill, 1859.

578. C. M.

1 With tears of anguish I lament,
Here, at thy feet, my God,
My passion, pride, and discontent,
And vile ingratitude.

2 Sure, there was ne'er a heart so base,
So false as mine has been;
So faithless to its promises,
So prone to every sin!

3 How long, dear Saviour, shall I feel
These struggles in my breast?
When wilt thou bow my stubborn will
And give my conscience rest?

4 Break, sovereign Grace, oh, break the charm,
And set the captive free!
Reveal, almighty God, thine arm,
And haste to rescue me.

Samuel Stennett, 1772.

THE CHRISTIAN LIFE,—PENITENCE.

HEBER. C. M.

L. Approach, my soul, the mer-cy-seat Where Jesus answers prayer; There humbly fall before his feet, For none can perish there.

579.

1 APPROACH, my soul, the mercy-seat
  Where Jesus answers prayer;
  There humbly fall before his feet,
  For none can perish there.

2 Thy promise is my only plea,
  With this I venture nigh;
  Thou callest burdened souls to thee,
  And such, O Lord, am I.

3 Bowed down beneath a load of sin,
  By Satan sorely prest,
  By war without, and fear within,
  I come to thee for rest.

4 Be thou my Shield and Hiding-place,
  That, sheltered near thy side,
  I may my fierce accuser face,
  And tell him, thou hast died.

5 Oh wondrous love, to bleed and die,
  To bear the cross and shame,
  That guilty sinners, such as I,
  Might plead thy gracious Name!

John Newton, 1779.

580.

1 LORD, I have sinned; but oh forgive,
  Nor cast me quite away;
  Renew my soul and bid me live,
  And be my future stay.

2 Oh let me from my fall arise,
  More watchful and more strong;
  Light up my dim and tearful eyes,
  And fill my mouth with song.

3 On Christ's prevailing sacrifice
  I all my hopes recline,
  A broken spirit thou dost prize,
  And such, O Lord, be mine.

4 Give me a meek dependent heart
  For all my days to come;
  Nor let thy Spirit e'er depart,
  Till I am safe at home.

H. F. Lyte, 1834.

581.

1 How oft, alas! this wretched heart
  Has wandered from the Lord!
  How oft my roving thoughts depart
  Forgetful of his word!

2 Yet sovereign mercy calls, return!
  Dear Lord! and may I come?
  My vile ingratitude I mourn;
  Oh! take the wanderer home.

3 And canst thou, wilt thou yet forgive,
  And bid my crimes remove?
  And shall a pardoned rebel live
  To speak thy wondrous love?

4 Almighty grace! thy healing power
  How glorious — how divine!
  That can to life and bliss restore
  So vile a heart as mine!

5 Thy pard'ning love, so free, so sweet,
  Dear Saviour! I adore;
  Oh! keep me at thy sacred feet,
  And let me rove no more.

Anne Steele, 1760.

582. C. M.

1 O THOU, whose tender mercy hears
Contrition's humble sigh,
Whose hand indulgent wipes the tears
From sorrow's weeping eye;

2 See, low before thy throne of grace,
A wretched wanderer mourn;
Hast thou not bid me seek thy face?
Hast thou not said, return?

3 And shall my guilty fears prevail
To drive me from thy feet?
Oh! let not this dear refuge fail,
This only safe retreat!

4 Absent from thee, my Guide, my Light,
Without one cheering ray, [night,
Through dangers, fears, and gloomy
How desolate my way!

5 Oh shine on this benighted heart,
With beams of mercy shine!
And let thy healing voice impart
A taste of joys divine.

6 Thy presence only can bestow
Delights which never cloy:
Be this my solace here below,
And my eternal joy!
Anne Steele, 1760.

583. C. M.

1 THE Lord will happiness divine
On contrite hearts bestow;
Then tell me, gracious God! is mine
A contrite heart or no?

2 I hear, but seem to hear in vain,
Insensible as steel;
If aught is felt, 'tis only pain
To find I cannot feel.

3 I sometimes think myself inclined
To love thee if I could;
But often feel another mind,
Averse to all that's good.

4 My best desires are faint and few,
I fain would strive for more;
But, when I cry, "My strength renew,"
Seem weaker than before.

5 Thy saints are comforted, I know,
And love thy house of prayer;
I sometimes go where others go,
But find no comfort there.

6 Oh, make this heart rejoice or ache,
Decide this doubt for me;
And, if it be not broken, break;
And heal it if it be.
William Cowper, 1779.

584. PSALM 102. C. M.

1 HEAR me, O God, nor hide thy face.
But answer, lest I die!
Hast thou not built a throne of grace,
To hear when sinners cry?

2 As on some lonely building's top
The sparrow tells her moan,
Far from the tents of joy and hope,
I sit and grieve alone.

3 But thou forever art the same,
O my Eternal God!
Ages to come shall know thy name,
And spread thy works abroad.

4 Thou wilt arise and show thy face,
Nor will my Lord delay,
Beyond th' appointed hour of grace,
That long expected day.

5 He hears his saints, he knows their cry;
And by mysterious ways
Redeems the prisoners doomed to die,
And fills their tongues with praise
Isaac Watts, 1719.

585. C. M.

1 SWEET was the time when first I felt
The Saviour's pardoning blood
Applied to cleanse my soul from guilt,
And bring me home to God.

2 Soon as the morn the light revealed,
His praises tuned my tongue;
And, when the evening shade prevailed,
His love was all my song.

3 In prayer, my soul drew near the Lord,
And saw his glory shine;
And when I read his holy word,
I called each promise mine.

4 Now, when the evening shade prevails,
My soul in darkness mourns;
And, when the morn the light reveals,
No light to me returns.

5 Rise, Saviour! help me to prevail.
And make my soul thy care:
I know thy mercy cannot fail,
Let me that mercy share.
John Newton, 1779, a.

THE CHRISTIAN LIFE,—PENITENCE.

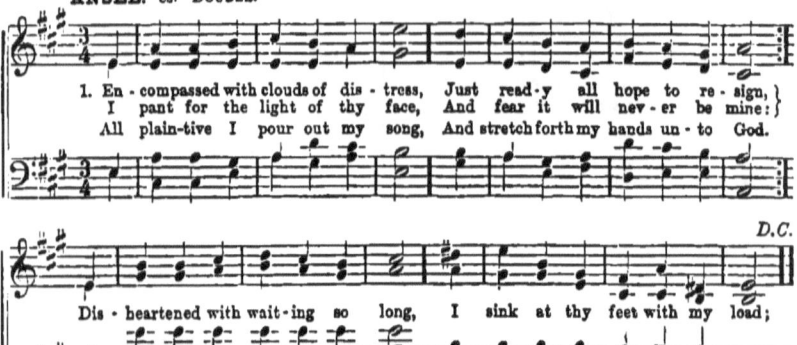

586.

1 ENCOMPASSED with clouds of distress,
  Just ready all hope to resign,
  I pant for the light of thy face,
  And fear it will never be mine:
  Disheartened with waiting so long,
  I sink at thy feet with my load;
  All plaintive I pour out my song,
  And stretch forth my hands unto God.

2 Shine, Lord, and my terror shall cease;
  The blood of atonement apply;
  And lead me to Jesus for peace,
  The rock that is higher than I:
  Speak, Saviour! for sweet is thy voice,
  Thy presence is fair to behold;
  I thirst for thy spirit with cries,
  And groanings that cannot be told.

3 If sometimes I strive, as I mourn,
  My hold of thy promise to keep,
  The billows more fiercely return,
  And plunge me again in the deep:
  While harassed and cast from thy sight,
  The tempter suggests, with a roar,
  "The Lord has forsaken thee quite;
  Thy God will be gracious no more."

4 Yet, Lord, if thy love hath designed
  No covenant blessing for me,
  Ah, tell me, how is it I find
  Some pleasure in waiting for thee?

Almighty to rescue thou art;
  Thy grace is my only resource:
  If e'er thou art Lord of my heart,
  Thy Spirit must take it by force.
  Augustus M. Toplady, 1772.

587. Tune, "Night," p. 239. 7s.

1 OH this soul how dark and blind!
  Oh this foolish, earthly mind!
  Oh this froward, selfish will,
  Which refuses to be still!

2 Oh these ever roaming eyes,
  Upward that refuse to rise!
  These still wayward feet of mine,
  Found in every path but thine!

3 Oh this stubborn, prayerless knee,
  Hands so seldom clasped to thee,
  Longings of the soul that go,
  Like the wild wind, to and fro!

4 To and fro, without an aim,
  Turning idly whence they came;
  Bringing in no joy, no bliss,
  Adding to my weariness.

5 Giver of the heavenly peace,
  Bid, oh, bid these tumults cease;
  Minister thy holy balm,
  Fill me with thy Spirit's calm.

6 Thou, the Life, the Truth, the Way,
  Leave me not in sin to stay;
  Bearer of the sinner's guilt,
  Lead me, lead me, as thou wilt!
  Horatius Bonar, 1861.

THE CHRISTIAN LIFE,—HUMILITY.

NIGHT. 7s.

588.

1 JESUS, cast a look on me;
 Give me sweet simplicity,
 Make me poor and keep me low,
 Seeking only thee to know;

2 Weaned from my lordly self,
 Weaned from the miser's pelf,
 Weaned from the scorner's ways,
 Weaned from the lust of praise.

3 All that feeds my busy pride,
 Cast it evermore aside;
 Bid my will to thine submit;
 Lay me humbly at thy feet.

4 Make me like a little child,
 Of my strength and wisdom spoiled,
 Seeing only in thy light,
 Walking only in thy might,

5 Leaning on thy loving breast,
 Where a weary soul may rest;
 Feeling well the peace of God
 Flowing from thy gracious blood!

6 In this posture let me live,
 And hosannas daily give;
 In this temper let me die,
 And hosannas ever cry!
John Berridge, 1785.

589. PSALM 131.

1 QUIET, Lord, my froward heart,
 Make me teachable and mild,
 Upright, simple, free from art,
 Make me as a weanèd child,
 From distrust and envy free,
 Pleased with all that pleases thee.

2 What thou shalt to-day provide,
 Let me as a child receive;
 What to-morrow may betide,
 Calmly to thy wisdom leave;
 'Tis enough that thou wilt care;
 Why should I the burden bear?

3 As a little child relies
 On a care beyond his own,
 Knows he's neither strong nor wise,
 Fears to stir a step alone;
 Let me thus with thee abide,
 As my Father, Guard, and Guide.

4 Thus preserved from Satan's wiles,
 Safe from dangers, free from fears,
 May I live upon thy smiles,
 Till the promised hour appears
 When the sons of God shall prove
 All their Father's boundless love.
John Newton, 1779.

DOXOLOGY.

To the Father and the Son,
And the Spirit, Three in One,
As of old, and as in heaven,
Now and here be glory given.
J. H. Newman, 1840.

THE CHRISTIAN LIFE,—ASPIRATION.

ST. FRANCIS. 8s & 7s. DOUBLE.

590.

1 HUMBLE, Lord, my haughty spirit,
  Bid my swelling thoughts subside;
 Strip me of my fancied merit;
  What have I to do with pride?
 Was my Saviour meek and lowly?
  And shall such a worm as I,
 Weak, and earthly, and un- | holy,
  Dare to lift my | head on | high?

2 Teach me, Lord, my true condition;
  Bring me childlike to thy knee;
 Stripped of every low ambition,
  Willing to be led by thee.
 Guide me by thy Holy Spirit;
  Feed me from thy blessèd word:
 All my wisdom, all my | merit,
  Borrowed from thy- | self, O | Lord.

3 Like a little babe, confiding,
  Simple, docile, let me be;
 Trusting still to thy providing,
  Willing to be led by thee.
 Thus my all to thee submitting,
  I am thine and not my own;
 And when earthly hopes are | flitting,
  Rest secure on | God a- | lone.

H. F. Lyte, 1834.

591.

1 LOVE divine, all love excelling,
  Joy of heaven, to earth come down,
 Fix in us thy humble dwelling;
  All thy faithful mercies crown.
 Jesus, thou art all compassion,
  Pure unbounded love thou art:
 Visit us with thy sal- | vation;
  Enter every | trembling | heart.

2 Breathe, oh breathe thy loving Spirit
  Into every troubled breast;
 Let us all in thee inherit;
  Let us find the promised rest.
 Come, almighty to deliver,
  Let us all thy life receive;
 Suddenly return, and | never,
  Never more thy | temples | leave.

3 Finish then thy new creation;
  Pure and spotless let us be;
 Let us see thy great salvation
  Perfectly restored in thee;
 Changed from glory into glory,
  Till in heaven we take our place,
 Till we cast our crowns be- | fore thee,
  Lost in **wonder**, | love, and | praise.

Charles Wesley, 1746.

THE CHRISTIAN LIFE,—ASPIRATION.

BALERMA. C. M.

1. Oh, for a closer walk with God, A calm and heav-enly frame; A light to shine up-on the road That leads me to the Lamb!

592.

1 Oh, for a closer walk with God,
A calm and heavenly frame,
A light to shine upon the road
That leads me to the Lamb!

2 Where is the blessedness I knew
When first I saw the Lord?
Where is the soul-refreshing view
Of Jesus and his word?

3 What peaceful hours I once enjoyed!
How sweet their memory still!
But they have left an aching void
The world can never fill.

4 Return, O Holy Dove, return,
Sweet messenger of rest;
I hate the sins that made thee mourn,
And drove thee from my breast.

5 The dearest idol I have known,
Whate'er that idol be,
Help me to tear it from thy throne,
And worship only thee.

6 So shall my walk be close with God,
Calm and serene my frame;
So purer light shall mark the road
That leads me to the Lamb.
William Cowper, 1779.

593.

1 My God! the spring of all my joys,
The life of my delights,
The glory of my brightest days,
And comfort of my nights!

2 In darkest shades if he appear,
My dawning is begun;
He is my soul's sweet morning star,
And he my rising sun.

3 The opening heavens around me shine
With beams of sacred bliss,
While Jesus shows his heart is mine,
And whispers, I am his!

4 My soul would leave this heavy clay
At that transporting word,
Run up with joy the shining way,
T' embrace my dearest Lord.

5 Fearless of hell and ghastly death,
I'd break through every foe;
The wings of love and arms of faith
Should bear me conqueror through.
Isaac Watts, 1709.

594.

1 I THINK of thee, my God, by night,
And talk of thee by day;
Thy love my treasure and delight,
Thy truth my strength and stay.

2 The day is dark, the night is long,
Unblest with thoughts of thee,
And dull to me the sweetest song,
Unless its theme thou be.

3 So all day long, and all the night,
Lord, let thy presence be.
Mine air, my breath, my shade, my light,
Myself absorbed in thee.
John S. B. Monsell, 1863.

242 THE CHRISTIAN LIFE,—ASPIRATION.

DELAY. 7s.

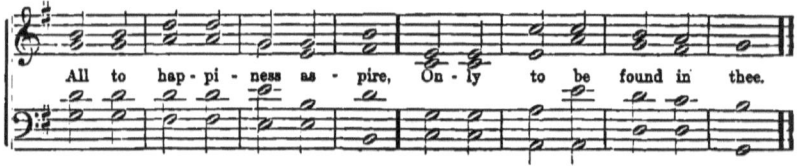

1. Object of my first desire, Jesus crucified for me, All to happiness aspire, Only to be found in thee.

595.

1 Object of my first desire,
Jesus crucified for me!
All to happiness aspire,
Only to be found in thee.

2 Thee to please and thee to know,
Constitute our bliss below;
Thee to see and thee to love,
Constitute our bliss above.

3 Lord, it is not life to live,
If thy presence thou deny;
Lord, if thou thy presence give,
'T is no longer death to die.

4 Source and giver of repose,
Singly from thy smile it flows;
Peace and happiness are thine,
Mine they are, if thou art mine.
A. M. Toplady, 1774.

596.

1 Jesus, Jesus, visit me,
How my soul longs after thee!
When, my best, my dearest friend,
Shall our separation end?

2 Lord, my longings never cease,
Without thee I find no peace;
'T is my constant cry to thee,
Jesus, Jesus, visit me.

3 Mean the joys of earth appear,
All below is dark and drear;
Nought but thy beloved voice
Can my wretched heart rejoice.

4 Thou alone, my gracious Lord,
Art my shield and great reward:
All my hope, my Saviour thou,
To thy sovereign will I bow.

5 Come, inhabit then my heart,
Purge its sin, and heal its smart;
See, I ever cry to thee,
Jesus, Jesus, visit me.

6 Patiently I wait thy day;
For this gift alone I pray,
That when death shall visit me
Thou my Light and Life wilt be.
J. Angelus, 1660; tr. by R. P. Dunn, 1852.

597.

1 Holy Lamb, who thee receive,
Who in thee begin to live,
Day and night they cry to thee,
As thou art so let us be!

2 Jesus, see my panting breast;
See, I pant in thee to rest;
Gladly would I now be clean;
Cleanse me now from every sin.

3 Fix, oh fix my wav'ring mind,
To thy cross my spirit bind;
Earthly passions far remove;
Swallow up my soul in love.

4 Dust and ashes though we be,
Full of sin and misery,
Thine we are, thou Son of God;
Take the purchase of thy blood!
Anna Dober, 1735; tr. by John Wesley, 1740.

THE CHRISTIAN LIFE,—ASPIRATION.

COMMUNION. C. M.

1. My God! though cleaving to the dust, My soul cries out for thee: Oh come, confirm my humble trust, And dwell thyself in me.

598.

1 My God! though cleaving to the dust,
    My soul cries out for thee:
  Oh come, confirm my humble trust,
    And dwell thyself in me.

2 No shadow now can give me peace,
    No image fading still,
  Me with the substance of thy grace,
    Thyself, thy Spirit, fill!

3 Henceforth to me this blessing give,
    This only needful thing —
  In thee, by thee, for thee to live,
    Who art my God and King.

4 Yet how, if sins my heart defile,
    Can I be one with thee?
  Lord, thou art pure, and I am vile,
    And righteous thou must be.

5 Jesus, behold! I plead thy blood;
    Thou hast the ransom given:
  Oh fill my heart, blest Lamb of God,
    With love, and peace, and heaven.

Adrien Bossier; tr. by Henry Downton, 1870.

599.

1 I knew thee in the land of drought,
    Thy comfort and control,
  Thy truth encompassed me about,
    Thy love refreshed my soul.

2 I knew thee when the world was waste,
    And thou alone wast fair,
  On thee my heart its fondness placed,
    My soul reposed its care.

3 And if thine altered hand doth now
    My sky with sunshine fill,
  Who amid all so fair as thou?
    Oh let me know thee still;

4 Still turn to thee in days of light,
    As well as nights of care,
  Thou brightest amid all that's bright!
    Thou fairest of the fair!

5 My sun is, Lord, where'er thou art,
    My cloud, where self I see,
  My drought in an ungrateful heart,
    My freshest springs in thee.

J. S. B. Monsell, 1863.

600.

1 Oh, could I find, from day to day,
    A nearness to my God;
  Then should my hours glide sweet away,
    And live upon his word.

2 Lord, I desire with thee to live
    Anew from day to day;
  In joys the world can never give,
    Nor ever take away.

3 O Jesus, come and rule my heart,
    And make me wholly thine:
  That I may never more depart,
    Nor grieve thy love divine.

4 Thus, till my last expiring breath,
    Thy goodness I'll adore:
  And when my flesh dissolves in death,
    My soul shall love thee more.

Benjamin Cleaveland, 1792, a.

THE CHRISTIAN LIFE,—ASPIRATION.

BARBY. C. M.

601.   Psalm 119.

1 My soul lies cleaving to the dust;
  Lord, give me life divine;
  From vain desires and every lust
  Turn off these eyes of mine.

2 I need the influence of thy grace
  To speed me in thy way,
  Lest I should loiter in my race,
  Or turn my feet astray.

3 Are not thy mercies sovereign still,
  And thou a faithful God?
  Wilt thou not grant me warmer zeal
  To run the heavenly road?

4 Does not my heart thy precepts love,
  And long to see thy face?
  And yet how slow my spirits move,
  Without enlivening grace.

5 Then shall I love thy gospel more,
  And ne'er forget thy word,
  When I have felt its quickening power
  To draw me near the Lord.
    Isaac Watts, 1719.

602.

1 Oh for a heart to praise my God,
  A heart from sin set free;
  A heart that always feels thy blood
  So freely spilt for me!

2 A heart resigned, submissive, meek,
  My great Redeemer's throne;
  Where only Christ is heard to speak,
  Where Jesus reigns alone!

3 An humble, lowly, contrite heart,
  Believing, true, and clean!
  Which neither life nor death can part
  From him that dwells within.

4 A heart in every thought renewed,
  And filled with love divine;
  Perfect, and right, and pure, and good;
  A copy, Lord, of thine!

5 Thy nature, gracious Lord, impart;
  Come quickly from above;
  Write thy new name upon my heart,
  Thy new, best name of Love.
    Charles Wesley, 1742.

603.

1 Jesus, my Saviour, bind me fast,
  In cords of heavenly love;
  Then sweetly draw me to thy breast,
  Nor let me thence remove.

2 Draw me from all created good,
  From self, the world, and sin,
  To the dear fountain of thy blood,
  And make me pure within.

3 Oh lead me to thy mercy-seat,
  Attract me nearer still;
  Draw me, like Mary, to thy feet,
  To sit and learn thy will.

4 Oh draw me by thy providence,
  Thy Spirit and thy word,
  From all the things of time and sense,
  To thee, my gracious Lord.
    Benjamin Beddome, 1790.

THE CHRISTIAN LIFE,—ASPIRATION.

RELIANCE. 7s & 6s.

1. I need thee, precious Jesus, For I am full of sin; My soul is dark and guilty, My heart is dead within: I need the cleansing fountain Where I can always flee, The blood of Christ most precious, The sinner's perfect plea.

604.

1 I NEED thee, precious Jesus,
 For I am full of sin;
 My soul is dark and guilty,
 My heart is dead within:
 I need the cleansing fountain
 Where I can always flee,
 The blood of Christ most precious,
 The sinner's perfect plea.

2 I need thee, blessèd Jesus,
 For I am very poor;
 A stranger and a pilgrim,
 I have no earthly store:
 I need the love of Jesus
 To cheer me on my way,
 To guide my doubting footsteps,
 To be my strength and stay.

3 I need thee, blessèd Jesus;
 I need a friend like thee,—
 A friend to soothe and pity,
 A friend to care for me.
 I need the heart of Jesus
 To feel each anxious care,
 To tell my every trial,
 And all my sorrows share.

4 I need thee, blessèd Jesus,
 And hope to see thee soon,
 Encircled with the rainbow,
 And seated on thy throne!
 There, with thy blood-bought children,
 My joy shall ever be,
 To sing thy praise, Lord Jesus,
 To gaze, my Lord, on thee.
  Frederick Whitfield, 1861.

605.

1 To thee, O dear, dear Saviour!
 My spirit turns for rest,
 My peace is in thy favor,
 My pillow on thy breast.

2 Though all the world deceive me,
 I know that I am thine,
 And thou wilt never leave me,
 O blessèd Saviour mine.

3 O thou whose mercy found me,
 From bondage set me free,
 And then forever bound me,
 With threefold cords to thee:

4 Oh for a heart to love thee
 More truly as I ought;
 And nothing place above thee,
 In deed, or word, or thought.

5 Oh for that choicest blessing
 Of living in thy love,
 And thus on earth possessing
 The peace of heaven above!
  J. S. B. Monsell, 1863.

THE CHRISTIAN LIFE,—ASPIRATION.

BETHANY. 6s & 4s.

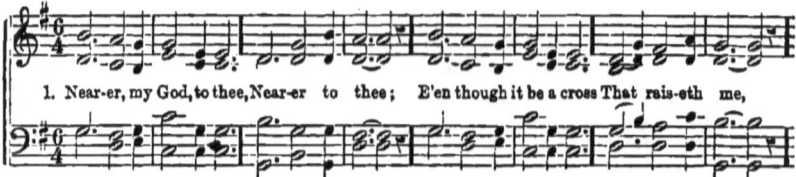
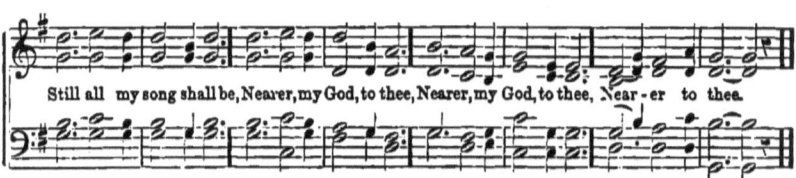

1. Near-er, my God, to thee, Near-er to thee; E'en though it be a cross That rais-eth me, Still all my song shall be, Nearer, my God, to thee, Nearer, my God, to thee, Near-er to thee.

606.

2 Though like the wanderer,
  The sun gone down,
 Darkness be over me,
  My rest a stone,
 Yet in my dreams I'd be
  Nearer, my God, to thee,
  Nearer to thee.

3 There let the way appear
  Steps unto heaven;
 All that thou sendest me
  In mercy given,
 Angels to beckon me
  Nearer, my God, to thee,
  Nearer to thee.

4 Then with my waking thoughts,
  Bright with thy praise,
 Out of my stony griefs,
  Bethel I'll raise;
 So by my woes to be
  Nearer, my God, to thee,
  Nearer to thee.

5 Or if on joyful wing,
  Cleaving the sky,
 Sun, moon, and stars forgot,
  Upward I fly,
 Still all my song shall be,
  Nearer, my God, to thee,
  Nearer to thee.

  Sarah Flower Adams, 1841.

ASPIRATION CHANT. 6s.

607.

1 My spirit longs for thee
  Within my | trou-bled | breast;
 Unworthy though I be
  Of | so di- | vine a | guest!

2 Of so divine a guest
  Unworthy | though I | be,
 Yet hath my heart no rest
  Un- | til it | come to | thee!

3 Unless it come from thee,
  In vain I | look a- | round;
 In all that I can see,
  No | rest is | to be | found!

4 No rest is to be found,
  But in thy | bless-ed | love,
 Oh, let my wish be crowned,
  And | send it | from a- | bove!

  John Byrom, 1773.

THE CHRISTIAN LIFE,—ASPIRATION.

ATKINS. C. M.

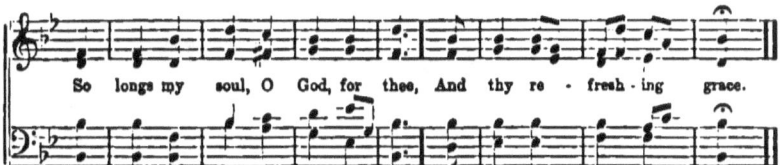

1. As pants the hart for cooling streams, When heated in the chase,
So longs my soul, O God, for thee, And thy refreshing grace.

608.
Psalm 42.

1 As pants the hart for cooling streams
When heated in the chase,
So longs my soul, O God, for thee,
And thy refreshing grace.

2 For thee, my God, the living God,
My thirsty soul doth pine;
Oh when shall I behold thy face,
Thou Majesty Divine?

3 Why restless, why cast down, my soul?
Trust God, who will employ
His aid for thee, and change those sighs
To thankful hymns of joy.

4 God of my strength, how long shall I,
Like one forgotten, mourn;
Forlorn, forsaken, and exposed
To my oppressor's scorn?

5 Why restless, why cast down, my soul?
Hope still, and thou shalt sing
The praise of him who is thy God,
Thy health's eternal spring.

Tate and Brady, 1696.

609.

1 In vain I trace creation o'er
In search of sacred rest;
The whole creation is too poor,
Too mean, to make me blest.

2 Let earth and all her charms depart,
Unworthy of the mind;

In God alone this restless heart
An equal bliss can find.

3 Thy favor, Lord, is all I want;
Here would my spirit rest;
Oh, send the rich, the boundless grant,
And make me fully blest!

Anne Steele, 1760.

610.

1 Why is my heart so far from thee,
My God, my chief delight?
Why are my thoughts no more by day
With thee, no more by night?

2 Why should my foolish passions rove?
Where can such sweetness be,
As I have tasted in thy love,
As I have found in thee?

3 Trifles of nature, or of art,
With fair, deceitful charms,
Intrude into my thoughtless heart,
And thrust me from thy arms.

4 Wretch that I am, to wander thus,
In chase of false delight!
Let me be fastened to thy cross,
Rather than lose thy sight.

5 Make haste, my days, to reach the goal,
And bring my heart to rest
On the dear centre of my soul,
My God, my Saviour's breast!

Isaac Watts, 1709.

THE CHRISTIAN LIFE,—PRAYER.

RETREAT. L. M.

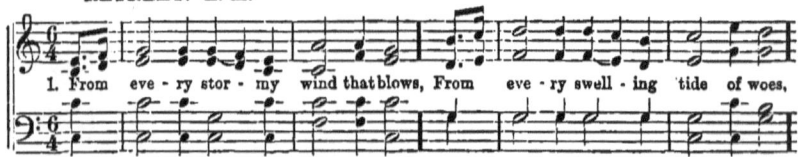

611.

1 From every stormy wind that blows,
From every swelling tide of woes,
There is a calm, a sure retreat,
'T is found beneath the mercy-seat.

2 There is a place where Jesus sheds
The oil of gladness on our heads,
A place than all beside more sweet;
It is the blood-stained mercy-seat.

3 There is a spot where spirits blend,
Where friend holds fellowship with friend;
Though sundered far, by faith they meet
Around the common mercy-seat.

4 Ah! whither could we flee for aid,
When tempted, desolate, dismayed?
Or how the hosts of hell defeat,
Had suffering saints no mercy-seat?

5 There, there, on eagle wings we soar,
And time, and sense, seem all no more;
And heaven comes down our souls to greet,
And glory crowns the mercy-seat.

6 Oh let my hand forget her skill,
My tongue be silent, cold and still,
This bounding heart forget to beat,
If I forget the mercy-seat!
Hugh Stowell, 1831.

612.

1 Hast thou within a care so deep,
It chases from thine eyelids sleep?
To thy Redeemer take that care,
And change anxiety to prayer.

2 Hast thou a hope with which thy heart
Would almost feel it death to part?
Entreat thy God that hope to crown,
Or give thee strength to lay it down.

3 Hast thou a friend whose image dear
May prove an idol worshipped here?
Implore the Lord that nought may be
A shadow between heaven and thee.

4 Whate'er the care that breaks thy rest,
Whate'er the wish that swells thy breast,
Spread before God that wish, that care,
And change anxiety to prayer.
Ryle's Collection.

613.

1 God of my life, to thee I call,
Afflicted at thy feet I fall;
When the great water-floods prevail,
Leave not my trembling heart to fail!

2 Friend of the friendless and the faint,
Where should I lodge my deep complaint?
Where but with thee, whose open door
Invites the helpless and the poor?

3 Did ever mourner plead with thee,
And thou refuse that mourner's plea?
Does not the word still fixed remain,
That none shall seek thy face in vain?

4 Poor though I am, despised, forgot,
Yet God, my God, forgets me not;
And he is safe, and must succeed,
For whom the Lord vouchsafes to plead.
William Cowper, 1779.

THE CHRISTIAN LIFE,—PRAYER.

SHIRLAND. S. M.

1. Jesus, who knows full well
The heart of every saint,
Invites us all our griefs to tell,
To pray and never faint.

614. Luke xviii. 1-7.

1 Jesus, who knows full well
 The heart of every saint,
 Invites us all our griefs to tell,
 To pray and never faint.

2 He bows his gracious ear,
 We never plead in vain;
 Yet we must wait till he appear,
 And pray, and pray again.

3 Though unbelief suggest,
 Why should we longer wait?
 He bids us never give him rest,
 But be importunate.

4 And shall not Jesus hear
 His chosen when they cry?
 Yes, though he may awhile forbear,
 He'll help them from on high.

5 His nature, truth, and love,
 Engage him on their side;
 When they are grieved, his mercies move,
 And can they be denied?

6 Then let us earnest be,
 And never faint in prayer;
 He loves our importunity,
 And makes our cause his care.
 John Newton, 1779.

615.

1 Behold the throne of grace!
 The promise calls me near;
 There Jesus shows a smiling face,
 And waits to answer prayer.

2 That rich atoning blood,
 Which sprinkled round I see,
 Provides for those who come to God
 An all-prevailing plea.

3 My soul! ask what thou wilt;
 Thou canst not be too bold;
 Since his own blood for thee he spilt,
 What else can he withhold?

4 Thine image, Lord, bestow,
 Thy presence and thy love;
 I ask to serve thee here below,
 And reign with thee above.

5 Teach me to live by faith;
 Conform my will to thine;
 Let me victorious be in death,
 And then in glory shine.
 John Newton, 1779.

616. Matt. vi. 9-15. Tune, "Ward," p. 250. L. M.

1 Father of heaven! whose gracious hand
 Dispenses good in boundless store,
 May every breath thy praise expand,
 And every heart thy name adore.

2 Great God! may all our wakened powers
 To spread thy sway exulting join;
 Till we shall dare to think thee ours,
 And thou shalt deign to make us thine.

3 Whate'er thy will, may we display
 Hearts that submit without a sigh;
 Whate'er thy law, may we obey,
 Like raptured saints, and feel its joy.

250 — THE CHRISTIAN LIFE,—PRAYER.

WARD. L. M.

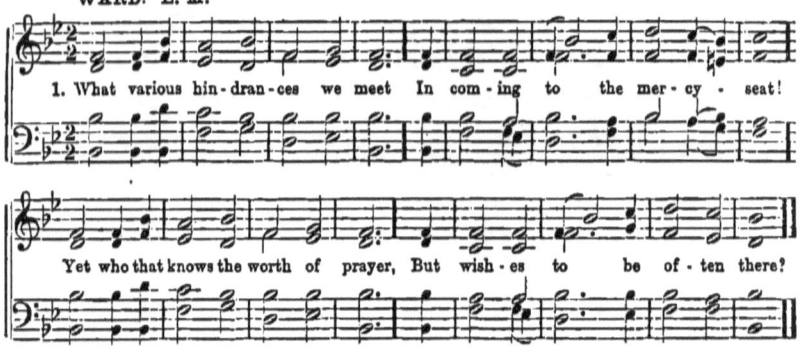

1. What various hin-dran-ces we meet In com-ing to the mer-cy-seat! Yet who that knows the worth of prayer, But wish-es to be of-ten there?

4 Vouchsafe us what our wants require
This fleeting life in peace to spend,
But bid our wishes, Lord, aspire
To grasp the life that cannot end.

5 Our countless crimes with mercy view,
For Jesus' sake their guilt remove,
And teach us, Lord, to pardon too,
That thou may'st see a world of love.

6 Protect us when temptation's near,
Keep us from pride and passion free;
Shield us from sin and sorrow here,
And bring us, Lord, at length to thee.
J. D. Carlyle, 1805.

617.

1 What various hindrances we meet
In coming to the mercy-seat!
Yet who that knows the worth of prayer,
But wishes to be often there?

2 Prayer makes the darkened cloud withdraw,
Prayer climbs the ladder Jacob saw,
Gives exercise to faith and love,
Brings every blessing from above.

3 Restraining prayer, we cease to fight,
Prayer makes the Christian's armor bright;
And Satan trembles when he sees
The weakest saint upon his knees.

4 While Moses stood with arms spread wide,
Success was found on Israel's side;
But when through weariness they failed,
That moment Amalek prevailed.

5 Have you no words? Ah! think again;
Words flow apace when you complain,
And fill your fellow-creature's ear
With the sad tale of all your care.

6 Were half the breath thus vainly spent
To Heaven in supplication sent,
Your cheerful song would oftener be,
"Hear what the Lord has done for me."
William Cowper, 1779.

618.

1 Children of God! in all your need,
Remember him who died for you;
Ye suppliants, think, whene'er you plead,
The Lord of Love is pleading too.

2 Nor pleads in vain; the Father hears
The voice of his beloved Son;
'Tis music in Jehovah's ears;
He pleads, and lo! the suit is won.

3 "Father, forgive them!" Jesus cried,
When bleeding on th' accursed tree,
"Bless, bless them, Lord, for this I died!"
Is still his all-prevailing plea.

4 Come, brethren, then; our feeblest prayer,
Perfumed with Jesus' blessed name,
Is heard on high, is treasured there;
And all that heaven can give may claim.

5 From everlasting we are his,
In love's eternal counsel given;
And he himself our portion is,
The glory of our promised heaven.
Sir Edward Denny, 1839.

THE CHRISTIAN LIFE,—PRAYER.

DEDHAM. C. M.

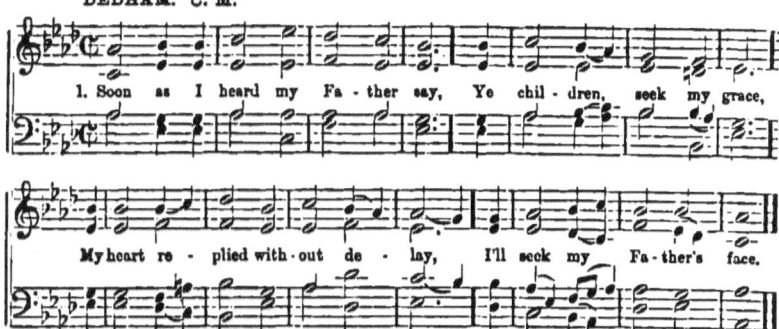

1. Soon as I heard my Father say, Ye children, seek my grace, My heart replied without delay, I'll seek my Father's face.

619.
PSALM 27.

1 Soon as I heard my Father say,
"Ye children, seek my grace,"
My heart replied without delay,
"I'll seek my Father's face."

2 Let not thy face be hid from me,
Nor frown my soul away;
God of my life, I fly to thee
In a distressing day.

3 Should friends and kindred near and dear
Leave me to want or die,
My God would make my life his care,
And all my need supply.

4 My fainting flesh had died with grief,
Had not my soul believed
To see thy grace provide relief;
Nor was my hope deceived.

5 Wait on the Lord, ye trembling saints,
And keep your courage up;
He'll raise your spirit when it faints,
And far exceed your hope.
Isaac Watts, 1719.

620.

1 For mercies, countless as the sands,
Which daily I receive
From Jesus my Redeemer's hands,
My soul, what canst thou give?

2 Alas! from such an heart as mine,
What can I bring him forth?
My best is stained and dyed with sin,
My all is nothing worth.

3 Yet this acknowledgment I'll make
For all he has bestowed;
Salvation's sacred cup I'll take,
And call upon my God.

4 The best return for one like me,
So wretched and so poor,
Is from his gifts to draw a plea,
And ask him still for more.
William Cowper, 1779.

621.
Tune, "Seymour," p. 193.

1 Come, my soul, thy suit prepare;
Jesus loves to answer prayer;
He himself has bid thee pray;
Therefore will not say thee nay.

2 Thou art coming to a King,
Large petitions with thee bring;
For his grace and power are such,
None can ever ask too much.

3 With my burden I begin;
Lord, remove this load of sin;
Let thy blood, for sinners spilt,
Set my conscience free from guilt.

4 Lord, I come to thee for rest;
Take possession of my breast;
There thy blood-bought right maintain,
And without a rival reign.

5 Show me what I have to do;
Every hour my strength renew;
Let me live a life of faith;
Let me die thy people's death.
John Newton, 1779.

THE CHRISTIAN LIFE,—PRAYER.

COME, YE DISCONSOLATE. 11s & 10s.

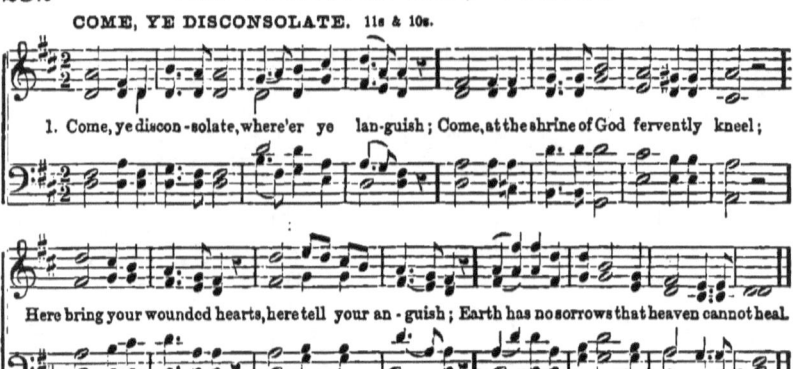

1. Come, ye discon-solate, where'er ye lan-guish; Come, at the shrine of God fervently kneel;
Here bring your wounded hearts, here tell your an-guish; Earth has no sorrows that heaven cannot heal.

622.

1 COME, ye disconsolate, where'er ye languish;
  Come, at the shrine of God fervently kneel;
  Here bring your wounded hearts, here tell your anguish;
  Earth has no sorrows that heaven cannot heal.

2 Joy of the desolate, light of the straying,
  Hope of the penitent, fadeless and pure;
  Here speaks the Comforter, in mercy saying,
  Earth has no sorrows that heaven cannot cure:

3 Here see the bread of life; see waters flowing
  Forth from the throne of God, boundless in love;
  Come to the feast of love, come, ever knowing
  Earth has no sorrows but heaven can remove.

Thomas Moore, 1816.

DOXOLOGY.

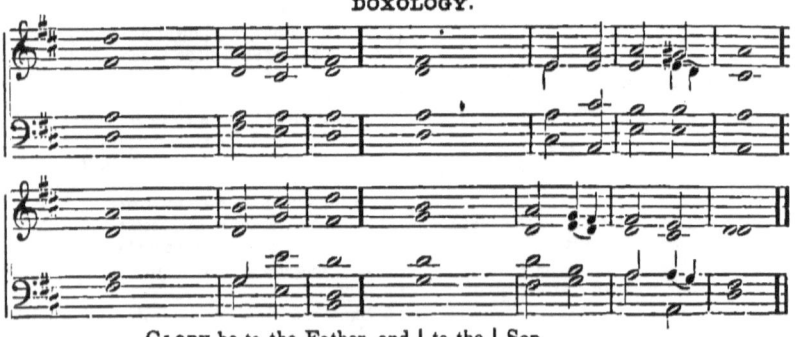

GLORY be to the Father, and | to the | Son,
And | to the | Holy | Ghost;

As it was in the beginning, is now, and | ever | shall be,
World | without | end. A- | men.

THE CHRISTIAN LIFE,—PRAYER.

DEVIZES. C. M.

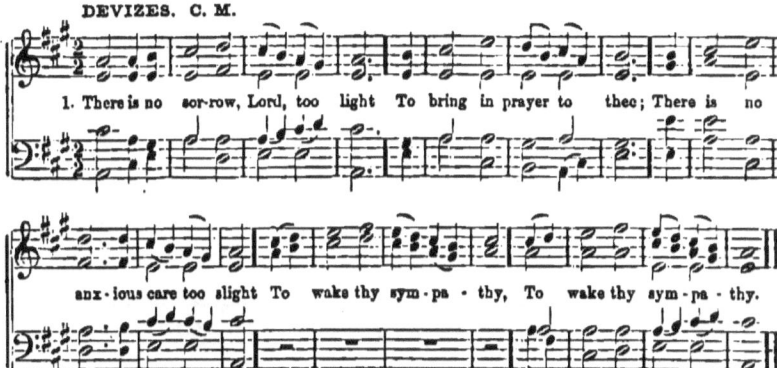

1. There is no sorrow, Lord, too light To bring in prayer to thee; There is no anx-ious care too slight To wake thy sym-pa-thy, To wake thy sym-pa-thy.

623.

1 THERE is no sorrow, Lord, too light
  To bring in prayer to thee;
  There is no anxious care too slight
  To wake thy sympathy.

2 Thou who hast trod the thorny road
  Wilt share each small distress;
  The love which bore the greater load
  Will not refuse the less.

3 There is no secret sigh we breathe
  But meets thine ear divine;
  And every cross grows light beneath
  The shadow, Lord, of thine.

4 Life's ills without, sin's strife within,
  The heart would overflow,
  But for that love which died for sin,
  That love which wept with woe.
  Jane Crewdson, 1860; *alt. by B. H. Kennedy*, 1863.

624.

1 OH that I knew the secret place
  Where I might find my God;
  I'd spread my wants before his face,
  And pour my woes abroad.

2 I'd tell him how my sins arise,
  What sorrows I sustain;
  How grace decays, and comfort dies,
  And leaves my heart in pain.

3 He knows what arguments I'd take,
  To wrestle with my God;
  I'd plead for his own mercy's sake,
  And for my Saviour's blood.

4 Arise, my soul, from deep distress,
  And banish every fear;
  He calls thee to his throne of grace,
  To spread thy sorrows there.
  Isaac Watts, 1720.

625. GEN. xxxii. 24-29.

1 SHEPHERD Divine, our wants relieve
  In this our evil day;
  To all thy tempted followers give
  The power to trust and pray.

2 Long as our fiery trials last,
  Long as the cross we bear,
  Oh let our souls on thee be cast,
  In never-ceasing prayer.

3 Thy Spirit's interceding grace
  Give us in faith to claim;
  To wrestle till we see thy face,
  And know thy hidden Name.

4 Till thou the Father's love impart,
  Till thou thyself bestow,
  Be this the cry of every heart —
  I will not let thee go:

5 I will not let thee go, unless
  Thou tell thy name to me:
  With all thy great salvation bless,
  And make me all like thee.

6 Then let me on the mountain-top
  Behold thine open face.
  Till faith in sight is swallowed up,
  And prayer in endless praise.
  Charles Wesley, 1742.

254 THE CHRISTIAN LIFE,—PRAYER.

PENIEL. L. M. (Omit repeat for 4 lines.)

1. Come, O thou trav-el - ler un - known, Whom still I hold, but can - not see,
My compan-y be - fore is gone, And I am left a - lone with thee;
With thee all night I mean to stay, And wres-tle till the break of day.

626. Gen. xxxii. 24-29.

1 Come, O thou traveller unknown,
  Whom still I hold, but cannot see,
My company before is gone,
  And I am left alone with thee;
With thee all night I mean to stay,
And wrestle till the break of day.

2 I need not tell thee who I am,
  My misery or sin declare;
Thyself hast called me by my name;
  Look on thy hands, and read it there!
But who, I ask thee, who art thou?
Tell me thy name, and tell me now.

3 In vain thou strugglest to get free,
  I never will unloose my hold;
Art thou the Man that died for me?
  The secret of thy love unfold.
Wrestling, I will not let thee go,
Till I thy name, thy nature know.

4 Yield to me now, for I am weak,
  But confident in self-despair;
Speak to my heart, in blessings speak,
  Be conquered by my instant prayer!
Speak, or thou never hence shalt move,
And tell me, if thy name is Love?

5 'Tis Love! 'tis Love! Thou diedst for
  I hear thy whisper in my heart; [me!
The morning breaks, the shadows flee;
Pure universal Love thou art!

To me, to all, thy bowels move;
  Thy nature, and thy name, is Love!

6 My prayer hath power with God; the
  Unspeakable I now receive; [grace
Through faith I see thee face to face,
  I see thee face to face, and live:
In vain I have not wept and strove;
Thy nature, and thy name, is Love.

Charles Wesley, 1742.

627.

1 My God, is any hour so sweet,
  From blush of morn to evening star,
As that which calls me to thy feet—
  The hour of prayer?

2 Then is my strength by thee renewed;
  Then are my sins by thee forgiven;
Then dost thou cheer my solitude,
  With hopes of heaven.

3 No words can tell what sweet relief
  Here for my every want I find;
What strength for warfare, balm for grief,
  What peace of mind!

4 Hushed is each doubt, gone every fear;
  My spirit seems in heaven to stay;
And e'en the penitential tear
  Is wiped away.

5 Lord, till I reach yon blissful shore,
  No privilege so dear shall be
As thus my inmost soul to pour
  In prayer to thee.

Charlotte Elliott, 1854.

THE CHRISTIAN LIFE,—PRAYER.

CORINTH. C. M.

1. Far from the world, O Lord, I flee, From strife and tumult far; From scenes where Satan wages still His most successful war.

628.

1 FAR from the world, O Lord, I flee,
From strife and tumult far;
From scenes where Satan wages still
His most successful war.

2 The calm retreat, the silent shade,
With prayer and praise agree,
And seem by thy sweet bounty made
For those who follow thee.

3 There, if thy Spirit touch the soul,
And grace her mean abode,
Oh with what peace, and joy, and love,
She communes with her God!

4 There, like the nightingale, she pours
Her solitary lays,
Nor asks a witness of her song,
Nor thirsts for human praise.

5 Author and Guardian of my life,
Sweet Source of light divine,
And, all harmonious names in one,
My Saviour! thou art mine!

6 What thanks I owe thee, and what love,
A boundless, endless store,
Shall echo through the realms above
When time shall be no more!

William Cowper, 1779.

629.

1 PRAYER is the soul's sincere desire,
Uttered or unexpressed;
The motion of a hidden fire
That trembles in the breast.

2 Prayer is the burden of a sigh,
The falling of a tear,
The upward glancing of an eye,
When none but God is near.

3 Prayer is the simplest form of speech
That infant lips can try;
Prayer the sublimest strains that reach
The Majesty on high.

4 Prayer is the contrite sinner's voice,
Returning from his ways,
While angels in their songs rejoice,
And cry, "Behold he prays!"

5 Prayer is the Christian's vital breath,
The Christian's native air;
His watchword at the gates of death,
He enters heaven with prayer.

6 Nor prayer is made by man alone;
The Holy Spirit pleads,
And Jesus, on th' eternal throne,
For sinners intercedes.

7 O thou, by whom we come to God,
The life, the truth, the way,
The path of prayer thyself hast trod;
Lord, teach us how to pray.

James Montgomery, 1819.

DOXOLOGY.

ALL glory to the Father be,
All glory to the Son,
All glory, Holy Ghost, to thee,
While endless ages run.

Hymns Ancient and Modern.

THE CHRISTIAN LIFE,—FAITH.

ILLA. L. M.

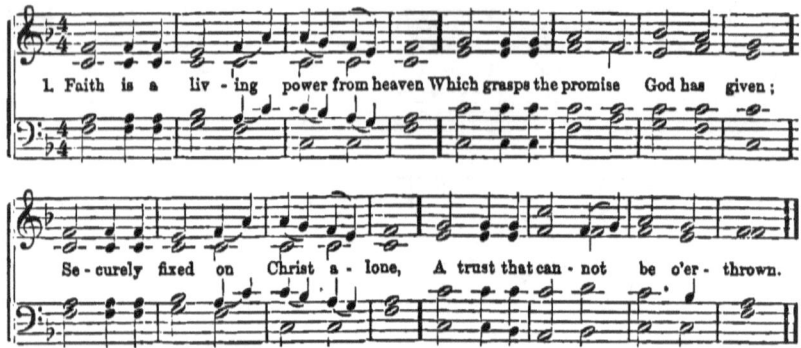

1. Faith is a liv-ing power from heaven Which grasps the promise God has given;
Se-curely fixed on Christ a-lone, A trust that can-not be o'er-thrown.

630.

1 FAITH is a living power from heaven
Which grasps the promise God has given;
Securely fixed on Christ alone,
A trust that cannot be o'erthrown.

2 Faith finds in Christ whate'er we need
To save and strengthen, guide and feed;
Strong in his grace it joys to share
His cross, in hope his crown to wear.

3 Faith to the conscience whispers peace,
And bids the mourner's sighing cease;
By faith the children's right we claim,
And call upon our Father's name.

4 Faith feels the Spirit's kindling breath
In love and hope that conquer death;
Faith blesses e'en his smiting rod,
And brings us to delight in God.

5 Such faith in us, O God, implant,
And to our prayers thy favor grant
In Jesus Christ, thy saving Son,
Who is our fount of health alone.

6 In him may every trusting soul
Press onward to the heavenly goal,
The blessedness no foes destroy,
Eternal love and light and joy.
Bohemian Brethren, 1531; *Hymnologia Christiana*, 1863.

631.

1 SEE a poor sinner, dearest Lord,
Whose soul, encouraged by thy word,
At mercy's footstool would remain,
And then would look, and look again.

2 Take courage then, my trembling soul,
One look from Christ will make thee whole;
Trust thou in him, 'tis not in vain,
But wait, and look, and look again.

3 Look to the Lord, his word, his throne;
Look to his grace, and not your own:
There wait and look, and look again;
You shall not wait nor look in vain.

4 Ere long that happy day will come,
When I shall reach my blissful home;
And when to glory I attain,
Oh then I'll look, and look again.
Samuel Medley, 1789.

632.

1 'TIS by the faith of joys to come
We walk through deserts dark as night;
Till we arrive at heaven our home,
Faith is our guide, and faith our light.

2 The want of sight she well supplies,
She makes the pearly gates appear;
Far into distant worlds she pries,
And brings eternal glories near.

3 Cheerful we tread the desert through,
When faith inspires a heavenly ray,
Though lions roar, and tempests blow,
And rocks and dangers fill the way.
Isaac Watts, 1709.

DOXOLOGY.

PRAISE God, from whom all blessings flow;
Praise him, all creatures here below;
Praise him above, ye heavenly host;
Praise Father, Son, and Holy Ghost.
Thomas Ken, 1697.

THE CHRISTIAN LIFE,—FAITH.

FAITH. C. M.

1. O faith, thou workest miracles Upon the hearts of men, Choosing thy home in those same hearts We know not how or when.

633.

1 O FAITH, thou workest miracles
Upon the hearts of men,
Choosing thy home in those same hearts
We know not how or when.

2 O gift of gifts! O grace of faith!
My God, how can it be
That thou, who hast discerning love,
Shouldst give that gift to me?

3 There was a place, there was a time,
Whether by night or day,
Thy Spirit came and left that gift,
And went upon his way.

4 Ah, Grace! into unlikeliest hearts
It is thy boast to come,
The glory of thy light to find
In darkest spots a home.

5 The crowd of cares, the weightiest cross,
Seem trifles less than light,
Earth looks so little and so low,
When faith shines full and bright.

6 Oh happy, happy that I am!
If thou canst be, O Faith,
The treasure that thou art in life,
What wilt thou be in death?

F. W. Faber, 1840.

634.

1 FAITH adds new charms to earthly bliss,
And saves me from its snares;
Its aid in every duty brings,
And softens all my cares.

2 The wounded conscience knows its power
The healing balm to give;
That balm the saddest heart can cheer,
And make the dying live.

3 Wide it unveils celestial worlds,
Where deathless pleasures reign,
And bids me seek my portion there,
Nor bids me seek in vain.

4 Faith shows the precious promise sealed
With the Redeemer's blood,
And helps my feeble hope to rest
Upon a faithful God.

5 There, there unshaken would I rest,
Till this frail body dies;
And then, on faith's triumphant wings,
To endless glory rise.

Isaac Watts, 1709.

635.   PSALM 125.   C. M.

1 UNSHAKEN as the sacred hill,
And fixed as mountains be,
Firm as a rock the soul shall rest,
That leans, O Lord, on thee!

2 Not walls nor hills could guard so well
Old Salem's happy ground,
As those eternal arms of love,
That every saint surround.

3 Deal gently, Lord, with souls sincere,
And lead them safely on
To the bright gates of paradise,
Where Christ, their Lord, is gone.

Isaac Watts, 1719.

THE CHRISTIAN LIFE,—FAITH.

PETERBORO'. C. M.

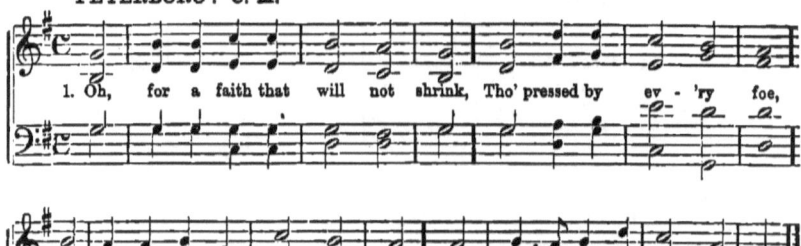

1. Oh, for a faith that will not shrink, Tho' pressed by ev-'ry foe, That will not tremble on the brink Of an-y earth-ly woe.

636.

1 Oh for a faith that will not shrink,
 Though pressed by every foe,
 That will not tremble on the brink
 Of any earthly woe! —

2 That will not murmur nor complain
 Beneath the chastening rod,
 But in the hour of grief or pain
 Will lean upon its God; —

3 A faith that shines more bright and clear
 When tempests rage without;
 That when in danger knows no fear,
 In darkness feels no doubt; —

4 That bears unmoved the world's dread
 Nor heeds its scornful smile; [frown,
 That seas of trouble cannot drown,
 Nor Satan's arts beguile; —

5 A faith that keeps the narrow way
 Till life's last hour is fled,
 And with a pure and heavenly ray
 Lights up the dying bed.

6 Lord, give us such a faith as this,
 And then whate'er may come,
 We'll taste, e'en here, the hallowed bliss
 Of an eternal home.
William H. Bathurst, 1831.

637.
HAB. iii. 17-18.,

1 What though no flowers the fig-tree
 Though vines their fruit deny, [clothe,
 The labor of the olive fail,
 And fields no meat supply; —

2 Though from the fold, with sad surprise,
 My flock cut off I see;
 Though famine pine in empty stalls,
 Where herds were wont to be; —

3 Yet in the Lord will I be glad,
 And glory in his love;
 In him I'll joy, who will the God
 Of my salvation prove.

4 God is the treasure of my soul,
 The source of lasting joy,
 A joy which want shall not impair,
 Nor death itself destroy.
William Cameron, 1781.

638.

1 Firm as the earth thy gospel stands,
 My Lord, my hope, my trust!
 If I am found in Jesus' hands,
 My soul can ne'er be lost.

2 His honor is engaged to save
 The meanest of his sheep;
 All whom his heavenly Father gave,
 His hands securely keep.

3 Nor death nor hell shall e'er remove
 His favorites from his breast;
 In the dear bosom of his love
 They must forever rest.
Isaac Watts, 1709.

DOXOLOGY.

Let God the Father, and the Son,
 And Spirit, be adored,
Where there are works to make him known,
 Or saints to love the Lord.
Isaac Watts, 1709.

THE CHRISTIAN LIFE,—FAITH.

BRADFORD. C. M.

I know that my Redeemer lives, And ever prays for me;
A token of his love he gives, A pledge of liberty.

639.

1 I KNOW that my Redeemer lives,
  And ever prays for me:
  A token of his love he gives,
  A pledge of liberty.

2 I find him lifting up my head;
  He brings salvation near;
  His presence makes me free indeed,
  And he will soon appear.

3 He wills that I should holy be;
  What can withstand his will?
  The counsel of his grace in me
  He surely shall fulfil.

4 Jesus, I hang upon thy word;
  I steadfastly believe
  Thou wilt return, and claim me, Lord,
  And to thyself receive.

5 When God is mine, and I am his,
  Of paradise possessed,
  I taste unutterable bliss,
  And everlasting rest.
  Charles Wesley. 1747.

640.

1 ARISE, my soul, my joyful powers,
  And triumph in my God;
  Awake, my voice, and loud proclaim
  His glorious grace abroad.

2 The arms of everlasting love
  Beneath my soul he placed,
  And on the Rock of ages set
  My slippery footsteps fast.

3 The city of my blest abode
  Is walled around with grace;
  Salvation for a bulwark stands
  To shield the sacred place.

4 Arise, my soul! awake my voice,
  And tunes of pleasure sing;
  Loud hallelujahs shall address
  My Saviour and my King.
  Isaac Watts, 1709.

641.

1 WALK in the light! and thou shalt own
  Thy darkness pass'd away,
  Because that light hath on thee shone
  In which is perfect day.

2 Walk in the light! so shalt thou know
  That fellowship of love,
  His Spirit only can bestow
  Who reigns in light above.

3 Walk in the light! and thou shalt find
  Thy heart made truly his
  Who dwells in cloudless light enshrined,
  In whom no darkness is.

4 Walk in the light! and e'en the tomb
  No fearful shade shall wear;
  Glory shall chase away its gloom,
  For Christ hath conquered there.

5 Walk in the light! thy path shall be
  Peaceful, serene, and bright;
  For God, by grace, shall dwell in thee,
  And God himself is light.
  Bernard Barton, 1826.

THE CHRISTIAN LIFE,—FAITH.

GOSHEN. 10s & 11s.

1. Be-gone, un-be-lief! my Saviour is near, And for my re-lief will sure-ly ap-pear; By prayer let me wrestle, and he will perform; With Christ in the ves-sel, I smile at the storm.

642.

1 BEGONE, unbelief! my Saviour is near,
  And for my relief will surely appear;
  By prayer let me wrestle, and he will perform;
  With Christ in the vessel, I smile at the storm.

2 Though dark be my way, since he is my guide,
  'Tis mine to obey, 't is his to provide;
  Though cisterns be broken, and creatures all fail,
  The word he has spoken shall surely prevail.

3 His love in time past forbids me to think
  He'll leave me at last in trouble to sink;
  Each sweet Ebenezer I have in review,
  Confirms his good pleasure to help me quite through.

4 Determined to save, he watched o'er my path,
  When, Satan's blind slave, I sported with death;
  And can he have taught me to trust in his name,
  And thus far have brought me to put me to shame?

5 Why should I complain of want or distress,
  Temptation or pain?—he told me no less;
  The heirs of salvation, I know from his word,
  Through much tribulation must follow their Lord.

6 How bitter that cup no heart can conceive,
  Which he drank quite up that sinners might live!
  His way was much rougher and darker than mine;
  Did Jesus thus suffer, and shall I repine?

7 Since all that I meet shall work for my good,
  The bitter is sweet, the med'cine is food;
  Though painful at present, 'twill cease before **long**,
  And then oh how pleasant the conqueror's song.

John Newton, 1779.

THE CHRISTIAN LIFE,—SUFFERING AND TRUST. 261

NAOMI. C. M.

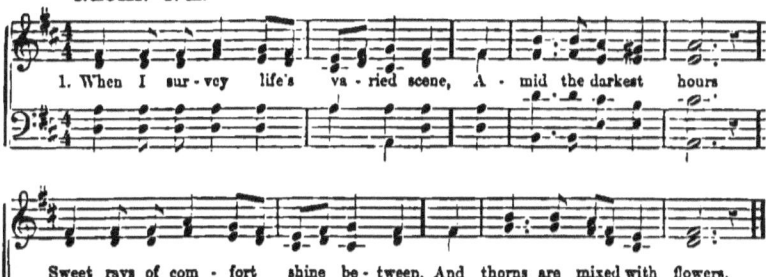

1. When I survey life's varied scene, Amid the darkest hours Sweet rays of comfort shine between, And thorns are mixed with flowers.

643.

1 WHEN I survey life's varied scene,
  Amid the darkest hours
  Sweet rays of comfort shine between,
  And thorns are mixed with flowers.

2 Lord, teach me to adore thy hand,
  From whence my comforts flow,
  And let me in this desert land
  A glimpse of Canaan know.

3 And oh! whate'er of earthly bliss
  Thy sovereign hand denies,
  Accepted at thy throne of grace
  Let this petition rise:

4 Give me a calm, a thankful heart,
  From every murmur free;
  The blessings of thy grace impart,
  And let me live to thee.

5 Let the sweet hope that thou art mine
  My path of life attend.
  Thy presence through my journey shine,
  And bless its happy end!
  Anne Steele, 1760.

644. PSALM 66.

1 Now shall my solemn vows be paid
  To that Almighty Power,
  Who heard the long requests I made
  In my distressful hour.

2 My lips and cheerful heart prepare
  To make his mercies known;
  Come, ye that fear my God, and hear
  The wonders he hath done.

3 When on my head huge sorrows fell,
  I sought his heavenly aid;
  He saved my sinking soul from hell,
  And death's eternal shade.

4 If sin lay covered in my heart,
  While prayer employed my tongue,
  The Lord had shown me no regard,
  Nor I his praises sung.

5 But God, his name be ever blest,
  Hath set my spirit free,
  Nor turned from him my poor request,
  Nor turned his heart from me.
  Isaac Watts, 1719.

645. PSALM 40.

1 I WAITED patient for the Lord,
  He bowed to hear my cry;
  He saw me resting on his word,
  And brought salvation nigh.

2 He raised me from a horrid pit
  Where mourning long I lay,
  And from my bonds released my feet,
  Deep bonds of miry clay.

3 Firm on a rock he made me stand,
  And taught my cheerful tongue
  To praise the wonders of his hand,
  In a new thankful song.

4 I'll spread his works of grace abroad;
  The saints with joy shall hear,
  And sinners learn to make my God
  Their only hope and fear.
  Isaac Watts, 1719.

262 THE CHRISTIAN LIFE,—SUFFERING AND TRUST.

APPLETON. L. M.

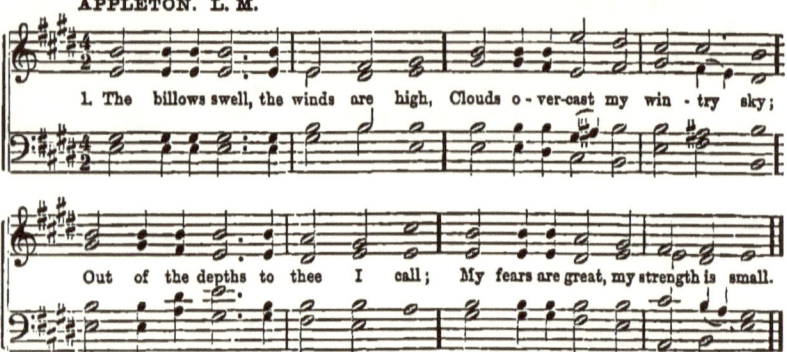

646.

1 THE billows swell, the winds are high,
   Clouds overcast my wintry sky;
   Out of the depths to thee I call;
   My fears are great, my strength is small.

2 O Lord, the pilot's part perform,
   And guide and guard me through the storm!
   Defend me from each threatening ill;
   Control the waves; say, "Peace, be still!"

3 Amidst the roaring of the sea,
   My soul still hangs her hopes on thee;
   Thy constant love, thy faithful care,
   Is all that saves me from despair.

4 Tho' tempest-tossed, and half a wreck,
   My Saviour through the floods I seek;
   Let neither winds nor stormy main
   Force back my shattered bark again.
   William Cowper, 1779.

647.

1 THUS far my God hath led me on,
   And made his truth and mercy known;
   My hopes and fears alternate rise,
   And comforts mingle with my sighs.

2 Through this wide wilderness I roam,
   Far distant from my blissful home;
   Lord, let thy presence be my stay,
   And guard me in this dangerous way.

3 My soul, with various tempests tossed,
   Her hopes o'erturned, her projects crossed,
   Sees every day new straits attend,
   And wonders where the scene will end.

4 Is this, dear Lord, that thorny road
   Which leads us to the mount of God?
   Are these the toils thy people know,
   While in the wilderness below?

5 'T is even so thy faithful love
   Doth all thy children's graces prove;
   'T is thus our pride and self must fall,
   That Jesus may be All in All.
   John Fawcett, 1782.

648.

1 GOD of my life, whose gracious power
   Through varied deaths my soul hath led,
   Or turned aside the fatal hour,
   Or lifted up my sinking head;

2 In all my ways thy hand I own,
   Thy ruling providence I see;
   Assist me still my course to run,
   And still direct my paths to thee.

3 Whither, oh whither should I fly,
   But to my loving Saviour's breast,
   Secure within thine arms to lie,
   And safe beneath thy wings to rest?

4 I have no skill the snare to shun,
   But thou, O Christ, my wisdom art;
   I ever into ruin run,
   But thou art greater than my heart.

5 Foolish, and impotent, and blind,
   Lead me a way I have not known;
   Bring me where I my heaven may find—
   The heaven of loving thee alone.
   Charles Wesley, 1740.

THE CHRISTIAN LIFE,—SUFFERING AND TRUST. 263

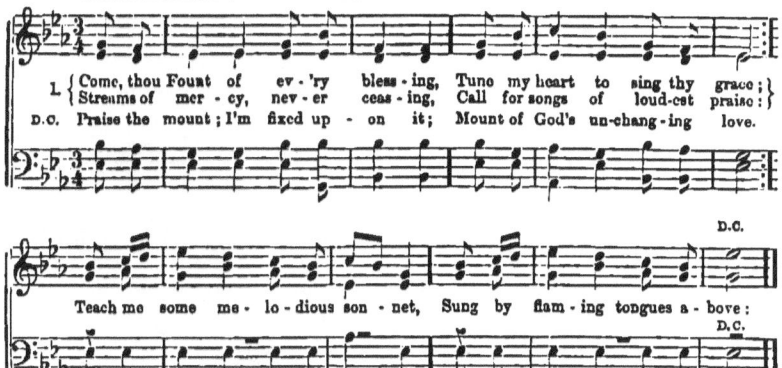

649.

1 COME, thou Fount of every blessing,
  Tune my heart to sing thy grace;
Streams of mercy never ceasing
  Call for songs of loudest praise.
Teach me some melodious sonnet,
  Sung by flaming tongues above:
Praise the mount; I'm fixed upon it;
  Mount of God's unchanging love.

2 Here I raise my Ebenezer;
  Hither by thy help I'm come;
And I hope, by thy good pleasure,
  Safely to arrive at home.
Jesus sought me when a stranger,
  Wandering from the fold of God;
He, to rescue me from danger,
  Interposed with precious blood.

3 Oh to grace how great a debtor
  Daily I'm constrained to be!
Let that grace now, like a fetter,
  Bind my wandering heart to thee:
Prone to wander, Lord, I feel it;
  Prone to leave the God I love;
Here's my heart, oh, take and seal it;
  Seal it from thy courts above.

Robert Robinson, 1757.

650.

1 GENTLY, Lord, oh, gently lead us
  Through this lonely vale of tears;
Through the changes thou 'st decreed us,
  Till our last great change appears:
When temptation's darts assail us,
  When in devious paths we stray,
Let thy goodness never fail us;
  Lead us in thy perfect way.

2 In the hour of pain and anguish,
  In the hour when death draws near,
Suffer not our hearts to languish,
  Suffer not our souls to fear:
And, when mortal life is ended,
  Bid us on thy bosom rest;
Till, by angel-bands attended,
  We awake among the blest.

Thomas Hastings, 1832.

DOXOLOGY.

PRAISE the God of all creation:
  Praise the Father's boundless love;
Praise the Lamb, our expiation,
  Priest and King enthroned above:
Praise the Fountain of salvation,
  Him by whom our spirits live;
Undivided adoration
  To the One Jehovah give.

Josiah Conder, 1836.

264 THE CHRISTIAN LIFE,—SUFFERING AND TRUST.

ZONG. 6s.

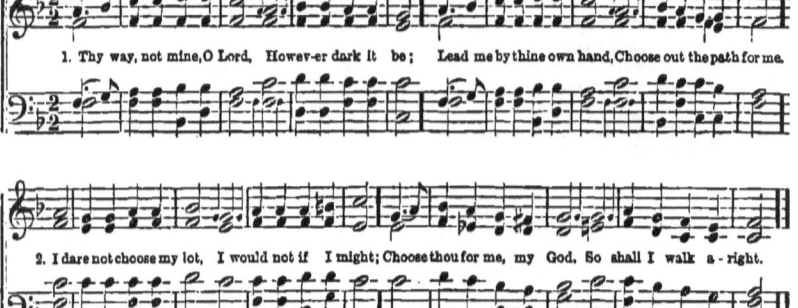

1. Thy way, not mine, O Lord, Howev-er dark it be; Lead me by thine own hand, Choose out the path for me.

2. I dare not choose my lot, I would not if I might; Choose thou for me, my God, So shall I walk a-right.

651.

1 Thy way, not mine, O Lord,
　However dark it be;
　Lead me by thine own hand,
　Choose out the path for me.

2 I dare not choose my lot,
　I would not if I might;
　Choose thou for me, my God;
　So shall I walk aright.

3 The kingdom that I seek
　Is thine, so let the way
　That leads to it be thine,
　Else I must surely stray.

4 Choose thou for me my friends,
　My sickness or my health;
　Choose thou my cares for me,
　My poverty or wealth.

5 Not mine, not mine the choice,
　In things or great or small;
　Be thou my guide, my strength,
　My wisdom and my all.
　　　　　Horatius Bonar, 1856.

652.

1 My Jesus, as thou wilt!
　Oh, may thy will be mine!
　Into thy hand of love
　I would my all resign:
Through sorrow, or through joy,
　Conduct me as thine own,
And help me still to say,
　My Lord, thy will be done!

2 My Jesus, as thou wilt!
　If needy here and poor,
　Give me thy people's bread,
　Their portion rich and sure.
The manna of thy word
　Let my soul feed upon;
And if all else should fail,
　My Lord, thy will be done!

3 My Jesus, as thou wilt!
　Though seen through many a tear,
　Let not my star of hope
　Grow dim or disappear:
Since thou on earth hast wept
　And sorrowed oft alone,
If I must weep with thee,
　My Lord, thy will be done!

4 My Jesus, as thou wilt!
　All shall be well for me:
　Each changing future scene
　I gladly trust with thee.
Straight to my home above
　I travel calmly on,
And sing, in life or death,
　My Lord, thy will be done!
　　　B. Schmolke, 1714; tr. by Jane Borthwick, 1853.

THE CHRISTIAN LIFE,—SUFFERING AND TRUST. 265

RESIGNATION. 8s & 4s, and 8s & 6s.

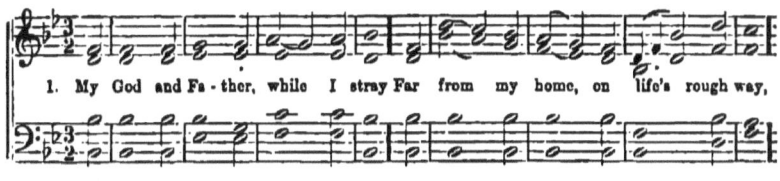

1. My God and Fa-ther, while I stray Far from my home, on life's rough way,

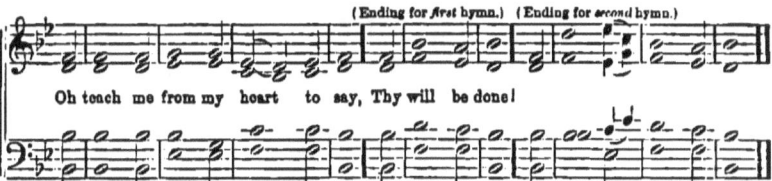

(Ending for first hymn.) (Ending for second hymn.)

Oh teach me from my heart to say, Thy will be done!

653.

1 My God and Father, while I stray
 Far from my home, on life's rough way,
 Oh teach me from my heart to say,
  Thy will be done!

2 Though dark my path and sad my lot,
 Let me be still and murmur not,
 Or breathe the prayer divinely taught,
  Thy will be done!

3 What though in lonely grief I sigh
 For friends beloved, no longer nigh,
 Submissive still would I reply,
  Thy will be done!

4 Should grief or sickness waste away
 My life in premature decay,
 My Father! still I strive to say,
  Thy will be done!

5 Though thou hast called me to resign
 What most I prized, it ne'er was mine,
 I have but yielded what was thine ;
  Thy will be done!

6 Let but my fainting heart be blest
 With thy sweet Spirit for its guest,
 My God, to thee I'll leave the rest;
  Thy will be done!

7 Renew my will from day to day;
 Blend it with thine, and take away
 All that now makes it hard to say,
  Thy will be done!

8 Then when on earth I breathe no more,
 The prayer oft mixed with tears before
 I'll sing upon a happier shore:
  Thy will be done!
   Charlotte Elliott, 1834.

654.

1 O HOLY Saviour, Friend unseen,
 The faint, the weak, on thee may lean :
 Help me, throughout life's varying scene,
  By faith to cling to thee !

2 Blest with communion so divine,
 Take what thou wilt, shall I repine,
 When, as the branches to the vine,
  My soul may cling to thee ?

3 Far from her home, fatigued, opprest,
 Here she has found a place of rest,
 An exile still, yet not unblest
  While she can cling to thee !

4 Though faith and hope awhile be tried,
 I ask not, need not, aught beside :
 How safe, how calm, how satisfied,
  The souls that cling to thee!

5 They fear not life's rough storms to brave,
 Since thou art near, and strong to save;
 Nor shudder e'en at death's dark wave,
  Because they cling to thee !

6 Blest is my lot, whate'er befall :
 What can disturb me, who appall,
 While, as my strength, my rock, my all,
  Saviour, I cling to thee ?
   Charlotte Elliott, 1834.

266 THE CHRISTIAN LIFE,—SUFFERING AND TRUST.

SALISBURY. L. M. 6 LINES.

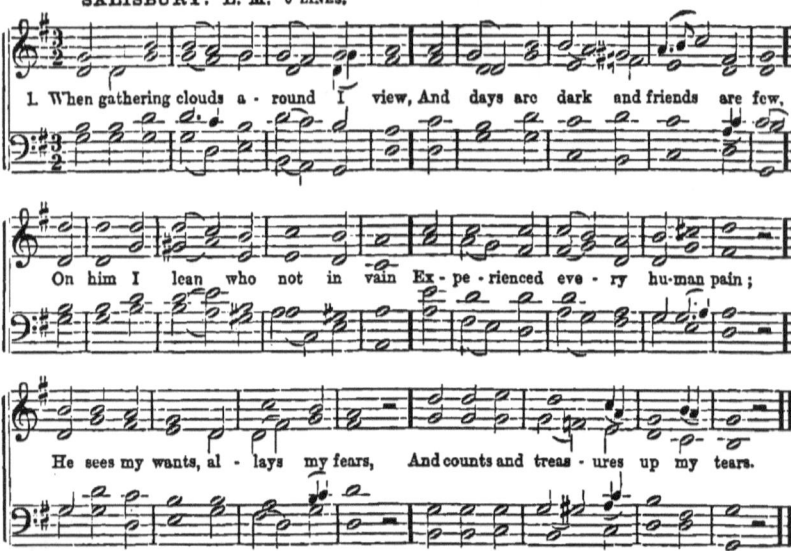

655.

1 WHEN gathering clouds around I view,
And days are dark and friends are few,
On him I lean who not in vain
Experienced every human pain;
He sees my wants, allays my fears,
And counts and treasures up my tears.

2 If aught should tempt my soul to stray
From heavenly wisdom's narrow way,
To fly the good I would pursue,
Or do the sin I would not do,
Still he who felt temptation's power
Shall guard me in that dangerous hour.

3 If wounded love my bosom swell,
Deceived by those I prized too well,
He shall his pitying aid bestow
Who felt on earth severer woe,—
At once betrayed, denied, or fled,
By those who shared his daily bread.

4 When sorrowing o'er some stone I bend
Which covers what was once a friend,
And from his voice, his hand, his smile,
Divides me for a little while,
Thou, Saviour, mark'st the tears I shed,
For thou didst weep o'er Lazarus dead.

5 And oh, when I have safely past
Through every conflict but the last,
Still, still unchanging, watch beside
My painful bed, for thou hast died;
Then point to realms of cloudless day,
And wipe the latest tear away.

Sir Robert Grant, 1812.

656.

1 HE sendeth sun, he sendeth shower,
Alike they're needful for the flower;
And joys and tears alike are sent
To give the soul fit nourishment:
As comes to me or cloud or sun,
Father, thy will, not mine, be done.

2 Can loving children e'er reprove
With murmurs whom they trust and love?
Creator, I would ever be
A trusting, loving child to thee:
As comes to me or cloud or sun,
Father, thy will, not mine, be done.

3 Oh ne'er will I at life repine;
Enough that thou hast made it mine;
When fall the shadows cold of death,
I yet will sing with parting breath,—
As comes to me or shade or sun,
Father, thy will, not mine, be done.

Sarah Flower Adams, 1841.

THE CHRISTIAN LIFE,—SUFFERING AND TRUST.

BRATTLE STREET. C. M. DOUBLE.

1. When languor and disease invade This trembling house of clay,
   'Tis sweet to look beyond the cage, And long to fly away: Sweet to look inward, and attend The whispers of his love; Sweet to look upward to the place Where Jesus pleads above.

657.

2 Sweet to look back, and see my name
   In life's fair book set down ;
   Sweet to look forward, and behold
   Eternal joys my own ;
   Sweet to reflect how grace divine
   My sins on Jesus laid ;
   Sweet to remember that his blood
   My debt of sufferings paid.

3 Sweet on his faithfulness to rest,
   Whose love can never end ;
   Sweet on his covenant of grace
   For all things to depend.
   Sweet in the confidence of faith
   To trust his firm decrees ;
   Sweet to lie passive in his hand,
   And know no will but his.

4 Sweet to rejoice in lively hope,
   That, when my change shall come,
   Angels will hover round my bed,
   And waft my spirit home.
   There shall my disimprisoned soul
   Behold him, and adore ;
   Be with his likeness satisfied,
   And grieve and sin no more ;

5 Shall see him wear that very flesh
   On which my guilt was laid ;
   His love intense, his merit fresh,
   As though but newly slain.
   If such the sweetness of the stream,
   What must the fountain be,
   Where saints and angels draw their bliss
   Immediately from thee !

   Augustus M. Toplady, 1780.

658.

1 GREAT Source of boundless power and
   Attend my mournful cry ;   [grace,
   In the dark hour of deep distress,
   To thee, to thee I fly.

2 Thou art my strength, my life, my stay,
   Assist my feeble trust ;
   Drive these distressing fears away,
   And raise me from the dust.

3 Oh let me call thy grace to mind,
   And trust thy glorious name ;
   Jehovah, powerful, wise, and kind,
   Forever is the same.

4 Here let me rest, on thee depend,
   My God, my hope, my all ;
   Be thou my everlasting friend,
   And I can never fall.

   Anne Steele, 1760.

THE CHRISTIAN LIFE,—SUFFERING AND TRUST.

NICHOLS. C. M.

1. Almighty Father of mankind, On thee my hopes remain; And when the day of trouble comes, I shall not trust in vain.

659.

1 Almighty Father of mankind,
    On thee my hopes remain;
  And when the day of trouble comes,
    I shall not trust in vain.

2 In early days thou wast my guide,
    And of my youth the friend;
  And as my days began with thee,
    With thee my days shall end.

3 I know the power in whom I trust,
    The arm on which I lean;
  He will my Saviour ever be,
    Who has my Saviour been.

4 My God, who madest me to hope
    When life began to beat,
  And when a stranger in the world
    Didst guide my wandering feet;

5 Thou wilt not cast me off when age
    And evil days descend;
  Thou wilt not leave me in despair,
    To mourn my latter end.

6 Therefore in life I'll trust to thee,
    In death I will adore;
  And after death I'll sing thy praise,
    When time shall be no more.
            Michael Bruce, 1781.

660.

1 O Lord, my best desire fulfil,
    And help me to resign
  Life, health, and comfort to thy will,
    And make thy pleasure mine.

2 Why should I shrink at thy command,
    Whose love forbids my fears,
  Or tremble at the gracious hand
    That wipes away my tears?

3 No; let me rather freely yield
    What most I prize to thee,
  Who never hast a good withheld,
    Nor wilt withhold from me.
            William Cowper, 1779.

661.

1 Eternal God, we look to thee,
    To thee for help we fly;
  Thine eye alone our wants can see,
    Thy hand alone supply.

2 Lord, let thy fear within us dwell,
    Thy love our footsteps guide;
  That love will all vain love expel,
    That fear all fear beside.

3 Not what we wish, but what we want,
    Oh let thy grace supply;
  The good unasked, in mercy grant;
    The ill, though asked, deny.
            James Merrick, 1765.

662.

1 I worship thee, sweet will of God,
    And all thy ways adore,
  And every day I live I seem
    To love thee more and more.

2 I love to kiss each print where thou
    Hast set thine unseen feet;
  I cannot fear thee, blessed will,
    Thine empire is so sweet.

3 When obstacles and trials seem
   Like prison-walls to be,
   I do the little I can do,
   And leave the rest to thee.

4 I have no cares, O blessed will,
   For all my cares are thine;
   I live in triumph, Lord, for thou
   Hast made thy triumphs mine.

5 And when it seems no chance nor change
   From grief can set me free,
   Hope finds its strength in helplessness,
   And patient waits on thee.

6 Ride on, ride on triumphantly,
   Thou glorious will, ride on;
   Faith's pilgrim sons behind thee take
   The road that thou hast gone.
   F. W. Faber, 1832.

663. C. M.

1 My God, my Father, blissful name!
   Oh may I call thee mine?
   May I with sweet assurance claim
   A portion so divine?

2 This only can my fears control,
   And bid my sorrows fly;
   What harm can ever reach my soul
   Beneath my Father's eye?

3 Whate'er thy providence denies,
   I calmly would resign,
   For thou art good and just and wise:
   Oh bend my will to thine.

4 Whate'er thy sacred will ordains,
   Oh give me strength to bear;
   And let me know my Father reigns,
   And trust his tender care.

5 Thy sovereign ways are all unknown
   To my weak, erring sight;
   Yet let my soul adoring own
   That all thy ways are right.

6 My God, my Father, be thy name
   My solace and my stay;
   Oh wilt thou seal my humble claim,
   And drive my fears away?
   Anne Steele, 1760.

664. C. M.

1 Lord, it belongs not to my care
   Whether I die or live;
   To love and serve thee is my share,
   And this thy grace must give.

2 If life be long I will be glad,
   That I may long obey;
   If short, yet why should I be sad
   To soar to endless day?

3 Christ leads me through no darker rooms
   Than he went through before;
   He that into God's kingdom comes
   Must enter by this door.

4 Come, Lord, when grace hath made me
   Thy blessèd face to see; [meet
   For if thy work on earth be sweet,
   What will thy glory be!

5 Then shall I end my sad complaints,
   And weary, sinful days,
   And join with the triumphant saints
   To sing Jehovah's praise.

6 My knowledge of that life is small;
   The eye of faith is dim;
   But 't is enough that Christ knows all,
   And I shall be with him.
   Richard Baxter, 1681. a.

665. C. M.

1 Dear Refuge of my weary soul,
   On thee, when sorrows rise,
   On thee, when waves of trouble roll,
   My fainting hope relies.

2 To thee I tell each rising grief,
   For thou alone canst heal;
   Thy word can bring a sweet relief
   For every pain I feel.

3 But oh, when gloomy doubts prevail,
   I fear to call thee mine;
   The springs of comfort seem to fail,
   And all my hopes decline.

4 Yet, gracious God, where shall I flee?
   Thou art my only trust;
   And still my soul would cleave to thee,
   Though prostrate in the dust.

5 Thy mercy-seat is open still;
   Here let my soul retreat,
   With humble hope attend thy will,
   And wait beneath thy feet.
   Anne Steele, 1760.

270. THE CHRISTIAN LIFE,—SUFFERING AND TRUST.

EASTON. L. M.

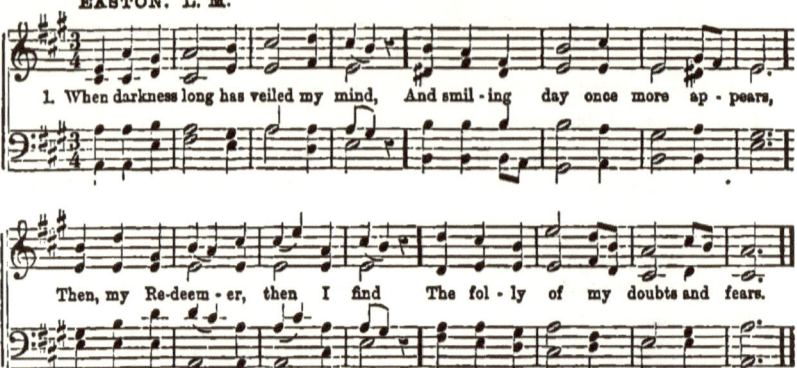

1. When darkness long has veiled my mind, And smiling day once more appears, Then, my Redeemer, then I find The folly of my doubts and fears.

666.

1 When darkness long has veiled my mind,
  And smiling day once more appears,
  Then, my Redeemer, then I find
  The folly of my doubts and fears.

2 Straight I upbraid my wandering heart,
  And blush that I should ever be
  Thus prone to act so base a part,
  Or harbor one hard thought of thee.

3 Oh let me then at length be taught,
  What I am still so slow to learn,
  That God is love, and changes not,
  Nor knows the shadow of a turn.

4 Sweet truth, and easy to repeat;
  But when my faith is sharply tried,
  I find myself a learner yet,
  Unskilful, weak, and apt to slide.

5 But, O my Lord, one look from thee
  Subdues my disobedient will,
  Drives doubt and discontent away,
  And thy rebellious worm is still.

6 Thou art as ready to forgive
  As I am ready to repine;
  Thou, therefore, all the praise receive;
  Be shame and self-abhorrence mine.
  William Cowper, 1779.

667.

1 I asked the Lord that I might grow
  In faith, and love, and every grace;
  Might more of his salvation know,
  And seek more earnestly his face.

2 'T was he who taught me thus to pray,
  And he, I trust, has answered prayer;
  But it has been in such a way
  As almost drove me to despair.

3 I hoped that in some favored hour
  At once he'd answer my request,
  And by his love's constraining power
  Subdue my sins and give me rest.

4 Instead of this, he made me feel
  The hidden evils of my heart,
  And let the angry powers of hell
  Assault my soul in every part.

5 Yea, more; with his own hand he seemed
  Intent to aggravate my woe;
  Crossed all the fair designs I schemed,
  Blasted my gourds, and laid me low.

6 "Lord, why is this?" I trembling cried;
  "Wilt thou pursue this worm to death?"
  "'T is in this way," the Lord replied,
  "I answer prayer for grace and faith:

7 "These inward trials I employ,
  From self and pride to set thee free,
  And break thy schemes of earthly joy,
  That thou may'st seek thy all in me."
  John Newton, 1779.

DOXOLOGY.

Praise God, from whom all blessings flow;
Praise him, all creatures here below;
Praise him above, ye heavenly host;
Praise Father, Son, and Holy Ghost.
Thomas Ken, 1697.

THE CHRISTIAN LIFE.—SUFFERING AND TRUST.

WATTS. L. M.

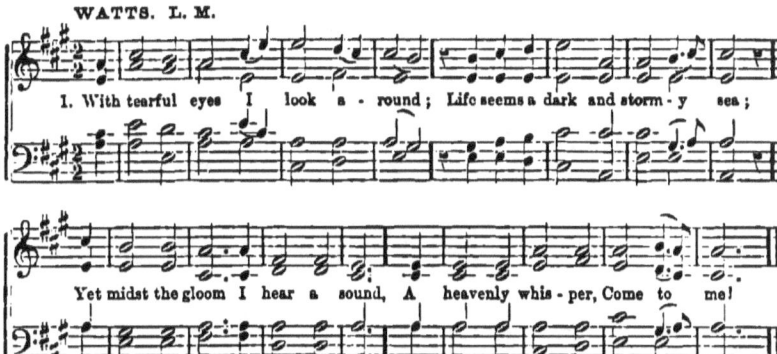

1. With tearful eyes I look around; Life seems a dark and stormy sea; Yet midst the gloom I hear a sound, A heavenly whisper, Come to me!

668.

1 WITH tearful eyes I look around;
Life seems a dark and stormy sea;
Yet midst the gloom I hear a sound,
A heavenly whisper, Come to me!

2 It tells me of a place of rest;
It tells me where my soul may flee:
Oh to the weary, faint, opprest,
How sweet the bidding, Come to me!

3 When nature shudders, loth to part
From all I love, enjoy, and see;
When a faint chill steals o'er my heart,
A sweet voice utters, Come to me!

4 Come, for all else must fail and die;
Earth is no resting-place for thee;
Heavenward direct thy weeping eye;
I am thy portion; Come to me!

5 O voice of mercy, voice of love!
In conflict, grief, and agony,
Support me, cheer me from above,
And gently whisper, Come to me!

Hugh White, 1841.

669. PSALM 3.

1 LORD, how the troublers of my peace
Within me and around increase!
What faithless doubts my heart assail,
That thou wilt slight, and they prevail!

2 But, Lord, my spirit flies to thee;
My hope, my shelter, thou shalt be:
O thou who from thy holy hill
Hast heard, oh hear me, help me still!

3 Beneath thy wing secure I sleep;
What foe can harm while thou dost keep?
I wake and find thee at my side,
My omnipresent guard and guide!

4 Oh why should earth or hell distress,
With God so strong, so nigh to bless?
From him alone salvation flows;
On him alone, my soul, repose!

H. F. Lyte, 1834. a.

670. ISAIAH xliii. 1, 2; DAN. iii. 19.

1 LET Jacob to his Maker sing,
And praise his great redeeming King:
Called by a new, a gracious name,
Let Israel loud his God proclaim.

2 He knows our souls in all their fears,
And gently wipes our falling tears;
Forms trembling voices to a song,
And bids the feeble heart be strong.

3 Then let the rivers swell around,
And rising floods o'erflow the ground;
Rivers and floods and seas divide,
And homage pay to Israel's guide.

4 Then let the fires their rage display,
And flaming terrors bar the way;
Untouched, unharmed, he leads them through,
And makes the flames refreshing too.

5 The fires but on their bonds shall prey;
The floods but wash their stains away;
And grace divine new trophies raise
Amid the deluge and the blaze.

Philip Doddridge, 1755. a.

272 THE CHRISTIAN LIFE,—SUFFERING AND TRUST.

OLMUTZ. S. M.

1. Com-mit thou all thy griefs And ways in-to his hands, To his sure truth and ten-der care, Who earth and heaven commands.

671.

1 Commit thou all thy griefs
 And ways into his hands,
To his sure truth and tender care,
 Who earth and heaven commands.

2 Give to the winds thy fears;
 Hope, and be undismayed;
God hears thy sighs and counts thy tears,
 God shall lift up thy head.

3 Through waves and clouds and storms,
 He gently clears thy way;
Wait thou his time; so shall this night
 Soon end in joyous day.

4 What though thou rulest not?
 Yet heaven and earth and hell
Proclaim, God sitteth on the throne,
 And ruleth all things well.

5 Leave to his sovereign sway
 To choose and to command;
So shalt thou wondering own, his way
 How wise, how strong his hand!

6 Far, far above thy thought
 His counsel shall appear,
When fully he the work hath wrought
 That caused thy needless fear.

7 Thou seest our weakness, Lord;
 Our hearts are known to thee;
Oh, lift thou up the sinking hand,
 Confirm the feeble knee.
  Paul Gerhard, 1666; tr. by *J. Wesley*, 1739.

672.

1 Oh what, if we are Christ's,
 Is earthly shame or loss?
Bright shall the crown of glory be,
 When we have borne the cross.

2 Keen was the trial once,
 Bitter the cup of woe,
When martyred saints, baptized in blood,
 Christ's sufferings shared below.

3 Bright is their glory now,
 Boundless their joy above,
Where, on the bosom of their God,
 They rest in perfect love.

4 Lord, may that grace be ours,
 Like them in faith to bear
All that of sorrow, grief, or pain
 May be our portion here.

5 Enough if thou at last
 The word of blessing give,
And let us rest beneath thy feet,
 Where saints and angels live.

6 All glory, Lord, to thee,
 Whom heaven and earth adore;
To Father, Son, and Holy Ghost,
 One God for evermore.
  Sir Henry W. Baker, 1857.

DOXOLOGY.
Give to the Father praise,
 Give glory to the Son,
And to the Spirit of his grace
 Be equal honor done.
  Isaac Watts, 1709.

673. S. M.

1 How gentle God's commands!
How kind his precepts are!
Come, cast your burdens on the Lord,
And trust his constant care.

2 While Providence supports,
Let saints securely dwell;
That hand which bears all nature up
Shall guide his children well.

3 Why should this anxious load
Press down your weary mind?
Haste to your heavenly Father's throne,
And sweet refreshment find.

4 His goodness stands approved,
Down to the present day;
I 'll drop my burden at his feet,
And bear a song away.
Philip Doddridge, 1755.

674. PSALM 61. S. M.

1 WHEN, overwhelmed with grief,
My heart within me dies,
Helpless, and far from all relief,
To heaven I lift mine eyes.

2 Oh lead me to the rock
That's high above my head,
And make the covert of thy wings
My shelter and my shade.

3 Within thy presence, Lord,
Forever I'll abide;
Thou art the tower of my defence,
The refuge where I hide.

4 Thou givest me the lot
Of those that fear thy name;
If endless life be their reward,
I shall possess the same.
Isaac Watts, 1719.

675. S. M.

1 My spirit on thy care,
Blest Saviour, I recline;
Thou wilt not leave me to despair,
For thou art love divine.

2 In thee I place my trust;
On thee I calmly rest;
I know thee good, I know thee just,
And count thy choice the best.

3 Whate'er events betide,
Thy will they all perform;

Safe in thy breast my head I hide,
Nor fear the coming storm.

4 Let good or ill befall,
It must be good for me,
Secure of having thee in all,
Of having all in thee.
H. F. Lyte, 1834.

676. S. M.

1 YOUR harps, ye trembling saints,
Down from the willows take;
Loud, to the praise of love divine,
Bid every string awake.

2 Though in a foreign land,
We are not far from home,
And nearer to our house above
We every moment come.

3 His grace will to the end
Stronger and brighter shine;
Nor present things, nor things to come,
Shall quench the spark divine.

4 The people of his choice
He will not cast away;
Yet do not always here expect
On Tabor's mount to stay.

5 When we in darkness walk,
Nor feel the heavenly flame,
Then is the time to trust our God,
And rest upon his name.

6 Soon shall our doubts and fears
Subside at his control;
His loving-kindness shall break through
The midnight of the soul.

7 Wait till the shadows flee;
Wait thy appointed hour;
Wait till the bridegroom of thy soul
Reveal his love with power.

8 The time of love will come,
When thou shalt clearly see,
Not only that he shed his blood,
But that it flowed for thee.

9 Blest is the man, O God,
That stays himself on thee:
Who wait for thy salvation, Lord,
Shall thy salvation see.
Augustus Montague Toplady, 1772.

274. THE CHRISTIAN LIFE,—SUFFERING AND TRUST.

ORTONVILLE. C. M.

1. He who on earth as man was known, And bore our sins and pains, Now, seated on th' eternal throne, The God of glory reigns, The God of glory reigns.

677.

1 He who on earth as man was known,
   And bore our sins and pains,
   Now, seated on th' eternal throne,
   The God of glory reigns.

2 His hands the wheels of nature guide
   With an unerring skill;
   And countless worlds, extended wide,
   Obey his sovereign will.

3 While harps unnumbered sound his praise
   In yonder world above,
   His saints on earth admire his ways,
   And glory in his love.

4 This land through which his pilgrims go
   Is desolate and dry;
   But streams of grace from him o'erflow
   Their thirst to satisfy.

5 When troubles, like a burning sun,
   Beat heavy on their head,
   To this almighty rock they run,
   And find a pleasing shade.

6 How glorious he, how happy they
   In such a glorious friend,
   Whose love secures them all the way,
   And crowns them at the end!
   John Newton, 1779.

678.

1 O Lord, I would delight in thee,
   And on thy care depend;
   To thee in every trouble flee,
   My best, my only friend.

2 When all created streams are dried,
   Thy fulness is the same;
   May I with this be satisfied,
   And glory in thy name.

3 No good in creatures can be found,
   But may be found in thee;
   I must have all things, and abound,
   While God is God to me.

4 Oh that I had a stronger faith
   To look within the veil,
   To credit what my Saviour saith,
   Whose word can never fail!

5 He that has made my heaven secure,
   Will here all good provide;
   While Christ is rich, can I be poor?
   What can I want beside?

6 O Lord, I cast my care on thee;
   I triumph and adore;
   Henceforth my great concern shall be
   To love and praise thee more.
   John Ryland, 1777.

DOXOLOGY.

The God of mercy be adored,
Who calls our souls from death,
Who saves by his redeeming word
And new-creating breath.

To praise the Father, and the Son,
And Spirit all divine,
The One in Three, and Three in One,
Let saints and angels join.
Isaac Watts, 1709.

THE CHRISTIAN LIFE,—SUFFERING AND TRUST. 275

AUTUMN. 8s & 7s. Double.

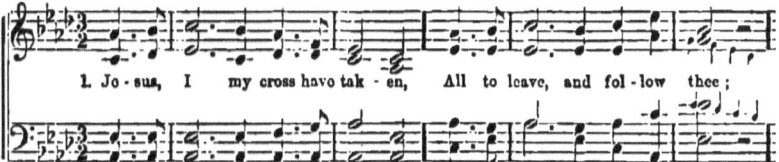
1. Jesus, I my cross have tak-en, All to leave, and fol-low thee;

Des-ti-tute, despised, for-sak-en, Thou from hence my all shalt be:
Yet how rich is my con-di-tion! God and heaven are still my own!

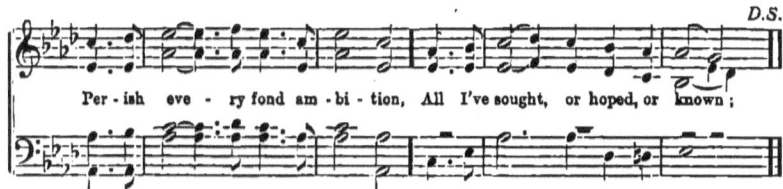
Per-ish eve-ry fond am-bi-tion, All I've sought, or hoped, or known;

679.

1 Jesus, I my cross have taken,
  All to leave, and follow thee;
Destitute, despised, forsaken,
  Thou from hence my all shalt be:
Perish every fond ambition,
  All I've sought, or hoped, or known;
Yet how rich is my condition!
  God and heaven are still my own!

2 Let the world despise and leave me,
  They have left my Saviour too;
Human hearts and looks deceive me;
  Thou art not, like them, untrue;
And while thou shalt smile upon me,
  God of wisdom, love, and might,
Foes may hate, and friends may shun me,
  Show thy face, and all is bright.

3 Man may trouble and distress me,
  'T will but drive me to thy breast;
Life with trials hard may press me,
  Heaven will bring me sweeter rest:
Oh, 'tis not in grief to harm me,
  While thy love is left to me,
Oh, 'twere not in joy to charm me,
  Were that joy unmixed with thee!

4 Take, my soul, thy full salvation;
  Rise o'er sin, and fear, and care;
Joy to find, in every station,
  Something still to do or bear:
Think what Spirit dwells within thee;
  What a Father's smile is thine;
What a Saviour died to win thee;
  Child of heaven, shouldst thou repine?

5 Haste then on from grace to glory,
  Armed by faith, and winged by prayer,
Heaven's eternal day's before thee,
  God's own hand shall guide thee there:
Soon shall close thy earthly mission,
  Swift shall pass thy pilgrim days;
Hope soon change to full fruition,
  Faith to sight, and prayer to praise.

Henry F. Lyte, 1833.

276 THE CHRISTIAN LIFE, — SUFFERING AND TRUST.

HORTON. 7s.

1. Sovereign Rul-er of the skies, Ev-er gra-cious, ev-er wise, All my times are in thy hand, All e-vents at thy command.

680.

1 SOVEREIGN Ruler of the skies,
Ever gracious, ever wise,
All my times are in thy hand,
All events at thy command.

2 His decree, who formed the earth,
Fixed my first and second birth;
Parents, native place, and time,
All appointed were by him.

3 He that formed me in the womb,
He shall guide me to the tomb;
All my times shall ever be
Ordered by his wise decree.

4 Times of sickness, times of health,
Times of penury and wealth;
Times of trial and of grief,
Times of triumph and relief,

5 Times the tempter's power to prove,
Times to taste a Saviour's love, —
All must come, and last, and end,
As shall please my heavenly Friend.

6 O thou gracious, wise, and just,
In thy hands my life I trust:
Have I something dearer still?
I resign it to thy will.

7 May I always own thy hand;
Still to the surrender stand;
Know that thou art God alone;
I and mine are all thy own.

8 Thee at all times will I bless;
Having thee, I all possess;
How can I bereavéd be,
Since I cannot part with thee?
John Ryland, 1777.

681.

1 DAY by day the manna fell;
Oh to learn this lesson well:
Still by constant mercy fed,
Give me, Lord, my daily bread.

2 "Day by day" the promise reads;
Daily strength for daily needs;
Cast foreboding fears away;
Take the manna of to-day.

3 Lord, my times are in thy hand;
All my sanguine hopes have planned,
To thy wisdom I resign,
And would make thy purpose mine.

4 Thou my daily task shalt give;
Day by day to thee I live:
So shall added years fulfil,
Not mine own, my Father's will.

5 Fond ambition, whisper not;
Happy is my humble lot:
Anxious, busy cares, away;
I'm provided for to-day.

6 Oh to live exempt from care,
By the energy of prayer,
Strong in faith, with mind subdued,
Yet elate with gratitude!
Josiah Conder, 1837.

THE CHRISTIAN LIFE,—SUFFERING AND TRUST.

PRAYER. S. M. DOUBLE.

Thou ve-ry pre-sent aid In suffering and distress, The soul which still on thee is stayed Is kept in per-fect peace. The soul by faith re-clined On his Re-deem-er's breast, Midst rag-ing storms ex-ults to find An ev-er-last-ing rest.

682.

1 Thou very present aid
  In suffering and distress,
 The soul which still on thee is stayed,
  Is kept in perfect peace.
 The soul by faith reclined
  On his Redeemer's breast,
 Midst raging storms exults to find
  An everlasting rest.

2 Sorrow and fear are gone
  Whene'er thy face appears;
 It stills the sighing orphan's moan,
  And dries the widow's tears.
 It hallows every cross;
  It sweetly comforts me,
 And makes me now forget my loss,
  And lose myself in thee.
        Charles Wesley, 1749.

683.   Psalm 55.

1 Let sinners take their course,
  And choose the road to death;
 But in the worship of my God
  I'll spend my daily breath.

2 My thoughts address his throne
  When morning brings the light;
 I seek his blessing every noon,
  And pay my vows at night.

3 Thou wilt regard my cries,
  O my eternal God,
 While sinners perish in surprise,
  Beneath thine angry rod.

4 Because they dwell at ease,
  And no sad changes feel,
 They neither fear nor trust thy name,
  Nor learn to do thy will.

5 But I, with all my cares,
  Will lean upon the Lord;
 I'll cast my burden on his arm,
  And rest upon his word.

6 His arm shall well sustain
  The children of his love;
 The ground on which their safety stands
  No earthly power can move.
        Isaac Watts, 1719.

THE CHRISTIAN LIFE,—SUFFERING AND TRUST.

SYDENHAM. C. M.

1. Come, let us to the Lord our God With contrite hearts return; Our God is gracious, nor will leave The desolate to mourn.

684.

1 Come, let us to the Lord our God
  With contrite hearts return;
 Our God is gracious, nor will leave
  The desolate to mourn.

2 His voice commands the tempest forth,
  And stills the stormy wave;
 And though his arm be strong to smite,
  'T is also strong to save.

3 Long hath the night of sorrow reigned;
  The dawn shall bring us light;
 God shall appear, and we shall rise
  With gladness in his sight.

4 Our hearts, if God we seek to know,
  Shall know him and rejoice;
 His coming like the morn shall be,
  Like morning songs his voice.

5 As dew upon the tender herb,
  Diffusing fragrance round;
 As showers that usher in the spring,
  And cheer the thirsty ground;

6 So shall his presence bless our souls,
  And shed a joyful light;
 That hallowed morn shall chase away
  The sorrows of the night.
    John Morrison, 1781.

685.

1 A Friend there is; your voices join,
  Ye saints, to praise his name,
 Whose truth and kindness are divine,
  Whose love's a constant flame.

2 When most we need his helping hand,
  This friend is always near;
 With heaven and earth at his command,
  He waits to answer prayer.

3 His love no end or measure knows,
  No change can turn its course;
 Immutably the same it flows
  From one eternal source.

4 When frowns appear to veil his face,
  And clouds surround his throne,
 He hides the purpose of his grace,
  To make it better known.

5 And if our dearest comforts fall
  Before his sovereign will,
 He never takes away our all,—
  Himself he gives us still.

6 Our sorrows in the scale he weighs,
  And measures out our pains;
 The wildest storm his word obeys,
  His word its rage restrains.
    Joseph Swain, 1792.

686.

1 O thou whose sacred feet have trod
  The thorny path of woe;
 Forbid that I should slight the rod,
  Or faint beneath the blow.

2 My spirit to its chastening stroke
  I meekly would resign,
 Nor murmur at the heaviest yoke
  That tells me I am thine.

3 Give me the spirit of thy trust,
   To suffer as a son,
To say, though lying in the dust,
   My Father's will be done.

4 I know that trial works for ends
   Too high for sense to trace,
That oft in dark attire he sends
   Some embassy of grace.

5 May none depart till I have gained
   The blessing which it bears,
And learn, though late, I entertained
   An angel unawares.

6 So shall I bless the hour that sent
   The mercy of the rod,
And build an altar by the tent
   Where I have met with God.
                                James D. Burns, 1858.

687. Nehemiah xiii. 31.   C. M.

1 O THOU from whom all goodness flows,
   I lift my heart to thee;
In all my sorrows, conflicts, woes,
   Dear Lord, remember me.

2 When on my groaning burdened heart
   My sins lie heavily,
My pardon speak, new peace impart,
   In love remember me.

3 Temptations sore obstruct my way,
   And ills I cannot flee;
Oh, give me strength, Lord, as my day;
   For good remember me.

4 Distressed with pain, disease, and grief,
   This feeble body see;
Grant patience, rest, and kind relief;
   Hear, and remember me.

5 If on my face, for thy dear name,
   Shame and reproaches be,
All hail reproach, and welcome shame,
   If thou remember me.

6 The hour is near; consigned to death,
   I own the just decree:
"Saviour!" with my last parting breath,
   I'll cry, "remember me!"
                                Thomas Haweis, 1792.

688.   C. M.

1 THE world can neither give nor take,
   Nor can they comprehend,
That peace of God which Christ hath
   That peace which knows no end.[bought,

2 The burning bush was not consumed,
   Whilst God remained there;
The three, when Jesus made the fourth,
   Found fire as soft as air.

3 God's furnace doth in Zion stand;
   But Zion's God sits by,
As the refiner views his gold
   With an observant eye.

4 His thoughts are high, his love is wise,
   His wounds a cure intend;
And, though he doth not always smile,
   He loves unto the end.

5 His love is constant as the sun,
   Though clouds come oft between;
And, could my faith but pierce these
   It might be always seen.   [clouds,

6 Yet I shall ever, ever sing,
   And thou forever shine;
I have thine own dear pledge for this:
   Lord, thou art ever mine.
                        Selina, Countess of Huntingdon, 1780.

689.   C. M.

1 MY soul, triumphant in the Lord,
   Shall tell its joys abroad,
And march with holy vigor on,
   Supported by its God.

2 Through all the winding maze of life
   His hand hath been my guide,
And in that long-experienced care
   My heart shall still confide.

3 His grace through all the desert flows
   An unexhausted stream;
That grace on Zion's sacred mount
   Shall be my endless theme.

4 Beyond the choicest joys of earth
   These distant courts I love;
But oh, I burn with strong desire
   To view thy house above.

5 Mingled with all the shining band,
   My soul would there adore,
A pillar in thy temple fixed,
   To be removed no more.
                                Philip Doddridge, 1755.

280 THE CHRISTIAN LIFE,—SUFFERING AND TRUST.

ALL SAINTS. L. M.

690.

1 Jesus, my Lord, 'tis sweet to rest
Upon thy tender, loving breast,
Where deep compassions ever roll
Towards my helpless, weary soul.

2 Thy love, my Saviour, dries my tears,
Expels my griefs, and calms my fears;
Sheds light and gladness o'er my heart,
And bids each anxious thought depart.

3 Blest foretaste this of joys to come
In thy eternal, heavenly home;
Where I shall see thy smiling face,
And know thy rich, unfathomed grace.

4 That grace sustains my spirit now,
Though still a pilgrim here below;
That grace suffices, comforts, guides,
Upholds, defends, preserves, provides.

5 Yes, thou art with me, O my God,
To bear me on to thy abode,
Where I shall never cease to prove
Thy deep, divine, unfailing love.

6 Help me to praise thee day by day,
Till earth's dark scenes are passed away,
Till in thy own unclouded light
Thy glory satisfies my sight.

H. B. in Lyra Sacra, 1865.

691.   Psalm 42.

1 My spirit sinks within me, Lord;
But I will call thy grace to mind,
And times of past distress record,
When I have found my God was kind.

2 Yet will the Lord command his love
When I address his throne by day,
Nor in the night his grace remove;
The night shall hear me sing and pray.

3 I'll chide my heart, that sinks so low;
Why should my soul indulge in grief?
Hope in the Lord, and praise him too;
He is my rest, my sure relief.

4 Thy light and truth shall guide me still;
Thy words shall my best thoughts em-
And lead me to thy heavenly hill, [ploy,
My God, my most exceeding joy.

Isaac Watts, 1719.

692.   Psalm 1.

1 Uphold me, Lord, too prone to stray,
Uphold me in thy narrow way;
From sin and folly bid me flee,
And turn from all who turn from thee.

2 The cloud and pillar of thy word,
Be this my guide, my comfort, Lord,
By day, by night at hand to bless,
And lead me through the wilderness.

3 So shall I flourish like a tree
Planted, and watched, and nursed by thee,
With streams of grace around its roots,
And bending low with holy fruits.

4 So shall I go from light to light,
Till prayer is praise, and faith is sight;
And while the sinner's doom I see,
Adore the grace that rescued me.

H. F. Lyte, 1834.

693. L. M.

1 ETERNAL beam of light divine,
Fountain of unexhausted love,
In whom the Father's glories shine
Through earth beneath and heaven above;

2 Jesus, the weary wanderer's rest,
Give me thy easy yoke to bear;
With steadfast patience arm my breast,
With spotless love and lowly fear.

3 Thankful I take the cup from thee,
Prepared and mingled by thy skill;
Though bitter to the taste it be,
Powerful the wounded soul to heal.

4 Be thou, O Rock of ages, nigh; [gone,
So shall each murmuring thought be
And grief, and fear, and care shall fly
As clouds before the midday sun.

5 Speak to my warring passions peace;
Say to my trembling heart, be still:
Thy power my strength and fortress is,
For all things serve thy sovereign will.

6 O death, where is thy sting? where now
Thy boasted victory, O grave?
Who shall contend with God, or who
Can hurt whom God delights to save?

Charles Wesley, 1740.

694. L. M.

1 WHEN in the hour of lonely woe
I give my sorrow leave to flow,
And anxious fear and dark distrust
Weigh down my spirit to the dust;

2 When not e'en friendship's gentle aid
Can heal the wounds the world has made,
Oh, this shall check each rising sigh,
That Jesus is forever nigh.

3 His counsels and upholding care
My safety and my comfort are;
And he shall guide me all my days,
Till glory crown the work of grace.

4 Jesus, in whom but thee above
Can I repose my trust, my love?
And shall an earthly object be
Loved in comparison with thee?

5 My flesh is hastening to decay;
Soon shall the world have passed away;
And what can mortal friends avail, [fail?
When heart and strength and life shall

6 But oh, be thou, my Saviour, nigh,
And I will triumph while I die;
My strength, my portion, is divine,
And Jesus is forever mine.

Josiah Conder, 1855.

695. L. M.

1 O THOU to whose all-searching sight
The darkness shineth as the light,
Search, prove my heart; it pants for thee;
Oh, burst these bonds, and set it free.

2 Wash out its stains, refine its dross;
Nail my affections to the cross;
Hallow each thought; let all within
Be clean, as thou, my Lord, art clean.

3 If in this darksome wild I stray,
Be thou my light, be thou my way;
No foes, no violence I fear,
No fraud, while thou, my God, art near.

4 When rising floods my soul o'erflow,
When sinks my heart in waves of woe,
Jesus, thy timely aid impart,
And raise my head and cheer my heart.

5 Saviour, where'er thy steps I see,
Dauntless, untired, I follow thee;
Oh let thy hand support me still,
And lead me to thy holy hill.

6 If rough and thorny be the way,
My strength proportion to my day,
Till toil, and grief, and pain shall cease,
Where all is calm and joy and peace.

Tr. from German by John Wesley, 1739-1743.

696. L. M.

1 OH for a beam of heavenly light
To guide my roving steps aright,
And lead me to the blest abode
Where dwells my Father and my God.

2 Lord, I am weak and prone to stray;
Oh keep me in thy holy way;
What nature wants let grace supply,
And smooth my progress to the sky.

3 Trusting in Jesus, let me go
In safety through this vale of woe;
And may his gracious presence cheer
My heart in all its wanderings here.

4 And when my pilgrimage is o'er,
Oh let me rest upon that shore
Where sin shall never more molest,
Nor drive me from my Saviour's breast.

W. H. Bathurst, 1830.

282 THE CHRISTIAN LIFE,—SUFFERING AND TRUST.

ST. PAULS. L. M.

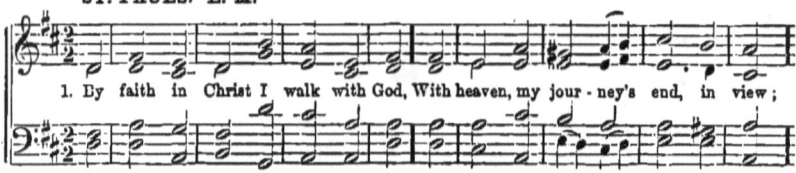

697.

1 By faith in Christ I walk with God,
   With heaven, my journey's end, in view;
   Supported by his staff and rod,
   My road is safe, and pleasant too.

2 I travel through a desert wide,
   Where many round me blindly stray;
   But he vouchsafes to be my guide,
   And will not let me miss my way.

3 Though snares and dangers throng my path,
   And earth and hell my course with-
   I triumph over all by faith,   [stand,
   Guarded by his almighty hand.

4 The wilderness affords no food;
   But God for my support prepares,
   Provides me every needful good,
   And frees my soul from want and cares.

5 With him sweet converse I maintain;
   Great as he is, I dare be free;
   I tell him all my grief and pain,
   And he reveals his love to me.

6 Some cordial from his word he brings
   Whene'er my feeble spirit faints;
   At once my soul revives and sings,
   And yields no more to sad complaints.

7 I pity all that worldlings talk
   Of pleasures, that will quickly end;
   Be this my choice, O Lord, to walk
   With thee, my guide, my guard, my friend!

John Newton, 1779.

698.   Luke x. 42.

1 Beset with snares on every hand,
   In life's uncertain path I stand;
   Saviour divine, diffuse thy light
   To guide my doubtful footsteps right.

2 Engage this roving, treacherous heart
   To fix on Mary's better part;
   To scorn the trifles of a day,
   For joys that none can take away.

3 Then let the wildest storms arise;
   Let tempests mingle earth and skies;
   No fatal shipwreck shall I fear,
   But all my treasures with me bear.

4 If thou, my Jesus, still be nigh,
   Cheerful I live, and joyful die;
   Secure, when mortal comforts flee,
   To find ten thousand worlds in thee.

Philip Doddridge, 1755.

699.   2 Cor. xii. 7-10.

1 Let me but hear my Saviour say,
   "Strength shall be equal to thy day,"
   Then I rejoice in deep distress,
   Leaning on all-sufficient grace.

2 I can do all things, or can bear
   All suffering, if my Lord be there;
   Sweet pleasures mingle with the pains,
   While he my sinking head sustains.

3 I glory in infirmity,
   That Christ's own power may rest on me;
   When I am weak, then am I strong;
   Grace is my shield, and Christ my song.

Isaac Watts, 1709. a.

THE CHRISTIAN LIFE,—SUFFERING AND TRUST. 283
SUPPLICATION. 7s & 6s.

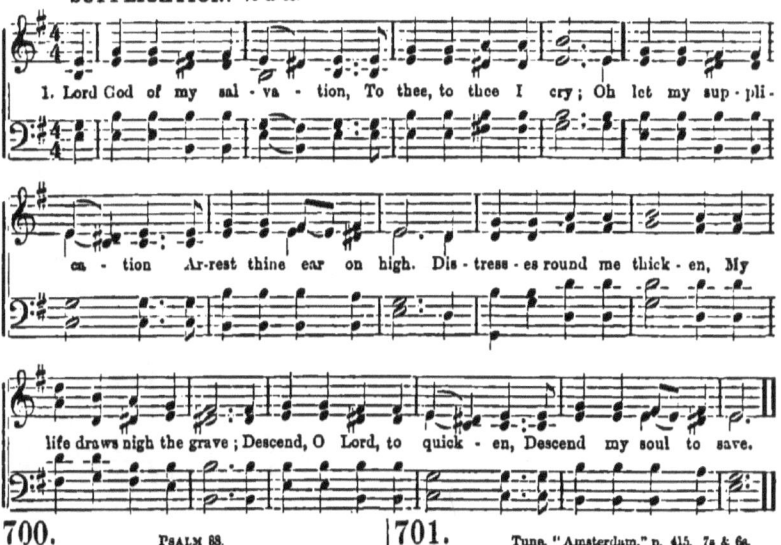

1. Lord God of my sal-va-tion, To thee, to thee I cry; Oh let my sup-pli-ca-tion Ar-rest thine ear on high. Dis-tress-es round me thick-en, My life draws nigh the grave; Descend, O Lord, to quick-en, Descend my soul to save.

700.   PSALM 88.

1 LORD God of my salvation,
    To thee, to thee I cry;
  Oh let my supplication
    Arrest thine ear on high.
  Distresses round me thicken,
    My life draws nigh the grave;
  Descend, O Lord, to quicken,
    Descend my soul to save.

2 Thy wrath lies hard upon me,
    Thy billows o'er me roll;
  My friends all seem to shun me,
    And foes beset my soul;
  Where'er on earth I turn me,
    No comforter is near;
  Wilt thou too, Father, spurn me?
    Wilt thou refuse to hear?

3 No; banished and heart-broken,
    My soul still clings to thee;
  The promise thou hast spoken
    Shall still my refuge be.
  So present ills and terrors
    My future joy increase,
  And scourge me from my errors
    To duty, hope, and peace.
        H. F. Lyte, 1834.

701.   Tune, "Amsterdam," p. 415. 7s & 6s.

1 FULL of weakness and of sin,
    We look to thee for life;
  Lord, thy gracious work begin,
    And calm the inward strife.

2 Though our hearts are prone to stray,
    Oh be thou a constant friend;
  Though we know not how to pray,
    Thy saving mercy send.

3 Let thy Spirit, gracious Lord,
    Our souls with love inspire.
  Strength and confidence afford,
    And breathe celestial fire.

4 Teach us first to feel our need,
    And then all need supply;
  When we hunger, deign to feed,
    And hear us when we cry.

5 When we cleave to earthly things,
    Send thy reviving grace;
  Raise our souls, and give them wings
    To reach thy holy place.
        William Hiley Bathurst, 1831.
        DOXOLOGY.

  FATHER, Son, and Holy Ghost,
    Blessing, honor, glory be
  Given by all the heavenly host,
    And all on earth, to thee.

284 THE CHRISTIAN LIFE,—SUFFERING AND TRUST.

BENTON. 6s & 10s.

1. Thou who didst stoop below
To drain the cup of woe,
Wearing the form of frail mortality,
Thy bless-èd labors done,
Thy crown of victory won,
Hast passed from earth, passed to thy home on high.

702.

2   Our eyes behold thee not,
    Yet hast thou not forgot
Those who have placed their hope, their trust in thee;
   Before thy Father's face
    Thou hast prepared a place,
That where thou art, there they may also be.

3   It was no path of flowers
    Through this dark world of ours,
Belovéd of the Father, thou didst tread:
   And shall we in dismay
    Shrink from the narrow way,
When clouds and darkness are around it spread?

4   O thou who art our life,
    Be with us through the strife;
Thy holy head by earth's fierce storms was bowed;
   Raise thou our eyes above,
    To see a Father's love
Beam, like the bow of promise, through the cloud.

5   E'en through the awful gloom
    Which hovers o'er the tomb,
That light of love our guiding star shall be;
   Our spirits shall not dread
    The shadowy way to tread,
Friend, Guardian, Saviour, which doth lead to thee.

Sarah Appleton Miles, 1840.

THE CHRISTIAN LIFE,—SUFFERING AND TRUST. 285

HOLLEY. 7s.

1. Thine for-ev-er! God of love, Hear us from thy throne a-bove; Thine for-ev-er may we be, Here and in e-ter-ni-ty.

703.

1 Thine forever! God of love,
Hear us from thy throne above;
Thine forever may we be,
Here and in eternity.

2 Thine forever! Lord of life,
Shield us through the earthly strife;
Thou, the Life, the Truth, the Way,
Guide us to the realms of day.

3 Thine forever! oh, how blest
They who find in thee their rest;
Saviour, Guardian, heavenly Friend,
Oh, defend us to the end.

4 Thine forever! Saviour, keep
These thy frail and trembling sheep;
Safe alone beneath thy care,
Let us all thy goodness share.

5 Thine forever! thou our Guide,
All our wants by thee supplied,
All our sins by thee forgiven,
Lead us, Lord, from earth to heaven.
Mary F. Maude, 1848.

704.

1 Heavenly Father, to whose eye
Future things unfolded lie,
Through the desert, where I stray,
Let thy counsels guide my way.

2 Lead me not, for flesh is frail,
Where fierce trials would assail;
Leave me not, in darkened hour,
To withstand the tempter's power.

3 Help thy servant to maintain
A profession free from stain;
That my sole reproach may be
Following Christ and fearing thee.

4 Should thy wisdom, Lord, decree
Trials long and sharp for me,
Pain or sorrow, care or shame,
Father, glorify thy name.

5 Let me neither faint nor fear,
Feeling still that thou art near,
In the course my Saviour trod,
Tending still to thee, my God.
Josiah Conder, 1855.

705.

1 'Tis my happiness below
Not to live without the cross,
But the Saviour's power to know,
Sanctifying every loss:
Trials must and will befall;
But with humble faith to see
Love inscribed upon them all,
This is happiness to me.

2 Did I meet no trials here,
No chastisement by the way,
Might I not with reason fear
I should prove a castaway?
Trials make the promise sweet;
Trials give new life to prayer;
Trials bring me to his feet,
Lay me low, and keep me there.
William Cowper, 1779.

286 THE CHRISTIAN LIFE,—SUFFERING AND TRUST.

RELIANCE. 7s & 6s.

1. God is my strong salvation; What foe have I to fear? In darkness and temptation, My light, my help, is near: Tho' hosts encamp around me, Firm in the fight I stand; What terror can confound me, With God at my right hand?

706.

1 God is my strong salvation;
  What foe have I to fear?
In darkness and temptation,
  My light, my help, is near:
Though hosts encamp around me,
  Firm in the fight I stand;
What terror can confound me,
  With God at my right hand?

2 Place on the Lord reliance;
  My soul, with courage wait;
His truth be thine affiance,
  When faint and desolate;
His might thy heart shall strengthen,
  His love thy joy increase;
Mercy thy days shall lengthen;
  The Lord will give thee peace.
James Montgomery, 1825.

707.

1 Sometimes a light surprises
  The Christian while he sings;
It is the Lord who rises
  With healing on his wings;
When comforts are declining,
  He grants the soul again
A season of clear shining,
  To cheer it after rain.

2 In holy contemplation,
  We sweetly then pursue
The theme of God's salvation,
  And find it ever new:
Set free from present sorrow,
  We cheerfully can say,
Let the unknown to-morrow
  Bring with it what it may.

3 It can bring with it nothing
  But he will bear us through;
Who gives the lilies clothing,
  Will clothe his people too:
Beneath the spreading heavens
  No creature but is fed;
And he who feeds the ravens
  Will give his children bread.

4 Though vine nor fig-tree neither
  Their wonted fruit should bear,
Though all the fields should wither,
  Nor flocks nor herds be there;
Yet God the same abiding,
  His praise shall tune my voice;
For while in him confiding,
  I cannot but rejoice.
William Cowper, 1779.

THE CHRISTIAN LIFE,—SUFFERING AND TRUST.

LUX BENIGNA. 10s, 4s & 10s.

708.

1 LEAD, kindly Light, amid the encircling gloom,
    Lead thou me on;
The night is dark, and I am far from home,
    Lead thou me on;
Keep thou my feet; I do not ask to see
The distant scene; one step enough for me.

2 I was not ever thus, nor prayed that thou
    Shouldst lead me on;
I loved to choose and see my path; but now
    Lead thou me on:
I loved the garish day, and, spite of fears,
Pride ruled my will. Remember not past years.

3 So long thy Power has blest me, sure it still
    Will lead me on
O'er moor and fen, o'er crag and torrent, till
    The night is gone;
And with the morn those angel faces smile
Which I have loved long since, and lost awhile!

John Henry Newman, 1833.

288 THE CHRISTIAN LIFE,—SUFFERING AND TRUST.

OLIVET. 6s & 4s.

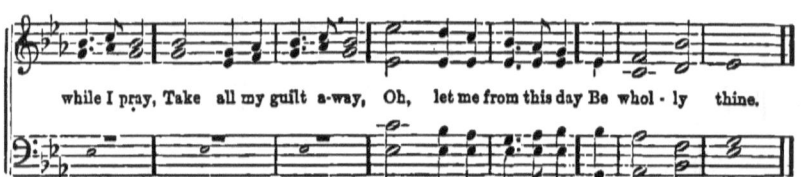

1. My faith looks up to thee, Thou Lamb of Calvary, Saviour divine! Now hear me while I pray, Take all my guilt away, Oh, let me from this day Be wholly thine.

709.

1 My faith looks up to thee,
   Thou Lamb of Calvary,
      Saviour divine!
   Now hear me while I pray,
   Take all my guilt away,
   Oh, let me from this day
      Be wholly thine.

2 May thy rich grace impart
   Strength to my fainting heart,
      My zeal inspire;
   As thou hast died for me,
   Oh, may my love to thee
   Pure, warm, and changeless be,
      A living fire.

3 While life's dark maze I tread,
   And griefs around me spread,
      Be thou my guide;
   Bid darkness turn to day,
   Wipe sorrow's tears away,
   Nor let me ever stray
      From thee aside.

4 When ends life's transient dream,
   When death's cold, sullen stream
      Shall o'er me roll,
   Blest Saviour, then, in love,
   Fear and distrust remove;
   Oh, bear me safe above,
      A ransomed soul.

Ray Palmer, 1830.

710.

1 O THOU best gift of heaven,
   Thou who thyself hast given,
      For thou hast died,
   This thou hast done for me:
   ‖ What have I done for thee, ‖
      Thou crucified?

2 I long to serve thee more:
   Reveal an open door,
      Saviour, to me;
   Then, counting all but loss,
   ‖ I'll glory in thy cross, ‖
      And follow thee.

3 Do thou but point the way,
   And give me strength t'obey;
      Thy will be mine;
   Then can I think it joy
   ‖ To suffer or to die, ‖
      Since I am thine.

Anon.

DOXOLOGY.

To God the Father, Son,
And Spirit, three in one,
   All praise be given:
Crown him in every song;
To him your hearts belong;
Let all his praise prolong,
   On earth, in heaven!

THE CHRISTIAN LIFE,—SUFFERING AND TRUST.

HARWOOD. C. P. M.

1. O Lord! how happy should we be If we could cast our care on thee— If we from self could rest; And feel at heart, that one above, In perfect wisdom, perfect love, Is working for the best.

711. LUKE xii. 22.

1 O LORD! how happy should we be
If we could cast our care on thee —
If we from self could rest;
And feel at heart, that one above,
In perfect wisdom, perfect love,
Is working for the best.

2 How far from this our daily life,
Ever disturbed by anxious strife,
By sudden, wild alarms;
Oh, could we but relinquish all
Our earthly props, and simply fall
On thine almighty arms!

3 Could we but kneel, and cast our load,
E'en while we pray, upon our God,
Then rise with lightened cheer,
Sure that the Father, who is nigh
To still the famished raven's cry,
Will hear in that we fear!

4 Lord, make these faithless hearts of ours
Such lesson learn from birds and flowers;
Make them from self to cease;
Leave all things to a Father's will,
And taste, before him lying still,
E'en in affliction, peace.

Joseph Anstice, 1836.

712.

1 CHILDREN of light, arise and shine!
Your birth, your hopes, are all divine,
Your home is in the skies.
Oh! then, for heavenly glory born,
Look down on all with holy scorn
That earthly spirits prize.

2 With Christ, with glory full in view,
Oh! what is all the world to you?
What is it all but loss?
Come on, then, cleave no more to earth
Nor wrong your high celestial birth,
Ye pilgrims of the cross.

3 The cross is ours; we bear it now:
But did not he beneath it bow,
And suffer there at last?
All that we feel can Jesus tell;
His gracious soul remembers well
The sorrows of the past.

4 O blessed Lord, we yet shall reign,
Redeemed from sorrow, sin, and pain,
And walk with thee in white.
We suffer now; but oh! at last
We'll bless the Lord for all the past,
And own our cross was light.

Sir Edward Denny, 1839.

290 THE CHRISTIAN LIFE,—SUFFERING AND TRUST.

GUIDANCE. 5s & 8s.

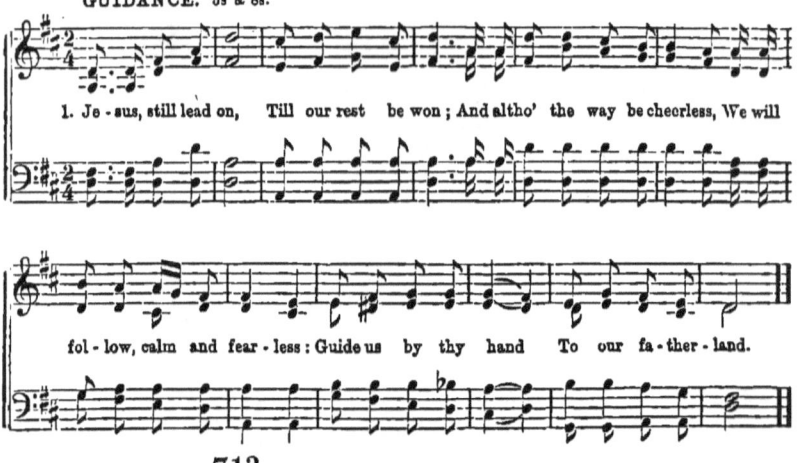

713

1   Jesus, still lead on,
    Till our rest be won;
And although the way be cheerless,
We will follow, calm and fearless:
    Guide us by thy hand
    To our fatherland.

2   If the way be drear,
    If the foe be near,
Let not faithless fears o'ertake us,
Let not faith and hope forsake us;
    For, through many a foe,
    To our home we go.

3   When we seek relief
    From a long-felt grief,
When temptations come alluring,
Make us patient and enduring;
    Show us that bright shore
    Where we weep no more.

4   Jesus, still lead on,
    Till our rest be won;
Heavenly Leader, still direct us,
Still support, console, protect us,
    Till we safely stand
    In our fatherland.

Count Zinzendorf, 1721; tr. by Jane Borthwick, 1853.

GENNESARET. 6s & 4s.

714.

1 Fierce was the wild billow,
　　Dark was the night,
　　Oars labored heavily,
　　Foam glittered white,
　　Trembled the mariners,
　　Peril was nigh;
　　Then said the God of God,
　　"Peace! It is I."

2 Ridge of the mountain-wave,
　　Lower thy crest;
　　Wail of Euroclydon,
　　Be thou at rest;
　　Sorrow can never be,
　　Darkness must fly,
　　Where saith the Light of Light,
　　"Peace! It is I!"

3 Jesus, Deliverer,
　　Come thou to me;
　　Soothe thou my voyaging
　　Over life's sea:
　　Thou, when the storm of death
　　Roars, sweeping by,
　　Whisper, thou Truth of Truth,
　　"Peace! It is I!"

Anatolius, died 458; tr. by J. M. Neale, 1862.

THE CHRISTIAN LIFE,—CONSECRATION.

TALLIS. C. M.

1. Thou art my por-tion, O my God; Soon as I know thy way,

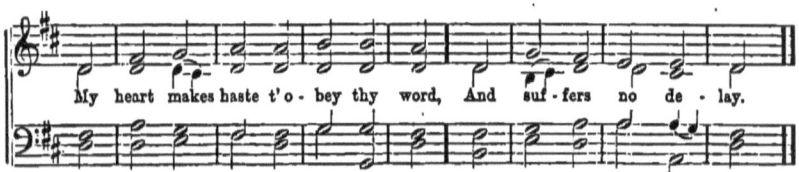
My heart makes haste t' o-bey thy word, And suf-fers no de-lay.

715. PSALM 119.

1 Thou art my portion, O my God;
  Soon as I know thy way,
  My heart makes haste t' obey thy word,
  And suffers no delay.

2 I choose the path of heavenly truth,
  And glory in my choice;
  Not all the riches of the earth
  Could make me so rejoice.

3 The testimonies of thy grace
  I set before mine eyes;
  Thence I derive my daily strength,
  And there my comfort lies.

4 If once I wander from thy path,
  I think upon my ways;
  Then turn my feet to thy commands,
  And trust thy pardoning grace.

5 Now I am thine, forever thine,
  Oh save thy servant, Lord!
  Thou art my shield, my hiding-place;
  My hope is in thy word.
  Isaac Watts, 1719.

716.

1 How can I sink with such a prop
  As my eternal God,
  Who bears the earth's huge pillars up,
  And spreads the heavens abroad?

2 How can I die while Jesus lives,
  Who rose and left the dead?
  Pardon and grace my soul receives
  From mine exalted Head.

3 All that I am, and all I have,
  Shall be forever thine;
  Whate'er my duty bids me give,
  My cheerful hands resign.

4 Yet if I might make some reserve,
  And duty did not call,
  I love my God with zeal so great,
  That I should give him all.
  Isaac Watts, 1709.

717.

1 Oh not to fill the mouth of fame
  My longing soul is stirred;
  Oh give me a diviner name,—
  Call me thy servant, Lord.

2 Sweet title that delighteth me,
  Rank earnestly implored;
  Oh what can reach the dignity
  Of thy true servants, Lord?

3 No longer would my soul be known
  As self-sustained and free;
  Oh, not mine own, oh, not mine own,
  Lord, I belong to thee.

4 In each aspiring burst of prayer,
  Sweet leave my soul would ask
  Thine every burden, Lord, to bear,
  To do thine every task.

5 In life, in death, on earth, in heaven,
  No other name for me;
  The same sweet style and title given
  Through all eternity.
  Thomas H. Gill, 1859.

718. C. M.

1 LET worldly minds the world pursue;
   It has no charms for me:
   Once I admired its trifles too,
   But grace hath set me free.

2 Its pleasures now no longer please,
   No more content afford;
   Far from my heart be joys like these,
   Now I have seen the Lord.

3 As by the light of opening day
   The stars are all concealed,
   So earthly pleasures fade away
   When Jesus is revealed.

4 Creatures no more divide my choice;
   I bid them all depart:
   His name, and love, and gracious voice,
   Have fixed my roving heart.

5 Now, Lord, I would be thine alone,
   And wholly live to thee;
   But may I hope that thou wilt own
   A worthless worm like me?

6 Yes; though of sinners I'm the worst,
   I cannot doubt thy will;
   For if thou hadst not loved me first,
   I had refused thee still.
   John Newton, 1779.

719. C. M.

1 LORD, as to thy dear cross we flee,
   And plead to be forgiven,
   So let thy life our pattern be,
   And form our souls for heaven.

2 Help us, through good report and ill,
   Our daily cross to bear,
   Like thee to do our Father's will,
   Our brethren's grief to share.

3 Let grace our selfishness expel,
   Our earthliness refine,
   And kindness in our bosoms dwell,
   As free and true as thine.

4 If joy shall at thy bidding fly,
   And grief's dark day come on,
   We, in our turn, would meekly cry,
   Father, thy will be done.

5 Should friends misjudge, or foes defame,
   Or brethren faithless prove,
   Then, like thine own, be all our aim
   To conquer them by love.

6 Kept peaceful in the midst of strife,
   Forgiving and forgiven,
   Oh may we lead the pilgrim's life,
   And follow thee to heaven!
   J. H. Gurney, 1838.

720. PSALM 119. C. M.

1 OH that the Lord would guide my ways,
   To keep his statutes still;
   Oh that my God would grant me grace
   To know and do his will.

2 Oh send thy Spirit down to write
   Thy law upon my heart;
   Nor let my tongue indulge deceit,
   Nor act the liar's part.

3 From vanity turn off my eyes;
   Let no corrupt design,
   Nor covetous desire, arise
   Within this soul of mine.

4 Order my footsteps by thy word,
   And make my heart sincere;
   Let sin have no dominion, Lord,
   But keep my conscience clear.

5 Make me to walk in thy commands,
   'T is a delightful road,
   Nor let my head, nor heart, nor hands,
   Offend against my God.
   Isaac Watts, 1719.

721. C. M.

1 OH wherefore, Lord, doth thy dear praise
   But tremble on my tongue?
   Why lack my lips sweet skill to raise
   A full, triumphant song?

2 Oh make me, Lord, thy statutes learn;
   Keep in thy ways my feet;
   Then shall my lips divinely burn;
   Then shall my songs be sweet.

3 Each sin I cast away shall make
   My soul more strong to soar;
   Each work I do for thee shall wake
   A strain divine the more.

4 My voice shall more delight thine ear,
   The more I wait on thee;
   Thy service bring my song more near
   The angelic harmony.

5 Oh when shall perfect holiness
   Make this poor voice divine,
   And all harmonious heaven confess
   No sweeter song than mine?
   Thomas H. Gill, 1849.

294 THE CHRISTIAN LIFE,—CONSECRATION.

WINCHESTER. L. M.

1. Oh that I could for-ev-er dwell De-light-ed at the Sa-viour's feet,

Be-hold the form I love so well, And all his ten-der words re-peat!

722.

1 OH that I could forever dwell
    Delighted at the Saviour's feet,
Behold the form I love so well,
    And all his tender words repeat!

2 The world shut out from all my soul,
    And heaven brought in with all its bliss,
Oh! is there aught, from pole to pole,
    One moment to compare with this?

3 This is the hidden life I prize,
    A life of penitential love,
When most my follies I despise,
    And raise my highest thoughts above;

4 When all I am I clearly see,
    And freely own with deepest shame;
When the Redeemer's love to me
    Kindles within a deathless flame.

5 Thus would I live till nature fail,
    And all my former sins forsake;
Then rise to God within the veil,
    And of eternal joys partake.
        Andrew Reed, 1841.

723.

1 MY gracious Lord, I own thy right
    To every service I can pay,
And call it my supreme delight
    To hear thy dictates and obey.

2 What is my being but for thee,
    Its sure support, its noblest end,
Thine ever-smiling face to see.
    And serve the cause of such a friend!

3 I would not breathe for worldly joy,
    Or to increase my worldly good;
Nor future days nor powers employ
    To spread a sounding name abroad.

4 'T is to my Saviour I would live,
    To him who for my ransom died;
Nor could the bowers of Eden give
    Such bliss as blossoms at his side.

5 His work my hoary age shall bless,
    When youthful vigor is no more;
And my last hour of life confess
    His dying love, his saving power.
        Philip Doddridge, 1755.

724.

1 O THOU, who camest from above,
    The pure celestial fire t' impart,
Kindle a flame of sacred love
    On the mean altar of my heart.

2 There let it for thy glory burn
    With inextinguishable blaze,
And, trembling, to its source return,
    In humble prayer and fervent praise.

3 Jesus, confirm my heart's desire
    To work and speak and think for thee;
Still let me guard the holy fire,
    And still stir up thy gift in me;

4 Ready for all thy perfect will,
    My acts of faith and love repeat;
Till death thy endless mercies seal,
    And make the sacrifice complete.
        Charles Wesley, 1762.

THE CHRISTIAN LIFE,—CONSECRATION.

HOWLAND. L. M.

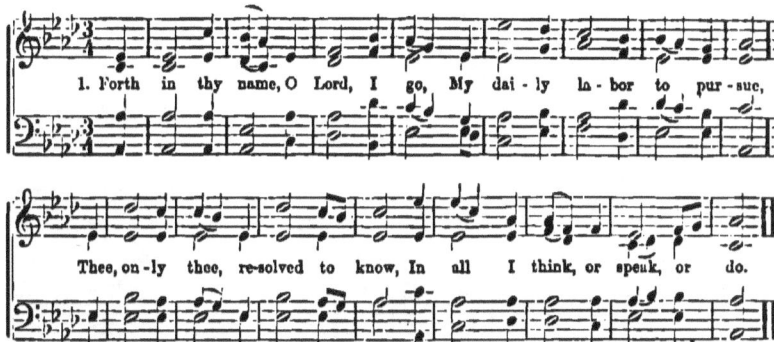

1. Forth in thy name, O Lord, I go, My daily labor to pursue, Thee, only thee, resolved to know, In all I think, or speak, or do.

725.

1 FORTH in thy name, O Lord, I go,
My daily labor to pursue,
Thee, only thee, resolved to know,
In all I think, or speak, or do.

2 The task thy wisdom hath assigned
Oh let me cheerfully fulfil;
In all my works thy presence find,
And prove thy good and perfect will.

3 Preserve me from my calling's snare,
And hide my simple heart above, —
Above the thorns of choking care,
And gilded baits of worldly love.

4 Thee may I set at my right hand,
Whose eyes my inmost substance see,
And labor on at thy command,
And offer all my works to thee.

5 Give me to bear thy easy yoke,
And every moment watch and pray;
And still to things eternal look,
And hasten to thy glorious day:

6 For thee delightfully employ [given,
Whate'er thy bounteous grace hath
And run my course with even joy,
And closely walk with thee to heaven.

Charles Wesley, 1749.

726.

1 MY Saviour, how shall I proclaim,
How pay the mighty debt I owe?
Let all I have, and all I am,
Ceaseless to all thy glory show.

2 Too much to thee I cannot give;
Too much I cannot do for thee;
Let all thy love and all thy grief
Grav'n on my heart forever be.

3 The meek, the still, the lowly mind,
Oh may I learn from thee, my God,
And love, with softest pity joined,
For those that trample on thy blood.

4 Still let thy tears, thy groans, thy sighs
O'erflow my eyes and heave my breast;
Till loose from flesh and earth I rise,
And ever in thy bosom rest.

John Wesley, 1703-1791.

727. PSALM 116.

1 REDEEMED from guilt, redeemed from fears,
My soul enlarged, and dried my tears,
What can I do, oh love divine,
What, to repay such gifts as thine?

2 What can I do, so poor, so weak,
But from thy hand new blessings seek,
A heart to feel thy mercies more,
A soul to know thee, and adore?

3 Oh teach me at thy feet to fall,
And yield thee up myself, my all;
Before thy saints my debts to own,
And live and die to thee alone.

4 Thy Spirit, Lord, at large impart,
Expand and raise and fill my heart;
So may I hope my life shall be
Some faint return, O Lord, to thee.

Henry F. Lyte, 1834.

THE CHRISTIAN LIFE,—CONSECRATION.

GOLDEN HILL. S. M.

1. My Maker and my King, To thee my all I owe; Thy sovereign bounty is the spring From whence my blessings flow.

728.

1 My Maker and my King,
   To thee my all I owe;
Thy sovereign bounty is the spring
   From whence my blessings flow.

2 The creature of thy hand,
   On thee alone I live;
My God, thy benefits demand
   More praise than life can give.

3 Oh, what can I impart,
   When all is thine before?
Thy love demands a thankful heart;
   The gift, alas, how poor!

4 Shall I withhold thy due?
   And shall my passions rove?
Lord, form this wretched heart anew,
   And fill it with thy love.
Anne Steele, 1760.

729.

1 Teach me, my God and King,
   In all things thee to see;
And what I do in anything,
   To do it as for thee:

2 To scorn the senses' sway,
   While still to thee I tend;
In all I do, be thou the way,
   In all be thou the end.

3 All may of thee partake;
   Nothing so small can be
But draws, when acted for thy sake,
   Greatness and worth from thee.

4 If done beneath thy laws
   E'en servile labors shine;
Hallowed is toil, if this the cause;
   The meanest work, divine.
George Herbert, 1632. a.

730.

1 Dear Lord and Master mine,
   Thy happy servant see;
My Conqu'ror, with what joy divine
   Thy captive clings to thee!

2 I love thy yoke to wear,
   To feel thy gracious bands,
Sweetly restrained by thy care,
   And happy in thy hands.

3 No bar would I remove;
   No bond would I unbind;
Within the limits of thy love
   Full liberty I find.

4 I would not walk alone,
   But still with thee, my God,
At every step my blindness own,
   And ask of thee the road.

5 Dear Lord and Master mine,
   Still keep thy servant true;
My Guardian and my Guide divine,
   Bring, bring thy pilgrim through.

6 My Conqu'ror and my King,
   Still keep me in thy train;
And with thee thy glad captive bring,
   When thou return'st to reign.
Thomas H. Gill, 1859.

THE CHRISTIAN LIFE,—CONFLICT.

PRAGUE. S. M.

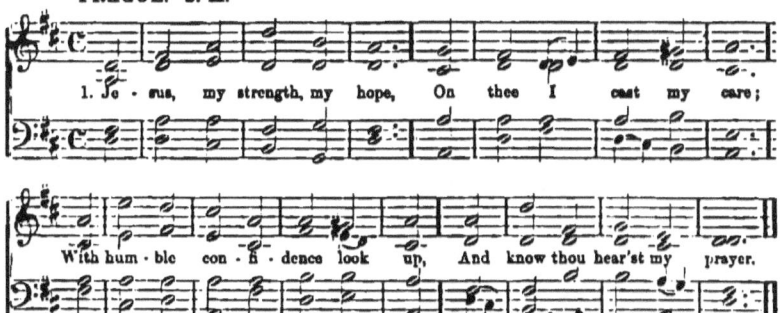

1. Jesus, my strength, my hope, On thee I cast my care; With humble confidence look up, And know thou hear'st my prayer.

731.

1 JESUS, my strength, my hope,
    On thee I cast my care;
  With humble confidence look up,
    And know thou hear'st my prayer.

2 Give me on thee to wait,
    Till I can all things do;
  On thee, almighty to create,
    Almighty to renew.

3 I want a godly fear,
    A quick discerning eye,
  That looks to thee when sin is near,
    And sees the tempter fly:

4 A spirit still prepared,
    And armed with jealous care;
  Forever standing on its guard,
    And watching unto prayer.

5 I want a heart to pray,
    To pray and never cease;
  Never to murmur at thy stay,
    Or wish my suff'rings less.

6 This blessing, above all,
    Always to pray, I want;
  Out of the deep on thee to call,
    And never, never faint.

7 I want a true regard,
    A single, steady aim,
  Unmoved by threat'ning or reward,
    To thee and thy great name;

8 A jealous, just concern
    For thine immortal praise;

  A pure desire that all may learn
    And glorify thy grace.

9 I rest upon thy word, —
    The promise is for me;
  My succor and salvation, Lord,
    Shall surely come from thee.

10 But let me still abide,
    Nor from my hope remove,
  Till thou my patient spirit guide
    Into thy perfect love.

Charles Wesley, 1742.

732.

1 YE servants of the Lord,
    Each in his office wait,
  Observant of his heavenly word,
    And watchful at his gate.

2 Let all your lamps be bright,
    And trim the golden flame;
  Gird up your loins, as in his sight,
    For awful is his name.

3 Watch; 't is your Lord's command;
    And while we speak he's near;
  Mark the first signal of his hand,
    And ready all appear.

4 Oh happy servant he,
    In such a posture found;
  He shall his Lord with rapture see,
    And be with honor crowned.

5 Christ shall the banquet spread
    With his own royal hand,
  And raise that fav'rite servant's head
    Amid the angelic band

Philip Doddridge, 1755. a.

THE CHRISTIAN LIFE,—CONFLICT.

PILESGROVE. L. M.

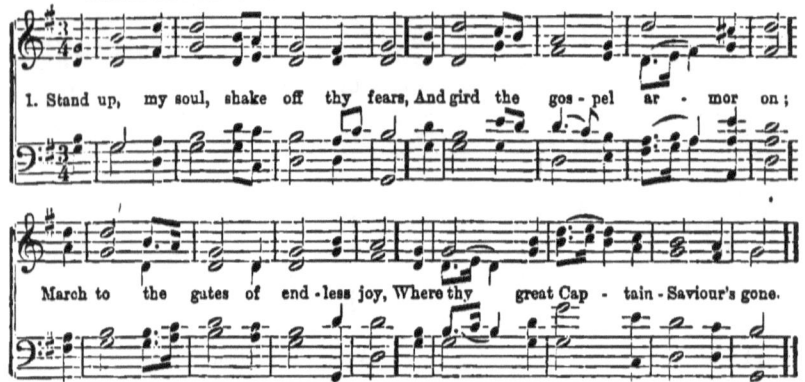

1. Stand up, my soul, shake off thy fears, And gird the gos-pel ar-mor on; March to the gates of end-less joy, Where thy great Cap-tain-Saviour's gone.

733.

1 STAND up, my soul, shake off thy fears,
  And gird the gospel armor on;
  March to the gates of endless joy, [gone.
  Where thy great Captain-Saviour's

2 Hell and thy sins resist thy course;
  But hell and sin are vanquished foes;
  Thy Jesus nailed them to the cross,
  And sung the triumph when he rose.

3 Then let my soul march boldly on,
  Press forward to the heavenly gate;
  There peace and joy eternal reign, [wait.
  And glittering robes for conquerors

4 There shall I wear a starry crown,
  And triumph in almighty grace,
  While all the armies of the skies
  Join in my glorious leader's praise.
          Isaac Watts, 1709.

734.

1 AWAKE, our souls; away, our fears;
  Let every trembling thought be gone;
  Awake, and run the heavenly race,
  And put a cheerful courage on.

2 True, 't is a strait and thorny road,
  And mortal spirits tire and faint;
  But they forget the mighty God,
  Who feeds the strength of every saint,—

3 The mighty God, whose matchless power
  Is ever new and ever young,
  And firm endures, while endless years
  Their everlasting circles run.

4 From thee, the overflowing spring,
  Our souls shall drink a fresh supply;
  While such as trust their native strength
  Shall melt away, and droop, and die.

5 Swift as an eagle cuts the air,
  We'll mount aloft to thine abode;
  On wings of love our souls shall fly,
  Nor tire amid the heavenly road!
          Isaac Watts, 1709.

735.

1 O ISRAEL, to thy tents repair:
  Why thus secure on hostile ground?
  Thy King commands thee to beware,
  For many foes thy camp surround.

2 The trumpet gives a martial strain:
  O Israel, gird thee for the fight!
  Arise, the combat to maintain,
  And put thine enemies to flight.

3 Thou shouldst not sleep, as others do;
  Awake; be vigilant; be brave!
  The coward, and the sluggard too,
  Must wear the fetters of the slave.

4 A nobler lot is cast for thee;
  A kingdom waits thee in the skies:
  With such a hope, shall Israel flee,
  Or yield, through weariness, the prize?

5 No; let a careless world repose, [day,
  And slumber on through life's short
  While Israel to the conflict goes,
  And bears the glorious prize away!
          Thomas Kelly, 1806.

THE CHRISTIAN LIFE,—CONFLICT.

ARLINGTON. C. M.

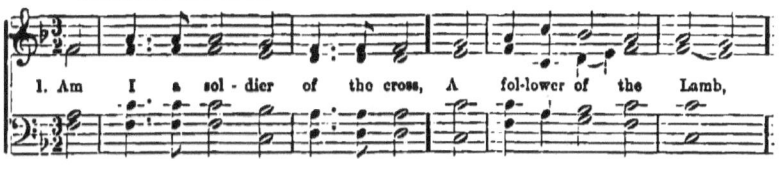
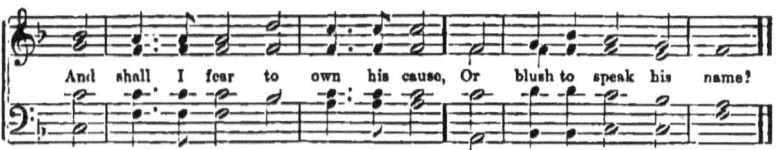

1. Am I a sol-dier of the cross, A fol-lower of the Lamb, And shall I fear to own his cause, Or blush to speak his name?

736.

1 Am I a soldier of the cross,
   A follower of the Lamb,
And shall I fear to own his cause,
   Or blush to speak his name?

2 Must I be carried to the skies
   On flowery beds of ease,
While others fought to win the prize,
   And sailed through bloody seas?

3 Are there no foes for me to face?
   Must I not stem the flood?
Is this vile world a friend to grace,
   To help me on to God?

4 Sure I must fight if I would reign;
   Increase my courage, Lord;
I'll bear the toil, endure the pain,
   Supported by thy word.

5 Thy saints, in all this glorious war,
   Shall conquer, though they die;
They view the triumph from afar,
   And seize it with their eye.

6 When that illustrious day shall rise,
   And all thy armies shine
In robes of victory through the skies,
   The glory shall be thine.
                    Isaac Watts, 1709.

737.

1 THE Son of God goes forth to war,
   A kingly crown to gain,

His blood-red banner streams afar;
   Who follows in his train?

2 Who best can drink his cup of woe,
   Triumphant over pain,
Who patient bears his cross below,
   He follows in his train.

3 The martyr first, whose eagle eye
   Could pierce beyond the grave,
Who saw his Master in the sky,
   And called on him to save;

4 Like him, with pardon on his tongue,
   In midst of mortal pain,
He prayed for them that did the wrong:
   Who follows in his train?

5 A glorious band, the chosen few
   On whom the Spirit came,   [knew,
Twelve valiant saints, their hope they
   And mocked the cross and flame.

6 They climbed the steep ascent of heaven,
   Through peril, toil, and pain;
O God, to us may grace be given
   To follow in their train!
                    Reginald Heber, 1827.

DOXOLOGY.

LET God the Father, and the Son,
   And Spirit, be adored,   [known,
Where there are works to make him
   Or saints to love the Lord!
                    Isaac Watts, 1719.

THE CHRISTIAN LIFE,—CONFLICT.

HEBRON. L. M.

1. Je-sus, and shall it ev-er be, A mor-tal man a-shamed of thee? A-shamed of thee, whom an-gels praise, Whose glo-ries shine through endless days?

738.

1 JESUS, and shall it ever be,
A mortal man ashamed of thee?
Ashamed of thee, whom angels praise,
Whose glories shine through endless days?

2 Ashamed of Jesus! sooner far
Let evening blush to own a star;
He sheds the beams of light divine
O'er this benighted soul of mine.

3 Ashamed of Jesus! just as soon
Let midnight be ashamed of noon;
'T is midnight with my soul till he,
Bright Morning Star, bid darkness flee.

4 Ashamed of Jesus! that dear friend
On whom my hopes of heaven depend?
No; when I blush be this my shame,
That I no more revere his name.

5 Ashamed of Jesus! yes, I may,
When I've no guilt to wash away,
No tear to wipe, no good to crave,
No fears to quell, no soul to save.

6 Till then — nor is my boasting vain —
Till then I boast a Saviour slain;
And oh may this my glory be,
That Christ is not ashamed of me!
Joseph Grigg, 1765; alt. by Benj. Francis, 1787.

739.

1 AWAKE, my soul, lift up thine eyes,
See where thy foes against thee rise,
In long array, a numerous host;
Awake, my soul! or thou art lost.

2 Here giant danger threatening stands,
Mustering his pale terrific bands;
There pleasure's silken banners spread,
And willing souls are captive led.

3 Thou tread'st upon enchanted ground;
Perils and snares beset thee round;
Beware of all, guard every part,
But most the traitor in thy heart.

4 The terror and the charm repel,
And powers of earth, and powers of hell;
The man of Calvary triumphed here:
Why should his faithful followers fear?
Anna Lætitia Barbauld, 1773.

740.

1 So let our lips and lives express
The holy gospel we profess,
So let our works and virtues shine,
To prove the doctrine all divine.

2 Thus shall we best proclaim abroad
The honors of our Saviour God,
When his salvation reigns within,
And grace subdues the power of sin.

3 Our flesh and sense must be denied,
Passion and envy, lust and pride;
While justice, temperance, truth, and love,
Our inward piety approve.

4 Religion bears our spirits up,
While we expect that blessed hope,
The bright appearance of the Lord,
And faith stands leaning on his word.
Isaac Watts, 1709.

THE CHRISTIAN LIFE,—CONFLICT.

CHRISTMAS. C. M.

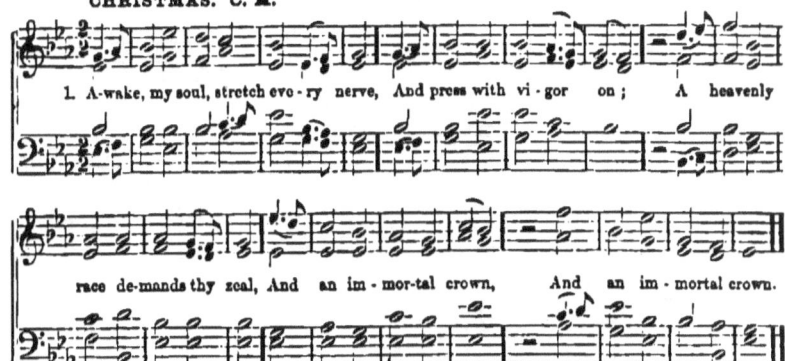

1. A-wake, my soul, stretch eve-ry nerve, And press with vi-gor on; A heavenly race demands thy zeal, And an im-mor-tal crown, And an im-mortal crown.

741.

1 AWAKE, my soul, stretch every nerve,
And press with vigor on;
A heavenly race demands thy zeal,
And an immortal crown.

2 A cloud of witnesses around
Hold thee in full survey;
Forget the steps already trod,
And onward urge thy way.

3 'T is God's all-animating voice
That calls thee from on high;
'T is his own hand presents the prize
To thine aspiring eye;

4 That prize, with peerless glories bright,
Which shall new lustre boast, [gems
When victors' wreaths and monarchs'
Shall blend in common dust.

5 Blest Saviour, introduced by thee,
Have I my race begun;
And, crowned with victory, at thy feet
I 'll lay my honors down.
Philip Doddridge, 1755.

742.   GEN. xxiv. 56.

1 IN all my Lord's appointed ways
My journey I 'll pursue;
Hinder me not, ye much-loved saints,
For I must go with you.

2 Through floods and flames, if Jesus lead,
I 'll follow where he goes;
Hinder me not! shall be my cry,
Though earth and hell oppose.

3 Through duty, and through trials too,
I 'll go at his command;
Hinder me not, for I am bound
To my Immanuel's land.

4 And when my Saviour calls me home,
Still this my cry shall be,
Hinder me not! come, welcome death;
I 'll gladly go with thee!
John Ryland, 1773.

743.

1 I 'M not ashamed to own my Lord,
Or to defend his cause;
Maintain the honor of his word,
The glory of his cross.

2 Jesus, my God! I know his name,
His name is all my trust;
Nor will he put my soul to shame,
Nor let my hope be lost.

3 Firm as his throne his promise stands,
And he can well secure
What I've committed to his hands,
Till the decisive hour.

4 Then will he own my worthless name
Before his Father's face,
And in the New Jerusalem
Appoint my soul a place.
Isaac Watts, 1707.

DOXOLOGY.

To Father, Son, and Holy Ghost,
One God, whom we adore,
Be glory as it was, is now
And shall be evermore!
Tate and Brady, 1696.

302. THE CHRISTIAN LIFE, — CONFLICT.

MAITLAND. C. M.

1. Must Jesus bear the cross alone, And all the world go free? No, there's a cross for every one, And there's a cross for me.

744.

2 This consecrated cross I'll bear
   Till death shall set me free,
And then go home my crown to wear,
   For there's a crown for me.

3 Upon the crystal pavement, down
   At Jesus' piercéd feet,
Joyful I'll cast my golden crown,
   And his dear name repeat.

4 And palms shall wave, and harps shall ring,
   Beneath heaven's arches high;
The Lord that lives, the ransomed sing,
   That lives no more to die.

5 Oh, precious cross! oh, glorious crown!
   Oh, resurrection day!
Ye angels, from the stars come down,
   And bear my soul away!
                                G. N. Allen, 1852.

745.   ISAIAH xl. 27-31.

1 WHENCE do our mournful thoughts arise,
   And where's our courage fled?
Has restless sin or raging hell
   Struck all our comforts dead?

2 Have we forgot th' almighty Name
   That formed the earth and sea?
And can an all-creating arm
   Grow weary or decay?

3 Treasures of everlasting might
   In our Jehovah dwell;
He gives the conquest to the weak,
   And treads their foes to hell.

4 Mere mortal power shall fade and die,
   And youthful vigor cease;
But we who wait upon the Lord
   Shall feel our strength increase.

5 The saints shall mount on eagles' wings,
   And taste the promised bliss,
Till their unwearied feet arrive
   Where perfect pleasure is.
                                Isaac Watts, 1709.

746.

1 ALAS, what hourly dangers rise!
   What snares beset my way!
To heaven oh let me lift my eyes,
   And hourly watch and pray.

2 How oft my mournful thoughts complain,
   And melt in flowing tears;
My weak resistance, ah, how vain;
   How strong my foes and fears!

3 O gracious God, in whom I live,
   My feeble efforts aid;
Help me to watch, and pray, and strive,
   Though trembling and afraid.

4 Increase my faith, increase my hope,
   When foes and fears prevail;
And bear my fainting spirit up,
   Or soon my strength will fail.

5 Oh keep me in thy heavenly way,
   And bid the tempter flee;
And let me never, never stray
   From happiness and thee.
                                Anne Steele, 1760.

THE CHRISTIAN LIFE,—CONFLICT.   303

LABAN. S. M.

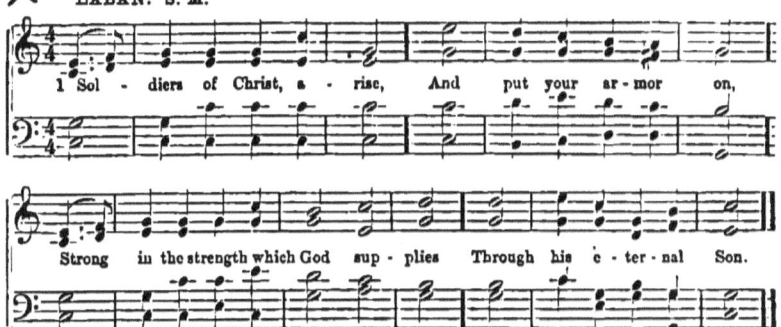

Soldiers of Christ, arise, And put your armor on,
Strong in the strength which God supplies Through his eternal Son.

747.

1 SOLDIERS of Christ, arise,
  And put your armor on,
Strong in the strength which God supplies
  Through his eternal Son.

2 Strong in the Lord of hosts
  And in his mighty power,
Who in the strength of Jesus trusts
  Is more than conqueror.

3 Stand then in his great might,
  With all his strength endued,
And take, to arm you for the fight,
  The panoply of God:

4 That, having all things done,
  And all your conflicts past,
You may o'ercome through Christ alone,
  And stand entire at last.

5 From strength to strength go on;
  Wrestle, and fight, and pray;
Tread all the powers of darkness down,
  And win the well-fought day.

6 Still let the Spirit cry
  In all his soldiers, come!
Till Christ the Lord descend from high,
  And take the conquerors home.
    Charles Wesley, 1745.

748.

1 MY soul, be on thy guard;
  Ten thousand foes arise,
And hosts of sin are pressing hard
  To draw thee from the skies.

2 Oh watch, and fight, and pray;
  The battle ne'er give o'er;
Renew it boldly every day,
  And help divine implore.

3 Ne'er think the victory won,
  Nor once at ease sit down;
Thine arduous work will not be done
  Till thou obtain thy crown.

4 Fight on, my soul, till death
  Shall bring thee to thy God;
He'll take thee at thy parting breath
  To his divine abode.
    Heath.

749.

1 A CHARGE to keep I have,
  A God to glorify,
A never-dying soul to save,
  And fit it for the sky.

2 To serve the present age,
  My calling to fulfil,—
Oh may it all my powers engage
  To do my Master's will!

3 Arm me with jealous care,
  As in thy sight to live;
And oh, thy servant, Lord, prepare
  A strict account to give.

4 Help me to watch and pray,
  And on thyself rely,
Assured, if I my trust betray,
  I shall forever die.
    Charles Wesley, 1767.

THE CHRISTIAN LIFE, — CONFLICT.

PAUL. 10s, 11 & 12.

1. Breast the wave, Christian, when it is strongest; Watch for day, Christian, when the night's long-est; Onward and onward still be thine endeavor; The rest that remaineth, endureth forever.

750.

2 Fight the fight, Christian; Jesus is o'er thee;
Run the race, Christian; heaven is before thee;
He who hath promised faltereth never;
The love of eternity flows on forever.

3 Lift the eye, Christian, just as it closeth;
Raise the heart, Christian, ere it reposeth:
Thee from the love of Christ nothing shall sever;
Mount when thy work is done, and praise him forever.

Joseph Stammers, 1844.

751.   Tune, "Meribah," p. 414.   C. P. M.

1 Fear not, O little flock, the foe
  Who madly seeks your overthrow;
    Dread not his rage and power; [faints,
What though your courage sometimes
This seeming triumph o'er God's saints
    Lasts but a little hour.

2 Fear not! be strong! your cause belongs
  To him who can avenge your wrongs;
    Leave it to him, our Lord;
Though hidden yet from mortal eyes,
Salvation shall for you arise;
    He girdeth on his sword.

3 As sure as God's own promise stands,
  Not earth, nor hell, with all their bands,
    Against us shall prevail: [throne;
The Lord shall mock them from his
God is with us, we are his own;
    Our victory cannot fail.

4 Amen! Lord Jesus, grant our prayer;
  Great Captain, now thine arm make bare,
    Thy church with strength defend:
So shall all saints and martyrs raise
A joyful chorus to thy praise
    Through ages without end!

Altenburg, 1631; tr. by C. *Winkworth*, 1855, a.

THE CHRISTIAN LIFE,—CONFLICT.

CORONA. 7,7; 8,7; 7,7; 8,7.

752.

1 HEAD of the Church triumphant,
 We joyfully adore thee;
Till thou appear, thy members here
 Shall sing like those in glory:
We lift our hearts and voices
 With blest anticipation,
And cry aloud, and give to God
 The praise of our salvation.

2 Thou dost conduct thy people
 Through torrents of temptation;
Nor will we fear, while thou art near,
 The fire of tribulation:
The world, with sin and Satan,
 In vain our march opposes;
By thee we shall break through them all,
 And sing the song of Moses.

3 While in affliction's furnace,
 And passing through the fire,
Thy love we praise, that knows our days,
 And ever brings us nigher.
We'll lift our hands exulting
 In thine almighty favor;
The love divine, that made us thine,
 Shall keep us thine forever.

4 By faith we see the glory
 To which thou shalt restore us;
The cross despise for that high prize
 Which thou hast set before us:
And if thou count us worthy,
 We each, as dying Stephen,
Shall see thee stand at God's right hand,
 To take us up to heaven.
 Charles Wesley, 1745.

306 CHRISTIAN LIFE,—FELLOWSHIP AND CHARITY.

PENN. 7s. DOUBLE. (Omit repeat for Hymn 754.)

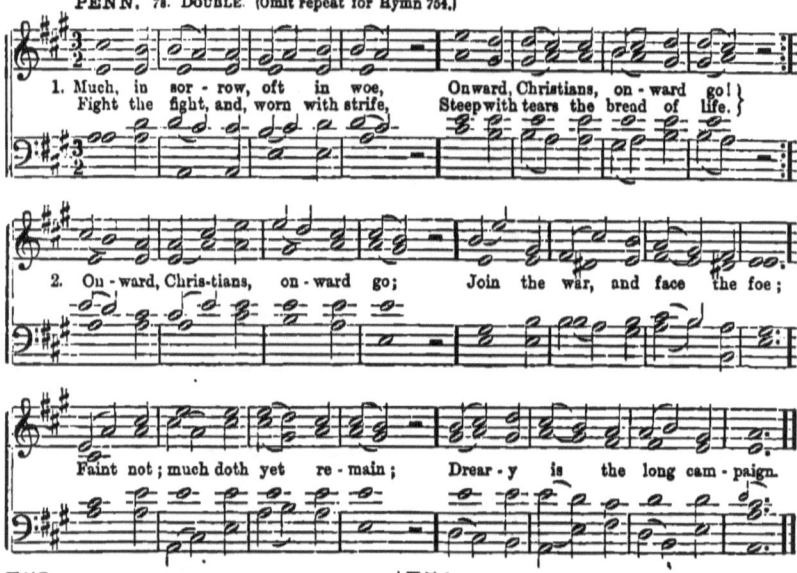

1. Much, in sorrow, oft in woe,
Fight the fight, and, worn with strife,
Onward, Christians, onward go!
Steep with tears the bread of life.

2. Onward, Christians, onward go;
Join the war, and face the foe;
Faint not; much doth yet remain;
Dreary is the long campaign.

753.

2 Onward, Christians, onward go;
Join the war, and face the foe;
Faint not; much doth yet remain;
Dreary is the long campaign.

3 Shrink not, Christians: will ye yield?
Will ye quit the painful field?
Will ye flee in danger's hour?
Know ye not your Captain's power?

4 Let your drooping hearts be glad;
March, in heavenly armor clad;
Fight, nor think the battle long;
Victory soon shall tune your song.

5 Let not sorrow dim your eye,
Soon shall every tear be dry;
Let not woe your course impede;
Great your strength, if great your need.

6 Onward then to battle move!
More than conquerors ye shall prove;
Though opposed by many a foe,
Christian soldiers, onward go!

Henry Kirke White, 1806; completed by Fanny Fuller Maitland, 1827.

754. PSALM 133.

1 'T is a pleasant thing to see
Brethren in the Lord agree;
Children of a God of love
Live as they should live above;
Acting each a Christian part,
One in lip and one in heart.

2 As the precious ointment shed
Upon Aaron's hallowed head,
Downward through his garments stole,
Spreading odor o'er the whole;
So from our High Priest above
To his church flows heavenly love.

3 Gently as the dews distil
Down on Zion's holy hill,
Dropping gladness where they fall,
Bright'ning and refreshing all,
Such is Christian union, shed
Through the members from the Head.

4 Where divine affection lives,
There the Lord his blessing gives;
Where on earth his will is done,
There his heaven is half begun:
Lord, our great example prove;
Teach us all like thee to love.

Henry F. Lyte, 1834.

CHRISTIAN LIFE,—FELLOWSHIP AND CHARITY. 307
BOYLSTON. S. M.

1. Blest be the tie that binds Our hearts in Christian love: The fellowship of kindred minds Is like to that above.

755.
1 BLEST be the tie that binds
   Our hearts in Christian love:
   The fellowship of kindred minds
   Is like to that above.

2 Before our Father's throne
   We pour our ardent prayers;
   Our fears, our hopes, our aims are one,
   Our comforts and our cares.

3 We share our mutual woes,
   Our mutual burdens bear,
   And often for each other flows
   The sympathizing tear.

4 When we asunder part,
   It gives us inward pain;
   But we shall still be joined in heart,
   And hope to meet again.

5 This glorious hope revives
   Our courage by the way;
   While each in expectation lives,
   And longs to see the day.

6 From sorrow, toil, and pain,
   And sin, we shall be free,
   And perfect love and friendship reign
   Through all eternity.
                    John Fawcett, 1772.

756.   PSALM 133.
1 BLEST are the sons of peace
   Whose hearts and hopes are one;
   Whose kind designs to serve and please
   Through all their actions run.

2 Blest is the pious house
   Where zeal and friendship meet;
   Their songs of praise, their mingled vows,
   Make their communion sweet.

3 Thus when on Aaron's head
   They poured the rich perfume,
   The oil through all his raiment spread,
   And pleasure filled the room.

4 Thus on the heavenly hills
   The saints are blest above,
   Where joy like morning dew distils,
   And all the air is love.
                    Isaac Watts, 1719.

757.
1 JESUS, our faith increase;
   Fast knit, O Lord, to thee,
   Around us bind the bond of peace,
   The Spirit's unity.

2 One God and Father ours,
   One Christ his gift of love,
   One Spirit shed in living showers,
   One home prepared above.

3 To one glad hope we cling,
   Through Jesus' life and death;
   One theme of saving grace we sing,
   And ours one common faith.

4 Then grant us, Lord, one mind,
   One will in all our ways,
   One heart to thine own truth inclined,
   One mouth to speak thy praise.
                    Bristol Hymns, 1870.

308 CHRISTIAN LIFE,—FELLOWSHIP AND CHARITY.

ZEPHYR. L. M.

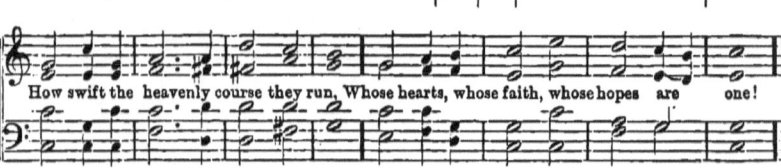

1. How blest the sacred tie that binds In union sweet according minds; How swift the heavenly course they run, Whose hearts, whose faith, whose hopes are one!

758.

1 How blest the sacred tie that binds
In union sweet according minds;
How swift the heavenly course they run,
Whose hearts, whose faith, whose hopes
are one!

2 To each the soul of each how dear;
What jealous love, what holy fear;
How doth the generous flame within
Refine from earth and cleanse from sin.

3 Their streaming tears together flow
For human guilt and mortal woe;
Their ardent prayers together rise
Like mingling flames in sacrifice.

4 Together both they seek the place
Where God reveals his awful face;
How high, how strong their raptures swell,
There's none but kindred souls can tell.

5 Nor shall the glowing flame expire
When nature droops her sickening fire;
Then shall they meet in realms above,
A heaven of joy because of love.
A. L. Barbauld, 1773.

759.

1 O Lord, how joyful 'tis to see
The brethren join in love to thee;
On thee alone their heart relies,
Their only strength thy grace supplies.

2 How sweet, within thy holy place,
With one accord to sing thy grace,
Besieging thine attentive ear
With all the force of fervent prayer.

3 Oh may we love the house of God,
Of peace and joy the blest abode;
Oh may no angry strife destroy
That sacred peace, that holy joy.

4 The world without may rage, but we
Will only cling more close to thee,
With hearts to thee more wholly given,
More weaned from earth, more fixed on heaven.

5 Lord, shower upon us from above
The sacred gift of mutual love;
Each other's wants may we supply,
And reign together in the sky.
John Chandler, 1837.

760.

1 Had I the tongues of Greeks and Jews,
And nobler speech than angels use,
If love be absent, I am found,
Like tinkling brass, an empty sound.

2 Were I inspired to preach and tell
All that is done in heaven or hell,
Or could my faith the world remove,
Still am I nothing without love.

3 Should I distribute all my store
To feed the hungry, clothe the poor,
Or give my body to the flame
To gain a martyr's glorious name,

4 If love to God and love to men
Be absent, all my hopes are vain;
Nor tongues, nor gifts, nor fiery zeal,
The work of love can e'er fulfil.
Isaac Watts, 1709. a.

CHRISTIAN LIFE,—FELLOWSHIP AND CHARITY. 309
BEETHOVEN. L. M.

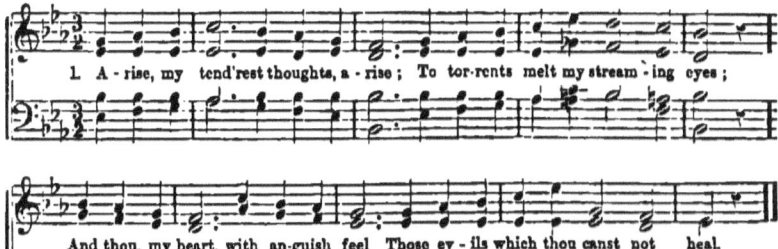

1. A-rise, my tend'rest thoughts, a-rise; To torrents melt my streaming eyes;
And thou, my heart, with an-guish feel Those ev-ils which thou canst not heal.

761.

1 ARISE, my tend'rest thoughts, arise;
To torrents melt my streaming eyes;
And thou, my heart, with anguish feel
Those evils which thou canst not heal.

2 See human nature sunk in shame;
See scandals poured on Jesus' name;
The Father wounded through the Son;
The world abused, the soul undone.

3 My God, I feel the mournful scene;
My spirit yearns o'er dying men;
And fain my pity would reclaim
And snatch the firebrands from the flame.

4 But feeble my compassion proves,
And can but weep where most it loves:
Thine own all-saving arm employ,
And turn these drops of grief to joy.
Philip Doddridge, 1719.

762. MATT. V. 3-10.

1 BLEST are the humble souls that see
Their emptiness and poverty;
Treasures of grace to them are given,
And crowns of joy laid up in heaven.

2 Blest are the meek, who stand afar
From rage and passion, noise and war;
God will secure their happy state,
And plead their cause against the great.

3 Blest are the souls that thirst for grace,
Hunger and long for righteousness;
They shall be well supplied and fed
With living streams and living bread.

4 Blest are the men whose pities move
And melt with sympathy and love;
From Christ the Lord shall they obtain
Like sympathy and love again.

5 Blest are the men of peaceful life,
Who quench the coals of growing strife;
They shall be called the heirs of bliss,
The sons of God, the God of peace.

6 Blest are the sufferers, who partake
Of pain and shame for Jesus' sake;
Their souls shall triumph in the Lord;
Glory and joy are their reward.
Isaac Watts, 1709.

763.

1 BLEST is the man whose spirit shares
A suffering brother's wants and cares;
The Lord will visit him in grief,
And bring his trials sweet relief.

2 The sinner's Friend delights to see
His people kind and good as he.
And bids them each with each unite
To make their common burden light.

3 That burden well the Saviour knows;
He bore on earth our sins and woes;
By friends betrayed, by foes assailed,
Yet love divine o'er all prevailed.

4 That love, O Lord, still let us share,
Still lead us on through foe and snare,
Till we thy face unclouded see,
And lose ourselves and earth in thee.
H. F. Lyte, 1834.

310 CHRISTIAN LIFE,—FELLOWSHIP AND CHARITY.

EXETER. C. M.

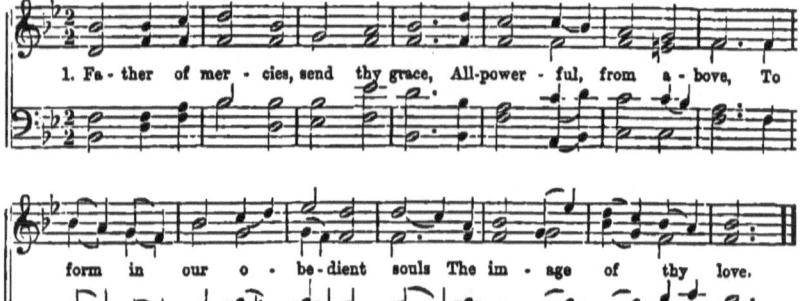

1. Father of mercies, send thy grace, All-powerful, from above, To form in our obedient souls The image of thy love.

764.

1 Father of mercies, send thy grace,
  All-powerful, from above,
 To form in our obedient souls
  The image of thy love.

2 Oh, may our sympathizing breasts
  That generous pleasure know,
 Kindly to share in others' joy,
  And weep for others' woe.

3 When poor and helpless sons of grief
  In deep distress are laid,
 Soft be our hearts their pains to feel,
  And swift our hands to aid.

4 So Jesus looked on dying men,
  When throned above the skies,
 And, 'midst the embraces of his God,
  He felt compassion rise.

5 On wings of love the Saviour flew
  To raise us from the ground,
 And made the richest of his blood
  A balm for every wound.
            Philip Doddridge, 1755.

765.

1 Bright Source of everlasting love,
  To thee our souls we raise,
 And to thy sovereign bounty rear
  A monument of praise.

2 Thy mercy gilds the path of life
  With every cheering ray,
 And kindly checks the rising tear,
  Or wipes that tear away.

3 What shall we render, bounteous Lord
  For all the grace we see?
 The goodness feeble worms can yield
  Extendeth not to thee.

4 To tents of woe, to beds of pain,
  We cheerfully repair,
 And, with the gift thy hand bestows,
  Relieve the mourners there.

5 The widow's heart shall sing for joy;
  The orphan shall be glad;
 And hungering souls we'll gladly point
  To Christ, the living bread.

6 Thus passing through the vale of tears,
  Our useful light shall shine,
 And others learn to glorify
  Our Father's name divine.
            James Boden, 1798.

766.

1 Jesus, my Lord, how rich thy grace,
  Thy bounties how complete!
 How shall I count the matchless sum,
  How pay the mighty debt!

2 High on a throne of radiant light
  Dost thou exalted shine;
 What can my poverty bestow,
  When all the worlds are thine?

3 But thou hast brethren here below,
  The partners of thy grace,
 And wilt confess their humble names
  Before thy Father's face.

THE CHRISTIAN LIFE,—ITS BLESSEDNESS.

4 In them thou may'st be clothed and fed,
  And visited and cheered;
  And in their accents of distress
  My Saviour's voice is heard.

5 Thy face, with reverence and love,
  I in thy poor would see;
  Oh rather let me beg my bread
  Than hold it back from thee!
    Philip Doddridge, 1755.

767. C. M.

1 How sweet, how heavenly is the sight,
  When those that love the Lord
  In one another's peace delight,
  And so fulfil his word!

2 When each can feel his brother's sigh,
  And with him bear a part;
  When sorrow flows from eye to eye,
  And joy from heart to heart!

3 When, free from envy, scorn, and pride,
  Our wishes all above,
  Each can his brother's failings hide,
  And show a brother's love!

4 When love, in one delightful stream,
  Through every bosom flows,
  And union sweet, and dear esteem,
  In every action glows!

5 Love is the golden chain that binds
  The happy souls above;
  And he's an heir of heaven who finds
  His bosom glow with love.
    Joseph Swain, 1792.

768. C. M.

1 HAPPY the souls to Jesus joined,
  And saved by grace alone;
  Walking in all his ways they find
  Their heaven on earth begun.

2 The church triumphant in thy love,
  Their mighty joys we know;
  They sing the Lamb in hymns above,
  And we in hymns below.

3 Thee, in thy glorious realm, they praise,
  And bow before thy throne;
  We, in the kingdom of thy grace:
  The kingdoms are but one.

4 The holy to the holiest leads;
  From hence our spirits rise;
  And he that in thy statutes treads
  Shall meet thee in the skies.
    Charles Wesley, 1745.

769. ISAIAH XXXV. 8-10. C. M.

1 SING, ye redeemed of the Lord,
  Your great Deliverer sing;
  Pilgrims for Zion's city bound,
  Be joyful in your King.

2 See the fair way his hand has raised,
  How holy, and how plain;
  Nor shall the simplest traveller err,
  Nor ask the track in vain.

3 No roaring lion shall destroy,
  Nor lurking serpent wound;
  Pleasure and safety, peace and praise,
  Through all the path are found.

4 A hand divine shall lead you on
  Through all the blissful road,
  Till to the sacred mount you rise,
  And see your smiling God.

5 There garlands of immortal joy
  Shall bloom on every head;
  While sorrow, sighing, and distress,
  Like shadows all are fled.

6 March on in your Redeemer's strength;
  Pursue his footsteps still;
  And let the prospect cheer your eye
  While laboring up the hill.
    Philip Doddridge, 1755.

770. PSALM 91. C. M.

1 THERE is a safe and secret place
  Beneath the wings divine,
  Reserved for all the heirs of grace;
  Oh be that refuge mine!

2 The least and feeblest there may bide,
  Uninjured and unawed;
  While thousands fall on every side,
  He rests secure in God.

3 The angels watch him on his way,
  And aid with friendly arm;
  And Satan, roaring for his prey,
  May hate, but cannot harm.

4 He feeds in pastures large and fair
  Of love and truth divine:
  O child of God, O glory's heir,
  How rich a lot is thine!

5 A hand almighty to defend,
  An ear for every call,
  An honored life, a peaceful end,
  And heaven to crown it all!
    Henry F. Lyte, 1834.

THE CHRISTIAN LIFE,—ITS BLESSEDNESS.

ST. MARTIN'S. C. M.

771. Col. iii. 3.

1 O HAPPY soul that lives on high,
  While men lie grovelling here!
  His hopes are fixed above the sky,
  And faith forbids his fear.

2 His conscience knows no secret stings,
  While peace and joy combine
  To form a life whose holy springs
  Are hidden and divine.

3 He waits in secret on his God;
  His God in secret sees:
  Let earth be all in arms abroad,
  He dwells in heavenly peace.

4 His pleasures rise from things unseen,
  Beyond this world and time,
  Where neither eyes nor ears have been,
  Nor thoughts of sinners climb.

5 He wants no pomp nor royal throne
  To raise his figure here;
  Content and pleased to live unknown,
  Till Christ, his life, appear.

6 He looks to heaven's eternal hill
  To meet that glorious day,
  But patient waits his Saviour's will
  To fetch his soul away.
  Isaac Watts, 1709.

772.

1 THRICE happy souls, who, born from
    While yet they sojourn here, [heaven,
  Thus all their days with God begin,
  And spend them in his fear!

2 'Midst hourly cares may love present
  Its incense to thy throne,
  And while the world our hands employs,
  Our hearts be thine alone.

3 As sanctified to noblest ends,
  Be each refreshment sought,
  And by each various providence
  Some wise instruction brought.

4 When to laborious duties called,
  Or by temptations tried,
  We'll seek the shelter of thy wings,
  And in thy strength confide.

5 As different scenes of life arise,
  Our grateful hearts would be
  With thee amidst the social band,
  In solitude with thee.

6 At night we lean our weary heads
  On thy paternal breast,
  And, safely folded in thine arms,
  Resign our powers to rest.

7 In solid, pure delights like these,
  Let all my days be passed;
  Nor shall I then impatient wish,
  Nor shall I fear the last.
  Philip Doddridge, 1737.

DOXOLOGY.

Honor to the Almighty Three
  And everlasting One;
All glory to the Father be,
  The Spirit and the Son.
  Isaac Watts, 1709.

THE CHRISTIAN LIFE,—ITS BLESSEDNESS.   313
HAVERHILL. S. M.

1. Oh bless-ed souls are they Whose sins are cov-ered o'er!
Di-vine-ly blest, to whom the Lord Im-putes their guilt no more.

773.   PSALM 32.

1 OH blessed souls are they
Whose sins are covered o'er!
Divinely blest, to whom the Lord
Imputes their guilt no more.

2 They mourn their follies past,
And keep their hearts with care;
Their lips and lives, without deceit,
Shall prove their faith sincere.

3 While I concealed my guilt,
I felt the festering wound,
Till I confessed my sins to thee,
And ready pardon found.

4 Let sinners learn to pray,
Let saints keep near the throne;
Our help in times of deep distress
Is found in God alone.
Isaac Watts, 1719.

774.

1 WHAT cheering words are these,
Their sweetness who can tell?—
In time and to eternal days,
'T is with the righteous well.

2 Well when they see his face,
Or sink amidst the flood;
Well in affliction's thorny maze,
Or on the mount with God.

3 'T is well when joys arise,
'T is well when sorrows flow;
'T is well when darkness veils the skies,
And strong temptations blow.

4 'T is well when at his throne
They wrestle, weep, and pray,
'T is well when at his feet they groan,
Yet bring their wants away.

5 'T is well when they can sing
As sinners bought with blood,
And when they touch the mournful string,
And mourn an absent God.

6 'T is well when on the mount
They feast on dying love,
And 't is as well, in God's account,
When they the furnace prove.
John Kent, 1803.

775.

1 BLEST are the pure in heart,
For they shall see their God:
The secret of the Lord is theirs;
Their soul is Christ's abode.

2 The Lord, who left the heavens,
Our life and peace to bring,
To dwell in lowliness with men,
Their pattern and their King;

3 He to the lowly soul
Doth still himself impart,
And for his dwelling and his throne
Chooseth the pure in heart.

4 Lord, we thy presence seek;
May ours this blessing be;
Oh, give the pure and lowly heart,
A temple meet for thee.
John Keble, 1827, a.

THE CHRISTIAN LIFE,—ITS BLESSEDNESS.

PLEYEL'S HYMN. 7s.

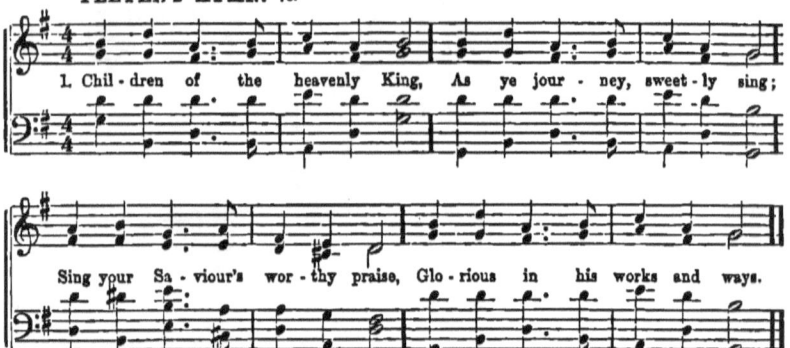

1. Children of the heavenly King, As ye journey, sweetly sing; Sing your Saviour's worthy praise, Glorious in his works and ways.

776.

1 CHILDREN of the heavenly King,
As ye journey, sweetly sing;
Sing your Saviour's worthy praise,
Glorious in his works and ways.

2 We are travelling home to God,
In the way the fathers trod;
They are happy now, and we
Soon their happiness shall see.

3 Shout, ye little flock, and blest;
You on Jesus' throne shall rest;
There your seat is now prepared,
There your kingdom and reward.

4 Lift your eyes, ye sons of light;
Zion's city is in sight;
There our endless home shall be,
There our Lord we soon shall see.

5 Lord, obediently we go,
Gladly leaving all below;
Only thou our leader be,
And we still will follow thee!
John Cennick, 1742.

777. PSALM 15.

1 WHO, O Lord, when life is o'er,
Shall to heaven's blest mansions soar?
Who, an ever-welcome guest,
In thy holy place shall rest?

2 He whose heart thy love has warmed;
He whose will, to thine conformed,
Bids his life unsullied run;
He whose words and thoughts are one;

3 He who shuns the sinner's road,
Loving those who love their God;
Who, with hope and faith unfeigned,
Treads the path by thee ordained;

4 He who trusts in Christ alone,
Not in aught himself hath done:
He, great God, shall be thy care,
And thy choicest blessings share.
H. F. Lyte, 1834.

778.

1 REST, my soul, the work is done,
Done by God's almighty Son;
This to faith is now so clear,
There's no place for doubt or fear.

2 Not through works of weary toil
Comes the sunshine of God's smile;
One with Christ, and found in him,
Brightly falls the glorious beam.

3 Now, with faith in Jesus blest,
We are entering into rest;
He, who full salvation brought,
In us all our works hath wrought.

4 Come, my soul, take up the cross,
Count the gain, despise the loss;
Labor for and with the Lord
Brings exceeding great reward.

5 Free from every fear of wrath,
Choose the laborer's happy path;
Tread the way which Christ hath trod,
Till the Sabbath of thy God.
Bristol Hymns, 1870.

THE CHRISTIAN LIFE,—ITS BLESSEDNESS. 315

ROSEFIELD. 7s. 6 LINES. (Omit repeat for 4 lines.)

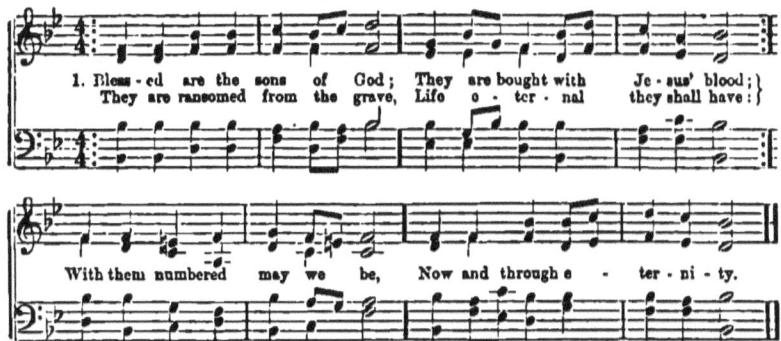

779.

1 BLESSED are the sons of God;
They are bought with Jesus' blood;
They are ransomed from the grave,
Life eternal they shall have;
　With them numbered may we be,
　Now and through eternity.

2 God did love them in his Son
Long before the world begun;
They the seal of this receive
When on Jesus they believe:
　With them, &c.

3 They are justified by grace,
They enjoy a solid peace;
All their sins are washed away,
They shall stand in God's great day.
　With them, &c.

4 They are harmless, meek, and mild,
Holy, humble, undefiled;
They are lights upon the earth,
Children of a heavenly birth.
　With them, &c.

5 They have fellowship with God,
Through the Mediator's blood;
One with God, through Jesus one,
Glory is in them begun.
　With them, &c.

6 They alone are truly blest—
Heirs with God, joint heirs with Christ;
They with love and peace are filled;
They are by his Spirit sealed.
　With them, &c.

Joseph Humphreys, 1743, a.

780.

1 As the sun's enlivening eye
　Shines on every place the same;
So the Lord is always nigh
　To the souls that love his name.

2 When they move at duty's call,
　He is with them by the way;
He is ever with them all,
　Those who go and those who stay.

3 From his holy mercy-seat
　Nothing can their souls confine,
Still in spirit they may meet,
　And in sweet communion join.

4 For a season called to part,
　Let us then ourselves commend
To the gracious eye and heart
　Of our ever-present Friend.

5 Jesus, hear our humble prayer;
　Tender Shepherd of thy sheep,
Let thy mercy and thy care
　All our souls in safety keep.

6 In thy strength may we be strong;
　Sweeten every cross and pain;
Give us, if we live, e'er long.
　Here to meet in peace again.

John Newton, 1779.

THE CHRISTIAN LIFE,—ITS BLESSEDNESS.

ST. THOMAS. S. M.

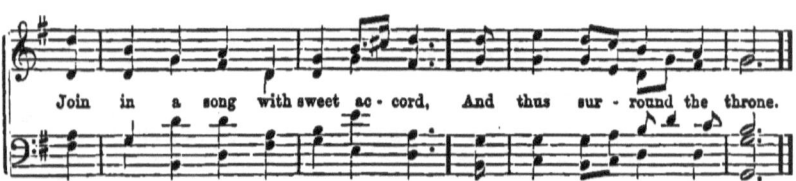

781.

1 Come, we that love the Lord,
  And let our joys be known;
  Join in a song with sweet accord,
  And thus surround the throne.

2 Let those refuse to sing
  That never knew our God;
  But favorites of the heavenly King
  May speak their joys abroad.

3 The hill of Zion yields
  A thousand sacred sweets,
  Before we reach the heavenly fields,
  Or walk the golden streets.

4 Then let our songs abound,
  And every tear be dry;   [ground
  We're marching through Immanuel's
  To fairer worlds on high.
                    Isaac Watts, 1709.

782.   1 John iii. 1-3.

1 Behold what wondrous grace
  The Father hath bestowed
  On sinners of a mortal race,
  To call them sons of God!

2 Nor doth it yet appear
  How great we must be made;
  But when we see our Saviour here,
  We shall be like our Head.

3 A hope so much divine
  May trials well endure,
  May purge our souls from sense and sin,
  As Christ the Lord is pure.

4 If in my Father's love
  I share a filial part,
  Send down thy Spirit like a dove
  To rest upon my heart.

5 We would no longer lie
  Like slaves beneath the throne;
  Our faith shall Abba, Father! cry,
  And thou the kindred own.
                    Isaac Watts, 1709.

783.

1 To God, the only wise,
  Our Saviour and our King,
  Let all the saints below the skies
  Their humble praises bring.

2 'T is his almighty love,
  His counsel and his care,
  Preserves us safe from sin and death,
  And every hurtful snare.

3 He will present our souls,
  Unblemished and complete,
  Before the glory of his face,
  With joys divinely great.

4 Then all the chosen seed
  Shall meet around the throne,
  Shall bless the conduct of his grace,
  And make his wonders known.

5 To our Redeemer, God,
  Wisdom and power belong,
  Immortal crowns of majesty,
  And everlasting song.
                    Isaac Watts, 1709.

THE CHURCH. 317

SHIRLAND. S. M.

1. I love thy kingdom, Lord, The house of thine abode, The church our blest Redeemer saved With his own precious blood.

784. PSALM 137.

1 I LOVE thy kingdom, Lord,
  The house of thine abode,
The church our blest Redeemer saved
  With his own precious blood.

2 I love thy church, O God;
  Her walls before thee stand,
Dear as the apple of thine eye,
  And graven on thy hand.

3 For her my tears shall fall,
  For her my prayers ascend;
To her my cares and toils be given
  Till toils and cares shall end.

4 Beyond my highest joy
  I prize her heavenly ways,
Her sweet communion, solemn vows,
  Her hymns of love and praise.

5 Jesus, thou Friend divine,
  Our Saviour and our King,
Thy hand from every snare and foe
  Shall great deliverance bring.

6 Sure as thy truth shall last,
  To Zion shall be given
The brightest glories earth can yield,
  And brighter bliss of heaven.
  Timothy Dwight, 1800.

785. PSALM 48.

1 GREAT is the Lord our God,
  And let his praise be great;
He makes his churches his abode,
  His most delightful seat.

2 These temples of his grace,
  How beautiful they stand!
The honors of our native place,
  The bulwarks of our land.

3 In Zion God is known
  A refuge in distress;
How bright has his salvation shone
  Through all her palaces!

4 Oft have our fathers told,
  Our eyes have often seen,
How well our God secures the fold
  Where his own sheep have been.

5 In every new distress
  We'll to his house repair,
We'll think upon his wondrous grace,
  And seek deliverance there.
  Isaac Watts, 1719.

DOXOLOGY.

JESUS, eternal Son,
  We praise thee and adore,
Who art with God the Father one,
  And Spirit evermore.

THE CHURCH.

LONDON NEW. C. M.

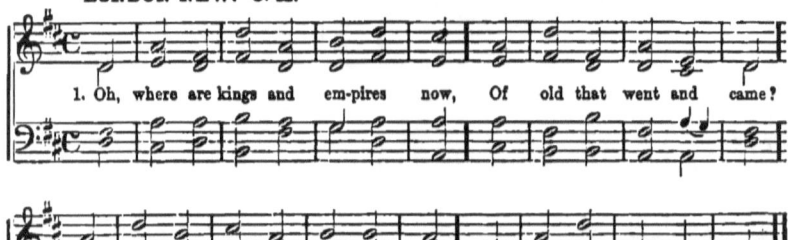
1. Oh, where are kings and em-pires now, Of old that went and came?

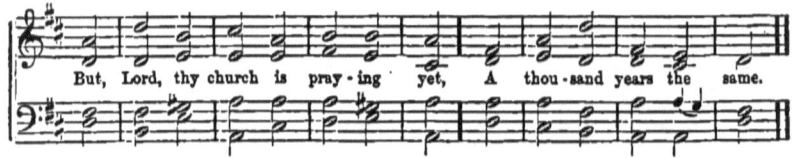
But, Lord, thy church is pray-ing yet, A thou-sand years the same.

786.

1 Oh, where are kings and empires now,
  Of old that went and came?
  But, Lord, thy church is praying yet,
  A thousand years the same.

2 We mark her goodly battlements,
  And her foundations strong;
  We hear within the solemn voice
  Of her unending song.

3 For not like kingdoms of the world
  Thy holy church, O God;
  Though earthquake shocks are threat'-[ning her,
  And tempests are abroad,

4 Unshaken as eternal hills
  Immovable she stands,
  A mountain that shall fill the earth,
  A house not made with hands.
  A. C. Coxe, 1850.

787.

1 How honorable is the place
  Where we adoring stand,
  Zion, the glory of the earth,
  And beauty of the land!

2 Bulwarks of mighty grace defend
  The city where we dwell,
  The walls, of strong salvation made,
  Defy the assaults of hell.

3 Lift up the everlasting gates,
  The doors wide open fling,
  Enter, ye nations, that obey
  The statutes of our King.

4 Here shall you taste unmingled joys,
  And live in perfect peace,
  You that have known Jehovah's name,
  And ventured on his grace.

5 Trust in the Lord, forever trust,
  And banish all your fears;
  Strength in the Lord Jehovah dwells,
  Eternal as his years.
  Isaac Watts, 1709.

788.

1 Inquire, ye pilgrims, for the way
  That leads to Zion's hill,
  And thither set your steady face,
  With a determined will.

2 Invite the strangers all around
  Your pious march to join;
  And spread the sentiments you feel
  Of faith and love divine.

3 Oh come, and to his temple haste,
  And seek his favor there;
  Before his footstool humbly bow,
  And pour your fervent prayer.

4 Oh come, and join your souls to God
  In everlasting bands;
  Accept the blessings he bestows,
  With thankful hearts and hands.
  Philip Doddridge, 1755.

DOXOLOGY.

To Father, Son, and Holy Ghost,
  One God, whom we adore,
  Be glory as it was, is now,
  And shall be evermore.
  Tate and Brady, 1696.

THE CHURCH. 319

789. Heb. xii. 18. C. M.
1 NOT to the terrors of the Lord,
  The tempest, fire, and smoke;
  Not to the thunder of that word
  Which God on Sinai spoke;
2 But we are come to Zion's hill,
  The city of our God,
  Where milder words declare his will,
  And spread his love abroad.
3 Behold the innumerable host
  Of angels clothed in light;
  Behold the spirits of the just,
  Whose faith is turned to sight;
4 Behold the blest assembly there,
  Whose names are writ in heaven;
  And God the judge of all declares
  Their vilest sins forgiven.
5 The saints on earth, and all the dead,
  But one communion make;
  All join in Christ their living head,
  And of his grace partake.
6 In such society as this
  My weary soul would rest;
  The man that dwells where Jesus is
  Must be forever blest.
  Isaac Watts, 1709.

790. Psalm 102. C. M.
1 LET Zion and her sons rejoice;
  Behold the promised hour;
  Her God hath heard her mourning voice,
  And comes t' exalt his power.
2 Her dust and ruins that remain
  Are precious in our eyes:
  Those ruins shall be built again,
  And all that dust shall rise.
3 The Lord will raise Jerusalem,
  And stand in glory there;
  Nations shall bow before his name,
  And kings attend with fear.
4 He sits a sovereign on his throne,
  With pity in his eyes;
  He hears the dying prisoners' groan,
  And sees their sighs arise.
5 He frees the souls condemned to death,
  Nor, when his saints complain,
  Shall it be said that praying breath
  Was ever spent in vain.
6 This shall be known when we are dead,
  And left on long record,
  That nations yet unborn may read,
  And trust and praise the Lord.
  Isaac Watts, 1719.

791. C. M.
1 CHURCH of the ever-living God,
  The Father's gracious choice,
  Amid the voices of this earth
  How feeble is thy voice.
2 A little flock — so calls he thee
  Who bought thee with his blood;
  A little flock, disowned of men,
  But owned and loved of God.
3 Not many rich or noble called,
  Not many great or wise;   [priests
  They whom God makes his kings and
  Are poor in human eyes.
4 But the chief Shepherd comes at length;
  Their feeble days are o'er,
  No more a handful in the earth,
  A little flock no more.
5 No more a lily among thorns,
  Weary and faint and few,
  But countless as the stars of heaven,
  Or as the early dew.
6 Then entering the eternal halls,
  In robes of victory,
  That mighty multitude shall keep
  The joyous jubilee.
  Horatius Bonar, 1857.

792. C. M.
1 DAUGHTER of Zion, from the dust
  Exalt thy fallen head;
  Again in thy Redeemer trust,
  He calls thee from the dead.
2 Awake, awake, put on thy strength,
  Thy beautiful array;
  Thy day of freedom dawns at length,
  The Lord's appointed day.
3 Rebuild thy walls, thy bounds enlarge,
  And send thy heralds forth;
  Say to the south, "Give up thy charge,
  And keep not back, O north!"
4 They come, they come! thine exiled bands,
  Where'er they rest or roam,
  Have heard thy voice in distant lands,
  And hasten to their home.
5 Thus, though the universe shall burn,
  And God his works destroy,
  With songs thy ransomed shall return,
  And everlasting joy.
  James Montgomery, 1825.

THE CHURCH.

ZION. 8s, 7s & 4s.

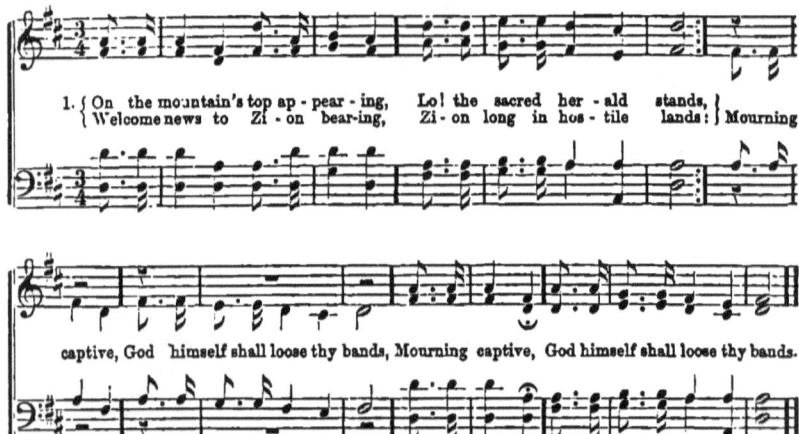

1. { On the mountain's top appearing, Lo! the sacred herald stands, / Welcome news to Zion bearing, Zion long in hostile lands: } Mourning captive, God himself shall loose thy bands, Mourning captive, God himself shall loose thy bands.

793.

1 On the mountain's top appearing,
   Lo! the sacred herald stands,
Welcome news to Zion bearing,
   Zion long in hostile lands:
      Mourning captive,
   God himself shall loose thy bands.

2 Has thy night been long and mournful?
   Have thy friends unfaithful proved?
Have thy foes been proud and scornful,
   By thy sighs and tears unmoved?
      Cease thy mourning:
   Zion still is well beloved.

3 God, thy God, will now restore thee;
   He himself appears thy friend;
All thy foes shall flee before thee;
   Here their boasts and triumphs end:
      Great deliverance
   Zion's King vouchsafes to send.

4 Enemies no more shall trouble;
   All thy wrongs shall be redressed;
For thy shame thou shalt have double,
   In thy Maker's favor blest:
      All thy conflicts
   End in everlasting rest.

Thomas Kelly, 1804.

794.

1 Zion stands with hills surrounded,
   Zion, kept by power divine;
All her foes shall be confounded,
   Though the world in arms combine;
      Happy Zion,
   What a favored lot is thine!

2 Every human tie may perish;
   Friend to friend unfaithful prove;
Mothers cease their own to cherish;
   Heaven and earth at last remove;
      But no changes
   Can attend Jehovah's love.

3 If thy God should show displeasure,
   'Tis to save, and not destroy:
If he punish, 'tis in measure;
   'Tis to rid thee of alloy.
      Be thou patient;
   Soon thy grief shall turn to joy.

Thomas Kelly, 1806.

THE CHURCH.

HAMPTON. H. M.

1. O Zion, tune thy voice, And raise thy hands on high; Tell all the earth thy joys, And boast salvation nigh. Cheerful in God, Arise and shine, While rays divine Stream all abroad.

795.

1 O Zion, tune thy voice,
    And raise thy hands on high;
   Tell all the earth thy joys,
    And boast salvation nigh.
   Cheerful in God, | While rays divine
   Arise and shine, | Stream all abroad.

2 He gilds thy mourning face
    With beams that cannot fade;
   His all-resplendent grace
    He pours around thy head;
   The nations round | With lustre new
   Thy form shall view, | Divinely crowned.

3 In honor to his name
    Reflect that sacred light;
   And loud that grace proclaim,
    Which makes thy darkness bright.
   Pursue his praise, | In worlds above
   Till sovereign love | The glory raise.

4 There on his holy hill
    A brighter Sun shall rise,
   And with his radiance fill
    Those fairer, purer skies;
   While round his throne | In nobler spheres,
   Ten thousand stars, | His influence own.

Philip Doddridge, 1755.

796.

1 One sole baptismal sign,
    One Lord, below, above,
   One faith, one hope divine,
    One only watchword, love:
   From different temples though it rise,
   One song ascendeth to the skies.

2 Our sacrifice is one;
    One Priest before the throne,
   The slain, the risen Son,
    Redeemer, Lord alone;
   And sighs from contrite hearts that spring,
   Our chief, our choicest offering.

3 Head of thy church beneath,
    The catholic, the true,
   On all her members breathe,
    Her broken frame renew:
   Then shall thy perfect will be done,
   When Christians love and live as one.

Robert Robinson, 1780.

DOXOLOGY.

To God the Father's throne
 Perpetual honors raise;
Glory to God the Son,
 And to the Spirit praise:
With all our powers, eternal King,
Thy name we sing, while faith adores.

Isaac Watts, 1709.

THE CHURCH.

ASHWELL. L. M.

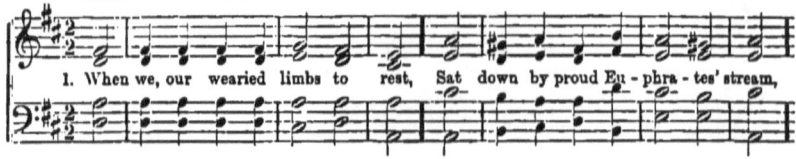
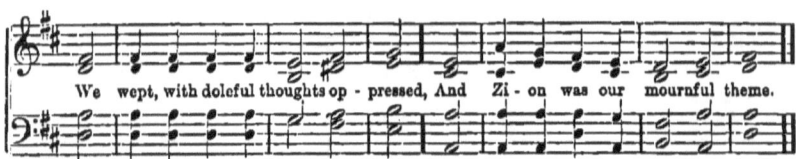

1. When we, our wearied limbs to rest, Sat down by proud Eu-phra-tes' stream, We wept, with doleful thoughts op-pressed, And Zi-on was our mournful theme.

797. Psalm 137.

1 When we, our wearied limbs to rest,
　Sat down by proud Euphrates' stream,
　We wept, with doleful thoughts oppressed,
　And Zion was our mournful theme.

2 Our harps that, when with joy we sung,
　Were wont their tuneful parts to bear,
　With silent strings neglected hung
　On willow trees that withered there.

3 How shall we tune our voice to sing,
　Or touch our harps with skilful hands?
　Shall hymns of joy, to God our King,
　Be sung by slaves in foreign lands?

4 O Salem! our once happy seat,
　When I of thee forgetful prove,
　Let then my trembling hand forget
　The speaking string with art to move.
　　　　　　　　Tate and Brady, 1696.

798.

1 Why, on the bending willows hung,
　O Israel, sleeps thy tuneful string?
　Still mute remains thy sullen tongue,
　And Zion's song declines to sing?

2 Awake! thy sweetest raptures raise;
　Let harp and voice unite their strains;
　Thy promised King his sceptre sways,
　And Jesus, thy Messiah, reigns.

3 No taunting foes the song require;
　No strangers mock thy captive chain;
　But friends invite the silent lyre,
　And brethren ask the holy strain.

4 Nor fear thy Salem's hills to wrong,
　If other lands thy triumph share;
　A heavenly city claims thy song,
　A brighter Salem rises there.

5 By foreign streams no longer roam,
　Nor, weeping, think of Jordan's flood;
　In every clime behold a home,
　In every temple see thy God.
　　　　　　　　Anon.

799.

1 O Saviour, is thy promise fled?
　Nor longer might thy grace endure
　To heal the sick, and raise the dead,
　And preach the gospel to the poor?

2 Come, Jesus, come; return again;
　With brighter beam thy servants bless,
　Who long to feel thy perfect reign,
　And share thy kingdom's happiness.

3 A feeble race, by passion driven,
　In darkness and in doubt we roam,
　And lift our anxious eyes to heaven,
　Our hope, our harbor, and our home.

4 Come, Jesus, come, and as of yore
　The prophet went to clear thy way,
　A harbinger thy feet before,
　A dawning to thy brighter day;

5 So now may grace, with heavenly shower,
　Our stony hearts for truth prepare;
　Sow in our souls the seed of power,
　Then come, and reap thy harvest there.
　　　　　　　　Reginald Heber, 1827.

THE CHURCH.

ANVERN. L. M.

1. Tri-umph-ant Zi - on, lift thy head From dust, and darkness, and the dead; Tho' humbled long, a-wake at length, And gird thee with thy Sa-viour's strength, And gird thee with thy Saviour's strength.

800.

1 TRIUMPHANT Zion. lift thy head
From dust, and darkness, and the dead;
Though humbled long, awake at length,
And gird thee with thy Saviour's strength.

2 Put all thy beauteous garments on,
And let thy various charms be known;
The world thy glories shall confess,
Decked in the robes of righteousness.

3 No more shall foes unclean invade,
And fill thy hallowed walls with dread;
No more shall hell's insulting host
Their victory and thy sorrows boast.

4 God, from on high, thy groans will hear;
His hand thy ruins shall repair;
Reared and adorned by love divine,
Thy towers and battlements shall shine.
Philip Doddridge, 1775.

801.

1 HAPPY the church, thou sacred place,
The seat of thy Creator's grace;
Thy holy courts are his abode,
Thou earthly palace of our God.

2 Thy walls are strength; and at thy gates
A guard of heavenly warriors waits;
Nor shall thy deep foundation move,
Fixed on his counsels and his love.

3 Thy foes in vain designs engage;
Against thy throne in vain they rage,
Like rising waves with angry roar,
That dash and die upon the shore.

4 God is our shield, and God our sun;
Swift as the fleeting moments run,
On us he sheds new beams of grace;
And we reflect his brightest praise.
Isaac Watts, 1709.

802.

1 WE are a garden walled around,
Chosen and made peculiar ground,
A little spot enclosed by grace
Out of the world's wide wilderness.

2 Like trees of myrrh and spice we stand
Planted by God the Father's hand;
And all his springs in Zion flow
To make the young plantation grow.

3 Awake, O heavenly wind, and come,
Blow on this garden of perfume;
Spirit divine, descend and breathe
A gracious gale on plants beneath.

4 Make our best spices flow abroad
To entertain our Saviour-God;
And faith, and love, and joy appear,
And every grace be active here.
Isaac Watts, 1709.

DOXOLOGY.

To God the Father, God the Son,
And God the Spirit, Three in One,
Be honor, praise, and glory given,
By all on earth, and all in heaven!
Isaac Watts, 1709.

324 THE CHURCH.

LATTER DAY. 8s & 7s.

1. Glorious things of thee are spo-ken, Zi-on, ci-ty of our God; He whose word can-not be broken, Formed thee for his own a-bode: On the Rock of A-ges founded, What can shake thy sure repose? With salvation's walls sur-rounded, Thou may'st smile at all thy foes.

803.

1 GLORIOUS things of thee are spoken,
　Zion, city of our God ;
He whose word cannot be broken,
　Formed thee for his own abode :
On the Rock of Ages founded,
　What can shake thy sure repose?
With salvation's walls surrounded,
　Thou may'st smile at all thy foes.

2 See, the streams of living waters,
　Springing from eternal love,
Well supply thy sons and daughters,
　And all fear of want remove.
Round each habitation hovering,
　See the cloud of fire appear
For a glory and a covering,
　Showing that the Lord is near.

3 Saviour, if of Zion's city
　I, through grace, a member am,
Let the world deride or pity,
　I will glory in thy name.

Fading is the worldling's pleasure,
　All his boasted pomp and show :
Solid joys and lasting treasure
　None but Zion's children know.
　　　　　　　John Newton, 1779.

804.

1 SAVIOUR, visit thy plantation ;
　Grant us, Lord, a gracious rain :
All will come to desolation,
　Unless thou return again.
Keep no longer at a distance,
　Shine upon us from on high,
Lest, for want of thine assistance,
　Every plant should droop and die.

2 Let our mutual love be fervent ;
　Make us prevalent in prayer ;
Let each one esteemed thy servant
　Shun the world's bewitching snare.
Break the tempter's fatal power,
　Turn the stony heart to flesh,
And begin from this good hour
　To revive thy work afresh.
　　　　　　　John Newton, 1779.

THE CHURCH.

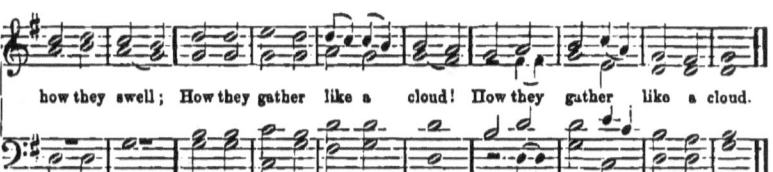

HENDON. 7s.

1. "Give us room, that we may dwell," Zion's children cry aloud; See their numbers, how they swell; How they gather like a cloud! How they gather like a cloud.

805.

1 "Give us room, that we may dwell,"
Zion's children cry aloud;
See their numbers, how they swell;
How they gather like a cloud!

2 Oh, how bright the morning seems!
Brighter from so dark a night;
Zion is like one that dreams,
Filled with wonder and delight.

3 Lo, thy sun goes down no more;
God himself will be thy light;
All that caused thee grief before
Buried lies in endless night.

4 Zion, now arise and shine;
Lo, thy light from heaven is come;
These that crowd from far are thine;
Give thy sons and daughters room.
Anon.

806.

1 People of the living God,
I have sought the world around,
Paths of sin and sorrow trod,
Peace and comfort nowhere found.

2 Now to you my spirit turns,
Turns a fugitive unblest;
Brethren, where your altar burns,
Oh receive me into rest.

3 Lonely I no longer roam,
Like the cloud, the wind, the wave;
Where you dwell shall be my home,
Where you die shall be my grave;

4 Mine the God whom you adore,
Your Redeemer shall be mine;
Earth can fill my soul no more,
Every idol I resign.

5 Tell me not of gain or loss,
Ease, enjoyment, pomp and power;
Welcome poverty and cross,
Shame, reproach, affliction's hour.

6 "Follow me!"—I know thy voice;
Jesus, Lord, thy steps I see;
Now I take thy yoke by choice;
Light thy burden now to me.
James Montgomery, 1825.

807.

1 Come, and let us sweetly join,
Christ to praise in hymns divine;
Give we all, with one accord,
Glory to our common Lord.

2 We for Christ, our Master, stand,
Lights in a benighted land;
We our dying Lord confess;
We are Jesus' witnesses.

3 Jesus, we thy promise claim;
We are met in thy great name;
In the midst do thou appear;
Manifest thy presence here.

4 Make us all in thee complete;
Make us all for glory meet;
Meet to' appear before thy sight,
Partners with the saints in light.
Charles Wesley, 1741.

THE CHURCH.

ST. CLEMENT'S DANE. C. M.

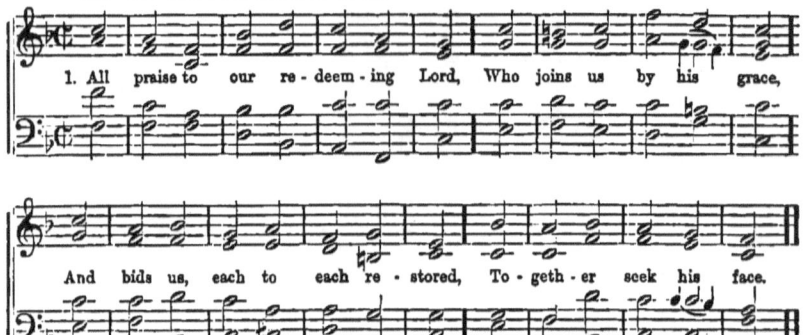

1. All praise to our redeeming Lord, Who joins us by his grace, And bids us, each to each restored, Together seek his face.

808.

1 ALL praise to our redeeming Lord,
   Who joins us by his grace,
   And bids us, each to each restored,
   Together seek his face.

2 He bids us build each other up;
   And gathered into one,
   To our high calling's glorious hope,
   We hand in hand go on.

3 Try us, O God, and search the ground
   Of every sinful heart;
   Whate'er of sin in us is found,
   Oh bid it all depart.

4 Help us to help each other, Lord,
   Each other's cross to bear;
   Let each his friendly aid afford,
   And feel his brother's care.

5 Up into thee, our living Head,
   Let us in all things grow,
   Till thou hast made us free indeed,
   And spotless here below.

6 Then when the mighty work is wrought,
   Receive thy ready bride;
   Give us in heaven a happy lot
   With all the sanctified.
                    Charles Wesley, 1750.

809.

1 PLANTED in Christ, the living vine,
   This day, with one accord,
   Ourselves, with humble faith and joy,
   We yield to thee, O Lord.

2 Joined in one body may we be;
   One inward life partake;
   One be our heart, one heavenly hope
   In every bosom wake.

3 In prayer, in effort, tears, and toils,
   One wisdom be our guide;
   Taught by one Spirit from above,
   In thee may we abide.

4 Then, when among the saints in light
   Our joyful spirits shine,
   Shall anthems of immortal praise,
   O Lamb of God, be thine!
                    S. F. Smith, 1843.

810.

1 WITNESS, ye men and angels, now
   Before the Lord we speak;
   To him we make our solemn vow,
   A vow we dare not break:—

2 That, long as life itself shall last,
   Ourselves to Christ we yield;
   Nor from his cause will we depart,
   Or ever quit the field.

3 We trust not in our native strength,
   But on his grace rely,
   That with returning wants the Lord
   Will all our need supply.

4 Oh guide our doubtful feet aright,
   And keep us in thy ways;
   And, while we turn our vows to prayers,
   Turn thou our prayers to praise.
                    Benjamin Beddome, 1818.

BAPTISM.

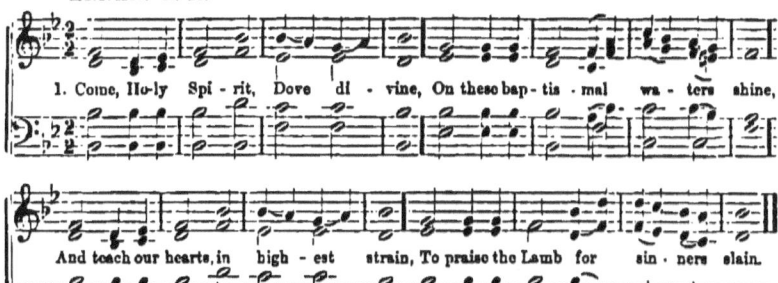

811.

1 COME, Holy Spirit, Dove divine,
On these baptismal waters shine,
And teach our hearts, in highest strain,
To praise the Lamb for sinners slain.

2 We love thy name, we love thy laws,
And joyfully embrace thy cause ;
We love thy cross, the shame, the pain,
O Lamb of God, for sinners slain !

3 We plunge beneath thy mystic flood,
Oh, plunge us in thy cleansing blood ;
We die to sin, and seek a grave
With thee, beneath the yielding wave.

4 And as we rise, with thee to live,
Oh, let the Holy Spirit give
The sealing unction from above,
The breath of life, the fire of love !

Adoniram Judson.

812.

1 OUR Saviour bowed beneath the wave,
And meekly sought a watery grave ;
Come, see the sacred path he trod,
A path well pleasing to our God.

2 His voice we hear, his footsteps trace,
And hither come to seek his face,
To do his will, to feel his love,
And join our songs with songs above.

3 Hosanna to the Lamb divine !
Let endless glories round him shine !
High o'er the heavens forever reign,
O Lamb of God, for sinners slain !

Adoniram Judson.

813.

1 IN thine assembly here we stand,
Obedient to thy great command ;
The sacred flood is full in view,
And thy sweet voice invites us through.

2 The word, the Spirit, and the bride,
Must not invite and be denied ;
Was not the Lord, who came to save,
Interred in such a liquid grave ?

3 Thus we, dear Saviour, own thy name ;
Receive us rising from the stream ;
Then to thy table let us come,
And dwell in Zion as our home.

Rippon's Selection, 1778.

814. Tune, "Dundee," p. 333. C. M.

1 BURIED beneath the yielding wave,
The great Redeemer lies ;
Faith views him in the watery grave,
And thence beholds him rise.

2 Thus it becomes his saints, to-day,
Their ardent zeal t' express,
And, in the Lord's appointed way,
Fulfil all righteousness.

3 With joy we in his footsteps tread,
And would his cause maintain,
Like him be numbered with the dead,
And with him rise and reign.

4 Now we, dear Jesus, would to thee
Our grateful voices raise ;
Washed in the fountain of thy blood,
Our lives shall be thy praise.

Benjamin Beddome, 1787.

BAPTISM

ST. BRIDE'S. S. M.

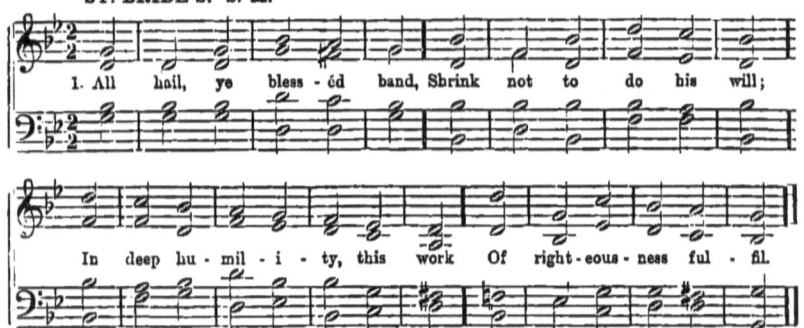

1. All hail, ye blessèd band, Shrink not to do his will; In deep humility, this work Of righteousness fulfil.

815. *See Note, p. 460.*

Congregation.

1 ALL hail, ye blessèd band,
   Shrink not to do his will;
   In deep humility, this work
   Of righteousness fulfil.

2 Tread in the Saviour's steps,
   Invoke his Spirit free,
   And as he burst the gates of death,
   So may your rising be.
   L. H. Sigourney, 1832.

Choir.

3 SAVIOUR, thy law we love,
   Thy pure example bless,
   And with a firm, unwavering zeal,
   Would in thy footsteps press.

Choir.

4 We love thy holy word,
   Thy precepts we obey,
   Buried with Christ, our dying Lord,
   We seek to be, this day.
   L. H. Sigourney, 1832.

Choir.

5 HERE we behold the grave
   Which held our buried Head;
   We claim a burial in the wave
   Because with Jesus dead.

Choir.

6 Here, too, we see him rise,
   And live no more to die;
   And one with him by sacred ties,
   We rise to live on high.
   C. H. Spurgeon, 1860.

Choir.

7 OH, what, if we are Christ's,
   Is earthly shame or loss?
   Bright shall the crown of glory be,
   When we have borne the cross.
   H. W. Baker, 1852.

Choir.

8 Ashamed who now can be
   To own the Crucified?
   Nay, rather be our glory this,
   To die with him who died.

Congregation.

9 COME, sinners, wash away
   Your sins of crimson dye;
   Buried with him, your vilest sins
   Shall in oblivion lie.

10 Rise and ascend with him,
    A heavenly life to lead,
    Who came to ransom guilty men
    From regions of the dead.
    Anon.

816.

1 DOWN to the sacred wave
   The Lord of life was led,
   And he who came our souls to save
   In Jordan bowed his head.

2 He taught the solemn way;
   He fixed the holy rite;
   He bade his ransomed ones obey,
   And keep the path of light.

3 Blest Saviour, we will tread
   In thy appointed way;
   Let glory o'er these scenes be shed,
   And smile on us to-day.
   S. F. Smith, 1843.

BAPTISM.

FEDERAL STREET. L. M.

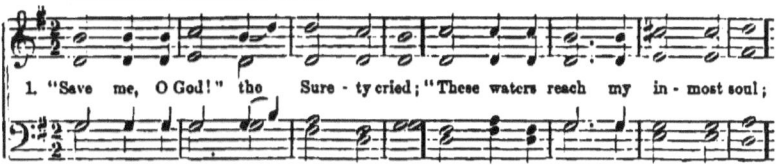

1. "Save me, O God!" the Sure-ty cried; "These waters reach my in-most soul;

In mi-ry deeps my foot-steps slide, Un-fathomed bil-lows o'er me roll."

817.

1 "Save me, O God!" the Surety cried;
 "These waters reach my inmost soul;
In miry deeps my footsteps slide,
 Unfathomed billows o'er me roll."

2 Ah, Lord, our sins upon thee laid
 Forbade deliverance in that hour;
The cup was drained, our debt is paid,
 And thou art raised to die no more.

3 And here baptizing, Lord, we own
 For us thou bor'st the wrathful flood;
This water saves not; thou alone
 Hast wrought salvation by thy blood.

4 Buried with thee, beneath this wave,
 As one with thee in death we go;
And, rising from this watery grave,
 Our union in thy life we show.

5 As dead with thee, oh may we die
 Daily to self, the world, and sin;
And, living now with thee on high,
 The heavenly life on earth begin.
   Bristol Hymns, 1870.

818.

1 While we thy ways, blest Saviour, tread,
 We think what thou for us hast done,
Rejoice in thee, our glorious Head,
 And sing the triumphs thou hast won.

2 While through the watery grave we go,
 Thee to remembrance may it bring,
Baptized for us in bitterest woe, [spring.
 Whence all our joys and blessings

3 When rising, also, from the wave,
 Thy resurrection meets our eyes,
We see how thou didst spoil the grave,
 And as our Head triumphant rise.

4 Here we with rapture see portrayed
 With thee, O Lord. our union sure,
Where grace its riches has displayed,
 Which shall for evermore endure.

5 Lord, may we ever live to prove
 Thy cleansing blood hath set us free,
In willing services of love
 To consecrate our lives to thee.
   Bristol Hymns, 1870.

819.

1 Come, happy souls, adore the Lamb,
 Who loved our race ere time began,
Who veiled his Godhead in our clay,
 And in an humble manger lay.

2 To Jordan's stream the Spirit led
 To mark the path the saints should tread;
With joy they trace the sacred way,
 To see the place where Jesus lay.

3 Baptized by John in Jordan's wave,
 The Saviour left his watery grave; [way,
Heaven owned the deed, approved the
 And blessed the place where Jesus lay.

4 Come, all who love his precious name,
 Come, tread his steps, and learn of him;
Happy beyond expression they
 Who find the place where Jesus lay.
   Thomas Baldwin, 1819.

BAPTISM.

ST. JOHN BAPTIST'S. 11s.

1. O thou who in Jordan didst bow thy meek head, And 'whelmed in our sorrow didst sink to the dead, Then rose from the darkness to glory above, And claimed for thy chosen the kingdom of love;

820.

1 O thou who in Jordan didst bow thy meek head,
And whelmed in our sorrow didst sink to the dead,
Then rose from the darkness to glory above,
And claimed for thy chosen the kingdom of love;

2 Thy footsteps we follow, to bow in the tide,
And are buried with thee in the death thou hast died,
Then wake with thy likeness to walk in the way
That brightens and brightens to shadowless day.

3 O Jesus, our Saviour, O Jesus, our Lord,
By the life of thy passion, the grace of thy word,
Accept us, redeem us, dwell ever within,
To keep, by thy Spirit, our spirits from sin;

4 Till, crowned with thy glory, and waving the palm,
Our garments all white from the blood of the Lamb,
We join the bright millions of saints gone before,
And bless thee, and wonder, and praise evermore.

George W. Bethune, 1857.

DOXOLOGY.

O FATHER Almighty, to thee be addressed,
With Christ and the Spirit, one God ever bless'd,
All glory and worship, from earth and from heaven,
As was, and is now, and shall ever be given.

BAPTISM. 331

1. Hast thou said, exalted Jesus, "Take thy cross and follow me"?
Shall the word with terror seize us? Shall we from the burden flee?
Lord, I'll take it, Lord, I'll take it, And, rejoicing, follow thee.

821.

2 Sweet the sign that thus reminds me,
   Saviour, of thy love for me ;
Sweeter still the love that binds me
   In its deathless bonds to thee :
Oh what pleasure,
Buried with my Lord to be !

3 Should it rend some fond connection,
   Should I suffer shame or loss,
Yet the fragrant, blest reflection,
   I have been where Jesus was,
Will revive me
When I faint beneath the cross.

4 Fellowship with him possessing,
   Let me die to all around,
So I rise to enjoy the blessing,
   Kept for those in Jesus found,
When the archangel
Wakes the sleepers under ground.

5 Then, baptized in love and glory,
   Lamb of God, thy praise I 'll sing ;
Loudly, with the immortal story,
   All the harps of heaven shall ring :
Saints and seraphs
Sound it loud from every string.
John E. Giles, 1844.

822.

1 JESUS, mighty King in Zion,
   Thou alone our Guide shalt be :
Thy commission we rely on ;
   We would follow none but thee.

2 As an emblem of thy passion,
   And thy victory o'er the grave,
We, who know thy great salvation,
   Are baptized beneath the wave.

3 Fearless of the world's despising,
   We the ancient path pursue,
Buried with our Lord, and rising
   To a life divinely new.
John Fellows, 1773.

823.

1 LORD, in humble, sweet submission,
   Here we meet to follow thee ;
Trusting in thy great salvation,
   Which alone can make us free.

2 Nought have we to claim as merit ;
   All the duties we can do
Can no crown of life inherit :
   All the praise to thee is due.

3 Yet we come in Christian duty,
   Down beneath the wave to go ;
Oh the bliss ! the heavenly beauty !
   Christ the Lord was buried so.

4 Come, ye children of the kingdom,
   Follow him beneath the wave ;
Rise, and show his resurrection,
   And proclaim his power to save.

5 Welcome, all ye friends of Jesus,
   Welcome to his church below ;
Venture wholly on the Saviour ;
   Come and with his people go.
Robert T. Daniel, 1832.

BAPTISM.

SPANISH HYMN. 7s. DOUBLE.

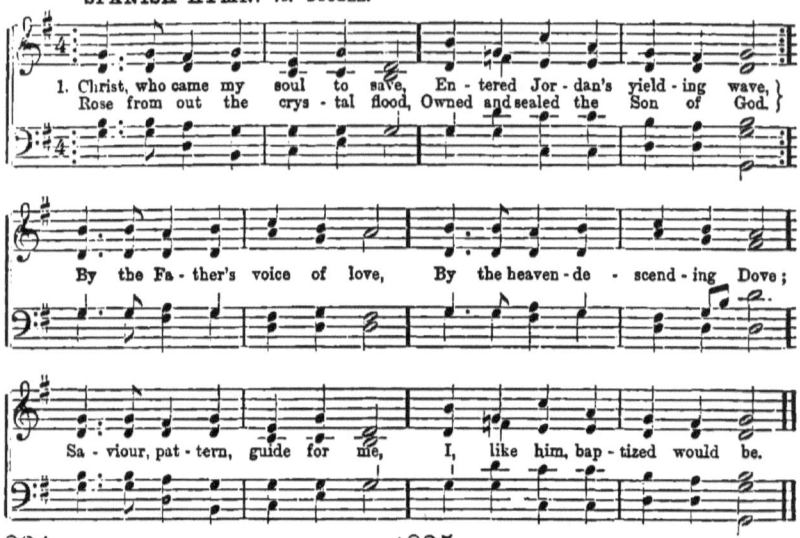

824.

1 CHRIST, who came my soul to save,
　Entered Jordan's yielding wave,
Rose from out the crystal flood,
　Owned and sealed the Son of God,
By the Father's voice of love,
　By the heaven-descending Dove;
Saviour, Pattern, Guide for me,
　I like him baptized would be.

2 In the garden, o'er his soul
　Sorrow's whelming waves did roll;
Ah, on Calvary's cruel tree,
　Jesus bowed in death for me.
I with him am crucified;
　All my hope is, He hath died;
At his feet my place I take,
　Bear the cross for his dear sake.

3 In the new-made tomb he lay,
　Taking all its dread away;
Burst he through its rock-bound door,
　Glorious now, and evermore.
I with Christ would buried be
In this rite required of me,
Rising from the mystic flood,
Living hence anew to God.

S. D. Phelps, 1857.

825.

1 CHILDREN of the King of grace,
　As from earth to heaven ye go,
Your Redeemer's footsteps trace,
　Follow him in all ye do.

2 His sweet presence you will find
　Shining on you as you go;
Cast your fears and cares behind,
　Trust him, he will bring you through.

3 You are buried with the Lord;
　In the Lord you rise again;
Now you live upon his word,
　Who, to ransom you, was slain.

4 Hear the voice that speaks from heaven,
　"This is my appointed way;"
You, whose sins he has forgiven,
　Follow him without delay.

5 Mighty Saviour, we obey
　Thy divine, commanding voice;
Thou hast taught our feet the way,
　In thy mandate we rejoice.

6 On thy promise we rely,
　Hear us from thy lofty throne;
Shine upon us from on high,
　Bless and seal us as thy own.

Joseph Swain, 1792.

BAPTISM.

DUNDEE. C. M.

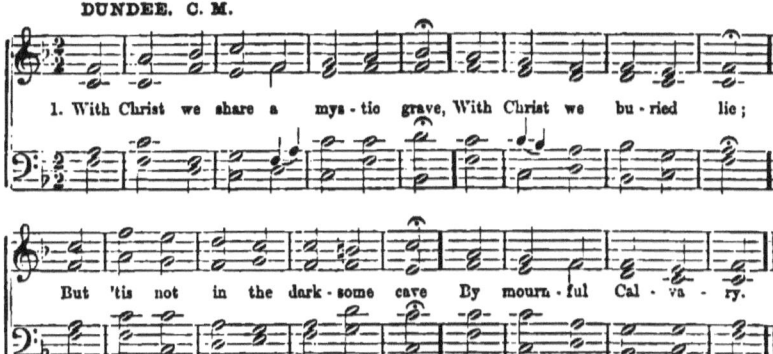

1. With Christ we share a mys-tic grave, With Christ we bu-ried lie;
But 'tis not in the dark-some cave By mourn-ful Cal-va-ry.

826.

1 WITH Christ we share a mystic grave,
 With Christ we buried lie;
 But 't is not in the darksome cave
 By mournful Calvary.

2 The pure and bright baptismal flood
 Entombs our nature's stain;
 New creatures from the cleansing wave
 With Christ we rise again.

3 Thrice blest, if, through this world of sin,
 And lust, and selfish care,
 Our resurrection-mantle white
 And undefiled we wear.

4 Thrice blest, if, through the gate of death,
 Glorious at last and free,
 We to our joyful rising pass,
 O risen Lord, with thee.
 John Mason Neale, 1851.

827.

1 O LORD, while we confess the worth
 Of this the outward seal,
 Do thou the truths herein set forth
 To every heart reveal.

2 Death to the world we here avow,
 Death to each fleshly lust;
 Newness of life our calling now,
 A risen Lord our trust.

3 And we, O Lord, who now partake
 Of resurrection-life,
 With every sin, for thy dear sake,
 Would be at constant strife.

4 Baptized into the Father's name,
 We 'd walk as sons of God;
 Baptized in thine, we own thy claim
 As ransomed by thy blood.

5 Baptized into the Holy Ghost,
 We 'd keep his temple pure,
 And make thy grace our only boast,
 And by thy strength endure.
 Mary Bowly, 1845, a.

828.

1 'T IS the great Father we adore
 In this baptismal sign;
 'T is he whose voice on Jordan's shore
 Proclaimed the Son divine.

2 The Father hailed him; let our breath
 In answering praise ascend,
 As in the image of his death
 We own our heavenly Friend.

3 We seek the consecrated grave
 Along the path he trod:
 Receive us in the hallowed wave,
 Thou holy Son of God.

4 Blest Spirit, with intense desire
 Solicitous we bow;
 Baptize us in renewing fire,
 And ratify the vow.

5 Let earth and heaven our pledge record,
 And future witness bear.
 That we to Zion's mighty Lord
 Our full allegiance swear.
 Maria G. Saffery, 1828.

BAPTISM.

ST. PETERSBURG. L. M. 6 LINES. (Omit repeat for 4 lines.)

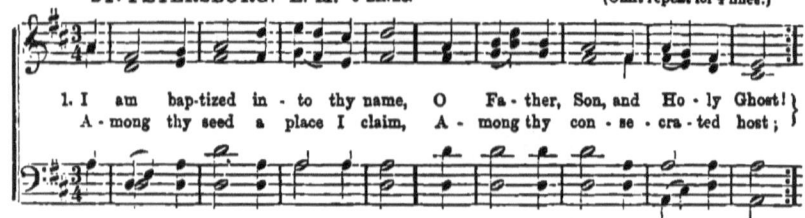

1. I am baptized into thy name, O Father, Son, and Holy Ghost!
Among thy seed a place I claim, Among thy consecrated host;

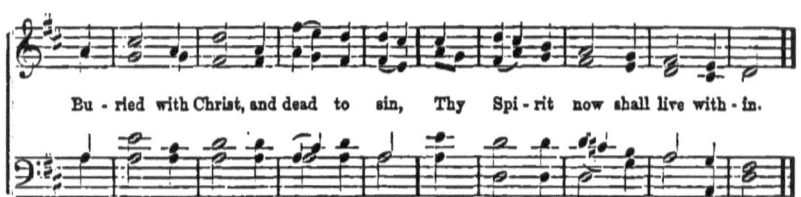

Buried with Christ, and dead to sin, Thy Spirit now shall live within.

829.

1 I AM baptized into thy name,
 O Father, Son, and Holy Ghost!
Among thy seed a place I claim,
 Among thy consecrated host;
Buried with Christ, and dead to sin,
Thy Spirit now shall live within.

2 My loving Father, here dost thou
 Proclaim me as thy child, and heir;
My faithful Saviour bidd'st me now
 The fruit of all thy sorrows share;
Thou, Holy Ghost, wilt comfort me
When darkest clouds around I see.

3 Hence, Prince of darkness, hence, my foe!
 Another Lord hath purchased me;
My conscience tells of sin, yet know,
 Baptized in Christ, I fear not thee:
Away, vain world; sin, leave me now;
I turn from you: God hears my vow.

4 And never let me waver more,
 O Father, Son, and Holy Ghost;
Till at thy will this life is o'er,
 Still keep me in thy faithful host,
So unto thee I live and die,
And praise thee evermore on high.

Rambach, 1720; tr. by C. Winkworth, 1858.

830.

1 Do we not know that solemn word,
That we are buried with the Lord?
Baptized into his death, and then
Put off the body of our sin?

2 Our souls receive diviner breath,
Raised from corruption, guilt, and death;
So from the grave did Christ arise,
And lives to God above the skies.

3 No more let sin or Satan reign
Within our mortal flesh again;
The various lusts we served before
Shall have dominion now no more.

Isaac Watts, 1709.

831.

1 BURIED in baptism with our Lord,
We rise with him, to life restored;
Not the bare life in Adam lost,
But richer far, for more it cost.

2 Water can cleanse the flesh, we own,
But Christ well knows, and Christ alone,
How dear to him our cleansing stood,
Baptized in fire, and bathed in blood.

3 He by his blood atoned for sin,
This precious blood can wash us clean,
And he arrays us in the dress
Of his unspotted righteousness.

Moravian Collection.

BAPTISM.

832.

1 AROUND thy grave, Lord Jesus,
  Thine empty grave, we stand,
With hearts all full of praises,
  To keep thy blest command;
By faith our souls rejoicing
  To trace thy path of love,
Through death's dark, angry billows,
  Up to the throne above.

2 Lord Jesus, we remember
  The travail of thy soul,
When, in thy love's deep pity,
  The waves did o'er thee roll.
Baptized in death's cold waters,
  For us thy blood was shed;
For us the Lord of glory
  Was numbered with the dead.

3 O Lord, thou now art risen,
  Thy travail all is o'er;
For sin thou once hast suffered,
  Thou liv'st to die no more;
Sin, death and hell are vanquished
  By thee, thy church's Head;
And lo! we share thy triumph,
  Thou first-born from the dead!

4 Into thy death baptizéd,
  We own with thee we died;
With thee, our Life, are risen,
  And shall be glorified.
From sin, the world, and Satan,
  We're ransomed by thy blood,
And now would walk as strangers,
  Alive with thee, to God.

James G. Deck, 1845.

BAPTISM.

HEBER. C. M.

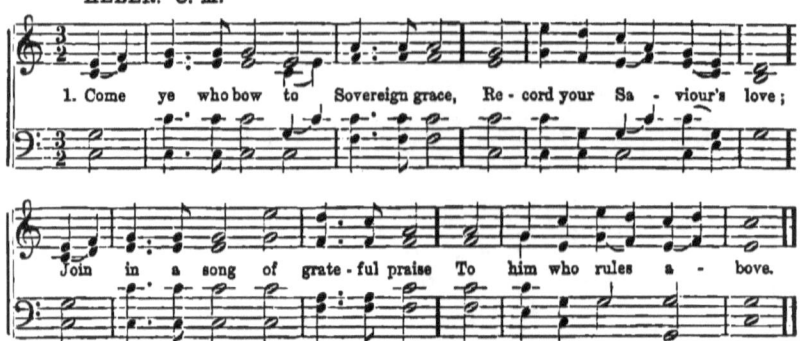

833.

1 Come ye who bow to Sovereign grace,
Record your Saviour's love;
Join in a song of grateful praise
To him who rules above.

2 Once in the gloomy grave he lay,
But, by his rising power,
He bore the gates of death away:
Hail, mighty Conqueror!

3 Here we declare, in emblem plain,
Our burial in his grave;
And since in him we rose again,
We rise from out the wave.
James Upton, 1814.

834.

1 Hearken, ye children of your God;
Ye heirs of glory, hear;
For accents so divine as these
Might charm the dullest ear.

2 Baptized into your Saviour's death,
Your souls to sin must die;
With Christ your Lord ye live anew,
With Christ ascend on high.

3 Rise from these earthly trifles, rise
On wings of faith and love;
Above your choicest treasure lies,
And be your hearts above.

4 But earth and sin will drag us down,
When we attempt to fly;
Lord, send thy strong attractive power
To raise and fix us high.
Philip Doddridge, 1755.

835.

1 O Lord, we see thy work set forth
In this thine own command,
And here confess the wondrous worth
Of all God's love hath planned.

2 Here we recall, O blessed Lord,
Thy agonizing death,
When o'er thy holy soul were poured
The floods of righteous wrath.

3 In thee we died, — our Surety thou, —
No judgment need we fear;
The burial of our sins we now
With joy remember here.

4 Nor that alone, for we were raised
In thee, the risen Lord;
And in this act thy work is praised,
And thou thyself adored.

5 As one with thee, oh! may we know
The old things passed away;
Live the new life, and here below
The heavenly mind display.
Bristol Hymns, 1870.

836.

1 Let plenteous grace descend on those
Who, hoping in thy word,
This day have solemnly declared
That Jesus is their Lord.

2 With cheerful feet may they advance,
And run the christian race,
And, through the troubles of the way,
Find all-sufficient grace.
James Newton, 1800.

THE LORD'S SUPPER.

WIRTH. C. M.

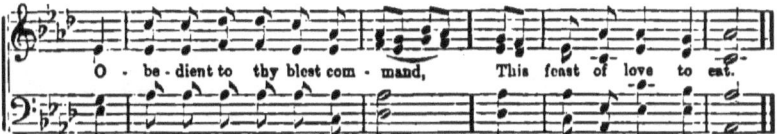

837.

1 AROUND thy table, holy Lord,
  In fellowship we meet;
  Obedient to thy blest command,
  This feast of love to eat.

2 By faith we take the bread of life,
  With which our souls are fed;
  And cup, in token of thy blood
  That was for sinners shed.

3 Under thy banner thus we sing
  The wonders of thy love,
  While we anticipate by faith
  The heavenly feast above.
  Thomas Cotterill, 1819. a.

838.

1 O GOD, unseen, yet ever near,
  Thy presence may we feel;
  And thus, inspired with holy fear,
  Before thine altar kneel.

2 Here may thy faithful people know
  The blessings of thy love;
  The streams that through the desert flow,
  The manna from above.

3 We come, obedient to thy word,
  To feast on heavenly food;
  Our meat, the body of the Lord;
  Our drink, his precious blood.

4 Thus may we all thy words obey,
  For we, O God, are thine,
  And go rejoicing on our way,
  Renewed with strength divine!
  Edmund Osler, 1835.

839.

1 ACCORDING to thy gracious word,
  In meek humility,
  This will I do, my dying Lord,
  I will remember thee.

2 Thy body, broken for my sake,
  My bread from heaven shall be;
  Thy testamental cup I take,
  And thus remember thee.

3 Gethsemane can I forget?
  Or there thy conflict see,
  Thine agony and bloody sweat,
  And not remember thee?

4 When to the cross I turn mine eyes,
  And rest on Calvary,
  O Lamb of God, my sacrifice,
  I must remember thee:

5 Remember thee, and all thy pains,
  And all thy love to me;
  Yea, while a breath, a pulse remains,
  Will I remember thee.

6 And when these failing lips grow dumb,
  And mind and memory flee,
  When thou shalt in thy kingdom come,
  Jesus, remember me.
  James Montgomery, 1825.

DOXOLOGY.

To God the Father glory be,
  And to his only Son,
And to the Spirit, One and Three,
  While endless ages run.
  J. H. Newman, 1842.

THE LORD'S SUPPER.

COVENTRY. C. M.

1. "The pro-mise of my Fa-ther's love Shall stand for-ev-er good:"

He said, and gave his soul to death, And sealed the grace with blood.

840.

1 "The promise of my Father's love
   Shall stand forever good:"
   He said, and gave his soul to death,
   And sealed the grace with blood.

2 To this dear covenant of thy word
   I set my worthless name;
   I seal the engagement to my Lord,
   And make my humble claim.

3 I call that legacy my own,
   Which Jesus did bequeath;
   'Twas purchased with a dying groan,
   And ratified in death.

4 Sweet is the memory of his name
   Who blest us in his will,
   And to the test'ment of his love
   Made his own life the seal.
   Isaac Watts, 1709.

841.

1 If human kindness meets return,
   And owns the grateful tie;
   If tender thoughts within us burn
   To feel a friend is nigh;

2 Oh, shall not warmer accents tell
   The gratitude we owe
   To him who died our fears to quell,
   Our more than orphan's woe?

3 While yet his anguished soul surveyed
   Those pangs he would not flee,
   What love his latest words displayed! —
   "Meet and remember me."

4 Remember thee, thy death, thy shame,
   Our sinful hearts to share!
   O memory! leave no other name
   But his recorded there.
   Gerard T. Noel, 1813.

842.

1 How sweet and awful is the place,
   With Christ within the doors;
   While everlasting love displays
   The choicest of her stores!

2 While all our hearts and all our songs
   Join to admire the feast,
   Each of us cries, with thankful tongue,
   "Lord, why was I a guest?

3 "Why was I made to hear thy voice,
   And enter while there's room,
   When thousands make a wretched choice,
   And rather starve than come?"

4 'Twas the same love that spread the feast,
   That sweetly drew us in;
   Else we had still refused to taste,
   And perished in our sin.

5 Pity the nations, O our God!
   Constrain the earth to come;
   Send thy victorious word abroad,
   And bring the strangers home.

6 We long to see thy churches full,
   That all the chosen race
   May, with one voice and heart and soul,
   Sing thy redeeming grace.
   Isaac Watts, 1709.

THE LORD'S SUPPER.

ASHWELL. L. M.

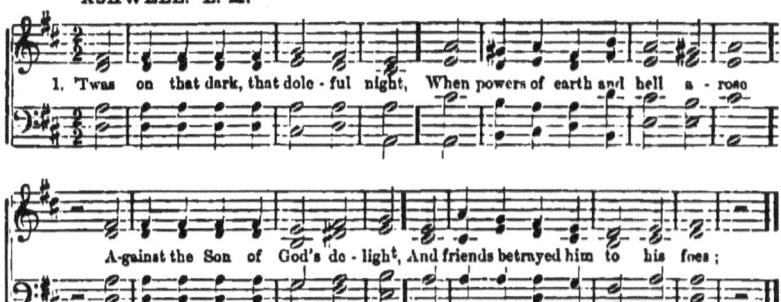

843.

1 'Twas on that dark, that doleful night,
  When powers of earth and hell arose
  Against the Son of God's delight,
  And friends betrayed him to his foes;

2 Before the mournful scene began,
  He took the bread, and blessed, and brake;
  What love through all his actions ran!
  What wondrous words of grace he spake!

3 "This is my body, broke for sin;
  Receive and eat the living food;"
  Then took the cup, and blessed the wine;
  "'T is the new covenant in my blood."

4 "Do this," he cried, "till time shall end,
  In memory of your dying Friend;
  Meet at my table, and record
  The love of your departed Lord."

5 Jesus, thy feast we celebrate;
  We show thy death, we sing thy name,
  Till thou return, and we shall eat
  The marriage supper of the Lamb.
  Isaac Watts, 1709.

844.

1 At thy command, our dearest Lord,
  Here we attend thy dying feast;
  Thy blood, like wine, adorns thy board,
  And thine own flesh feeds every guest.

2 Our faith adores thy bleeding love,
  And trusts for life in one that died;
  We hope for heavenly crowns above
  From a Redeemer crucified.

3 Let the vain world pronounce it shame,
  And fling their scandals on thy cause;
  We come to boast our Saviour's name,
  And make our triumphs in his cross.

4 With joy we tell the scoffing age,
  He that was dead has left his tomb;
  He lives above their utmost rage,
  And we are waiting till he come.
  Isaac Watts, 1709.

845.

1 Amidst us our Belovéd stands,
  And bids us view his piercéd hands;
  Points to the wounded feet and side,
  Blest emblems of the Crucified.

2 What food luxurious loads the board,
  When at his table sits the Lord!
  The wine how rich, the bread how sweet,
  When Jesus deigns the guests to meet!

3 If now, with eyes defiled and dim,
  We see the signs but see not him,
  Oh may his love the scales displace,
  And bid us see him face to face!

4 Our former transports we recount,
  When with him in the holy mount;
  These cause our souls to thirst anew,
  His marred but lovely face to view.

5 Thou glorious Bridegroom of our hearts,
  Thy present smile a heaven imparts:
  Oh lift the veil, if veil there be,
  Let every saint thy beauties see!
  Charles H. Spurgeon, 1866.

THE LORD'S SUPPER.

LOUVAN. L. M.

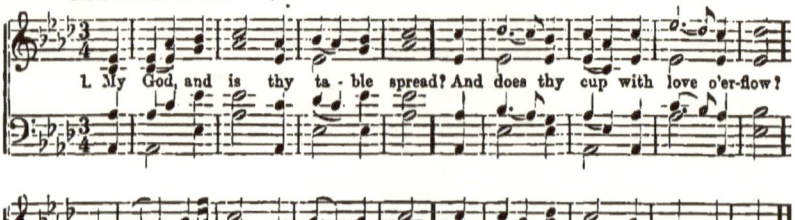

846.

1 My God, and is thy table spread?
 And does thy cup with love o'erflow?
 Thither be all thy children led,
 And let them all its sweetness know.

2 Hail, sacred feast, which Jesus makes!
 Rich banquet of his flesh and blood;
 Thrice happy he who here partakes
 That sacred stream, that heavenly food.

3 Why are its dainties all in vain
 Before unwilling hearts displayed?
 Was not for you the victim slain?
 Are you forbid the children's bread?

4 Oh let thy table honored be,
 And furnished well with joyful guests;
 And may each soul salvation see,
 That here its sacred pledges tastes.

5 Let crowds approach, with hearts prepared;
 With hearts inflamed let all attend;
 Nor, when we leave our Father's board,
 The pleasure or the profit end.

6 Revive thy dying churches, Lord,
 And bid our drooping graces live,
 And more that energy afford
 · A Saviour's love alone can give.
Philip Doddridge, 1775.

847.

1 Jesus, thou everlasting King,
 Accept the tribute which we bring,
 Accept the well-deserved renown,
 And wear our praises as thy crown.

2 Let every act of worship be
 Like our espousals, Lord, to thee;
 Like the dear hour when from above
 We first received thy pledge of love.

3 The gladness of that happy day,
 Our hearts would wish it long to stay;
 Nor let our faith forsake its hold,
 Nor comfort sink, nor love grow cold.

4 Oh let each minute, as it flies,
 Increase thy praise, improve our joys;
 Till we are raised to sing thy name
 At the great supper of the Lamb.
Isaac Watts, 1709.

848.

1 Far from my thoughts, vain world, be gone;
 Let my religious hours alone;
 Fain would my eyes my Saviour see,
 I wait a visit, Lord, from thee.

2 My heart grows warm with holy fire,
 And kindles with a pure desire:
 Come, my dear Jesus, from above,
 And feed my soul with heavenly love.

3 Blest Jesus, what delicious fare!
 How sweet thy entertainments are!
 Never did angels taste above
 Redeeming grace and dying love.

4 Hail, great Immanuel, all divine!
 In thee thy Father's glories shine;
 Thou brightest, sweetest, fairest one
 That eyes have seen or angels known.
Isaac Watts, 1709.

THE LORD'S SUPPER. 341

849.

1 O BREAD to pilgrims given,
O food that angels eat,
O manna sent from heaven,
For heaven-born natures meet!
Give us, for thee long pining,
To eat till richly filled;
Till, earth's delights resigning,
Our every wish is stilled.

2 O water, life-bestowing,
From out the Saviour's heart,
A fountain purely flowing,
A fount of love thou art!
Oh let us, freely tasting,
Our burning thirst assuage;
Thy sweetness, never wasting,
Avails from age to age.

3 Jesus, this feast receiving,
We thee unseen adore;
Thy faithful word believing,
We take, and doubt no more.
Give us, thou true and loving,
On earth to live in thee;
Then, death the veil removing,
Thy glorious face to see!

Thomas Aquinas, 1260; tr. by Ray Palmer, 1858.

850. *Tune, "Amsterdam," p. 415. 7s & 6s.*

1 LAMB of God, whose bleeding love
We now recall to mind,
Send the answer from above,
And let us mercy find;
Think on us, who think on thee,
Every burdened soul release;
Oh remember Calvary,
And bid us go in peace!

2 By thine agonizing pain
And bloody sweat, we pray;
By thy dying love to man,
Take all our sins away:
Burst our bonds and set us free,
From iniquity release;
Oh remember Calvary,
And bid us go in peace!

3 Let thy blood, by faith applied,
The sinner's pardon seal;
Speak us freely justified,
And all our sickness heal;
By thy passion on the tree,
Let our griefs and troubles cease;
Oh remember Calvary,
And bid us go in peace!

Charles Wesley, 1745.

THE LORD'S SUPPER.

OLNEY. S. M.

851.

1 SWEET feast of love divine!
'Tis grace that makes us free
To feed upon this bread and wine,
In memory, Lord, of thee.

2 Here every welcome guest
Waits, Lord, from thee to learn
The secrets of thy Father's breast,
And all thy grace discern.

3 Here conscience ends its strife,
And faith delights to prove
The sweetness of the bread of life,
The fulness of thy love.

4 That blood that flowed for sin
In symbol here we see,
And feel the blessed pledge within,
That we are loved of thee.

5 Oh, if this glimpse of love
Is so divinely sweet,
What will it be, O Lord, above,
Thy gladd'ning smile to meet!

6 To see thee face to face,
Thy perfect likeness wear,
And all thy ways of wondrous grace
Through endless years declare!

Sir Edward Denny, 1839.

852.

1 WITH Jesus in the midst,
We gather round the board;
Though many, we are one in Christ,
One body in the Lord.

2 Our sins were laid on him,
When bruised on Calvary;
With Christ we died and rose again,
And sit with him on high.

3 Faith eats the bread of life,
And drinks the living wine;
Thus we, in love together knit,
On Jesus' breast recline.

4 Soon shall the night be gone,
The Morning Star appear,
Soon shall the day of glory dawn
Our longing hearts to cheer.

Bristol Hymns, 1870.

853.

1 WE bless our Saviour's name,
Our sins are all forgiven;
To suffer once, to earth he came,
See now he's crowned in heaven.

2 His precious blood was shed,
His body bruised for sin;
Rememb'ring this, we break the bread,
And, thankful, drink the wine.

3 While we remember thee,
Lord, in the midst appear;
Let each by faith thy body see,
While we assemble here.

4 We never would forget
Thy rich, thy precious love,
Our theme of joy and wonder here,
Our endless song above.

Bristol Hymns, 1870.

THE LORD'S SUPPER. 343

SACRAMENTAL HYMN. 9s & 8s. DOUBLE.

1. Bread of the world in mercy broken, Wine of the soul in mercy shed,
By whom the words of life were spoken, And in whose death our sins are dead;

2. Look on the heart by sorrow broken, Look on the tears by sinners shed,
And be thy feast to us a token, That by thy grace our souls are fed. Amen. A-men.

854.

1 BREAD of the world in mercy broken,
  Wine of the soul in mercy shed,
  By whom the words of life were spoken,
  And in whose death our sins are dead;

2 Look on the heart by sorrow broken,
  Look on the tears by sinners shed,
  And be thy feast to us the token
  That by thy grace our souls are fed.
  Reginald Heber, 1820.

855.

1 BODY of Jesus, oh sweet food!
  Blood of my Saviour, precious blood!
  On these thy gifts. Eternal Priest.
  Grant thou my soul in faith to feast.

2 Weary and faint, I thirst and pine
  For thee my bread, for thee my wine,
  Till strengthened, as Elijah trod,
  I journey to the mount of God.

3 Then clad in white, with crown and palm,
  At the great supper of the Lamb,
  Be mine with all thy saints to rest.
  Like him that leaned upon thy breast.

4 Saviour, till then I fain would know
  That feast above by this below,
  This bread of life, this wondrous food,
  Thy body and thy precious blood.
  A. C. Coxe, 1852.

THE LORD'S SUPPER.

HORTON. 7s.   (Repeat for 6 lines.)

856.

1 At the Lamb's high feast we sing
Praise to our victorious King,
Who hath washed us in that tide
Flowing from his piercéd side.

2 Praise we him whose love divine
Gives his sacred blood for wine,
Gives his body for the feast,
Christ the victim, Christ the Priest.

3 Where the paschal blood is poured
Death's dark angel sheathes his sword;
Israel's hosts triumphant go
Through the wave that drowns the foe.

4 Praise we Christ whose blood was shed,
Paschal victim, paschal bread;
With sincerity and love,
Eat we manna from above.

5 Mighty victim from the sky,
Hell's fierce powers beneath thee lie;
Thou hast conquered in the fight,
Thou hast brought us life and light.

6 Now no more can death appal,
Now no more the grave enthrall;
Thou hast opened paradise,
And in thee thy saints shall rise.

Tr. from the Latin by Robert Campbell, 1850.

857.

1 "Till he come!" oh, let the words
Linger on the trembling chords;
Let the little while between
In their golden light be seen;
Let us think how heaven and home
Lie beyond that "till he come."

2 Clouds and conflicts round us press;
Would we have one sorrow less?
All the sharpness of the cross,
All that tells the world is loss,
Death, and darkness, and the tomb,
Only whisper "till he come."

3 When the weary ones we love
Enter on their rest above,
Seems the earth so poor and vast,
All our life-joy overcast?
Hush! be every murmur dumb;
It is only "till he come."

4 See the feast of love is spread;
Drink the wine and break the bread,
Sweet memorials, till the Lord
Call us round the heavenly board;
Some from earth, from glory some,
Severed only "till he come."

Edward Henry Bickersteth, 1866.

THE LORD'S SUPPER.

HOLLEY. 7s.

1. Father, while we break this bread, And our Lord remember thus, Make us one with him our Head, Thou in him, and he in us.

858. John vi. 56.

1 Father, while we break this bread,
And our Lord remember thus,
Make us one with him our Head,
Thou in him and he in us.

2 While to lips with praise that glow
This communion cup we press,
Holy Father, make us grow
More like him we thus confess.

3 Reconciled in Christ thy Son,
In whose name on thee we call;
Make us perfect, all in one,
We in him and thou in all.
John Pierpont.

859.

1 Bread of heaven, on thee we feed,
For thy flesh is meat indeed;
Ever let our souls be fed
With this true and living bread.

2 Vine of heaven, thy blood supplies
This blest cup of sacrifice;
Lord, thy wounds our healing give,
To thy cross we look and live.

3 Day by day, with strength supplied
Through the life of him who died,
Lord of life, oh let us be
Rooted, grafted, built in thee.
Josiah Conder, 1824.

BENEDICTION CHANT. 10s.

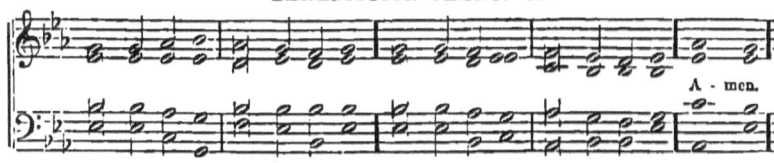

A - men.

860.

1 And now we rise; the symbols|disappear;
The feast, though not the love, is|past
and gone, [art here,
The bread and wine remove; but| thou
Nearer than ever; still my|shield and
sun.

2 Feast after feast thus comes and|passes by,
And passing points to the glad|feast
above,
Giving sweet foretaste of the|festal joy,
The Lamb's great bridal feast of|bliss
and love.
Horatius Bonar, 1856.

THE MINISTRY

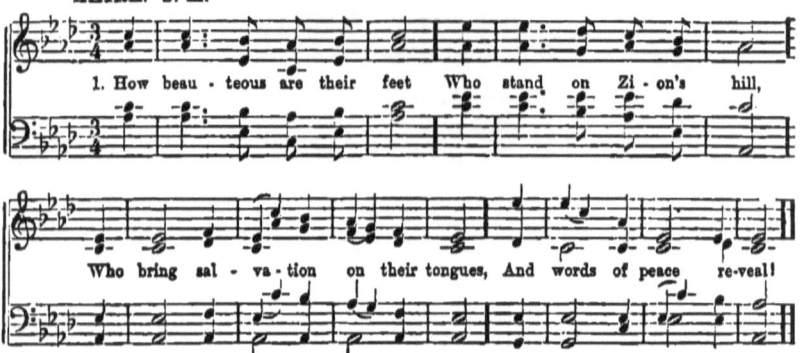

AHIRA. S. M.

1. How beauteous are their feet Who stand on Zion's hill,
Who bring salvation on their tongues, And words of peace reveal!

861. ISAIAH LII. 7-10.

1 How beauteous are their feet
  Who stand on Zion's hill,
Who bring salvation on their tongues,
  And words of peace reveal!

2 How charming is their voice!
  How sweet the tidings are!
" Zion, behold thy Saviour King;
  He reigns and triumphs here."

3 How happy are our ears,
  That hear this joyful sound,
Which kings and prophets waited for,
  And sought, but never found!

4 How blessèd are our eyes,
  That see this heavenly light!
Prophets and kings desired it long,
  But died without the sight.

5 The watchmen join their voice,
  And tuneful notes employ;
Jerusalem breaks forth in songs,
  And deserts learn the joy.

6 The Lord makes bare his arm
  Through all the earth abroad;
Let every nation now behold
  Their Saviour and their God!
          Isaac Watts, 1709.

862. Tune, "Coventry," p. 333.   C. M.

1 LET Zion's watchmen all awake,
  And take the alarm they give;
Now let them, from the mouth of God,
  Their awful charge receive.

2 'T is not a cause of small import
  The pastor's care demands,
But what might fill an angel's heart,
  And filled a Saviour's hands.

3 They watch for souls for which the Lord
  Did heavenly bliss forego;
For souls which must forever live
  In raptures or in woe.

4 May they that Jesus whom they preach,
  Their own Redeemer see;
And watch thou daily o'er their souls,
  That they may watch for thee.
          Philip Doddridge, 1736.

863. Tune, "Coventry," p. 333.   C. M.

1 Lord, thou hast taught our hearts to glow
  With love's undying flame;
But more of thee we long to know,
  And more would love thy name.

2 Thou bid'st us go, with thee to stand
  Against hell's marshalled powers,
And heart to heart, and hand to hand,
  To make thine honor ours.

3 With thine own pity, Saviour, see
  The thronged and darkening way!
We go to win the lost to thee,
  Oh help us, Lord, we pray!

4 Teach thou our lips of thee to speak,
  Of thy sweet love to tell,
Till they who wander far shall seek
  And find and serve thee well.
          Ray Palmer.

THE MINISTRY. 847

WAREHAM. L. M.

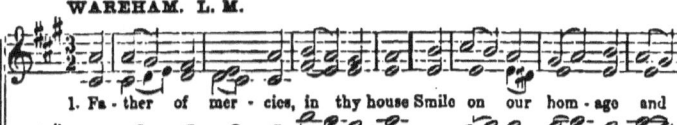

1. Fa-ther of mer-cies, in thy house Smile on our hom-age and our vows;

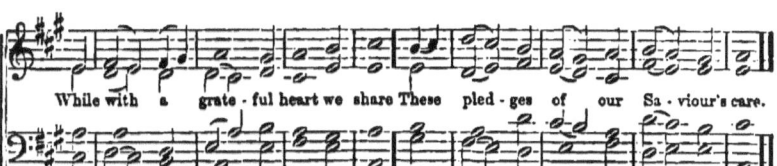

While with a grate-ful heart we share These pled-ges of our Sa-viour's care.

864.

1 FATHER of mercies, in thy house
Smile on our homage and our vows,
While with a grateful heart we share
These pledges of our Saviour's care.

2 The Saviour, when to heaven he rose
In splendid triumph o'er his foes,
Scattered his gifts on men below,
And wide his royal bounties flow.

3 Hence sprung the Apostles' honored name,
Sacred beyond heroic fame;
In lowlier forms to bless our eyes,
Pastors from hence, and teachers rise.

4 So shall the bright succession run
Through the last courses of the sun;
While unborn churches by their care
Shall rise and flourish large and fair.

5 Jesus our Lord, their hearts shall know,
The spring whence all these blessings
Pastors and people shout his praise [flow;
Through the long round of endless days.
Philip Doddridge, 1755.

865.

1 GREAT Lord of angels, we adore
The grace that builds thy courts below,
And through ten thousand sons of light
Stoops to regard what mortals do.

2 Amidst the wastes of time and death
Successive pastors thou dost raise,
Thy charge to keep, thy house to guide,
And form a people for thy praise.

3 The heavenly natives with delight
Hover around the sacred place,
Nor scorn to learn from mortal tongues
The wonders of redeeming grace.

4 At length dismissed from feeble clay
Thy servants join the angelic band,
With them through distant worlds they fly,
With them before thy presence stand.

5 Yet while these labors we pursue,
Thus distant from thy heavenly throne,
Give us a zeal and love like theirs,
And half their heaven shall here be
known.
Philip Doddridge, 1755.

866.

1 WE bid thee welcome in the name
Of Jesus, our exalted Head;
Come as a servant: so he came,
And we receive thee in his stead.

2 Come as a shepherd; guard and keep
This fold from hell, and earth, and sin;
Nourish the lambs, and feed the sheep,
The wounded heal, the lost bring in.

3 Come as a teacher, sent from God,
Charged his whole counsel to declare;
Lift o'er our ranks the prophet's rod,
While we uphold thy hands with prayer.

4 Come as a messenger of peace,
Filled with the Spirit, fired with love!
Live to behold our large increase,
And die to meet us all above.
James Montgomery, 1825.

THE MINISTRY.

HARMONY GROVE. L. M.

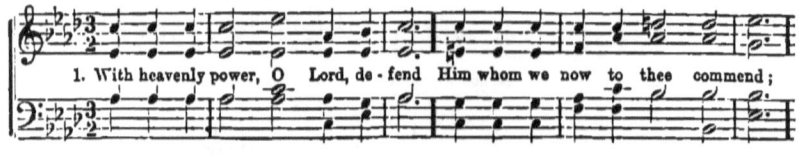
1. With heavenly power, O Lord, de-fend Him whom we now to thee commend;

Thy faith-ful mes - sen - ger se - cure, And make him to the end en - dure.

867.

1 WITH heavenly power, O Lord, defend
Him whom we now to thee commend;
Thy faithful messenger secure,
And make him to the end endure.

2 Gird him with all-sufficient grace;
Direct his feet in paths of peace;
Thy truth and faithfulness fulfil
And arm him to obey thy will.

3 Before him thy protection send,
Oh love him, save him to the end;
Nor let him as a pilgrim rove
Without the convoy of thy love.

4 Enlarge, inflame, and fill his heart;
In him thy mighty power exert;
That thousands yet unborn may praise
The wonders of redeeming grace.
Rowland Hill, 1774.

868.

1 FATHER of mercies, bow thy ear,
Attentive to our earnest prayer;
We plead for those who plead for thee,
Successful pleaders may they be!

2 How great their work, how vast their charge!
Do thou their anxious souls enlarge;
Their best acquirements are our gain,
We share the blessings they obtain.

3 Clothe, then, with energy divine,
Their words, and let those words be thine;
To them thy sacred truth reveal,
Suppress their fear, inflame their zeal.

4 Teach them to sow the precious seed;
Teach them thy chosen flock to feed;
Teach them immortal souls to gain —
Souls that will well reward their pain.

5 Let thronging multitudes around
Hear from their lips the joyful sound,
In humble strains thy grace implore,
And feel thy new-creating power.
Benjamin Beddome, 1787.

869.

1 POUR out thy Spirit from on high;
Lord, thine assembled servants bless;
Graces and gifts to each supply, [ness.
And clothe thy priests with righteous-

2 Within thy temple when we stand
To teach the truth, as taught by thee,
Saviour, like stars in thy right hand
The angels of the churches be!

3 Wisdom, and zeal, and faith impart,
Firmness, with meekness from above,
To bear thy people on our heart, [love;
And love the souls whom thou dost

4 To watch, and pray, and never faint,
By day and night strict guard to keep,
To warn the sinner, cheer the saint,
Nourish thy lambs, and feed thy sheep.

5 Then, when our work is finished here,
In humble hope our charge resign!
When the Chief Shepherd shall appear,
O God! may they and we be thine!
James Montgomery, 1825.

870. L. M.

1 O Lord of hosts, whose glory fills
The bounds of the eternal hills,
And yet vouchsafes, in Christian lands,
To dwell in temples made with hands;

2 Grant that all we who here to-day
Rejoicing this foundation lay,
May be in very deed thine own,
Built on the precious Corner-stone.

3 Endue the creatures with thy grace
That shall adorn thy dwelling-place;
The beauty of the oak and pine,
The gold and silver, make them thine.

4 To thee they all pertain; to thee
The treasures of the earth and sea;
And when we bring them to thy throne
We but present thee with thine own.

5 The heads that guide endue with skill;
The hands that work preserve from ill;
That we, who these foundations lay,
May raise the topstone in its day.

6 Both now and ever, Lord, protect
The temple of thine own elect;
Be thou in them, and they in thee,
Oh ever-blessèd Trinity!

John Mason Neale, 1851.

871. L. M.

1 Jesus, where'er thy people meet,
There they behold thy mercy-seat;
Where'er they seek thee thou art found,
And every place is hallowed ground.

2 For thou, within no walls confined,
Inhabitest the humble mind;
Such ever bring thee where they come,
And going, take thee to their home.

3 Dear Shepherd of thy chosen few,
Thy former mercies here renew;
Here, to our waiting hearts, proclaim
The sweetness of thy saving name.

4 Here may we prove the power of prayer
To strengthen faith and sweeten care;
To teach our faint desires to rise,
And bring all heaven before our eyes.

5 Behold, at thy commanding word
We stretch the curtain and the cord;
Come thou, and fill this wider space,
And bless us with a large increase.

6 Lord, we are few, but thou art near;
Nor short thine arm, nor deaf thine ear;
Oh rend the heavens, come quickly down,
And make a thousand hearts thine own.

William Cowper, 1779.

872. L. M.

1 Enthroned in light, eternal God,
The highest heaven is thy abode;
Yet thou with us wilt deign to dwell;
Thou lov'st the gates of Zion well:
On Salem's peaceful hill we raise
A sacred temple to thy praise.

2 Here let the pilgrim find the road
That leads the wandering soul to God;
Here sorrow lift her tearful eye,
Allured to brighter scenes on high;
The weary spirit find repose,
And at the cross forget her woes.

3 Our God, our fathers' God, we raise
This sacred temple to thy praise;
Here, safe beneath thy sheltering wing,
Shall contrite souls their offerings bring,
Till called to soar and join the song
Which swells amid the heavenly throng.

Thomas Harris, 1792.

873. L. M.

1 And will the great, eternal God
On earth establish his abode?
And will he, from his radiant throne,
Avow our temples for his own?

2 We bring the tribute of our praise,
And sing that condescending grace
Which to our notes will lend an ear,
And call us, sinful mortals, near.

3 These walls we to thy honor raise;
Long may they echo with thy praise,
And thou, descending, fill the place
With choicest tokens of thy grace.

4 Here let the great Redeemer reign,
With all the graces of his train;
While power divine his words attends,
To conquer foes and cheer his friends.

5 And in the great, decisive day,
When God the nations shall survey,
May it before the world appear
That crowds were born to glory here.

Philip Doddridge, 1755.

THE SANCTUARY.

FLETCHER. C. M.

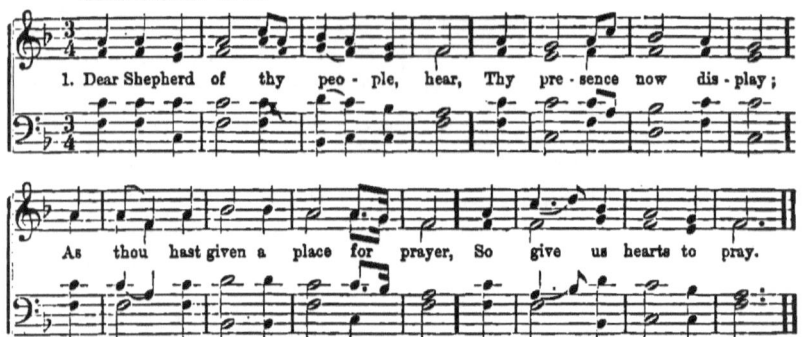

1. Dear Shepherd of thy peo-ple, hear, Thy pre-sence now dis-play;
As thou hast given a place for prayer, So give us hearts to pray.

874.

1 Dear Shepherd of thy people, hear,
  Thy presence now display;
  As thou hast given a place for prayer,
  So give us hearts to pray.

2 Within these walls let holy peace,
  And love, and concord, dwell;
  Here give the troubled conscience ease,
  The wounded spirit heal.

3 The feeling heart, the melting eye,
  The humbled mind bestow;
  And shine upon us from on high,
  To make our graces grow.

4 May we in faith receive thy word,
  In faith present our prayers,
  And in the presence of our Lord
  Unbosom all our cares.

5 And may the gospel's joyful sound,
  Enforced by mighty grace,
  Awaken many sinners round,
  To come and fill the place.
  John Newton, 1779.

875.

1 Spirit divine, attend our prayers,
  And make this house thy home;
  Descend with all thy gracious powers;
  Oh, come, great Spirit, come.

2 Come as the light: to us reveal
  Our sinfulness and woe,
  And lead us in those paths of life,
  Where all the righteous go.

3 Come as the dew and sweetly bless
  This consecrated hour;
  May barrenness rejoice to own
  Thy fertilizing power.

4 Come, as the wind, with rushing sound,
  And pentecostal grace,
  That all of woman born may see
  The glory of thy face.

5 Spirit divine, attend our prayers,
  Make a lost world thy home;
  Descend with all thy gracious powers,
  Oh, come, great Spirit, come.
  Andrew Reed, 1841.

876. Psalm 132.

1 Arise! O King of grace, arise!
  And enter to thy rest;
  Lo! thy church waits with longing eyes
  Thus to be owned and blest!

2 Enter with all thy glorious train,
  Thy Spirit and thy word;
  All that the ark did once contain
  Could no such grace afford.

3 Here, mighty God, accept our vows;
  Here let thy praise be spread;
  Bless the provisions of thy house,
  And fill thy poor with bread.

4 Here let the Son of David reign;
  Let God's Anointed shine:
  Justice and truth his court maintain
  With love and power divine.

5 Here let him hold a lasting throne,
  And as his kingdom grows,
  Fresh honors shall adorn his crown,
  And shame confound his foes.
  Isaac Watts, 1719.

THE SANCTUARY.

CLAREMONT. H. M.

877.

2 Oh, then, with hymns of praise
  These hallowed courts shall ring!
Our voices we will raise,
  The Three in One to sing;
And thus proclaim | Both loud and long,
In joyful song, | That glorious Name.

3 Here, gracious God, do thou
  Forevermore draw nigh;
Accept each faithful vow,
  And mark each suppliant sigh:
In copious shower, | Each holy day,
On all who pray, | Thy blessings pour.

4 Here may we gain from heaven
  The grace which we implore,
And may that grace, once given,
  Be with us evermore, —
Until that day | To endless rest
When all the blest | Are called away.

Tr. from the Latin by John Chandler, 1837.

878.

1 GREAT King of glory, come,
  And with thy favor crown
This temple as thy dome,
  This people as thy own;
Beneath this roof, | How God can dwell
Oh deign to show | With men below!

2 Here may thine ears attend
  Our interceding cries,
And grateful praise ascend,
  All fragrant, to the skies.
Here may the word | And spread celestial
Melodious sound, | Joys around!

3 Here may our unborn sons
  And daughters sound thy praise,
And shine, like polished stones,
  Through long succeeding days;
Here, Lord, display | While temples stand,
Thy saving power, | And men adore.

Benjamin Francis, 1774.

SILOAM. C. M.

879.
PSALM 78.

1 LET children hear the mighty deeds
   Which God performed of old,
Which in our younger years we saw,
   And which our fathers told.

2 He bids us make his glories known,
   His works of power and grace;
And we'll convey his wonders down
   Through every rising race.

3 Our lips shall tell them to our sons,
   And they again to theirs,
That generations yet unborn
   May teach them to their heirs.

4 Thus shall they learn, in God alone
   Their hope securely stands,
That they may ne'er forget his works,
   But practise his commands.

Isaac Watts, 1719.

880.

1 SEE Israel's gentle Shepherd stand,
   With all-engaging charms;
Hark! how he calls the tender lambs,
   And folds them in his arms!

2 "Permit them to approach," he cries,
   "Nor scorn their humble name;
For 't was to bless such souls as these
   The Lord of angels came."

3 We bring them, Lord, in thankful hands,
   And yield them up to thee;
Joyful that we ourselves are thine
   Thine let our offspring be!

4 If orphans they are left behind,
   Thy guardian care we trust;
That care shall heal our bleeding hearts,
   While weeping o'er their dust.

Philip Doddridge, 1755.

881.

1 BY cool Siloam's shady rill
   How sweet the lily grows!
How sweet the breath, beneath the hill,
   Of Sharon's dewy rose!

2 Lo! such the child, whose early feet
   The paths of peace have trod,
Whose secret heart, with influence sweet,
   Is upward drawn to God.

3 By cool Siloam's shady rill
   The lily must decay;
The rose that blooms beneath the hill
   Must shortly fade away.

4 And soon, too soon, the wint'ry hour
   Of man's maturer age
Will shake the soul with sorrow's power,
   And stormy passion's rage.

5 O thou, whose infant feet were found
   Within thy Father's shrine, [crowned,
Whose years, with changeless virtue
   Were all alike divine, —

6 Dependent on thy bounteous breath,
   We seek thy grace alone,
In childhood, manhood, age, and death,
   To keep us still thine own.

Reginald Heber, 1827.

CHILDREN. 353

WOODWORTH. L. M.

1. Hark! 'tis your heavenly Father's call, How soft the charming ac-cents fall; "Ask and re-ceive, my son," he cries, With lov-ing heart and melt-ing eyes

882.

1 HARK! 'tis your heavenly Father's call,
How soft the charming accents fall;
"Ask and receive, my son," he cries,
With loving heart and melting eyes.

2 Lord, I accept thine offered grace,
I come to seek my Father's face,
Nor will he turn his ear away
Who taught my heart and lips to pray.

3 One thing I ask, and wilt thou hear,
And grant my soul a gift so dear?
Wisdom, descending from above,
The sweetest token of thy love;

4 Wisdom betimes to know the Lord,
To fear his name and keep his word;
To lead my feet in paths of truth,
And guide and guard my wandering youth.

5 Then shouldst thou grant a length of days,
My life shall still proclaim thy praise;
Or early death my soul convey
To realms of everlasting day.
Ottiwell Heginbotham, 1799.

883.

1 A LITTLE child the Saviour came,
The mighty God was still his name,
And angels worshipped as he lay,
The seeming infant of a day.

2 He who, a little child, began
The life divine to show to man,
Proclaims from heaven the message free,
" Let little children come to me."

3 We bring them, Lord, and would resign
Their care to thee: oh, call them thine;
Their souls with saving grace endow,
Renew them by thy Spirit now.

4 Oh give thine angels charge, good Lord,
Them safely in thy way to guard;
Thy blessing on their lives command,
And write their names upon thy hand.
Scottish Hymnal, 1868. a.

884.

1 SAVIOUR, who didst from heaven come
A little child awhile to be, [down,
Whose precious blood and thorny crown
From death and sin have ransomed me:

2 Teach me, dear Saviour, some return
Of lowly service for thy love,
Such as a thankful child may learn,
Such as thy Spirit shall approve.

3 Young hearts, I hear them say, are claimed
For God's own altar by thy word:
May I lay there my own, unblamed,
And wilt thou lift it heavenward, Lord!
Count Zinzendorf; tr. by James B. Tomalin, 1860.

DOXOLOGY.

To God the Father, God the Son,
And Holy Spirit, Three in One.
May every tongue and nation raise
An endless song of thankful praise.
Tr. from Latin by J. Chandler, 1837.

CHILDREN.

CHILDREN'S PRAISE. C. M.

1. Around the throne of God in heaven Thousands of children stand, Children whose sins are all forgiven, A

CHORUS.

holy, happy band, Singing Glory, glory, glory be to God on high.

885.

2 In flowing robes of spotless white
　See every one arrayed,
　Dwelling in everlasting light,
　And joys that never fade.

3 What brought them to that world above,
　That heaven so bright and fair,
　Where all is peace and joy and love?
　How came those children there?

4 Because the Saviour shed his blood
　To wash away their sin:
　Bathed in that precious purple flood,
　Behold them white and clean.

5 On earth they sought the Saviour's grace,
　On earth they loved his name;
　So now they see his blessed face,
　And stand before the Lamb.
　　　　　　Anne Shepherd, 1841.

ADAMS. C. M.

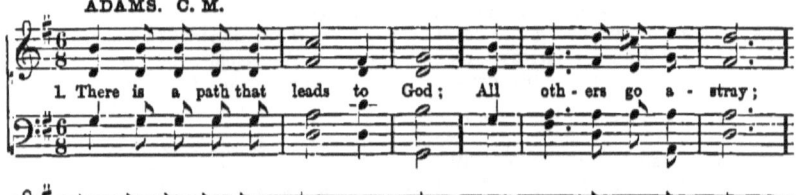

1. There is a path that leads to God; All others go astray;

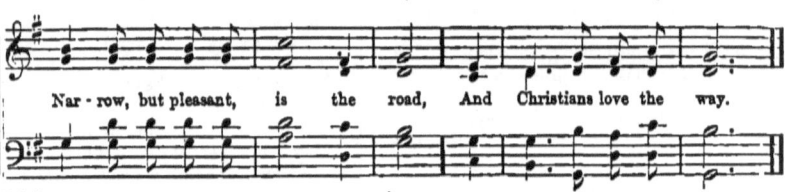

Narrow, but pleasant, is the road, And Christians love the way.

886.

2 It leads straight through this world of sin,
　And dangers must be passed;
　But those who boldly walk therein
　Will get to heaven at last.

3 How shall an infant pilgrim dare
　This dangerous path to tread?
　For on the way is many a snare,
　For youthful travellers spread;

4 While the broad road, where thousands go,
　Lies near and opens fair,
　And many turn aside I know
　To walk with sinners there.

5 But, lest my feeble steps should slide
　Or wander from the way,
　Lord, condescend to be my guide,
　And I shall never stray.
　　　　　　Jane Taylor, 1825.

CHILDREN.

BLESSING. 11s & 8s.

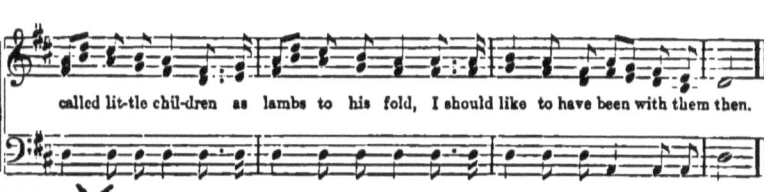

1. I think when I read that sweet story of old, When Jesus was here among men, How he called little children as lambs to his fold, I should like to have been with them then.

887.

2 I wish that his hands had been placed on my head,
    That his arm had been thrown around [me,
And that I might have seen his kind look when he said,
    "Let the little ones come unto me."

3 Yet still to his footstool in prayer I may go,
    And ask for a share in his love;
And if I thus earnestly seek him below,
    I shall see him and hear him above,

4 In that beautiful place he is gone to prepare
    For all who are washed and forgiven;
And many dear children are gathering there,
    "For of such is the kingdom of heaven."

5 But thousands and thousands who wander and fall,
    Never heard of that heavenly home;
I should like them to know there is room for them all,
    And that Jesus has bid them to come.

6 I long for the joy of that glorious time,
    The sweetest and brightest and best,
When the dear little children of every clime
    Shall crowd to his arms and be blest.

Jemima Luke, 1841.

888. Tune, "Clarion," p. 360. 6s & 4s.

1 SHEPHERD of tender youth,
  Guiding in love and truth,
    Through devious ways;
Christ, our triumphant King,
We come thy name to sing,
And here our children bring,
    To shout thy praise.

2 Thou art our holy Lord;
  The all-subduing Word,
    Healer of strife;
Thou didst thyself abase,
  That from sin's deep disgrace
Thou mightest save our race,
    And give us life.

3 Ever be thou our Guide,
  Our Shepherd and our pride,
    Our staff and song;
Jesus, thou Christ of God,
By thy perennial word,
Lead us where thou hast trod,
    Make our faith strong.

4 So now, and till we die,
  Sound we thy praises high,
    And joyful sing:
Let all the holy throng,
Who to thy church belong,
Unite and swell the song
    To Christ our King!

Clemens Alexandrinus, before 212.

COMMISSION. L. M.

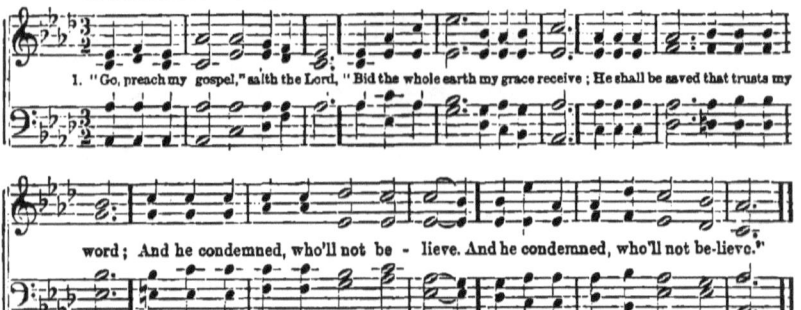

889.

1 " Go, preach my gospel," saith the Lord;
" Bid the whole earth my grace receive:
He shall be saved that trusts my word;
And he condemned, who'll not believe.

2 " I'll make your great commission known,
And ye shall prove my gospel true,
By all the works that I have done,
By all the wonders ye shall do.

3 " Teach all the nations my commands;
I'm with you till the world shall end!
All power is trusted in my hands;
I can destroy, and I defend."

4 He spake, and light shone round his head,
On a bright cloud to heaven he rode;
They to the farthest nations spread
The grace of their ascended God.
Isaac Watts, 1709.

890.

1 Awake! all-conquering arm, awake!
And lift the Saviour's standard high;
Oh cause thy cheering face to shine,
And call thy chosen people nigh.

2 Baptize benighted nations, Lord,
And let thy saving truth be known;
Arise, thy royal power assume,
And claim the kingdoms for thine own.

3 Bless those who now in distant lands
Bid the untutored heathen live;
Be thou their guard, their God, their friend;
Success to every effort give. [friend;

4 Eternal God, their hearts inspire;
Let each thy sacred presence prove;
Bid them go forth with holy zeal,
And loud proclaim thy dying love.

5 Mountains of unbelief and sin
Shall fall before thy sacred word;
And millions, saved from death and hell,
Shall own the Saviour as their Lord.
Aaron C. H. Seymour, 1805.

891.

1 O Spirit of the living God,
In all thy plenitude of grace,
Where'er the foot of man hath trod,
Descend on our apostate race.

2 Give tongues of fire and hearts of love,
To preach the reconciling word;
Give power and unction from above,
Where'er the joyful sound is heard.

3 Be darkness, at thy coming, light;
Confusion, order in thy path;
Souls without strength inspire with might,
Bid mercy triumph over wrath.

4 O Spirit of the Lord, prepare
All the round earth her God to meet;
Breathe thou abroad like morning air,
Till hearts of stone begin to beat.

5 Baptize the nations; far and nigh
The triumphs of the cross record;
The name of Jesus glorify,
Till every kindred call him Lord.
James Montgomery, 1825.

MISSIONS.

MISSIONARY CHANT. L. M.

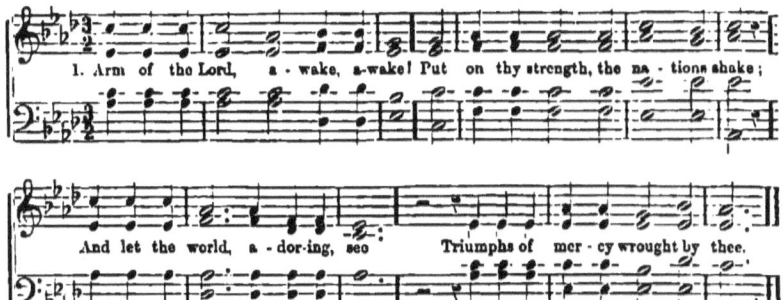

1. Arm of the Lord, a-wake, a-wake! Put on thy strength, the na-tions shake; And let the world, a-dor-ing, see Triumphs of mer-cy wrought by thee.

892.
1 ARM of the Lord, awake, awake!
Put on thy strength, the nations shake;
And let the world, adoring, see
Triumphs of mercy wrought by thee.

2 Say to the heathen, from thy throne,
I am Jehovah, God alone:
Thy voice their idols shall confound,
And cast their altars to the ground.

3 No more let human blood be spilt —
Vain sacrifice for human guilt!
But to each conscience be applied
The blood that flowed from Jesus' side.

4 Almighty God, thy grace proclaim,
In every clime, of every name;
Let adverse powers before thee fall,
And crown the Saviour Lord of all.
William Shrubsole, 1795.

893.
1 SOVEREIGN of worlds, display thy power;
Be this thy Zion's favored hour:
Oh, bid the morning star arise;
Oh, point the heathen to the skies.

2 Set up thy throne where Satan reigns,
In western wilds and eastern plains;
Far let the gospel's sound be known;
Make thou the universe thine own.

3 Speak, and the world shall hear thy voice;
Speak, and the desert shall rejoice:
Dispel the gloom of heathen night;
Bid every nation hail the light.
Baptist Magazine, 1816.

894.
1 YE Christian heralds, go, proclaim
Salvation through Immanuel's name:
To distant climes the tidings bear,
And plant the rose of Sharon there.

2 He'll shield you with a wall of fire,
With flaming zeal your breasts inspire,
Bid raging winds their fury cease,
And hush the tempest into peace.

3 And when your labors all are o'er,
Then we shall meet to part no more;
Meet with the blood-bought throng, to fall,
And crown our Jesus Lord of all!
Anon.

895. *Isaiah lxii. 6, 7.*
1 INDULGENT Sovereign of the skies,
And wilt thou bow thy gracious ear?
While feeble mortals raise their cries,
Wilt thou, the great Jehovah, hear?

2 How shall thy servants give thee rest,
Till Zion's mouldering walls thou raise;
Till thine own power shall stand confessed,
And make Jerusalem a praise?

3 Look down, O God, with pitying eye,
And view the desolation round:
See what wide realms in darkness lie,
And hurl their idols to the ground.

4 Loud let the gospel trumpet blow,
And call the nations from afar:
Let all the isles their Saviour know,
And earth's remotest ends draw near.
Philip Doddridge, 1763.

MISSIONS.

NORTHFIELD. C. M.

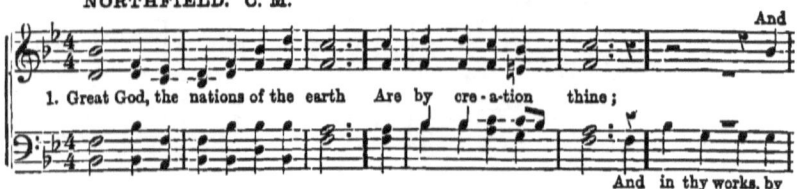

896.

1 GREAT God, the nations of the earth
  Are by creation thine;
  And in thy works, by all beheld,
  Thy radiant glories shine.

2 But, Lord, thy greater love has sent
  Thy gospel to mankind,
  Unveiling what rich stores of grace
  Are treasured in thy mind.

3 Lord, when shall these glad tidings spread
  The spacious earth around,
  Till every tribe and every soul
  Shall hear the joyful sound?

4 Send forth thy word, and let it fly,
  Armed with thy Spirit's power;
  Ten thousand shall confess its sway,
  And bless the saving hour.

5 Beneath the influence of thy grace
  The barren wastes shall rise
  With sudden green and fruits arrayed,
  A blooming Paradise.

6 Peace, with her olive crowned, shall stretch
  Her wings from shore to shore;
  No trump shall rouse the rage of war,
  Nor murderous cannon roar.

7 Lord, for those days we wait; those days
  Are in thy word foretold;
  Fly swifter, sun and stars, and bring
  This promised age of gold.
  Thomas Gibbons, 1767.

897.

1 BEHOLD, the mountain of the Lord
  In latter days shall rise
  On mountain tops, above the hills,
  And draw the wondering eyes.

2 To this the joyful nations round,
  All tribes and tongues, shall flow;
  Up to the hill of God, they'll say,
  And to his house we'll go.

3 The beam that shines from Zion's hill
  Shall lighten every land;
  The King who reigns in Salem's towers
  Shall all the world command.

4 No strife shall vex Messiah's reign,
  Or mar the peaceful years; [swords,
  To ploughshares men shall beat their
  To pruning-hooks their spears.

5 No longer hosts encountering hosts
  Their millions slain deplore;
  They hang the trumpet in the hall,
  And study war no more.

6 Come, then, oh, come, from every land,
  To worship at his shrine;
  And, walking in the light of God,
  With holy beauties shine.
  Michael Bruce, 1768.

MISSIONS.

DUKE STREET. L. M.

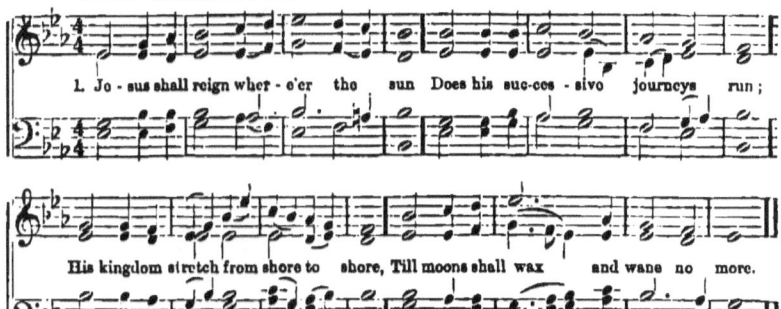

1. Jesus shall reign where'er the sun Does his successive journeys run; His kingdom stretch from shore to shore, Till moons shall wax and wane no more.

898. Psalm 72.

1 JESUS shall reign where'er the sun
Does his successive journeys run;
His kingdom stretch from shore to shore,
Till moons shall wax and wane no more.

2 For him shall endless prayer be made,
And praises throng to crown his head;
His name like sweet perfume shall rise
With every morning sacrifice.

3 People and realms of every tongue
Dwell on his love with sweetest song;
And infant voices shall proclaim
Their early blessings on his name.

4 Blessings abound where'er he reigns;
The prisoner leaps to lose his chains;
The weary find eternal rest,
And all the sons of want are blest.

5 Where he displays his healing power,
Death and the curse are known no more;
In him the tribes of Adam boast
More blessings than their father lost.

6 Let every creature rise and bring
Peculiar honors to our King;
Angels descend with songs again,
And earth repeat the loud Amen!
Isaac Watts, 1719.

899.

1 THOUGH now the nations sit beneath
The darkness of o'erspreading death,
God will arise with light divine,
On Zion's holy towers to shine.

2 That light shall shine on distant lands,
And wandering tribes, in joyful bands,
Shall come, thy glory, Lord, to see,
And in thy courts to worship thee.

3 O light of Zion, now arise!
Let the glad morning bless our eyes!
Ye nations, catch the kindling ray,
And hail the splendors of the day.
Leonard Bacon, 1823, a.

900. Psalm 72.

1 GREAT God, whose universal sway
The known and unknown worlds obey;
Now give the kingdom to thy Son,
Extend his power, exalt his throne.

2 As rain on meadows newly mown,
So shall he send his influence down;
His grace on fainting souls distils
Like heavenly dew on thirsty hills.

3 The heathen lands, that lie beneath
The shade of overspreading death,
Revive at his first dawning light,
And deserts blossom at the sight.

4 The saints shall flourish in his days,
Dressed in the robes of joy and praise;
Peace, like a river, from his throne
Shall flow to nations yet unknown.
Isaac Watts, 1719.

DOXOLOGY.

To God the Father, God the Son,
And Holy Spirit, Three in One,
May every tongue and nation raise
An endless song of thankful praise.
Tr. from Latin by J. Chandler, 1837.

MISSIONS.

CLARION. 6s & 4s.

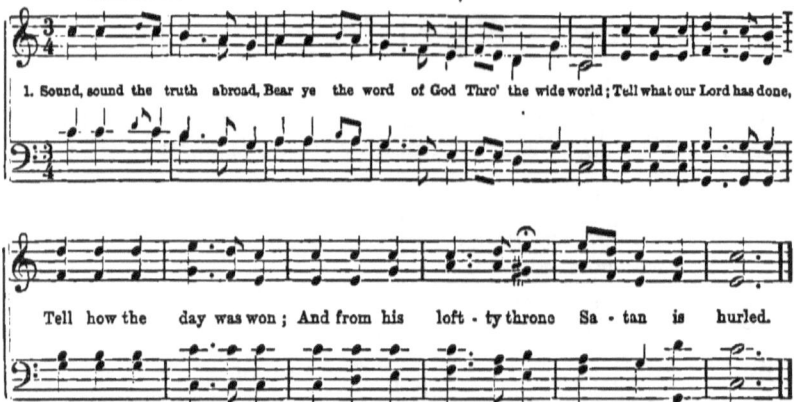

1. Sound, sound the truth abroad, Bear ye the word of God Thro' the wide world; Tell what our Lord has done, Tell how the day was won; And from his lofty throne Satan is hurled.

901.

1 SOUND, sound the truth abroad,
  Bear ye the word of God
    Through the wide world;
  Tell what our Lord has done,
  Tell how the day was won;
    And from his lofty throne
      Satan is hurled.

2 Far over sea and land,
  'Tis our Lord's own command,
    Bear ye his name;
  Bear it to every shore,
  Regions unknown explore,
  Enter at every door —
    Silence is shame.

3 When on the mighty deep,
  He will their spirits keep,
    Stayed on his word;
  When in a foreign land,
  No other friend at hand,
  Jesus will by them stand —
    Jesus, their Lord.

4 Ye who, forsaking all
  At your loved Master's call,
    Comforts resign;
  Soon will the work be done;
  Soon will the prize be won;
  Brighter than yonder sun
    Then shall ye shine.

Thomas Kelly, 1820.

902. Tune, "Stockwell," p. 391. 8s & 7s.

1 LIGHT of those whose dreary dwelling
  Borders on the shades of death,
  Come, and, by thy love revealing,
  Dissipate the clouds beneath.

2 The new heaven and earth's Creator,
  In our deepest darkness rise,
  Scattering all the night of nature,
  Pouring day upon our eyes.

3 Still we wait for thine appearing,
  Life and joy thy beams impart,
  Chasing all our fears, and cheering
  Every poor, benighted heart.

4 Come and manifest the favor
  God hath for our ransomed race;
  Come, thou universal Saviour,
  Come, and bring the gospel grace.

5 Save us in thy great compassion
  O thou mild, pacific Prince;
  Give the knowledge of salvation,
  Give the pardon of our sins.

6 By thy all-restoring merit,
  Every burdened soul release;
  Every weary, wandering spirit
  Guide into thy perfect peace.

Charles Wesley, 1744.

MISSIONS.

ZION. 8s, 7s & 4s.

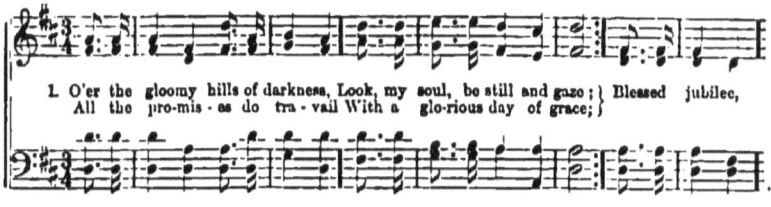

1. O'er the gloomy hills of darkness, Look, my soul, be still and gaze; } Blessed jubilee,
All the promises do travail With a glorious day of grace; }

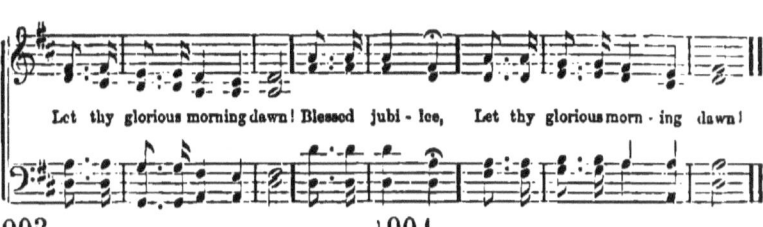

Let thy glorious morning dawn! Blessed jubi-lee, Let thy glorious morn-ing dawn!

903.

1 O'er the gloomy hills of darkness,
   Look, my soul, be still and gaze;
   All the promises do travail
   With a glorious day of grace;
      Blessed jubilee,
   Let thy glorious morning dawn!

2 Let the Indian, let the negro,
   Let the rude barbarian see
   That divine and glorious conquest,
   Once obtained on Calvary;
      Let the gospel
   Loud resound from pole to pole.

3 Kingdoms wide that sit in darkness —
   Grant them, Lord, the saving light;
   And from eastern coast to western
   May the morning chase the night;
      And redemption,
   Freely purchased, win the day!

4 Fly abroad, thou mighty gospel,
   Win and conquer, never cease;
   May thy lasting, wide dominion
   Multiply and still increase;
      Sway thy sceptre,
   Saviour, all the world around!
                William Williams, 1772.

904.

1 O'er the realms of pagan darkness
   Let the eye of pity gaze;
   See the kindreds of the people
   Lost in sin's bewildering maze:
      Darkness brooding
   O'er the face of all the earth.

2 Light of them that sit in darkness,
   Rise and shine; thy blessings bring:
   Light to lighten all the Gentiles,
   Rise with healing in thy wing:
      To thy brightness
   Let all kings and nations come.

3 May the heathen, now adoring
   Idol gods of wood and stone,
   Come, and, worshipping before him,
   Serve the living God alone:
      Let thy glory
   Fill the earth as floods the sea.

4 Thou, to whom all power is given,
   Speak the word; at thy command,
   Let the company of heralds
   Spread thy name from land to land;
      Lord, be with them,
   Alway, to the end of time.
                Thomas Cotterill, 1819.

MISSIONS.

OLIPHANT. 8s, 7s & 4s.

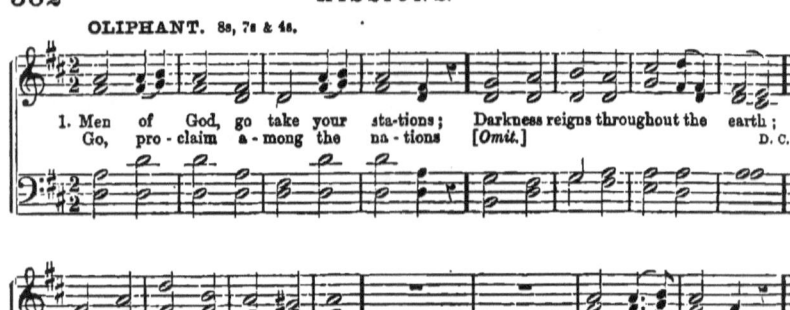

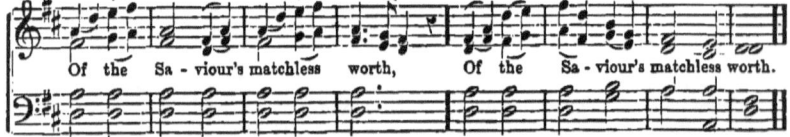

905.

1 MEN of God, go take your stations;
   Darkness reigns throughout the earth;
   Go, proclaim among the nations
   Joyful news of heavenly birth;
     Bear the tidings
     Of the Saviour's matchless worth.

2 Of his gospel not ashaméd,
   As the power of God to save,
   Go, where Christ was never naméd,
   Publish freedom to the slave!
     Blesséd freedom!
     Such as Zion's children have.

3 When exposed to fearful dangers,
   Jesus will his own defend;
   Borne afar 'midst foes and strangers,
   Jesus will appear your friend,
     And his presence
     Shall be with you to the end.
         Thomas Kelly, 1806.

906.

1 YES, we trust the day is breaking;
   Joyful times are near at hand;
   God, the mighty God, is speaking
   By his word in every land:
     When he chooses,
     Darkness flies at his command.

2 Let us hail the joyful season;
   Let us hail the dawning ray;
   When the Lord appears, there's reason
   To expect a glorious day:
     At his presence
     Gloom and darkness flee away.

3 While the foe becomes more daring,
   While he enters like a flood,
   God, the Saviour, is preparing
   Means to spread his truth abroad;
     Every language
     Soon shall tell the love of God.

4 God of Jacob, high and glorious,
   Let thy people see thy hand!
   Let the gospel be victorious
   Through the world, in every land,
     And the idols
     Perish, Lord, at thy command!
         Thomas Kelly, 1806.

907. 8s, 7s & 4s.

1 Mighty Lord, extend thine empire!
  Be thy truth with triumph crowned!
 Let the lands that sit in darkness
  Hear the glorious gospel's sound,
    From our borders,
  To the world's remotest bound.

2 By thine arm, eternal Father,
  Scatter far the shades of night!
 Let the great Immanuel's kingdom
  Open like the morning light,
    And the future
  Realize our visions bright.

3 Come, too long to earth a stranger,
  Once again thy reign restore!
 In thy strength, ride forth and conquer,
  Still advancing more and more,
    Till the heathen
  Shall the Lord supreme adore.
            Joseph Cottle, 1828.

908. 8s, 7s & 4s.

1 Who but thou, almighty Spirit,
  Can the heathen world reclaim?
 Men may preach, but, till thou favor,
  Heathens will be still the same:
    Mighty Spirit,
  Witness to the Saviour's name.

2 Thou hast promised, by the prophets,
  Glorious light in latter days:
 Come, and bless bewildered nations;
  Change our prayers and tears to praise:
    Promised Spirit,
  Round the world diffuse thy rays.

3 All our hopes, and prayers, and labors
  Must be vain without thy aid;
 But thou wilt not disappoint us;
  All is true that thou hast said:
    Gracious Spirit,
  O'er the world thy influence shed.
      "*Eriphas*," *Evangelical Magazine*, 1821.

909. 8s, 7s & 4s.

1 Yes, my native land, I love thee;
  All thy scenes, I love them well:
 Friends, connections, happy country,
  Can I bid you all farewell?
    Can I leave you,
  Far in heathen lands to dwell?

2 Home, thy joys are passing lovely —
  Joys no stranger-heart can tell:
 Happy home, indeed I love thee:
  Can I, can I say, Farewell?
    Can I leave thee,
  Far in heathen lands to dwell?

3 Scenes of sacred peace and pleasure,
  Holy days and Sabbath bell,
 Richest, brightest, sweetest treasure,
  Can I say a last farewell?
    Can I leave you,
  Far in heathen lands to dwell?

4 Yes! I hasten from you gladly,
  From the scenes I loved so well:
 Far away, ye billows, bear me;
  Lovely, native land, farewell!
    Pleased I leave thee,
  Far in heathen lands to dwell.

5 In the deserts let me labor;
  On the mountains let me tell
 How he died, the blessèd Saviour,
  To redeem a world from hell:
    Let me hasten,
  Far in heathen lands to dwell.

6 Bear me on, thou restless ocean;
  Let the winds my canvas swell:
 Heaves my heart with warm emotion,
  While I go far hence to dwell:
    Glad I bid thee,
  Native land, farewell, farewell!
            S. F. Smith, 1833.

MISSIONS.

CHAMBER ST. CHANT. L. M.

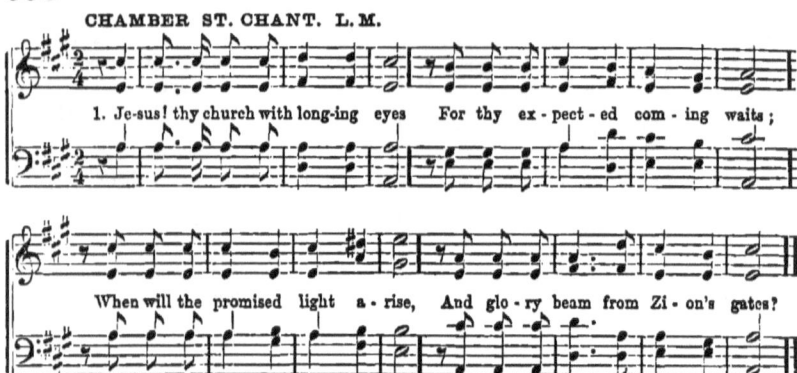

1. Jesus! thy church with longing eyes For thy expected coming waits; When will the promised light arise, And glory beam from Zion's gates?

910.

1 JESUS! thy church with longing eyes
   For thy expected coming waits;
   When will the promised light arise,
   And glory beam from Zion's gates?

2 E'en now, when tempests round us fall,
   And wintry clouds o'ercast the sky,
   Thy words with pleasure we recall,
   And deem that our redemption's nigh.

3 Come, gracious Lord, our hearts renew,
   Our foes repel, our wrongs redress,
   Man's rooted enmity subdue,
   And crown thy gospel with success.

4 Oh come, and reign o'er every land;
   Let Satan from his throne be hurled;
   All nations bow to thy command,
   And grace revive a dying world!

5 Yes, thou wilt speedily appear!
   The smitten earth already reels;
   And not far off we seem to hear
   The thunder of thy chariot wheels.

6 Teach us in watchfulness and prayer
   To wait for the appointed hour;
   And fit us by thy grace to share
   The triumphs of thy conquering power.
       William Hiley Bathurst, 1831.

911.

1 SOON may the last glad song arise,
   Through all the myriads of the skies —
   That song of triumph which records
   That all the earth is now the Lord's.

2 Let thrones, and powers, and kingdoms
   Obedient, mighty God, to thee; [be
   And over land, and stream, and main,
   Now wave the sceptre of thy reign.

3 Oh, let that glorious anthem swell;
   Let host to host the triumph tell,
   That not one rebel heart remains,
   But over all the Saviour reigns.
       Anon.

912.

1 BEHOLD the expected time draw near,
   The shades disperse, the dawn appear;
   Behold the wilderness assume
   The beauteous tints of Eden's bloom.

2 *Events with prophecies conspire
   To raise our faith, our zeal to fire;
   The ripening fields, already white,
   Present a harvest to our sight.

3 The untaught heathen waits to know
   The joy the gospel will bestow;
   The exiled slave waits to receive
   The freedom Jesus has to give.

4 Come, let us, with a grateful heart,
   In the blest labor share a part;
   Our prayers and offerings gladly bring
   To aid the triumphs of our King.
       Mrs. Voke, 1806.

DOXOLOGY.

To thee, Eternal Three in One,
Let homage meet by all be done;
As by the cross thou dost restore,
So rule and guide us evermore.
       Tr. from the Latin, by J. M. Neale, 1851.

MISSIONS.

913.

2 See heathen nations bending
   Before the God we love,
   And thousand hearts ascending
   In gratitude above;
   While sinners, now confessing,
   The gospel call obey,
   And seek the Saviour's blessing —
   A nation in a day.

3 Blest river of salvation,
   Pursue thy onward way;
   Flow thou to every nation,
   Nor in thy richness stay :
   Stay not till all the lowly
   Triumphant reach their home ;
   Stay not till all the holy
   Proclaim, "The Lord is come!"
   S. F. Smith, 1843.

914.   PSALM 72.

1 HAIL to the Lord's Anointed,
   Great David's greater Son!
   Hail, in the time appointed,
   His reign on earth begun!
   He comes to break oppression,
   To set the captive free ;
   To take away transgression,
   And rule in equity.

2 He comes with succor speedy
   To those who suffer wrong;
   To help the poor and needy,
   And bid the weak be strong :
   To give them songs for sighing,
   Their darkness turn to light,
   Whose souls, condemned and dying,
   Were precious in his sight.

3 He shall come down like showers
   Upon the fruitful earth,
   And love, joy, hope, like flowers,
   Spring in his path to birth ;
   Before him, on the mountains,
   Shall peace, the herald, go,
   And righteousness, in fountains,
   From hill to valley flow.

4 Kings shall fall down before him,
   And gold and incense bring,
   All nations shall adore him,
   His praise all people sing :
   For him shall prayer unceasing
   And daily vows ascend ;
   His kingdom still increasing,
   A kingdom without end.
   James Montgomery, 1822.

MISSIONS

HARWELL. 8s & 7s. (Repeat first two lines for Hymn 916.)

915.

1 Lo! he comes! let all adore him!
'T is the God of grace and truth!
Go! prepare the way before him,
Make the rugged places smooth!
Lo! he comes, the mighty Lord!
Great his work, and his reward.

2 Let the valleys all be raiséd;
Go, and make the crooked straight;
Let the mountains be abaséd;
Let all nature change its state;
Through the desert mark a road,
Make a highway for our God.

3 Through the desert God is going,
Through the desert waste and wild,
Where no goodly plant is growing,
Where no verdure ever smiled;
But the desert shall be glad,
And with verdure soon be clad.

4 Where the thorn and brier flourished,
Trees shall there be seen to grow,
Planted by the Lord and nourished,
Stately, fair, and fruitful too;
They shall rise on every side,
They shall spread their branches wide.

5 From the hills and lofty mountains
Rivers shall be seen to flow,
There the Lord will open fountains,
Thence supply the plains below;
As he passes, every land
Shall confess his powerful hand.

Thomas Kelly, 1809.

916.

1 With my substance I will honor
My Redeemer and my Lord;
Were ten thousand worlds my manor,
All were nothing to his word.

2 While the heralds of salvation
His abounding grace proclaim,
Let his friends, of every station,
Gladly join to spread his fame.

3 Be his kingdom now promoted,
Let the earth her Monarch know!
Be my all to him devoted;
To my Lord my all I owe.

4 Praise the Saviour, all ye nations!
Praise him, all ye hosts above!
Shout, with joyful acclamations,
His divine, victorious love!

Benjamin Francis, 1774.

MISSIONS.

ROYALTY. 12s, 11s & 4s.

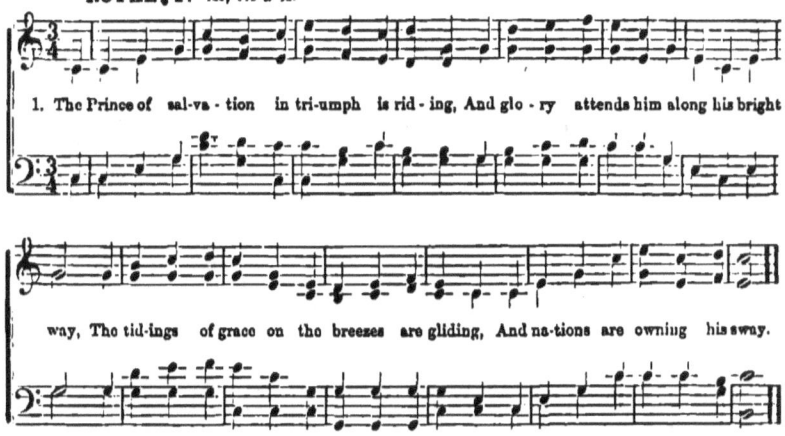

917.

1 THE Prince of salvation in triumph is riding,
   And glory attends him along his bright way ;
   The tidings of grace on the breezes are gliding,
      And nations are owning his sway.

2 Ride on in thy greatness, thou conquering Saviour ;
   Let thousands of thousands submit to thy reign,
   Acknowledge thy goodness, entreat for thy favor,
      And follow thy glorious train.

3 Then loud shall ascend, from each sanctified nation,
   The voice of thanksgiving, the chorus of praise ;
   And heaven shall reëcho the song of salvation
      In rich and melodious lays.

S. F. Smith, 1843.

918.   Tune, "Petersburg," p. 334.   8s & 4s.

1 HARK! how the gospel trumpet sounds!
   Through all the world the echo bounds!
   And Jesus, by redeeming blood,
   Is bringing sinners back to God,
   And guides them safely by his word
      To endless day.

2 Hail, Jesus! all victorious Lord!
   Be thou by all mankind adored!
   For us didst thou the fight maintain,
   And o'er our foes the victory gain,
   That we with thee might ever reign
      In endless day.

3 Fight on, ye conquering souls, fight on,
   And when the conquest you have won,
   Then palms of victory you shall bear,
   And in his kingdom have a share,
   And crowns of glory ever wear,
      In endless day.

4 There we shall in full chorus join,
   With saints and angels all combine
   To sing of his redeeming love,
   When rolling years shall cease to move,
   And this shall be our theme above,
      In endless day.

Samuel Medley, 1789.

MISSIONS

BELLAK. 7s. (Repeat for six lines.)

1. Hark! the distant isles proclaim Glory to Messiah's name; Hymns of praise unheard before, Echo from the farthest shore.

919.

1 Hark! the distant isles proclaim
Glory to Messiah's name;
Hymns of praise unheard before,
Echo from the farthest shore.

2 Hearts that once were taught to own
Idol gods of wood and stone,
Now to light and life restored,
Honor Jesus as their Lord.

3 Blessed Saviour, still proceed;
Bid the glorious conquest speed;
Let this first refreshing ray
Brighten to a perfect day.

4 At thy gospel's solemn call,
Bid the towers of Satan fall,
And his wretched slaves obtain
Freedom from their galling chain.

5 Let the messengers of peace
Raise their voice and never cease,
Till the world, from sin made free,
Shall unite to worship thee.
William H. Bathurst, 1831.

920. Psalm 72.

1 Hasten, Lord, the glorious time,
When, beneath Messiah's sway,
Every nation, every clime,
Shall the gospel call obey.

2 Then shall wars and tumults cease,
Then be banished grief and pain;

Righteousness and joy and peace,
Undisturbed shall ever reign.

3 Mightiest kings his power shall own;
Heathen tribes his name adore;
Satan and his host o'erthrown,
Bound in chains shall hurt no more.

4 Bless we then our gracious Lord;
Ever praise his glorious name;
All his mighty acts record,
All his wondrous love proclaim.
Harriet Auber, 1829.

921. Psalm 67.

1 God of mercy, God of grace,
Show the brightness of thy face:
Shine upon us, Saviour, shine;
Fill thy church with light divine;
And thy saving health extend
To the earth's remotest end.

2 Let the people praise thee, Lord;
Be by all that live adored:
Let the nations shout and sing,
Glory to their Saviour King;
At thy feet their tribute pay,
And thy holy will obey.

3 Let the people praise thee, Lord:
Earth shall then her fruits afford;
God to man his blessings give;
Man to God devoted live;
All below, and all above,
One in joy, and light, and love.
Henry F. Lyte, 1834.

MISSIONS.

HUMMEL. C. M.

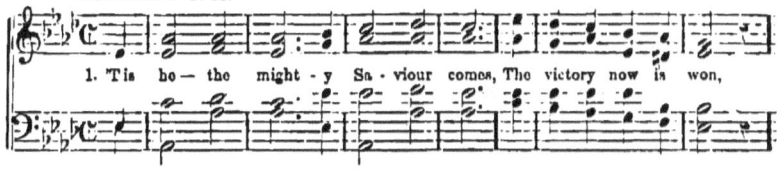

1. 'Tis he—the mighty Saviour comes, The victory now is won,

And lo, the throne of David waits For David's royal Son.

922.

1 'Tis he—the mighty Saviour comes,
  The victory now is won,
And lo, the throne of David waits
  For David's royal Son.

2 Thou blessed heir of all the earth,
  Ascend thine ancient throne,
And bid the willing nations now
  Thy peaceful sceptre own.

3 Shine forth in all thy glory, Lord,
  That man at length may see
That joy, so long estranged from earth,
  Can only spring from thee.

4 O happy day! 't is come at last,
  The reign of death is o'er;
And sin, that marred our sweetest joys,
  Shall grieve our hearts no more.

5 Washed in thy blood, the tribes of earth,
  With all the blest above,
Shall dwell in peace, united now,
  One family of love.

6 Fruit of thy toil, thou bleeding Lamb!
  These joys we owe to thee;
Then take the glory, Lord; 't is thine,
  And shall forever be.
      Sir Edward Denny, 1848.

923.   PSALM 96.

1 SING to the Lord, ye distant lands,
  Ye tribes of every tongue;
His new-discovered grace demands
  A new and nobler song.

2 Say to the nations, Jesus reigns,
  God's own almighty Son;
His power the sinking world sustains,
  And grace surrounds his throne.

3 Let heaven proclaim the joyful day,
  Joy through the earth be seen;
Let cities shine in bright array,
  And fields in cheerful green.

4 Let an unusual joy surprise
  The islands of the sea;
Ye mountains sink, ye valleys rise,
  Prepare the Lord his way.

5 Behold he comes! He comes to bless
  The nations as their God;
To show the world his righteousness,
  And send his truth abroad.
      Isaac Watts, 1719.

924.

1 SHINE, mighty God, on Zion shine,
  With beams of heavenly grace;
Reveal thy power through every land,
  And show thy smiling face.

2 When shall thy name, from shore to shore,
  Sound all the earth abroad,
And distant nations know and love
  Their Saviour and their God?

3 Sing to the Lord, ye distant lands;
  Sing loud, with solemn voice;
Let every tongue exalt his praise,
  And every heart rejoice.
      Isaac Watts, 1709, a.

MISSIONS.

HENRY. C. M.

1. Je-sus, im-mor-tal King, a-rise! As-sume, as-sert thy sway, Till earth, sub-dued, its tri-bute brings, And dis-tant lands o-bey.

925.

1 Jesus, immortal King, arise!
  Assume, assert thy sway,
  Till earth, subdued, its tribute brings,
  And distant lands obey.

2 Ride forth, victorious conqueror, ride,
  Till all thy foes submit,
  And all the powers of hell resign
  Their trophies at thy feet!

3 Send forth thy word, and let it fly
  This spacious earth around,
  Till every soul beneath the sun
  Shall hear the joyful sound.

4 Oh may the dear Redeemer's name
  Through every clime be known,
  And heathen gods, like Dagon, fall,
  And Jesus reign alone.

5 Oh hasten, Lord, that happy time,
  That long-expected day,
  When every kingdom, tribe and tongue
  Shall own thy gentle sway;

6 When all th' untutored heathen tribes
  Shall the Redeemer own,
  And crowds of willing converts come
  To worship at thy throne.

7 From sea to sea, from shore to shore,
  May Jesus be adored!
  And earth, with all her millions, shout
  Hosannas to the Lord.
  A. C. H. Seymour, 1810.

926.

1 Light of the lonely pilgrim's heart,
  Star of the coming day,
  Arise, and with thy morning beams
  Chase all our griefs away!

2 Come, blessèd Lord, bid every shore
  And answering island sing
  The praises of thy royal name,
  And own thee as their King.

3 Bid the whole earth, responsive now
  To the bright world above,
  Break forth in sweetest strains of joy,
  In memory of thy love.

4 Lord, Lord, thy fair creation groans,
  The air, the earth, the sea,
  In unison with all our hearts,
  And calls aloud for thee.

5 Come, then, with all thy quickening power,
  With one awakening smile,
  And bid the serpent's trail no more
  Thy beauteous realms defile.

6 Thine was the Cross, with all its fruits
  Of grace and peace divine;
  Be thine the crown of glory now,
  The palm of victory thine.
  Sir Edward Denny, 1848.

DOXOLOGY.

Honor and glory, power and praise,
  To Father and to Son,
And Holy Ghost, be paid always,
  The Eternal Three in One.
  John Henry Newman, 1849.

MISSIONS.

MISSIONARY HYMN. 7s & 6s.

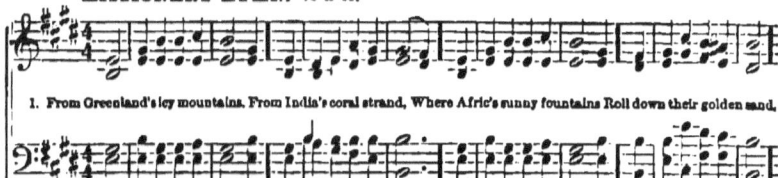

1. From Greenland's icy mountains, From India's coral strand, Where Afric's sunny fountains Roll down their golden sand,

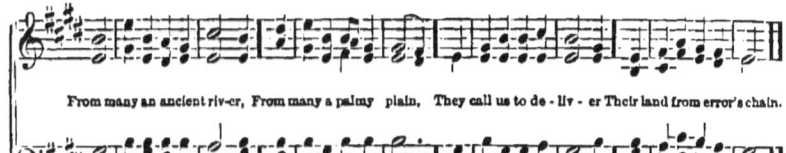

From many an ancient river, From many a palmy plain, They call us to de-liv-er Their land from error's chain.

927.

1 From Greenland's icy mountains,
From India's coral strand,
Where Afric's sunny fountains
Roll down their golden sand,
From many an ancient river,
From many a palmy plain,
They call us to deliver
Their land from error's chain.

2 What though the spicy breezes
Blow soft o'er Ceylon's isle;
Though every prospect pleases,
And only man is vile;
In vain with lavish kindness
The gifts of God are strown;
The heathen in his blindness
Bows down to wood and stone.

3 Can we, whose souls are lighted
With wisdom from on high,
Can we to men benighted
The lamp of life deny?
Salvation! O salvation!
The joyful sound proclaim,
Till each remotest nation
Has learnt Messiah's name.

4 Waft, waft, ye winds, his story,
And you, ye waters, roll,
Till like a sea of glory
It spreads from pole to pole;
Till o'er our ransomed nature
The Lamb for sinners slain,
Redeemer, King, Creator,
In bliss returns to reign.
Reginald Heber. 1819.

928. Psalm 14.

1 On that the Lord's salvation
Were out of Zion come,
To heal his ancient nation,
To lead his outcasts home!
How long the holy city
Shall heathen feet profane?
Return, O Lord, in pity;
Rebuild her walls again.

2 Let fall thy rod of terror;
Thy saving grace impart;
Roll back the veil of error;
Release the fettered heart;
Let Israel, home returning,
Their lost Messiah see;
Give oil of joy for mourning,
And bind thy church to thee.
Henry F. Lyte, 1833.

872   SEAMEN.

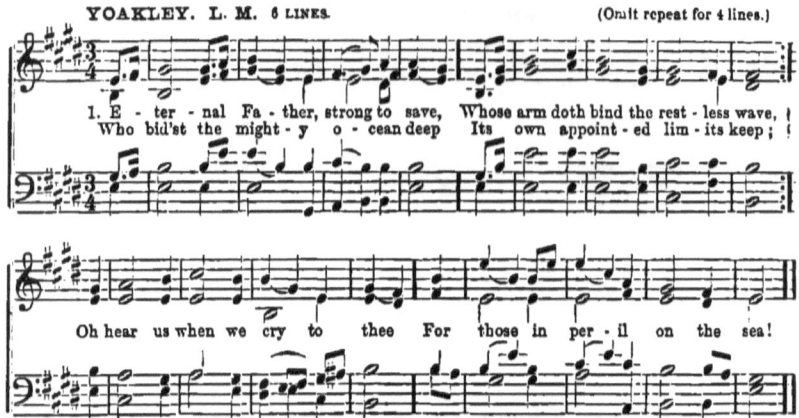

YOAKLEY. L. M. 6 LINES.   (Omit repeat for 4 lines.)

929.

1 Eternal Father, strong to save,
   Whose arm doth bind the restless wave,
   Who bid'st the mighty ocean deep
   Its own appointed limits keep;
   Oh hear us when we cry to thee
   For those in peril on the sea!

2 O Saviour, whose almighty word
   The winds and waves submissive heard,
   Who walkedst on the foaming deep,
   And calm amid its rage didst sleep;
   Oh hear us when we cry to thee
   For those in peril on the sea!

3 O sacred Spirit, who didst brood
   Upon the chaos dark and rude,
   Who bad'st its angry tumult cease,
   And gavest light, and life, and peace;
   Oh hear us when we cry to thee
   For those in peril on the sea!

4 O Trinity of love and power,
   Our brethren shield in danger's hour;
   From rock and tempest, fire and foe,
   Protect them whereso'er they go:
   Thus evermore shall rise to thee
   Glad hymns of praise from land and sea!
                   W. Whiting, 1860.

930.

1 While o'er the deep thy servants sail,
   Send thou, O Lord, the prosperous gale;
   And on their hearts, where'er they go,
   Oh let thy heavenly breezes blow.

2 If on the morning's wings they fly,
   They will not pass beyond thine eye;
   The wanderer's prayer thou bend'st to hear,
   And faith exults to know thee near.

3 When tempests rock the groaning bark,
   Oh hide them safe in Jesus' ark;
   When in the tempting port they ride,
   Oh keep them safe at Jesus' side.

4 If life's wide ocean smile or roar,
   Still guide them to the heavenly shore;
   And grant their dust in Christ may sleep,
   Abroad, at home, or in the deep.
                   George Burgess, a.

931.

1 Lord of the ocean, hear our cry,
   As o'er the trackless deep we roam;
   Be thou our haven always nigh;
   On homeless waters thou our home.

2 O Jesus, Saviour, at whose voice
   The tempest sank to perfect rest,
   Bid thou the mourner's heart rejoice,
   And cleanse and calm the troubled breast.

3 O Holy Ghost, beneath whose power
   Creation woke to life and light,
   Command thy blessing in this hour,
   Thy fostering warmth, thy quickening might.

4 Great God, Triune Jehovah, thee
   We love, we worship, we adore;
   Our refuge on time's changeful sea,
   Our joy on heaven's eternal shore.
               Edward Henry Bickersteth, 1869.

SEAMEN. 373

SCOTLAND. 12s.

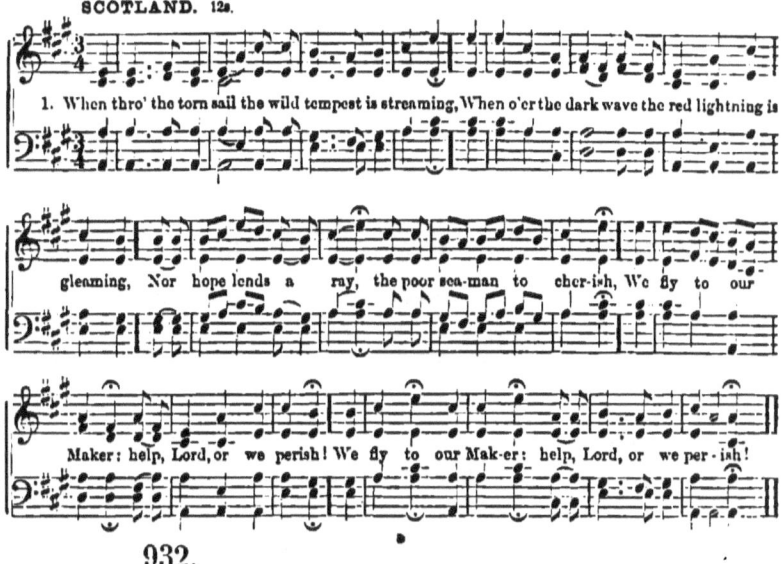

932.

1 When through the torn sail the wild tempest is streaming,
When o'er the dark wave the red lightning is gleaming,
Nor hope lends a ray, the poor seaman to cherish,
We fly to our Maker: help, Lord, or we perish!

2 O Jesus, once tossed on the breast of the billow,
Aroused by the shriek of despair from thy pillow,
Now seated in glory, the mariner cherish,
Who cries in his danger, "Help, Lord, or we perish!"

3 And, oh! when the whirlwind of passion is raging,
When hell in our hearts its wild warfare is waging,
Arise in thy strength, thy redeemed to cherish,
Rebuke the destroyer, — help, Lord, or we perish!

Reginald Heber, 1827.

933. Tune, "Yoakley." p. 372. L. M.

1 Glory to thee, whose powerful word
Bids the tempestuous wind arise;
Glory to thee, the sovereign Lord
Of air, and earth, and seas, and skies.

2 Let air, and earth, and skies obey,
And seas thy awful will perform;
From them we learn to own thy sway,
And shout to meet the gathering storm.

3 What though the floods lift up their voice!
Thou hearest, Lord, our louder cry;
They cannot damp thy children's joys,
Or shake the soul, when God is nigh.

4 Roar on, ye waves, our souls defy
Your roaring to disturb our rest;
In vain t' impair the calm ye try,
The calm in a believer's breast.

5 Rage, while our faith the Saviour tries,
Thou sea, the servant of his will!
Rise, while our God permits thee, rise;
But fall when he shall say, "Be still!"

Charles Wesley, 1740.

THE NATION.

AMERICA. 6s & 4s.

1. My country, 'tis of thee, Sweet land of liberty, Of thee I sing: Land where my fathers died, Land of the pilgrims' pride, From every mountain side Let freedom ring!

934.

1 My country, 't is of thee,
 Sweet land of liberty,
  Of thee I sing :
 Land where my fathers died,
 Land of the pilgrims' pride,
  From every mountain side
   Let freedom ring!

2 My native country, thee,
 Land of the noble free,
  Thy name I love :
 I love thy rocks and rills,
 Thy woods and templed hills ;
 My heart with rapture thrills
  Like that above.

3 Let music swell the breeze,
 And ring from all the trees
  Sweet freedom's song ;
 Let mortal tongues awake,
 Let all that breathe partake,
 Let rocks their silence break,
  The sound prolong.

4 Our fathers' God, to thee,
 Author of liberty,
  To thee we sing ;
 Long may our land be bright
 With freedom's holy light,
 Protect us with thy might,
  Great God, our King!

S. F. Smith, 1833.

935.

1 GOD bless our native land!
 Firm may she ever stand,
  Through storm and night :
 When the wild tempests rave,
 Ruler of wind and wave,
 Do thou our country save
  By thy great might !

2 For her our prayer shall rise
 To God, above the skies ;
  On him we wait :
 Thou who art ever nigh,
 Guarding with watchful eye,
 To thee aloud we cry,
  God save the State !

John S. Dwight, 1844.

THE NATION.

KENT. L. M.

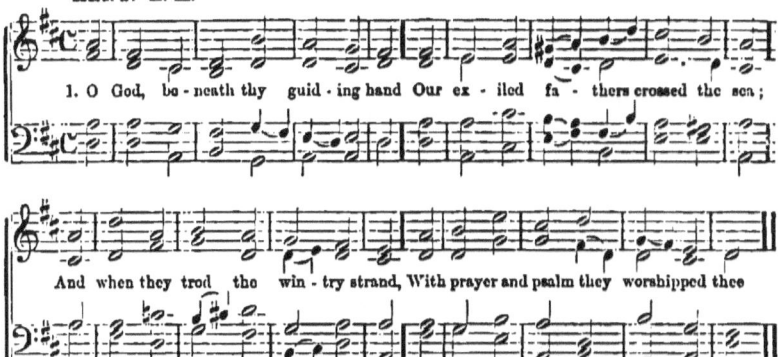

1. O God, be-neath thy guid-ing hand Our ex-iled fa-thers crossed the sea; And when they trod the win-try strand, With prayer and psalm they worshipped thee

936.

1 O GOD, beneath thy guiding hand,
Our exiled fathers crossed the sea ;
And when they trod the wintry strand,
With prayer and psalm they worship-
  ped thee.

2 Thou heard'st, well-pleased, the song, the
  prayer ;
Thy blessing came ; and still its power
Shall onward through all ages bear
The memory of that holy hour.

3 Laws, freedom, truth, and faith in God
Came with those exiles o'er the waves ;
And where their pilgrim feet have trod,
The God they trusted guards their
  graves.

4 And here thy name, O God of love,
Their children's children shall adore,
Till these eternal hills remove,
And spring adorns the earth no more.
Leonard Bacon, 1838.

937.

1 WHEN Israel, of the Lord beloved,
Out from the land of bondage came,
Her fathers' God before her moved,
An awful guide, in smoke and flame.

2 By day, along th' astonished lands,
The cloudy pillar glided slow ;
By night, Arabia's crimsoned sands
Returned the fiery column's glow.

3 Thus present still, though now unseen,
O Lord, when shines the prosperous
Be thoughts of thee a cloudy screen, [day,
To temper the deceitful ray !

4 And, oh ! when gathers on our path,
In shade and storm, the frequent night,
Be thou long suffering, slow to wrath,
A burning and a shining light.
Sir Walter Scott, 1820.

938. PSALM 44. Tune, "Dundee," p. 377. C. M.

1 O LORD, our fathers oft have told,
In our attentive ears,
Thy wonders in their days performed,
And elder times than theirs.

2 For, not their courage, nor their sword,
To them salvation gave ;
Nor strength that from unequal force
Their fainting troops could save :

3 But thy right hand and powerful arm,
Whose succor they implored ;
Thy presence with the chosen race,
Who thy great name adored.

4 As thee, their God, our fathers owned,
Thou art our sovereign King :
Oh, therefore, as thou didst to them,
To us deliverance bring !

5 To thee the triumph we ascribe,
From whom the conquest came ;
In God we will rejoice all day,
And ever bless his name.
Tate and Brady, 1696.

FAST

BONO. 8, 8, 8, 6.

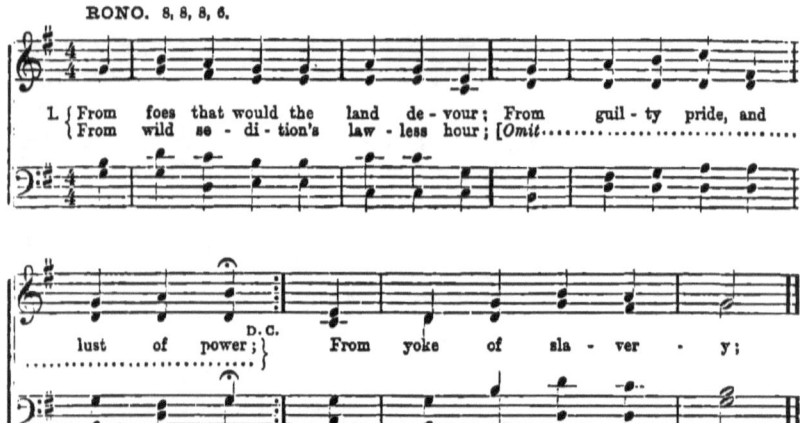

1. From foes that would the land devour; From guilty pride, and lust of power; From wild sedition's lawless hour; [Omit...] From yoke of slavery;

939.

1 From foes that would the land devour;
From guilty pride, and lust of power;
From wild sedition's lawless hour;
From yoke of slavery;

2 From blinded zeal, by faction led;
From giddy change, by fancy bred;
From poisoned error's serpent head,
Good Lord, preserve us free!

3 Defend, O God, with guardian hand,
The laws and rulers of our land,
And grant thy churches grace to stand
In faith and unity!

4 Thy Spirit's help of thee we crave,
That thy Messiah, sent to save,
Returning to the world, might have
A people serving thee!
Reginald Heber, [1827] a.

940. Tune, "Autumn," p. 275. 8s & 7s.

1 Dread Jehovah! God of nations!
From thy temple in the skies,
Hear thy people's supplications;
Now for their deliverance rise.

2 Though our sins, our hearts confounding,
Long and loud for vengeance call,
Thou hast mercy more abounding:
Jesus' blood can cleanse them all.

3 Let that love veil our transgression;
Let that blood our guilt efface:
Save thy people from oppression;
Save from spoil thy holy place.

4 Lo! with deep contrition turning,
Humbly at thy feet we bend;
Hear us, fasting, praying, mourning,
Hear us, spare us, and defend!
C— F— 1804.

941. Tune, "Kent," p. 375. L. M.

1 O God of love, O King of peace,
Make wars throughout the world to cease;
The wrath of sinful man restrain,
Give peace, O God, give peace again.

2 Remember, Lord, thy works of old,
The wonders that our fathers told.
Remember not our sin's dark stain,
Give peace, O God, give peace again.

3 Whom shall we trust but thee, O Lord?
Where rest but on thy faithful word?
None ever called on thee in vain,
Give peace, O God, give peace again.

4 Where saints and angels dwell above,
All hearts are knit in holy love;
O bind us in that heavenly chain,
Give peace, O God, give peace again.
Sir H. W. Baker, 1861.

FAST. 377

DUNDEE. C. M.

1. See, gra-cious God, be - fore thy throne, Thy mourn-ing peo-ple bend!
'T is on thy sov-reign grace a - lone Our humble hopes do - pend.

942.
1 SEE, gracious God, before thy throne,
   Thy mourning people bend!
   'T is on thy sovereign grace alone
   Our humble hopes depend.

2 Tremendous judgments from thy hand
   Thy dreadful power display;
   Yet mercy spares this guilty land,
   And still we live to pray.

3 How changed, alas! are truths divine
   For error, guilt, and shame!
   What impious numbers, bold in sin,
   Disgrace the Christian name!

4 Oh turn us, turn us, mighty Lord,
   By thy resistless grace;
   Then shall our hearts obey thy word,
   And humbly seek thy face.

5 Then should insulting foes invade,
   We shall not sink in fear;
   Secure of never-failing aid,
   If God, our God, is near.
   Isaac Watts, 1709.

943.   PSALM 60.
1 LORD, thou hast scourged our guilty land,
   Behold thy people mourn;
   Shall vengeance ever guide thy hand?
   Shall mercy ne'er return?

2 Beneath the terrors of thine eye,
   Earth's haughty towers decay;
   Thy frowning mantle spreads the sky,
   And mortals melt away.

3 Our Zion trembles at the stroke,
   And dreads thy lifted hand;
   Oh heal the people thou hast broke,
   And save the sinking land.

4 Attend our armies to the fight,
   And be their guardian God;
   In vain shall numerous powers unite
   Against thy lifted rod.

5 Our troops, beneath thy guiding hand,
   Shall gain a glad renown:
   'T is God who makes the feeble stand,
   And treads the mighty down.
   Isaac Watts, 1719. a.

944.
1 IN grief and fear, to thee, O Lord,
   For succor now we fly;
   Thine awful judgments are abroad,
   Oh shield us lest we die.

2 The fell disease on every side
   Walks forth with tainted breath;
   And pestilence, with rapid stride,
   Bestrews the land with death.

3 Oh look with pity on the scene
   Of sadness and of dread,
   And let thine angel stand between
   The living and the dead.

4 With contrite hearts to thee, our King,
   We turn, who oft have strayed;
   Accept the sacrifice we bring,
   And let the plague be stayed.
   William Bullock, 1854.

THANKSGIVING.

HARVEST HOME. 7s. Double.

1. Come, ye thankful people, come, Raise the song of Harvest-home! All is safely gathered in, Ere the winter storms begin; God our Maker doth provide For our wants to be supplied: Come to God's own temple, come, Raise the song of Harvest-home!

945.

2 We ourselves are God's own field,
Fruit unto his praise to yield;
Wheat and tares together sown,
Unto joy or sorrow grown:
First the blade, and then the ear,
Then the full corn shall appear:
Grant, O harvest Lord, that we
Wholesome grain and pure may be!

3 For the Lord our God shall come,
And shall take his harvest home;
From his field shall in that day
All offences purge away;
Give his angels charge at last
In the fire the tares to cast;
But the fruitful ears to store
In his garner evermore.

4 Then, thou church triumphant come,
Raise the song of Harvest-home!
All are safely gathered in,
Free from sorrow, free from sin,
There, forever purified,
In God's garner to abide:
Come, ten thousand angels, come,
Raise the glorious Harvest-home!

Henry Alford, 1865.

946.

1 Praise to God, immortal praise,
For the love that crowns our days!
Bounteous source of every joy,
Let thy praise our tongues employ.

2 For the blessings of the field,
For the stores the gardens yield;
For the fruits in full supply,
Ripened 'neath the summer sky,

3 Flocks that whiten all the plain;
Yellow sheaves of ripened grain;
Clouds that drop their fattening dews;
Suns that temperate warmth diffuse:

4 All that spring with bounteous hand
Scatters o'er the smiling land;
All that liberal autumn pours
From her rich o'erflowing stores:

5 These to thee, my God, we owe,
Source whence all our blessings flow;
And for these my soul shall raise
Grateful vows and solemn praise.

Anna Lætitia Barbauld, 1773. a.

THANKSGIVING.

SHOEL. L. M.

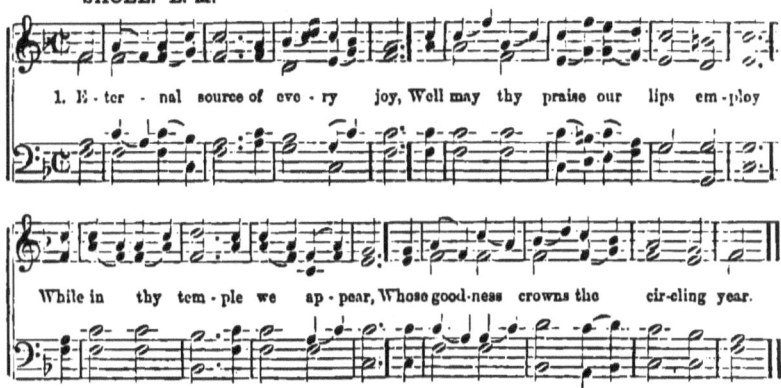

1. E-ter-nal source of eve-ry joy, Well may thy praise our lips em-ploy
While in thy tem-ple we ap-pear, Whose good-ness crowns the cir-cling year.

947.

1 ETERNAL Source of every joy,
Well may thy praise our lips employ
While in thy temple we appear,
Whose goodness crowns the circling year.

2 The flowery spring, at thy command,
Embalms the air and paints the land;
The summer rays with vigor shine,
To raise the corn and cheer the vine.

3 Thy hand in autumn richly pours
Through all our coasts redundant stores;
And winters, softened by thy care,
No more a face of horror wear.

4 Seasons, and months, and weeks, and days,
Demand successive songs of praise;
Still be the cheerful homage paid,
With opening light and evening shade.

5 Oh may our more harmonious tongue
In worlds unknown pursue the song;
And in those brighter courts adore,
Where days and years revolve no more!

Philip Doddridge, 1755.

948.

1 GOD of the world, near and afar
Thy glories shine in earth and star;
We see thy love in opening flower,
In distant orb thy wondrous power.

2 God of the harvest, sun and shower
Own the high mandate of thy power;
Plenty her rich profusion strews
When thou dost bid or want her woes.

3 God of our lives, the throbbing heart
Doth at thy beck its action start,
Throbs on, obedient to thy will,
Or ceases at thy fatal chill.

4 God of eternal life, thy love
Doth every stain of sin remove;
To thine exalted Son shall come [home.
Earth's wandering tribes to find their

5 God of all goodness, to the skies
Our hearts in grateful anthems rise;
And to thy service shall be given
The rest of life, the whole of heaven.

S. S. Cutting, 1835.

949. Tune, "America," p. 374. 6s & 4s.

1 THE God of harvest praise;
Hands, hearts, and voices raise,
With sweet accord;
From field to garner throng,
Bearing your sheaves along,
And in your harvest song
Bless ye the Lord.

2 Yea, bless his holy name,
And your souls' thanks proclaim,
Through all the earth;
To glory in your lot
Is duty; but be not
God's benefits forgot
Amidst your mirth.

James Montgomery, 1825.

THE YEAR.

VARINA. C. M. DOUBLE.

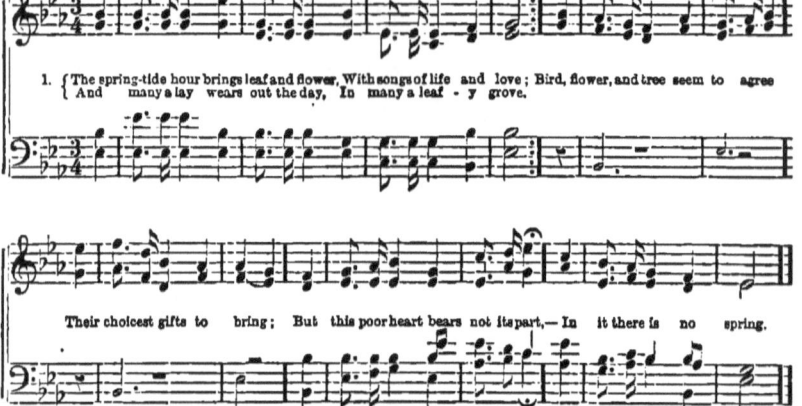

1. The spring-tide hour brings leaf and flower, With songs of life and love; Bird, flower, and tree seem to agree
   And many a lay wears out the day, In many a leaf-y grove.
   Their choicest gifts to bring; But this poor heart bears not its part,— In it there is no spring.

950.

1 The spring-tide hour brings leaf and
   With songs of life and love; [flower,
   And many a lay wears out the day
   In many a leafy grove.
   Bird, flower, and tree seem to agree
   Their choicest gifts to bring;
   But this poor heart bears not its part,—
   In it there is no spring.

2 Dews fall apace, the dews of grace,
   Upon this soul of sin,
   And love divine delights to shine
   Upon the waste within:
   Yet, year by year, fruits, flowers, appear,
   And birds their praises sing;
   But this poor heart bears not its part,—
   Its winter has no spring.

3 Lord, let thy love, fresh from above,
   Soft as the south-wind blow;
   Call forth its bloom, wake its perfume,
   And bid its spices flow:
   And when thy voice makes earth rejoice,
   And nature laugh and sing,
   Lord, make this heart to bear its part,
   And join the praise of spring.
   John S. B. Monsell, 1850.

951. Tune, "Ariel," p. 220. C. P. M.

1 Thy mighty working, mighty God,
   Wakes all my powers; I look abroad,
     And can no longer rest;
   I, too, must sing when all things sing,
   And from my heart the praises ring
     The Highest loveth best.

2 If thou, in thy great love to us,
   Wilt scatter joy and beauty thus
     O'er this poor earth of ours;
   What nobler glories shall be given
   Hereafter in thy shining heaven,
     Set round with golden towers!

3 What thrilling joy, when on our sight
   Christ's garden beams in cloudless light,
     Where all the air is sweet;
   Still laden with th' unwearied hymn
   From all the thousand seraphim
     Who God's high praise repeat!

4 Oh were I there! oh that I now
   Before thy throne, my God, could bow,
     And bear my heavenly palm!
   Then, like the angels, would I raise
   My voice, and sing thine endless praise
     In many a sweet-toned psalm.
   Paul Gerhardt, 1659; tr. by C. Winkworth, 1855.

THE YEAR.

NEWBOLD. C. M.

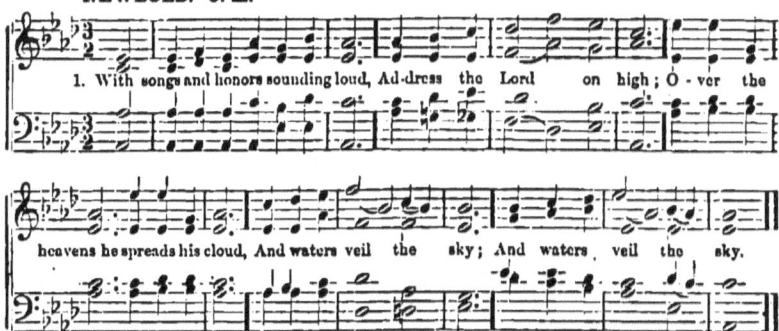

1. With songs and honors sounding loud, Address the Lord on high; Over the heavens he spreads his cloud, And waters veil the sky; And waters veil the sky.

952. Psalm 147.

1 WITH songs and honors sounding loud,
  Address the Lord on high;
  Over the heavens he spreads his cloud,
  And waters veil the sky.

2 He sends his showers of blessings down
  To cheer the plains below;
  He makes the grass the mountains crown,
  And corn in valleys grow.

3 His hoary frost, his fleecy snow,
  Descend and clothe the ground;
  The liquid streams forbear to flow,
  In icy fetters bound.

4 He sends his word and melts the snow,
  The fields no longer mourn;
  He calls the warmer gales to blow,
  And bids the spring return.

5 The changing wind, the flying cloud,
  Obey his mighty word:
  With songs and honors sounding loud,
  Praise ye the sovereign Lord!
  Isaac Watts, 1719.

953.

1 FOUNTAIN of mercy, God of love,
  How rich thy bounties are!
  The rolling seasons, as they move,
  Proclaim thy constant care.

2 When in the bosom of the earth
  The sower hid the grain,
  Thy goodness marked its secret birth,
  And sent the early rain.

3 The spring's sweet influence was thine,
  The plants in beauty grew;
  Thou gav'st refulgent suns to shine,
  And mild refreshing dew.

4 These various mercies from above
  Matured the swelling grain;
  A yellow harvest crowns thy love,
  And plenty fills the plain.

5 Seed-time and harvest, Lord, alone
  Thou dost on man bestow;
  Let him not then forget to own
  From whom his blessings flow.

6 Fountain of love, our praise is thine;
  To thee our songs we'll raise,
  And all created nature join
  In sweet harmonious praise.
  Anne Flowerdew, 1811.

954.

1 LORD, in thy name thy servants plead,
  And thou hast sworn to hear;
  Thine is the harvest, thine the seed,
  The fresh and fading year.

2 The former and the latter rain,
  The summer sun and air,
  The green ear and the golden grain,
  All thine, are ours by prayer.

3 Thine too by right, and ours by grace,
  The wondrous growth unseen, [brace,
  The hopes that soothe, the fears that
  The love that shines serene.

4 So grant the precious things brought forth
  By sun and shade below,
  That thee in thy new heaven and earth
  We never may forego.
  John Keble, 1857.

THE YEAR

STONEFIELD. L. M.

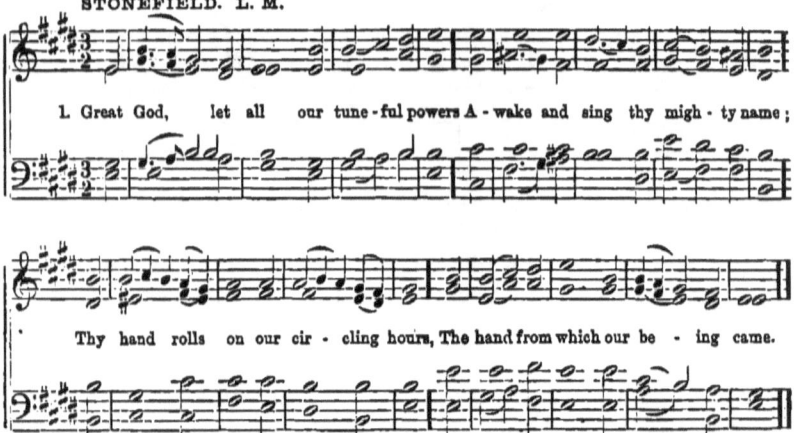

1. Great God, let all our tune-ful powers A-wake and sing thy migh-ty name;
Thy hand rolls on our cir-cling hours, The hand from which our be-ing came.

955.

1 Great God, let all our tuneful powers
  Awake and sing thy mighty name;
  Thy hand rolls on our circling hours,
  The hand from which our being came.

2 Seasons and moons, revolving round
  In beauteous order, speak thy praise,
  And years, with smiling mercy crowned,
  To thee successive honors raise.

3 Each changing season on our souls
  Its sweetest, kindest influence sheds;
  And every period, as it rolls, [heads.
  Showers countless blessings on our

4 Our lives, our health, our friends, we owe
  All to thy vast, unbounded love;
  Ten thousand precious gifts below,
  And hopes of nobler joys above.
  Ottiwell Heginbotham, 1768-1794.

956.

1 My helper, God, I bless his name;
  The same his power, his grace the same;
  The tokens of his friendly care
  Open, and crown, and close the year.

2 I 'midst ten thousand dangers stand,
  Supported by his guardian hand;
  And see, when I survey my ways,
  Ten thousand monuments of praise.

3 Thus far his arm has led me on,
  Thus far I make his mercy known;
  And while I tread this desert land,
  New mercies shall new songs demand.

4 My grateful soul on Jordan's shore
  Shall raise one sacred pillar more;
  Then bear, in his bright courts above,
  Inscriptions of immortal love.
  Philip Doddridge, 1755.

957.

1 Great God, we sing that mighty hand
  By which supported still we stand:
  The opening year thy mercy shows;
  That mercy crowns it till it close.

2 By day, by night, at home, abroad,
  Still are we guarded by our God;
  By his incessant bounty fed,
  By his unerring counsel led.

3 With grateful hearts the past we own;
  The future, all to us unknown,
  We to thy guardian care commit,
  And peaceful leave before thy feet.

4 In scenes exalted or deprest,
  Thou art our joy, and thou our rest;
  Thy goodness all our hopes shall raise,
  Adored through all our changing days.
  Philip Doddridge, 1755.

THE YEAR.

MORTALITY. C. M.

1. Thee we adore, Eternal Name, And humbly own to thee
How feeble is our mortal frame, What dying worms are we.

958.

1 THEE we adore, Eternal Name,
    And humbly own to thee
How feeble is our mortal frame,
    What dying worms are we.

2 The year rolls round, and steals away
    The breath that first it gave;
Whate'er we do, where'er we be,
    We're travelling to the grave.

3 Great God, on what a slender thread
    Hang everlasting things!
The eternal state of all the dead
    Upon life's feeble strings!

4 Infinite joy or endless woe
    Attends on every breath;
And yet how unconcerned we go
    Upon the brink of death!

5 Waken, O Lord, our drowsy sense,
    To walk this dangerous road;
And if our souls are hurried hence,
    May they be found with God.
Isaac Watts, 1709.

959.

1 AWAKE, ye saints, and raise your eyes,
    And raise your voices high;
Awake, and praise that sovereign love
    That shows salvation nigh.

2 On all the wings of time it flies;
    Each moment brings it near:
Then welcome each declining day,
    Welcome each closing year.

3 Not many years their rounds shall run,
    Nor many mornings rise,
Ere all its glories stand revealed
    To our admiring eyes.

4 Ye wheels of nature, speed your course!
    Ye mortal powers, decay!
Fast as ye bring the night of death,
    Ye bring eternal day!
Philip Doddridge, 1755.

960.

1 Now, gracious Lord, thine arm reveal,
    And make thy glory known;
Now let us all thy presence feel,
    And soften hearts of stone.

2 Help us to venture near thy throne,
    And plead a Saviour's name;
For all that we can call our own
    Is vanity and shame.

3 From all the guilt of former sin
    May mercy set us free;
And let the year we now begin,
    Begin and end with thee.

4 Send down thy Spirit from above,
    That saints may love thee more,
And sinners now may learn to love
    Who never loved before.

5 And when before thee we appear,
    In our eternal home,
May growing numbers worship here,
    And praise thee in our room.
John Newton, 1779.

THE YEAR.

BENEVENTO. 7s. DOUBLE.

1. While with cease-less course the sun Hasted through the for-mer year,
Ma-ny souls their race have run, Nev-er more to meet us here:
We a lit-tle lon-ger wait, But how lit-tle, none can know.
Fixed in an e-ter-nal state, They have done with all be-low;

961.

1 WHILE with ceaseless course the sun
　Hasted through the former year,
Many souls their race have run,
　Never more to meet us here:
Fixed in an eternal state,
　They have done with all below;
We a little longer wait,
　But how little, none can know.

2 As the wingéd arrow flies
　Speedily the mark to find;
As the lightning from the skies
　Darts, and leaves no trace behind;
Swiftly thus our fleeting days
　Bear us down life's rapid stream:
Upward, Lord, our spirits raise!
　All below is but a dream.

3 Thanks for mercies past receive;
　Pardon of our sins renew;
Teach us, henceforth, how to live
　With eternity in view.
Bless thy word to young and old;
　Fill us with a Saviour's love;
And, when life's short tale is told,
　May we dwell with thee above!
　　　　　　　John Newton, 1779.

962.

1 FOR thy mercy and thy grace,
　Faithful through another year,
Hear our songs of thankfulness,
　Father and Redeemer, hear.

2 In our weakness and distress,
　Rock of strength, be thou our stay;
In the pathless wilderness
　Be our true and living way.

3 Who of us death's awful road
　In the coming year shall tread?
With thy rod and staff, O God,
　Comfort thou his dying head.

4 Keep us faithful, keep us pure;
　Keep us evermore thine own;
Help, oh help us to endure;
　Fit us for the promised crown.

5 So within thy palace gate
　We shall praise, on golden strings,
Thee, the only Potentate,
　Lord of lords and King of kings!
　　　　　　Henry Downton, 1851.

DOXOLOGY.

SING we to our God above
Praise eternal as his love;
Praise him, all ye heavenly host;
Father, Son, and Holy Ghost.

THE YEAR.

NEW YEAR'S HYMN. 11s & 6s.

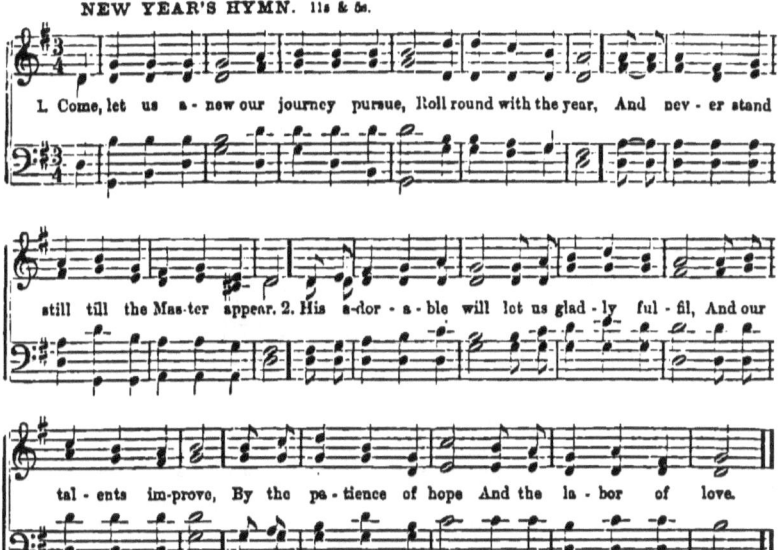

1. Come, let us anew our journey pursue, Roll round with the year, And never stand still till the Master appear. 2. His adorable will let us gladly fulfil, And our talents improve, By the patience of hope And the labor of love.

963.

1 COME, let us anew our journey pursue,
    Roll round with the year,
And never stand still till the Master appear.

2 His adorable will let us gladly fulfil,
    And our talents improve,
By the patience of hope and the labor of love.

3 Our life is a dream; our time as a stream
    Glides swiftly away,
And the fugitive moment refuses to stay.

4 The arrow is flown, the moment is gone;
    The millennial year
Rushes on to our view, and eternity's here.

5 Oh that each in the day of his coming may say,
    "I have fought my way through;
I have finished the work thou didst give me to do."

6 Oh that each from his Lord may receive the glad word,
    "Well and faithfully done!
Enter into my joy, and sit down on my throne."

Charles Wesley, 1750.

LIFE AND DEATH.

HAMBURG. L. M.

1. Through every age, eternal God, Thou art our rest, our safe abode; High was thy throne ere heaven was made, Or earth, thy humble footstool, laid.

964. PSALM 90.

1 THROUGH every age, eternal God,
Thou art our rest, our safe abode;
High was thy throne ere heaven was made,
Or earth, thy humble footstool, laid.

2 Long hadst thou reigned ere time began,
Or dust was fashioned into man;
And long thy kingdom shall endure,
When earth and time shall be no more.

3 But man, weak man, is born to die,
Made up of guilt and vanity:
Thy dreadful sentence, Lord, was just,
"Return, ye sinners, to your dust."

4 Teach us, O Lord, how frail is man!
And kindly lengthen out our span,
Till a wise care of piety
Fit us to die and dwell with thee.
Isaac Watts, 1719.

965.

1 GOD of Eternity, from thee
Did infant time his being draw; [years,
Moments, and days, and months, and
Revolve by thy unvaried law.

2 Silent and slow they glide away;
Steady and strong the current flows;
Lost in eternity's wide sea,
The boundless gulf from whence it rose.

3 With it the thoughtless sons of men
Before the rapid streams are borne
On to that everlasting home,
Whence not one soul can e'er return.

4 Yet, while the shore on either side
Presents a gaudy, flattering show,
We gaze, in fond amazement lost,
Nor think to what a world we go.

5 Great Source of wisdom! teach my heart
To know the price of every hour;
That time may bear me on to joys
Beyond its measure and its power.
Philip Doddridge, 1755.

966. PSALM 39.

1 ALMIGHTY Maker of my frame,
Teach me the measure of my days;
Teach me to know how frail I am,
And spend the remnant to thy praise.

2 My days are shorter than a span,
A little point my life appears;
How frail at best is dying man!
How vain are all his hopes and fears!

3 Vain his ambition, noise, and show!
Vain are the cares which rack his mind!
He heaps up treasures mixed with woe,
And dies, and leaves them all behind.

4 Oh be a nobler portion mine!
My God! I bow before thy throne;
Earth's fleeting treasures I resign,
And fix my hope on thee alone.

5 Oh, spare me, and my strength restore,
Ere my few hasty minutes flee!
And when my days on earth are o'er,
Let me forever dwell with thee.
Anne Steele, 1760.

LIFE AND DEATH.

COMPTON. S. M.

1. To-morrow, Lord, is thine, Lodged in thy sovereign hand; And if its sun arise and shine, It shines by thy command.

967.

1 To-morrow, Lord, is thine,
  Lodged in thy sovereign hand;
  And if its sun arise and shine,
  It shines by thy command.

2 The present moment flies,
  And bears our life away;
  Oh make thy servants truly wise,
  That they may live to-day.

3 Since on this wingèd hour
  Eternity is hung,
  Waken by thine almighty power
  The aged and the young.

4 One thing demands our care:
  Oh be it still pursued;
  Lest, slighted once, the season fair
  Should never be renewed.

5 To Jesus may we fly,
  Swift as the morning light,
  Lest life's young golden beams should die
  In sudden, endless night.
  Philip Doddridge, 1755.

968.

1 One sweetly solemn thought
  Comes to me o'er and o'er,
  Nearer my parting hour am I
  Than e'er I was before.

2 Nearer my Father's house,
  Where many mansions be;
  Nearer the throne where Jesus reigns,
  Nearer the crystal sea;

3 Nearer my going home,
  Laying my burden down,

Leaving my cross of heavy grief,
  Wearing my starry crown;

4 Nearer that hidden stream,
  Winding through shades of night,
  Rolling its cold, dark waves between
  Me and the world of light.

5 Jesus! to thee I cling:
  Strengthen my arm of faith;
  Stay near me while my way-worn feet
  Press through the stream of death.
  Phœbe Cary, 1854. a.

969.

1 How swift the torrent rolls
  That bears us to the sea;
  The tide that bears our thoughtless souls
  To vast eternity!

2 Our fathers, where are they,
  With all they called their own?
  Their joys and griefs and hopes and cares,
  Their wealth and honor gone.

3 There, where the fathers lie,
  Must all their children dwell;
  Nor other heritage possess
  But such a gloomy cell.

4 God of our fathers, hear,
  Thou everlasting friend,
  While we as on life's utmost verge
  Our souls to thee commend.

5 Of all the pious dead
  May we the footsteps trace,
  Till, with them in the land of light,
  We dwell before thy face.
  Philip Doddridge, 1755.

LIFE AND DEATH.

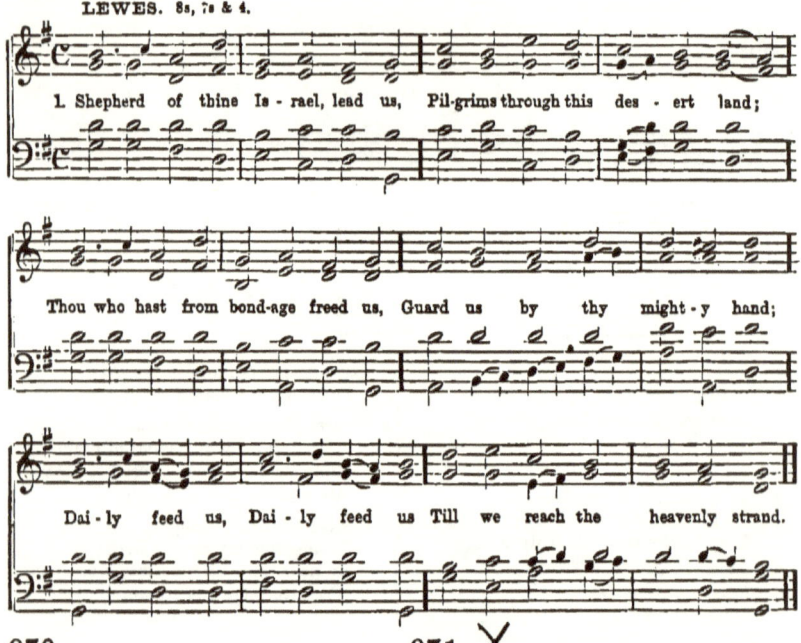

LEWES. 8s, 7s & 4.

1. Shepherd of thine Israel, lead us, Pilgrims through this desert land;
Thou who hast from bondage freed us, Guard us by thy mighty hand;
Daily feed us, Daily feed us Till we reach the heavenly strand.

970.

1 SHEPHERD of thine Israel, lead us,
    Pilgrims through this desert land;
Thou who hast from bondage freed us,
    Guard us by thy mighty hand;
        Daily feed us
Till we reach the heavenly strand.

2 As thou didst in wondrous manner
    Guide thy chosen flock aright,
Let thy presence be our banner,
    Cloud by day and fire by night;
        Thy protection
Be our shield, thy word our light.

3 When we come to Death's dark river,
    Should we dread the swelling tide,
Death of death, life's Source and Giver!
    Bid the narrow stream divide:
        Joyful praises
We will sing on Canaan's side.
Josiah Conder, 1854.

971. X

1 GUIDE me, O thou great Jehovah,
    Pilgrim through this barren land;
I am weak, but thou art mighty;
    Hold me with thy powerful hand;
        Bread of heaven!
Feed me now and evermore.

2 Open now the crystal fountain
    Whence the healing streams do flow;
Let the fiery cloudy pillar
    Lead me all my journey through;
        Strong deliverer!
Be thou still my Strength and Shield.

3 When I tread the verge of Jordan,
    Bid my anxious fears subside;
Death of death, and hell's Destruction,
    Land me safe on Canaan's side;
        Songs of praises
I will ever give to thee.
William Williams, 1773.

LIFE AND DEATH. 389

SHINING SHORE. P. M.

972.

1 My days are gliding swiftly by,
And I, a pilgrim stranger,
Would not detain them as they fly,
Those hours of toil and danger;
For now we stand on Jordan's strand;
Our friends are passing over,
And just before, the shining shore
We may almost discover.

2 Our absent King the watchword gave,
" Let every lamp be burning ; "
We look afar across the wave,
Our distant home discerning.
For now we stand on Jordan's strand, etc.

3 Should coming days be dark and cold,
We will not yield to sorrow,
For hope will sing, with courage bold,
" There's glory on the morrow :"
For now we stand on Jordan's strand, etc.

4 Let storms of woe in whirlwinds rise,
Each cord on earth to sever,
There, bright and joyous in the skies,
There, is our home forever :
For now we stand on Jordan's strand, etc.

David Nelson, a.

LIFE AND DEATH.

EVENTIDE. 10s.

1. Abide with me! Fast falls the even-tide; The darkness deepens; Lord, with me abide! When other helpers fail, and comforts flee, Help of the helpless, oh abide with me! Amen.

973.

1 ABIDE with me! Fast falls the eventide;
The darkness deepens; Lord, with me abide!
When other helpers fail, and comforts flee,
Help of the helpless, oh abide with me!

2 Swift to its close ebbs out life's little day;
Earth's joys grow dim, its glories pass away;
Change and decay in all around I see;
O thou who changest not, abide with me!

3 Come not in terrors, as the King of kings,
But kind and good, with healing in thy wings;
Tears for all woes, a heart for every plea:
Come, Friend of sinners, thus abide with me!

4 I need thy presence every passing hour;
What but thy grace can foil the tempter's power?
Who like thyself my guide and stay can be?
Through cloud and sunshine, oh abide with me!

5 I fear no foe, with thee at hand to bless;
Ills have no weight, and tears no bitterness:
Where is death's sting? where, grave, thy victory?
I triumph still, if thou abide with me.

6 Hold thou thy cross before my closing eyes;
Shine through the gloom, and point me to the skies;
Heaven's morning breaks, and earth's vain shadows flee!
In life, in death, O Lord, abide with me!

Henry F. Lyte, 1847.

CHANT.

LIFE AND DEATH.

STOCKWELL. 8s & 7s.

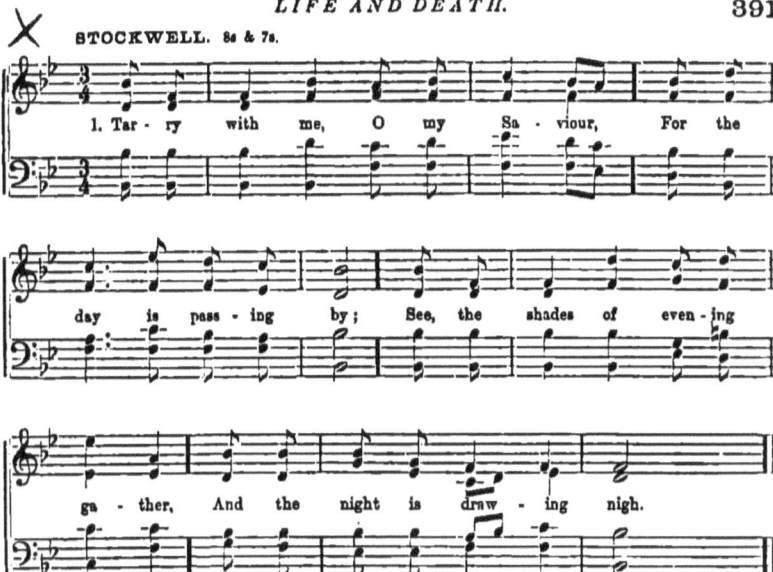

1. Tarry with me, O my Saviour, For the day is passing by; See, the shades of evening gather, And the night is drawing nigh.

974.

1 TARRY with me, O my Saviour,
For the day is passing by;
See, the shades of evening gather,
And the night is drawing nigh.

2 Deeper, deeper grow the shadows,
Paler now the glowing west;
Swift the night of death advances;
Shall it be the night of rest?

3 Feeble, trembling, fainting, dying,
Lord, I cast myself on thee;
Tarry with me through the darkness;
While I sleep, still watch by me.

4 Tarry with me, O my Saviour!
Lay my head upon thy breast
Till the morning, then awake me —
Morning of eternal rest!
Anon, 1858.

975.

1 HAPPY soul! thy days are ended,
All thy mourning days below;
Go, by angel guards attended,
To the sight of Jesus go!

2 Waiting to receive thy spirit,
Lo! the Saviour stands above;
Shows the purchase of his merit,
Reaches out the crown of love.

3 Struggle through thy latest passion
To thy dear Redeemer's breast,
To his uttermost salvation,
To his everlasting rest:

4 For the joy he sets before thee,
Bear a momentary pain;
Die, to live a life of glory;
Suffer, with thy Lord to reign.
Charles Wesley, 1747.

DOXOLOGY.

1 PRAISE the God of our salvation,
Praise the Father's boundless love;
Praise the Lamb, our expiation;
Praise the Spirit from above;

2 Praise the Fountain of salvation,
Him by whom our spirits live;
Undivided adoration
To the one Jehovah give!
Josiah Conder, 1836.

LIFE AND DEATH.

FREDERICK. 11s.

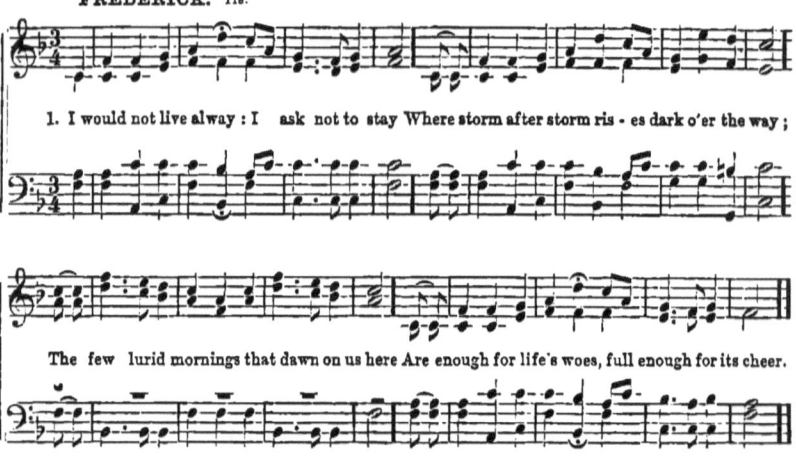

1. I would not live alway: I ask not to stay Where storm after storm ris-es dark o'er the way; The few lurid mornings that dawn on us here Are enough for life's woes, full enough for its cheer.

976.

1 I WOULD not live alway: I ask not to stay
  Where storm after storm rises dark o'er the way;
  The few lurid mornings that dawn on us here
  Are enough for life's woes, full enough for its cheer.

2 I would not live alway, thus fettered by sin —
  Temptation without and corruption within:
  E'en the rapture of pardon is mingled with fears,
  And the cup of thanksgiving with penitent tears.

3 I would not live alway; no, welcome the tomb;
  Since Jesus hath lain there, I dread not its gloom;
  There sweet be my rest, till he bid me arise
  To hail him in triumph descending the skies.

4 Who, who would live alway, away from his God,
  Away from yon heaven, that blissful abode,
  Where the rivers of pleasure flow o'er the bright plains,
  And the noontide of glory eternally reigns;

5 Where the saints of all ages in harmony meet,
  Their Saviour and brethren transported to greet;
  While the anthems of rapture unceasingly roll,
  And the smile of the Lord is the feast of the soul?

W. A. Muhlenberg, 1823.

LIFE AND DEATH.

WESTMINSTER ABBEY. L. M.

1. The hour of my departure's come; I hear the voice that calls me home; At last, O Lord, let trouble cease, And let thy servant die in peace.

977.

1 THE hour of my departure's come;
I hear the voice that calls me home;
At last, O Lord, let trouble cease,
And let thy servant die in peace.

2 The race appointed I have run,
The combat's o'er, the prize is won;
And now my witness is on high,
And now my record's in the sky.

3 Not in mine innocence I trust;
I bow before thee in the dust;
And through my Saviour's blood alone
I look for mercy at thy throne.

4 I leave the world without a tear,
Save for the friends I held so dear;
To heal their sorrows, Lord, descend,
And to the friendless prove a friend.

5 I come, I come, at thy command,
I yield my spirit to thy hand;
Stretch forth thine everlasting arms,
And shield me in the last alarms.

6 The hour of my departure's come:
I hear the voice that calls me home;
Now, O my God, let trouble cease!
Now let thy servant die in peace!
Michael Bruce, 1766.

978.

1 WHY should we start and fear to die?
What timorous worms we mortals are!
Death is the gate of endless joy,
And yet we dread to enter there.

2 The pains, the groans, and dying strife,
Fright our approaching souls away;
Still we shrink back again to life,
Fond of our prison and our clay.

3 Oh, if my Lord would come and meet,
My soul should stretch her wings in haste,
Fly fearless through death's iron gate,
Nor feel the terrors as she passed.

4 Jesus can make a dying bed
Feel soft as downy pillows are,
While on his breast I lean my head,
And breathe my life out sweetly there.
Isaac Watts, 1709.

979.

1 O GOD, thy grace and blessing give
To us, who on thy name attend,
That we this mortal life may live
Regardful of our journey's end.

2 Teach us to know that Jesus died,
And rose again, our souls to save;
Teach us to take him as our guide,
Our help from childhood to the grave.

3 Then shall not death with terror come,
But welcome as a bidden guest,
The herald of a better home,
The messenger of peace and rest.

4 And when the awful signs appear
Of judgment, and the throne above,
Our hearts still fixed, we shall not fear;
God is our trust, and God is love.
Anon. 1853.

LIFE AND DEATH.

NORTHAMPTON. C. M.

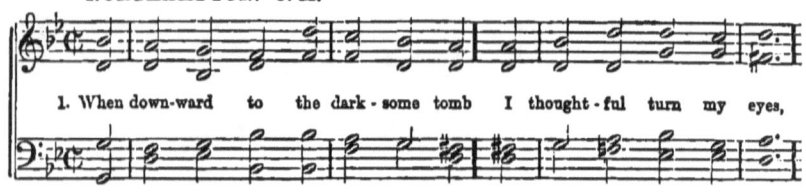
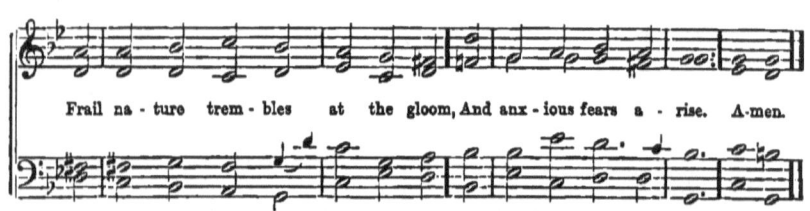

1. When downward to the darksome tomb I thoughtful turn my eyes, Frail nature trembles at the gloom, And anxious fears arise. A-men.

980.

1 When downward to the darksome tomb
　.I thoughtful turn my eyes,
Frail nature trembles at the gloom,
　And anxious fears arise.

2 Why shrinks my soul? In death's em-
　Once Jesus captive slept;　　[brace
And angels, hovering o'er the place,
　His lowly pillow kept.

3 Thus shall they guard my sleeping dust,
　And, as the Saviour rose,
The grave again shall yield her trust,
　And end my deep repose.

4 My Lord, before to glory gone,
　Shall bid me come away;　　[dawn
And calm and bright shall break the
　Of heaven's eternal day.

5 Then let my faith each fear dispel,
　And gild with light the grave;
To him my loftiest praises swell,
　Who died from death to save.
　　　　　　　Ray Palmer, 1858.

981.

1 When bending o'er the brink of life
　My trembling soul shall stand,
Waiting to pass death's awful flood,
　Great God, at thy command;

2 O thou great source of joy supreme,
　Whose arm alone can save,
Dispel the darkness that surrounds
　The entrance to the grave.

3 Lay thy supporting, gentle hand
　Beneath my sinking head,
And with a ray of love divine
　Illume my dying bed.
　　　　　　William B. Collyer, 1812.

982.

1 Oh for an overcoming faith
　To cheer my dying hours,
To triumph o'er the monster death,
　And all his frightful powers.

2 Joyful, with all the strength I have,
　My quivering lips should sing,
"Where is thy boasted victory, grave?
　And where the monster's sting?"

3 If sin be pardoned, I'm secure;
　Death hath no sting beside;
The law gives sin its damning power;
　But Christ, my ransom, died.

4 Now to the God of victory
　Immortal thanks be paid,
Who makes us conquerors while we die,
　Through Christ, our living head.
　　　　　　　Isaac Watts, 1709.

LIFE AND DEATH.

TRIUMPH. 7s & 6s.

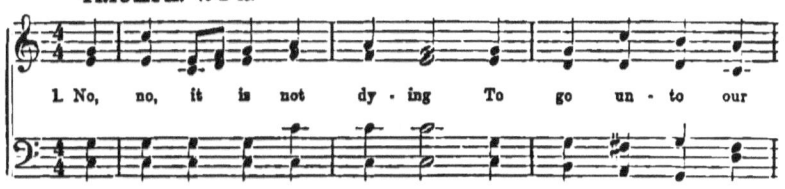
1. No, no, it is not dy-ing To go un-to our

God, This gloom-y earth for-sak-ing, Our

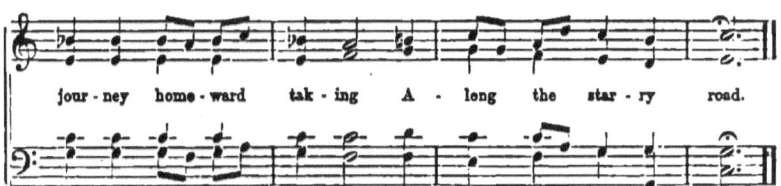
jour-ney home-ward tak-ing A-long the star-ry road.

983.

1 No, no, it is not dying
   To go unto our God,
   This gloomy earth forsaking,
   Our journey homeward taking
   Along the starry road.

2 No, no, it is not dying
   Heaven's citizen to be;
   A crown immortal wearing,
   And rest unbroken sharing,
   From care and conflict free.

3 No, no, it is not dying
   To hear this gracious word,
   "Receive a Father's blessing,
   For evermore possessing
   The favor of the Lord."

4 No, no, it is not dying
   The Shepherd's voice to know;
   His sheep he ever leadeth,
   His peaceful flock he feedeth,
   Where living pastures grow.

5 No, no, it is not dying
   To wear a lordly crown;
   Among God's people dwelling,
   The glorious triumph swelling
   Of him whose sway we own.

6 Oh, no, this is not dying,
   Thou Saviour of mankind!
   There streams of love are flowing,
   No hindrance ever knowing;
   Here, drops alone we find.

Cæsar Malan; tr. by R. P. Dunn, 1852.

LIFE AND DEATH.

PRAYER. S. M. DOUBLE.

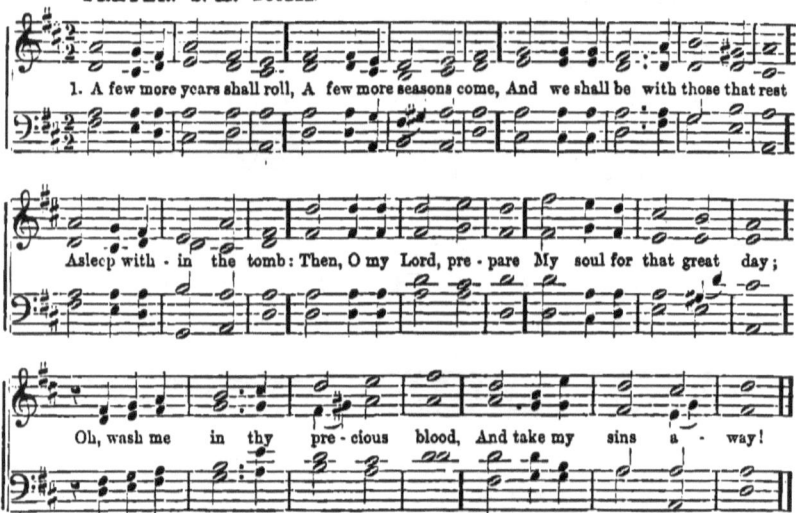

984.

1 A FEW more years shall roll,
   A few more seasons come,
And we shall be with those that rest
   Asleep within the tomb:
Then, O my Lord, prepare
   My soul for that great day;
Oh, wash me in thy precious blood,
   And take my sins away!

2 A few more suns shall set
   O'er these dark hills of time,
And we shall be where suns are not,
   A far serener clime.
Then, O my Lord, prepare
   My soul for that blest day;
Oh, wash me in thy precious blood,
   And take my sins away!

3 A few more struggles here,
   A few more partings o'er,
A few more toils, a few more tears,
   And we shall weep no more:
Then, O my Lord, prepare
   My soul for that bright day;
Oh, wash me in thy precious blood,
   And take my sins away!

4 'T is but a little while
   And he shall come again,
Who died that we might live, who lives
   That we with him may reign:
Then, O my Lord, prepare
   My soul for that glad day;
Oh, wash me in thy precious blood,
   And take my sins away!
                        Horatius Bonar, 1857.

985.

1 IT is not death to die —
   To leave this weary road,
And, 'mid the brotherhood on high,
   To be at home with God.

2 It is not death to close
   The eye long dimmed by tears,
And wake, in glorious repose
   To spend eternal years.

3 It is not death to fling
   Aside this sinful dust,
And rise, on strong exulting wing,
   To live among the just.

4 Jesus, thou Prince of life,
   Thy chosen cannot die;
Like thee, they conquer in the strife,
   To reign with thee on high.
                        George W. Bethune, 1847.

LIFE AND DEATH. 897

REST. L. M.

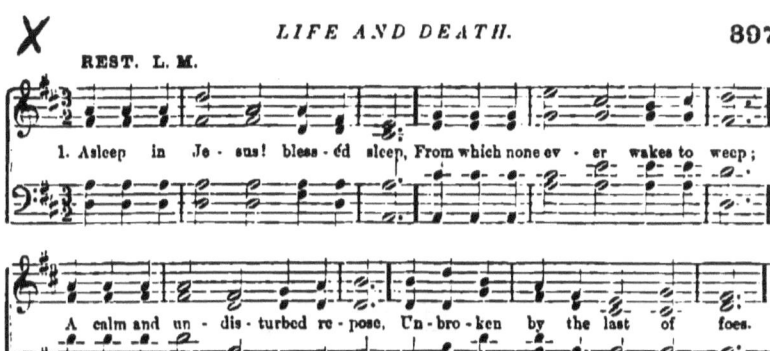

1. Asleep in Jesus! blessèd sleep, From which none ever wakes to weep; A calm and undisturbed repose, Unbroken by the last of foes.

986.

1 ASLEEP in Jesus! blessèd sleep,
From which none ever wakes to weep;
A calm and undisturbed repose,
Unbroken by the last of foes.

2 Asleep in Jesus! Oh, how sweet
To be for such a slumber meet!
With holy confidence to sing
That Death hath lost his venomed sting!

3 Asleep in Jesus! peaceful rest,
Whose waking is supremely blest:
No fear, no woe, shall dim that hour
That manifests the Saviour's power.

4 Asleep in Jesus! Oh, for me
May such a blissful refuge be:
Securely shall my ashes lie,
And wait the summons from on high.
Margaret Mackay, 1832.

987.

1 DEAREST of names, our Lord, our King!
Jesus, thy praise we humbly sing:
In cheerful songs we'll spend our breath,
And in thee triumph over death.

2 Death is no more among our foes,
Since Christ, the mighty Conqueror, rose;
Both power and sting the Saviour broke;
He died, and gave the finished stroke.

3 Saints die, and we should gently weep;
Sweetly in Jesus' arms they sleep;
Far from this world of sin and woe,
Nor sin, nor pain, nor grief, they know.

4 Death is a sleep; and oh how sweet
To souls prepared its stroke to meet!
Their dying beds, their graves, are blest,
For all to them is peace and rest.

5 Oh may I live with Jesus nigh,
And sleep in Jesus when I die!
Then, joyful, when from death I wake,
I shall eternal bliss partake.
Samuel Medley, 1790.

988.

1 GENTLY, my Saviour, let me down,
  To slumber in the arms of death;
I rest my soul on thee alone.
  E'en till my last expiring breath.

2 Soon will the storm of life be o'er,
  And I shall enter endless rest;
There I shall live to sin no more,
  And bless thy name, forever blest.

3 Bid me possess sweet peace within;
  Let childlike patience keep my heart;
Then shall I feel my heaven begin,
  Before my spirit hence depart.

4 Oh, speed thy chariot. God of love,
  And take me from this world of woe!
I long to reach those joys above,
  And bid farewell to all below.

5 There shall my raptured spirit raise
  Still louder notes than angels sing.
High glories to Immanuel's grace.
  My God, my Saviour, and my King!
Rowland Hill, 1796.

LIFE AND DEATH.

WYMAN'S CHANT. C. M.

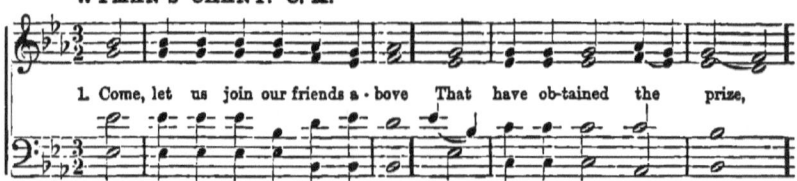

1. Come, let us join our friends above That have obtained the prize,

And on the ea-gle wings of love To joys ce-les-tial rise.

989.

1 COME, let us join our friends above,
   That have obtained the prize,
   And on the eagle wings of love
   To joys celestial rise.

2 Let all the saints terrestrial sing
   With those to glory gone,
   For all the servants of our King,
   In earth and heaven, are one.

3 One family, we dwell in him,
   One church, above, beneath,
   Though now divided by the stream,
   The narrow stream of death.

4 One army of the living God,
   To his command we bow;
   Part of his host hath crossed the flood,
   And part is crossing now.

5 His militant embodied host,
   With wishful looks we stand,
   And long to see that happy coast,
   And reach that heavenly land.

6 Oh that we now might grasp our Guide!
   Oh that the word were given!
   Come, Lord of hosts, the waves divide,
   And land us all in heaven!

Charles Wesley, 1759.

990.

1 YE golden lamps of heaven, farewell,
   With all your feeble light;
   Farewell, thou ever-changing moon,
   Pale empress of the night.

2 And thou, refulgent orb of day,
   In brighter flames arrayed;
   My soul, that springs beyond thy sphere,
   No more demands thine aid.

3 Ye stars are but the shining dust
   Of my divine abode,
   The pavement of those heavenly courts
   Where I shall reign with God.

4 The Father of eternal light
   Shall there his beams display,
   Nor shall one moment's darkness mix
   With that unvaried day.

5 No more the drops of piercing grief
   Shall swell into mine eyes,
   Nor the meridian sun decline
   Amid those brighter skies.

6 There all the millions of his saints
   Shall in one song unite,
   And each the bliss of all shall view
   With infinite delight.

Philip Doddridge, 1755.

LIFE AND DEATH.

MALDEN. S. M.

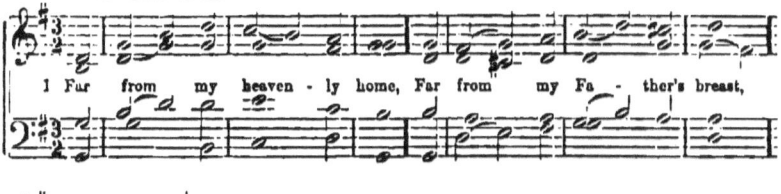
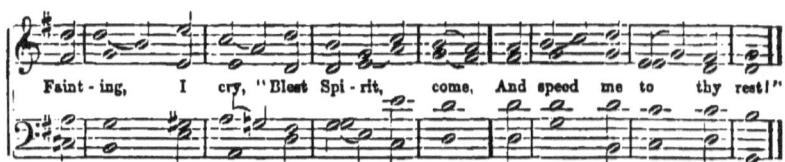

1 Far from my heaven-ly home, Far from my Fa-ther's breast,
Faint-ing, I cry, "Blest Spi-rit, come, And speed me to thy rest!"

991. PSALM 137.

1 FAR from my heavenly home,
　Far from my Father's breast,
Fainting, I cry, "Blest Spirit, come,
　And speed me to my rest!"

2 Upon the willows long
　My harp has silent hung;
How should I sing a cheerful song,
　Till thou inspire my tongue?

3 My spirit homeward turns,
　And fain would thither flee;
My heart, O Zion, droops and yearns,
　When I remember thee.

4 To thee, to thee I press,
　A dark and toilsome road:
When shall I pass the wilderness,
　And reach the saints' abode?

5 God of my life, be near;
　On thee my hopes I cast:
Oh, guide me through the desert here,
　And bring me home at last!
　　　　Henry F. Lyte, 1834.

992.

1 OH for the death of those
　Who slumber in the Lord!
Oh be like theirs my last repose,
　Like theirs my last reward!

2 Their bodies in the ground,
　In silent hope, may lie.
Till the last trumpet's joyful sound
　Shall call them to the sky.

3 Their ransomed spirits soar,
　On wings of faith and love.
To meet the Saviour they adore,
　And reign with him above.

4 With us their names shall live
　Through long-succeeding years,
Embalmed with all our hearts can give.
　Our praises and our tears.

5 Oh for the death of those
　Who slumber in the Lord!
Oh be like theirs my last repose,
　Like theirs my last reward!
　　　　Anon.

993.

1 FOR all thy saints, O God,
　Who strove in Christ to live,
Who followed him, obeyed, adored,
　Our grateful hymn receive.

2 For all thy saints, O God,
　Accept our thankful cry,
Who counted Christ their great reward,
　And yearned for him to die.

3 They all, in life and death,
　With him, their Lord, in view,
Learned from thy Holy Spirit's breath
　To suffer and to do.

4 For this thy name we bless,
　And humbly pray that we
May follow them in holiness,
　And live and die in thee.
　　　　Richard Mant, 1849. a.

LIFE AND DEATH.

CHINA. C. M.

1. Why do we mourn departing friends, Or shake at death's alarms? 'Tis but the voice that Jesus sends To call them to his arms.

994.

1 Why do we mourn departing friends,
  Or shake at death's alarms?
  'Tis but the voice that Jesus sends
  To call them to his arms.

2 Are we not tending upward too,
  As fast as time can move?
  Nor would we wish the hours more slow,
  To keep us from our Love.

3 Why should we tremble to convey
  Their bodies to the tomb?
  There the dear flesh of Jesus lay,
  And left a long perfume.

4 The graves of all his saints he blessed,
  And softened every bed;
  Where should the dying members rest
  But with the dying Head?

5 Thence he arose, ascending high,
  And showed our feet the way:
  Up to the Lord our flesh shall fly
  At the great rising day.

6 Then let the last loud trumpet sound,
  And bid our kindred rise;
  Awake, ye nations under ground,
  Ye saints, ascend the skies!
  Isaac Watts, 1709.

995.

1 Now let our mourning hearts revive,
  And all our tears be dry;   [grief,
  Why should those eyes be drowned in
  Which view a Saviour nigh?

2 What though the arm of conquering death
  Does God's own house invade?
  What though the prophet and the priest
  Be numbered with the dead?

3 Though earthly shepherds dwell in dust,
  The aged and the young,
  The watchful eye in darkness closed,
  And mute th' instructive tongue:

4 Th' eternal Shepherd still survives,
  New comfort to impart;
  His eye still guides us, and his voice
  Still animates our heart.

5 Lo, I am with you! saith the Lord;
  My church shall safe abide;
  For I will ne'er forsake my own,
  Whose souls in me confide.
  Philip Doddridge, 1736.

996.   Rev. xiv. 13.

1 Hear what the voice from heaven pro-
  For all the pious dead;   [claims
  Sweet is the savor of their names,
  And soft their sleeping bed.

2 They die in Jesus, and are blessed;
  How kind their slumbers are!
  From sufferings and from sin released,
  And freed from every snare.

3 Far from this world of toil and strife,
  They're present with the Lord;
  The labors of their mortal life
  End in a large reward.
  Isaac Watts, 1707.

LIFE AND DEATH.

TRANQUILLITY. S. H. M.

1. Friend af-ter friend de-parts; Who hath not lost a friend?

There is no un-ion here of hearts That finds not here an end:

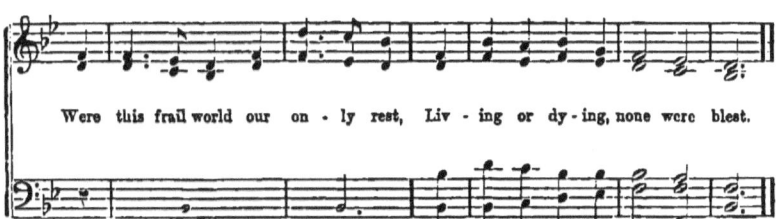

Were this frail world our on-ly rest, Liv-ing or dy-ing, none were blest.

997.

1 FRIEND after friend departs;
  Who hath not lost a friend?
There is no union here of hearts
  That finds not here an end:
Were this frail world our only rest,
Living or dying, none were blest.

2 Beyond the flight of time,
  Beyond this vale of death,
There surely is some blessed clime,
  Where life is not a breath,
Nor life's affections transient fire,
Whose sparks fly upwards to expire.

3 There is a world above,
  Where parting is unknown;
A whole eternity of love,
  Formed for the good alone:
And faith beholds the dying here
Translated to that happier sphere.

4 Thus star by star declines
  Till all are passed away,
As morning high and higher shines
  To pure and perfect day:
Nor sink those stars in empty night;
They hide themselves in heaven's own
  light!

James Montgomery, 1824.

LIFE AND DEATH.

STATE STREET. S. M.

1. Servant of God, well done! Rest from thy loved employ; The battle fought, the victory won, Enter thy Master's joy!

998.

1 Servant of God, well done!
  Rest from thy loved employ;
  The battle fought, the victory won,
  Enter thy Master's joy!

2 The voice at midnight came;
  He started up to hear;
  A mortal arrow pierced his frame;
  He fell, but felt no fear.

3 At midnight came the cry,
  "To meet thy God prepare!"
  He woke, and caught his Captain's eye;
  Then, strong in faith and prayer,

4 His spirit with a bound
  Left its encumbering clay:
  His tent, at sunrise, on the ground
  A darkened ruin lay.

5 The pains of death are past,
  Labor and sorrow cease,
  And, life's long warfare closed at last,
  His soul is found in peace.

6 Soldier of Christ, well done!
  Praise be thy new employ;
  And, while eternal ages run,
  Rest in thy Saviour's joy!

James Montgomery, 1825.

999. Tune, "Scotland," p. 373. 12s & 11s.

1 Thou art gone to the grave! but we will not deplore thee,
  Though sorrows and darkness encompass the tomb,
  The Saviour hath passed through its portals before thee,
  And the lamp of his love is thy guide through the gloom.

2 Thou art gone to the grave! we no longer behold thee,
  Nor tread the rough paths of the world by thy side;
  But the wide arms of mercy are spread to enfold thee,
  And sinners may hope, for the Sinless hath died.

3 Thou art gone to the grave! and, its mansion forsaking,
  Perchance thy weak spirit in doubt lingered long;
  But the sunshine of glory beamed bright on thy waking,
  And full on thy ear burst the seraphim's song.

4 Thou art gone to the grave! but we will not deplore thee,
  Since God was thy ransom, thy guardian, and guide:
  He gave thee, he took thee, and he will restore thee;
  And death has no sting, for the Saviour hath died.

Reginald Heber, 1812.

LIFE AND DEATH. 403

SAUL. L. M. 6 lines.

1. Un-veil thy bo-som, faith-ful tomb, Take this new trea-sure to thy trust, And give these sa-cred rel-ics room To seek a slum-ber in the dust, And give these sacred rel-ics room To seek a slumber in the dust.

1000.

1 UNVEIL thy bosom, faithful tomb,
  Take this new treasure to thy trust;
  And give these sacred relics room
  To seek a slumber in the dust.

2 Nor pain, nor grief, nor anxious fear
  Invades thy bounds; no mortal woes
  Can reach the peaceful sleepers here,
  And angels watch their soft repose.

3 So Jesus slept; God's dying Son
  Passed through the grave and blessed the bed;
  Rest here, dear saint, till from his throne
  The morning break, and pierce the shade.

4 Break from his throne, illustrious morn!
  Attend, O earth, his sovereign word;
  Restore thy trust, a glorious form;
  He must ascend to meet his Lord.
  Isaac Watts, 1734.

1001.

1 WE sing his love who once was slain,
  Who soon o'er death revived again,
  That all his saints through him might
  Eternal conquests o'er the grave: [have
    Soon shall the trumpet sound, and we
    Shall rise to immortality.

2 The saints who now with Jesus sleep,
  His own almighty power shall keep,
  Till dawns the bright illustrious day
  When death itself shall die away:
    Soon shall the trumpet sound, and we
    Shall rise to immortality.

3 How loud shall our glad voices sing
  When Christ his risen saints shall bring,
  From beds of dust and silent clay,
  To realms of everlasting day!
    Soon shall the trumpet sound, and we
    Shall rise to immortality.

4 When Jesus we in glory meet,
  Our utmost joys shall be complete;
  When landed on that heavenly shore,
  Death and the curse will be no more:
    Soon shall the trumpet sound, and we
    Shall rise to immortality.

5 Hasten, dear Lord, the glorious day,
  And this delightful scene display,
  When all thy saints from death shall rise
  Raptured in bliss beyond the skies!
    Soon shall the trumpet sound, and we
    Shall rise to immortality.
  Rowland Hill, 1796.

LIFE AND DEATH.

MEINHOLD. 7s, 8s & 7s.

1. Tender Shepherd, thou hast stilled Now thy little lamb's brief weeping: Ah, how peaceful, pale, and mild, In its narrow bed 't is sleeping, And no sigh of anguish sore Heaves that little bosom more!

1002.

1 TENDER Shepherd, thou hast stilled
  Now thy little lamb's brief weeping:
Ah, how peaceful, pale, and mild,
  In its narrow bed 't is sleeping,
And no sigh of anguish sore
Heaves that little bosom more!

2 In this world of care and pain,
  Lord, thou wouldst no longer leave it;
To the sunny heavenly plain
  Thou dost now with joy receive it:
Clothed in robes of spotless white,
Now it dwells with thee in light.

3 Ah, Lord Jesus, grant that we
  Where it lives may soon be living,
And the lovely pastures see
  That its heavenly food are giving:
Then the gain of death we prove,
Though thou take what most we love.

J. W. Meinhold, 1797-1851; tr. by C. Winkworth, 1856.

1003. Tune, "Pilgrimage," p. 416. L. M.

1 How blest the righteous when he dies,
  When sinks a weary soul to rest,
How mildly beam the closing eyes,
  How gently heaves the expiring breast!

2 So fades a summer cloud away;
  So sinks the gale when storms are o'er;
So gently shuts the eye of day;
  So dies a wave along the shore.

3 A holy quiet reigns around,
  A calm which life nor death destroys;
And naught disturbs that peace profound
  Which his unfettered soul enjoys.

4 Farewell, conflicting hopes and fears,
  Where lights and shades alternate dwell;
How bright the unchanging morn appears!
  Farewell, inconstant world, farewell!

5 Life's labor done, as sinks the clay,
  Light from its load the spirit flies,
While heaven and earth combine to say,
  " How blest the righteous when he dies!"

Anna L. Barbauld, 1773.

LIFE AND DEATH.

HOPE. 7s. 6 lines.

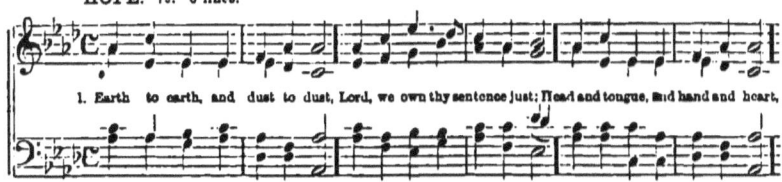

1004.

1 Earth to earth, and dust to dust, —
Lord, we own thy sentence just:
Head and tongue, and hand and heart,
All in guilt have borne their part;
Righteous is the common doom, —
All must moulder in the tomb.

2 Lord, from nature's gloomy night
Turn we to the gospel's light;
Thou didst triumph o'er the grave,
Thou wilt all thy people save;
Ransomed by thy blood, the just
Rise immortal from the dust.

John H. Gurney, 1838.

1005.

1 Thou whose never-failing arm
Led me all my earthly way,
Brought me out of every harm
Safely to my closing day;
  Thou in whom I now believe,
  Jesus, Lord, my soul receive.

2 From this state of sin and pain,
From this world of grief and strife,
From this body's mortal chain.
From this weak, imperfect life;
  Thou in whom I now believe,
  Jesus, Lord, my soul receive.

3 To the mansions of thy love,
To the spirits of the just,
To the angel hosts above,
To thyself, my only trust;
  Thou in whom I now believe,
  Jesus, Lord, my soul receive.

Henry F. Lyte, 1834.

1006.   Tune, "Pleyel's," p. 314.   7s.

1 Christ will gather in his own
To the place where he is gone.
Where the heart and treasure lie,
Where our life is hid on high.

2 Day by day the voice saith, "Come,
Enter thine eternal home;"
Asking not if we can spare
This dear soul it summons there.

3 Had he asked us, well we know
We should cry, "Oh spare this blow!"
Yes, with streaming tears should pray,
"Lord, we love him, let him stay."

4 But the Lord doth naught amiss,
And, since he has ordered this,
We have naught to do but still
Rest in silence on his will.

5 Many a heart no longer here,
Ah! was all too inly dear;
Yet, O Love, 't is thou dost call,
Thou wilt be our All in all.

Count Zinzendorf; tr. by C. Winkworth, 1853.

CHRIST'S SECOND COMING.

BRIDEGROOM. C. M.

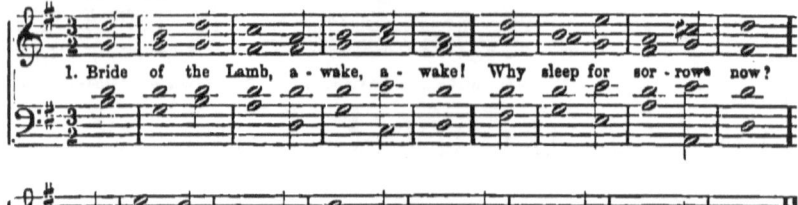
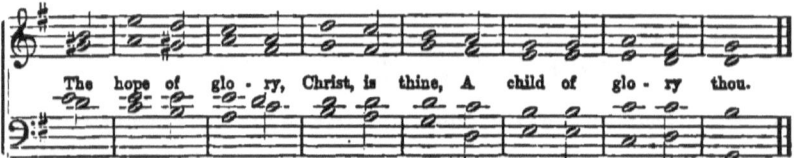

1. Bride of the Lamb, a-wake, a-wake! Why sleep for sor-rows now? The hope of glo-ry, Christ, is thine, A child of glo-ry thou.

1007.

1 BRIDE of the Lamb, awake, awake!
 Why sleep for sorrow now?
 The hope of glory, Christ, is thine,
 A child of glory thou.

2 Thy spirit, through the lonely night,
 From earthly joy apart,
 Hath sighed for one that's far away,—
 The Bridegroom of thy heart.

3 But see! the night is waning fast,
 The breaking morn is near;
 And Jesus comes, with voice of love,
 Thy drooping heart to cheer.

4 He comes — for, oh, his yearning heart
 No more can bear delay —
 To scenes of full unmingled joy
 To call his bride away.

5 Then weep no more; 't is all thine own,
 His crown, his joy divine;
 And, sweeter far than all beside,
 He, he himself is thine!
 Sir Edward Denny, 1839.

1008.

1 WHEN came in flesh the Incarnate Word,
 The heedless world slept on,
 And only simple shepherds heard
 That God had sent his Son.

2 When comes the Saviour at the last,
 From west to east shall shine
 The awful pomp, and earth aghast
 Shall tremble at the sign.

3 Lord, who could dare see thee descend
 In state, unless he knew
 Thou art the sorrowing sinner's Friend,
 The gracious and the true?

4 Dwell in our hearts, O Saviour blest!
 So shall thine advent dawn
 'Twixt us and thee, our bosom Guest,
 Be but the veil withdrawn.
 Joseph Anstice, 1836.

1009.

1 Lo, what a glorious sight appears
 To our believing eyes!
 The earth and seas are passed away,
 And the old rolling skies.

2 From the third heaven, where God resides,
 That holy, happy place,
 The New Jerusalem comes down,
 Adorned with shining grace.

3 Attending angels shout for joy,
 And the bright armies sing,
 "Mortals, behold the sacred seat
 Of your descending King.

4 " The God of glory down to men
 Removes his blest abode;
 Men, the dear objects of his grace,
 And he their loving God.

5 " His own soft hand shall wipe the tears
 From every weeping eye;
 And pains, and groans, and griefs, and fears,
 And death itself, shall die!"

6 How long, dear Saviour, oh how long
 Shall this bright hour delay?
 Fly swifter round, ye wheels of time,
 And bring the welcome day.
 Isaac Watts, 1709.

CHRIST'S SECOND COMING.

DAY DAWN. 7s & 6s.

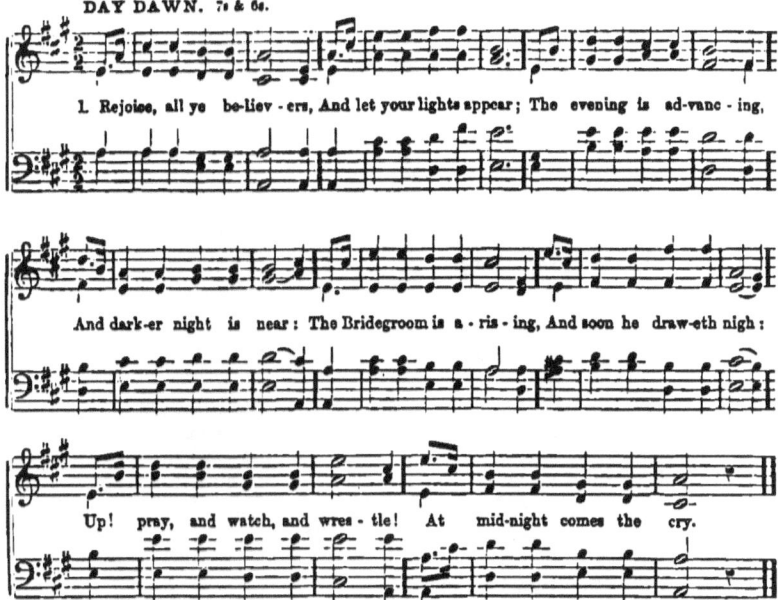

1. Rejoice, all ye believ-ers, And let your lights appear; The evening is ad-vanc-ing, And dark-er night is near: The Bridegroom is a-ris-ing, And soon he draw-eth nigh: Up! pray, and watch, and wres-tle! At mid-night comes the cry.

1010.

1 REJOICE, all ye believers,
    And let your lights appear;
The evening is advancing,
    And darker night is near:
The Bridegroom is arising,
    And soon he draweth nigh:
Up! pray, and watch, and wrestle!
    At midnight comes the cry.

2 The watchers on the mountain
    Proclaim the Bridegroom near;
Go meet him as he cometh,
    With hallelujahs clear:
The marriage-feast is waiting,
    The gates wide-open stand;
Up, up, ye heirs of glory!
    The Bridegroom is at hand!

3 Our hope and expectation,
    O Jesus, now appear;
Arise, thou Sun so longed for,
    O'er this benighted sphere!
With heart and hands uplifted,
    We plead, O Lord, to see
The day of earth's redemption,
    That brings us unto thee!

Laurentius Laurenti, 1700; tr. by Jane Borthwick, 1853.

1011.

1 LORD Jesus, thy returning,
    Thy people to receive,
Will end the days of mourning
    To all who then believe;
And since thy hands are keeping
    The spirits of the just,
Thy voice shall raise from sleeping
    The forms returned to dust.

2 Beneath thy safe protection
    We travel through the waste;
The joys of resurrection
    E'en here by faith we taste;
The words that prove so cheering
    Thy gracious lips let fall,
And thy desired appearing
    Shall prove the truth of all.

Bristol Hymns, 1870.

CHRIST'S SECOND COMING.

ST. BRIDE'S. S. M.

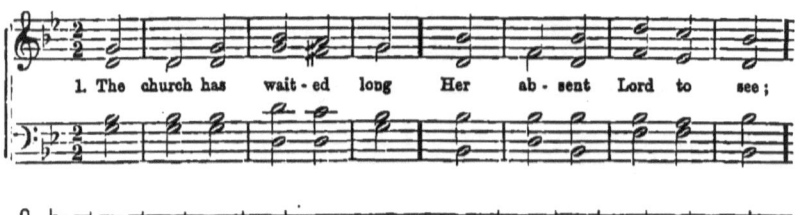

1. The church has wait-ed long Her ab-sent Lord to see;

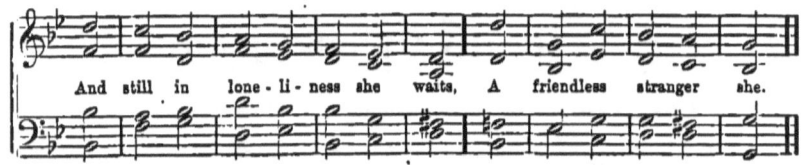

And still in lone-li-ness she waits, A friendless stranger she.

1012.

1 THE church has waited long
  Her absent Lord to see;
  And still in loneliness she waits,
  A friendless stranger she.

2 How long, O Lord our God,
  Holy and true and good,
  Wilt thou not judge thy suffering church,
  Her sighs and tears and blood?

3 Saint after saint on earth
  Has lived and loved and died;
  And as they left us one by one,
  We laid them side by side.

4 We laid them down to sleep,
  But not in hope forlorn;
  We laid them but to ripen there,
  Till the last glorious morn.

5 We long to hear thy voice,
  To see thee face to face,
  To share thy crown and glory then,
  As now we share thy grace.

6 Come, Lord, and wipe away
  The curse, the sin, the stain,
  And make this blighted world of ours
  Thine own fair world again.

  Horatius Bonar, 1856.

1013.

1 COME, Lord, and tarry not;
  Bring the long-looked-for day;
  Oh why these years of waiting here,
  These ages of delay?

2 Come, for thy saints still wait;
  Daily ascends their sigh;
  The Spirit and the bride say, Come!
  Dost thou not hear the cry?

3 Come, for creation groans,
  Impatient of thy stay,
  Worn out with these long years of ill,
  These ages of delay.

4 Come, for the corn is ripe;
  Put in thy sickle now;
  Reap the great harvest of the earth,
  Sower and reaper thou.

5 Come in thy glorious might,
  Come with the iron rod,
  Scattering thy foes before thy face,
  Most mighty Son of God.

6 Come, and make all things new;
  Build up this ruined earth,
  Restore our faded Paradise,
  Creation's second birth.

7 Come, and begin thy reign
  Of everlasting peace;
  Come, take the kingdom to thyself,
  Great King of righteousness!

  Horatius Bonar, 1857.

DOXOLOGY.

GIVE to the Father praise,
  Give glory to the Son,
And to the Spirit of his grace
  Be equal honor done.

  Isaac Watts, 1709.

RESURRECTION AND JUDGMENT.

AUGUSTUS. C. M.

1. Through sorrow's night and danger's path, A-midst the deepening gloom, We, sol-diers of an injured King, Are marching to the tomb.

1014.

1 THROUGH sorrow's night and danger's
  Amidst the deepening gloom,   [path,
We, soldiers of an injured King,
Are marching to the tomb.

2 There, when the turmoil is no more,
  And all our powers decay,
Our cold remains in solitude
  Shall sleep the years away.

3 Our labors done, securely laid
  In this our last retreat,
Unheeded o'er our silent dust
  The storms of life shall beat.

4 Yet not thus lifeless, thus inane,
  The vital spark shall lie;
For o'er life's wreck that spark shall rise
  To seek its kindred sky.

5 These ashes too, this little dust,
  Our Father's care shall keep,
Till the last angel rise and break
  The long and dreary sleep.

6 Then love's soft dew o'er every eye
  Shall shed its mildest rays,
And the long silent dust shall burst
  With shouts of endless praise!
    Henry Kirke White, 1807.

1015.   Job xix. 25, 26.

1 MY faith shall triumph o'er the grave,
  And trample on the tomb;
I know that my Redeemer lives,
  And on the clouds shall come.

2 I know that he shall soon appear
  In power and glory meet,
And death, the last of all his foes,
  Lie vanquished at his feet.

3 Then, though the grave my flesh devour,
  And hold me for its prey,
I know my sleeping dust shall rise
  On the last judgment-day.

4 I in my flesh shall see my God,
  When he on earth shall stand;
I shall with all his saints ascend
  To dwell at his right hand.
      Anon, 1858.

1016.

1 BLEST be the everlasting God,
  The Father of our Lord;
Be his abounding mercy praised,
  His majesty adored.

2 When from the dead he raised his Son,
  And called him to the sky,
He gave our souls a lively hope
  That they should never die.

3 What though our inbred sins require
  Our flesh to see the dust;
Yet, as the Lord our Saviour rose,
  So all his followers must.

4 There's an inheritance divine
  Reserved against that day;
'Tis uncorrupted, undefiled,
  And cannot waste away.

5 Saints by the power of God are kept
  Till the salvation come;
We walk by faith as strangers here,
  Till Christ shall call us home.
    Isaac Watts, 1709.

RESURRECTION AND JUDGMENT.

UTICA. S. M.

1. And must this body die, This mortal frame decay? And must these active limbs of mine Lie mouldering in the clay?

1017.

1 AND must this body die,
  This mortal frame decay?
And must these active limbs of mine
  Lie mouldering in the clay?

2 God my Redeemer lives,
  And often from the skies
Looks down, and watches all my dust,
  Till he shall bid it rise.

3 Arrayed in glorious grace
  Shall these vile bodies shine,
And every shape and every face
  Look heavenly and divine.

4 These lively hopes we owe
  To Jesus' dying love;
We would adore his grace below,
  And sing his power above.
      Isaac Watts, 1709.

1018.

1 THOU Judge of quick and dead,
  Before whose bar severe,
With holy joy or guilty dread,
  We all shall soon appear;

2 Our cautioned souls prepare
  For that tremendous day,
And fill us now with watchful care,
  And stir us up to pray:

3 To pray, and wait the hour,
  The awful hour unknown,
When, robed in majesty and power,
  Thou shalt from heaven come down,

4 The immortal Son of Man,
  To judge the human race,
With all thy Father's dazzling train,
  With all thy glorious grace.

5 Oh may we thus be found,
  Obedient to his word,
Attentive to the trumpet's sound,
  And looking for our Lord.

6 Oh may we thus insure
  Our lot among the blest,
And watch a moment, to secure
  An everlasting rest!
      Charles Wesley, 1749.

1019.

1 AND will the Judge descend,
  And must the dead arise,
And not a single soul escape
  His all-discerning eyes?

2 How will my heart endure
  The terrors of that day,
When earth and heaven before his face
  Astonished shrink away?

3 But, ere the trumpet shakes
  The mansions of the dead,
Hark! from the gospel's gentle sound
  What joyful tidings spread!

4 Ye sinners, seek his grace,
  Whose wrath ye cannot bear;
Fly to the shelter of his cross,
  And find salvation there!
      Philip Doddridge, 1755.

RESURRECTION AND JUDGMENT.

DOOMSDAY. L. M.

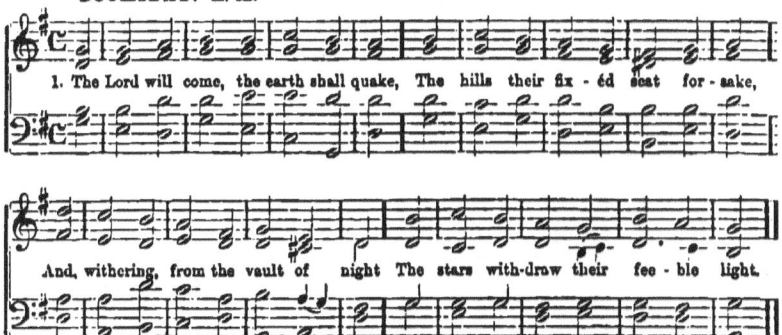

1020.

1 THE Lord will come, the earth shall
  The hills their fixéd seat forsake, [quake,
  And, withering, from the vault of night
  The stars withdraw their feeble light.

2 The Lord will come, but not the same
  As once in lowly form he came,
  A silent Lamb to slaughter led,
  The bruised, the suffering, and the dead.

3 The Lord will come, a dreadful form,
  With wreath of flame and robe of storm,
  On cherub wings and wings of wind,
  Anointed Judge of human kind.

4 Can this be he who wont to stray
  A pilgrim on the world's highway,
  By power oppressed, and mocked by pride,
  The Nazarene, the Crucified?

5 While sinners in despair shall call,
  " Rocks, hide us! mountains, on us fall!"
  The saints, ascending from the tomb,
  Shall sing for joy, " The Lord is come!"
  Reginald Heber, 1811.

1021.

1 THAT day of wrath, that dreadful day,
  When heaven and earth shall pass away!
  What power shall be the sinner's stay?
  How shall he meet that dreadful day?

2 When, shriveling like a parchéd scroll,
  The flaming heavens together roll;
  When louder yet, and yet more dread,
  Swells the high trump that wakes the
    dead!

3 Oh, on that day, that wrathful day,
  When man to judgment wakes from clay,
  Be thou the trembling sinner's stay,
  Though heaven and earth shall pass away!
  Tr. from Latin by Sir Walter Scott, 1805.

1022. PSALM 97.

1 HE reigns! the Lord, the Saviour reigns!
  Praise him in evangelic strains;
  Let the whole earth in songs rejoice,
  And distant islands join their voice!

2 Deep are his counsels, and unknown;
  But grace and truth support his throne:
  Though gloomy clouds his ways surround,
  Justice is their eternal ground.

3 In robes of judgment, lo! he comes,
  Shakes the wide earth, and cleaves the
  Before him burns devouring fire; [tombs;
  The mountains melt, the seas retire!

4 His enemies, with sore dismay,
  Fly from the sight, and shun the day;
  Then lift your heads, ye saints, on high,
  And sing, for your redemption's nigh!
  Isaac Watts, 1719.

RESURRECTION AND JUDGMENT.

JUDGMENT HYMN. 8s & 7s.

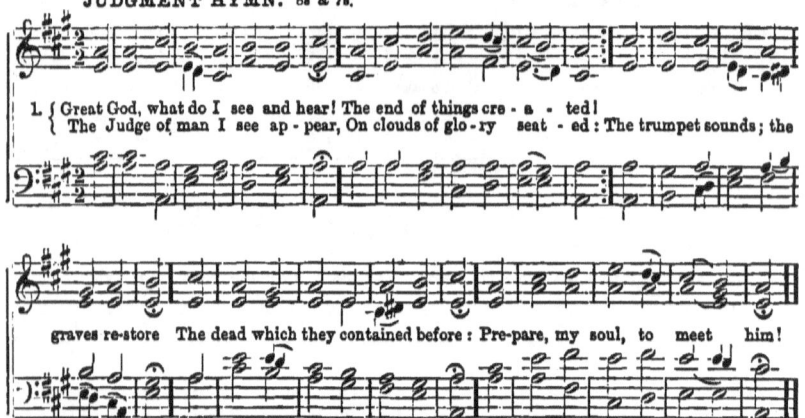

1. { Great God, what do I see and hear! The end of things cre - a - ted!
   { The Judge of man I see ap - pear, On clouds of glo - ry seat - ed : The trumpet sounds; the graves re-store The dead which they contained before : Pre-pare, my soul, to meet him!

1023.

1 GREAT God, what do I see and hear!
  The end of things created!
  The Judge of man I see appear,
  On clouds of glory seated:
  The trumpet sounds; the graves restore
  The dead which they contained before:
  Prepare, my soul, to meet him!

2 The dead in Christ shall first arise
  And greet the archangel's warning,
  To meet the Saviour in the skies
  On this auspicious morning:
  No gloomy fears their souls dismay,
  His presence sheds eternal day
  On those prepared to meet him.

3 Far over space, to distant spheres,
  The lightnings are prevailing:
  The ungodly rise, and all their tears
  And sighs are unavailing:
  The day of grace is past and gone;
  They shake before the Judge's throne,
  All unprepared to meet him.

4 Stay, fancy, stay, and drop thy wings,
  Repress thy flight too daring!
  One wondrous sight my comfort brings,
  The Judge my nature wearing.
  Beneath his cross I view the day
  When heaven and earth shall pass away,
  And thus prepare to meet him.

William Bengo Collyer, 1812.
(First Stanza Anon., from Bartholomew Ringwaldt, 1585.*)*

1024. Tune, "Helmsley," p. 413. 8s, 7s & 4.

1 DAY of Judgment, day of wonders!
  Hark! the trumpet's awful sound,
  Louder than a thousand thunders,
  Shakes the vast creation round:
    How the summons
  Will the sinner's heart confound!

2 See the Judge, our nature wearing,
  Clothed in majesty divine!
  Ye, who long for his appearing,
  Then shall say, this God is mine!
    Gracious Saviour,
  Own me in that day for thine.

3 At his call the dead awaken,
  Rise to life from earth and sea;
  All the powers of nature, shaken
  By his look, prepare to flee:
    Careless sinner,
  What will then become of thee!

4 But to those who have confessèd,
  Loved and served the Lord below,
  He will say, "Come near, ye blessèd!
  See the kingdom I bestow:
    You forever
  Shall my love and glory know."

John Newton, 1779.

RESURRECTION AND JUDGMENT. 413

HELMSLEY. 8s, 7s & 4.

1. Lo, he com-eth! countless trumpets Blow to
   'Mid ten thousand saints and angels, See their
   raise the sleeping dead; } Hal - le - lu - jah!
   great ex - alt - ed Head!
   Hal - le - lu - jah! Wel - come, wel - come, Son of God!

1025.

2 Now his merit, by the harpers,
   Through the eternal deep resounds;
   Now resplendent shine his nail-prints,
   Every eye shall see his wounds;
      They who pierced him
   Shall at his appearance wail.

3 Full of joyful expectation,
   Saints behold the Judge appear;
   Truth and justice go before him;
   Now the royal sentence hear:
      Hallelujah!
   Welcome, welcome, Judge divine.

4 " Come, ye blessèd of my Father,
   Enter into life and joy;
   Banish all your fears and sorrows;
   Endless praise be your employ:"
      Hallelujah!
   Welcome, welcome to the skies.
                    John Cennick, 1752.

1026.

1 Lo, he comes, with clouds descending,
   Once for favored sinners slain;
   Thousand thousand saints attending
   Swell the triumph of his train:
      Hallelujah!
   God appears on earth to reign.

2 Every eye shall now behold him
   Robed in dreadful majesty;
   Those who set at nought, and sold him,
   Pierced and nailed him to the tree,
      Deeply wailing,
   Shall the true Messiah see.

3 Every island, sea, and mountain,
   Heaven and earth, shall flee away;
   All who hate him must, confounded,
   Hear the trump proclaim the day;
      Come to judgment!
   Come to judgment, come away!

4 Answer thine own Bride and Spirit,
   Hasten, Lord, and quickly come:
   The new heaven and earth to inherit,
   Take thy pining exiles home:
      All creation
   Travails, groans, and bids thee come!

5 Yea, amen; let all adore thee,
   High on thine eternal throne;
   Saviour, take the power and glory,
   Claim the kingdoms for thine own:
      Oh, come quickly,
   Everlasting God, come down.

           John Cennick, 1752; *Charles Wesley*, 1758.
              Varied by Martin Madan, 1760.

RESURRECTION AND JUDGMENT.

MERIBAH. C. P. M.

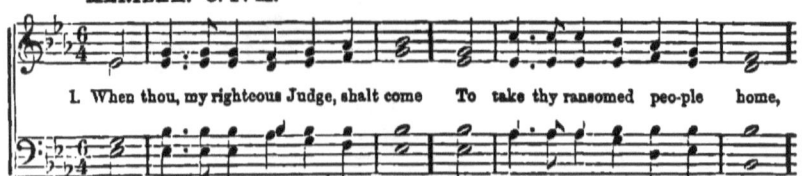
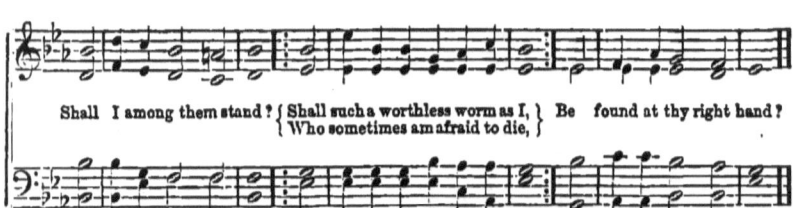

1027.

1 When thou, my righteous Judge, shalt come
To take thy ransomed people home,
Shall I among them stand?
Shall such a worthless worm as I,
Who sometimes am afraid to die,
Be found at thy right hand?

2 I love to meet among them now,
Before thy gracious feet to bow,
Though vilest of them all;
But — can I bear the piercing thought?
What if my name should be left out,
When thou for them shalt call!

3 Prevent, prevent it by thy grace;
Be thou, dear Lord, my hiding-place,
In this th' accepted day;
Thy pardoning voice, oh, let me hear,
To still my unbelieving fear;
Nor let me fall, I pray.

4 Let me among thy saints be found,
Whene'er th' archangel's trump shall sound,
To see thy smiling face;
Then loudest of the throng I'll sing,
While heaven's resounding mansions ring
With shouts of sovereign grace.

Selina, Countess of Huntingdon, 1772. a.

1028. Matt. xxv. 41. Tune, "Augustus," p. 409. C. M.

1 That awful day will surely come,
Th' appointed hour makes haste.
When I must stand before my Judge,
And pass the solemn test.

2 Thou lovely Chief of all my joys,
Thou Sovereign of my heart,
How could I bear to hear thy voice
Pronounce the sound, "Depart!"

3 Oh, wretched state of deep despair!
To see my God remove,
And fix my doleful station where
I must not taste his love!

4 Jesus, I throw my arms around
And hang upon thy breast;
Without a gracious smile from thee,
My spirit cannot rest.

5 Oh, tell me that my worthless name
Is graven on thy hands!
Show me some promise in thy book,
Where my salvation stands!

6 Give me one kind, assuring word,
To sink my fears again;
And cheerfully my soul shall wait
Her threescore years and ten.

Isaac Watts, 1709.

HEAVEN.

AMSTERDAM. 7s & 6s.

1. Rise, my soul, and stretch thy wings, Thy better portion trace ; Sun and moon and stars de-cay;
Rise from transi-to-ry things Towards heaven, thy native place :
Time shall soon this earth remove ; Rise, my soul, and haste away To seats prepared a-bove.

1029. ✗

1 RISE, my soul, and stretch thy wings,
　Thy better portion trace ;
Rise from transitory things
　Towards heaven, thy native place :
Sun and moon and stars decay ;
　Time shall soon this earth remove ;
Rise, my soul, and haste away
　To seats prepared above.

2 Rivers to the ocean run,
　Nor stay in all their course ;
Fire, ascending, seeks the sun ;
　Both speed them to their source :
So my soul, derived from God,
　Pants to view his glorious face,
Forward tends to his abode,
　To rest in his embrace.

3 Cease, ye pilgrims, cease to mourn,
　Press onward for the prize ;
Soon our Saviour will return
　Triumphant in the skies :
Yet a season, and you know
　Happy entrance will be given,
All our sorrows left below,
　And earth exchanged for heaven.

Robert Seagrave, 1742.

1030.　　Tune, "Jenner," p. 335.　7s & 6s.

1 OH for the robes of whiteness !
　Oh for the tearless eyes !
Oh for the glorious brightness
　Of the unclouded skies !

2 Oh for the no more weeping
　Within the land of love,
The endless joy of keeping
　The bridal feast above !

3 Oh for the bliss of dying,
　My risen Lord to meet !
Oh for the rest of lying
　Forever at his feet !

4 Oh for the hour of seeing
　My Saviour face to face,
The hope of ever being
　In that sweet meeting-place !

5 Jesus, thou King of glory,
　I soon shall dwell with thee ;
I soon shall sing the story
　Of thy great love to me.

6 Meanwhile my thoughts shall enter,
　E'en now, before thy throne,
That all my love may centre
　On thee, and thee alone.

Charitie Lees Smith, 1861.

HEAVEN.

PILGRIMAGE. L. M.

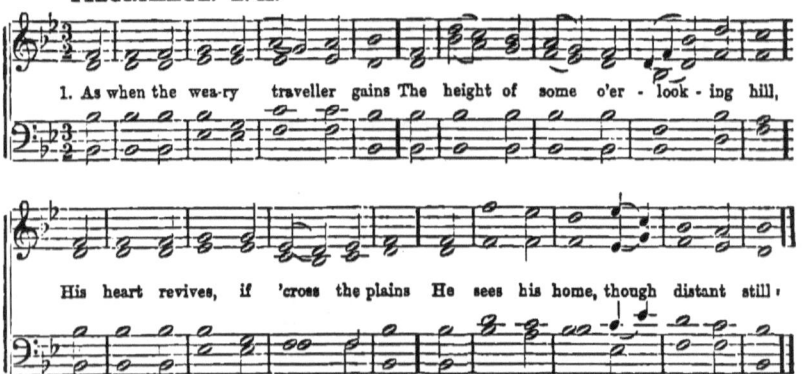

1. As when the wea-ry traveller gains The height of some o'er-look-ing hill, His heart revives, if 'cross the plains He sees his home, though distant still:

1031.

1 As when the weary traveller gains
  The height of some o'erlooking hill,
  His heart revives, if 'cross the plains
  He sees his home, though distant still:

2 While he surveys the much-loved spot,
  He slights the space that lies between;
  His past fatigues are now forgot,
  Because his journey's end is seen.

3 Thus when the Christian pilgrim views
  By faith his mansion in the skies,
  The sight his fainting strength renews,
  And wings his speed to reach the prize.

4 The thought of home his spirit cheers;
  No more he grieves for troubles past,
  Nor any future trial fears,
  So he may safe arrive at last.

5 'T is there, he says, I am to dwell
  With Jesus in the realms of day;
  Then I shall bid my cares farewell,
  And he shall wipe my tears away.
   John Newton, 1779.

1032.

1 Now let our souls, on wings sublime,
  Rise from the vanities of time,
  Draw back the parting veil, and see
  The glories of eternity.

2 Twice born by a celestial birth;
  Why should we grovel here on earth?
  Why grasp at transitory toys,
  So near to heaven's eternal joys?

3 Shall aught beguile us on the road,
  While we are travelling back to God?
  For strangers into life we come,
  And dying is but going home.

4 Welcome, sweet hour of full discharge,
  That sets my longing soul at large,
  Unbinds my chains, breaks up my cell,
  And gives me with my God to dwell.

5 To dwell with God, to feel his love,
  Is the full heaven enjoyed above;
  And the sweet expectation now
  Is the young dawn of heaven below.
   Thomas Gibbons, 1762.

1033.

1 Thou vain, deceitful world, farewell,
  Thine idle joys no more we love:
  By faith in brighter worlds we dwell,
  In spirit find our home above.

2 Jesus, we go with thee to taste
  Of joy supreme, that never dies;
  Our feet still press the weary waste,
  Our heart, our home, are in the skies.

3 And, oh! while unto heaven's high hill
  The toilsome path of life we tread,
  Around us, loving Father, still
  Thy circling wings of mercy spread.

4 From day to day, from hour to hour,
  Oh let our rising spirits prove
  The strength of thine almighty power,
  The sweetness of thy saving love!
   Sir Edward Denny, 1839.

HEAVEN.

1034. Heb. xiii. 14. L. M.

1 "We 've no abiding city here,"—
  This may distress the worldling's mind,
  But should not cost the saint a tear,
  Who hopes a better rest to find.

2 "We 've no abiding city here,"—
  Sad truth, were this to be our home;
  But let this thought our spirits cheer,
  "We seek a city yet to come."

3 "We 've no abiding city here;"
  Then let us live as pilgrims do;
  Let not the world our rest appear,
  But let us haste from all below.

4 "We 've no abiding city here,"
  We seek a city out of sight;
  Zion its name, the Lord is there,
  It shines with everlasting light.

5 Oh sweet abode of peace and love,
  Where pilgrims freed from toil are blest;
  Had I the pinions of the dove,
  I 'd fly to thee and be at rest!
  Thomas Kelly, 1812-1836.

1035. L. M.

1 On for a sight, a pleasing sight,
  Of our almighty Father's throne!
  There sits our Saviour crowned with light,
  Clothed in a body like our own.

2 Adoring saints around him stand, [fall;
  And thrones and powers before him
  The God shines gracious through the Man,
  And sheds sweet glories on them all.

3 Oh! what amazing joys they feel,
  While to their golden harps they sing,
  And sit on every heavenly hill,
  And spread the triumphs of their King!

4 When shall the day, dear Lord, appear,
  That I shall mount to dwell above;
  And stand, and bow, among them there,
  And view thy face, and sing, and love!
  Isaac Watts, 1709.

1036. L. M.

1 On for a sweet, inspiring ray,
  To animate our feeble strains,
  From the bright realms of endless day,
  The blissful realms where Jesus reigns!

2 There. low before his glorious throne,
  Adoring saints and angels fall.
  And, with delightful worship, own [all.
  His smile their bliss, their heaven, their

3 Immortal glories crown his head,
  While tuneful hallelujahs rise,
  And love and joy and triumph spread
  Through all th' assemblies of the skies.

4 He smiles, and seraphs tune their songs
  To boundless rapture while they gaze;
  Ten thousand thousand joyful tongues
  Resound his everlasting praise.

5 There all the favorites of the Lamb
  Shall join at last the heavenly choir:
  Oh, may the joy-inspiring theme
  Awake our faith and warm desire!
  Anne Steele, 1760.

1037. Psalm 17. L. M.

1 What sinners value, I resign;
  Lord, 't is enough that thou art mine:
  I shall behold thy blissful face,
  And stand complete in righteousness.

2 This life 's a dream, an empty show;
  But the bright world to which I go
  Hath joys substantial and sincere;
  When shall I wake and find me there?

3 Oh glorious hour! Oh blest abode!
  I shall be near and like my God!
  And flesh and sin no more control
  The sacred pleasures of the soul.

4 My flesh shall slumber in the ground
  Till the last trumpet's joyful sound;
  Then burst the chains with sweet surprise,
  And in my Saviour's image rise!
  Isaac Watts, 1719.

1038. L. M.

1 Let me be with thee where thou art,
  My Saviour, my eternal Rest;
  Then only will this longing heart
  Be fully and forever blest.

2 Let me be with thee where thou art,
  Thy unveiled glory to behold;
  Then only will this wandering heart
  Cease to be treacherous, faithless, cold.

3 Let me be with thee where thou art,
  Where spotless saints thy name adore;
  Then only will this sinful heart
  Be evil and defiled no more.

4 Let me be with thee where thou art,
  Where none can die, where none remove;
  There neither death nor life will part
  Me from thy presence and thy love.
  Charlotte Elliott, 1837.

HEAVEN.

JORDAN. C. M. Double.

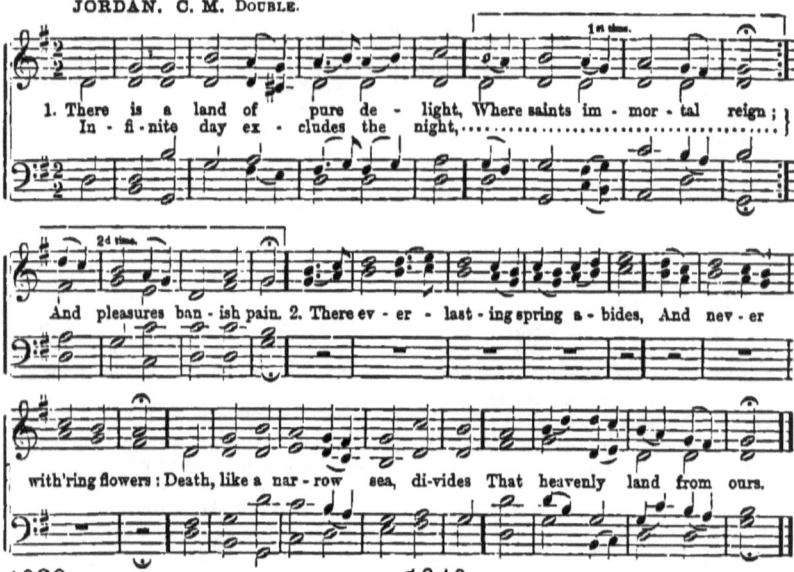

1039.

1 There is a land of pure delight,
   Where saints immortal reign;
   Infinite day excludes the night,
   And pleasures banish pain.

2 There everlasting spring abides,
   And never-withering flowers:
   Death, like a narrow sea, divides
   This heavenly land from ours.

3 Sweet fields beyond the swelling flood
   Stand dressed in living green;
   So to the Jews old Canaan stood,
   While Jordan rolled between.

4 But timorous mortals start and shrink
   To cross this narrow sea,
   And linger, shivering, on the brink,
   And fear to launch away.

5 Oh, could we make our doubts remove,
   Those gloomy doubts that rise,
   And see the Canaan that we love
   With unbeclouded eyes!—

6 Could we but climb where Moses stood,
   And view the landscape o'er,   [flood
   Not Jordan's stream nor death's cold
   Should fright us from the shore.
   Isaac Watts, 1709.

1040.

1 On Jordan's stormy banks I stand,
   And cast a wishful eye
   To Canaan's fair and happy land,
   Where my possessions lie.

2 Oh the transporting, rapturous scene
   That rises to my sight!
   Sweet fields arrayed in living green,
   And rivers of delight.

3 All o'er those wide-extended plains
   Shines one eternal day;
   There God the Son forever reigns,
   And scatters night away.

4 No chilling winds or poisonous breath
   Can reach that healthful shore;
   Sickness and sorrow, pain and death,
   Are felt and feared no more.

5 When shall I reach that happy place,
   And be forever blest?
   When shall I see my Father's face,
   And in his bosom rest?

6 Filled with delight, my raptured soul
   Can here no longer stay;
   Though Jordan's waves around me roll,
   Fearless I'd launch away.
   Samuel Stennett, 1787.

1041. C. M.

1 Come, Lord, and warm each languid heart,
Inspire each lifeless tongue;
And let the joys of heaven impart
Their influence to our song.

2 Sorrow and pain, and every care,
And discord, there shall cease;
And perfect joy, and love sincere,
Adorn the realms of peace.

3 There on a throne, how dazzling bright!
The exalted Saviour shines,
And beams ineffable delight
On all the heavenly minds.

4 There shall the followers of the Lamb
Join in immortal songs,
And endless honors to his name
Employ their tuneful tongues.

5 Lord, tune our hearts to praise and love,
Our feeble notes inspire,
Till in thy blissful courts above
We join the angelic choir.

Anne Steele, 1760.

1042. C. M.

1 Father, I long, I faint to see
The place of thine abode;
I'd leave thy earthly courts and flee
Up to thy seat, my God!

2 Here I behold thy distant face,
And 't is a pleasing sight;
But to abide in thine embrace
Is infinite delight.

3 I'd part with all the joys of sense
To gaze upon thy throne;
Pleasure springs fresh forever thence,
Unspeakable, unknown.

4 There all the heavenly hosts are seen,
In shining ranks they move,
And drink immortal vigor in
With wonder and with love.

5 There at thy feet with awful fear
The adoring armies fall;
With joy they shrink to nothing there,
Before the eternal All.

6 The more thy glories strike my eyes,
The humbler I shall lie;
Thus, while I sink, my joys shall rise
Unmeasurably high.

Isaac Watts, 1709.

1043. C. M.

1 From thee, my God, my joys shall rise,
And run eternal rounds,
Beyond the limits of the skies,
And all created bounds.

2 The holy triumphs of my soul
Shall death itself outbrave,
Leave dull mortality behind,
And fly beyond the grave.

3 There, where my blessèd Jesus reigns,
In heaven's unmeasured space,
I'll spend a long eternity
In pleasure and in praise.

4 Millions of years my wondering eyes
Shall o'er thy beauties rove,
And endless ages I'll adore
The glories of thy love.

5 My Saviour, every smile of thine
Shall fresh endearments bring,
And thousand tastes of new delight
From all thy graces spring.

6 Haste, my Beloved! raise my soul
Up to thy blest abode;
Fly, for my spirit longs to see
My Saviour and my God!

Isaac Watts, 1709.

1044. C. M.

1 My thoughts surmount these lower skies,
And look within the veil:
There springs of endless pleasure rise;
The waters never fail.

2 There I behold, with sweet delight,
The blessèd Three in One;
And strong affections fix my sight
On God's incarnate Son.

3 His promise stands forever firm;
His grace shall ne'er depart:
He binds my name upon his arm,
And seals it on his heart.

4 Light are the pains that nature brings,
How short our sorrows are,
When with eternal future things
The present we compare!

5 I would not be a stranger still
To that celestial place,
Where I forever hope to dwell
Near my Redeemer's face.

Isaac Watts, 1709.

HEAVEN.

JERUSALEM THE GOLDEN. 7s & 6s.

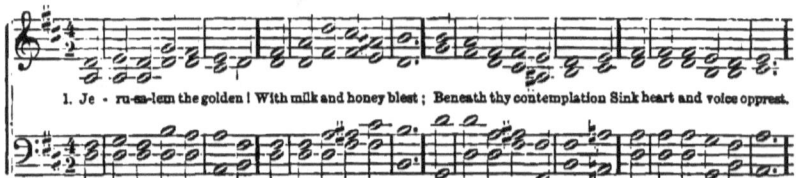
1. Je-ru-sa-lem the golden! With milk and honey blest; Beneath thy contemplation Sink heart and voice opprest.

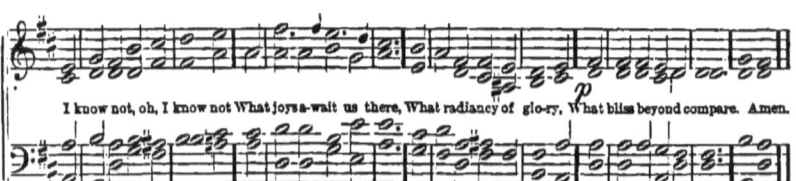
I know not, oh, I know not What joys a-wait us there, What radiancy of glo-ry, What bliss beyond compare. Amen.

1045.

1 JERUSALEM the golden!
  With milk and honey blest,
  Beneath thy contemplation
  Sink heart and voice opprest.
  I know not, oh, I know not
  What joys await us there,
  What radiancy of glory,
  What bliss beyond compare.

2 They stand, those halls of Zion,
  All jubilant with song,
  And bright with many an angel,
  And all the martyr throng.
  The Prince is ever in them,
  The daylight is serene;
  The pastures of the blessèd
  Are decked in glorious sheen.

3 There is the throne of David;
  And there, from care released,
  The shout of them that triumph,
  The song of them that feast.
  And they who, with their Leader,
  Have conquered in the fight,
  Forever and forever
  Are clad in robes of white.
  Bernard, 1150; tr. by J. M. Neale, 1851.

1046.

1 FOR thee, O dear, dear country,
  Mine eyes their vigils keep;
  For very love, beholding
  Thy happy name, they weep.
  The mention of thy glory
  Is unction to the breast,
  And medicine in sickness,
  And love, and life, and rest.

2 O one, O only mansion!
  O Paradise of joy!
  Where tears are ever banished,
  And smiles have no alloy;
  The Lamb is all thy splendor,
  The Crucified thy praise;
  His laud and benediction
  Thy ransomed people raise.

3 Thou hast no shore, fair ocean!
  Thou hast no time, bright day!
  Dear fountain of refreshment
  To pilgrims far away!
  Upon the Rock of ages
  They raise thy holy tower;
  Thine is the victor's laurel,
  And thine the golden dower.

4 O sweet and blessèd country,
  The home of God's elect!
  O sweet and blessèd country,
  That eager hearts expect!
  Jesus, in mercy bring us,
  To that dear land of rest;
  Who art, with God the Father,
  And Spirit, ever blest.
  Bernard, 1150; tr. by J. M. Neale, 1851.

HEAVEN.

JERUSALEM ON HIGH. H. M.

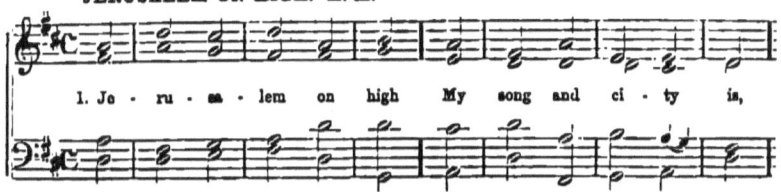
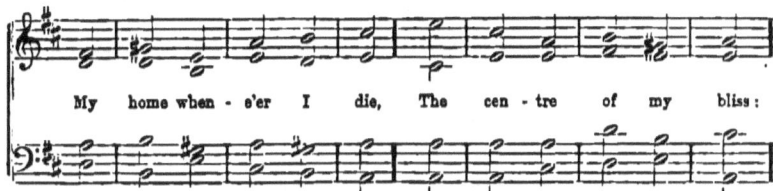
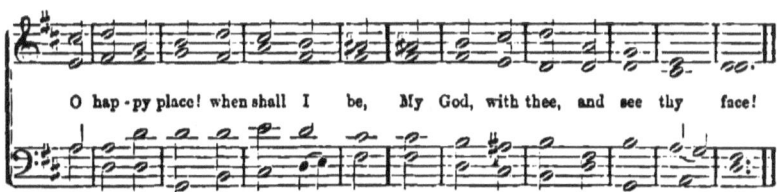

1047.

1 JERUSALEM on high
  My song and city is,
My home whene'er I die,
  The centre of my bliss:
O happy place! when shall I be,
My God, with thee, and see thy face!

2 There dwells my Lord, my King,
  Judged here unfit to live;
There angels to him sing,
  And lowly homage give:
O happy place! when shall I be,
My God, with thee, and see thy face!

3 The patriarchs of old
  There from their travels cease;
The prophets there behold
  Their longed-for Prince of peace:
O happy place! when shall I be,
My God, with thee, to see thy face!

4 The Lamb's apostles there
  I might with joy behold,
The harpers I might hear
  Harping on harps of gold:
O happy place! when shall I be,
My God, with thee, to see thy face!

5 The bleeding martyrs, they
  Within those courts are found,
Clothed in pure array,
  Their scars with glory crowned:
O happy place! when shall I be,
My God, with thee, to see thy face!

6 Ah me, ah me! that I
  In Kedar's tents here stay;
No place like that on high;
  Lord, thither guide my way:
O happy place! when shall I be,
My God, with thee, to see thy face!

Samuel Crossman, 1664.

HEAVEN.

RHINE. C. M.

1. Je-ru-sa-lem! my happy home! Name ever dear to me! When shall my labors have an end, In joy, and peace, and thee! In joy, and peace, and thee?

1048.

1 JERUSALEM! my happy home!
  Name ever dear to me!
 When shall my labors have an end,
  In joy, and peace, and thee?

2 When shall these eyes thy heaven-built [walls
  And pearly gates behold?
 Thy bulwarks with salvation strong,
  And streets of shining gold?

3 Oh when, thou city of my God,
  Shall I thy courts ascend,
 Where congregations ne'er break up,
  And Sabbaths have no end?

4 There happier bowers than Eden's bloom,
  Nor sin nor sorrow know: [scenes
 Blest seats! through rude and stormy
  I onward press to you.

5 Why should I shrink at pain and woe,
  Or feel at death dismay?
 I've Canaan's goodly land in view,
  And realms of endless day.

6 Apostles, martyrs, prophets, there,
  Around my Saviour stand;
 And soon my friends in Christ below
  Will join the glorious band.

7 Jerusalem! my happy home!
  My soul still pants for thee;
 Then shall my labors have an end
  When I thy joys shall see.
  Tr. from Latin hymn of 8th century, in Eckington Coll., 1790.

1049.

1 FAR from these narrow scenes of night
  Unbounded glories rise,
 And realms of infinite delight,
  Unknown to mortal eyes.

2 Fair distant land! could mortal eyes
  But half its joys explore,
 How would our spirits long to rise,
  And dwell on earth no more!

3 There pain and sickness never come,
  And grief no more complains;
 Health triumphs in immortal bloom,
  And endless pleasure reigns.

4 No cloud those blissful regions know,
  Forever bright and fair;
 For sin, the source of mortal woe,
  Can never enter there.

5 There no alternate night is known,
  Nor sun's faint sickly ray;
 But glory from the sacred throne
  Spreads everlasting day.

6 The glorious Monarch there displays
  His beams of wondrous grace;
 His happy subjects sing his praise,
  And bow before his face.

7 Oh may the heavenly prospect fire
  Our hearts with ardent love,
 Till wings of faith and strong desire
  Bear every thought above!
  Anne Steele, 1760.

HEAVEN. C. DOUBLE.

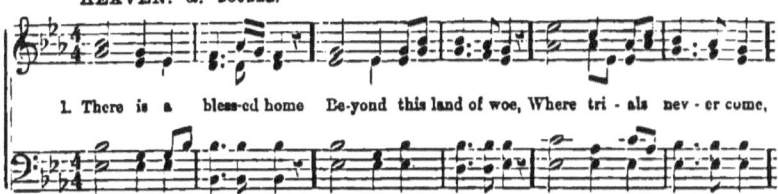
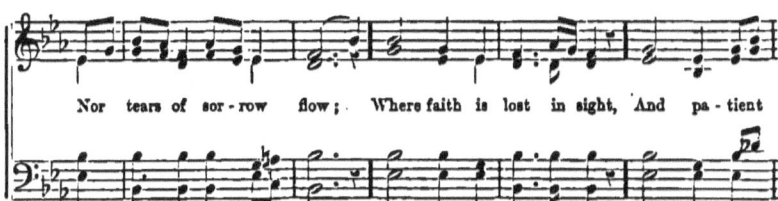
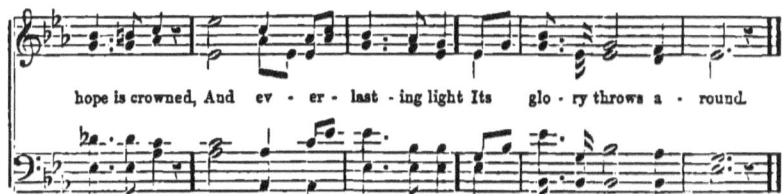

1050.

1 There is a blessed home
 Beyond this land of woe,
Where trials never come,
 Nor tears of sorrow flow;
Where faith is lost in sight,
 And patient hope is crowned,
And everlasting light
 Its glory throws around.

2 There is a land of peace,
 Good angels know it well;
Glad songs that never cease
 Within its portals swell;
Around its glorious throne
 Ten thousand saints adore
Christ, with the Father one,
 And Spirit, evermore.

3 Oh joy all joys beyond,
 To see the Lamb who died,
And count each sacred wound
 In hands, and feet, and side;
To give to him the praise
 Of every triumph won,
And sing through endless days
 The great things he hath done.

4 Look up, ye saints of God,
 Nor fear to tread below
The path your Saviour trod
 Of daily toil and woe;
Wait but a little while
 In uncomplaining love;
His own most gracious smile
 Shall welcome you above.

Sir H. W. Baker, 1861.

HEAVEN.

PARNELL. S. M.

1. For-ev-er with the Lord! A-men! so let it be! Life from the dead is in that word! 'T is im-mor-tal-i-ty.

1051.

1 FOREVER with the Lord!
 Amen! so let it be!
Life from the dead is in that word,
 'T is immortality.

2 Here in the body pent,
 Absent from him I roam,
Yet nightly pitch my moving tent
 A day's march nearer home.

3 My Father's house on high,
 Home of my soul, how near,
At times, to faith's foreseeing eye,
 Thy golden gates appear!

4 Ah! then my spirit faints
 To reach the land I love,
The bright inheritance of saints,
 Jerusalem above!

5 "Forever with the Lord!"
 Father, if 't is thy will,
The promise of that faithful word
 E'en here to me fulfil.

6 Be thou at my right hand,
 Then I can never fail;
Uphold thou me, and I shall stand,
 Fight, and I must prevail.

7 So when my latest breath
 Shall rend the veil in twain,
By death I shall escape from death,
 And life eternal gain.

8 Knowing as I am known,
 How shall I love that word,
And oft repeat before the throne,
 "Forever with the Lord!"
 James Montgomery, 1825.

1052.

1 FROM Egypt lately come,
 Where death and darkness reign,
We seek our new, our better home,
 Where we our rest shall gain.

2 To Canaan's sacred bound
 We haste, with songs of joy,
Where peace and liberty are found,
 And sweets that never cloy.

3 There sin and sorrow cease,
 And every conflict's o'er;
We there shall dwell in endless peace,
 And never hunger more.

4 There, in celestial strains,
 Enraptured myriads sing;
There love in every bosom reigns,
 For God himself is King.

5 We soon shall join the throng,
 Their pleasures we shall share,
And sing the everlasting song
 With all the ransomed there.

6 How sweet the prospect is!
 It cheers the pilgrim's breast;
We're journeying through the wilder-
 But soon shall gain our rest. [ness,
 Thomas Kelly, 1812.

HEAVEN. 425

BALDWIN. C. M.

1. Hope of our hearts, O Lord, ap-pears, Thou glo-rious Star of day!
Shine forth, and chase the drea-ry night, With all our tears, a-way.

1053.

1 Hope of our hearts, O Lord, appear,
Thou glorious Star of day!
Shine forth, and chase the dreary night,
With all our tears, away.

2 No resting place we seek on earth,
No loveliness we see;
Our eye is on the royal crown,
Prepared for us and thee.

3 But, dearest Lord, however bright
That crown of joy above,
What is it to the brighter hope
Of dwelling in thy love?

4 What to the joy, the deeper joy,
Unmingled, pure, and free,
Of union with our living Head,
Of fellowship with thee?

5 This joy e'en now on earth is ours;
But only, Lord, above,
Our hearts, without a pang, shall know
The fulness of thy love.

6 There, near thy heart, upon the throne,
Thy ransomed bride shall see
What grace was in the bleeding Lamb,
Who died to make her free.
Sir Edward Denny, 1839.

1054.

1 How bright those glorious spirits shine!
Whence all their white array?
How came they to the blissful seats
Of everlasting day?

2 Lo, these are they from suffering great
Who came to realms of light,
And in the blood of Christ have washed
Those robes which shine so bright.

3 Now with triumphal palms they stand
Before the throne on high,
And serve the God they love amidst
The glories of the sky.

4 His presence fills each heart with joy,
Tunes every mouth to sing;
By day, by night, the sacred courts
With glad hosannas ring.

5 Hunger and thirst are felt no more,
Nor suns with scorching ray;
God is their sun whose cheering beams
Diffuse eternal day.

6 The Lamb, which dwells amidst the throne,
Shall o'er them still preside,
Feed them with nourishment divine,
And all their footsteps guide.

7 'Mong pastures green he 'll lead his flock,
Where living streams appear;
And God the Lord from every eye
Shall wipe off every tear.
Isaac Watts, 1707; varied by William Cameron, 1770.

DOXOLOGY.

Honor to the Almighty Three
And everlasting One;
All glory to the Father be,
The Spirit, and the Son!
Isaac Watts, 1709.

BEMERTON. C. M.

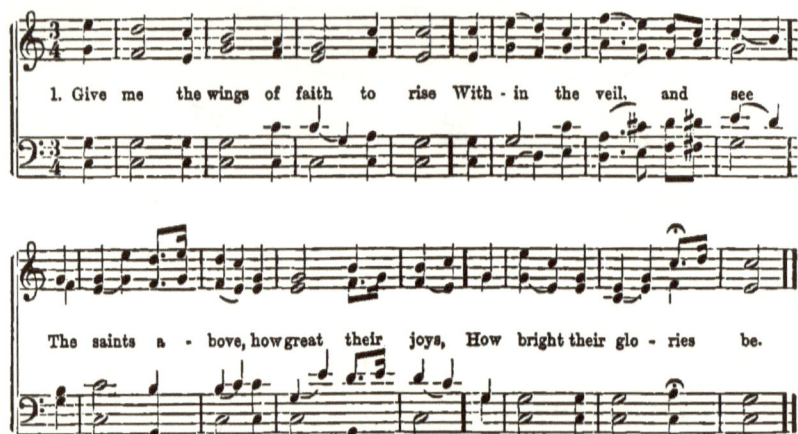

1. Give me the wings of faith to rise With-in the veil, and see
The saints a-bove, how great their joys, How bright their glo-ries be.

1055.

1 GIVE me the wings of faith to rise
   Within the veil, and see
The saints above, how great their joys,
   How bright their glories be.

2 Once they were mourning here below,
   And bathed their couch with tears;
They wrestled hard, as we do now,
   With sins, and doubts, and fears.

3 I ask them whence their victory came;
   They, with united breath,
Ascribe their conquest to the Lamb,
   Their triumph to his death.

4 They marked the footsteps that he trod;
   His zeal inspired their breast;
And, following their incarnate God,
   Possessed the promised rest.

5 Our glorious Leader claims our praise,
   For his own pattern given;
While the long cloud of witnesses
   Show the same path to heaven.
                        Isaac Watts, 1709.

1056.

1 THERE is a fold whence none can stray,
   And pastures ever green,
Where sultry sun, or stormy day,
   Or night, is never seen.

2 Far up the everlasting hills,
   In God's own light it lies;
His smile its vast dimension fills
   With joy that never dies.

3 There congregate the sons of light,
   Fair as the morning sky,
And taste of infinite delight
   Beneath their Saviour's eye.

4 One narrow vale, one darksome wave,
   Divides that land from this:
I have a Shepherd pledged to save
   And bear me home to bliss.

5 Soon at his feet my soul will lie
   In life's last struggling breath;
But I shall only seem to die,
   I shall not taste of death.

6 Far from this guilty world to be
   Exempt from toil and strife,
To spend eternity with thee,
   My Saviour, this is life!
                        Bishop East.

DOXOLOGY.

To Father, Son, and Holy Ghost,
   One God, whom we adore,
Be glory as it was, is now,
   And shall be evermore.
                        Tate and Brady, 1696.

HEAVEN.

CONSOLATION. C. M.

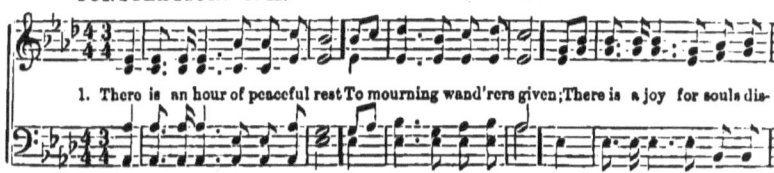
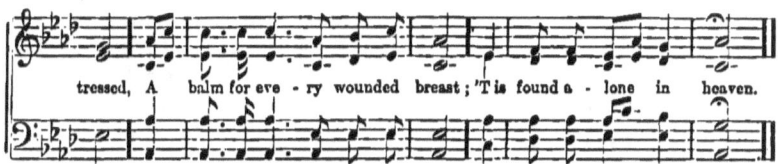

1. There is an hour of peaceful rest To mourning wand'rers given; There is a joy for souls distressed, A balm for eve - ry wounded breast; 'T is found a - lone in heaven.

1057.

1 THERE is an hour of peaceful rest
  To mourning wanderers given;
There is a joy for souls distressed,
  A balm for every wounded breast;
    'T is found alone in heaven.

2 There is a home for weary souls,
  By sins and sorrows driven,
When tossed on life's tempestuous shoals,
Where storms arise, and ocean rolls,
  And all is drear — 't is heaven.

3 There faith lifts up the tearless eye, —
  The heart no longer riven, —
And views the tempest passing by,
Sees evening shadows quickly fly,
  And all serene in heaven.

4 There fragrant flowers immortal bloom,
  And joys supreme are given;
There rays divine disperse the gloom;
Beyond the dark and narrow tomb
  Appears the dawn of heaven.
    William B. Tappan, 1829.

1058.

1 RISE, O my soul, pursue the path
  By ancient worthies trod;
Aspiring, view those holy men,
  Who lived and walked with God.

2 Though dead, they speak in reason's ear,
  And in example live;
Their faith, and hope, and mighty deeds
  Still fresh instruction give.

3 'T was through the Lamb's most precious
  They conquered every foe,   [blood
And to his power and matchless grace
  Their crowns of life they owe.

4 Lord, may I ever keep in view
  The patterns thou hast given,
And ne'er forsake the blessèd road
  That led them safe to heaven.
    John Needham, 1768.

1059.

1 WHEN I can read my title clear
  To mansions in the skies,
I bid farewell to every fear,
  And wipe my weeping eyes.

2 Should earth against my soul engage,
  And fiery darts be hurled,
Then I can smile at Satan's rage,
  And face a frowning world.

3 Let cares like a wild deluge come,
  And storms of sorrow fall,
May I but safely reach my home,
  My God, my heaven, my all!

4 There shall I bathe my weary soul
  In seas of heavenly rest,
And not a wave of trouble roll
  Across my peaceful breast.
    Isaac Watts, 1709.

HEAVEN

PARADISE. 8s, 6s & 6s.

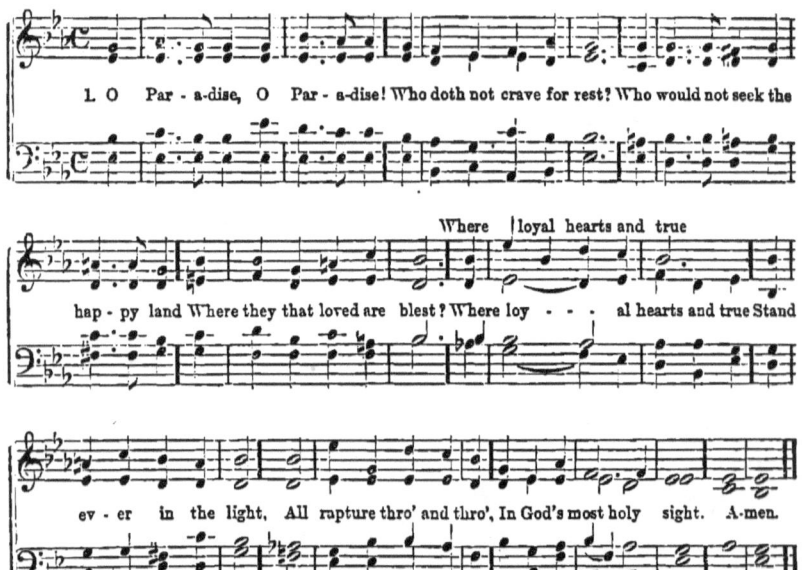

1. O Paradise, O Paradise! Who doth not crave for rest? Who would not seek the happy land Where they that loved are blest? Where loyal hearts and true Stand ever in the light, All rapture thro' and thro', In God's most holy sight. A-men.

1060.

1 O Paradise, O Paradise!
   Who doth not crave for rest?
   Who would not seek the happy land
   Where they that loved are blest?
     Where loyal hearts and true
      Stand ever in the light,
     All rapture through and through,
      In God's most holy sight.

2 O Paradise, O Paradise!
   'T is weary waiting here;
   I long to be where Jesus is,
   To feel, to see him near;
     Where loyal hearts and true
      Stand ever in the light,
     All rapture through and through,
      In God's most holy sight.

3 O Paradise, O Paradise!
   I want to sin no more;
   I want to be as pure on earth
   As on thy spotless shore,
     Where loyal hearts and true
      Stand ever in the light,
     All rapture through and through,
      In God's most holy sight.

4 O Paradise, O Paradise!
   I greatly long to see
   The special place my dearest Lord
   In love prepares for me;
     Where loyal hearts and true
      Stand ever in the light,
     All rapture through and through,
      In God's most holy sight.

5 Lord Jesus, King of Paradise,
   Oh keep me in thy love,
   And guide me to that happy land
   Of perfect rest above,
     Where loyal hearts and true
      Stand ever in the light,
     All rapture through and through,
      In God's most holy sight.
                Frederick W. Faber. 1862.

HEAVEN.

GLORY. 7s. Double.

1. What are these arrayed in white, Brighter than the noon-day sun, Foremost of the sons of light, [Omit.] Nearest the eternal throne? These are they that bore the cross, Faithful to their Master died, Sufferers in his righteous cause, Followers of the Cru-ci-fied.

1061.   Rev. vii. 13.

1 What are these arrayed in white,
  Brighter than the noonday sun,
Foremost of the sons of light,
  Nearest the eternal throne?

2 These are they that bore the cross,
  Faithful to their Master died;
Sufferers in his righteous cause,
  Followers of the Crucified.

3 Out of great distress they came,
  And their robes by faith below,
In the blood of Christ the Lamb,
  They have washed as white as snow.

4 More than conquerors at last,
  Here they find their trials o'er:
They have all their sufferings passed,
  Hunger now and thirst no more.

5 He that on the throne doth reign
  Them for evermore shall feed,
With the tree of life sustain,
  To the living fountains lead.

6 He shall all their griefs remove,
  He shall all their wants supply;
God himself, the God of love,
  Tears shall wipe from every eye.
                Charles Wesley, 1745, a.

1062.

1 Palms of glory, raiment bright,
  Crowns that never fade away,
Gird and deck the saints in light;
  Priests, and kings, and conquerors, they.

2 Yet the conquerors bring their palms
  To the Lamb amid the throne,
And proclaim in joyful psalms,
  Victory through his cross alone.

3 Kings for harps their crowns resign,
  Crying, as they strike the chords,
"Take the kingdom; it is thine,
  King of kings, and Lord of lords."

4 Round the altar priests confess,
  If their robes are white as snow,
'T was their Saviour's righteousness
  And his blood that made them so.

5 Who were these? On earth they dwelt,
  Sinners once of Adam's race;
Guilt, and fear, and suffering felt,
  But were saved by sovereign grace.

6 They were mortal, too, like us:
  And when we, like them, shall die,
May our souls, translated thus,
  Triumph, reign, and shine on high!
               James Montgomery, 1827.

HEAVEN.

BEULAH. 7s. DOUBLE.

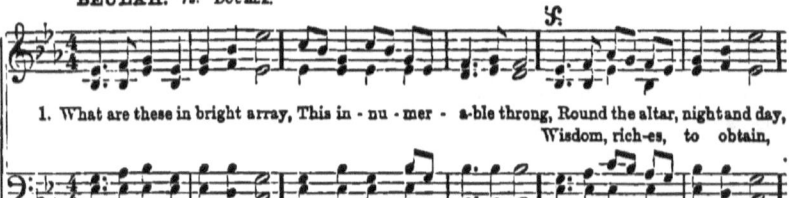

1. What are these in bright array, This in-nu-mer-a-ble throng, Round the altar, night and day,
Wisdom, rich-es, to obtain,

Hymning one triumphant song? "Worthy is the Lamb, once slain, Blessing, honor, glory, power,
New do-min-ion every hour."

1063.
REV. vii. 13.

1 WHAT are these in bright array,
  This innumerable throng,
Round the altar, night and day,
  Hymning one triumphant song?
"Worthy is the Lamb, once slain,
  Blessing, honor, glory, power,
Wisdom, riches, to obtain,
  New dominion every hour."

2 These through fiery trials trod,
  These from great affliction came;
Now, before the throne of God,
  Sealed with his almighty name,
Clad in raiment pure and white,
  Victor-palms in every hand,
Through their dear Redeemer's might,
  More than conquerors they stand.

3 Hunger, thirst, disease unknown,
  On immortal fruits they feed;
Them the Lamb amidst the throne
  Shall to living fountains lead:
Joy and gladness banish sighs;
  Perfect love dispels all fear;
And forever from their eyes
  God shall wipe away the tear.
James Montgomery, 1819.

1064.

1 HIGH in yonder realms of light
  Dwell the raptured saints above,
Far beyond our feeble sight,
  Happy in Immanuel's love:
Pilgrims in this vale of tears,
  Once they knew, like us below,
Gloomy doubts, distressing fears,
  Torturing pain and heavy woe.

2 But these days of weeping o'er,
  Passed this scene of toil and pain,
They shall feel distress no more,
  Never, never weep again:
'Mid the chorus of the skies,
  'Mid the angelic lyres above,
Hark, their songs melodious rise,
  Songs of praise to Jesus' love!

3 All is tranquil and serene,
  Calm and undisturbed repose;
There no cloud can intervene,
  There no angry tempest blows:
Every tear is wiped away,
  Sighs no more shall heave the breast,
Night is lost in endless day,
  Sorrow, in eternal rest.
Thomas Raffles, 1812.

HEAVEN.

HAVEN. L. M.

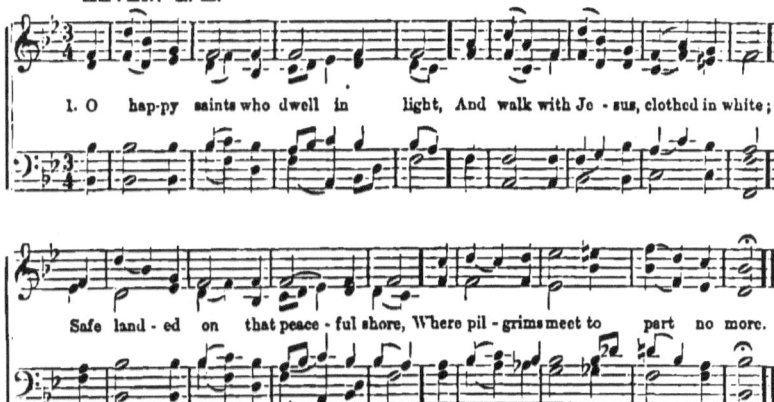

1. O happy saints who dwell in light, And walk with Jesus, clothed in white;
Safe landed on that peaceful shore, Where pilgrims meet to part no more.

1065.

1 O HAPPY saints who dwell in light,
And walk with Jesus, clothed in white;
Safe landed on that peaceful shore,
Where pilgrims meet to part no more.

2 Released from sin, and toil, and grief,
Death was their gate to endless life, —
An opened cage, to let them fly
And build their happy nest on high.

3 And now they range the heavenly plains,
And sing their hymns in melting strains;
And now their souls begin to prove
The heights and depths of Jesus' love.

4 He cheers them with eternal smile;
They sing hosannas all the while,
Or, overwhelmed with raptures sweet,
Sink down adoring at his feet.

5 Ah, Lord, with tardy steps I creep,
And sometimes sing, and sometimes weep;
Yet strip me of this house of clay,
And I will sing as loud as they.

John Berridge, 1785.

1066.

1 EXALTED high at God's right hand,
Nearer the throne than cherubs stand,
With glory crowned, in white array,
My wondering soul says, who are they?

2 These are the saints beloved of God;
Washed are their robes in Jesus' blood;
More spotless than the purest white,
They shine in uncreated light.

3 Brighter than angels, lo! they shine,
Their glories great, and all divine:
Tell me their origin, and say,
Their order what, and whence came they?

4 Through tribulation great they came,
They bore the cross, and scorned the shame:
Within the living temple blest, [
In God they dwell, and on him rest.

5 Unknown to mortal ears, they sing
The secret glories of their King:
Tell me the subject of their lays,
And whence their loud exalted praise?

6 Jesus, the Saviour, is their theme;
They sing the wonders of his name;
To him ascribing power and grace,
Dominion, and eternal praise.

7 Amen! they cry, to him alone,
Who dares to fill his Father's throne;
They give him glory, and again
Repeat his praise, and say, Amen!

Rowland Hill, 1783.

HEAVEN.

DEVOTION. 8s.

1. My Saviour, whom absent I love; Whom, not having seen, I adore;
Whose name is exalted above All glory, dominion, and power;

1067.

2 Dissolve thou these bands that detain
My soul from her portion in thee,
Ah, strike off this adamant chain,
And make me eternally free.

3 When that happy era begins,
When arrayed in thy glories I shine,
Nor grieve any more, by my sins,
The bosom on which I recline;

4 Oh then shall the veil be removed,
And round me thy brightness be poured;
I shall meet him whom absent I loved,
I shall see whom unseen I adored.

William Cowper, 1800.

1068.

1 OH when shall we sweetly remove,
Oh when shall we enter our rest,
Return to the Zion above,
The mother of spirits distrest;
That city of God the great King,
Where sorrow and death are no more,
Where saints our Immanuel sing,
And cherub and seraph adore?

2 Thou know'st in the spirit of prayer
We long thy appearing to see,
Resigned to the burden we bear,
But longing to triumph with thee:
'T is good at thy word to be here;
'T is better in thee to be gone,
And see thee in glory appear,
And rise to a share in thy throne.

3 To mourn for thy coming is sweet.
To weep at thy longer delay;
But thou, whom we hasten to meet,
Shalt chase all our sorrows away.
The tears shall be wiped from our eyes
When thee we behold in the cloud,
And echo the joys of the skies,
And shout to the trumpet of God.

Charles Wesley.

1069.

1 WE speak of the realms of the blest,
That country so bright and so fair,
And oft are its glories confessed;
But what must it be to be there!

2 We speak of its pathways of gold,
Its walls decked with jewels so rare,
Its wonders and pleasures untold;
But what must it be to be there!

3 We speak of its freedom from sin,
From sorrow, temptation, and care,
From trials without and within;
But what must it be to be there!

4 We speak of its service of love,
The robes which the glorified wear,
The church of the first-born above;
But what must it be to be there!

5 Then let us, 'midst pleasure or woe,
For heaven our spirits prepare,
And shortly we also shall know
And feel what it is to be there.

Elizabeth Mills, 1829.

SELECTIONS FOR CHANTING.

DOXOLOGIES.

1. GLORIA IN EXCELSIS. Ascribed to *Telesphorus*, A.D. 128-139.

1 GLORY be to | God on | high, ‖ and on earth | peace, good- | will toward | men.
2 We praise thee, we bless thee, we | worship | thee, ‖ we glorify thee, we give thanks to | thee for | thy great | glory,

3 O Lord God, | heavenly | King, ‖ God the | Father | Al- | mighty.
4 O Lord, the only-begotten Son, | Jesus | Christ ; ‖ O Lord God, Lamb of | God, Son | of the | Father,

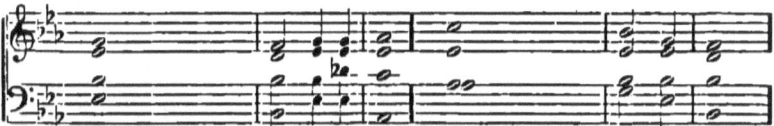

5 That takest away the | sins · of the | world, ‖ have mercy | upon | us.
6 Thou that takest away the | sins · of the | world ‖ have mercy | upon | us.
7 Thou that takest away the | sins · of the | world, ‖ re- | ceive our | prayer.
8 Thou that sittest at the right hand of | God the | Father. ‖ have mercy | upon | us.

9 For Thou | only · art | holy ; ‖ Thou | only | art the | Lord ;
10 Thou only. O Christ, with the | Holy | Ghost, ‖ art most high in the | glory of | God the | Father. ‖ A- | men.

2. TE DEUM LAUDAMUS.

1 We praise | thee, O | God ; ‖ we acknowledge | thee to | be the | Lord ; (2)

3 To thee all angels | cry a- | loud, ‖ the heavens, and | all the | powers · there- | in. (4)

6 The glorious company of the apostles | praise — | thee ; ‖ the goodly fellow- ship of the | prophets | praise — | thee ; (7)

8 The Father of an | infi-nite | majesty ; ‖ thine adorable, | true, and | only | Son ; (9)

2 All the earth doth | worship | thee, ‖ the | Father | ever- | lasting. (3)

4 To thee cherubim and | sera- | phim ‖ con- | tinual- | ly do | cry, (5)

7 The noble army of martyrs | praise — | thee ; ‖ the Holy Church throughout all the world | doth ac- | knowledge | thee, (8)

9 Also the | Holy | Ghost, ‖ the | Com- | fort- | er. (10)

5 Ho - ly, Ho - ly, Ho - ly, Lord God of Sab - a - oth,

Heaven and earth are full of the maj - es-ty of thy glo - ry. (6)

DOXOLOGIES. 435

TE DEUM LAUDAMUS. Concluded.

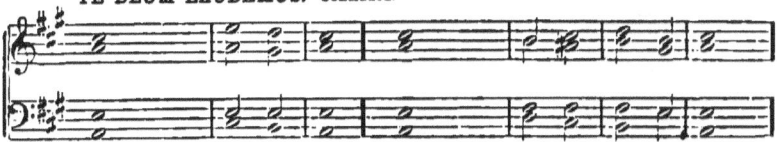

10 Thou art the King of | glory, · O | Christ; ‖ thou art the ever- | lasting | Son · of the | Father.

11 When thou tookest upon thee to de- | liver | man, ‖ thou didst humble thyself to be | born — | of a | virgin.

12 When thou hadst overcome the | sharpness · of | death, ‖ thou didst open the kingdom of | heaven · to | all be- | lievers.

13 Thou sittest at the right | hand of | God, ‖ in the | glory | of the | Father.

14 We believe that | thou shalt | come, ‖ shalt | come to | be our | Judge.

15 We therefore pray thee | help thy | servants, ‖ whom thou hast redeemed | with thy | precious | blood.

16 Make them to be numbered | with thy | saints, ‖ in | glory | ever- | lasting.

17 O Lord, save thy people, and | bless thine | heritage; ‖ govern them, and | lift them | up for- | ever.

18 Day by day we | magni-fy | thee, ‖ and we worship thy name ever, | world with- | out — | end.

19 Vouch- | safe, O | Lord. ‖ to keep us | this day | without | sin.

20 O Lord, have | mercy · up- | on us, ‖ have | mercy | upon | us.

21 O Lord, let thy mercy | be up- | on us, ‖ as our | trust — | is in | thee.

22 O Lord, in thee, in thee have I trust-ed; let me nev-er be confounded, let me nev-er be con-found-ed.

DOXOLOGIES.

3. TRISAGION.

1 HOLY, Holy, Holy Lord God of Sabaoth; Heaven and earth are full | of thy | glory.

2 Hosanna in the highest! Blessed is he that cometh in the name of the Lord. Ho- | sanna | in the | highest!

4. TERSANCTUS.

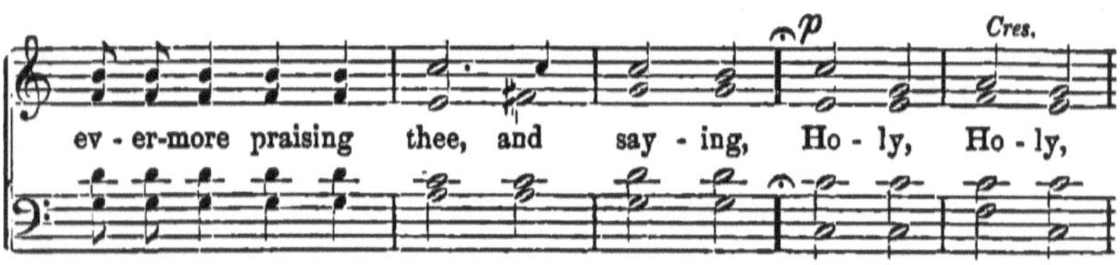

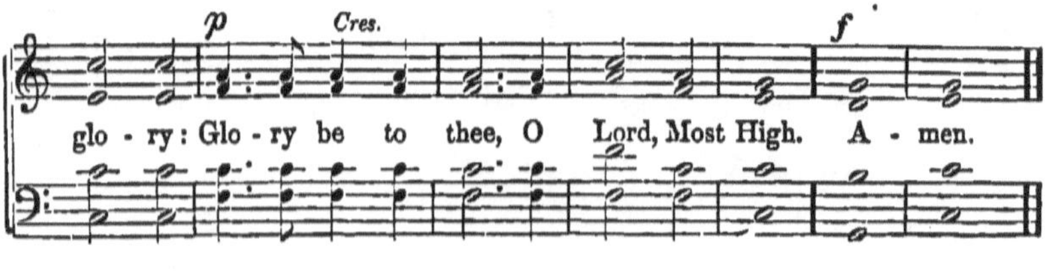

THEREFORE with angels, and archangels, and with all the company of.. } heaven, { we laud and magnify thy glorious.... } name, evermore praising thee, and saying, Holy, Holy, Holy Lord God of hosts; Heaven and earth are full of.... thy glory: Glory be to thee, O Lord, Most High. A-men.

DOXOLOGIES. 437

5. GLORIA PATRI. No. 1.

Glo - ry be to the Fa - ther, and to the Son, and to the Ho - ly Ghost; As it was in the be - gin - ning, is now, and ev - er shall be, world without end. A - men. A - men.

6. GLORIA PATRI. No. 2.

Glo - ry be to the Fa - ther, and to the Son, and to the Ho - ly Ghost; As it was in the be - gin - ning, is now, and ev - er shall be, world with-out end. A - men. A - men.

7. RESPONSE. No. 1.

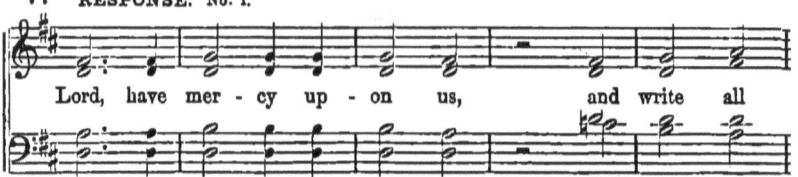

Lord, have mer-cy up-on us, and write all these thy laws in our hearts, we be-seech thee.

8. RESPONSE. No. 2.

A-men.

1 THE law of the Lord is perfect, con- | verting · the | soul:
  The testimony of the Lord is sure, making | wise the | simple.

2 The statutes of the Lord are right, re- | joicing · the | heart:
  The commandment of the Lord is pure, en- | lightening · the | eyes.

3 The fear of the Lord is clean, en- | during · for- | ever:
  The judgments of the Lord are true and righteous | alto-gether.

4 More to be desired are they than gold, yea, than | much fine | gold:
  Sweeter also than honey and the | honey- | comb.

5 Moreover by them is thy | servant | warned:
  And in keeping of them there is | great re- | ward.

9. RESPONSE. No. 3.

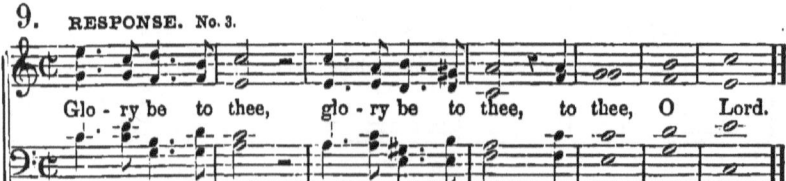

Glo-ry be to thee, glo-ry be to thee, to thee, O Lord.

10. THE HEAVENS DECLARE.

PSALM XIX. (Responsive.)

1 THE heavens declare the glory of God; —
    and the firmament showeth his | handy — work.
2 *Day unto day uttereth speech, —
    and night unto | night . . showeth | knowledge.*
3 There is no speech nor language where
    their | voice . . is not | heard.
4 *Their line is gone out through all the earth, —
    and their words to the | end . . of the | world.*
5 In them hath he set a tabernacle for the sun,
    which is as a bridegroom coming out of his chamber,
    and rejoiceth as a strong man to | run . . a | race.
6 *His going forth is from the end of the heaven, —
    and his circuit to the ends of it, —
    and there is nothing hid from the | heat . . there- | of.*
7 The law of the Lord is perfect, —
    con- | verting . . the | soul.
  *The testimony of the Lord is sure, —
    making | wise . . the | simple.*
8 The statutes of the Lord are right, —
    re- | joicing . . the | heart.
  *The commandment of the Lord is pure, —
    en- | lightening . . the | eyes.*
9 The fear of the Lord is clean, —
    en- | during . . for- | ever.
  *The judgments of the Lord are true, —
    and | righteous . . alto- | gether.*
10 More to be desired are they than gold, —
    yea, than much fine gold; —
    sweeter also than honey and the | honey — | comb.
11 *Moreover, by them is thy servant warned; —
    and in keeping of them there is | great . . re- | ward.*
12 Who can understand his errors? |
    cleanse thou me from | se . . cret | faults.
13 *Let the words of my mouth,
    and the meditations of my heart, —
    be acceptable in thy sight, O Lord, —
    my strength and my Re- | deemer. . . A | men.*

11. THE LORD IS MY SHEPHERD.

PSALM 23.

1 THE Lord is my Shepherd; — I | shall .. not | want.
2 He maketh me to lie down in green pastures; —
   He leadeth me beside the | still= | waters.
3 He restoreth my soul; — he leadeth me in the paths of righteousness
   for his | name's =sake. —
4 Yea, — though I walk through the valley of the shadow of death,
   I will fear no evil; — for thou art with me; —
   thy rod and thy | staff .. they | comfort me.
5 Thou preparest a table before me in the presence of mine enemies: —
   thou anointest my head with oil; — my | cup .. runneth | over.
6 Surely goodness and mercy shall follow me all the days of my life; —
   and I shall dwell in the house of the | Lord .. for- | ever.

12. GOD BE MERCIFUL.

PSALM 67.

1 GOD be merciful unto | us, and | bless us;
   And cause his | face to | shine up- | on us;
2 That thy way may be known upon | earth,
   Thy saving | health a- | mong all | nations.
3 Let the people | praise thee, · O | God;
   Let | all the | people | praise thee.
4 Oh let the nations be glad and | sing for | joy:
   For thou shalt judge the people righteously, and govern the | na-
   tions | upon | earth.
5 Let the people | praise thee, · O | God;
   Let | all the | people | praise thee.
6 Then shall the earth | yield her | increase;
   And God, even | our own | God, shall | bless us.
7 God | shall — | bless us;
   And all the ends of the | earth shall | fear — | him.
   Glory be to the Father, etc.

13. LORD, OUR DWELLING PLACE.

PSALM 90. (Responsive.)

1 LORD, thou hast been our | dwelling- | place
In | all — | gene- | rations.

2 *Before the mountains were brought forth, or ever thou hadst formed the | earth*
and the | world,
Even from everlasting to ever- | lasting, | thou art | God.

3 Thou turnest man | to de- | struction;
And sayest, re- | turn, ye | children · of | men.

4 *For a thousand years in thy sight are but as yesterday | when · it is | past,*
And as a | watch — | in the | night.

5 Thou carriest them away as with a flood; they are | as a | sleep:
In the morning they are like | grass which | groweth | up.

6 *In the morning it flourisheth, and | groweth | up;*
In the evening it is cut | down, and | wither- | eth.

7 For we are consumed | by thine | anger,
And by thy | wrath — | are we | troubled.

8 *Thou hast set our iniquities | before | thee,*
Our secret sins in the | light · of thy | counte- | nance.

9 For all our days are passed away | in thy | wrath:
We spend our years as a | tale — | that is | told.

10 *The days of our years are three-score years and ten; and if by reason of strength*
they be | four-score | years,
Yet is their strength labor and sorrow; for it is soon cut off, | and we | fly
| away.

11 Who knoweth the power | of thine | anger?
Even according to thy fear, | so— | is thy | wrath.

12 *So teach us to | number · our | days,*
That we may apply our | hearts — | unto | wisdom.

Glory be to the Father, and | to the | Son,
And | to the | Holy | Ghost;

As it was in the beginning, is now, and | ever | shall be,
World | without | end. A- | men.

14. O COME LET US SING.

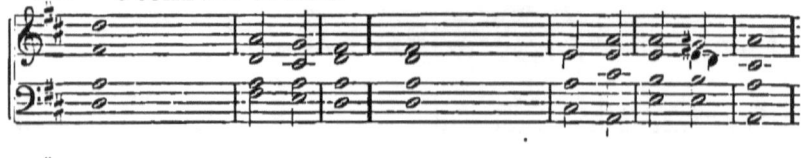

PSALM 95.

1 Oh come, let us sing un- | to the | Lord ;
Let us heartily rejoice in the | strength of | our sal- | vation.

2 Let us come before his presence | with thanks- | giving ;
And show ourselves | glad in | him with | psalms.

3 For the Lord is a | great — | God ;
And a great | King a- | bove all | gods.

4 In his hands are all the corners | of the | earth ;
And the strength of the | hills is | his — | also.

5 The sea is his, | and he | made it ;
And his hands pre- | pared the | dry — | land.

6 Oh come, let us worship, | and fall | down,
And kneel be- | fore the | Lord our | Maker :

7 For he is the | Lord our | God ;
And we are the people of his pasture and the | sheep of | his — | hand.

8 Oh worship the Lord in the | beauty of | holiness ;
Let the whole earth | stand in | awe of | him :

9 For he cometh, for he cometh to | judge the | earth ;
And with righteousness to judge the world, and the | peo-ple | with his | truth.

10 Glory be to the Father, and | to the | Son,
And | to the | Holy | Ghost ;
As it was in the beginning, is now, and | ev-er | shall be,
World | with-out | end. A- | men.

15.

PSALM 121.

1 I will lift up mine eyes unto the hills, from whence | cometh · my | help.
My help cometh from the Lord, | which made | heaven · and | earth.

2 He will not suffer thy foot to be moved: he that keepeth thee | will not | slumber.
Behold, he that keepeth Israel shall | neither | slumber · nor | sleep.

3 The Lord is thy keeper : the Lord is thy shade upon | thy right | hand :
The sun shall not smite thee by day, | nor the | moon by | night.

4 The Lord shall preserve thee from all evil : he shall pre- | serve thy | soul.
The Lord shall preserve thy going out and thy coming in from this time forth,
and | even · for | ev-er | more.

Glory be to the Father, &c.

16. ARISE, O LORD.

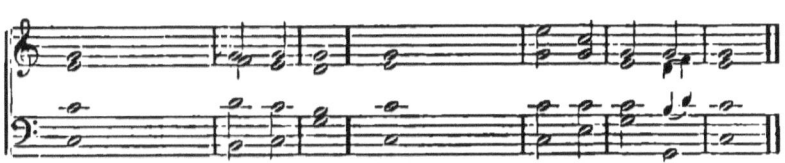

PSALMS 132 and 24. (Dedication.)

1 Arise, O Lord, | into · thy | rest;
Thou, and the | ark — | of thy | strength.

2 Let thy priests be clothed with | right-eous-| ness;
And let thy | saints — | shout for | joy.

3 Who shall ascend into the hill | of the | Lord,
Or who shall stand | in his | ho-ly | place?

4 He that hath clean hands, and a | pure — | heart;
Who hath not lifted up his soul unto | vanity, · nor | sworn de- | ceitfully,

5 He shall receive the blessing | from the | Lord,
And righteousness from the | God of | his sal- | vation.

6 Lift up your heads, O ye gates; and be ye lift up, ye ever- | last-ing | doors:
And the King of | glo-ry | shall come | in.

7 Who is this | King of | glory?
The Lord, strong and mighty, the | Lord — | mighty · in | battle.

8 Lift up your heads, O ye gates: even lift them up, ye ever- | last-ing | doors,
And the King of | glo-ry | shall come | in.

9 Who is this | King of | glory?
The Lord of hosts, | he · is the | King of | glory.

Glory be to the Father, and | to the | Son,
And | to the | Ho-ly | Ghost;

As it was in the beginning. is now, and | ever | shall be,
World | with-out | end. A- | men.

17. HE IS DESPISED AND REJECTED.

ISAIAH 53.

1 HE is despised and re- | jected of | men;
  A man of sorrows, | and ac- | quainted with | grief:
2 And we hid as it were our | faces | from him;
  He was despised, and | we es- | teemed · him | not.
3 Surely he hath borne our griefs and | carried · our | sorrows;
  Yet we did esteem him stricken, | smitten · of | God, · and af- | flicted.
4 But he was wounded for | our trans- | gressions,
  He was | bruised · for | our in- | iquities;
5 The chastisement of our peace | was up- | on him;
  And with | his stripes | we are | healed.
6 All we like sheep have | gone a- | stray;
  We have turned every | one to | his own | way;
7 And the Lord hath | laid on | him
  The in- | iqui-ty | of us | all.
8 When thou shalt make his soul an | offering · for | sin,
  He shall see his seed, he | shall pro- | long his | days;
9 And the pleasure of the Lord shall prosper | in his | hand.
  He shall see of the travail of his soul, and | shall be | satis- | fied.
  Glory be to the Father, &c.

18. BLESSED BE THE LORD.

LUKE I. 68-71.

1 BLESSED be the Lord | God of | Israel,
  For he hath visited | and re- | deemed his | people;
2 And hath raised up a horn of sal- | vation | for us,
  In the house | of his | servant | David;
3 As he spake by the mouth of his | holy | prophets,
  Which have been | since the | world be- | gan;
4 That we should be saved | from our | enemies,
  And from the | hand of | all that | hate us.
5 Glory be to the Father, and | to the | Son,
  And | to the | Holy | Ghost;
6 As it was in the beginning, is now, and | ever | shall be,
  World | without | end. A- | men.

19. BURIED WITH CHRIST.

1 BURIED with Christ by | baptism · unto | death, —
We rise in the | likeness · of his | res-ur- | rection.

2 If ye then be | risen · with | Christ,
Seek those things which are above, where Christ sitteth at the | right — | hand of | God.

3 For as many as have been baptized into Christ, have | put on | Christ.
Therefore glorify God in your body, and in your | spir-it, | which are | God's.

4 Reckon ye yourselves to be dead in- | deed ·· unto | sin, —
But alive unto God through | Je-sus | Christ our | Lord.

5 If we be dead with him, we shall also | live with | him;
If we suffer with him, we shall | al-so | reign with | him.

6 Blessed is he whose transgression is forgiven, whose | sin is | covered.
Blessed is the man to whom the Lord im- | pu-teth | not in- | iquity.

20.

1 Go ye therefore, and | teach all | nations, —
Baptizing them in the name of the Father, and of the Son, and | of the | Ho-ly | — Ghost.

2 Repent, and be baptized every | one of | you
In the name of Christ, for the re- | mis-sion | of — | sins.

3 Arise, and be baptized, and wash away thy sins, calling on the | name · of the |
For thus it becometh us to ful- | fil all | right-eous- | ness.   [Lord.

4 Glory be to the Father, and | to the | Son, —
And | to the | Ho-ly | Ghost;

5 As it was in the beginning, is now, and | ev-er | shall be,
World — | with-out | end. A- | men.

21. BLESSED ARE THE DEAD.

1 BLESSED are the dead, who die in the | Lord, from | henceforth;

Yea, saith the Spirit, that they may rest from their labors, | and their | works do | follow them.

2 For if we believe that Jesus died and | rose a- | gain,

Even so them also which sleep in Jesus | will God | bring with | him.

3 For the Lord himself shall descend from heaven with a shout, with the voice of the archangel, and with the | trump of | God:

And the dead in | Christ — | shall rise | first.

4 Blessed and holy is he that hath part in the first resurrection:

On such the second death | hath no | power;

But they shall be priests of God and of Christ,

And shall reign with | him a | thou-sand | years.

5 Unto him that loved us,

And washed us from our sins in | his own | blood,

And hath made us kings and priests to God and his Father;

To him be glory and do- | minion ·· for- | ever ·· and | ever. A- | men.

BLESSED ARE THE DEAD.

22. I AM THE RESURRECTION.

1 Man that is born of a woman, is of few days, and | full of | trouble;
He cometh forth like a flower, and is cut down; he fleeth as a shadow | and con- | tinu · eth | not.

2 It is appointed unto men | once to | die —
But | af - ter | this the | judgment.

3 I am the Resurrection | and the | Life;
He that believeth in me, though he were | dead, yet | shall he | live.

4 And whosoever liveth, and believeth in me, shall | nev - er | die.
Be- | liev - est | thou — | this?

5 Death is swallowed | up in | victory.
O death, where is thy sting? O | grave, where | is thy | victory?

6 The sting of death is sin, and the strength of | sin · is the | law.
But thanks be to God, who giveth us the victory through our | Lord —|Je - sus | Christ. | A- | men.

23. THY WILL BE DONE.

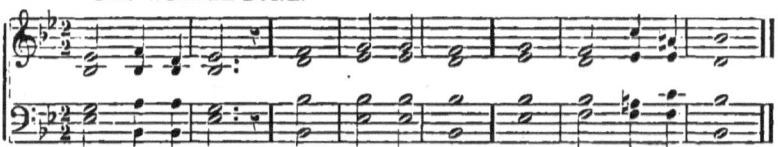

1 "Thy will be | done!" | In devious way
The hurrying stream of | life may | run; |
Yet still our grateful hearts shall say, |
   "Thy will be | done."

2 "Thy will be | done!" | If o'er us shine
A gladd'ning and a | ·prosperous | sun, |
This prayer will make it more divine : |
   "Thy will be | done."

3 "Thy will be|done!" || Though shrouded o'er
Our | path with | gloom, || one comfort — one
Is ours: to breathe, while we adore, |
   "Thy will be | done!"

(Close by repeating the first two measures — "Thy will be done.")

24. CAST THY BURDEN ON THE LORD.

Ps. lv. 22.

Cast thy burden on the Lord, and he shall sustain thee; he shall never suffer the righteous to be moved.

INDEX OF FIRST LINES.

	HYMN		HYMN
Abide with me! fast falls the eventide	973	Arise, my tenderest thoughts, arise	767
According to thy gracious word	839	Arm of the Lord, awake, awake!	892
A charge to keep I have	749	Around thy grave, Lord Jesus	832
A debtor to mercy alone	428	Around thy table, holy Lord	837
A few more years shall roll	984	Around the throne of God in heaven	885
A Friend there is: your voices join	685	Asleep in Jesus! blessed sleep	986
Again returns the day of holy rest	49	As o'er the past my memory strays	479
Again the Lord of life and light	68	As pants the hart for cooling streams	608
Ah! how shall fallen man	411	As the sun's enlivening eye	780
Ah, what avails my strife	474	As when the weary traveller gains	1031
Alas! and did my Saviour bleed	244	As with gladness men of old	223
Alas! what hourly dangers rise	746	At thy command, our dearest Lord	844
A little child the Saviour came	883	At the Lamb's high feast we sing	856
All hail, Incarnate God	308	Author of faith, to thee I cry	502
All hail the power of Jesus' name	301	Awaked by Sinai's awful sound	433
All hail, ye blessed band	815	Awake, all-conquering arm, awake	890
All praise to thee, eternal Lord	230	Awake and sing the song	351
All praise to our redeeming Lord	808	Awake, awake the sacred song	213
All praise to thee, my God, this night	85	Awake, our drowsy souls	56
All that I was, my sin and guilt	480	Awake our souls, away our fears	734
Almighty Father of mankind	659	Awake, my soul, and with the sun	80
Almighty God, thy word is cast	37	Awake, my soul, awake, my tongue	181
Almighty Maker of my frame	966	Awake, my soul, in joyful lays	322
Amazing grace! how sweet the sound	421	Awake, my soul, lift up thine eyes	739
Am I a soldier of the cross?	736	Awake, my soul, stretch every nerve	741
Amidst us our Belovéd stands	845	Awake, my tongue, thy tribute bring	154
And have I measured half my days?	476	Awake, ye saints, and raise your eyes	959
And must this body die	1017	Before Jehovah's awful throne	2
And now we rise; the symbols disappear	860	Before the throne of God above	284
And will the great eternal God	873	Before thy throne, O Lord of heaven	92
And will the Judge descend	1019	Begin, my tongue, some heavenly theme	187
Angels, from the realms of glory	218	Begone, unbelief! my Saviour is near	642
Angels, roll the rock away	261	Behold, a Stranger's at the door	443
Another six days' work is done	58	Behold the amazing sight	242
Approach, my soul, the mercy seat	579	Behold the expected time draw near	912
Arise, O King of grace, arise!	876	Behold the glories of the Lamb	280
Arise, my soul, arise	306	Behold, the morning sun	407
Arise, my soul, my joyful powers	640	Behold the mountain of the Lord	897

449

INDEX OF FIRST LINES.

HYMN		HYMN	
Behold the throne of grace	615	Church of the ever-living God	791
Behold what wondrous grace	782	Come, all ye saints of God	362
Behold where in the friend of man	234	Come, and let us sweetly join	807
Be joyful in God, all ye lands of the earth	113	Come, blessed Spirit, source of light	391
Beneath thy cross I lay me down	498	Come, dearest Lord, descend and dwell	43
Beset with snares on every hand	698	Come, every pious heart	266
Beyond the glittering starry globe	278	Come, happy souls, adore the Lamb	819
Bless, O my soul, the living God	136	Come, heavenly Love, inspire my song	329
Blessed are the sons of God	779	Come hither, all ye weary souls	442
Blest are the humble souls that see	762	Come, Holy Ghost, in love	394
Blest are the pure in heart	775	Come, Holy Ghost, in us arise	368
Blest are the sons of peace	756	Come, Holy Ghost, who ever one	373
Blest be the everlasting God	1016	Come, Holy Spirit, come	373
Blest be the Father and his love	103	Come, Holy Spirit, Dove divine	811
Blest be thy love, dear Lord	526	Come, Holy Spirit, heavenly Dove, My	390
Blest be the tie that binds	755	Come, Holy Spirit, heavenly Dove, With	366
Blest Comforter divine	372	Come, humble sinner, in whose breast	455
Blest hour when mortal man retires	59	Come, let our voices join to raise	9
Blest is the man whose spirit shares	763	Come, let us anew our journey pursue	963
Blest morning, whose young dawning rays	67	Come, let us join our cheerful songs	279
Blow ye the trumpet, blow	425	Come, let us join our friends above	989
Body of Jesus, O sweet food	855	Come, let us sing the song of songs	357
Bread of heaven, on thee we feed	859	Come, let us to the Lord our God	684
Bread of the world, in mercy broken	854	Come, Lord, and tarry not	1013
Breast the wave, Christian	750	Come, Lord, and warm each languid	1041
Brethren, let us join to bless	300	Come, my fond, fluttering heart	466
Bride of the Lamb! awake! awake!	1007	Come, my soul, thy suit prepare	621
Brightest and best of the sons of the	219	Come, O Creator Spirit blest	371
Bright Source of everlasting love	765	Come, O my soul, in sacred lays	119
Bright was the guiding star that led	215	Come, O thou traveller unknown	626
Broad is the road that leads to death	453	Come, our indulgent Saviour, come	271
Buried beneath the yielding wave	814	Come, sacred Spirit, from above	370
Buried in baptism with our Lord	831	Come, said Jesus' sacred voice	445
By cool Siloam's shady rill	881	Come, sound his praise abroad	89
By faith in Christ I walk with God	697	Come, thou almighty King	103
		Come, thou Desire of all thy saints	24
Call Jehovah thy salvation	201	Come, thou Fount of every blessing	649
Child of sin and sorrow	447	Come, thou long-expected Jesus	217
Children of God, in all your need	618	Come, weary souls, with sin distressed	441
Children of light, arise and shine	712	Come, we that love the Lord	781
Children of the heavenly King	776	Come, ye disconsolate, where'er ye	622
Children of the King of grace	825	Come, ye sinners, poor and wretched	449
Christ is our Corner-stone	877	Come, ye thankful people, come	945
Christ, the Lord, is risen again	263	Come, ye that love the Saviour's name	15
Christ, the Lord, is risen to-day	264	Come, ye who bow to sovereign grace	833
Christ, who came my soul to save	824	Commit thou all thy griefs	671
Christ, whose glory fills the sky	326	Compared with Christ in all beside	523
Christ will gather in his own	1006	Crown his head with endless blessing	295

INDEX OF FIRST LINES. 451

Daughter of Zion, from the dust	792
Day by day the manna fell	681
Day of Judgment! Day of wonders!	1024
Dearest of names, our Lord, our King	987
Dear Lord and Master mine	730
Dear Refuge of my weary soul	665
Dear Saviour! I am thine	515
Dear Saviour, when my thoughts recall	573
Dear Shepherd of thy people, hear	874
Depth of mercy, can there be	559
Descend from heaven, celestial Dove	380
Descend, immortal Dove	383
Did Christ o'er sinners weep	438
Dismiss us with thy blessing, Lord	45
Do not I love thee, O my Lord	542
Do we not know that solemn word	830
Down to the sacred wave	816
Dread Jehovah! God of nations	940
Dread Sovereign, let my evening song	88
Early, my God, without delay	21
Earth to earth, and dust to dust	1004
Encompassed with clouds of distress	586
Enthroned in light, eternal God	872
Enthroned on high, Almighty Lord	367
Ere another Sabbath's close	71
Eternal beam of light divine	693
Eternal Father, strong to save	929
Eternal God, we look to thee	661
Eternal light! eternal light	147
Eternal Source of every joy	947
Eternal Spirit, we confess	369
Exalted high at God's right hand	1066
Faith adds new charms to earthly bliss	634
Faith is a living power from heaven	630
Faithful, O Lord, thy mercies are	198
Far as thy name is known	40
Far from my heavenly home	991
Far from my thoughts, vain world, begone	848
Far from these narrow scenes of night	1040
Far from the world, O Lord, I flee	628
Father, how wide thy glory shines	424
Father! if I may call thee so	490
Father, I long, I faint to see	1042
Father of heaven! whose gracious hand	616
Father of heaven! whose love profound	104
Father of love and power	99
Father of mercies, bow thine ear	868
Father of mercies, in thy house	864
Father of mercies! in thy word	402
Father of mercies, send thy grace	764
Father, while we break this bread	658
Fear not, O little flock, the foe	751
Fierce was the wild billow	714
Firm as the earth thy gospel stands	638
For all thy saints, O God	993
Forever with the Lord	1051
For mercies countless as the sands	620
For thee, O God, our constant praise	4
For thee, O dear, dear country	1046
For thy mercy and thy grace	962
Forth from the dark and stormy sky	26
Forth in thy name, O Lord, I go	725
Fountain of mercy! God of love	953
Frequent the day of God returns	61
Friend after friend departs	907
From all that dwell below the skies	139
From deep distress and troubled thoughts	551
From Egypt lately come	1052
From every stormy wind that blows	611
From foes that would the land devour	939
From Greenland's icy mountains	927
From the cross uplifted high	444
From thee, my God, my joys shall rise	1043
From thy dear pierced side	439
Full of weakness and of sin	701
Gently, gently lay thy rod	560
Gently, Lord! oh, gently lead us	650
Gently, my Saviour, let me down	988
Gird on thy conquering sword	313
Give me the wings of faith to rise	1055
Give thanks to God: he reigns above	173
Give to our God immortal praise	172
Give us room that we may dwell	805
Glorious things of thee are spoken	803
Glory, glory to our King	296
Glory to God on high	361
Glory to thee, whose powerful word	933
God bless our native land	935
God calling yet! shall I not hear?	452
God in the gospel of his Son	409
God is love: his mercy brightens	202
God is my strong salvation	706
God is the refuge of his saints	175

INDEX OF FIRST LINES.

HYMN		
God moves in a mysterious way	160	
God, my supporter and my hope	170	
God of Eternity, from thee	965	
God of mercy! God of grace!	921	
God of my life, through all its days	135	
God of my life, to thee I call	613	
God of my life, whose gracious power	648	
God of the morning, at whose voice	78	
God of the world! near and afar	948	
Go, preach my gospel, saith the Lord	889	
Go to dark Gethsemane	239	
Grace! 'tis a charming sound	436	
Great Father of each perfect gift	363	
Great God, attend while Zion sings	10	
Great God, how infinite art thou	140	
Great God, indulge my humble claim	130	
Great God, let all our tuneful powers	955	
Great God of wonders! all thy ways	430	
Great God, the nations of the earth	896	
Great God, to thee my evening song	86	
Great God! we sing that mighty hand	957	
Great God, what do I see and hear	1023	
Great God, whose universal sway	900	
Great is the Lord our God	785	
Great King of glory, come	878	
Great Lord of angels, we adore	865	
Great Ruler of all nature's frame	145	
Great Source of boundless power	658	
Guide me, O thou great Jehovah	971	
Had I the tongues of Greeks and Jews	760	
Hail, sovereign love, that first began	323	
Hail the day that sees him rise	272	
Hail, thou once despised Jesus	294	
Hail to the Lord's Anointed	914	
Hail to the Prince of life and peace	310	
Hallelujah! raise, oh raise	156	
Happy soul! thy days are ended	975	
Happy the church, thou sacred place	801	
Happy the souls to Jesus joined	768	
Hark! how the gospel trumpet sounds	918	
Hark! my soul, it is the Lord	530	
Hark! ten thousand harps and voices	315	
Hark! the distant isles proclaim	919	
Hark! the glad sound, the Saviour comes	208	
Hark! the herald angels sing	224	
Hark! the voice of love and mercy	252	
Hark! 'tis your heavenly Father's call	882	

HYMN		
Hark! what mean those holy voices	216	
Hast thou said, exalted Jesus	821	
Hast thou within a care so deep	612	
Haste, traveller, haste! the night comes on	461	
Hasten, Lord, the glorious time	920	
Hasten, sinner, to be wise	462	
Head of the church triumphant	752	
Hear, gracious God, a sinner's cry	492	
Hear me, O God, nor hide thy face	584	
Hear what the voice from heaven	996	
Hearken, ye children of your God	834	
Hearts of stone, relent, relent	483	
Heavenly Father, to whose eye	704	
He dies! the friend of sinners dies	269	
He lives, the great Redeemer lives	286	
Here at thy cross, my dying God	499	
He reigns, the Lord, the Saviour reigns	1022	
He sendeth sun, he sendeth shower	656	
He who on earth as man was known	677	
High in the heavens, eternal God	178	
High in yonder realms of light	1064	
Holy Bible! book divine	398	
Holy Father, whom we praise	73	
Holy Ghost! the Infinite	375	
Holy Ghost, with light divine	384	
Holy Jesus, Saviour blest	325	
Holy Lamb, who thee receive	597	
Holy Spirit, from on high	385	
Holy Spirit, heavenly Dove	386	
Hope of our hearts, O Lord, appear	1053	
Hosanna to the living Lord	42	
Hosanna to the Prince of light	268	
How are thy servants blessed, O Lord	193	
How beauteous are their feet	861	
How beauteous were the marks divine	233	
How blest the righteous when he dies	1003	
How blest the sacred tie that binds	758	
How bright those glorious spirits shine	1054	
How can I sink with such a prop	716	
How charming is the place	33	
How did my heart rejoice to hear	14	
How firm a foundation, ye saints	183	
How gentle God's commands	673	
How heavy is the night	412	
How helpless guilty nature lies	420	
How honorable is the place	787	
How is our nature spoiled by sin	416	
How lost was my condition	482	

INDEX OF FIRST LINES. 453

	HYMN
How oft, alas! this wretched heart	581
How pleasant, how divinely fair	16
How pleased and blest was I	13
How precious is the book divine	406
How rich thy favors, God of grace	191
How sad our state by nature is	417
How shall I praise the eternal God	162
How shall the young secure their hearts	399
How sweet and awful is the place	842
How sweet, how heavenly is the sight	767
How sweetly flowed the gospel sound	229
How sweet the name of Jesus sounds	327
How swift the torrent rolls	969
Humble, Lord, my haughty spirit	590
I am baptized into thy name	829
I asked the Lord that I might grow	667
I bless the Christ of God	349
I give immortal praise	105
I hear a voice that comes from far	429
I heard the voice of Jesus say	511
I knew thee in the land of drought	599
I know that my Redeemer lives	639
I lay my sins on Jesus	481
I left the God of truth and light	494
I love the volume of thy word	397
I love thy kingdom, Lord	784
I love to steal a while away	90
I need thee, precious Jesus	604
I send the joys of earth away	508
I think of thee, my God, by night	594
I think, when I read that sweet story	887
I thirst, thou wounded Lamb of God	562
I waited patient for the Lord	645
I was a wandering sheep	473
I worship thee, sweet will of God	662
I would love thee, God and Father	533
I would not live alway: I ask not to stay	976
If human kindness meets return	841
I'll praise my Maker with my breath	126
I'm not ashamed to own my Lord	743
In all my Lord's appointed ways	742
In all my vast concerns with thee	146
In evil long I took delight	243
In grief and fear to thee, O Lord	944
In my distress I sought my God	144
In the cross of Christ I glory	256
In thine assembly here we stand	813

	HYMN
In thy name, O Lord, assembling	46
In vain I trace creation o'er	609
Indulgent God! how kind	426
Indulgent Sovereign of the skies	895
Infinite excellence is thine	345
Inquire, ye pilgrims, for the way	788
In sleep's serene oblivion laid	82
Inspirer and Hearer of prayer	94
Is this the kind return	557
It is not death to die	985
I've found the pearl of greatest price	334
Jerusalem on high	1047
Jerusalem, my happy home	1048
Jerusalem, the golden	1045
Jesus, and shall it ever be	738
Jesus, cast a look on me	588
Jesus Christ is risen to-day	262
Jesus demands this heart of mine	550
Jesus, full of all compassion	485
Jesus, God of love, attend	35
Jesus, I love thy charming name	540
Jesus, I my cross have taken	679
Jesus, I sing thy matchless grace	521
Jesus, immortal King, arise	925
Jesus, immutably the same	520
Jesus, Jesus, visit me	596
Jesus, Lamb of God, for me	484
Jesus lives! no longer now	292
Jesus, lover of my soul	254
Jesus, mighty King in Zion	822
Jesus, my all, to heaven is gone	343
Jesus, my Lord, how rich thy grace	766
Jesus, my Lord! my life! my all!	496
Jesus, my Lord 'tis sweet to rest	690
Jesus, my Saviour, bind me fast	603
Jesus, my strength, my hope	731
Jesus, our faith increase	757
Jesus, our fainting spirits cry	572
Jesus, our souls' delightful choice	554
Jesus shall reign where'er the sun	898
Jesus, still lead on	713
Jesus, the Lamb of God	350
Jesus, the Lord our souls adore	287
Jesus, the name high over all	330
Jesus, the Shepherd of the sheep	341
Jesus, the sinner's Friend, to thee	497
Jesus! the very thought of thee	539
Jesus, thou art my Righteousness	332

INDEX OF FIRST LINES.

HYMN		HYMN	
Jesus, thou everlasting King	847	Long have I sat beneath the sound	38
Jesus, thou joy of loving hearts	524	Look, ye saints, the sight is glorious	296
Jesus, thy blood and righteousness	335	Lord, a better heart bestow	468
Jesus, thy boundless love to me	534	Lord, as to thy dear cross we flee	719
Jesus, thy church with longing eyes	910	Lord, at thy feet we sinners lie	576
Jesus, we look to thee	32	Lord, didst thou die, but not for me	507
Jesus, where'er thy people meet	871	Lord, dismiss us with thy blessing	47
Jesus, who knows full well	614	Lord God of morning and of night	79
Jesus, whom angel hosts adore	336	Lord God of my salvation	700
Join all the glorious names	307	Lord God, the Holy Ghost	382
Joy to the world! the Lord is come	209	Lord, how mysterious are thy ways	163
Just as I am, without one plea	487	Lord, how secure my conscience was	478
		Lord, how the troublers of my peace	669
Keep silence, all created things	161	Lord, I am thine, entirely thine	510
		Lord, I am vile, conceived in sin	410
Laden with guilt, and full of fears	401	Lord, I have made thy word my choice	400
Lamb of God, whose bleeding love	850	Lord, I have sinned, but oh, forgive	580
Lamp of our feet, whereby we trace	405	Lord, I hear of showers of blessing	486
Lead, kindly light, amid the encircling	708	Lord, in humble, sweet submission	828
Let all the earth their voices raise	127	Lord, in the morning thou shalt hear	22
Let all the just to God with joy	188	Lord, in the temples of thy grace	11
Let children hear the mighty deeds	879	Lord, in thy name, thy servants plead	954
Let everlasting glories crown	408	Lord, in thy people dost thou dwell	518
Let every mortal ear attend	454	Lord, it belongs not to my care	664
Let Jacob to his Maker sing	670	Lord Jesus, are we one with thee	517
Let me be with thee where thou art	1038	Lord Jesus, thy returning	1011
Let me but hear my Saviour say	699	Lord, my weak thought in vain would	167
Let plenteous grace descend on those	836	Lord, now we part in thy blest name	44
Let sinners take their course	683	Lord of my life, whose tender care	96
Let the earth now praise the Lord	222	Lord of the ocean, hear our cry	931
Let them neglect thy glory, Lord	109	Lord of the Sabbath, hear our vows	74
Let us sing the King Messiah	297	Lord of the worlds above	19
Let us with a gladsome mind	157	Lord, thou hast formed mine every part	149
Let worldly minds the world pursue	718	Lord, thou hast scourged our guilty land	943
Let Zion and her sons rejoice	790	Lord, thou hast searched and seen	148
Let Zion in her songs record	432	Lord, thou hast taught our hearts to glow	863
Let Zion's watchmen all awake	862	Lord, thou hast won, at length I yield	501
Lift up your heads, ye mighty gates	228	Lord, we adore thy vast designs	166
Light of the lonely pilgrim's heart	926	Lord, we come before thee now	80
Light of those whose dreary dwelling	902	Lord, when thou didst ascend on high	270
Like Noah's weary dove	470	Lord, when we bend before thy throne	29
Lo! God is here! let us adore	27	Lord, with a grieved and aching heart	549
Lo! he cometh, countless trumpets	1025	Loud hallelujahs to the Lord	128
Lo! he comes, let all adore	915	Love divine, all love excelling	591
Lo! he comes, with clouds descending	1026		
Lo! on a narrow neck of land	503	Men of God, go take your stations	905
Lo! what a glorious sight appears	1009	Mighty God, while angels bless thee	120
Long as I live I'll bless thy name	111	Mighty Lord, extend thine empire	907

INDEX OF FIRST LINES. 455

	HYMN
Mine eyes and my desire	556
Morning breaks upon the tomb	260
Mortals, awake, with angels join,	212
Much in sorrow, oft in woe	753
Must Jesus bear the cross alone	744
My country, 'tis of thee	934
My days are gliding swiftly by	972
My dear Redeemer, and my Lord	231
My faith looks up to thee	709
My faith shall triumph o'er the grave	1015
My former hopes are fled	472
My God, accept my early vows	12
My God and Father, while I stray	653
My God, and is thy table spread	846
My God, how endless is thy love	88
My God, how wonderful thou art	124
My God, I love thee; not because	541
My God, in whom are all the springs	138
My God, is any hour so sweet	627
My God, my Father, blissful name	663
My God, my King, thy various praise	118
My God, my Life, my Love	528
My God, permit me not to be	568
My God, permit my tongue	527
My God, the covenant of thy love	190
My God! the spring of all my joys	593
My God! though cleaving to the dust	598
My God, what monuments I see	180
My gracious Lord, I own thy right	723
My helper God, I bless his name	956
My Jesus, as thou wilt	652
My Lord, my love, was crucified	69
My Maker and my King	728
My never-ceasing song shall show	189
My only Saviour! when I feel	567
My Saviour, how shall I proclaim	726
My Saviour, my Almighty Friend	331
My Saviour, whom absent I love	1067
My Shepherd will supply my need	206
My soul before thee prostrate lies	570
My soul, be on thy guard	748
My soul, how lovely is the place	7
My soul, inspired with sacred love	179
My soul lies cleaving to the dust	601
My soul, repeat his praise	199
My soul shall praise thee, O my God	125
My soul, triumphant in the Lord	689
My spirit longs for thee	607

	HYMN
My spirit on thy care	675
My spirit sinks within me, Lord	691
My thoughts surmount these lower skies	1014
Nature with open volume stands	250
Nearer, my God, to thee	606
New every morning is the love	76
No change of times shall ever shock	176
No more, my God, I boast no more	495
No, no, it is not dying	983
Not all the blood of beasts	413
Not all the outward forms on earth	422
Not to condemn the sons of men	227
Not to the terrors of the Lord	789
Not unto us, almighty Lord	134
Not with our mortal eyes	529
Not yet, ye people of his grace	548
Now be my heart inspired to sing	311
Now begin the heavenly theme	324
Now for a tune of lofty praise	277
Now from the altar of my heart	91
Now, gracious Lord, thine arm reveal	960
Now let our cheerful eyes survey	282
Now let our mourning hearts revive	995
Now let our souls on wings sublime	1032
Now let us join with hearts and tongues	355
Now let us raise our cheerful strains	358
Now, my soul, thy voice uprising	251
Now shall my solemn vows be paid	644
Now to the Lord a noble song	303
Now to the Lord that makes us know	312
O blessing rich, for sons of men	519
O Bread to pilgrims given	849
O Christ! our King, Creator Lord	305
O Christ, our true and only light	310
O Christ, the Lord of heaven, to thee	356
O Christ, who hast prepared a place	275
O day of rest and gladness	54
O faith, thou workest miracles	633
O Father, though the anxious fear	62
O God! beneath thy guiding hand	936
O God, by whom the seed is given	36
O God, my God, my All thou art	545
O God of Bethel, by whose hand	196
O God of love! O King of peace	941
O God of mercy, hear my call	419
O God, thou art my God alone	544

	HYMN
O God, thy grace and blessing give	979
O God unseen, yet ever near	838
O happy saints, who dwell in light	1065
O happy soul that lives on high	771
O Holy Ghost who down dost come	377
O Holy Saviour, Friend unseen	654
O Holy Spirit, come	381
O Israel, to thy tents repair	735
O Jesus! King most wonderful	344
O Jesus! Lord of heavenly grace	81
O Jesus! sweet the tears I shed	247
O Jesus, thou the Beauty art	538
O Lord, and shall our fainting souls	388
O Lord, another day is flown	89
O Lord, how good, how great art thou	158
O Lord! how happy should we be	711
O Lord, how joyful 'tis to see	759
O Lord, I would delight in thee	678
O Lord, my best desire fulfil	660
O Lord of hosts, whose glory fills	870
O Lord, our fathers oft have told	938
O Lord, thy heavenly grace impart	564
O Lord, turn not thy face away	575
O Lord, we see thy work set forth	835
O Lord, when we the path retrace	235
O Lord, while we confess the worth	827
O love divine, how sweet thou art!	532
O love of God, how strong and true	318
O Paradise! O Paradise!	1060
O sacred Head, now wounded	253
O Saviour, is thy promise fled	799
O Saviour, who for man hast trod	290
O Spirit of the living God	891
O thou best gift of heaven	710
O thou, by long experience tried	546
O thou from whom all goodness flows	687
O thou my soul forget no more	547
O thou that hearest prayer	20
O thou that hearest the prayer of faith	500
O thou, the contrite sinner's Friend	291
O thou, to whose all-searching sight	695
O thou who camest from above	724
O thou who hast redeemed of old	321
O thou who hear'st when sinners cry	493
O thou who in Jordan didst bow thy meek	820
O thou, whose sacred feet have trod	686
O thou, whose tender mercy hears	582
O wondrous type, O vision fair	236

	HYMN
O Zion, tune thy voice	795
Object of my first desire	595
O'er the gloomy hills of darkness	903
O'er the realms of pagan darkness	904
O'erwhelmed in depths of woe	241
Oh blessed souls are they	773
Oh, bless the Lord, my soul	200
Oh, could I find, from day to day	600
Oh, could I speak the matchless worth	320
Oh for a beam of heavenly light	696
Oh for a closer walk with God	592
Oh for a faith that will not shrink	636
Oh for a heart to praise my God	602
Oh for an overcoming faith	982
Oh for a sight, a pleasing sight	1035
Oh for a strong, a lasting faith	182
Oh for a sweet inspiring ray	1036
Oh for a thousand tongues to sing	328
Oh for that tenderness of heart	574
Oh for the death of those	992
Oh for the robes of whiteness	1030
Oh happy day, that fixed my choice	509
Oh how I love thy holy law	404
Oh! mean may seem this house of clay	522
Oh not to fill the mouth of fame	717
Oh sweetly breathe the lyres above	504
Oh that I could forever dwell	722
Oh that I could repent	558
Oh that I knew the secret place	624
Oh that my load of sin were gone	552
Oh that the Lord's salvation	928
Oh that the Lord would guide my ways	720
Oh this soul how dark and blind	587
Oh, turn, great Ruler of the skies	571
Oh what, if we are Christ's	672
Oh when shall we sweetly remove	1068
Oh, wherefore, Lord, doth thy dear praise	721
Oh where are kings and empires now	786
Oh where is now that glowing love	555
Oh where shall rest be found	471
Oh, worship the King, all glorious above	112
On Jordan's bank, the Baptist's cry	226
On Jordan's stormy banks I stand	1040
On this day, the first of days	64
On the mountain's top appearing	793
Once more before we part	41
One sole baptismal sign	796
One sweetly solemn thought	968

INDEX OF FIRST LINES. 457

HYMN
One there is, above all others 316
Oppressed with noon day's scorching heat· 246
Our blest Redeemer, ere he breathed 393
Our Father! we adore and praise 379
Our God, our help in ages past 141
Our heavenly Father calls 516
Our Lord is risen from the dead 276
Our Saviour bowed beneath the wave.... 812
Palms of glory, raiment bright 1062
People of the living God 806
Planted in Christ, the living vine........ 809
Pleasant are thy courts above............ 34
Plunged in a gulf of dark despair 210
Pour out thy Spirit from on high........ 869
Praise, Lord, for thee in Zion waits 5
Praise the Lord, his glories show........ 132
Praise to God, immortal praise 946
Praise to the radiant source of bliss. 338
Praise to thee, thou great Creator....... 121
Praise waits in Zion, Lord, for thee 6
Praise ye the Lord; exalt his name...... 17
Praise ye the Lord; my heart shall join.. 137
Praises to him whose love has given..... 102
Prayer is the soul's sincere desire 629
Prince of peace, control my will 561
Prostrate, dear Jesus, at thy feet........ 418
Quiet, Lord, my froward heart.......... 589
Raise your triumphant songs 437
Redeemed from guilt, redeemed from fears 727
Rejoice, all ye believers................ 1010
Rejoice, the Lord is King 314
Rest, my soul, the work is done.......... 778
Resting from his work to-day............ 259
Return, my roving heart, return 569
Return, my soul, and sweetly rest....... 174
Return, O wanderer, return............ 451
Ride on! ride on in majesty............ 237
Rise, my soul, and stretch thy wings....1029
Rise, O my soul, pursue the path 1058
Rock of Ages, cleft for me............. 258
Safely through another week 63
Salvation! oh, the joyful sound!........ 423
Save me, O God, the Surety cried...... 817
Saviour, again to thy dear name we raise 48

HYMN
Saviour, breathe an evening blessing.... 95
Saviour, I lift my trembling eyes...... 285
Saviour, visit thy plantation 804
Saviour, when in dust to thee.......... 293
Saviour, who didst from heaven come.... 884
See, a poor sinner, dearest Lord 631
See, gracious God, before thy throne 942
See Israel's gentle Shepherd stands 880
See, Jesus stands with open arms 456
See, the ransomed millions stand........ 299
See, what a living stone 52
Servant of God! well done 998
Shall hymns of grateful love............ 359
Shepherd divine, our wants relieve...... 625
Shepherd of tender youth.............. 888
Shepherd of thine Israel, lead us........ 970
Shine, mighty God, on Zion shine....... 924
Show pity, Lord, O Lord, forgive 489
Since all the downward tracts of time ... 159
Sing, O heavens! O earth, rejoice 274
Sing to the Lord Jehovah's name 8
Sing to the Lord; ye distant lands....... 923
Sing, ye redeemed of the Lord.......... 769
Sinners, the voice of God regard...!.... 459
Sinners, turn, why will ye die 463
Sinners, will you scorn the message 450
So let our lips and lives express.......... 740
Softly fades the twilight ray 72
Softly now the light of day 100
Soldiers of Christ, arise................ 747
Sometimes a light surprises............. 707
Songs of praise the angels sang......... 131
Sons of God, triumphant rise........... 273
Sons we are through God's election 434
Soon as I heard my Father say 619
Soon may the last glad song arise 911
Sovereign of worlds, display thy power.. 893
Sovereign Ruler, Lord of all 464
Sovereign Ruler of the skies........... 680
Sound, sound the truth abroad.......... 901
Spirit divine, attend our prayer........ 875
Spirit of mercy, truth, and love......... 376
Spirit of power, and truth and love...... 389
Spirit of truth! on this thy day........ 365
Stand up, and bless the Lord........... 114
Stand up, my soul, shake off thy fears.. 733
Stay, thou insulted Spirit, stay.......... 887
Sun of my soul, thou Saviour dear...... 84

INDEX OF FIRST LINES.

HYMN		HYMN	
Sure the blest Comforter is nigh	392	The promise of my Father's love	840
Surely Christ thy griefs has borne	467	The race that long in darkness pined	211
Sweet feast of love divine	851	The Saviour calls; let every ear	457
Sweet is the light of Sabbath eve	75	The Son of God goes forth to war	737
Sweet is the memory of thy grace	169	The Son of God! the Lord of life	337
Sweet is the solemn voice that calls	18	The spacious firmament on high	155
Sweet is the work, my God, my King	57	The Spirit breathes upon the word	403
Sweet is the work, O Lord	51	The spring-tide hour brings leaf and flower	950
Sweet Saviour, bless us ere we go	93	The starry firmament on high	396
Sweet the moments, rich in blessing	257	The sun is sinking fast	101
Sweet was the time when first I felt	585	The wanderer no more will roam	488
		The world can neither give nor take	688
Talk with us, Lord, thyself reveal	536	Thee we adore, eternal Lord	117
Tarry with me, O my Saviour	974	Thee we adore, eternal Name	958
Teach me, my God and King	729	There is a blessed home	1050
Tender Shepherd, thou hast stilled	1002	There is a fold whence none can stray	1056
That awful day will surely come	1028	There is a fountain filled with blood	414
That day of wrath, that dreadful day	1021	There is an hour of peaceful rest	1037
The atoning work is done	309	There is a land of pure delight	1039
The billows swell, the winds are high	646	There is a path that leads to God	886
The church has waited long	1012	There is a safe and secret place	770
The day is past and gone	97	There is none other name than thine	319
The day of rest once more comes round	70	There is no sorrow, Lord, too light	623
The day, O Lord, is spent	98	Thine forever! God of love	703
The festal morn, my God is come	53	This is the day the Lord hath made	66
The God of Abraham praise	122	Thou art gone to the grave! but we will	999
The God of harvest praise	949	Thou art my portion, O my God	715
The happy morn is come	265	Thou art the Way! to thee alone	339
The head that once was crowned with	302	Thou hidden love of God, whose height	585
The heavens declare thy glory, Lord	395	Thou hidden source of calm repose	817
The Holy Ghost is here	374	Thou Judge of quick and dead	1018
The hour of my departure's come	977	Thou Lord of all above	475
The King of heaven his table spreads	458	Thou lovely Source of true delight	537
The Lord! how wondrous are his ways	177	Thou only Sovereign of my heart	566
The Lord is King! lift up thy voice	153	Thou Prince of glory, slain for me	363
The Lord Jehovah reigns; his throne	151	Thou vain, deceitful world, farewell	1033
The Lord Jehovah reigns, and royal state	152	Thou very present aid	682
The Lord my pasture shall prepare	204	Thou, who art enthroned above	133
The Lord my Shepherd is	205	Thou, who didst stoop below	702
The Lord of glory is my light	23	Thou, whose almighty word	107
The Lord our God is clothed with might	143	Thou, whose never-failing arm	1005
The Lord will come! the earth shall quake	1020	Though nature's strength decay	123
The Lord will happiness divine	583	Though now the nations sit beneath	899
The mercies of my God and King	192	Thrice happy souls, who born from heaven	772
The moment a sinner believes	427	Through all the changing scenes of life	197
The morning light is breaking	913	Through every age, eternal God	964
The Prince of salvation in triumph is riding	917	Through sorrow's night and danger's path	1014
The promises I sing	186	Thus far my God hath led me on	647

INDEX OF FIRST LINES. 459

	HYMN
Thus far the Lord hath led me on	87
Thy goodness, Lord, our souls confess	195
Thy mercy, O God, is the theme of my	184
Thy mighty working, mighty God	951
Thy name, almighty Lord	116
Thy way, not mine, O Lord	651
Thy ways, O Lord! with wise design	164
Thy works, not mine, O Christ	440
"Till he come," oh! let the words	857
'Tis a pleasant thing to see	754
'Tis a point I long to know	531
'Tis by the faith of joys to come	632
'Tis he — the mighty Saviour comes	922
'Tis midnight, and on Olive's brow	238
'Tis my happiness below	705
'Tis not that I did choose thee	435
'Tis the great Father we adore	828
To bless thy chosen race	115
To Calvary, Lord, in spirit now	243
To celebrate thy praise, O Lord	110
To Christ, the Lord, let every tongue	352
To-day thy mercy calls me	460
To-day the Saviour calls	448
To God, my Saviour and my King	506
To God, the only wise	783
To heaven I lift my waiting eyes	171
To him that chose us first	106
To him that loved the souls of men	346
To-morrow, Lord, is thine	967
To our Redeemer's glorious name	333
To praise our Shepherd's care	347
To thee, my Shepherd and my Lord	207
To thee, O dear, dear Saviour	605
To thy pastures fair and large	203
To thy temple I repair	31
Trembling before thine awful throne	503
Triumphant Zion, lift thy head	800
'Twas on that dark, that doleful night	843
Unshaken as the sacred hill	635
Unveil thy bosom, faithful tomb	1000
Up to the Lord that reigns on high	168
Uphold me, Lord, too prone to stray	692
Upward I lift mine eyes	185
Wait, O my soul, thy Maker's will	165
Walk in the light! and thou shalt own	641
Watchman, tell us of the night	221

	HYMN
We are a garden walled around	802
We bid thee welcome in the name	866
We bless our Saviour's name	853
We sing his love, who once was slain	1001
We sing the praise of him who died	249
We sing to thee, thou Son of God	353
We speak of the realms of the blest	1060
Weary of wandering from my God	553
Welcome, delightful morn	55
Welcome, sweet day of rest	50
Welcome, thou Victor in the strife	267
We've no abiding city here	1034
What are these arrayed in white	1061
What are these in bright array	1063
What cheering words are these	774
What equal honors shall we bring	304
What secret place, what distant star	150
What shall I render to my God	28
What sinners value, I resign	1037
What though no flowers the fig-tree clothe	637
What various hindrances we meet	617
When all thy mercies, O my God	194
When at thy footstool, Lord, I bend	565
When bending o'er the brink of life	981
When came in flesh the incarnate Word	1008
When darkness long has veiled my mind	666
When downward to the darksome tomb	980
When first o'erwhelmed with sin and shame	289
When gathering clouds around I view	635
When God revealed his gracious name	512
When I can read my title clear	1039
When life's varied scene	643
When I survey the wondrous cross	248
When in the hour of lonely woe	694
When Israel of the Lord beloved	937
When Jordan hushed his waters still	225
When languor and disease invade	657
When like a stranger on our sphere	232
When marshalled on the nightly plain	342
When on Sinai's top I see	235
When, overwhelmed with grief	674
When rising from the bed of death	477
When shall I, Lord, a journey take	577
When sins and fears prevailing rise	525
When streaming from the eastern skies	77
When the worn spirit wants repose	60
When thou, my righteous Judge, shalt	1027
When through the torn sail the wild	932

INDEX OF FIRST LINES.

HYMN		HYMN
When thy mortal life is fled	469	With joy we hail the sacred day 65
When we our wearied limbs to rest	797	With joy we meditate the grace 281
When wounded sore the stricken soul	415	With my substance I will honor 916
Whence do our mournful thoughts arise	745	With one consent, let all the earth 1
Where high the heavenly temple stands	283	With reverence let the saints appear.... 142
Where is my God? does he retire	288	With songs and honors sounding loud.... 952
While my Redeemer's near	348	With tearful eyes I look around 668
While o'er the deep thy servants sail	930	With tears of anguish, I lament......... 578
While shepherds watched their flocks by	214	Witness, ye men and angels now 810
While we thy ways, blest Saviour tread	818	Worthy the Lamb of boundless sway.... 354
While with ceaseless course the sun	961	Wouldst thou learn the depth of sin..... 240
Whilst thee I seek, protecting Power	25	
Who but thou, almighty Spirit	908	Ye Christian heralds, go, proclaim 894
Who can describe the joys that rise	513	Ye dying sons of men 465
Who can forbear to sing	514	Ye golden lamps of heaven, farewell 990
Who, O Lord, when life is o'er	777	Ye nations round the earth, rejoice...... 3
Who shall the Lord's elect condemn	431	Ye servants of God, your Master proclaim 360
Why do we mourn departing friends	994	Ye servants of the Lord................. 732
Why is my heart so far from thee	610	Ye souls for whom the Son did die...... 543
Why on the bending willows hung	798	Ye who in his courts are found.......... 446
Why should the children of a King	364	Yes, my native land! I love thee 909
Why should we start and fear to die	978	Yes, we trust the day is breaking....... 906
With all my powers of heart and tongue	129	Your harps, ye trembling saints......... 676
With broken heart and contrite sigh	491	
With Christ we share a mystic grave	826	Zion stands with hills surrounded....... 794
With heavenly power, O Lord, defend	867	Zion, the marvellous story be telling 220
With Jesus in the midst	852	

NOTE TO HYMN 815.

Stanzas 3 to 8 inclusive of this hymn are designed to be sung during the intervals of a baptism; one verse as each candidate goes down into the water, or comes forth from it, according to choice. As it is generally found difficult for a congregation to sing unitedly and at the right time in the administration, it has been suggested that a choir sing these stanzas, the congregation uniting in the first two and the last two, as indicated.

GENERAL INDEX OF SUBJECTS.

HYMNS.

I.—*WORSHIP* .... 1— 48

II.—*THE LORD'S DAY* .... 49— 75

III.—*MORNING AND EVENING* .... 76—101

IV.—*GOD:*

    1. The Trinity ....102—108
    2. His Praise ....110—139
    3. His Attributes ....140—155
    4. His Providence ....156—207

V.—*CHRIST:*

    1. His Advent ....208—230
    2. His Life ....231—237
    3. His Sufferings and Death ....238—259
    4. His Resurrection and Ascension ....260—277
    5. His Glory ....278—280
    6. His Intercession ....281—293
    7. His Reign ....294—316
    8. His Characters ....317—349
    9. His Praise ....350—362

VI.—*THE HOLY SPIRIT* ....363—394

VII.—*THE SCRIPTURES* ....395—410

VIII.—*SALVATION:*

    1. Man's Need ....411—421
    2. Of Grace ....422—440
    3. Its Calls ....441—468
    4. Sought and Found ....469—514

IX.—THE CHRISTIAN LIFE:

HYMNS.
1. Union with Christ .... 515—523
2. Love to Christ .... 524—548
3. Penitence .... 549—587
4. Humility .... 588—589
5. Aspiration .... 590—610
6. Prayer .... 611—631
7. Faith .... 632—644
8. Suffering and Trust .... 645—714
9. Consecration .... 715—730
10. Conflict .... 731—752
11. Fellowship and Charity .... 753—766
12. Its Blessedness .... 767—783

X.—THE CHURCH:

1. Its Honor and Work .... 784—810
2. Baptism .... 811—836
3. The Lord's Supper .... 837—860
4. The Ministry .... 861—869
5. The Sanctuary .... 870—878
6. Children .... 879—888
7. Missions .... 889—928
8. Seamen .... 929—933

XI.—THE NATION:

1. Fast and Thanksgiving .... 934—949

XII.—THE YEAR .... 950—963

XIII.—LIFE AND DEATH .... 964—1006

XIV.—CHRIST'S SECOND COMING .... 1007—1013

XV.—RESURRECTION AND JUDGMENT .... 1014—1028

XVI.—HEAVEN .... 1029—1069

———◆◆———

PAGE
XVII.—CHANTS AND SELECTIONS FOR CHANTING .... 433—448

PARTICULAR INDEX OF SUBJECTS.

[The figures designate Hymns.]

ABBA FATHER. 306, 375, 379, 535, 782.
Abiding of Christ, 84, 227, 518, 520, 536, 596, 690, 698, 973.
Abiding with Christ, 518, 520, 536, 546, 603.
Abraham. 122, 123, 335.
Absence from God, 470, 472, 476, 555, 584, 596, 607, 608, 774.
Accepted Time, 443, 447, 448, 450, 456, 458–462, 465, 460, 1027.
Access to God, 4, 5, 6, 7, 33, 53, 59, 130, 147, 283, 284, 487, 488, 500, 502, 516, 614, 615, 618, 621.
Activity, 732, 735, 739, 741, 747–749, 753, 764–766.
Adoption. 306, 379, 500, 782.
Advent of Christ;—
  At Birth. 208–220.
  To Judgment. 314, 1008, 1020, 1025–1028.
  To Kingdom, 243, 857, 1007–1013.
Advocate, Christ our, 77, 147, 286, 288, 289, 291, 294, 306, 516, 553.
Affliction;— 643–714.
  Appointed, 650, 752.
  Blessed. 656, 686, 690, 705, 752.
  Delivered from. 644. 645, 676, 714.
  Sanctified. 667, 670, 700.
  Submission under. 590, 651–653. 660, 663, 686, 693.
  Trust in, 659, 664–666, 669, 670, 671, 675, 678, 680–685, 689, 700, 706, 707, 711, 714.
Almost Christian, 459.
Angels. 237, 273, 279, 337, 355, 450, 504, 505, 513, 523, 657, 770, 789, 810, 865, 883, 1036, 1045, 1050.
Ascension of Christ, 270–278.
Ashamed of Jesus, 738, 743.
Asleep in Jesus, 986.
Aspiration, 591–610.
Assurance;—
  Expressed, 234, 286, 306, 335, 349, 525, 639, 752, 782.
  Prayed for, 364, 554.
  Urged. 776, 778.
Atonement;—
  Necessary, 410, 412, 413, 416, 417, 418, 419, 440, 500.
  Completed 273, 309, 312, 440.
  Sufficient. 230, 204, 307, 425, 427, 500.
Autumn, 133, 946, 947, 953.

Backsliding. 465, 493, 553, 554, 555, 556, 569, 571, 673, 578, 580, 581, 583, 585.

Baptism, 811–836.
Beatitudes, 762.
Benevolence, 763–766, 912, 916.
Blessedness of Christian, 768–783.
Brevity of Life, 964, 966, 967, 960, 972.
Brotherly Love, 754–759, 767.
Burial, 964–996.
  A Brother, 986, 987, 992, 993, 1000, 1003, 1006.
  A Child. 1002.
  A Sister, 986, 987, 992, 993.
  A Pastor. 992, 993, 995, 998, 999.
  A Friend, 986, 987, 992, 993, 994, 996, 997.

Calmness, 530, 643, 654, 656, 673, 675, 680, 683, 690, 711.
Calvary. 243, 252, 255, 336, 420.
Cares, 612, 623, 678, 683, 711, 772.
Charity, 760–767.
Cheerfulness, 645, 670, 676, 689, 771, 774.
Children. 879–888.
Childlike Spirit, 588, 590, 681, 686, 709, 711.
Christ;—
  Advent and Birth, 208–220.
  Advocate, 147, 286, 288, 290, 291, 306, 516, 55a.
  Ascension, 270–278.
  Baptism, 812, 813, 814, 815, 816, 819, 820, 822, 824, 825, 827, 829.
  Burial, 259.
  Blood, 335, 410–416, 460, 565.
  Captain of Salvation, 307.
  Characters, 316–349.
  Conqueror, 265–268, 270, 271, 276, 278, 296–299, 302, 305, 307, 344, 730.
  Corner-stone, 877.
  Crucified, 241, 101, 251, 252.
  Crowned, 295, 296, 298, 299, 301, 302, 847.
  Desire of Nations, 217, 224.
  Divinity, 213, 222, 224, 230, 295, 305, 311, 337, 350, 358.
  Example, 231–234, 719.
  Friend, 234, 253, 286, 316, 320, 322, 329, 497, 547, 604, 677, 695.
  Guide. 234, 348, 703, 708, 713.
  Hiding-place, 323, 327, 579.
  Humanity, 214, 219, 222, 224, 230, 305, 350, 353.
  Immanuel, 224, 451.
  Intercessor, 286, 291, 314, 431.
  Judge, 1013, 1020, 1025, 1026, 1027, 1088.

PARTICULAR INDEX OF SUBJECTS.

King, 209, 217, 218, 221, 228, 261, 262, 264, 269, 276, 294-315, 332, 344, 360, 446, 452, 548, 677.
Lamb, 263, 279, 280, 284, 294, 321, 335, 350, 354, 357, 361, 362, 413, 414, 424, 425, 439, 481, 484, 487, 488, 562, 707.
Life, Incidents of, 231, 236-240.
Light, 211, 222, 233, 326, 338, 340, 344, 511, 524, 538, 582.
Lord, 300, 301, 309, 310, 332, 335.
Love, 211, 303, 317, 318, 321, 322, 324, 331, 498, 523, 534, 602, 626.
Miracles, 232.
Mediator, 779.
Physician, 466, 482, 783.
Priest, 281-293, 307, 309, 312, 332, 425.
Prince, 208, 210, 211, 221, 225, 248, 268, 304, 308, 310, 345, 356, 443, 558.
Prophet, 307, 332.
Redeemer, 286, 289.
Refuge, 254, 258, 350, 500, 566, 665, 674.
Resurrection, 260-271, 1016.
Righteousness, 300, 330, 335, 412, 417, 440, 493, 495, 500.
Rock of Ages, 258, 319, 327.
Sacrifice, 413, 416, 446.
Saviour and Salvation, 295, 317, 333, 358, 448, 764.
Shepherd, 327, 341, 347-348, 473, 625, 791, 1002, 1056.
Sufferings, 238-245, 251.
Sun of Righteousness, 224, 494.
Surety, 306, 817.
Way, Truth, and Life, 325, 339, 343, 587, 703.
Word, 213.
Vine, 520.
Christian, The, 575-783.
Afflicted, 613, 646, 647, 658, 674, 676, 686, 691, 694, 699, 702, 705.
Aspiring, 591-610.
Backsliding, 493, 553-556, 569, 571, 573, 578, 580, 581, 582, 585.
Blessed, 773-775, 778, 779, 780.
Cheerful, 632, 645, 670, 676, 689, 771, 774.
Comforted, 642, 644, 645, 655, 656, 668, 678, 685, 688, 600, 697, 698, 699.
Consecrated, 103, 715-730, 708, 810.
Dying, 973-975, 977, 978, 980-982, 988, 991, 1005.
Faithful, 732, 747, 749.
Grateful, 248, 253, 432, 512, 526, 649, 733.
Happy, 763, 771, 772, 776, 780, 781.
Hoping, 314, 712, 963, 972, 980, 990, 991, 1001, 1012, 1013, 1047, 1050, 1051-1053, 1056, 1059.
Justified, 413, 495, 528.
Life of, 740, 777.
Loving, 524-548.
Obeying, 715, 716, 717, 720, 723, 724.
One with Christ, 515-523.
Patient, 580, 667, 652, 653, 663, 664, 681, 686.
Penitent, 773, 549-587.
Persevering, 733, 734, 741, 742, 750, 783.
Praying, 611-629.
Resigned, 589, 651, 652, 653, 663, 664, 681, 686.
Resisting, 748, 750, 1055, 1059.

Safe, 769, 770, 774, 778.
Steadfast, 743, 745.
Trusting, 646-648, 654, 658-660, 665, 671, 674, 675, 676, 678, 689, 696, 700, 701, 706, 707.
Watchful, 731, 732, 735, 739.
Church; — 784-810.
Afflicted, 797, 798.
Delight in, 784, 789, 797, 803, 806.
Deliverance of, 784, 785, 790, 791, 793, 800.
Fellowship with, 788, 806, 807, 808, 809, 810.
Founded on Christ, 414.
God in, 785, 794.
Glory of, 795, 803.
Increase of, 788, 792, 805.
One, 789, 796.
Revived, 363, 366, 368, 370, 373, 376, 381, 382, 386, 799, 802, 804, 805.
Safe, 794, 803.
Stable, 786, 787, 801, 802, 803.
Triumphant, 784, 790, 791, 792, 800.
Communion; —
With God, 379, 576, 578, 520, 624, 627, 697.
With Christians, 754-759, 789, 806, 807, 808, 809.
Confession, 410, 412, 418, 419, 549, 559, 572, 575, 576, 578, 580, 581, 587, 773.
Of Christ, 810.
Conflict, 731-753, 1055, 1059.
Consecration, 703, 715-730.
Contentment, 589, 680, 681, 707, 711.
Conversion, 501, 503-506, 508-514.
Conviction of Sin, 410-412, 415, 416, 420, 433, 468, 472, 475, 478.
Corner-stone, 870.
Coronation of Christ, 295, 296, 298, 299, 301, 302, 847
Covenant, 190, 192, 428.
Courage, 733, 734, 736, 737, 738, 747, 757, 753.
Creation, 155, 172, 395.
Cross; —
Attracting, 242, 243, 246, 247, 249, 251, 305, 444, 499.
Borne, 235, 552, 672, 679, 712, 744.
Gloried in, 248-251, 256, 257, 302, 708.
Salvation by, 244, 247, 352, 253, 257, 416, 499.
Crucifixion, 241-245, 251, 252, 253, 541.

Death, 973-1006.
Anticipated, 204, 500, 687, 702, 707, 714, 973, 974, 976, 977-981, 988, 1005.
Of Child, 1002.
Of Friends, 997, 1006.
Of Pastor, 995, 998, 999.
Overcome, 693, 694, 702, 982, 983, 985, 967, 1004.
Dedication, 871-873.
Personal, 501, 504, 509, 570, 574, 723, 725, 729.
Delivery, 443, 447, 448, 458, 461, 462.
Deliverance, 197, 644, 645, 676, 714, 700, 791, 793, 800.
Dependence, 30, 134, 161, 168, 176, 178, 193, 783, 956, 957, 958, 962, 970, 971.
Depravity, 410, 412, 416, 417, 420, 432.
Devotion, 1-48.
Dismission, 44, 45, 47, 48.

PARTICULAR INDEX OF SUBJECTS. 465

Election, 161. 428. 431, 434, 543, 718, 779.
Encouragement. 982. 995, 1010, 1015, 1020, 1034, 1043, 1049, 1050, 1052, 1058.
Eternity, 140. 141, 147, 490, 965, 1032, 1043, 1051.
Evening. 84–101.
Example;—
  Of Christ, 231–234, 719, 1055.
  Of Christians, 740, 1055, 1058.

Faith;—630–642, 697, 707.
  Exercised, 637, 639, 640, 778.
  In Christ, 481, 482, 485, 487, 488, 491, 495. 630, 639, 642.
  Of God, 502.
  Power of, 427. 632, 633, 634, 697.
  Prayer of. 500, 631.
  " for, 182, 502, 630, 636, 654, 678.
  Victorious. 639, 697, 752, 753, 980, 982, 1043, 1044, 1055, 1061, 1065.
  Weak, 665.
Faithfulness;—
  Of God and Christ, 182, 183, 187–192, 198, 638, 743.
Family, 879, 880.
Fast, 939–944.
Fear, 400, 714. 973–982, 1018, 1027, 1029.
Fellowship, 754–759, 767, 806–809, 852.
Forbearance, 719, 767.
Forgiveness. 450, 475, 719, 773.
Funeral, 964–1006.

Gentleness, 719, 726.
Gethsemane, 238–240, 336.
Glory of Christ, 261, 264, 268, 274, 276, 282, 294, 295, 296, 298. 299, 301–305, 310, 311, 314, 315, 326, 876, 917.
God;—102–207.
  Attributes, 140–154.
  Benevolence, 157, 159, 169, 171, 177–180, 194, 195, 199, 202–207, 426, 673.
  Compassion, 195, 197, 199, 200. 506, 516.
  Condescension, 151, 156–158, 168.
  Creator, 155, 172, 395, 424.
  Eternity. 140, 141.
  Faithfulness, 182, 183, 187–192, 198.
  Government, 142, 151–153.
  Holiness, 62.
  Incomprehensibleness, 150, 160, 167.
  Infinity, 140, 162.
  Justice, 142.
  Majesty, 142–145.
  Mercy. 145, 157, 172, 173, 174, 181, 184, 191, 429, 435, 441, 491, 492. 559, 575, 576.
  Omnipotence, 142–145, 193.
  Omniscience, 146–149, 162, 695.
  Presence, 146, 149, 150, 546.
  Promises, 152, 185, 186.
  Providence, 156–207.
  Sovereignty, 151–153, 671, 680.
  Trinity, 102–109.
  Truth, 175, 182.
  Unchangeableness, 140, 182, 183, 198, 530, 685, 658.
  Wisdom, 154, 159, 160, 164, 165, 202.

Gospel;—195.
  Its Freedom, 430, 439, 441, 444–446, 449, 450, 451 453–455.
  Its Power, 409, 501, 903. 905.
  Its Success, 192, 395, 397, 514, 898, 903, 925.
Grace, 191. 303, 436.
  In Adoption, 782.
  In Conversion. 421, 426, 432, 433, 480, 501, 512.
  In Election. 434.
  In Prayer, 625.
  In Preservation, 421, 426, 436, 690, 783.
  In Restoration. 465, 649.
  In Salvation. 184, 421, 423, 424, 428, 430, 432, 436, 551, 640, 649.
  In Sanctification, 422, 434, 436.
Gratitude, 121. 189, 172–174, 189, 194, 207, 504–506, 545, 547, 708. 726, 727, 728.
Guidance, 203–206, 695, 696, 697. 698, 704, 709, 713, 971.
Guilt, 410–413, 417–420, 433, 484, 485.

Harvest, 945–949, 953, 954.
Hearing. 31, 46.
Heart;—
  Broken, 419, 483, 484, 491, 493, 549, 558, 576, 578, 581.
  Changed, 420, 581.
  Deceitful, 531, 583, 610.
  Hard, 247, 531, 550, 557, 558.
  Pure. 602, 720, 775, 777.
  Surrendered, 501, 504, 509.
Heathen, 903, 904, 912.
Heaven; 1029–1069.
  Anticipated, 976, 984, 989. 990, 991, 1001, 1029, 1031, 1033, 1034, 1037, 1052, 1056, 1059, 1069.
  Blessedness of, 1001, 1039, 1040, 1041, 1043, 1044, 1049, 1056.
  Christ in. 448, 762, 1053.
  Desired. 1029, 1030, 1032, 1035, 1038, 1040, 1042, 1046 1051, 1058, 1060, 1067, 1068.
  Glory of, 1036, 1042, 1045, 1046, 1047.
  Home In, 1047, 1048, 1050.
  Hoped for. 1046.
  Rest in, 1049, 1054, 1057.
  Saints in, 885, 1054, 1061. 1062, 1063. 1064, 1065, 1066.
  Vision of, 1055, 1058, 1059, 1061–1065.
Hell, 471, 490, 571, 1028.
Holiness;—
  Of God, 62, 147.
  Desired. 367–369, 371–373, 375, 377, 379, 384, 385. 390, 391, 502, 535, 597, 602, 603, 653, 724, 746.
Holy Spirit; 363–394.
  Comforting, 364, 372, 377, 384, 386, 389, 392, 500.
  Earnest, 363. 364. 375, 392.
  Enlightening, 367, 369, 373, 375, 377, 384, 385, 390 391, 394, 449.
  Grieved. 377, 387, 388, 453, 592.
  Indwelling. 374, 375, 379, 384, 393.
  Interceding. 375, 380, 625, 629.
  Reviving and Renewing, 363, 366, 368, 370, 373, 375, 377, 380, 381, 389, 422, 427, 513, 903.
  Sanctifying, 365, 366, 369, 371, 373, 375, 378, 384, 382, 389, 390, 403, 875.

Witnessing, 383, 403.
" to Christ, 379, 381, 385, 386, 486.
Hope, 392, 755, 1053, 1059.
    In Affliction, 287, 671. 679, 691.
    In Death, 972, 974, 975. 983. 985, 991.
    Under Conviction, 287, 410, 412, 413, 416-418, 452, 453, 489.
Humility, 442, 485, 491, 492, 493, 588-590.

Immortality, 1001, 1004.
Ingratitude, 86, 88, 557, 573, 578, 581.
Intercession, 147, 286, 288, 289, 291, 294, 306, 431, 516, 553.
Invitation, 441-469.

Jerusalem, 1045-1047, 1048, 1051.
Jesus, 216, 247, 254, 287, 292, 325, 330, 334, 335, 336, 341, 343, 344, 350, 356, 481, 484, 485, 496, 497, 511, 517, 520, 521, 524, 534, 528-540, 550, 554, 572, 588, 596, 603, 604, 614, 679, 690, 713, 731, 738, 743, 757, 766, 823, 833, 847, 852, 855, 898, 910, 925, 1005, 1011.
Jews, 928.
Joy, 200, 362, 377, 529, 539, 769, 781, 795, 1043.
Jubilee, 425.
Judgment, 469, 477, 503, 1018-1028.
Justification, 265, 284, 309, 335, 431, 495.

Kingdom of Christ, 892, 893, 895, 898, 899, 900, 907, 910, 911, 914, 916, 917, 919, 920, 922, 923, 924, 925, 926, 927.
Knowledge, 760.

Lamb of God, 294, 353, 425, 439, 481, 484, 487, 488, 562, 707, 850.
Law of God, 395, 397, 399, 400, 404, 416, 433, 478, 489.
Life; — 964-972.
    Brevity of, 958, 959, 964, 966, 967, 969, 972.
    Importance of, 965, 967.
Lord's Day; — 49-75.
    Anticipated, 60, 63.
    Enjoyed, 49, 51, 52, 54, 57, 58, 62, 66, 69.
    Evening, 51, 71, 72, 73, 74, 75.
    Morning, 51, 62, 63.
    Resurrection, 54, 67, 68.
    Rest, 54, 57, 59, 60, 63.
    Welcomed, 50, 53, 55, 56, 65, 70.
Lord's Prayer, 616.
Lord's Supper; — 837-860.
    Appointed, 838, 839, 844, 846.
    Closed, 860.
    In Memory of Christ, 837, 839, 840, 841, 843, 850, 851, 853, 855, 859.
    Showing forth his death, 839, 850, 854.
Love; —
    Of Christ, 228, 232, 235, 242, 243, 244, 248, 254, 257, 266, 292, 312, 315, 316, 317, 321, 322, 324, 331, 334, 346, 441, 483, 484, 487, 530, 532, 534, 539, 541, 547, 642, 649, 690, 837, 839, 841, 843, 844, 848, 850.
    Of Christians, 754-767.
    Of God, 202, 501, 532, 535, 543, 626, 666,
    To Christ, 524-548, 550, 724.
    To Christians, 754-759.

To God, 716, 527, 529, 535, 544-546.
To Men, 760, 761, 763-767.

Man; —
    Fallen, 158, 410, 411, 416, 434, 497..
    Lost. 422, 423, 465.
    Mortal, 199, 469, 958, 964-969, 972, 977, 979.
    Saved, 421, 422, 423, 426, 432, 437.
    Sinful, 412, 417, 418, 419, 420.
Meditation, 90, 404, 568, 628, 848.
Meekness, 231, 234, 235, 588-590, 726, 779.
Mercy; — (See God.)
Ministers, 861-869.
Missionaries, 890, 894, 901, 905, 909.
Missions, 889-928.
Morning. 76-83, 593, 594.
Moses, 200, 230. 351, 617.
Mourners, 622, 994, 995.
Mystery, 150-154, 160-167, 663.

Nation, 934-938.
Nature, 78, 112, 119, 133, 142, 145, 155, 158, 172, 180, 195, 395, 396, 407, 947, 950-954.
Nearness to God, 379, 516, 518, 520, 592, 600, 601, 606, 610, 624, 627, 628, 722.
New Song, 279. 280, 351, 355, 357, 359.
New Year, 956, 963.

Obedience, 720, 721, 723, 725, 729, 730, 812, 813, 815, 816.
Omnipotence, 142-145, 193.
Omnipresence, 146, 149, 150, 546.
Omniscience, 146-149, 162, 895.
Ordination, 861, 869.

Pardon., 430, 437, 477, 551.
Parents, 879, 883, 888.
Parting, 43, 44, 45, 47, 48, 755, 780.
Pastors, 862, 864-866, 869, 995.
Patience, 589, 651, 652, 653, 663, 684, 681, 686.
Peace; —
    In Death, 970, 971, 973, 977, 978, 979, 986, 988, 1003.
    Of Conscience, 445, 561, 634, 688.
    Through Christ, 496, 561, 714.
    Of Nations, 896, 897, 914, 920, 941.
Penitence, 418, 491, 549-587, 773.
Perseverance, 733, 734, 741, 742, 750, 783.
Pestilence, 944.
Physician, 466, 482.
Pilot, 646.
Pisgah, 1039.
Poor, 762, 763, 764, 765, 766.
Praise; — 110-139.
    Adoring, 27, 117, 124, 130, 545.
    For Creation, 5, 9, 39, 112, 119, 120, 121, 127, 128, 131, 133, 137, 139, 172.
    For Preservation, 5, 9, 28, 80, 83, 88, 129, 168-174, 176, 185, 193, 197.
    For Daily Mercies, 10, 25, 76-77, 83, 85-89, 120, 137, 157, 169.

PARTICULAR INDEX OF SUBJECTS.

For Redemption, 6, 15, 17, 52, 66-68, 102, 109, 115, 120, 136, 172.
Of Angels, 04, 120, 131, 156, 212, 213, 216, 218, 220, 278, 279, 355.
Of Children, 153, 181, 879, 888.
Of all People, 1-3, 113, 115, 116, 118, 121, 132, 138, 139, 156, 176.
To Christ, 218, 219, 260, 262, 274, 277, 294, 297-301, 303-305, 350-362, 847, 848, 856.
To God, 110-139, 545.
To the Trinity, 102-108.
Prayer; 579, 611-631, 731.
   Answered, 626, 667, 790.
   Effectual, 614, 615.
   Enjoyed, 60.
   Hindrances to, 617.
   Invitation to, 612, 619, 621, 622.
   Lord's, 616.
   Nature of, 629.
   Privilege of, 627, 628.
   Secret, 25, 90, 592, 603, 612, 615, 621, 624, 628.
   Through Christ, 293, 327, 615, 618.
   Unceasing, 614.
Preaching, 334, 861-863.
Predestination, 434.
Priesthood; —
   Of Christ, 251-293, 307, 309, 312, 332, 425.
   Of Christians, 346.
Progress, 692, 733, 734, 741, 742, 753, 769.
Promises; 152, 182, 183, 186, 187, 189, 198, 743, 751.
Providence; —156-207.
   Mysterious, 160-167.
   Special, 120, 156, 157, 185, 194, 201, 656.
   Universal, 120, 126, 128, 137, 191, 193, 194, 198, 643, 670, 680, 947.
   Wise, 154, 159, 164, 651, 663, 671, 711.
Purity, 62, 695, 775.

Race, Christian, 741, 750, 977.
Redemption, 210, 226, 250, 258, 262, 264, 280, 286, 294, 299, 312, 321, 323, 328, 342, 350, 359, 413-419, 425, 432, 551, 856, 903, 918:
Refuge, 254, 258, 461, 665, 674.
Regeneration, 420, 422, 433.
Renunciation of World, 588.
Repentance, 477, 483, 484, 489-493, 549-587.
Resignation, 680, 682, 696.
Rest, 246, 350, 441, 442, 445, 470, 471, 498, 563, 567, 572, 607, 609, 610, 668, 690, 691, 693.
Restoration, 556, 573.
Resurrection; — 1014-1017.
   Of Christ, 1016, 260-277.
   Of Christians, 1014, 1015, 1017.
Return to God, 457, 553, 555, 569, 581, 684.
Revival, 363, 366, 368, 370, 373, 376, 381, 382, 389, 486, 512-514, 585, 701, 792, 799, 800, 804, 805.
Righteousness; —
   Of Christ, 300, 330, 335, 412, 417, 440, 493, 495, 500.
Rock of Ages; 258, 319, 327, 693.

Sabbath, 40-75.
Sacrifice of Christ, 413, 416, 446.
Salvation; 410-514.
   By Blood of Christ, 410-416.
   Found, 478-514.
   Needed, 400-420.
   Of Grace, 420-440, 508, 512, 514.
   Sought, 470-514.
Sanctuary; 871-878.
   Dedicated, 871-878.
   Loved, 7, 10, 11, 13, 14, 16, 18, 19, 21-27, 33, 34, 759, 871.
Scriptures, 395-409, 537, 715, 720.
Seamen, 929-933.
Seasons, 945-955.
Second Coming of Christ, 1007-1013, 1020, 1025-1028.
Secret Prayer, 25, 90, 592, 603, 612, 615, 621, 624, 628.
Self-dedication; 501, 509, 510, 564, 708, 715-730.
   Denial, 719, 723, 740.
   Examination, 568, 569.
   Renunciation, 510, 404, 570.
   Surrender, 474, 487, 501, 510, 515, 562.
Shepherd; —
   Christ, 341, 347, 348.
   God, 203-207, 473, 970.
Sickness, 657, 660.
Sin; 410-420.
   Conviction of, 245, 410, 478, 579.
   Confession of, 410, 476, 549, 559, 575, 582, 583, 587.
   Forgiveness of, 245, 450, 475, 563, 580, 581.
   Indwelling, 254, 258, 497, 549, 552, 576, 667.
   Original, 410.
   Punished, 471, 490, 571, 1028.
   Repented, 477, 483, 484, 489-493, 549-587.
Sinai, 255, 270, 523.
Soldiers, 736.
Song; —
   Of Angels, 212, 214, 216, 218, 224, 225, 261, 268, 270, 274, 278, 279, 294, 298, 301, 315, 355, 504, 505, 513.
   Of Moses, 351, 752.
   Of Redeemed, 262, 279, 280, 294, 295, 299, 324, 354, 359, 361, 362, 768, 769, 971, 1052, 1054, 1065, 1066.
Sons of God, 273, 379, 686, 782.
Sorrow, 622-624, 644, 653, 655, 665, 674, 684, 687, 694, 700, 713, 995, 1064.
Soul; —
   Its worth, 470, 471, 490, 505, 975, 983, 985, 990, 1014, 1037.
   Love for it, 438, 449, 457, 513, 514, 542, 761.
Sovereignty of God, 151-153.
Spring, 950.
Star of Bethlehem, 215, 219, 221, 222, 342.
Storm, 932, 933.
Strength, 699.
Submission, 159, 165, 651-653, 683, 680, 682, 686, 711.
Suffering, 643-714.
Summer, 951.
Temptation; —
   Christ in, 648, 650, 687, 713.
   Courage in, 706.
   Support in, 687, 600, 706, 1069.

Thanksgiving, 2, 5, 110-139, 155-158, 169,172, 173, 180, 193-196, 202, 945-949.
Time; —
  Accepted, 447, 448, 459-464, 476, 503.
  Brief, 141, 447, 462, 476, 479, 503, 958, 961-963, 964-972, 984.
Transfiguration, 236, 255.
Trials, 159, 647, 667, 686, 704, 705.
Trinity, 54, 64, 81, 99, 102-109, 123, 226, 236, 373, 378, 379, 380, 830, 929.
Trust, 201, 485, 643-714, 745.
  In Christ, 254, 282, 285, 317, 329, 335, 525, 638, 639, 675, 686, 694, 707, 1005, 1028.
  In God, 159, 160, 164-166, 170, 172, 196, 197, 201-207, 646, 651, 658, 659, 678, 706, 711, 745, 991.

Unbelief, 160, 476, 502, 554, 642.
Union; —
  Of Christians, 754-767, 796, 808, 809.
  To Christ, 515, 523, 1053.

Victory; —
  Of Christ, 208, 210, 236, 251, 263-271, 274, 276-279, 287, 296-299, 302, 305, 307, 308, 310, 313, 344, 354, 356, 357, 360, 376, 898, 903, 906, 907, 910, 911, 914, 917, 918, 922, 925.
  Of Christians, 736, 741, 745, 747, 751, 752, 975, 982, 985, 1001, 1015, 1045-1047, 1054, 1055, 1058, 1061-1066.
Vows, 196, 509, 510, 663.

Wandering, 473, 494, 553, 555, 556, 566, 569, 573, 581, 587.
Warfare, 733, 735, 736, 993, 998, 1052, 1055, 1061-1063.
Watchfulness, 731, 732, 735, 739, 746-748, 749, 972.
Work, 708, 723-725, 729.
World; —
  Converted, 139, 376, 395, 889, 891, 892, 896, 897, 908, 921, 922, 925.
  Renounced, 458, 466, 508, 568, 609, 1033, 1037.
  Vain, 466, 1033.
Worship; 1-48.
  Call to, 1, 3, 8, 9, 15, 19, 113, 114, 127, 128, 132, 139.
  Close of, 43-48, 61, 71-75.
  Enjoyed, 4, 7, 10, 11, 13-19, 21, 23, 24, 31, 33, 34, 50, 51, 53-55, 57-60, 65, 69, 70, 75, 90.
  Evening, 83-101.
  Lord's Day, 49-75.
  Morning, 21, 22, 53, 55, 67, 68, 76-84, 130.
  Opening, 1-42, 49-70.

Year; 950-963.
  Its Close, 956, 958, 959, 961, 962.
  New, 957, 960, 962, 963.
  Seasons, 947, 950-954.
Youth, 399, 879-898.

Zeal, 542, 724, 730, 741.
Zion, 13, 14, 220, 225, 785, 787, 789, 790, 792-795, 800, 803, 805, 861, 872, 895, 899, 924, 928, 1034, 1045, 1068.

INDEX OF SCRIPTURE.

[The figures designate Hymns.]

GENESIS.
1: 2. 3....64, 107, 929, 931
1: 9, 10................39
2: 3............49, 54, 64
3: 15..................274
3: 19.................1004
5: 24.............646, 592
6: 9...................592
8: 9...................470
8: 22..............953, 954
12: 1—4................632
19: 17.................461
22: 14.................642
24: 56.................742
24: 63.............90, 628
28: 12.................617
28: 17.............27, 59
28: 10—22........196, 606
32: 24—32.........625, 626
32: 28.................670
45: 5—7................160
49: 18.................676

EXODUS.
3: 2...................688
3: 14..................132
13: 21.................987
15: 1..................351
17: 11.................617
19: 18...........255, 759
20: 10, 11......49, 54, 64
25: 22.................611
28: 29.................282

LEVITICUS.
3: 2, 8................413
14: 4—7................410
25: 8—13...............425

NUMBERS.
10: 2..............54. 70
23: 10......621, 992. 1003
23: 19............186, 189

DEUTERONOMY.
3: 25.................1040
5: 12—14........49. 54. 64
11: 19............111, 879
26: 15.................935
26: 17, 18...509, 510, 810
32: 4.............176, 198
32: 15.................557
32: 20.................462
33: 25.................699
33: 27.................175
34: 1....54, 643, 1039, 1040

JOSHUA.
3: 17..................972
4: 21, 22........111, 879
23: 14.................977

RUTH.
1: 16..................806

1ST SAMUEL.
1: 27. 28.........880, 883
2: 2..............175, 198
2: 6—9........168, 171, 185
3: 1...................406
3: 4—10................458
3: 18....165, 651. 652. 653,
            660, 662, 863
4: 9..........733, 735, 747
6: 20..................411
7: 12.......477, 642, 649

2D SAMUEL.
12: 23..994, 997, 1002, 1014,
                    1036
22: 7—20....142, 144, 145,
                151, 152
22: 47............176, 197
23: 4..................707
23: 5..................190

1ST KINGS.
8: 22—54....870, 872, 873,
                    876
8: 27...................27
8: 37..................944
15: 4..................180
19: 8..................855

2D KINGS.
2: 6—14................989
2: 19..................988
4: 26..................774
5: 10......410, 439, 482
6: 16..................751
7: 14..................452
20: 1...962, 966, 967, 977,
                979, 981

1ST CHRONICLES.
16: 19—23........936—938
29: 15.................972

2D CHRONICLES.
1: 11, 12..............882
6: ....870—878
6: 41..................876
16: 9............146—149

EZRA.
9: 6......559, 571, 575, 576

NEHEMIAH.
1: 4—11....940, 942, 943
9: 5...................114
13: 31.................687

ESTHER.
4: 16....452, 487, 499, 507
5: 2....................55

JOB.
1: 21...150, 660, 680, 684,
                    686
3: 17—19..986, 996. 1000,
                1057, 1060
4: 17..................411
7: 6..............967, 969
7: 16..................976
7: 17..................158
9: 2.............147, 411
9: 5—8..........142, 143
9: 10..................154
9: 25, 26........967, 969
11: 7....150, 160, 163, 167
11: 19.................87
13: 15....452, 651—653,
            675, 680
18: 683
19: 25 .....286, 292, 1015.
                    1017
23: 3—10........150, 624
26: 7—14........154, 167
29: 2.....555, 585, 502
29: 11—13.....704—767
31: 14.................411
33: 13......163—165, 167
35: 15—17..............606
34: 21, 22.......146—149
35: 10..................94
37: 23.................102
38: 7..................131
38: 8—11.........142, 143
42: 5, 6....477, 478, 571,
            573, 578 587

PSALMS.
1: 2...................404
1: 5....................22
2: 1—6............751, 801
2: 669
3: 5...........80, 83, 97
4: 8.........87, 97, 99
5: 22
5: 3..........12, 76—81
6: 560
8: 158, 124
8: 3, 4................168
9: 110
14: 7..................028
15: 777
16: 2..................765
16: 8—11.1051, 1054. 1060
17: 1037
18: 144, 176
18: 7..................411
18: 11.................112
18: 35.................650
19: ...595, 396, 403, 407

19: 1..................155
19: 5, 6................78
20: 5, 7................988
23: ....203—207, 341. 348
24: 3—5................777
24: 7—10,...228, 261, 276
25: 556
25: 14.................775
27: 23, 619, 706
27: 4...................33
29: 10, 11.......143, 144
30: 5..................671
31: 5..................675
31: 15...........680, 681
32: 1—7................773
32: 7..................323
32: 11.................761
33: 188
34: 197
34: 7.............87. 94
36: 178
36: 6..................180
37: 6..................671
37: 37................1003
39: 4..................006
40: 1—3................645
41: 1..................763
42: 608
42: 5..................745
44: 933
45: 297, 311, 313
45: 2..................352
45: 3, 5................56
46: 175
46: 5..................803
46: 9..................941
46: 10.................185
48: 40, 785
48: 14.........970, 971
51: 410, 419, 489, 492,
        493, 549, 571, 575, 580
51: 7..................330
51: 8...................35
53: 6..................929
55: 673, 683
56: 13.................746
57: 139
60: 943
61: 674
61: 2..................596
63: 21....130, 627. 544,
                545, 599
63: 3..................322
65: 4, 5, 6. 9. 20
65: 7............920, 933
65: 11............947, 955
65: 13.................952
66: 144
66: 10.................809
67: 115. 921
68: 18......265, 270, 274
69: 817
71: 329

469

INDEX OF SCRIPTURE.

71: 9—17............659
72: 898, 900, 914, 920
73: ....,..... 170, 683
73: 24...696, 697, 713, 720
73: 25 ....,528, 533
75: 7.................161
77: 16—19............144
77: 19 ....160, 163
78: 879
80: 804. 936
84: ...7, 10, 16, 19, 33, 34
84: 10 50
84: 11 ....94. 801
85: 555, 592, 799, 800
87: 2.................672
87: 3 ....787. 803
87: 5..............,...873
87: 7.................593
89: 186, 189
89: 6—14............142
89: 34 ....190, 192
90: 140, 141. 064
90: 12 ....953. 967
91: 201, 770
91: 5, 6 .....95, 185. 944
91: 11, 12..........87, 94
92: 51. 57
92: 12, 14 602
93: 152
93: 3, 4........143, 145
95: 8, 9, 39, 113
95: 2....................945
95: 7......447, 448, 460
96: 127, 923
97: 151, 153, 1022
98: 113, 209
100: 1, 2. 3
100: 1, 2 113
102: 1. 2 584
102: 13................790
102: 25...............141
103: 136, 199. 200
103: 15, 16 ......141, 964
104: 112
104: 23................725
107: 173
107: 21—30...193, 929, 933
108: 943
110: 310, 313, 1013
112: 771
113: 156
115: 134
116: 28, 727
116: 7.................174
116: 13................620
116: 15 ......992. 993. 906
117: 116, 139
118: 22................52
119: 23................66
119: ....399, 400, 404, 601.
          715
119: 105 ....405. 406
120: 5.................1047
121: 95, 171, 185
122: 13, 14, 18, 53
122: 7.................65
125: 635
126: 512
127: 2 ....79. 84. 986
130: ....418, 551, 570. 646.
          638, 700
130: 3.................411
130: 5, 6 645
131: 588, 589, 500
132: 8...................876
132: 13................803
132: 16 ....968, 869
133: 754, 756
135: 17

136: 157, 172
137: 797, 798, 991
137: 5, 6 784
138: 129
139: 146, 148, 149
139: 9.................930
139: 23................808
141: 12
141: 2.............58. 88
143: 2.................411
143: 4..........607, 609
143: 5.................691
143: 8 ....76—83
143: 10................720
144: 3.................158
144: 11. 12 ......879—887
144: 15...............227
145: ...111, 118, 135, 169.
          481
145: 10................128
146: 126, 135, 137
147: 952
147: 2.................928
147: 4, 5 154
147: 5.................148
147: 14................941
147: 20 ....936. 938
148: 121, 128
149: 131
149: 2..........769, 781
150: 132

PROVERBS.
3: 5. 6 671
3: 13—18..............582
4: 7...................882
4: 23..................739
10: 7..................906
18: 24.................316
27: 1..................967

ECCLESIASTES.
9: 10..................462
11: 9..........477. 1018
12: 1..........476. 477
12: 7.................1004
12: 14................1018

CANTICLES.
1: 3...................345
2: 11—13..............950
4: 16..................802
5: 10—16..............352

ISAIAH
1: 18 ....430, 481
2: 1—4................697
3: 10..................774
6: 8...................717
9: 1—7................211
9: 2....208, 899, 902, 904
9: 6...................217
21: 11................221
25: 8..................982
26: 3............682. 771
26: 1—4...............787
26: 19..............1014
26: 16 ....52. 877
32: 15. 16 363
33: 17.........548. 1049
33: 24..............1049
35: 1..861, 893. 896. 900. 912
35: 8—10...769, 776, 1045.
          1046
38: 1..........977. 979
40: 3—5...............915
40: 9........793, 795, 800

40: 11...164, 203—207. 341,
          347, 704
40: 26.................154
40: 27—31......734, 745
41: 8.................335
42: 1—3..........232—235
42: 16........160, 163. 165
43: 1.2................670
43: 6.................793
43: 10.................807
46: 4..................183
48: 10.........868, 752
49: 10....1054, 1061. 1063
49: 15..........530, 794
49: 16.................428
49: 20.................805
50: 10.................676
51: 9..................892
51: 11..769, 776, 1045, 1046
51: 14.................912
52: 1..................800
52: 7—10..............861
53: 1..................450
53: 3, 4........283, 481
53* 4.................336
53: 6..................473
53: 7..........233, 234
54: 2..................871
54: 10.................427
55: 449, 451
55: 1, 2...............509
55: 7, 8.........456, 457
59: 1..........565, 871
60: 792
60: 1..........795, 899
60: 8..................805
60: 9..................919
61: 1. 2..........232—235
61: 7..................793
61: 11.................696
62: 6, 7...............895
62: 6............861, 862
64: 1..................871
65: 17........1009. 1013
66: 1..........872, 873
66: 8..................913

JEREMIAH.
2: 2..................555
3: 4..................886
3: 22...549, 552, 553. 558.
          580, 581, 582
8: 22..................460
9: 1............438. 761
9: 17............143—145
13: 23.....416, 420. 422
14: 8...........692.799
17: 9.......468. 578. 583
23: 6........330, 334, 335
23: 23, 24........146—149
23: 23. 29............408
31: 3.....318, 321, 322, 501

LAMENTATIONS.
3: 31—33....659, 676, 685

EZEKIEL.
18: 20, 21 463
33: 662
33: 11.................463
34: 12......341, 347, 473
36: 26........420, 558, 576
37, 38.................370
37: 3..........280. 908
37: 9..........386, 875

DANIEL.
2: 35, 44 786

3: 25..................685
7: 14, 27.306, 310. 813, 314
12: 2...........1017,1019

HOSEA.
6: 1, 2 684
11: 4.................603
14: 1, 2, 4......563, 582

JOEL.
2: 12—17............940
2: 23.................954
2: 28, 29........363, 382

AMOS.
4: 12...469, 477, 984, 998,
          1018
7: 2 791

JONAH.
2: 644, 645, 658
3: 9...................452

MICAH.
2: 10..................1034
4: 1—4.........897. 899
6: 6—8.................777
7: 18..................430

NAHUM.
1: 3.............142—145
1: 15..................861

HABAKKUK.
2: 14 ....000. 911. 914
3: 17, 18.........637, 707

HAGGAI.
2: 7....217, 222, 224, 290

ZECHARIAH.
1: 5 ....969, 995
9: 9....................236
13: 1 ....330, 414

MALACHI.
3: 1 ....218. 799
3: 2 ....411, 1018, 1019
3: 10..................916
3: 16........780. 807, 808
4: 2..77, 81, 326. 332. 340,
          707, 902, 903

MATTHEW.
1: 21...317. 319. 327, 323,
          334, 538, 539. 540
2: 9, 10 ....215. 219. 220.
          223, 225. 342
2: 11..................219
3: 1, 2 226
3: 13...412, 816, 819, 820.
          825
5: 3—13................762
5: 6...................775
5: 14..........779, 807
5: 18..................356
6: 6..............627. 623
6: 9—13................616
6: 11..................681
6: 13..................704
6: 25—34......707. 711
7: 7..........502.612.615
7: 11..................20
7: 13, 14.........459, 896

INDEX OF SCRIPTURE. 471

8: 23—27....642, 646, 932, 933
9: 12..............482
9: 35..............232
9: 37, 38,........912, 954
10: 25..........719, 737, 744
10: 32, 33.....730, 738, 743
10: 39..........679, 744
10: 42..............760
11: 25, 26..............633
11: 19..............316
11: 28—30...229, 441, 442, 445, 449, 552, 668, 693
11: 29........231—235, 800
13: 3—8............36, 37
13: 17..............861
13: 45, 46............332
14: 23..........627, 628
17: 1—9........233, 255
19: 1—5........588—590
19: 20..........18, 807
21: 1—10..............247
21: 9..............42
21: 42..............52
22: 2—10....451, 455, 842
24: 27..............1008
24: 30..312, 446, 1023, 1028
24: 33..............596
26: 42..............740
25: 6, 23..............998
25: 6..........1007, 1010
25: 21..............963
25: 31—46......1020—1028
25: 40..............766
20: 11..........764—766
26: 28—30......837—860
26: 36—46......238—240
26: 39, 42....651, 653, 656, 662
26: 64..312, 446, 1023, 1028
27: 33—50......241—257
27: 51—53......241, 305
27: 59—61...259, 824, 826
28: 67......260—277, 1016
28: 18—20 ...263, 822, 890, 894, 901, 905

MARK.
2: 17..............482
4: 3—9............36, 37
4: 37—41 ..646, 931, 932, 933
6: 47—50..............714
9: 2—10......236, 255
9:......642, 666, 667
9: 36, 37; 10:15..588—590
10: 13—16........880, 857
10: 21........719, 740, 744
10: 29—30..........679
11: 1—10..............237
11: 9—10..............42
11: 23..........930, 636
12: 10..............52
13: 24—27..312, 446, 1023, 1028
13: 31..............396
13: 33—43..............943
13: 45..............749
14: 7..........764—766
14: 12—26......837—860
14: 32—42......238—240
14: 36...631, 653, 656, 662
14: 62..312, 446, 1023, 1028
15: 22—37......241—257
15: 46......239, 824, 826
16: ....67, 260—277
16: 15..........800, 834

LUKE.
1: 31—33..............224
2: 7, 13..........210, 883
2: 8—14........214, 218
2: 13, 14...216, 218, 223, 225
2: 29..............988
2: 46..............881
2: 52..............004
3: 3..............225
3: 7..............472
3: 22........819, 825, 820
4: 18..........208, 232
5: 8....410, 418. 475, 476, 482—483, 497, 549, 570, 571, 578.
5: 11..........679, 713
6: 36........764, 765, 767
7: 34..............316
7: 47..............257
8: 4—8............36, 37
8: 22—24..............932
9: 28..........679, 744
9: 28—36......236, 255
9: 46—48......588—590
9: 57—62......723, 725
10: 2..........912, 954
10: 21..............633
10: 24..............861
10: 30—37..............764
10: 39, 42...532, 608, 722
11: 1..............629
11: 2—4..............616
11: 4..............681
11: 8........614, 625, 626
9, 10.......502, 615, 621
11: 15..............20
12: 8, 9......736, 738, 743
12: 27—28..............711
12: 32..............791
12: 35—40...732, 746, 749, 749, 908
13: 24..........459, 462
14: 16—24....451, 453, 435, 465, 842
15: 6..............473
15: 7, 10..............513
15: 11—24...443, 452, 456—458, 479, 483, 404, 508
16: 3, 4..............719
16: 5..............636
17: 5........61, 182, 746, 757
17: 24........1008, 1023
18: 1—7........614, 615
18: 10—14...491, 492, 575, 576
18: 16..........880, 887
18: 37..............433
19: 10......208, 210, 227
19: 41......233, 439, 761
20: 17..............52
21: 27....1020, 1023, 1024
21: 33..............396
21: 36..............740
22: 19........837—860
22: 39—46......238—240
22: 42...651, 653, 656, 662
23: 33..........241—257
23: 34..............618
23: 44, 45..............241
23: 46..............101
23: 53......239, 824, 826
23: 42, 43........414, 687
24: 1—12...67, 260—277
24: 29........84, 973, 974
24: 32..............31

24: 50, 51..............272

JOHN.
1: 12..............782
1: 13..............422
1: 14..............213
1: 29 ...413, 414, 487, 488
3: 3..........420, 433
3: 16, 17........210, 227
3: 30..............211
4: 13, 14..............524
5: 30........395—409
6: 17—20..............714
6: 53—59...824, 837—839, 840, 852, 854, 855, 858—860
6: 68....471, 474, 560, 610
7: 37..........451, 454
8: 12...93, 320, 340, 708, 902
9: 25..............450
10: 4, 5..............341
10: 9..............1056
10: 11......341, 347, 348
10: 20..............638
11: 26........933, 985
11: 35..............655
12: 8..........764—760
12: 12—15..............237
12: 32..............242
13: 9..............330
13: 23..............532
14: 2...275, 432, 1031, 1039
14: 6....325, 339, 587, 703
14: 16..............303
14: 19..............525
15: 1—6......515, 519, 520, 654, 809
15: 12..........754—767
15: 13..............316
15: 16..............435
16: 26..............393
16: 7—14........363—394
16: 16........857, 084
16: 23..........615, 618
16: 33..............475
17: 9..........618, 639
17: 9, 10..............703
17: 12..............638
17: 21......754—759, 796, 809, 858
17: 23..............515
17: 24........1038, 1051
18: 1..........238—240
19: 17—37......241—258
19: 30..............252
19: 34......251, 258, 439
19: 38—42..............250
20: 1—18....67, 260—277
21: 15—17...530, 542, 866, 860

ACTS.
1: 9—11..............273
2: 1—13......64, 382
2: 2, 3......265, 287, 303
4: 12..............310
4: 41...687, 736, 738, 743
7: 55—60....737, 752, 973
7: 59..............1005
9: 6...710, 723, 728, 729, 730
9: 11..............629
9: 18..............420
10: 33..............31
13: 48..............434

14: 22..........642, 752
16: 0..............027
16: 30........410—514

ROMANS.
3: 20..............411
3: 21, 22....412, 413, 416, 424
3: 23, 24...410, 417, 421, 427, 430, 434
5: 5....102, 366, 378, 380
6: 4....826, 829, 830, 831, 832, 834
7: 0..........478, 480
7: 24..........552, 578
8: 14, 15....366, 375, 379, 500, 535, 782
8: 17..............779
8: 18..........712, 1044
8: 19—23....1012, 1013, 1026
8: 24..............1030
8: 26......375, 380, 620
8: 28..............774
8: 29..............434
8: 31..............507
8: 32..............615
8: 33..............431
8: 34..........251—293
9: 1—3..............761
10: 14, 15..............861
11: 33—36......154, 167
12: 2..........724, 725
12: 4, 5....757, 808, 809
12: 12..............1010
13: 10, 11......030, 968
14: 7, 8....627, 528, 729
15: 30..........867—869

1st CORINTHIANS.
1: 26..............791
1: 30......330, 335, 412, 778, 779
2: 2..........243—250
3: 9..............945
5: 8..............856
6: 19....374, 587, 775
6: 20......510, 723, 725, 726
9: 24—27..............741
10: 4..............258
10: 16, 17....852, 858
10: 31............50, 729
11: 23—25....547, 841, 844
12: 33..............857
12: 38..............864
13:..............760
13: 8..............305
13: 12..............664
15: 20..........588—590
15: 20....202—216, 1016
15: 65...264, 269, 693, 973, 982, 987
15: 57......982, 985, 987
16: 13......732—737, 747—751

2D CORINTHIANS.
1: 3, 4......372, 657, 674, 684, 707
1: 20......166, 197, 428
1: 21......363, 364, 375
4: 6..............424
4: 17, 18........633, 1044
5: 1......953, 1050, 1061
5: 5......353, 364, 375
5: 7......166, 632

INDEX OF SCRIPTURE.

5: 8...976. 988. 991. 1032,
1038. 1042, 1050,
1051, 1060, 1067—
1069.
5: 14...331, 333, 532, 534,
542. 543
5: 17..............423
6: 10....:.......771, 772
6: 16............591. 775
8: 9..........336, 517, 522
9: 15..............626
10: 1............233—235
12: 9, 10............699

GALATIANS.
1: 12............408, 409
2: 20..............248
2: 28..............757
3: 15...........555, 592
4: 26..............1068
6: 14....246—251, 256, 257

EPHESIANS.
2: 6..............768
2: 20..............677
3: 8..............532
3: 17—21.....43, 333, 796
3: 19........318, 487, 562
4: 4..............757
4: 5..............796
4: 8..........265, 864
4: 30.........397, 388
5: 8..............712
5: 19.......131, 133, 761
5: 27..............521
6: 10, 13......733, 747, 753
6: 18, 20.......1067—1069

PHILIPPIANS.
1: 6..............191
1: 21....595, 723, 975. 963,
985. 987
1: 23....976. 977. 978. 1031,
1042, 1043, 1047, 1051,
1067. 1068
2: 2...........754, 759
2: 3..............767
2: 5—11...213, 231, 234,
235, 336, 517, 522, 764
2: 10....301, 302, 310. 311,
313, 319, 334. 898, 925
2: 15..............779
3: 1........769, 776, 781
3: 7—9...248, 495, 523, 533,
535
3: 13, 14....741, 750, 753,
1029
3: 20—21..1007—1011, 1015
4: 4........769, 776, 781
4: 8........740, 777, 779

COLOSSIANS.
1: 7..............867
1: 13..........1051, 1059
1: 16. 17......120, 213, 333
2: 12......826, 829, 830, 832,
834
3: 1—3....771, 834, 1029
3: 3.........284, 349, 1006
3: 4.........782, 1010, 1011
3: 12—14........758—767
3: 16.........131, 133, 781

3: 17..............729
4: 2...........731, 749
4: 3............867—869

1st THESSALONIANS.
4: 13, 14.....986. 987. 994,
996, 1000, 1001. 1004,
1014—1017
4: 16....1019, 1023, 1024,
1026
4: 17......1042—1044, 1051
5: 5...........641, 712
5: 11..............808
5: 17..........614, 731

2d THESSALONIANS.
1: 7—10...1018, 1020—1028
3: 1............867—869

1st TIMOTHY.
1: 15....208—210, 220, 335,
423, 425, 429
1: 17..........162, 783
1: 18..............749
2: 5..............350
3: 16....150, 213, 230, 268,
275—280
4: 8............768—783
6: 6—8.....643, 660, 651,
664, 681, 711
6: 12...735, 736, 747, 748,
750, 751, 753, 810
6: 15, 16..........120, 353

2d TIMOTHY.
1: 8............738, 743
1: 9....426, 428, 429, 435,
842
1: 12..........639, 743
2: 3....736, 747, 749, 753
2: 13..........187—189
2: 19..........163, 638
3: 15......399, 881, 882
3: 16....398, 405, 406, 408,
409
4: 6—8.....963, 977, 998

TITUS.
2: 10—13...........740
2: 13....844, 857, 1007,
1010, 1011, 1053
3: 5—7.............440

HEBREWS.
1: 2..............409
1: 3.....120, 277, 290, 302,
305, 677
1: 8, 9.............311
1: 14..........94, 450
2: 3.....449, 462, 463, 469
2: 6—9.............158
2: 9......29, 4—305, 310, 677
2: 11..............316
2: 15..............355
2: 17, 18....281, 283, 517,
518, 522
3: 13....447, 448, 460, 462
4: 9.....58, 74, 1034, 1038,
1050, 1057, 1060
4: 13..........146—149
4: 14—16....281—283, 289,
290, 309, 615, 618

6: 12.....993. 1055, 1058
6: 19....287. 290. 678, 1059
7: 24, 25...284—286, 291—
293, 306
7: 26..........231—235
9: 12, 14..........413
9: 24........281—2d3
9: 27........1018—1028
10: 19—22....283, 343, 615
10: 24, 25....759, 807, 608
10: 37............1013
11:................1058
11: 1.........630—634
11: 10, 14....1031, 1034,
1047
11: 13...........972
11: 16......1042, 1046
11: 25............1037
12: 1.......741, 1055
12: 2....467, 631, 700
12: 3....233, 234, 235, 744
12: 4.........672, 737
12: 5....656, 667, 680, 686
12: 12............671
12: 18—24...768, 789, 980
13: 14....1031, 1034, 1047
13: 17............662

JAMES.
1: 5...20, 363, 390, 391, 882
1: 17....173, 198, 363, 666
1: 22............36—38
1: 27......760, 763—767
2: 14, 17.......740, 700
2: 23............335
4: 6, 10........588—590
4: 14......958, 964—967
5: 8........1007—1013
5: 10......1055, 1058
5: 16.........611—626

1st PETER.
1: 3, 4............1016
1: 8...529, 537, 538, 539, 849
1: 13.............732
1: 17...731, 739, 746, 748
1: 19....320, 335, 413—415
1: 24........141, 964—967
1: 25............396
2: 6...........52, 577
2: 7....317, 320, 327, 328,
332, 333, 334, 345,
539, 540
2: 21.......231—235, 719
2: 24......336, 413, 481
2: 25............473
3: 14............679
3: 18....242, 244, 245, 247,
253, 284
3: 21............826
3: 22....268, 287, 294, 296,
310, 314, 315
4: 12, 13............672
4: 17, 18..........469
5: 4............869
5: 7...25, 612, 643, 669,
671, 673, 675, 681,
682, 683, 707, 711
5: 8......739, 746, 748

2d PETER.
1: 19....326, 405, 406, 593
3: 10........1021, 1022

3: 12...1007—1013, 1021—
1024

1st JOHN.
1: 3............516, 536
1: 5..............641
1: 7.....414, 415, 439, 481,
487, 641
2: 1...35, 77, 147, 283—291
294, 553
2: 2..............335
3: 1, 2..........779, 782
4: 8..........202, 249
4: 0..........424, 437
4: 10.........435, 542
4: 19.........435, 541
5: 3..............673
5: 4...........636, 962
5: 7..........102—109

JUDE.
1: 14, 15......1018—1028
1: 22, 23............761
1: 24, 25............783

REVELATION.
1: 5, 6...312, 315, 346. 355
1: 7.............1026
1: 18......310, 314, 356
1: 20............869
2: 7............1000
3: 12............689
3: 20............443
4: 10............591
5: 9..........280, 350
5: 12...279, 304, 310, 354,
357, 361, 362, 1035,
1036, 1062.
6: 9, 10...........1047
6: 16....1020, 1022, 1028
7: 9—12...299, 360, 1035,
1036. 1042
7: 13—17.1054, 1055, 1061,
1062, 1063—1065
8: 3, 4............260
11: 15..........314, 611
14: 3........123, 290, 315
14: 13....992, 993, 906, 1003
14: 15.............1013
15: 3.........351. 752
17: 14.....297, 313, 918
19: 6............153
19: 9......847, 855, 860
19: 10............290
19: 16.........302, 332
20: 11—15....42, 1013, 1021,
1022, 1023, 1024,
1026
20: 12............161
21: 1—5......131, 1099
21: 4........1049, 1064
21: 6.........446, 849
21: 9............1007
21: 10—27....1045—1048
21: 23......223, 1035, 1036
22: 3............951
22: 4............851
22: 5............1049
22: 13............446
22: 16....226, 593, 738, 852,
803, 926, 1053
22: 17....445, 446, 448, 443,
451—455, 460
22: 20......243, 299, 799,
1012, 1013

ALPHABETICAL INDEX OF TUNES.

[Tunes marked (*) are prepared expressly for this work. Others have been contributed, or purchased, and cannot be used without permission.]

A.

		PAGE
Abridge..........C. M.	*Isaac Smith*...........	151
Adams..........C. M.	*C. Kingsley*...........	354
Adrian..........S. M.	*Geo. Hews*...........	162
Advent....⅃......7s 61.	*W. H. Birch*...........	96
Agnus Dei......6s & 4s.	*W. H. Birch*...........	203
Ahira (Leighton) S. M.	*H. W. Greatorex*.......	346
Aletta...............7s.	*Bradbury*.............	168
Alfreton......⅃..L. M.	*Beasteed*.............	119
All Saints....⅃...L. M.	*Wm. Knapp*...........	280
Almin............L. M.	*Arr. by Conrad Kocher*	68
America........6s & 4s.	*Alt. to Purcell*........	874
Amos............L. M.	*Neukomm*............	13
Amoy..........6s & 4s.	*L. Mason*............	187
Amsterdam....7s & 6s.	*English*.............	415
Ansel........8s Double.	*E. L. White*...........	238
Antioch..........C. M.	*Arr. by L. Mason*......	90
Anvern..........L. M.	" " " "	323
Appleton........L. M.	*Dr. Boyce*...........	262
Arcadia..........C. M.	*T. Hastings*...........	171
Ariel..........C. P. M.	*L. Mason*........138, 220
Arlington........C. M.	*Arne*............199, 299
Arnheim........L. M.	*S. Holyoke (a)*........	24
Ashwell..........L. M.	*L. Mason*.........322, 339
Aspiration Chant....6s.	....	246
Atkins..........C. M.	*Geo. Hews*...........	247
Atlantic..........L. M.	*Geo. Oates*...........	152
Augustus........C. M.	*W. W. Johnson*........	409
Autumn...⅃..8s & 7s D.	*Spanish*.............	275
Ava............6s & 4s.	*T. Hastings*...........	187
Avon........⅃...C. M.	*H. Wilson*............	212
Aylesbury........S. M.	*J. Chetham*...........	104

B.

Baldwin..........C. M.	*L. Marshall*...........	425
Balerma..........C. M.	*H. Wilson*............	241
Barby............C. M.	*Wm. Tansur*..........	244
Beethoven........L. M.	*Beethoven*...........	309
Belgrave..........C. M.	*Wm. Horsley*..........	76
Bellak..............7s.	*Mendelssohn*.........	368
Belmont......8s, 7s & 4.	*Anon*................	188
Demerton..........C. M.	*H. W. Greatorex*...18, 426
Benediction Chant..10s.	*English*.............	345

		PAGE
Benevento........7s D.	*S. Webbe*........... 126.	364
Benton........6s & 10s.	" *Shawm*"............	284
Bera............L. M.	*J. E. Gould*...........	207
Bethany........6s & 4s,	*L. Mason*............	246
Bethesda........H. M.	*Dr. Green*............	194
Beulah........⁓...7s D.	*E. Ives, Jr.*...........	430
Blendon..........L. M.	*Giardini*............	10
Blessing......11s & 8s.	....	355
Bloomfield Chant..L. M.	*Bradbury*............	61
Blumenthal......7s D.	*Blumenthal*...........	21
Bowdoin Square..C. M.	*S. Hill*.............	234
Bowen..........L. M.	*Haydn*.............	122
Boylston..........S. M.	*L. Mason*.........49, 307
Bradford ....C. M.	*Handel*..........223, 250
Brattle Street..C. M. D.	*Pleyel*.............	267
Bridegroom......C. M.	*S. Wesley*............	406
Bristol..........C. M.	*E. Hodges*............	82
Brown..........L. M.	*Bradbury*............	142
Brownell....L. M. (6l).	*Haydn*.............	17
Burlington........C. M.	*J. F. Burrows*........	215

C.

Caddo ....L. M.	*Bradbury*............	222
Calm ....C. M.	*J. E. Gould*...........	190
Cambridge......C. M.	*Dr. Randall*..........	12
Carey........L. M. (6l).	*Carey*..............	39
Chambers St.Chant.L.M.	*L. Marshall*...........	364
Chesterfield......C. M.	*Havels*.............	9
Chestnut Street..C. M.	*H. K. Oliver*.........	89
Children's Praise..C. M.	*Anon*...............	854
China............C. M.	*Swan*..............	400
Christmas........C. M.	*Handel*.............	301
Chrome......11s & 8s.	*T. Hastings*..........	54
Claremont........H. M.	" *Boston Academy*"....	351
Clarendon........C. M.	*I. Tucker*...........	65
Clarendon St..........7s.	*L. Marshall*..........	195
Clarion *........6s & 4s.	*Geo. Hews*...........	380
Colchester........C. M.	*Williams*............	92
Come, ye disconsolate 11s & 10s......	*Webbe*.............	252
Comforter ...7s & 5s D.	*Psalmodist*..........	159
Commission* ....L. M.	*Geo. Hews*...........	856
Communion ......C. M.	*S. Hill*.............	349

ALPHABETICAL INDEX OF TUNES.

			PAGE
Compton	S. M.	E. K. Prouty	387
Consolation	C. M.	from J. A. Neumann	427
Cooley	L. M.	H. K. Songs of Zion	189
Corinth	C. M.	L. Mason	255
Corona	7, 7, 8, 7, D.	Choral Harmony	305
Coronation	C. M.	O. Holden	130
Coronet*	8s & 7s D.	Geo. Hews	127
Coventry	C. M.	L. Mason	198, 338
Cowper	C. M.	T. Hastings	174
Creation	L. M.	Haydn	36
Culloden	H. M.	English Melody	135

D.

Dallas	7s.	Cherubini	71
Darwell	H. M.	Darwell	30, 133
Daydawn	7s & 6s.	Haydn	407
Dedham	C. M.	W. Gardner	251
Delay	7s.	L. Marshall	242
Denfield	C. M.	Glaser	224
Dennis	S. M.	Nageli	196
Devizes	C. M.	Tucker	253
Devotion	8s.	Walter's Coll.	432
Doomsday, (Old Commandments)	L. M.	J. B. Bonometti	411
Dort	6s & 4s.	L. Mason	154
Dover	S. M.	L. Mason	23
Downs	C. M.	L. Mason	35
Duke Street	L. M.	J. L. Hatton	8, 64, 359
Dundee	C. M.	Scottish	22, 333, 377

E.

Easter Hymn	H. M.	Anon	115
Easton	L. M.	Mozart	221, 270
Ecce Homo*	7s & 6s.	Arr. by Geo. Hews	109
Elizabethtown	C. M.	Kingsley	216
Emmaus*	L. M.	Geo. Hews	217
Enmore	C. M.	M. Harp	72
Ernan	L. M.	L. Mason	144, 210, 327
Essex (Sudbury)	7s.	T. Clark	62
Ethelberg	L. M.	Beethoven	225
Eucharist (St. Theodolph)	7s & 6s.	Hymns, Anc. & Mod.	341
Evan	C. M.	Havergal	101
Evening	L. M. (61)	J. E. Gould	45
Eventide	10s.	Hymns, Anc. & Mod.	390
Exeter	C. M.		310

F.

Faben	8s & 7s.	J. H. Wilcox	57
Faith	C. M.	S. P. Tuckerman	32, 257
Farrant	C. M.	R. Farrant	53
Federal Street	L. M.	H. K. Oliver	164, 206, 329
Fenworth	L. M. (61)	Anon	137
Fletcher	C. M.	W. Arnold	350
Folsom	11s & 10s.	From Mozart	94
Frederick	11s.	Geo. Kingsley	392

G.

			PAGE
Ganges	C. P. M.	Anon	181
Geer	C. M.	H. W. Greatorex	141
Geneva	C. M.	J. Cole	84
Gennesaret*	6s & 4s, Pec.	Geo. Hews	291
Gerar	S. M.	L. Mason	20
Germany	L. M.	Beethoven	38
Gethsemane	7s (61).	Walter's Coll.	103
Gilead	L. M.	Milgrove	40, 56
Glory	7s D.	Herold	429
Golan	8s & 6.	B. Academy (a)	125
Golden Hill	S. M.	Western Melody	296
Goshen	10s & 11s.	Old German	260
Grace Church	L. M.	From Pleyel	205
Gratitude	L. M.	Mendelssohn Coll.	233
Grostete	L. M.	H. W. Greatorex	134
Guardian	S. M.	A. Brown	149
Guidance*	5s & 8s.	Geo. Hews	290

H.

Habakkuk	C. P. M.	Dr. Hodges	209
Haddam	H. M.	L. Mason	14
Hamburg	L. M.	Gregorian Chant	74, 386
Hamden	8s, 7s & 4s.	L. Mason	108
Hampton	H. M.	From Haydn	321
Harmony Grove	L. M.	H. K. Oliver	348
Harvest Home	7s D.	English Melody	378
Harwell	8s & 7s D.	L. Mason	136, 366
Harwood	C. P. M.	Harwood	289
Hastings	8s & 6s & 8s.	Hastings	47
Haven*	L. M.	Geo. Hews	431
Haverhill	S. M.	L. Mason	313
Haydn's Hymn	8s,7s & 4.	Haydn	182
Heaven	6s D.	From Von Weber	423
Heber	C. M.	G. Kingsley	236, 336
Hebron	L. M.	L. Mason	100, 226, 300
Helmsley	8s, 7s & 4.	Rev. M. Madan	413
Hendon	7s.	From Malan	325
Henry	C. M.	S. B. Pond	370
Holley	7s.	Geo. Hews	49, 285, 345
Hope	7s (61)	P. H. Diemer	405
Horton	7s.	S. von Wartensee	276, 344
Howland	L. M.	N. Y. Choralist	205
Humility	L. M.	S. P. Tuckerman	185
Hummel	C. M.	Zeuner	16, 145, 309
Hursley	L. M.	German	41, 146, 232

I.

Illa	L. M.	Carmina Sacra	256
Imploring Chant	L. M.	L. Marshall	192
Israel	8s D.	Harp of Judah	179
Italian Hymn	6s & 4s.	E. Giardini	52

J.

Jerusalem on High	H. M.	Dr. Croft	421
Jenner	7s & 6s.	H. L. Jenner	29, 335
Jerusalem the Golden,	7s & 6s.	H. L. Jenner	420
Jordan	C. M. D.	Wm. Billings	415

ALPHABETICAL INDEX OF TUNES.

Tune			Page
Judah	S. P. M.	Jewish Melody	58
Judgment Hymn	8s & 7s.		
(2.)		M. Luther	412

K.

| Kedron Chant | C. M. | J. E. Gould | 43 |
| Kent | L. M. | G. Greene | 375 |

L.

Laban	S. M.	L. Mason	303
Lanesboro	C. M.	L. Mason	15
Langdon	7s (61).	Rev. W. E. Miller	186
Latter Day	8s & 7s.	Anon.	324
Lebanon	S. M. D.	J. Zundel	197
Leighton, (Ahira)	S. M.	H. W. Greatorex	27
Lenox	H. M.	Edson	132, 178
Lewes	8s, 7s & 4s.	Boosey's Coll.	388
Lischer	H. M.	L. Mason	81
London New	C. M.	Dr. Croft	66, 318
Louvan	L. M.	V. C. Taylor	50, 340
Lux Benigna	10s & 4s.	Hymns, Anc. & Mod.	287
Lyons	10s & 11s.	Haydn	54

M.

Maitland	C. M.	Western Tune	302
Malden	S. M.	W. H. Birch	399
Manoah	C. M.	H. W. Greatorex	105
Marlow	C. M.	L. Mason	177
Martyn	7s D.	Marsh	219
Martyrs	C. M.	Scottish	73
Mear	C. M.	Welsh Air	121
Meinhold	7s, 8s & 7s.	Hymns, Anc. & Mod.	404
Melchior	7s & 6s.	Melchior Teschner	192
Melcombe	L. M.	S. Webbe	180
Mendelssohn	L. M.	Mendelssohn	231
Mendon	L. M.	English	167
Meribah	C. P. M.	L. Mason	414
Merton	C. M.	H. K. Oliver	169
Migdol	L. M.	L. Mason	99
Milford	C. P. M.	Boosey's Coll.	161
Missionary Chant	L. M.	C. Zeuner	31, 357
Missionary Hymn	7s & 6s.	L. Mason	371
Mornington	S. M.	Earl of Mornington	150
Mortality	C. M.	Anon.	393
Mozart	7s.	Mozart	118
Mt. Calvary (Gethsemane)	7s (61)	Walter's Coll.	201

N.

Naomi	C. M.	L. Mason	175, 261
Nashville	L. P. M.	Gregorian	168
Nativity	7s D.	English	97
Nettleton	8s & 7s D.	Dr. Nettleton	263
Newbold	C. M.	Kingsley	381
Newcourt	L. P. M.	H. Bond	60
Newton	C. M.	T. Jackson	156
New Year's Hymn	11s & 5s.	Webbe	385

Nichols	C. M.	Geo. Hews	170, 268
Night	7s.	W. Beale (a)	230
Nightfall*	6s, 4s, 6s.	Geo. Hews	40
Northfield	C. M.	Ingalls	354
Northampton	C. M.	Hymns, Anc. & Mod.	394
Nottingham	C. M.	J. Clark	60
Nuremberg	7s.	J. S. Bach	19, 140

O.

Octavius	L. M.	G. F. Root	70
Old Hundred	L. M.	Martin Luther	7
Oliphant	8s, 7s, & 4.	B. Academy	362
Olivet	6s & 4s.	L. Mason	289
Olmutz	S. M.	From Gregorian Chant	273
Olney	S. M.	L. Mason	342
Opal	8s & 7s D.	J. Zundel	202
Ortonville	C. M.	T. Hastings	274
Owen	S. M.	Sweetser	173

P.

Paradise	8s, 6s, & 6s.	J. Barnby	423
Parnell	S. M.	Beethoven	424
Park Place	H. M.	S. B. Pond	69
Park Street	L. M.	Venua	139
Pascal	H. M.	Plymouth Coll.	184
Pastoral Hymn L. M. (61).		Mozart	88
Paul	10s, 11s & 12s.	Anon.	304
Pax Dei	10s.	Hymns, Anc. & Mod.	26
Peniel	L. M. (61).	Mendelssohn	254
Penn	7s (61).	W. H. Birch	306
Peterboro	C. M.	Webb	259
Peters	S. P. M.	B. Academy	11
Pilesgrove	L. M.	N. Mitchell	298
Pilgrimage	L. M.	Boosey's Coll.	416
Pleyel's Hymn	7s.	Pleyel	230, 314
Portuguese"	10s & 11s.	J. Reading	80
Prague	S. M.	Boosey's Coll.	297
Prayer	S. M. D.	L. Marshall	277, 396
Prince	L. M. (61).	Mendelssohn	229
Protection*	8s D.	Geo. Hews	46

R.

Rapture	C. P. M.	Harwood	29
Rathburn	8s & 7s.	J. Conkey	47, 111
Reliance*	7s & 6s.	Geo. Hews	245, 256
Resignation	8s & 4. or 8s & 6	Boosey's Coll.	265
Rest	L. M.	Bradbury	397
Retreat	L. M.	T. Hastings	249
Rhine	C. M.	German	422
Rockingham	L. M.	L. Mason	172
Rock of Ages	7s (61).	Hastings	112
Kono	8s & 6s.	Shawm	376
Rosefield	7s (6s).	Dr. Malan	129, 315
Rothwell	L. M.	L. Mason	123
Royalty	12s, 11s & 8s.	From German, L. Mason	367

ALPHABETICAL INDEX OF TUNES.

S.

		PAGE
Sabbath ....7s (61).	L. Mason	33
Sacramental Hymn ..9s & 8s D	W. H. Birch	343
Salisbury....L. M. (61).	Haydn	266
Saul...... ..L.M. (61).	Handel	403
Scotland.12s or 12s & 11s.	Dr. Clarke	373
Seir .... 8. M.	L. Mason	229
Selborne........7s & 6s.	Anon	200
Seymour ....7s.	H. W. Greatorex	193
Sheffield ....S. M.	T. Hastings...........	158
Shining Shore..8s & 7s.	G. F. Root	389
Shirland ....S. M.	Stanley 249, 317
Shoel ....L. M.	Shoel	379
Sicilian Hymn.8s, 7s, 4s.	Italian	25
Siloam.............C. M.	I. B. Woodbury 106, 352
Silver Street......8. M.	I. Smith	65
Solitude ....7s.	L. T. Downs	37
Spanish Hymn ....7s D.	Spanish 110, 332
Star of Bethlehem...... L. M. D	Scottish..............	147
State Street........S. M.	J. C. Woodman	402
Stephens..........C.M.	W. Jones	176
Sterling ....L. M.	Harrison	98
Stockwell..6s & 7s, Pec.	D. E. Jones	391
Stonefield ....L. M.	Stanley	382
St. Albinus ... 7s & 8s.	Hymns, Anc. & Mod....	125
St. Anns..............C. M.	Dr. Croft	155
St. Brides.........8. M.	Dr. Howard 328, 403
St. Clements Dane C. M.	W. H. Birch	326
St. Francis .. 8s & 7s D.	M. Harp...............	240
St. Gregorius .....C. M.	Tallis................	148
St. Johns ....C. M.	Anon..................	120
St. John Baptist's...11s.	Elvey.................	330
St. Martyns .. ... C. M.	Tansur	312
St. Mary's Abbey..8. M.	J. S. Bach	213
St. Paul's ....L. M.	Dr. Green.............	282
St. Petersburg L. M.(61).	Russian Air 124, 334
St. Thomas ....S. M.	Williams 213, 316
Sudbury (Essex).......7s.	T. Clark	114
Supplication (Ecce Homo).....7s & 6s D.	Arr. by Geo. Hews......	283
Sydenham ....C. M.	W. H. Birch	278

T.

Tallis..............C. M.	Tallis................	292
Tallis' Evening Hymn L. M.	Tallis................	42
Tamworth....8s, 7s & 4.	Lockhart	123
Tappan...........C. M.	Kingsley	116
Telleman's Chant....7s.	C. Zeuner.............	163
Thatcher..........S. M.	Handel	183
Theodora...........7s.	Handel	113
Tonica...........8s & 4s.	Harp of Judah (a).....	166
Tranquillity....S. H.M.	L. Marshall	401

		PAGE
Triumph* ......7s & 6s.	Geo. Hews........	395
Truro ....L. M.	C. Burney.............	131

U.

Utica .... S. M.	C. Zeuner.............	410
Uxbridge ....L. M.	L. Mason	78

V.

Vanhall's Hymn..L. M.	Vanhall	77
Varina ....C. M. D.	G. F. Root	380
Vesper Hymn 8s & 7s D. or 8s, 7s & 4s.........	Bortniansky 93, 331

W.

Ward ....L. M.	L. Mason............78, 250
Ware.............L. M.	N. D. Gould...........	63
Wareham ....L. M.	W. Knapp	347
Warrington .....L. M.	R. Harrison	102
Warsaw.........H. M.	T. Clark	51
Warwick ....C. M.	Stanley	34
Watchman........S. M.	Leach.................	86
Watchman tell us .7s D.	L. Mason	95
Watts ....L. M.	Arr. by M. Lord.......	271
Webb ....7s & 6s.	Webb	365
Wells ....L. M.	J. Holdroyd...........	227
Welton ....L. M.	Dr. Malan............	117
Westminster Abbey .... L. M.	Dr. Cooke	393
Williams........L. M.	Templi Carmina	107
Wilmot....8s & 7s or 7s.	L. Mason	87
Wimborne.......L. M.	Whittaker	157
Winchelsea......L. M.	Prelleur	160
Winchester......L. M.	Dr. Croft.............	294
Windham ....L. M.	Read ....,	204
Wirth ....C. M.	Bradbury 214, 337
Woodland........C. M.	N. D. Gould...........	67
Woodstock ......C. M.	Dutton................	44
Woodworth .....L. M.	Bradbury.............	353
Wyman's Chant ..C. M.	E. Hamilton	396

Y.

Yoakley .....L. M. (61).	Wm. Yoakley	372
York ....C. M.	John Milton (Father of poet)	65

Z.

Zalena.........C. P. M.	M. Harp...............	208
Zephyr .... L. M.	Bradbury 165, 308
Zerah...........C. M. (61).	L. Mason	91
Zion ....8s & 7s & 4s.	T. Hastings........320, 361
Zong ....6s D.	National Psalmist......	264

METRICAL INDEX OF TUNES.

L. M.

	PAGE		PAGE		PAGE
Alfreton	119	Grostete	134	Sterling	98
All Saints	280	Hamburg	74, 386	Stonefield	882
Almin	68	Harmony Grove	348	St. Paul's	282
Ames	13	Haven	431	St. Petersburg (61)	124, 334
Anvern	323	Hebron	100, 226, 300	Tallis' Evening Hymn	42
Appleton	262	Howland	295	Truro	131
Arnheim	24	Humility	185	Uxbridge	75
Ashwell	322, 339	Hursley	41, 146, 232	Vanhall's Hymn	77
Atlantic	152	Illa	256	Ward	78, 250
Beethoven	309	Imploring Chant	192	Ware	63
Bera	207	Kent	375	Wareham	347
Blendon	10	Louvan	50, 340	Warrington	102
Bloomfield Chant	61	Melcombe	180	Watts	271
Bowen	122	Mendelssohn	231	Wells	227
Brownell (61)	17	Mendon	167	Welton	117
Carey (61)	89	Migdol	99	Westminster Abbey	893
Chambers St. Chant	364	Missionary Chant	31, 357	Williams	107
Commission	356	Octavius	70	Wimborne	157
Cooley	189	Old Hundred	7	Winchelsea	160
Creation	36	Park Street	189	Winchester	294
Doomsday	411	Pastoral Hymn (61)	88	Windham	204
Duke St.	8, 64, 359	Peniel (61)	254	Woodworth	353
Easton	221, 270	Pilesgrove	298	Yoakley (61)	872
Emmaus	217	Pilgrimage	416	Zephyr	165, 308
Ernan	144, 210, 327	Prince (61)	228		
Ethelberg	225	Rest	397	L. P. M.	
Evening (61)	45	Retreat	248	Nashville	168
Federal St.	164, 206, 329	Rockingham	172	Newcourt	60
Fenworth (61)	137	Rothwell	123		
Germany	38	Salisbury (61)	266	C. M.	
Gilead	40, 66	Saul (61)	403	Abridge	151
Grace Church	205	Shoel	379	Adams	854
Gratitude	233	Star of Bethlehem (D)	147	Antioch	90

METRICAL INDEX OF TUNES.

	PAGE
Arcadia	171
Arlington	199, 299
Atkins	247
Augustus	409
Avon	212
Baldwin	425
Balerma	241
Barby	244
Belgrave	76
Bemerton	18, 426
Bowdoin Square	284
Bradford	223, 259
Brattle Street (D)	267
Bridegroom	406
Bristol	82
Brown	142
Burlington	215
Caddo	222
Calm	190
Cambridge	12
Chesterfield	9
Chestnut Street	89
Children's Praise	354
China	400
Christmas	301
Clarendon	85
Colchester	92
Communion	243
Consolation	427
Corinth	235
Coronation	130
Coventry	198, 338
Cowper	174
Dedham	251
Denfield	224
Devizes	253
Downs	35
Dundee	22, 333, 377
Elizabethtown	216
Enmore	72
Evan	101
Exeter	310
Faith	32, 257
Farrant	53
Fletcher	350
Geer	141
Geneva	84
Heber	236, 336

	PAGE
Henry	370
Hummel	16, 145, 369
Jordan (D)	418
Kedron Chant	43
Lanesboro'	15
London New	66, 318
Maitland	302
Manoah	105
Marlow	177
Martyrs	73
Mear	121
Merton	169
Mortality	383
Naomi	175, 261
Newbold	381
Newton	156
Nichols	170, 268
Northfield	358
Northampton	394
Nottingham	59
Ortonville	274
Peterboro'	258
Rhine	422
Siloam	106, 352
Stephens	176
St. Anns	155
St. Clements Dane	326
St. Gregorius	148
St. Johns	120
St. Martyns	312
Sydenham	278
Tallis	292
Tappan	116
Varina (D)	380
Warwick	34
Wirth	214, 337
Woodland	67
Woodstock	44
Wyman's Chant	398
York	65
Zerah (61)	91

C. P. M.

Ariel	138, 220
Ganges	181
Habakkuk	209
Harwood	289

	PAGE
Meribah	414
Milford	161
Rapture	28
Zalena	206

S. M.

Adrian	162
Ahira	346
Aylesbury	104
Boylston	48, 307
Compton	387
Dennis	196
Dover	23
Gerar	20
Golden Hill	296
Guardian	149
Haverhill	313
Laban	303
Lebanon (D)	197
Leighton	27
Malden	399
Mornington	150
Olmutz	272
Olney	342
Owen	173
Parnell	424
Prague	297
Prayer (D)	277, 396
Seir	229
Sheffield	158
Shirland	249, 317
Silver Street	55
State Street	402
St. Brides	328, 408
St. Mary's Abbey	218
St. Thomas	213, 316
Thatcher	183
Utica	410
Watchman	86

S. P. M.

Judah	58
Peters	11

S. H. M.

Tranquillity	401

METRICAL INDEX OF TUNES.

H. M.
Bethesda	194
Claremont	351
Culloden	135
Darwell	30, 133
Easter Hymn	115
Haddam	14
Hampton	321
Jerusalem on High	421
Lenox	132, 178
Lischer	81
Park Place	69
Pascal	184
Warsaw	51

5s & 8s.
Guidance	290

6s.
Aspiration Chant	246
Heaven (D)	423
Zong (D)	264

6s & 4s.
America	374
Amoy	187
Ava	187
Bethany	246
Clarion	360
Dort	154
Gennesaret (Pec.)	291
Italian Hymn	52
Olivet	288

6s, 4s, 6s.
Nightfall	49

6s, 10s.
Benton	284

7s.
Advent (Gl)	96
Aletta	168
Bellak	368
Benevento (D)	126, 384
Beulah (D)	430
Blumenthal (D)	21
Clarendon Street	195

Dallas	71
Delay	242
Essex	62
Gethsemane (Gl)	103
Glory (D)	429
Harvest Home (D)	378
Hendon	325
Holley	49, 285, 345
Hope (Gl)	405
Horton	276, 344
Jerusalem the Golden	420
Langdon (Gl)	186
Martyn	219
Mozart	118
Mt. Calvary (Gl)	201
Nativity (D)	97
Night	239
Nuremberg	19, 140
Penn (D)	306
Pleyel's Hymn	230, 314
Rock of Ages (Gl)	112
Rosefield (Gl)	129, 315
Sabbath (Gl)	33
Seymour	193
Solitude	37
Spanish Hymn (D)	110, 332
Sudbury	114
Telleman's Chant	163
Theodora	113
Watchman, tell us (D)	95

7s & 5s.
Comforter (D)	159

7s & 6s.
Amsterdam (Pec.)	415
Day Dawn	407
Ecce Homo	109
Eucharist	341
Jenner	29, 335
Jerusalem the Golden	420
Melchior	192
Missionary Hymn	371
Reliance	245, 286
Selborne	200
Supplication	283
Triumph	395
Webb	365

7s, 7s, 8s, 7s.
Corona (D)	305

7s & 8s.
St. Albinus	125

7s, 8s, 7s.
Meinhold	404

8s.
Ansel (D)	238
Devotion	432
Israel (D)	179
Protection (D)	46

8s & 4s.
Resignation	265
Tonica	166

8s & 6s.
Agnus Dei	203
Golan	125
Paradise	428
Resignation	265
Rono	376

8s, 6s & 8s.
Hastings	47

8s & 7s (D).
Autumn	275
Coronet	127
Faben	57
Harwell	136, 366
Judgment Hymn (71)	412
Latter Day	324
Nettleton	263
Opal	202
Rathbun (41)	47, 111
Shining Shore	389
Stockwell (Pec.)	391
St. Francis	240
Vesper Hymn	93, 331
Wilmot (or 7s)	87

8s, 7s & 4s.
Belmont	188
Hamden	108

	PAGE		PAGE		PAGE
Haydn's Hymn	182	**10s & 4s.**		**11s & 5s.**	
Helmsley	413	Lux Benigna	287	New Year's Hymn	385
Lewes	388				
Oliphant	362	**10s & 11s.**		**11s & 8s.**	
Sicilian Hymn	25	Goshen	260	Chrome	54
Tamworth	128	Lyons	54	Blessing	355
Zion	320, 361	Portuguese Hymn	80	**11s & 10s.**	
9s & 8s.				Come, ye disconsolate	252
Sacramental Hymn (D)	343	**10s, 11s & 12s.**		Folsom	94
		Paul	304	**12s, or 12s & 11s.**	
10s.				Scotland	373
Benediction Chant	345	**11s.**			
Eventide	390	Frederick	392	**12s, 11s & 4s.**	
Pax Dei	26	St. John Baptist's	330	Royalty	367

SELECTIONS FOR CHANTING.

	PAGE		PAGE
Arise, O Lord	443	Lord, our dwelling-place	441
Blessed are the dead	446	Oh come, let us sing	442
Blessed be the Lord	444	Responses I., II., III.	438
Buried with Christ	445	Te Deum	434
Cast thy burden on the Lord	448	Tersanctus	436
Gloria in excelsis	433	The heavens declare	439
Gloria Patri	437	The Lord is my Shepherd	440
God be merciful	440	Thy will be done	447
He is despised and rejected	444	Trisagion	436
am the Resurrection	447		

www.ingramcontent.com/pod-product-compliance
Lightning Source LLC
Chambersburg PA
CBHW051232300426
44114CB00011B/705